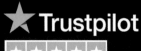

SELLING YOUR COINS & BANKNOTES?

Warwick and Warwick have an expanding requirement for coin and banknote collections, British and worldwide and for coins and notes of individual value. Our customer base is increasing dramatically and we need an ever larger supply of quality material to keep pace with demand. The market has never been stronger and if you are considering the sale of your collection, now is the time to act.

FREE VALUATIONS

We will provide a free, professional and without obligation valuation of your collection. Either we will make you a fair, binding private treaty offer, or we will recommend inclusion of your property in our next specialist public auction.

FREE TRANSPORTATION

We can arrange insured transportation of your collection to our Warwick offices completely free of charge. If you decline our offer, we ask you to cover the return carriage costs only.

FREE VISITS

Visits by our valuers are possible anywhere in the country or abroad, usually within 48 hours, in order to value larger collections. Please telephone for details.

VALUATION DAYS

We are staging a series of valuation days and will be visiting all areas of England, Scotland, Wales and Ireland during the coming months. Please visit our website or telephone for further details.

EXCELLENT PRICES

Because of the strength of our customer base we are in a position to offer prices that we feel sure will exceed your expectations.

ACT NOW

Telephone or email Richard Beale today with details of your property.

Buying and Selling Collectible Coins and Banknotes Made Easy

An authentic trading platform, tailored specifically to the needs of the Numismatic marketplace.

THE
COIN
Yearbook

2022

Edited by
John W. Mussell, FRGS
and the Editorial Team of COIN NEWS

ISBN 978 1 908828 57 6

Published by
TOKEN PUBLISHING LIMITED
40 Southernhay East, Exeter, Devon EX1 1PE
Telephone: 01404 46972
email: info@tokenpublishing.com. Website: www.tokenpublishing.com

Printed in Great Britain by Stephens & George Ltd.

Contents

Foreword

WELCOME to the 2022 edition of the COIN YEARBOOK, the best-selling collector's handbook and price guide for the fascinating hobby of numismatics. The chances are you already know a little bit about this book, but in case you are reading this introduction for the very first time you have in your hand (or on your screen, we just never know these days) a price guide to all English Scottish, Irish and Island coins stretching right back to Celtic times, through the Roman period (the book covers those Roman coins used in the British Isles) and on through the Iron Age coins, hammered coins, milled coins (they came in round about the time of the English Civil War and are so called because they were machine-made rather than handmade), right up to the present day. We have tried to include all coins used in the British Isles over time but we don't pretend the book is a full catalogue with every single variety listed. The COIN YEARBOOK will provide an overview—for a more in-depth look, other more specialist books are available.

Unfortunately, one of the areas that this, indeed every book on British Isles coins, will struggle with, is the "Island" coins. In recent years The Isle of Man and the Channel Islands have seen coins minted bearing their name that, in fact, will never see the light of day on any of the islands. The commemorative coin market is so vast these days, and the coins minted for it are so numerous, that keeping track of them all has been a mammoth task and one we simply haven't been able to keep up with. The fact is the numerous mints that issue coins of behalf of the Isle of Man and the Channel Islands do so not for use in everyday change but for the collector market. Often these coins are very limited in number and sold overseas, most of the time they're sold directly to marketing companies and their clients and we simply don't get to hear about them. We have done our best to include as many as we can but can only apologise for any omissions.

This past year has been an odd one for coin collecting, on the one hand the hobby itself has had something of a fillip thanks to lockdown; where people were unable to go out and socialise they turned inwards and back to more cloistered pastimes–the hobbies of their childhood once again grew in popularity. On the other hand the lack of cash use (those shops that did stay open tried desperately to get us to use cards, ostensibly "to keep us safe" but in reality because they didn't want to have to bank cash on a daily basis) has meant that fewer coins have been circulating. The "50p bounce" felt in the hobby thanks to the popularity amongst new collectors of first the Olympic and latterly the Beatrix Potter 50p coins, has all but disappeared, we await with interest to see whether it comes back again now that more places are open. Another reason why coin collecting has increased in popularity these past 18 months or so is the "investment" factor. With so much uncertainty around at the moment, with stock market volatility, with interest rates at ludicrously low levels and with traditional companies (and their shares) being so badly affected by lockdowns, more and more people have been turning to "assets", things they can physically hold, as somewhere to put their money (crypto currencies and Bitcoin et al aside—this book doesn't go down that road!) and consequently the demand for coins, if not the prices being asked for them, has noticeably increased in these past few months.

We don't look at coins as investments though, we steer well clear of the "I" word whenever we can, preferring instead to collect for enjoyment's sake rather than to make money—but we aren't so foolish as to think that money isn't a factor in our hobby, of course it is, a very big one and thus we produce this YEARBOOK and we know you want to know what your coins are worth! We also know that you want to know what you should be paying for coins to add to your collection—indeed that is the most important thing really, after all none of us want to feel we've overpaid for anything, and so the prices herein are buying prices, what you should expect to pay a dealer for the coin listed in the grade given. That said, please remember grading is very subjective: what you consider to be Very Fine+ someone else may see as Extremely Fine (for a simple introduction to grading see the table at the beginning of the Price Guide section), it is up to you to decide if you're happy with that. To get these prices we check dealers' lists and auction results then average everything out, so if a dealer has a coin for £195, another has it listed at £200 and a third for £220 then we will put it in the book at £205 even though none of those dealers has it up at that price! Dealers charge different prices for a number of reasons, depending on their overheads, what they paid for the coin, how long they've had it in stock, etc., so it's always worth shopping around. Also please remember that when you're selling a coin, dealers will often vary in their offers too, usually depending on whether they think they have a market for that particular coin (and don't forget that many dealers specialise and there's no point in offering a Royal Mint year set to a Roman and ancient coin dealer!).

When it comes to the valuations we don't just rely on checking lists and auctions to come up with our prices though, and we always get noted experts in their field to check things over too—we are thus indebted to the following people for their help and support. Chris Rudd and Elizabeth Cottam (Celtic); Stephen Mitchell of Studio Coins (Hammered); Royston Norbury of West Essex Coin Investments (Milled); Nick Swabey (Maundy); David Stuart (Scottish); Mike Southall (Isle of Man); Del Parker (Irish); and Charles Riley (Medals). We also express our gratitude to all the auction houses who have allowed access to their archives and given us permission to use their illustrations and of course the Royal Mint for their invaluable assistance.

Museum
archive

Engravings of the Queen and Prince Philip

When Charles Sigrist joined the Royal Mint in 1940, he was already 57 years old and not, therefore, an obvious recruit to help with a backlog of work that had built up in connection with the engraving of tooling for coins and medals. He was talented and experienced as an engraver and, after several years, he progressed from being a Craftsman to attain the formal rank of qualified Engraver. Following a long tradition of engravers who have worked for the Mint, he also carried out his own private work and it was in this capacity that the engraved silver medallic portraits illustrated here of the Queen and Prince Philip were prepared.

They form part of larger set of eight, dated between 1952 and 1953, that included George V, Queen Mary, George VI and Queen Elizabeth, and is also thought to include the Duke of Windsor and Winston Churchill. The portrait of Prince Philip, in particular, captures the character and bearing of the man. Its interest lies in that it is a much less well known medallic portrait of Prince Philip who, through his Presidency of the Royal Mint Advisory Committee, exercised a significant influence on numismatic design of the United Kingdom. The set is also, in and of itself, extremely rare and is testimony to the skill of a less-known Royal Mint engraver who, into his late 70s, carried on working on the nation's coins and medals.

Portrait of a sculptor

He may not be the most well-known figure in British numismatics but Francis Derwent Wood had an important part to play in the early years of the Royal Mint Advisory Committee. He was Professor of Sculpture at the Royal College of Art and was useful in suggesting young artists to become involved in coinage design. Those who have driven by Hyde Part Corner will have passed his Monument to the Machine Gunners and he was allowed to submit artwork for the re-design of the silver coinage in the 1920s, resulting in a beautifully composed rendering of a rose for the florin and thistle for the threepence which made it through to being struck as a pattern pieces.

The bronze portrait relief of Derwent Wood, illustrated here, has an added numismatic dimension because it is the work by Madge Kitchener. She was the artist responsible for the thrift design on the 12-sided threepence originally intended for the coinage of Edward VIII but later adapted for that of George VI. Born into a military family, she had as an uncle Lord Kitchener, and she later studied at the Slade School of Fine Art. She was known to the Royal Mint from a plaque she created for the British Empire Exhibition of 1924 but was strangely ignored by the Mint in its design commissioning through the 1920s. The connection between Madge Kitchener and Derwent Wood could be that she ran a gallery in Ashtead, Surrey, and it is known that he had strong links with that area. The portrait model now adds welcome evidence of this other dimension to her work as an artist, as well as providing a wonderful likeness of a past member of the Advisory Committee.

A bad penny

In August 1851 the Royal Mint received a coin in the post from Cork in Ireland. It was a penny dated the same year that had been tied to a card, fixed with a wax seal and addressed to Sir John Herschel, Master of the Mint. There was a message on the card: "One person has been transported for making this base counterfeit penny. Let us hope that another may not be transported for stealing of it". With transportation being phased out towards the end of the 1850s this will have been amongst the last such punishments for a coinage offence.

The individual who sent it to the Mint was performing a public service by taking the coin out of circulation and in this they certainly succeeded, since it has come down to the Royal Mint Museum essentially as despatched 170 years ago. Ireland, at the time, was a known source of counterfeits and Cork, in particular, was regarded as a hotbed of activity, so it should come as no surprise to see that city noted as the origin of the piece. The Museum has, for a long time, taken an interest in what happens to coins when they leave the factory and also in the nature of currency in circulation more generally. This must include counterfeits since the presence in the collection of an item such as the one illustrated here helps to build up a picture of what types of money were encountered in the markets and shops of everyday life.

Defaced copper penny

In 1860, a handsome new bronze coinage was introduced bearing the much-loved portrait of Queen Victoria by Leonard Wyon. It replaced coins that had been in circulation for some considerable time, dating back to the Cartwheel pennies of 1797, and the desirability of removing the cumbersome and fairly worn copper was widely acknowledged. The Master of the Royal Mint, Thomas Graham, provided scientific backing to these sentiments by means of a survey of the copper coinage carried out in 1857 which, although by no means perfect, set out a thorough justification for reform. Once the new coins had been introduced, though, the Mint was presented with the operational challenge of disposing of the old copper, the solution to which generated some odd looking pieces.

In this instance, the contract for melting down what was withdrawn was given to a firm in Swansea and to ensure there was no question of the coins being used again, the Mint arranged for them to be defaced prior to being shipped west. They were passed through a machine that imparted a ribbed or milled set of parallel lines and the penny of 1854 illustrated here shows the near complete coverage over the surface that was achieved. This specimen was not retained by the Mint at the time for the Museum's collection but was acquired in recent years. It illustrates an element in the story of how the copper was withdrawn and shows, quite clearly, that not all defaced coins reached their destination. Subjecting coins to this type of treatment was in one sense ironic since one of the justifications for withdrawing the old copper was the extent to which it had been contaminated by the presence of defaced coins bearing advertising slogans.

Prince Philip and the design of our money and medals

Prince Philip's life of long and distinguished public service included his Presidency of the Royal Mint Advisory Committee, the body that recommends designs for new United Kingdom coins and official medals. He served in this role from soon after the accession of Her Majesty the Queen in 1952 until 1999, when he stood down as part of a more general reduction in his commitments. The title President in relation to the Committee was created for him personally and may at first glance suggest an honorific role but the reality was quite different. He was an active and engaged chairman, taking a genuine interest in detailed questions of design and, as was reflected in other interests, in the technical implications of manufacture. He presided over many changes, including the design of the first coins of the new reign, the adoption of decimal currency in the 1960s and the ongoing reforms to the coinage over a number of decades, all guided by his breadth of knowledge, his clear thinking and his sharp wit.

After chairing his last meeting as President, which was held at St James's Palace, a lunch was arranged in his honour attended by current and former members of the Committee, artists who had designed coins and medals, and also a number of former Chancellors of the Exchequer, who are ex officio Master of the Mint. It was thought appropriate to give him a present in recognition of his long years of service and to this end Royal Mint engraver Robert Evans designed a beautiful object, around which were placed enlarged strikings of coin designed during the last 40 and more years. One in particular, a duplicate specimen of which is illustrated here, will have caught Prince Philip's eye—the effigy of the Queen by Mary Gillick. It was one of the first designs prepared under his time on the Committee and, perhaps more important, it was a portrait of his wife. It was an inspired likeness, defining a new beginning for the country and one that it is understood the Queen has always regarded with particular fondness. In April 2021, the country lost not only one of its foremost public figures but also someone who made a significant contribution to the numismatic history of the nation.

From the archive of decimal designs

The design of Britain's decimal coinage was a long-drawn-out affair, generating hundreds of designs from professionals and members of the public alike. Fortunately large numbers of these designs were retained and a substantial record of what was done and by whom still forms part of the Royal Mint Museum's archive of items relating to decimalisation. The whole story is fascinating, reaching right to the top of the British political and royal establishments and involving celebrated artists and designers of the time, such as Edward Bawden. The art historian Mark Stocker was commissioned some time ago to write an account of it all, making extensive use of the Museum's archive along the way, and the resulting book will be jointly published by the Museum and Spink.

One of those who submitted designs early on in the process was the young architect Andrew Anderson. He had been inspired by post-war Swedish coins and, as illustrated, although there are traditional motifs of roses, thistles, shamrock and lions, his approach was vigorously modern and markedly out of keeping with the largely conservative traditions of British circulating coinage design. Beyond the designs themselves, though, the archive contains commentaries by the artists and as a result we know that Anderson had considered the technical aspects of how well his designs might be produced and their resistance to wear in circulation. The 50th anniversary of decimalisation fell in February 2021 and Mark Stocker's book on how Britain decimalised its currency is a much-needed addition to the existing literature on the subject.

The end of the halfcrown and halfpenny

While there was a specific day on which Britain officially went decimal, February 15, 1971, the reality for those who lived through the changeover was a gradual withdrawal of the old pre-decimal coins and introduction of the new decimal money. It was all part of a grand plan to minimise disruption to businesses and to ease the passage of such a huge change for the British people. Five pence and ten pence pieces were accordingly introduced in 1968, with the fifty pence making its first appearance the following year. The same was true when it came to withdrawing some of the fondly remembered pre-decimal coins. The farthing had already ended its active life in 1960 for reasons not directly connected to decimalisation but, in the lead up to February 1971, the halfcrown and halfpenny were taken out of circulation.

Banks, in particular, were keen to inform their customers of the changeover and so if you had entered a branch towards the end of the 1960s you may well have encountered signs like the ones illustrated here. In an eye-catching manner these pop-up cardboard cut-outs specified precisely when the halfcrown and the halfpenny would cease to have any value in everyday exchange and urged the use of special bags so collecting in the coins could be handled in an orderly way. These signs are part of a large decimalisation collection held by the Royal Mint Museum, a proportion of which were placed on the Museum's website in the lead up to the 50th anniversary of decimalisation in February 2021.

THE ROYAL MINT®
THE ORIGINAL MAKER

Celebrate the People who Make us Proud

CELEBRATE A SUMMER OF BRITISH ICONS

Summer is here and we're celebrating the people who make us proud, from the influential and inspiring novelists Sir Walter Scott and H.G. Wells to the groundbreaking scientists Mary Anning and John Logie Baird, and the incredible athletes of Team GB. Join us in paying tribute to icons – past and present – who have made great contributions to the United Kingdom.

 Search: **A Summer of British Icons**

royalmint.com

CELEBRATE | COLLECT | INVEST | SECURE | DISCOVER

Monarchs
of England

Here we list the Kings and Queens from Anglo-Saxon times to the present, with the dates of their rule. Before Eadgar became the King of all England the country had been divided up into small kingdoms, each with their own ruler.

ANGLO-SAXON KINGS

The Anglo-Saxon monarchs ruled over the various kingdoms which existed in England following the withdrawal of the Romans in the 5th century AD. The most prominent kingdoms in the land were Kent, Sussex, Wessex, Mercia and Northumbria. Each kingdom produced its own coinage but in 973 Eadgar introduced a new coinage that became the standard for the whole of the country.

Eadgar (959–975)
Edward the Martyr (975–978)
Aethelred II (978–1016)
Cnut (1016–1035)
Harold I (1035–1040)
Harthacanut (1035–1042)
Edward the Confessor (1042–1066)
Harold II (1066)

NORMAN KINGS

The Normans came to Britain from their native France following the establishment of a kingdom in Sicily and southern Italy. An expedition led by the powerful Duke William of Normandy culminated in the battle of Hastings in 1066 where he defeated Harold II and was proclaimed King of All England. Their influence spread from these new centres to the Crusader States in the Near East and to Scotland and Wales in Great Britain, and to Ireland. Today their influence can be seen in their typical Romanesque style of architecture.

William I (1066–1087)
William II (1087–1100)
Henry I (1100–1135)
Stephen (1135–1154)

PLANTAGENETS

The Plantagenet kings of England were descended from the first House of Anjou who were established as rulers of England through the Treaty of Wallingford, which passed over the claims of Eustace and William, Stephen of Blois's sons, in favour of Henry of Anjou, son of the Empress Matilda and Geoffrey V, Count of Anjou.

Henry II (1154–1189)
Richard I (1189–1199)
John (1199–1216)
Henry III (1216–1272)
Edward I (1272–1307)
Edward II (1307–1327)
Edward III (1327–1377)
Richard II (1377–1399)

HOUSE OF LANCASTER

The House of Lancaster, a branch of the English royal House of Plantagenet, was one of the opposing factions involved in the Wars of the Roses, the civil war which dominated England and Wales during the 15th century. Lancaster provided England with three Kings

Henry IV (1399–1413)
Henry V (1413–1422)
Henry VI (1422–1461) and again 1470

HOUSE OF YORK

The House of York was the other branch of the House of Plantagenet involved in the disastrous Wars of the Roses. Edward IV was descended from Edmund of Langley, 1st Duke of York, the fourth surviving son of Edward III.

Edward IV (1461–1483 and again 1471–83)
Richard III (1483–1485)

TUDORS

The House of Tudor was an English royal dynasty that lasted 118 years, from 1485 to 1603. The family descended from the Welsh courtier Owen Tudor (Tewdwr). Following the defeat of Richard III at Bosworth, the battle that ended the Wars of the Roses, Henry Tudor, 2nd Earl of Richmond, took the throne as Henry VII.

Henry VII (1485–1509)
Henry VIII (1509–1547)
Edward VI (1547–1553)
Mary (1553–1558)
Philip & Mary (1554–1558)
Elizabeth I (1558–1603)

STUARTS

The House of Stuart ruled Scotland for 336 years, between 1371 and 1707. Elizabeth I of England's closest heir was James VI of Scotland via her grandfather Henry VII of England, who was founder of the Tudor dynasty. On Elizabeth's death, James Stuart ascended the thrones of England and Ireland and inherited the English claims to the French throne. The Stuarts styled themselves "Kings and Queens of Great Britain", although there was no parliamentary union until the reign of Queen Anne, the last monarch of the House of Stuart.

James I (1603–1625)
Charles I (1625–1649)
The Commonwealth (1653–1658)
Charles II (1660–1685)
James II (1685–1688)
William III & Mary (1688–1694)
William III (1694–1702)
Anne (1702–1714)

HOUSE OF HANOVER

The House of Hanover was a Germanic royal dynasty which ruled the Duchy of Brunswick-Lüneburg and the Kingdom of Hanover. George Ludwig ascended to the throne of the Kingdom of Great Britain and Ireland through the female line from Princess Elizabeth, sister of Charles I.

George I (1714–1727)
George II (1727–1760)
George III (1760–1820)
George IV (1820–1830)
William IV (1830–1837)
Victoria (1837–1901)

HOUSES OF SAXE-COBURG-GOTHA AND WINDSOR

The name Saxe-Coburg-Gotha was inherited by Edward VII from his father Prince Albert, the second son of the Duke of Saxe-Coburg-Gotha and husband of Victoria. During World War I the name was changed to Windsor to avoid the Germanic connotatiion.

Edward VII (1901–1910)
George V (1910–1936)
Edward VIII (1936)
George VI (1936–1952)
Elizabeth II (1952–)

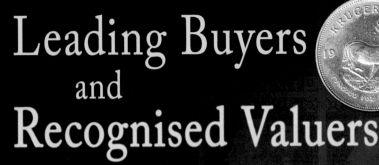

Dates
on coins

The vast majority of modern coins bear the date prominently on one side. In most cases dates are expressed in modified Arabic numerals according to the Christian calendar and present no problem in identification. There have been a few notable exceptions to this general rule, however. Morocco, for example, has used European numerals to express dates according to the Moslem calendar, so that a coin dated 1321 actually signifies 1903. Dates are almost invariably written from left to right—even in Arabic script which writes words from right to left. An exception, however, occurred in the Philippines quarto of 1822 where the date appeared as 2281, and the "2"s back to front for good measure.

	ARABIC-TURKISH	CHINESE, JAPANESE KOREAN, ANNAMESE (ORDINARY)	CHINESE, JAPANESE KOREAN, ANNAMESE (OFFICAL)	INDIAN	SIAMESE	BURMESE
1	١	一	壹	٩	๑	၁
2	٢	二	貳	٢	๒	၂
3	٣	三	叄	٣	๓	၃
4	٤	四	肆	٨	๔	၄
5	٥	五	伍	٤	๕	၅
6	٦	六	陸	٤	๖	၆
7	٧	七	柒	٥	๗	၇
8	٨	八	捌	٢	๘	၈
9	٩	九	玖	٩	๙	၉
0	٠			٥	๐	၀
10	١٠	十	拾		๑๐	
100	١٠٠	百			๑๐๐	
1000	١٠٠٠	千				

Dates in Roman numerals have been used since 1234 when this practice was adopted by the Danish town of Roskilde. Such Roman numerals were used sporadically throughout the Middle Ages and in later centuries and survive fitfully to this day. This was the system used in England for the first dated coins, the gold half-sovereigns of Edward VI struck at Durham House in 1548 (MDXLVIII). This continued till 1550 (MDL) but thereafter Arabic numerals were used, beginning with the half-crown of 1551. Notable exceptions of more recent times include the Gothic coinage of Queen Victoria (1847–87).

The first coin with the date in European numerals was a plappart of St Gallen, Switzerland dated 1424, but this was an isolated case. In 1477 Maria of Burgundy issued a guldiner which bore a date on the reverse, in the form of two pairs of digits flanking the crown at the top. The numerals in this instance were true Gothic, an interesting transition between true Arabic numerals and the modified Arabic figures now used in Europe. The Tyrolese guldengroschen of 1484–6 were the first coins to be regularly dated in European numerals and thereafter this custom spread rapidly.

For the numismatist, the problem arises when coins bear a date in the numerals of a different alphabet or computed according to a different era. Opposite is a table showing the basic numerals used in different scripts. The various eras which may be found in coin dates are as listed and explained opposite.

Hijra

The era used on Moslem coins dates from the flight of Mohammed from Mecca to Medina on July 15, 622 and is often expressed as digits followed by AH (Anno Hegirae). Moslems employ a lunar calendar of twelve months comprising 354 11/30 days. Tipu Sultan of Mysore in 1201 AH (the fifth year of his reign) introduced a new era dating from the birth of Mohammed in AD 570 and using a luni-solar system. Tipu also adopted the Hindu cycle of sixty years (the Tamil Brihaspate Cycle), but changed this two or three years later, from Hijra to Muludi.

Afghan coins used the lunar calendar until 1920 and during 1929–31, but at other times have used the solar calendar. Thus the Democratic Republic began issuing its coins in SH 1358 (1979).

To convert an AH date to the Christian calendar you must translate the Arabic into European numerals. Taking an Arabic coin dated 1320, for example, first deduct 3% (to convert from the Moslem lunar year to our solar year). This gives 39.6 which, rounded up to the nearest whole number, is 40. Deduct 40 from 1320 (1280), then add 622. The answer is 1902.

There have been a few notable exceptions. Thus the Khanian era of Ilkhan Ghazan Mahmud began on 1st Rajab 701 AH (1301). This era used a solar calendar, but was shortlived, being confined to coins of Mahmud and his nephew Abu Said down to year 34 (1333).

The era of Tarikh Ilahi was adopted by the Mughal emperor Akbar in the thirteenth year of his reign (922 AH). This era dated from his accession on 5th Rabi al-Sani 963 AH (February 19, 1556). The calendar had solar months and days but no weeks, so each day of the month had a different name. This system was used by Akbar, Jahangir and Shah Jahan, often with a Hijra date as well.

Saphar

The era of the Caesars began on January 1, 38 BC and dated from the conquest of Spain by Augustus. Its use on coinage, however, seems to have been confined to the marabotins of Alfonso VIII of Castile and was expressed in both Latin and Arabic.

Samvat

The era of Vikramaditya began in 57 BC and was a luni-solar system used in some Indian states. Coins may be found with both Samvat and Hijra dates. Conversion to the Christian date is simple; merely subtract 57 from the Samvat to arrive at the AD date.

Saka

This originated in the southwestern district of Northern India and began in AD 78. As it used the luni-solar system it converts easily by adding 78 to the Saka date.

Nepal

Nepalese coins have used four different date systems. All coins of the Malla kings were dated in Nepal Samvat (NS) era, year 1 beginning in 881. This system was also used briefly by the state of Cooch Behar. Until 1888 all coins of the Gurkha dynasty were dated in the Saka era (SE) which began in AD 78. After 1888 most copper coins were dated in the Vikram Samvat (VS) era from 57 BC. With the exception of some gold coins struck in 1890 and 1892, silver and gold coins only changed to the VS era in 1911, but now this system is used for all coins struck in Nepal. Finally, dates in the Christian era have appeared on some commemorative coins of recent years.

Ethiopian

This era dates from August AD 7, so that EE 1885 is AD 1892. Ethiopian dates are expressed in five digits using Amharic numerals. The first two are the digits of the centuries, the third is the character for 100, while the fourth and fifth are the digits representing the decade and year. On modern coins dates are rendered in Amharic numerals using the Christian era.

Thailand

Thai coins mainly use the Buddhist era (BE) which dates from 543 BC, but some coins have used dates from the Chula-Sakarat calendar (CS) which began in AD 638, while others use a Ratanakosin Sok (RS) date from the foundation of the Chakri dynasty in AD 1781.

Hebrew

The coins of Israel use the Jewish calendar dating from the beginning of the world (Adam and Eve in the Garden of Eden) in 3760 BC. Thus the year 1993 is rendered as 5753. The five millennia are assumed in dates, so that only the last three digits are expressed. 735 therefore equates with AD 1975. Dates are written in Hebrew letters, reading from right to left. The first two characters signify 400 and 300 respectively, totalling 700. The third letter denotes the decades (lamedh = 30) and the fourth letter, following the separation mark ("), represents the final digit (heh = 5). The Jewish year runs from September or October in the Christian calendar.

Dates from the creation of the world

This system was also used in Russia under Ivan IV. The dating system Anno Mundi (AM) was established by the Council of Constantinople in AD 680 which determined that the birth of Christ had occurred in 5508 AM. Ivan's coins expressed the date as 7055 (1447).

Dynastic dates

The system of dating coinage according to regnal years is a feature of Chinese and Japanese coins. Chinese coins normally have an inscription stating that they are coins of such and such a reign period (not the emperor's name), and during the Southern Sung dynasty this was joined by the numeral of the year of the reign. This system was continued under the republic and survives in Taiwan to this day, although the coins of the Chinese Peoples Republic are dated in western numerals using the Christian calendar.

Early Japanese coins bore a reference to the era (the title assumed by each emperor on his accession) but, like Chinese coins, could not be dated accurately. From the beginning of the Meiji era (1867), however, coins have included a regnal number. The Showa era, beginning in 1926 with the accession of Hirohito, eventually ran to sixty-three (expressed in western numerals on some denominations, in Japanese ideograms on others) to denote 1988, although the rest of the inscription was in Japanese characters.

Dynastic dates were used on Korean milled coins introduced in 1888. These bore two characters at the top Kae Kuk (founding of the dynasty) followed by quantitative numerals. The system dated from the founding of the Yi dynasty in 1392. Curiously enough, some Korean banknotes have borne dates from the foundation of the first dynasty in 2333 BC.

Iran adopted a similar system in 1975, celebrating the 15th anniversary of the Pahlavi regime by harking back to the glories of Darius. The new calendar dated from the foundation of the Persian Empire 2535 years earlier, but was abolished only three years later when the Shah was overthrown.

Political eras

France adopted a republican calendar in 1793 when the monarchy was abolished. Coins were then inscribed L'AN (the year) followed by Roman numerals, but later Arabic numerals were substituted. This continued to the year 14 (1806) but in that year the Emperor Napoleon restored the Christian calendar. The French system was emulated by Haiti whose coins dated from the revolution of 1803. The date appeared as AN followed by a number until AN 31 (1834) on some coins; others had both the evolutionary year and the Christian date from 1828 until 1850 (AN 47). Coins with a date in the Christian calendar appeared only in 1807–9 and then from 1850 onwards.

Mussolini introduced the Fascist calendar to Italy, dating from the seizure of power in October 1922. This system was widely employed on documents and memorials, but was first used on silver 20 lire coins of 1927 and then only in addition to the Christian date and appearing discreetly as Roman numerals. Subsequently it was extended to gold 50 lire and 100 lire coins in 1931 and the subsidiary coinage in 1936, being last used in the year XXI (1943).

Britain's Coin Shop - since 1955

45 Great Russell Street,
LONDON WC1B 3LU
(opposite the British Museum)
Tel: 020 7636 1188
Web www.coincraft.com
Email info@coincraft.com

C☉incraft

Britain's Coin Shop

$1,000,000+ Catalogue Value!

A unique opportunity for a company or individual to buy THE Original Hoard of Italy's First Banknotes 1746-1798. Purchased from the family that actually printed and issued these banknotes in 1746, they are guaranteed original and genuine. The notes were printed on oversized handmade paper, good for faming or reducing to banknote size, the choice is yours. We have been selling a few pieces from this hoard every year for the past 25 years. Ever since we bought them, through the good offices of Guido Crapanzano, Italy's leading banknote expert.

We have decided to offer them for sale, but only as one group. These antique Italian banknotes would make excellent prizes, wonderful historic pieces framed to hang on the wall, for re-sell or just to buy them and put them away. This hoard can be purchased at a very reasonable percentage of the catalogue price. The sale price is plus VAT if purchased in this county. All enquires will be treated in confidentiality.

Please serious enquires only, please note we will want to know a lot about you before we reveal too much more information. For now we can just say that this is THE hoard of Italy's first banknotes, the catalogue price is over a million dollars US, we have owned them for over 25 years and they can be bought by you at a reasonable price.

Thank you
Richard Lobel - Founder Coincraft – Britain's Coin Shop

WEAR HISTORY ON YOUR WRIST

Connecting two of the world's most sought-after collectables, our unique and exclusive range of watches feature some of the most storied coins in the history of numismatics.

Discover today by calling **0808 109 7836** quoting **92015046** or by visiting **londonmintoffice.org/watches**

THE
LONDON MINT
OFFICE

Trustpilot
★★★★★

Coin
inscriptions

This alphabetical listing is confined to inscriptions found on coins, mainly in the form of mottoes or of a commemorative nature. Names of rulers are, for the most part, excluded. Where the inscription is in a language other than English a translation is given, followed by the name of the issuing country or authority in parentheses.

A Deo et Caesare   From God and the Emperor (Frankfurt).

A Domino Factum est Istud et est Mirabile in Oculis Nostris   This is the Lord's doing and it is marvellous in our eyes (England, Mary).

A Solo Iehova Sapientia   From God alone comes true wisdom (Wittgenstein).

Ab Inimicis Meis Libera Me Deus   Free me from enemies (Burgundy).

Ad Legem Conventionis   According to the law of the Convention (Furstenberg).

Ad Normam Conventionis   According to the standard of the Convention (Prussia).

Ad Palmam Pressa Laeturo Resurgo   Pressed to the palm I rise more joyfully (Wittgenstein).

Ad Usam Luxemburgi CC Vallati   For the use of the besieged Luxembourgers (Luxembourg siege coins).

Adiuva Nos Deus Salutaris Noster   Help us, O God, our Saviour (Lorraine).

Adventus Optimi Principis   The coming of the noblest prince (Papacy).

Aes Usibus Aptius Auro   Bronze in its uses is more suitable than gold (Brazil).

Aeternum Meditans Decus   An ornament intended for all time (Alencon).

Aliis Inserviendo Consumor   I spend my life devoted to others (Brunswick-Wolfenbuttel).

Alles Mit Bedacht   All with reflection (Brunswick).

Amor Populi Praesidium Regis   The love of the people is the king's protection (England, Charles I).

Ang Fra Dom Hib & Aquit   (King) of England and France, Lord of Ireland and Aquitaine (England, Edward III).

Anno Regni Primo   In the first year of the reign (Britain, edge inscription on crowns).

Apres les Tenebres la Lumiere   After the shadows, the light (Geneva).

Archangelus Michael   Archangel Michael (Italy, Grimoald IV).

Ardua ad Gloriam Via   Struggles are the way to glory (Waldeck).

Arte Mea Bis Iustus Moneta Lud Iust   By my art I am twice the just coin of King Louis (France, 1641).

Aspera Oblectant   Wild places delight (Nassau-Weilburg).

Aspice Pisas Sup Omnes Specio   Behold the coin of Pisa, superior to all (Pisa).

Audiatur Altera Pars   Let the other part be heard (Stavelot).

Auf Gott Trawe Ich   In God I trust (Brunswick).

Ausen Gefaesen der Kirchen und Burger   From the vessels of the Church and citizens (Frankfurt siege, 1796).

Auspicio Regis et Senatus Angliae   By authority of the king and parliament of England (East India Company).

Auxilio fortissimo Dei   With the strongest help of God (Mecklenburg).

Auxilium de Sanctio   Aid from the sanctuary (Papacy).

Auxilium Meum a Dno Qui Fecit Celum e Terram   My help comes from God who made heaven and earth (Portugal).

Beata Tranquillatis   Blessed tranquillity (Rome, Licinius II).

Beatus Qui Speravit in dom   Blessed is he who has hoped in the Lord (Mansfeld).

Benedic Haereditati Tuae   Blessings on your inheritance (Savoy).

Benedicta Sit Sancta Trinitas   Blessed be the Holy Trinity (Albon).

Benedictio Domini Divites Facit   The blessing of the Lord makes the rich (Teschen).

Benedictus Qui Venit in Nomine Domini   Blessed is he who comes in the name of the Lord (Flanders).

Beschaw das Ziel Sage Nicht Viel   Consider the matter but say little (Quedlinburg).

Besser Land und Lud Verloren als ein Falscher Aid Geschworn Better to lose land and wealth than swear a false oath (Hesse).

Bey Gott ist Rath und That With God is counsel and deed (Mansfeld).

Britanniarum Regina Queen of the Britains (Britain, Victoria).

Britt Omn Rex King of all the Britains (i.e. Britain and the overseas dominions) (Britain, 1902–52).

Cal et Car Com de Fugger in Zin et Norn Sen & Adm Fam Cajetan and Carl, Counts of Fugger in Zinnenberg and Nordendorf, Lords and Administrators of the Family (Empire, Fugger).

Candide et Constanter Sincerely and steadfastly (Hesse-Cassel).

Candide sed Provide Clearly but cautiously (Osterwitz).

Candore et Amore With sincerity and love (Fulda).

Candore et Constantia With sincerity and constancy (Bavaria).

Capit Cath Ecclesia Monasteriensis Chapter of the Cathedral Church of Munster (Munster).

Capit Eccle Metropolit Colon Chapter of the Metropolitan Church of Cologne (Cologne).

Capitulum Regnans Sede Vacante Chapter governing, the See being vacant (Eichstadt).

Carola Magna Ducissa Feliciter Regnante Grand Duchess Charlotte, happily reigning (Luxembourg).

Carolus a Carolo Charles (I) to Charles (II) (England).

Cedunt Prementi Fata The fates yield to him who presses (Ploen, Hese-Cassel).

Charitate et Candore With charity and sincerity (East Frisia).

Charta Magna Bavariae The Great Charter of Bavaria (Bavaria).

Christo Auspice Regno I reign under the auspices of Christ (England, Charles I).

Christus Spes Una Salutis Christ is our one hope of salvation (Cleve).

Chur Mainz Electoral Principality of Mainz (Mainz).

Circumeundo Servat et Ornat It serves and decorates by going around (Sweden).

Civibus Quorum Pietas Coniuratione Die III Mai MDCCXCI Obrutam et Deletam Libertate Polona Tueri Conabatur Respublica Resurgens To the citizens whose piety the resurgent commonwealth tried to protect Poland overturned and deprived of liberty by the conspiracy of the third day of May 1791 (Poland).

Civitas Lucemborgiensis Millesimum Ovans Expletannum Completing the celebration of a thousand years of the city of Luxembourg (Luxembourg).

Civium Industria Floret Civitas By the industry of its people the state flourishes (Festival of Britain crown, 1951).

Cluniaco Cenobio Petrus et Paulus Peter and Paul from the Abbey of Cluny (Cluny).

Comes Provincie Fili Regis Francie Court of Provence and son of the King of France (Provence).

Communitas et Senatus Bonon City and senate of Bologna (Bologna).

Concordia Fratrum The harmony of the brothers (Iever).

Concordia Patriae Nutrix Peace, the nurse of the fatherland (Waldeck).

Concordia Res Parvae Crescunt Little things increase through harmony (Batavian Republic).

Concordia Res Parvae Crescunt, Discordia Dilabuntur By harmony little things increase, by discord they fall apart (Lowenstein-Wertheim-Virneburg).

Concordia Stabili With lasting peace (Hildesheim).

Confidens Dno Non Movetur He who trusts in God is unmoved (Spanish Netherlands).

Confidentia in Deo et Vigilantia Trust in God and vigilance (Prussian Asiatic Company).

Confoederato Helvetica Swiss Confederation (Switzerland)

Conjuncto Felix Fortunate in his connections (Solms).

Conservator Urbis Suae Saviour of his city (Rome, 4th century).

Consilio et Aequitate With deliberation and justice (Fulda).

Consilio et Virtutis With deliberation and valour (Hesse-Cassel).

Constanter et Sincere Steadfastly and sincerely (Lautern).

Crescite et Multiplicamini Increase and multiply (Maryland).

Cristiana Religio Christian religion (Germany, 11th century).

Crux Benedicat May the cross bless you (Oldenburg).

Cuius Cruore Sanati Sumus By His sacrifice are we healed (Reggio).

Cultores Sui Deus Protegit God protects His followers (England, Charles I).

Cum Deo et Die (Jure) With God and the day (Wurttemberg).

Cum Deo et Jure With God and the law (Wurttemberg).

Cum Deo et Labore With God and work (Wittgenstein).

Cum His Qui Orderant Pacem Eram Pacificus With those who order peace I was peaceful (Zug).

Curie Bonthon to so Doulo Protect his servant, o Lord (Byzantine Empire).

Custos Regni Deus God is the guardian of the kingdom (Naples and Sicily).

Da Gloriam Deo et Eius Genitrici Marie Give glory to God and His mother Mary (Wurttemberg).

Da Mihi Virtutem Contra Hostes Tuos Give me valour against mine enemies (Netherlands, Charles V).

Dat Wort is Fleis Gworden The word is made flesh (Muster).

Date Caesaris Caesari et Quae Sunt Dei Deo Render unto Caesar the things that are Caesar's and unto God the things that are God's (Stralsund).

De Oficina . . . From the mint of . . . (France, medieval).

Decreto Reipublicae Nexu Confoederationis Iunctae Die V Xbris MDCCXCII Stanislao Augusto Regnante By decree of the state in conjunction with the joint federation on the fifth day of December 1792, Stanislaus Augustus ruling (Poland).

Decus et Tutamen An ornament and a safeguard (Britain, pound).

Deducet Nos Mirabiliter Dextera Tua Thy right hand will guide us miraculously (Savoy).

Denarium Terrae Mariae Penny of Maryland (Maryland).

Deo Conservatori Pacis To God, preserver of peace (Brandenburg-Ansbach).

Deo OM Auspice Suaviter et Fortiter sed Luste nec Sibi sed Suis Under the auspices of God, greatest and best, pleasantly and bravely but justly, not for himself but for his people (Speyer).

Deo Patriae et Subditio For God, fatherland and neighbourhood (Mainz).

Der Recht Glaubt In Ewig Lebt Who believes in right will live in eternity (Linange-Westerburg).

Der Rhein ist Deutschlands Strom Nicht Deutschlands Grenze The Rhine is Germany's River not Germany's Frontier.

Deum Solum Adorabis You will venerate God alone (Hesse).

Deus Constituit Regna God establishes kingdoms (Ni jmegen).

Deus Dat Qui Vult God gives to him who wishes (Hanau-Munzenberg).

Deus et Dominus God and Lord (Rome, 3rd century).

Deus in Adiutorium Meum Intende God stretch out in my assistance (France).

Deus Providebit God will provide (Lowenstein-Wertheim-Virneburg).

Deus Refugium Meum God is my refuge (Cleve).

Deus Solatium Meum God is my comfort (Sweden).

Dextera Domini Exaltavit Me The right hand of God has raised me up (Modena, Spain).

Dextra Dei Exalta Me The right hand of God exalts me (Denmark).

Dieu et Mon Droit God and my right (Britain, George IV).

Dilexit Dns Andream The Lord delights in St Andrew (Holstein).

Dilexit Dominus Decorem Iustitiae The Lord is pleased with the beauty of justice (Unterwalden).

Dirige Deus Gressus Meos O God, direct my steps (Tuscany, Britain, Una £5).

Discerne Causam Meam Distinguish my cause (Savoy).

Divina Benedictiae et Caesarea Iustitia Sacrifice of blessings and imperial justice (Coblenz).

Dn Ihs Chs Rex Regnantium Lord Jesus Christ, King of Kings (Rome, Justinian II).

Dns Ptetor Ms Z Lib'ator Ms The Lord is my protector and liberator (Scotland, David II).

Dominabitur Gentium et Ipse He himself will also be lord of the nations (Austrian Netherlands).

Domine Conserva Nos in Pace O Lord preserve us in peace (Basle, Mulhausen).

Domine Elegisti Lilium Tibi O Lord Thou hast chosen the lily for Thyself (France, Louis XIV).

Domine ne in Furore Tuo Arguas Me O Lord rebuke me not in Thine anger (England, Edward III).

Domine Probasti Me et Congnovisti Me O Lord Thou hast tested me and recognised me (Mantua).

Domini est Regnum The Kingdom is the Lord's (Austrian Netherlands).

Dominus Deus Omnipotens Rex Lord God, almighty King (Viking coins).

Dominus Mihi Adiutor The Lord is my helper (Spanish Netherlands).

Dominus Providebit The Lord will provide (Berne).

Dominus Spes Populi Sui The Lord is the hope of his people (Lucerne).

Donum Dei ex Fodinis Vilmariens A gift of God from the Vilmar mines (Coblenz).

Duce Deo Fide et Justicia By faith and justice lead us to God (Ragusa).

Dum Praemor Amplior I increase while I die prematurely (Savoy).

Dum Spiro Spero While I live, I hope (Pontefract siege coins).

Dum Totum Compleat Orbem Until it fills the world (France, Henri II).

Dura Pati Virtus Valour endures hardships (Saxe-Lauenburg).

Durae Necessitatis Through force of necessity (Bommel siege, 1599).

Durum Telum Necessitas Hardship is a weapon of necessity (Minden).

Dux et Gubernatores Reip Genu Duke and governors of the republic of Genoa (Genoa).

E Pluribus Unum One out of more (USA).

Eccl S. Barbarae Patronae Fodin Kuttenbergensium Duo Flor Arg Puri The church of St Barbara, patron of the Kuttenberg mines, two florins of pure silver (Hungary).

Een en Ondelbaer Sterk One and indivisible (Batavian Republic).

Eendracht Mag Macht Unity makes strength (Belgium, South African Republic).

Einigkeit Recht und Freiheit Union, right and freedom (Germany).

Electorus Saxoniae Administrator Elector and administrator of Saxony (Saxony).

Elimosina   Alms (France, Pepin).

Ep Fris & Ratisb Ad Prum Pp Coad Aug   Bishop of Freising and Regensburg, administrator of Pruem, prince-provost, co-adjutant bishop of Augsburg (Trier).

Equa Libertas Deo Gratia Frat Pax in Virtute Tua et in Domino Confido   I believe in equal liberty by the grace of God, brotherly love in Thy valour and in the Lord (Burgundy).

Equitas Iudicia Tua Dom   Equity and Thy judgments O Lord (Gelderland).

Espoir Me Conforte   Hope comforts me (Mansfeld).

Espreuve Faicto Par Lexpres Commandement du Roy   Proof made by the express commandment of the King (France, piedforts).

Et in Minimis Integer   Faithful even in the smallest things (Olmutz).

Ex Auro Argentes Resurgit   From gold it arises, silver again (Sicily).

Ex Auro Sinico   From Chinese gold (Denmark).

Ex Flammis Orior   I arise from the flames (Hohenlohe-Neuenstein-Ohringen).

Ex Fodinis Bipontio Seelbergensibus   From the Seelberg mines of Zweibrucken (Pfalz-Birkenfeld).

Ex Metallo Novo   From new metal (Spain).

Ex Uno Omnis Nostra Salus   From one is all our salvation (Eichstadt, Mulhouse).

Ex Vasis Argent Cleri Mogunt Pro Aris et Focis   From the silver vessels of the clergy of Mainz for altars and for hearths (Mainz).

Ex Visceribus Fodinse Bieber   From the bowels of the Bieber mine (Hanau-Munzenberg).

Exaltabitur in Gloria   He shall be exalted in glory (England, quarter nobles).

Exemplum Probati Numismatis   An example of a proof coin (France, Louis XIII piedforts).

Exemtae Eccle Passau Episc et SRI Princ   Prince Bishop of the freed church of Passau, prince of the Holy Roman Empire (Passau).

Expectate Veni   Come, o expected one (Roman Britain, Carausius).

Extremum Subidium Campen   Kampen under extreme siege (Kampen, 1578).

Exurgat Deus et Dissipentur Inimici Eius   Let God arise and let His enemies be scattered (England, James I).

Faciam Eos in Gentem Unam   I will make them one nation (England, unites and laurels).

Faith and Truth I will Bear unto You   (UK £5, 1993).

Fata Consiliis Potiora   The fates are more powerful than councils (Hesse-Cassel).

Fata Viam Invenient   The fates will find a way (Gelderland).

Fecit Potentiam in Brachio Suo   He put power in your forearm (Lorraine).

Fecunditas   Fertility (Naples and Sicily).

Fel Temp Reparatio   The restoration of lucky times (Rome, AD 348).

Felicitas Perpetua   Everlasting good fortune (Rome, Constantius II).

Felix coniunctio   Happy Union (Brandenburg-Ansbach).

Fiat Misericordia Tua Dne   Let Thy mercy be O Lord (Gelderland).

Fiat Voluntas Domini Perpetuo   Let the goodwill of the Lord last for ever (Fulda).

Fidei Defensor   Defender of the Faith (Britain).

Fidelitate et Fortitudine   With fidelity and fortitude (Batthanyi).

Fideliter et Constanter   Faithfully and steadfastly (Saxe-Coburg-Gotha).

Fidem Servando Patriam Tuendo   By keeping faith and protecting the fatherland (Savoy).

Filius Augustorum   Son of emperors (Rome, 4th century).

Fisci Iudaici Calumnia Sublata   The false accusation of the Jewish tax lifted (Rome, Nerva).

Florent Concordia Regna   Through harmony kingdoms flourish (England, Charles I and II).

Fortitudo et Laus Mea Dominu   Fortitude and my praise in the Lord (Sardinia).

Free Trade to Africa by Act of Parliment *(Sic)* (Gold Coast).

Friedt Ernehrt Unfriedt Verzehrt   Peace nourishes, unrest wastes (Brunswick).

Fulgent Sic Littora Rheni   Thus shine the banks of the Rhine (Mannheim).

Fundator Pacis   Founder of peace (Rome, Severus).

Gaudium Populi Romani   The joy of the Roman people (Rome, 4th century).

Gen C Mar VI Dim Col USC & RAMAI Cons & S Conf M   General field marshal, colonel of the only dragoon regiment, present privy councillor of both their sacred imperial and royal apostolic majesties, and state conference minister (Batthanyi).

Gerecht und Beharrlich   Just and steadfast (Bavaria).

Germ Hun Boh Rex AAD Loth Ven Sal   King of Germany, Hungary and Bohemia, Archduke of Austria, Duke of Lorraine, Venice and Salzburg (Austria).

Germ Jero Rex Loth Bar Mag Het Dux   King of Germany, Jerusalem, Lorraine and Bar, Grand Duke of Tuscany (Austrian Netherlands).

Germania Voti Compos   Germany sharing the vows (Brandenburg-Ansbach).

Gloria ex Amore Patriae   Glory from love of country (Denmark).

Gloria in Excelsis Deo   Glory to God in the highest (France, Sweden).

Gloria Novi Saeculi   The glory of a new century (Rome, Gratian).

God With Us   (England, Commonwealth).

Godt Met Ons   God with us (Oudewater).

Gottes Freundt der Pfaffen Feindt   God's friend, the Pope's enemy (Brunswick, Christian).

Gratia Dei Sum Id Quod Sum   By the grace of God, I am what I am (Navarre).
Gratia Di Rex   By the grace of God, king (France, 8th century).
Gratitudo Concivibus Exemplum Posteritati   Gratitude to fellow Citizens, an example to posterity (Poland).
Gud och Folket   God and the people (Sweden).
Hac Nitimur Hanc Tuemur   With this we strive, this we shall defend (Batavian Republic).
Hac Sub Tutela   Under this protection (Eichstadt).
Haec Sunt Munera Minerae S Antony Eremitae   These are the rewards of the mine of St Antony the hermit (Hildesheim).
Hanc Deus Dedit   God has given this (Pontefract siege coins).
Hanc Tuemur Hac Nitimur   This we defend, by this we strive (Batavian Republic).
Has Nisi Periturus Mihi Adimat Nemo   Let no one remove these (Letters) from me under penalty of death (Commonwealth, edge inscription).
Henricus Rosas Regna Jacobus   Henry (united) the roses, James the kingdoms (England and Scotland, James VI and I).
Herculeo Vincta Nodo   Bound by a Herculean fetter (Savoy).
Herr Nach Deinem Willen   O Lord Thy will be done (Palatinate, Erbach).
Herre Gott Verleich Uns Gnade   Lord God grant us grace (Brunswick).
Hic Est Qui Multum Orat Pro Populo   Here is he who prays a lot for the people (Paderborn).
Hir Steid te Biscop   Here is represented the bishop (Gittelde).
His Ventis Vela Levantur   By these winds the sails are raised up (Hesse-Cassel).
Hispaniarum Infans   Infante of Spain and its dominions (Spain).
Hispaniarum et Ind Rex   King of Spain and the Indies.
Hispaniarum Rex   King of Spain (Spain).
Hoc Signo Victor Eris   With this sign you will be victor (Rome, Vetranio).
Honeste et Decenter   Honestly and decently (Nassau-Idstein).
Honi Soit Qui Mal y Pense   Evil to him who evil thinks (Britain, George III).
Honni Soit Qui Mal y Pense   (Hesse-Cassel).
Hospitalis et S Sepul Hierusal   Hospital and Holy Sepulchre of Jerusalem (Malta).
Hun Boh Gal Rex AA Lo Wi et in Fr Dux   King of Hungary, Bohemia and Galicia, Archduke of Austria, Dalmatia, Lodomeria, Wurzburg and Duke in Franconia (Austria).
Hung Boh Lomb et Ven Gal Lod III Rex Aa   King of Hungary, Bohemia, Lombardo-Venezia, Galicia, Lodomeria, Illyria, Archduke (Austria).
Ich Dien   I serve (Aberystwyth 2d, UK 2p).
Ich Getrawe Got in Aller Noth   I trust in God in all my needs (Hesse-Marburg).

Ich Habe Nur Ein Vaterland und das Heisst Deutschland   I have only one fatherland and that is called Germany (Germany).
Ielithes Penniae   Penny of Gittelde (Gittelde, 11th century).
Iesus Autem Transiens Per Medium Illorum Ibat   But Jesus, passing through the midst of them, went His way (England, Scotland, Anglo-Gallic).
Iesus Rex Noster et Deus Noster   Jesus is our king and our God (Florence).
Ihs Xs Rex Regnantium   Jesus Christ, King of Kings (Byzantine Empire).
Ihsus Xristus Basileu Baslie   Jesus Christ, King of Kings (Byzantine Empire).
Imago Sanch Regis Illustris Castelle Legionis e Toleto   The image of Sancho the illustrious king of Castile, Leon and Toledo.
In Casus Per Vigil Omnes   In all seasons through vigil (Wertheim).
In Deo Meo Transgrediar Murum   In my God I shall pass through walls (Teschen).
In Deo Spes Mea   In God is my hope (Gelderland).
In Domino Fiducia Nostra   In the Lord is our trust (Iever).
In Equitate Tua Vivificasti Me   In thy equity Thou hast vivified me (Gelderland).
In God We Trust   (USA).
In Hoc Signo Vinces   In this sign shalt thou conquer (Portugal).
In Honore Sci Mavrici Marti   In honour of the martyr St Maurice (St Maurice, 8th century).
In Manibus Domini sortes Meae   In the hands of the Lord are my fates (Mainz siege, 1688–9).
In Memor Vindicatae Libere ac Relig   In memory of the establishment of freedom and religion (Sweden).
In Memoriam Conjunctionis Utriusque Burgraviatus Norice   In memory of the union of both burgraviates in peace (Brandenburg-Ansbach).
In Memorian Connub Feliciaes Inter Princ Her Frider Carol et Dub Sax August Louis Frider Rodas D 28 Nov 1780 Celebrati   In memory of the most happy marriage between the hereditary prince Friedrich Karl and the Duchess of Saxony Augusta Louisa Frederika, celebrated on 28 Nov 1780 (Schwarzburg-Rudolstadt).
In Memorian Felicisssimi Matrimonii   In memory of the most happy marriage (Wied).
In Memoriam Pacis Teschinensis   Commemorating the Treaty of Teschen (Brandenburg-Ansbach).
In Nomine Domini Amen   In the name of the Lord amen (Zaltbommel).
In Omnem Terram Sonus Eorum   In to all the land their shall go sound (Chateau Renault, Papal States).
In Silencio et Spe Fortitudo Mea   In silence and hope is my fortitude (Brandenburg-Kustrin).
In Spe et Silentio Fortitudo Mea   In hope and silence is my fortitude (Vianen).

In Te Domine Confido   In you O Lord I place my trust (Hesse).

In Te Domine Speravi   In You, O Lord, I have hoped (Gurk).

In Terra Pax   Peace in the land (Papacy).

In Via Virtuti Nulla Via   There is no way for virtue on the way. (Veldenz).

Ind Imp, Indiae Imperator, Imperatrix   Emperor (Empress) of India (Britain).

India Tibi Cessit   India has yielded to thee (Portuguese India).

Infestus Infestis   Hostile to the troublesome (Savoy).

Inimicos Eius Induam Confusione   As for his enemies, I shall clothe them in shame (Sardinia, England, Edward VI).

Insignia Capituli Brixensis   The badge of the chapter of Brixen (Brixen).

Isti Sunt Patres Tui Verique Pastores   These are your fathers and true shepherds (Papacy).

Iudicium Melius Posteritatis Erit   Posterity's judgment will be better (Paderborn).

Iure et Tempore   By right and time (Groningen).

Iusques a Sa Plenitude   As far as your plenitude (France, Henri II).

Iuste et Constanter   Justly and constantly (Paderborn).

Iustirt   Adjusted (Hesse-Cassel).

Iustitia et Concordia   Justice and harmony (Zurich).

Iustitia et Mansuetudine   By justice and mildness (Bavaria, Cologne).

Iustitia Regnorum Fundamentum   Justice is the foundation of kingdoms (Austria).

Iustitia Thronum Firmat   Justice strengthens the throne (England, Charles I).

Iustus Non Derelinquitur   The just person is not deserted (Brandenburg-Calenberg).

Iustus Ut Palma Florebit   The just will flourish like the palm (Portugal).

L Mun Planco Rauracorum Illustratori Vetustissimo   To L Municius Plancus the most ancient and celebrated of the Rauraci (Basle).

Landgr in Cleggov Com in Sulz Dux Crum   Landgrave of Klettgau, count of Sulz, duke of Krumlau (Schwarzburg-Sonderhausen).

Latina Emeri Munita   Latin money of Merida (Suevi).

Lege et Fide   By law and faith (Austria).

Lex Tua Veritas   Thy law is the truth (Tuscany).

Liberta Eguaglianza   Freedom and equality (Venice)

Libertad en la Ley   Freedom within the law (Mexico).

Libertas Carior Auro   Freedom is dearer than gold (St Gall).

Libertas Vita Carior   Freedom is dearer than life (Kulenberg).

Libertas Xpo Firmata   Freedom strengthened by Christ (Genoa).

Liberte, Egalite, Fraternite   Liberty, equality, fraternity (France).

Lucerna Pedibus Meis Verbum Est   Thy word is a lamp unto mine feet (England, Edward VI).

Lumen ad Revelationem Gentium   Light to enlighten the nations (Papacy).

L'Union Fait la Force   The union makes strength (Belgium)

Macula Non Est in Te   There is no sin in Thee (Essen).

Magnus ab Integro Saeculorum Nascitur Ordo   The great order of the centuries is born anew (Bavaria).

Mandavit Dominus Palatie hanc Monetam Fiert   The lord of the Palatine ordained this coin to be made (Balath).

Manibus Ne Laedar Avaris   Lest I be injured by greedy hands (Sweden).

Mar Bran Sac Rom Imp Arcam et Elec Sup Dux Siles   Margrave of Brandenburg, archchamberlain of the Holy Roman Empire and elector, senior duke of Silesia (Prussia).

Maria Mater Domini Xpi   Mary mother of Christ the Lord (Teutonic Knights).

Maria Unxit Pedes Xpisti   Mary washes the feet of Christ (France, Rene d'Anjou).

Mater Castrorum   Mother of fortresses (Rome, Marcus Aurelius).

Matrimonio Conjuncti   Joined wedlock (Austria).

Me Coniunctio Servat Dum Scinditur Frangor   The relationship serves me while I am being torn to pieces (Lowenstein-Wertheim).

Mediolani Dux   Duke of Milan (Milan).

Mediolani et Man   Duke of Mantua and Milan (Milan).

Memor Ero Tui Iustina Virgo   I shall remember you, o maiden Justina (Venice).

Merces Laborum   Wages of work (Wurzburg).

Mirabilia Fecit   He wrought marvels (Viking coinage).

Misericordia Di Rex   King by the mercy of God (France, Louis II).

Mo Arg Ord Foe Belg D Gel & CZ   Silver coin of the order of the Belgian Federation, duchy of Guelder-land, county of Zutphen (Guelderland).

Moneta Abbatis   Coin of the abbey (German ecclesiastical coins, 13th–14th centuries).

Moneta Argentiae Ord Foed Belgii Holl   Silver coin of the federated union of Belgium and Holland (Batavian Republic).

Mo No Arg Con Foe Belg Pro Hol   New silver coin of the Belgian Federation, province of Holland (Holland).

Mo No Arg Pro Confoe Belg Trai Holl   New silver coin of the confederated Belgian provinces, Utrecht and Holland (Batavian Republic).

Mon Lib Reip Bremens   Coin of the free state of Bremen (Bremen).

Mon Nova Arg Duc Curl Ad Norma Tal Alb   New silver coin of the duchy of Courland, according to the standard of the Albert thaler (Courland).

Mon Nov Castri Imp   New coin of the Imperial free city of . . . (Friedberg).

Moneta Bipont   Coin of Zweibrucken (Pfalz-Birkenfeld-Zweibrucken).

Monet Capit Cathedr Fuld Sede Vacante   Coin of the cathedral chapter of Fulda, the see being vacant (Fulda).

Moneta in Obsidione Tornacensi Cusa   Coin struck during the siege of Tournai (Tournai, 1709).

Moneta Livosesthonica   Coin of Livonia (Estonia).

Moneta Nov Arg Regis Daniae   New silver coin of the king of Denmark (Denmark).

Moneta Nova Ad Norman Conventionis   New coin according to the Convention standard (Orsini-Rosenberg).

Moneta Nova Domini Imperatoris   New coin of the lord emperor (Brunswick, 13th century).

Moneta Nova Lubecensis   New coin of Lubeck.

Moneta Nova Reipublicae Halae Suevicae   New coin of the republic of Hall in Swabia.

Moneta Reipublicae Ratisbonensis   Coin of the republic of Regensburg.

Nach Alt Reichs Schrot und Korn   According to the old empire's grits and grain (Hesse).

Nach dem Conventions Fusse   According to the Convention's basis (German Conventionsthalers).

Nach dem Frankf Schlus   According to the Frankfurt standard (Solms).

Nach dem Schlus der V Staend   According to the standard of the union (Hesse).

Navigare Necesse Est   It is necessary to navigate (Germany).

Nec Aspera Terrent   Nor do difficulties terrify (Brunswick).

Nec Cito Nec Temere   Neither hastily nor rashlly (Cambrai).

Nec Numina Desunt   Nor is the divine will absent (Savoy).

Nec Temere Nec Timide   Neither rashly nor timidly (Danzig, Lippe).

Necessitas Legem Non Habet   Necessity has no law (Magdeburg).

Nemo Me Impune Lacessit   No one touches me with impunity (UK, Scottish pound edge inscription).

Nihil Restat Reliqui   No relic remains (Ypres).

Nil Ultra Aras   Nothing beyond the rocks (Franque-mont).

No Nobis Dne Sed Noi Tuo Da Gloriam   Not to us, o Lord but to Thy name be glory given (France, Francis I).

Nobilissimum Dom Ac Com in Lipp & St   Most noble lord and count in Lippe and Sternberg (Schaumburg-Lippe).

Nomen Domini Turris Fortissima   The name of the Lord is the strongest tower (Frankfurt).

Non Aes Sed Fides   Not bronze but trust (Malta).

Non Est Mortale Quod Opto   What I desire is not mortal. (Mecklenburg).

Non Mihi Sed Populo   Not to me but to the people (Bavaria).

Non Relinquam Vos Orphanos   I shall not leave you as orphans (Papacy).

Non Surrexit Major   None greater has arisen (Genoa, Malta).

Nullum Simulatum Diuturnum Tandem   Nothing that is feigned lasts long (Wittgenstein).

Nummorum Famulus   The servant of the coinage (England, tin halfpence and farthings).

Nunquam Retrorsum   Never backwards (Brunswick-Wolfenbuttel).

O Crux Ave Spes Unica   Hail, o Cross, our only hope (England half-angels, France, Rene d'Anjou).

O Maria Ora Pro Me   O Mary pray for me (Bavaria).

Ob Cives Servatos   On account of the rescued citizens (Rome, Augustus).

Oculi Domini Super Iustos   The eyes of the Lord look down on the just (Neuchatel).

Omnia Auxiliante Maria   Mary helping everything (Schwyz).

Omnia Cum Deo   Everything with God (Reuss-Greiz).

Omnia cum Deo et Nihil Sine Eo   Everthing with God and nothing without Him (Erbach).

Omnis Potestas a Deo Est   All power comes from God (Sweden).

Opp & Carn Dux Comm Rittb SCM Cons Int & Compi Mareschal   Duke of Troppau and Carniola, count of Rietberg, privy councillor of his sacred imperial majesty, field marshal (Liechtenstein).

Opp & Carn . . . Aur Velleris Eques   Duke of Troppau . . . knight of the Golden Fleece (Liechtenstein).

Opportune   Conveniently (Savoy).

Optimus Princeps   Best prince (Rome, Trajan).

Opulentia Salerno   Wealthy Salerno (Siculo-Norman kingdom).

Pace et Iustitia   With peace and justice (Spanish Netherlands).

Pacator Orbis   Pacifier of the world (Rome, Aurelian).

Palma Sub Pondere Crescit   The palm grows under its weight (Waldeck).

Pater Noster   Our Father (Flanders, 14th century).

Pater Patriae   Farther of his country (Rome, Caligula).

Patria Si Dreptul Meu   The country and my right (Roumania).

Patrimon Henr Frid Sorte Divisum   The heritage of Heinrich Friedrich divided by lot (Hohenlohe-Langenberg).

Patrimonia Beati Petri   The inheritance of the blessed Peter (Papacy).

Patrona Franconiae   Patron Franconia (Wurzburg).

Pax Aeterna   Eternal peace (Rome, Marcus Aurelius).

Pax et Abundantia   Peace and plenty (Burgundy, Gelderland).

Pax Missa Per Orbem   Peace sent throughout the world (England, Anne).

Pax Petrus   Peace Peter (Trier, 10th century).

Pax Praevalet Armis   May peace prevail by force of arms (Mainz).

Pax Quaeritur Bello   Peace is sought by war (Commonwealth, Cromwell).

Pecunia Totum Circumit Orbem   Money goes round the whole world (Brazil).

Per Aspera Ad Astra   Through difficulties to the stars (Mecklenburg-Schwerin).

Per Angusta ad Augusta   Through precarious times to the majestic (Solms-Roedelheim, a pun on the name of the ruler Johan August).

Per Crucem Tuam Salva Nos Christe Redemptor   By Thy cross save us, O Christ our Redeemer (England, angels).

Per Crucem Tuam Salva Nos Xpe Redemt   By Thy cross save us, O Christ our Redeemer (Portugal, 15th century).

Perdam Babillonis Nomen   May the name of Babylon perish (Naples).

Perennitati Iustissimi Regis   For the duration of the most just king (France, Louis XIII).

Perennitati Principis Galliae Restitutionis   For the duration of the restoration of the prince of the Gauls (France, Henri IV).

Perfer et Obdura Bruxella   Carry on and stick it out, Brussels (Brussels siege, 1579–80).

Perpetuus in Nemet Vivar   Hereditary count in Nemt-Ujvar (Batthanyi).

Pietate et Constantia   By piety and constancy (Fulda).

Pietate et Iustitia   By piety and justice (Denmark).

Plebei Urbanae Frumento Constituto   Free distribu-tion of grain to the urban working-class established (Rome, Nerva).

Pleidio Wyf Im Gwlad   True am I to my country (UK, Welsh pound edge inscription).

Plus Ultra   Beyond (the Pillars of Hercules) (Spanish America).

Point du Couronne sans Peine   Point of the crown without penalty (Coburg).

Pons Civit Castellana   The bridge of the town of Castellana (Papacy).

Populus et Senatus Bonon   The people and senate of Bologna (Bologna).

Post Mortem Patris Pro Filio   For the son after his father's death (Pontefract siege coins).

Post Tenebras Lux   After darkness light (Geneva).

Post Tenebras Spero Lucem   After darkness I hope for light (Geneva).

Posui Deum Adiutorem Meum   I have made God my helper (England, Ireland, 1351–1603).

Praesidium et Decus   Protection and ornament (Bologna).

Prima Sedes Galliarum   First see of the Gauls (Lyon).

Primitiae Fodin Kuttenb ab Aerari Iterum Susceptarum   First results dug from the Kuttenberg mines in a renewed undertaking (Austria).

Princps Iuventutis   Prince of youth (Roman Empire).

Pro Defensione Urbis et Patriae   For the defence of city and country (France, Louis XIV).

Pro Deo et Patria   For God and the fatherland (Fulda).

Pro Deo et Populo   For God and the people (Bavaria).

Pro Ecclesia et Pro Patria   For the church and the fatherland (Constance).

Pro Fausio PP Reitur VS   For happy returns of the princes of the Two Sicilies (Naples and Sicily).

Pro Lege et Grege   For law and the flock (Fulda).

Pro maximo Dei Gloria et Bono Publico   For the greatest glory of God and the good of the people (Wurttemberg).

Pro Patria   For the fatherland (Wurzburg).

Propitio Deo Secura Ago   With God's favour I lead a secure life. (Saxe-Lauenburg).

Protector Literis Literae Nummis Corona et Salus   A protection to the letters (on the face of the coin), the letters (on the edge) are a garland and a safeguard to the coinage (Commonwealth, Cromwell broad).

Protege Virgo Pisas   Protect Pisa, O Virgin (Pisa).

Provide et Constanter   Wisely and firmly (Wurttem-berg).

Providentia et Pactis   Through foresight and pacts (Brandenburg-Ansbach).

Providentia Optimi Principis   With the foresight of the best prince (Naples and Sicily).

Proxima Fisica Finis   Nearest to natural end (Orciano).

Proxima Soli   Nearest to the sun (Modena).

Pulcra Virtutis Imago   The beautiful image of virtue (Genoa).

Pupillum et Viduam Suscipiat   May he support the orphan and the widow (Savoy).

Quae Deus Conjunxit Nemo Separet   What God hath joined let no man put asunder (England, James I).

Quem Quadragesies et Semel Patriae Natum Esse Gratulamur   Whom we congratulate for the forty-first time for being born for the fatherland (Lippe-Detmold).

Qui Dat Pauperi Non Indigebit   Who gives to the poor will never be in need (Munster).

Quid Non Cogit Necessitas   To what does Necessity not drive. (Ypres).

Quin Matrimonii Lustrum Celebrant   They celebrate their silver wedding (Austria, 1879).

Quocunque Gesseris (Jeceris) Stabit   Whichever way you throw it it will stand (Isle of Man).

Quod Deus Vult Hoc Semper Fit   What God wishes always occurs. (Saxe-Weimar).

Reconduntur non Retonduntur   They are laid up in store, not thundered back (Savoy).

Recta Tueri   Defend the right (Austria).
Recte Constanter et Fortiter   Rightly, constantly and bravely (Bavaria).
Recte Faciendo Neminem Timeas   May you fear no one in doing right. (Solms-Laubach).
Rector Orbis   Ruler of the world (Rome, Didius Julianus).
Rectus et Immotus   Right and immovable (Hesse).
Redde Cuique Quod Suum Est   Render to each that which is his own (England, Henry VIII).
Redeunt antiqui Gaudia Moris   There return the joys of ancient custom (Regensburg).
Reg Pr Pol et Lith Saxon Dux   Royal prince of Poland and Lithuania and duke of Saxony (Trier).
Regia Boruss Societas Asiat Embdae   Royal Prussian Asiatic Society of Emden (Prussia).
Regier Mich Her Nach Deinen Wort   Govern me here according to Thy word (Palatinate).
Regnans Capitulum Ecclesiae Cathedralis Ratisbonensis Sede Vacante   Administering the chapter of the cathedral church at Regensburg, the see being vacant (Regensburg).
Regni Utr Sic et Hier   Of the kingdom of the Two Sicilies and of Jerusalem (Naples and Sicily).
Religio Protestantium Leges Angliae Libertas Parliamenti   The religion of the Protestants, the laws of England and the freedom of Parliament (England, Royalists, 1642).
Relinquo Vos Liberos ab Utroque Homine   I leave you as children of each man (San Marino).
Restauracao da Independencia   Restoration of inde-pendence (Portugal, 1990).
Restitutor Exercitus   Restorer of the army (Rome, Aurelian).
Restitutor Galliarum   Restorer of the Gauls (Rome, Gallienus).
Restitutor Generis Humani   Restorer of mankind (Rome, Valerian).
Restitutor et Libertatis   Restorer of freedom (Rome, Constantine).
Restitutor Orbis   Restorer of the world (Rome, Valerian).
Restitutor Orientis   Restorer of the east (Rome).
Restitutor Saeculi   Restorer of the century (Rome, Valerian).
Restitutor Urbis   Restorer of the city (Rome, Severus).
Rosa Americana Utile Dulci   The American rose, useful and sweet (American colonies).
Rosa Sine Spina   A rose without a thorn (England, Tudor coins).
Rutilans Rosa Sine Spina   A dazzling rose without a thorn (England, Tudor gold coins).
S Annae Fundgruben Ausb Tha in N Oe   Mining thaler of the St Anne mine in Lower Austria (Austria).
S Ap S Leg Nat Germ Primas   Legate of the Holy Apostolic See, born Primate of Germany (Salzburg).
S Carolus Magnus Fundator   Charlemagne founder (Munster).

S. Gertrudis Virgo Prudens Niviella   St Gertrude the wise virgin of Nivelles (Nivelles).
Sl Aul Reg Her & P Ge H Post Mag   General hereditary postmaster, supreme of the imperial court of the hereditary kingdom and provinces (Paar).
S. Ian Bapt F. Zachari   St John the Baptist, son of Zachary (Florence).
S. Kilianus Cum Sociis Francorum Apostoli   St Kilian and his companions, apostles to the Franks (Wurzburg).
S. Lambertus Patronus Leodiensis   St Lambert, patron of Liege (Liege).
Sac Nupt Celeb Berol   For the holy matrimony celebrated at Berlin (Brandenburg-Ansbach).
Sac Rom Imp   Holy Roman Empire (German states).
Sac Rom Imp Provisor Iterum   Administrator of the Holy Roman Empire for the second time (Saxony).
Salus Generis Humani   Safety of mankind (Rome, Vindex).
Salus Patriae   Safety of the fatherland (Italy).
Salus Populi   The safety of the people (Spain).
Salus Provinciarum   Safety of the provinces (Rome, Postumus).
Salus Publica Salus Mea   Public safety is my safety (Sweden).
Salus Reipublicae   The safety of the republic (Rome, Theodosius II).
Salus Reipublicae Suprema Lex   The safety of the republic is the supreme law (Poland).
Salvam Fac Rempublicam Tuam   Make your state safe (San Marino).
Sanctus Iohannes Innoce   St John the harmless (Gandersheim).
Sans Changer   Without changing (Isle of Man).
Sans Eclat   Without pomp (Bouchain siege, 1711).
Sapiente Diffidentia   Wise distrust (Teschen).
Scutum Fidei Proteget Eum / Eam   The shield of faith shall protect him / her (England, Edward VI and Elizabeth I).
Secundum Voluntatem Tuam Domine   Your favourable will o Lord (Hesse).
Securitati Publicae   For the public safety (Brandenburg-Ansbach).
Sede Vacante   The see being vacant (Papal states, Vatican and ecclesiastical coinage).
Sena Vetus Alpha et W Principum et Finis   Old Siena alpha and omega, the beginning and the end (Siena).
Senatus Populus QR   Senate and people of Rome (Rome, 1188).
Si Deus Nobiscum Quis Contra Nos   If God is with us who can oppose us (Hesse).
Si Deus Pro Nobis Quis Contra Nos   If God is for us who can oppose us (Roemhild).
Sieh Deine Seeligkeit Steht Fest Ins Vaters Liebe   Behold thy salvation stands surely in thy Father's love (Gotha).

Signis Receptis   When the standards had been recovered (Rome, Augustus).

Signum Crucis   The sign of the cross (Groningen).

Sincere et Constanter   Truthfully and steadfastly (Hesse-Darmstadt).

Sit Nomen Domini Benedictum   Blessed be the name of the Lord (Burgundy, Strasbourg).

St T X Adiuto Reg Iste Domba   Let it be to you, o Christ, the assistant to the king of Dombes (Dombes).

Sit Tibi Xpe Dat q'tu Regis Iste Ducat   May this duchy which Thou rulest be given to Thee, O Christ (Venice, ducat).

Sit Unio Haec Perennis   May this union last for ever (Hohenlohe-Langenberg).

Sola Bona Quae Honesta   The only good things are those which are honest (Brunswick).

Sola Facta Deum Sequor   Through deeds alone I strive to follow God (Milan).

Soli Deo Honor et Gloria   To God alone be honour and glory (Nassau).

Soli Reduci   To him, the only one restored (Naples and Sicily).

Solius Virtutis Flos Perpetuus   The flower of Virtue alone is perpetual (Strasbourg).

Spes Confisa Deo Nunquam Confusa Recedit   Hope entrusted in God never retreats in a disorderly fashion (Lippe).

Spes Nr Deus   God is our hope (Oudenarde siege, 1582).

Spes Rei Publicae   The hope of the republic (Rome, Valens).

Strena ex Argyrocopeo Vallis S Christoph   A New Year's gift from the silver-bearing valley of St Christopher (Wurttemberg, 1625).

Sub His Secura Spes Clupeus Omnibus in Te Sperantibus   Under these hope is safe, a shield for all who reside hope in Thee (Bavaria).

Sub Pondere   Under weight (Fulda).

Sub Protectione Caesarea   Under imperial protection (Soragna).

Sub Tuum Praesidium Confug   We flee to Thy protection (Salzburg).

Sub Umbra Alarum Tuarum   Under the shadow of Thy wings (Iever, Scotland, James V).

Subditorum Salus Felicitas Summa   The safety of the subjects is the highest happiness (Lubeck).

Suffict Mihi Gratia Tua Domine   Sufficient to me is Thy grace, o Lord (Ploen).

Supra Firmam Petram   Upon a firm rock (Papacy).

Susceptor Noster Deus   God is our defence (Tuscany).

Sydera Favent Industriae   The stars favour industry (Furstenberg).

Sylvarum Culturae Praemium   Prize for the culture of the forest (Brandenburg-Ansbach).

Tali Dicata Signo Mens Fluctuari Nequit   Consecrated by such a sign the mind cannot waver (England, Henry VIII George noble).

Tandem Bona Caus Triumphat   A good cause eventually triumphs (Dillenburg).

Tandem Fortuna Obstetrice   With good luck ultimately as the midwife (Wittgenstein).

Te Stante Virebo   With you at my side I shall be strong (Moravia).

Tene Mensuram et Respice Finem   Hold the measure and look to the end (Burgundy).

Tert Ducat Secular   Tercentenary of the duchy (Wurttemberg).

Thu Recht Schev Niemand   Go with right and fear no one (Saxe-Lauenburg).

Tibi Laus et Gloria   To Thee be praise and glory (Venice).

Timor Domini Fons Vitae   The fear of the Lord is a fountain of life (England, Edward VI shillings).

Tout Avec Dieu   Everything with God (Brunswick, 1626).

Traiectum ad Mosam   The crossing of the Maas (Maastricht).

Transvolat Nubila Virtus   Marriageable virtue soon flies past (Grueyeres).

Travail, Famille, Patrie   Work, family, country (Vichy France).

Triumphator Gent Barb   Victor over the barbarian people (Byzantine Empire, Arcadius).

Tueatur Unita Deus   May God guard these united (Kingdoms) (England, James I; Britain, 1847).

Turck Blegert Wien   Vienna besieged by the Turks (Vienna, 1531).

Tut Mar Gab Pr Vid de Lobk Nat Pr Sab Car et Aug Pr de Lobk   Regency of Maria Gabriela, widow of the prince of Lobkowitz, born princess of Savoy-Carignan, and August prince of Lobkowitz (Lobkowitz).

Tutela Italiae   The guardianship of Italy (Rome, Nerva).

Ubi Vult Spirat   He breathes where he will (Papacy).

Ubique Pax   Peace everywhere (Rome, Gallienus).

Union et Force   Union and strength (France).

Urbe Obsessa   The city under siege (Maastricht).

Urbem Virgo Tuam Serva   Protects thy city o virgin (Mary) (Strasbourg).

USC & RAM Cons Int Gen C Mar & Nob Praet H Turmae Capit   Privy councillor of both their holy imperial and royal apostolic majesties, general field marshal and captain of the noble praetorian Hungarian squadrons (Eszterhazy).

Veni Luumen Cordium   Come light of hearts (Vatican).

Veni Sancte Spiritus   Come Holy Ghost (Vatican).

Verbum Domini Manet in Aeternum   The word of the Lord abides forever (Hesse-Darmstadt, Veldenz).

Veritas Lex Tua   The truth is your law (Salzburg).

Veritas Temporis Filia   Truth is the daughter of time (England and Ireland, Mary Tudor).

Veritate et Labore   By truth and work (Wittgenstein).

Veritate et Iustitia   By truth and justice (German states).

Victoria Principum   The victory of princes (Ostrogoths).

Videant Pauperes et Laetentur   Let the poor see and rejoice (Tuscany).

Virgo Maria Protege Civitatem Savonae   Virgin Mary Protect the city of Savona (Savona).

Viribus Unitis   With united strength (Austria).

Virtute et Fidelitate   By virtue and faithfulness (Hesse-Cassel).

Virtute et Prudentia   With virtue and prudence (Auersperg).

Virtute Viam Dimetiar   I shall mark the way with valour (Waldeck).

Virtutis Gloria Merces   Glory is the reward of valour (Holstein-Gottorp).

Vis Unita Concordia Fratrum Fortior   United power is the stronger harmony of brothers (Mansfeld).

Visitavit Nos Oriens ex Alto   He has visited us arising on high (Luneburg).

Vivit Post Funera   He lives after death (Bremen).

Vota Optata Romae Fel   Vows taken for the luck of Rome (Rome, Maxentius).

Vox de Throno   A voice from the throne (Papacy).

Was Got Beschert Bleibet Unerwert   What God hath endowed leave undisturbed

Wider macht und List Mein Fels Gott Ist   Against might and trickery God is my rock (Hesse-Cassel).

Xpc Vincit Xpc Regnat   Christ conquers, Christ reigns (Scotland, Spain).

Xpc Vivet Xpc Regnat Xpc Impat   Christ lives, Christ reigns, Christ commands (Cambrai).

Xpe Resurescit   Christ lives again (Venice).

Xpistiana Religio   Christian religion (Carolingian Empire).

Xps Ihs Elegit me Regem Populo   Jesus Christ chose me as king to the people (Norway).

Zelator Fidei Usque ad Montem   An upholder of the faith through and through (Portugal).

Zum Besten des Vaterlands   To the best of the fatherland (Bamberg).

ABBREVIATIONS COMMONLY USED TO DENOTE METALLIC COMPOSITION

Cu	Copper
Cu/Steel	Copper plated Steel
Ag/Cu	Silver plated copper
Ae	Bronze
Cu-Ni	Cupro-Nickel
Ni-Ag	Nickel Silver (note-does not contain silver)
Brass/Cu-Ni	Brass outer, Cupro-Nickel inner
Ni-Brass	Nickel-Brass
Ag	Silver
Au/Ag	Gold plated silver
Au	Gold
Pt	Platinum

Care
of coins

There is no point in going to a great deal of trouble and expense in selecting the best coins you can afford, only to let them deteriorate in value by neglect and mishandling. Unless you give some thought to the proper care of your coins, your collection is unlikely to make a profit for you if and when you come to sell it. Housing your coins is the biggest problem of all, so it is important to give a lot of attention to this.

Storage

The ideal, but admittedly the most expensive, method is the coin cabinet, constructed of air-dried mahogany, walnut or rosewood *(never* oak, cedar or any highly resinous timber likely to cause chemical tarnish). These cabinets have banks of shallow drawers containing trays made of the same wood, with half-drilled holes of various sizes to accommodate the different denominations of coins. Such cabinets are handsome pieces of furniture but, being largely handmade, tend to be rather expensive. Occasionally good specimens can be picked up in secondhand furniture shops, or at the dispersal of house contents by auction, but the best bet is still to purchase a new cabinet, tailored to your own requirements. These collectors cabinets are hand-made using certified solid mahogany, as specified by leading museums, as mahogany does not contain any chemicals or resins that could result in the discolouration of the collection inside

For the coin connoisseur there are beautiful, hand-made mahogany cabinets such as this one from Peter Nichols Cabinet Makers.

the cabinet. The polish used on the outside of the cabinets is based on natural oils and hand applied then finished with bees wax. The trays are left as untreated mahogany so as not to introduce any harmful contaminants. The coin trays are available as single thickness or double thickness for holding thicker coins, capsules or artifacts.

Peter Nichols Cabinet Makers (telephone 0115 9224149, www.coincabinets.com) was established in 1967 and is now run by Geoff Skinner and Shirley Watts. Based in Nottingham, the family run business provides specialist and bespoke display and storage systems to suit every need from standard cabinets for the average collector all the way up to the massive 40-tray specials supplied to the British Museum. There are other makers of quality wooden coin cabinets such as **Rob Davis** of Ticknall, Derbyshire, who also provide a first-class bespoke product as well as a standard off-the-shelf range. All of these manufacturers use materials from sustainable sources and their products are exquisite examples of the cabinet maker's craft.

An excellent storage option is provided by a number of firms who manufacture coin trays in durable, felt-lined, man-made materials with shallow compartments to suit the various sizes of coins. Most of these trays interlock so that they build up into a cabinet of the desired size, and there are also versions designed as carrying cases, which are ideal for transporting coins.

The popular and extensive **Lighthouse** range is available from **Curtis Coin Care**. To view the current range of stock, go to www.curtiscoincare. com. This range includes a wide variety of cases and albums for the general collector in basic or deluxe styles as required, as well as printed albums

49

for the specialist. Their cases, including the popular aluminium range, are manufactured to the highest standards, lined with blue plush which displays any coin to its best advantage. The red-lined single trays come in deep or standard size and make an ideal cabinet when stacked together or housed in their attractive aluminium case, which is available separately. The trays themselves come with a variety of compartments for every size of coin. Their complete range can be viewed on-line.

The extensive **Lindner** range is supplied in the UK by Prinz Publications of 3A Hayle Industrial Park, Hayle, Cornwall TR27 5JR (telephone 01736 751914, www.prinz.co.uk). Well-known for their wide range of philatelic and numismatic accessories, but these include a full array of coin boxes, capsules, carrying cases and trays. The basic Lindner coin box is, in fact, a shallow tray available in a standard version or a smoked glass version. These trays have a crystal clear frame, red felt inserts and holes for various diameters of coins and medals. A novel feature of these trays is the rounded insert which facilitates the removal of coins from their spaces with the minimum of handling. These boxes are designed in such a manner that they interlock and can be built up into banks of trays, each fitted with a draw-handle and sliding in and out easily. Various types of chemically inert plastic capsules and envelopes have been designed for use in combination with plain shallow trays, without holes drilled. Lindner also manufacture a range of luxury cases lined in velvet and Atlas silk with padded covers and gold embossing on the spines, producing a most tasteful and elegant appearance.

Safe Albums of 16 Falcon Business Park, 38 Ivanhoe Road, Finchampstead, Berkshire RG40 4QQ (telephone 0118 932 8976, www.safealbums.co.uk) are the UK agents for the German

Stapel-Element, a drawer-stacking system with clear plasticiser-free trays that fit into standard bookshelves. The sliding coin compartments, lined with blue velvet, can be angled for display to best advantage. Stackable drawers can be built up to any height desired. A wide range of drawer sizes is available, with compartments suitable for the smallest coins right up to four-compartment trays designed for very large artefacts such as card-cases or cigarette cases. The Mobel-Element cabinet is a superb specialised cabinet constructed of the finest timber with a steel frame and steel grip bars which can be securely locked.

There are also various other storage systems, such as the simple cardboard or plastic box which is made specifically to hold coins stored in see-through envelopes of chemically-inert plastic of various sizes, or white acid-free envelopes, usually 50mm square.

An alternative to these is the card coin holder which has a window made of inert cellophane-type see-through material. The card is folded over with the coin inside and is then stapled or stuck together with its own self-adhesive lining. The cards are a standard 50mm square with windows of various sizes from 15 to 39mm and fit neatly into the storage box or album page.

Coin Albums

When coin collecting became a popular hobby in the 1960s, several firms marketed ranges of coin albums. They had clear plastic sleeves divided into tiny compartments of various sizes and had the merit of being cheap and taking up little room on a bookshelf.

They had several drawbacks, however, not the least being the tendency of the pages to sag with the weight of the coins, or even, in extreme cases, to pull away from the pegs or rings holding them on to the spine. They required very careful handling as

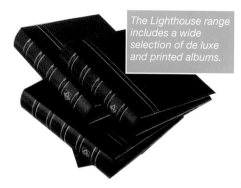

the coins could easily fall out of the top row as the pages were turned. The more expensive albums had little flaps that folded over the top of the coin to overcome this problem.

Arguably the worst aspect of these albums was the use of polyvinyl chloride (PVC) in the construction of the sleeves. Collectors soon discovered to their horror that this reacted chemically with their coins, especially those made of silver and many fine collections were ruined as a result.

Fortunately the lesson has been learned and the coin albums now on the market are quite safe. Lighthouse and Lindner offer a wide range of albums designed to house coins, medals or banknotes. The old problem about sagging pages is overcome by the use of a multi-ring binding welded to a very stout spine, while the sleeves contain neither Styrol nor PVC and will not affect any metals at all. In addition to pages with pockets of uniform size, the Karat range of albums operates on a slide principle which enables the user to insert vertical strips of different sizes on the same page, so that the coins of one country or series, or perhaps a thematic display of coins from different countries, can be displayed side by side.

Safe Albums offer a wide range of albums in the Coinholder System and Coin-Combi ranges. These, too, offer the choice of fixed pages with uniform-sized pockets, or interchangeable sliding inserts for different sizes side by side.

The "slab"

In the United States in the past few decades one of the preferred methods for keeping coins in pristine condition is the use of "slabs"—these tough plastic rectangles cannot be easily broken into, meaning that the coin inside remains in exactly the same condition as when it was placed in there. This has led to the rise of professional grading and encapsulation companies who not only "slab" your coin but also grade it and guarantee that grade.

This allows coins to be bought and sold with both vendor and purchaser knowing exactly what the grade is, thus taking out the subjectivity of dealer or collector—an issue that can mean a huge difference in the value of the coin. Slabbing in this way is essentially a tool to help a coin maintain a grade and thus more easily guarantee its value, however, many collectors prefer it as a method of protecting their coins as it allows them to be stored or transported easily with no fear of damage.

The biggest companies in the United States for the encapsulation of coins are **PCGS** (Professional Coin Grading Service) and **NGC** (Numismatic Gauaranty Corporation). They have been in business for some years and in America the "slabbed" coin is a common sight. It is less common in the UK, with many collectors still unsure about the benefits of the "slab", but undoubtedly with the US companies opening offices and grading centres throughout the world more and more collectors are using the service and the "slab" is becoming accepted everywhere. However, anyone wishing to photograph a coin undoubtedly has a problem, as can be seen in many auction catalogues offering such items. The tell-tale grips that hold the coin obscure part of the edge of the coin.

51

Cleaning
coins

This is like matrimony—it should not be embarked on lightly. Indeed, the advice given by the magazine *Punch* in regard to marriage is equally sound in this case—don't do it! It is far better to have a dirty coin than an irretrievably damaged one. Every dealer has horror stories of handling coins that previous owners have cleaned, to their detriment. Probably the worst example was a display of coins found by a metal detectorist who "improved" his finds by abrading them in the kind of rotary drum used by lapidarists to polish gemstones. If you really must remove the dirt and grease from coins, it is advisable to practise on coins of little value.

Warm water containing a mild household detergent or washing-up liquid will work wonders in removing surface dirt and grease from most coins, but silver is best washed in a weak solution of ammonia and warm water—one part ammonia to ten parts water. Gold coins can be cleaned with diluted citric acid, such as lemon juice. Copper or bronze coins present more of a problem, but patches of verdigris can usually be removed by careful washing in a 20 per cent solution of sodium sesquicarbonate. Wartime coins made of tin, zinc, iron or steel can be cleaned in a 5 per cent solution

of caustic soda containing some aluminium or zinc foil or filings, but they must be rinsed afterwards in clean water and carefully dried. Cotton buds are ideal for gently prising dirt out of coin legends and crevices in the designs. Soft brushes (with animal bristles—*never* nylon or other artificial bristles) designed for cleaning silver are most suitable for gently cleaning coins.

Coins recovered from the soil or the sea bed present special problems, due to chemical reaction between the metals and the salts in the earth or sea water. In such cases, the best advice is to take them to the nearest museum and let the professional experts decide on what can or should be done.

There are a number of proprietary coin-cleaning kits and materials on the market suitable for gold, silver, copper and other metals but all of these should be used with caution and always read the instructions that come with them. When using any type of chemical cleaner rubber gloves should be worn and care taken to avoid breathing fumes or getting splashes of liquid in your eyes or on your skin. Obviously, the whole business of cleaning is a matter that should not be entered into without the utmost care and forethought.

POLISHING: A WARNING

If cleaning should only be approached with the greatest trepidation, polishing is definitely OUT! Beginners sometimes fall into the appalling error of thinking that a smart rub with metal polish might improve the appearance of their coins. Short of actually punching a hole through it, there can hardly be a more destructive act. Polishing a coin may improve its superficial appearance for a few days, but such abrasive action will destroy the patina and reduce the fineness of the high points of the surface.

Even if a coin is only polished once, it will never be quite the same again, and an expert can tell this a mile off.

泰星コイン株式会社
TAISEI COINS CORPORATION

✕

THE ROYAL MINT®
THE ORIGINAL MAKER

Tokyo International Coin Convention

An exciting collaboration for the
Tokyo International Coin Convention (TICC)

Friday 29th April 2022
Royal Park Hotel

royalmint.com/auction

CELEBRATE | COLLECT | INVEST | SECURE | DISCOVER

Come and watch the UK's coins being made

The Royal Mint
Experience

THE EXPERIENCE OFFERS A GRAND DAY OUT FOR ALL THE FAMILY WHERE THE WORK AND ISSUES OF ONE OF THE OLDEST MINTS IN THE WORLD CAN BE EXPLORED AT IT'S PURPOSE-BUILT VISITORS' CENTRE IN LLANTRISANT.

Walk through Interactive Exhibition

Come and play, have fun and learn all about the history of coins

PENNY LANE

Strike your own coin

I struck this 50p coin

On the Royal Mint Experience tour you will learn more about the manufacturing process that goes into creating the coins in your pocket. As part of your tour, you will have the opportunity to strike your very own coin (the design of the coin alters, depending on what theme the Royal Mint are celebrating at the time of your visit). The opportunity to strike your own coin can be obtained for £6.90 and is limited to one coin per person. "Strike your own coin" can be purchased when pre-booking your visit and admission tickets.

WANT TO VISIT? see overleaf

And finally

The Royal Mint Experience is open but due to Covid-19 new guidelines are in operation and places must be booked prior to visiting. For full, up-to-date guidelines on how to book and the procedures in place for visiting please log onto www.royalmint.com/the-royal-mint-experience.

The Royal Mint Experience is a great day out for all the family—with a few special measures to make it a safe and relaxed experience for everyone.

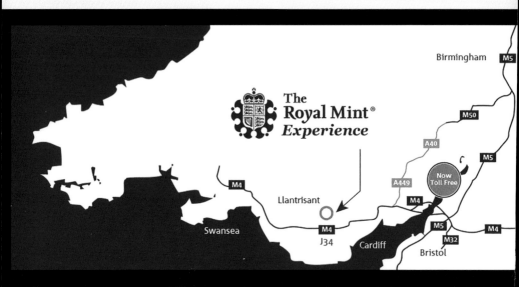

The Royal Mint is located 4 miles from Junction 34 of the M4. Drive past the main entrance to the Mint. The visitors' car park for The Royal Mint Experience is on the left opposite the Three Saints Hotel. The guided tour lasts 45 minutes, but allow a good couple of hours to explore the exhibits in the final exhibition hall. There are plenty of interactive exhibits to keep the children amused. There is a large cafeteria for visitors and a well-stocked shop selling souvenirs as well as coins.

Book your visit

Admission Prices:	Door £	Online £
Adult (16+)	13.50	13.00
Child (5-15 years)	11.00	10.00
Child under 5 years	Free	Free
Carer/Blue Peter Badge	Free	Free
Senior Citizens/Student	12.00	11.00
Family (1 adult/3 children		
Or 2 adults/2 children)	38.50	35.00
Exhibition only		£5.00

Tickets must be booked in advance by going online or by telephoning 0333 241 2223. Entry prices change throughout the year (the prices shown here are a guide) so when booking on-line select the date of your visit and see pricing for that day. Ticket prices include the guided factory experience and entry into the exhibition. An exhibition only option is available at £5.

The Royal Mint Experience is open 7 days a week from 9.45–17.00.

To plan your visit to the Royal Mint Experience go online at www.royalmint.com

Images courtesy of the Royal Mint. Information correct at time of going to press.

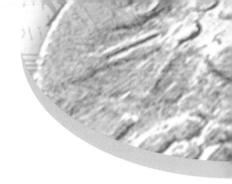

Celtic
coinage of Britain

Pritanic coins were the first coins made in Britain. They were issued for a century and a half before the Roman invasion, and possibly a little later in some areas. They were minted by the rulers of thirteen tribal groups or administrative authorities situated on the southeast of a line from the Humber to the Severn. In this short article Pritanic specialist CHRIS RUDD introduces this increasingly popular series.

Most folk call them British Celtic or Celtic coins of Britain. But I'll begin by letting you into a little known secret: most folk may be wrong. You see, there is no ancient textual evidence—none whatsoever—that anyone in iron age Britain called themselves a Celt. Neither is there a hint—not a whisper—that anyone else in the ancient world ever referred to the Brits as Celts. The Greeks didn't, the Gauls didn't, the Romans didn't. The correct name for iron age Britons is Pritani—well formed people or people of the forms. How do we know? Because a sailor from Marseilles said so.

The first coins made in Britain were made like this

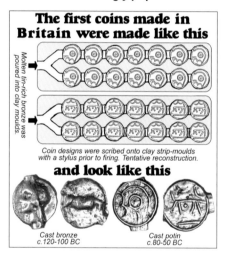

Molten tin-rich bronze was poured into clay moulds.

Coin designs were scribed onto clay strip-moulds with a stylus prior to firing. Tentative reconstruction.

and look like this

Cast bronze
c.120-100 BC

Cast potin
c.80-50 BC

Many Gaulish coins were imported to Britain, like this silver stater of the Coriosolites (ABC 70), typical of many in the huge Jersey hoard found in June 2012, containing an estimated 50,000 coins.

Around 330 BC an explorer, Pytheas of Marseilles, sailed to Britain in search of tin. His visit indicates early trade links with southern Gaul and that the Britons were called Pritani. Marseilles inspired Britain's first homemade coinage: potin coins cast in clay strip-moulds, with Apollo on one side and a bull on the other, plus MA for Massalia (Marseilles). Made in Kent c. 120–100 BC, these cast potins circulated alongside gold coins imported from Gaul. During the Gallic Wars (58–51 BC) many other Gaulish coins—gold, silver and bronze—came to Britain, some brought by refugees, others by British mercenaries, others by trade.

The most famous Gallic migrant was Commios "friend", a former ally of Caesar, who became king of the Regini and Atrebates in the south of England c. 50–25 BC. Commios was the first British ruler to place his name on coins. His three sons—Tincomarus (great in peace), Eppillus (little horse) and Verica (the high one), made the Commian dynasty one of the wealthiest and most powerful in Britain. Most of their coins adopted Roman imagery and archaeology indicates that they imported Roman luxury goods, especially Italian wine. Many coins of Verica show grapes, vine leaves and wine cups.

The main rivals of the Regini and Atrebates were the Catuvellauni of Hertfordshire. Their first known ruler was probably Cassivellaunos "bronze commander", leader of the British coalition against Caesar in 54 BC. Many of Britain's earliest gold coins were probably struck to fund resistance to Caesar and then to pay tribute to him. Cassivellaunos may have organised this war money. Addedomaros "great in chariots" (c. 45–25 BC) was the first ruler north of the Thames to inscribe his coins, perhaps copying Commios.

Thirteen possible tribal groups which were producing coins by c.50-40 BC (Cantiaci much earlier). By c.30 BC the Belgae, East Wiltshire and Berkshire group had apparently stopped minting independently.

Gold stater of Commios (ABC 1022) the first British king to place his name on coins. There are two hidden faces on the obverse.

Verica silver minim with wine cup (ABC 1331) and Verica gold stater with vine leaf (ABC 1193)—evidence of Britain's thirst for fine Italian wine and Roman silverware.

Catuvellaunian expansion continued under Tasciovanos "killer of badgers" whose coins became increasingly Roman in style. His son Cunobelinus "hound of Belenus"—Shakespeare's *Cymbeline*) was the most potent tribal king in Atlantic Europe. Suetonius called him "king of the Britons". During his thirty-year reign (c. AD 8–41) Cunobelinus may have minted well over a million gold staters, most of them displaying a corn ear and CAMV— short for *Camulodunon* (Colchester). When his brother Epaticcus "leader of horsemen" and his son Caratacus "the beloved"—both clad as Hercules on their silver coins—crossed the Thames and attacked the Atrebates, Verica fled to Claudius who invaded Britain in AD 43. The minting of tribal coins ceased shortly afterwards.

Other tribes that issued coins included the Cantiaci of Kent, the Belgae of Hampshire, the Durotriges of Dorset, the Dobunni of the West Midlands, the Trinovantes of Essex, the Iceni of East Anglia and the Corieltavi of Lincolnshire. However, only a minority of people in the British Isles used coins regularly—the moneyed minority in southeast England. Cornwall, Devon, Wales, northern England, Scotland and Ireland remained coinless. Which is why ancient British coins are relatively rare. For example, whereas Greek coins were minted for about 600 years, Roman for about 800 years and Gaulish for about 250 years, ancient British coins were produced for little more than 150 years, and often in much smaller runs.

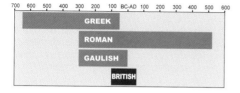

Ancient British coins weren't minted for as long as Greek, Roman or Gaulish coins were. That's one of the reasons they are so scarce.

This century and a half of Pritanic (not Celtic) coin production generated a remarkable flowering of insular creativity and insular technology, unmatched by any other northern European nation of the period. Though initially influenced by Gallic minting techniques and Gallic iconography, ancient British coinage rapidly developed its own denominational systems, its own gold standards and its own highly distinctive coin designs—often inspired by Roman prototypes, but invariably modified to suit local needs. Between c. 110 BC and c. AD 45 around a thousand different coin types were minted in Britain. Many if not most of these thousand types displayed what might loosely be described as "religious" imagery. Not surprisingly, really, when one recalls that Caesar says that Druidism originated in Britain. Moreover, Tasciovanos struck coins in no fewer than five different denominations, whereas most Gaulish rulers issued no more than two or three.

The history of late iron age Britain, particularly the century prior to the Claudian conquest, has largely been rewritten with the help of ancient British coins. Most of the recent advances in our knowledge of this period have been due to amateur metal detecting. As a direct result of coin finds made by metal detectorists since the 1970s four new coin-issuing groups and maybe ten new rulers, previously unknown or unrecognised, have been identified. Not bad for barely forty years of unfunded, unofficial fieldwork.

Unlike Gaul, most of the British Isles was virtually coinless throughout the late iron age (and later). Coin production was confined to south-east Britain. That's why, overall, ancient British coins are much rarer than Gaulish coins.

What is it about ancient British coins that is making them increasingly popular with collectors all over the world? Having been involved with them for many years (I excavated my first in 1952) I'll tell you why they appeal to me.

I love the *primal antiquity* of Pritanic coins. They were the first coins made in Britain over two thousand years ago. When you see the flamboyant freedom of their designs you realise that they are the most boisterously British coins ever minted, unlike the unsmiling Roman, Anglo-Saxon and Norman series that marched soberly in their dancing footsteps.

I love the *anarchic regality* of Pritanic coins. Like the rumbustious tribal kings that issued them, their personality is wild, strong and highly irregular. These coins were made by the first British rulers known by name to us—unruly, quarrelsome, beer-swilling, tribal warlords such as Cassivellaunos who fought Julius Caesar in 54 BC and Caratacus, the British resistance leader who opposed Claudius in AD 43.

I love the *imaginative imagery* you find on Pritanic coins: all the different gods and goddesses, armed warriors, chariot wheels, hidden faces, decapitated heads, suns, moons, stars, thunderbolts, floral motifs, magic signs and phallic symbols. Plus an amazing menagerie of wild animals, birds and mythical beasts.

I love the *myths, mystery and mysticism* behind Pritanic coins. Look closely at this late iron age money of Albion and you'll catch glimpses

Ancient British denominations

There was no national currency in pre-Roman Britain and little consistency from region to region. Different tribes issued different mixtures of low, medium and high value coins. Here are the most common denominations used by the ancient Brits. The names are ours, not theirs. We've no idea what they called their coins, shown here actual size.

GOLD STATERS
Can also be silver, billon or bronze

Norfolk Wolf, ABC 1393

GOLD QUARTER STATERS
Can also be silver or billon

Irstead Smiler, ABC 1480

SILVER UNITS

Norfolk God, ABC 1567

SILVER HALF UNITS

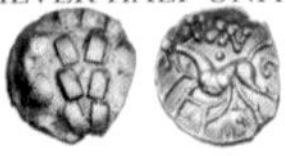

Aunt Cost Half, ABC 1953

SILVER MINIMS

Verica Sphinx, ABC 1340

BRONZE UNITS

Cunobelinus Centaur, ABC 2957

BRONZE HALF UNITS

Tasciovanos Goat, ABC 2709

CAST POTIN UNITS

Nipples, ABC 174

of long-lost legends and ancient pagan rituals such as head-hunting, bull sacrificing and shape-shifting. You'll marvel at the plethora of occult signs and arcane symbols and you may even feel the secret power of the Druids.

I love the *palpitating unpredictability* of Pritanic coins. Even after sixty years of heart-racing intimacy they are constantly and delightfully surprising me. Attributions, names and dates are always being revised. Not long ago the Coritani were renamed Corieltavi and Tincommios was rechristened Tincomarus. Almost every month exciting new types and new variants keep leaping out of the ground, thanks to metal detectorists. For example, on September 4, 2010 the late

Bronze units of Cunobelinus, son of Tasciovanos,showing a bull being sacrificed (ABC 2972) and a man—perhaps a Druid priest?—carrying a severed human head (ABC 2987).

Danny Baldock discovered the first recorded coin of Anarevitos, a Kentish ruler previously unknown to history.

I love the *uncommon scarcity* of Pritanic coins. Ask any metdet how many so-called Celtic coins he or she has found and you'll immediately realise that they are rarer than Roman coins—at least a thousand times rarer on average—for the reasons stated above.

Finally I love the *galloping good value* of this horsey money (some Pritanic horses have three tails, some breathe fire, others have a human torso). Their greater rarity doesn't mean they are

Silver unit of freedom-fighter Caratacus (ABC 1376) who defied the Roman invaders for eight years until he was betrayed by Cartimandua, queen of the Brigantes.

costlier than other ancient coins. In fact, they are often cheaper because demand determines price and because there are far fewer collectors of ancient British coins than there are, say, of Greek or Roman coins. For example, a very fine British gold stater typically costs less than half the price—sometimes even a third the price of a Roman aureus or English gold noble of comparable quality and rarity. But the disparity is gradually diminishing as more and more canny collectors are appreciating the untamed beauty and undervalued scarcity of Pritanic coins.

Coin Yearbook provides a great guide to current prices of commoner Pritanic types, but because new types keep turning up and because big hoards are sometimes found (causing values to fluctuate temporarily) you'd be well advised to also keep an eye on dealers' catalogues and prices realised at auction. If you're buying in Britain, buy from people who are members of the BNTA (British Numismatic Trade Association). If you're buying overseas, check that your suppliers

A unique gold stater of Anarevitos, a previously unknown ruler of the Cantiaci, probably a son of Eppillus, king of Calleva (Silchester). Sold by Elizabeth Cottam of Chris Rudd for £21,000, a record price for an ancient British coin (Coin News, December 2010).

belong to the IAPN (International Association of Professional Numismatists). And, if you're a beginner, beware of dodgy traders on the internet, or you could end up with a fistful of fakes and no refund.

I'd also counsel you to spend a day at the British Museum. Its collection of almost 7,000 ancient British coins is the most comprehensive, publicly accessible collection of its kind in the world. As their curator, Ian Leins, says: "They're public coins . . . your coins, and they're here for you to see. So come and see them. We'll be pleased to show them to you". Access to the collection is free for everyone. But you'll need to make an appointment before you go, and take some photo ID and proof of address. Email: coins@thebritishmuseum.ac.uk or telephone: 020 7323 8607.

Before you buy coins—any coins of any period—it always pays to read about them first. As an old adman I'm not shy about blowing my own trumpet. The best little introduction to Pritanic coins is *Britain's First Coins* by Chris Rudd (expected late 2012) and the most comprehensive catalogue of the series is *Ancient British Coins* also by Chris Rudd (2010), known in the trade as ABC. If you have even half the fun I've had with ancient British coins (and am still having)—I can promise you that you'll be a very happy person indeed. Never bored, and never with a complete collection.

Chris Rudd started studying ancient British coins sixty years ago and has written a hundred articles about them, many published by COIN NEWS. "I've still got a lot to learn" he says.

Collecting
ancient coins

Ancient coins differ from most other series which are collected in Britain in that every piece has spent the major part of the last two thousand years in the ground. As JOHN CUMMINGS, dealer in ancient coins and antiquities explains here, the effect that burial has had on the surface of the coin determines more than anything else the value of a particular piece. With more modern coins, the only things which affect price are rarity and grade. There may be a premium for coins exhibiting particularly fine tone, or with outstanding pedigrees, but an 1887 crown in "extremely fine" condition has virtually the same value as every other piece with the same grade and of the same date. With ancient coins the story is very different.

A large number of different criteria affect the price of an ancient coin. Factors affecting prices can be broken down into several categories:

Condition
The most important factor by far in determining price. Ancient coins were struck by hand and can exhibit striking faults. Value suffers if the coin is struck with the designs off-centre, is weakly struck, or if the flan is irregular in shape. Many of the Celtic tribes issued coins of varying fineness and those made from low quality gold or silver are worth less than similar specimens where the metal quality is better. Conversely, coins on exceptional flans, particularly well struck, or with fine patinas command a premium.

Many ancient coins have suffered during their stay in the ground. It must be borne in mind that the prices given in the price guide are for uncorroded, undamaged examples. A Roman denarius should be graded using the same criteria as those used for grading modern coins. The surfaces must be good, and the coin intact. The fact that the coin is 2,000 years old is irrelevant as far as grading is concerned. Coins which are not perfectly preserved are certainly not without value, however, the value for a given grade decreases with the degree of fault.

Rarity
As with all other series, rare coins usually command higher prices than common ones. A unique variety of a small fourth century Roman bronze coin, even in perfect condition, can be worth much less than a more worn and common piece from an earlier part of the empire. In the Celtic series, there is an almost infinite variety of minor types and a unique variety of an uninscribed type will rarely outbid an inscribed issue of a known king.

Historical and local significance
Types which have historical or local interest can command a price far above their scarcity value. Denarii of the emperor Tiberius are believed to have been referred to in the New Testament and command a far higher price than a less interesting piece of similar rarity. Similarly, pieces which have British reverse types such as the "VICT BRIT" reverse of the third century AD are more expensive than their scarcity would indicate. The 12 Caesars remain ever popular especially in the American market and this affects prices throughout the world. In the Celtic series, coins of Cunobelin or Boudicca are far more popular than pieces which have no historical interest but which may be far scarcer.

Reverse types

All Roman emperors who survived for a reasonable time issued coins with many different reverse types. The most common of these usually show various Roman gods. When a coin has an unusual reverse it always enhances the value. Particularly popular are architectural scenes, animals, references to Judaism, and legionary types.

Artistic merit

The Roman coinage is blessed with a large number of bust varieties and these can have a startling effect on price. For example, a common coin with the bust facing left instead of right can be worth several times the price of a normal specimen. Like many of the emperors, the coinage of Hadrian has a large number of bust varieties, some of which are extremely artistic and these, too, can command a premium.

The coinage used in Britain from the time of the invasion in AD 43 was the same as that introduced throughout the Empire by the emperor Augustus around 20 BC. The simple divisions of 2 asses equal to one dupondius, 2 dupondii equal to 1 sestertius, 4 sestertii equal to one denarius and 25 denarii equal to one aureus continued in use until the reformation of the coinage by Caracalla in AD 214.

Aureus (gold)

Denarius (silver)

Dupondius (copper)

Sestertius (bronze)

As (copper)

Hammered
coinage

The hammered currency of medieval Britain is among some of the most interesting coinage in the world. The turbulent history of these islands is reflected in the fascinating changes in size, design, fineness and workmanship, culminating in the many strange examples that emanated from the strife of the Civil War.

The Norman Conquest of England in 1066 and succeeding years had far-reaching effects on all aspects of life. Surprisingly, however, it had little impact on the coinage. William the Conqueror was anxious to emphasise the continuity of his reign, so far as the ordinary people were concerned, and therefore he retained the fabric, size and general design pattern of the silver penny. Almost 70 mints were in operation during this reign, but by the middle of the 12th century the number was reduced to 55 and under Henry II (1154–89) it fell to 30 and latterly to only eleven. By the early 14th century the production of coins had been centralised on London and Canterbury, together with the ecclesiastical mints at York and Canterbury. The silver penny was the principal denomination throughout the Norman period, pieces cut along the lines of the cross on the reverse continuing to serve as halfpence and farthings.

Eight types of penny were struck under William I and five under his son William Rufus, both profiles (left and right) and facing portraits being used in both reigns allied to crosses of various types. Fifteen types were minted under Henry I (1100–35), portraiture having now degenerated to crude caricature, the lines engraved on the coinage dies being built up by means of various punches. Halfpence modelled on the same pattern were also struck, but very sparingly and are very rare.

On Henry's death the succession was contested by his daughter Matilda and his nephew Stephen of Blois. Civil war broke out in 1138 and continued till 1153. Stephen controlled London and its mint, but Matilda and her supporters occupied the West Country and struck their own coins at Bristol. Several of the powerful barons struck their own coins, and there were distinct regional variants of the regal coinage. Of particular interest are the coins

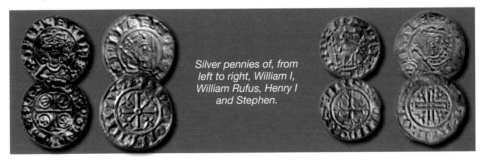

Silver pennies of, from left to right, William I, William Rufus, Henry I and Stephen.

struck from obverse dies with Stephen's portrait erased or defaced, believed to date from 1148 when the usurper was under papal interdict.

Peace was restored in 1153 when it was agreed that Matilda's son Henry should succeed Stephen. On the latter's death the following year, Henry II ascended the throne. Coins of Stephen's last type continued to be minted till 1158, but Henry then took the opportunity to overhaul the coinage which had become irregular and sub-standard during the civil war. The new "Cross Crosslet" coins, usually known as the Tealby coinage (from the hoard of over 5,000 pennies found at Tealby, Lincolnshire in 1807), were produced at 30 mints, but when the recoinage was completed this number was reduced to a dozen. The design of Henry's coins remained virtually the same throughout more than two decades, apart from minor variants. Then, in 1180, a new type, known as the Short Cross coinage, was introduced. This was a vast improvement over the poorly struck Cross Crosslet coins and continued without alteration, not only to the end of the reign of Henry II in 1189, but throughout the reigns of his sons Richard (1189–99) and John (1199–1216) and the first half of the reign of his grandson Henry III (1216–46). Throughout that 66 year period, however, there were minor variations in portraits and lettering which enable numismatists to attribute the HENRICUS coins to specific reigns and periods.

"Tealby" type penny (top), and
"Short Cross" penny of Henry II.

The style and workmanship of the Short Cross coinage deteriorated in the reign of Henry III. By the 1220s coin production was confined to the regal mints at London and Canterbury, the sole exception being the ecclesiastical mint maintained by the Abbot of Bury St Edmunds.

Halfpence and farthings were briefly struck in 1221–30, though halfpence are now extremely rare and so far only a solitary farthing has been discovered.

By the middle of this reign the coinage was in a deplorable state, being poorly struck, badly worn and often ruthlessly clipped. In 1247 Henry ordered a new coinage and in this the arms of the cross on the reverse were extended to the rim as a safeguard against clipping. This established a pattern of facing portrait and long cross on obverse and reverse respectively that was to continue till the beginning of the 16th century. Several provincial mints were re-activated to assist with the recoinage but they were all closed down again by 1250, only the regal mints at London and Canterbury and the ecclesiastical mints at Durham and Bury St Edmunds remaining active.

"Long Cross" pennies of Henry III (top),
and Edward I.

In 1257 Henry tentatively introduced a gold penny (worth 20 silver pence and twice the weight of a silver penny). The coin was undervalued and soon disappeared from circulation.

The Long Cross coinage of Henry III continued under Edward I till 1279 when the king introduced a new coinage in his own name. The penny continued the style of its predecessors, though much better designed and executed; but new denominations were now added. Henceforward halfpence and farthings became a regular issue and, at the same time, a fourpenny coin known as the groat (from French *gros*) was briefly introduced (minting ceased in 1282 and was not revived till 1351). Due to the centralisation of coin production the name of the moneyer was now generally dropped, although it lingered on a few years at Bury St Edmunds. The provincial mints were again revived in 1299–1302 to recoin the lightweight foreign imitations of pennies which had flooded in from the Continent.

The coinage of Edward II (1307–27) differed only in minor respects from that of his father, and a similar pattern prevailed in the first years of Edward III. In 1335 halfpence and farthings below the sterling fineness were struck. More

Pre-Treaty Noble of Edward III which contained reference to France in the legend.

importantly, further attempts were made to introduce gold coins. In 1344 the florin or double leopard of six shillings was introduced, along with its half and quarter. This coinage was not successful and was soon replaced by a heavier series based on the noble of 80 pence (6s. 8d.), half a mark or one third of a pound. The noble originally weighed 138.5 grains but it was successively reduced to 120 grains, at which weight it continued from 1351. During this reign the protracted conflict with France known as the Hundred Years' War erupted. Edward III, through his mother, claimed the French throne and inscribed this title on his coins. By the

Noble of Edward IV, issued before he was forced to abandon the throne of England.

Treaty of Bretigny (1361) Edward temporarily gave up his claim and the reference to France was dropped from the coins, but when war was renewed in 1369 the title was resumed, and remained on many English coins until the end of the 18th century. The silver coinage followed the pattern of the previous reign, but in 1351 the groat was re-introduced and with it came the twopence or half-groat. Another innovation was the use of mintmarks at the beginning of the inscriptions. Seven types of cross and one crown were employed from 1334 onwards and their sequence enables numismatists to date coins fairly accurately.

The full range of gold (noble, half-noble and quarter-noble) and silver (groat, half-groat, penny, halfpenny and farthing) continued under Richard II (1377–99). Little attempt was made to alter the facing portrait on the silver coins,

Noble of Henry IV which was reduced in weight due to the shortage of gold.

by now little more than a stylised caricature anyway.

Under Henry IV (1399–1413) the pattern of previous reigns prevailed, but in 1412 the weights of the coinage were reduced due to a shortage of bullion. The noble was reduced to 108 grains and its sub-divisions lightened proportionately. The penny was reduced by 3 grains, and its multiples and sub-divisions correspondingly reduced. One interesting change was the reduction of the fleur de lis of France from four to three in the heraldic shield on the reverse of the noble; this change corresponded with the alteration in the arms used in France itself. The Calais mint, opened by Edward III in 1363, was closed in 1411. There was no change in the designs used for the coins of Henry V (1413–22) but greater use was now made of mintmarks to distinguish the various periods of production. Coins were by now produced mainly at London, although the episcopal mints at Durham and York were permitted to strike pennies.

The supply of gold dwindled early in the reign of Henry VI and few nobles were struck after 1426. The Calais mint was re-opened in 1424 and struck a large amount of gold before closing finally in 1440. A regal mint briefly operated at York in 1423–24. Mintmarks were now much more widely used and tended to correspond more closely to the annual trials of the Pyx. The series of civil upheavals known as the Wars of the Roses erupted in this period.

In 1461 Henry VI was deposed by the Yorkist Earl of March after he defeated the Lancastrians at Mortimer's Cross. The Yorkists advanced on London where the victor was crowned Edward IV. At first he continued the gold series of his predecessor, issuing nobles and quarter-nobles, but in 1464 the weight of the penny was reduced

Groat of Richard III (1483–85).

to 12 grains and the value of the noble was raised to 100 pence (8s. 4d.). The ryal or rose-noble of 120 grains, together with its half and quarter, was introduced in 1465 and tariffed at ten shillings or half a pound. The need for a coin worth a third of a pound, however, led to the issue of the angel of 80 grains, worth 6s. 8d., but this was initially unsucessful and very few examples are now extant. The angel derived its name from the figure of the Archangel Michael on the obverse; a cross surmounting a shield appeared on the reverse.

In 1470 Edward was forced to flee to Holland and Henry VI was briefly restored. During this brief period (to April 1471) the ryal was discontinued but a substantial issue of angels and half-angels was made both at London and Bristol. Silver coins were struck at York as well as London and Bristol, the issues of the provincial mints being identified by the initials B or E (Eboracum, Latin for York). Edward

defeated the Lancastrians at Tewkesbury and deposed the luckless Henry once more. In his second reign Edward struck only angels and half-angels as well as silver from the groat to halfpenny. In addition to the three existing mints, silver coins were struck at Canterbury, Durham and the archiepiscopal mint at York. Mintmarks were now much more frequent and varied. Coins with a mark of a halved sun and rose are usually assigned to the reign of Edward IV, but they were probably also struck in the nominal reign of Edward V, the twelve-year-old prince held in the Tower of London under the protection of his uncle Richard, Duke of Gloucester. Coins with this mark on the reverse had an obverse mark of a boar's head, Richard's personal emblem. The brief reign of Richard III (1483–5) came to an end with his defeat at Bosworth and the relatively scarce coins of this period followed the pattern of the previous reigns, distinguished by the sequence of mint marks and the inscription RICAD or RICARD.

In the early years of Henry VII's reign the coinage likewise followed the previous patterns, but in 1489 the first of several radical changes was effected, with the introduction of the gold sovereign of 20 shillings showing a full-length portrait of the monarch seated on an elaborate throne. For reverse, this coin depicted a Tudor rose surmounted by a heraldic shield. A similar reverse appeared on the ryal of 10 shillings, but the angel and angelet retained previous motifs. The silver coins at first adhered to the medieval pattern, with the stylised facing portrait and long cross, but at the beginning of the 16th century a large silver coin, the testoon or shilling of 12 pence, was introduced and adopted a realistic profile of the king, allied to a reverse showing a cross surmounted by the royal arms. The same design was also used for the later issue of groat and half groat.

First coinage Angel of Henry VIII which retained the traditional 23.5 carat fineness.

This established a pattern which was to continue till the reign of Charles I. In the reign of Henry VIII, however, the coinage was subject to considerable debasement. This led to the eventual introduction of 22 carat (.916 fine) gold for the crown while the traditional 23 1/2 carat gold was retained for the angel and ryal. This dual system continued until the angel was discontinued at the outset of the Civil War in 1642; latterly it had been associated with the ceremony of touching for "King's Evil" or scrofula, a ritual used by the early Stuart monarchs to bolster their belief in the divine right of kings.

Under the Tudors and Stuarts the range and complexity of the gold coinage increased, but it was not until the reign of Edward VI that the silver series was expanded. In 1551 he introduced the silver crown of five shillings, the first English coin to bear a clear date on the obverse. Under Mary dates were extended to the shilling and sixpence.

The mixture of dated and undated coins continued under Elizabeth I, a reign remarkable for the range of denominations—nine gold and eight silver. The latter included the sixpence, threepence, threehalfpence and threefarthings,

The magnificent second coinage Rose-Ryal of James I (1603–25).

distinguished by the rose which appeared behind the Queen's head.

The coinage of James I was even more complex, reflecting the king's attempts to unite his dominions. The first issue bore the legend ANG: SCO (England and Scotland), but from 1604 this was altered to MAG: BRIT (Great Britain). This period witnessed new denominations, such as the rose-ryal and spur-ryal, the unite, the Britain crown and the thistle crown, and finally the laurel of 20 shillings and its sub-divisions.

In the reign of Elizabeth experiments began with milled coinage under Eloi Mestrell. These continued sporadically in the 17th century, culminating in the beautiful coins struck by Nicholas Briot (1631–39). A branch mint was established at Aberystwyth in 1637 to refine and coin silver from the Welsh mines. Relations between King and Parliament deteriorated in the reign of Charles I and led to the Civil War (1642). Parliament controlled London but continued to strike coins in the King's name. The Royalists struck coins, both in pre-war and new types, at Shrewsbury, Oxford, Bristol, Worcester, Exeter, Chester, Hereford and other Royalist strongholds, while curious siege pieces were pressed into service at Newark, Pontefract and Scarborough.

After the execution of Charles I in 1649 the Commonwealth was proclaimed and gold and silver coins were now inscribed in English instead of Latin. Patterns portraying Cromwell and a crowned shield restored Latin in 1656. Plans for milled coinage were already being considered before the Restoration of the monarchy in 1660. Hammered coinage appeared initially, resuming the style of coins under Charles I, but in 1662 the hand-hammering of coins was abandoned in favour of coins struck on the mill and screw press. The hammered coins of 1660–62 were undated and bore a crown mintmark, the last vestiges of medievalism in British coinage.

Coin
grading

Condition is the secret to the value of virtually anything, whether it be antiques, jewellery, horses or second-hand cars—and coins are certainly no exception. When collecting coins it is vital to understand the recognised standard British system of grading, i.e. accurately assessing a coin's condition or state of wear. Grading is an art which can only be learned by experience and so often it remains one person's opinion against another's, therefore it is important for the beginner or inexperienced collector to seek assistance from a reputable dealer or knowledgeable numismatist when making major purchases.

The standard grades as used in the Price Guide are as follows:

UNC	**Uncirculated** A coin that has never been in circulation, although it may show signs of contact with other coins during the minting process.
EF	**Extremely Fine** A coin in this grade may appear uncirculated to the naked eye but on closer examination will show signs of minor friction on the highest surface.
VF	**Very Fine** A coin that has had very little use, but shows signs of wear on the high surfaces.
F	**Fine** A coin that has been in circulation and shows general signs of wear, but with all legends and date clearly visible.

Other grades used in the normal grading system are:

BU	**Brilliant Uncirculated** As the name implies, a coin retaining its mint lustre.
Fair	A coin extensively worn but still quite recognisable and legends readable.
Poor	A coin very worn and only just recognisable.

Other abbreviations used in the Price Guide are:

Obv	**Obverse**
Rev	**Reverse**

Other abbreviations, mintmarks, etc. can be identified under the appropriate section of this Yearbook.

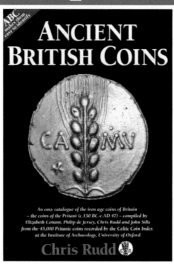

A SIMPLIFIED PRICE GUIDE TO
ANCIENT COINS USED IN BRITAIN

PART I
Ancient British

The prices given in this section are those that you would expect to pay from a reputable dealer and not the prices at which you could expect to sell coins.

The list below, which has been generously provided by Celtic coin dealer Elizabeth Cottam of Chris Rudd, contains most of the commonly available types: a fully comprehensive guide is beyond the scope of this book. Prices are for coins with good surfaces which are not weakly struck or struck from worn dies. Examples which are struck from worn or damaged dies can be worth considerably less. Particularly attractive examples of bronze Celtic coins command a very high premium. Where a price is given for an issue of which there are many varieties, the price is for the most common type. The illustrations are representative examples only and are not shown actual size.

UNINSCRIBED COINAGE

	F	VF	EF
GOLD STATERS			
Broad Flan	£700	£1775	£5750
Gallic War Uniface	£225	£400	£1000
Remic types	£250	£400	£800
Wonersh types	£250	£450	£2200
Chute	£200	£300	£750
Cheriton	£250	£450	£975
Iceni (various types)	£300	£500	£1350
Norfolk "wolf" type			
fine gold	£250	£475	£1500
brassy gold	£175	£300	£695
very debased	£120	£200	£475
Corieltauvi (various types)	£200	£400	£1000
Dobunni	£250	£500	£1500
Whaddon Chase types	£275	£475	£1300

Cheriton Smiler gold stater

	F	VF	EF
GOLD QUARTER STATERS			
Gallic Imported Types	£80	£175	£395
Kent types	£200	£300	£550
Southern types	£125	£200	£375
Iceni	£150	£250	£500
Corieltauvi	£125	£200	£500
Dobunni	£175	£300	£700
East Wiltshire	£300	£500	£1,000
Durotriges	£120	£225	£500
North Thames types	£220	£300	£550

Cranborne Chase silver stater

	F	VF	EF
SILVER COINAGE			
Armorican billion staters	£125	£250	£500
Kent Types	£150	£300	£675
South Thames types	£120	£175	£375

	F	VF	EF
Iceni ('crescent' types)	£35	£85	£185
Iceni ('Norfolk God' types)	£60	£100	£295
Corieltavi	£50	£110	£225
Dobunni	£85	£125	£295
Durotriges full stater			
fine silver	£80	£175	£350
base silver	£30	£55	£175
Durotriges quarter silver	£25	£35	£95

(Note—most examples are for base coins as better quality items are appreciably higher)

| North Thames types | £110 | £195 | £375 |

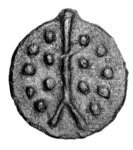

POTIN COINAGE

Hengistbury cast bronze

| Kent | £25 | £50 | £150 |

BRONZE COINAGE

Durotriges debased stater	£30	£75	£125
Durotriges cast bronze	£65	£125	£225
North Thames types. Various issues from:	£45	£110	£450

INSCRIBED CELTIC COINAGE

CANTIACI

Dubnovellaunos			
stater	£320	£600	£1500
silver unit	£135	£220	£575
bronze unit	£65	£175	£395
Vosenos			
stater	£1100	£2500	£5200
quarter stater	£295	£585	£1250
silver unit	£140	£300	£675
Sam			
stater (unique)	—	—	—
silver unit	£185	£350	£800
bronze unit	£110	£275	£550
Eppillus			
stater	£1100	£2000	£4575
quarter stater	£150	£265	£575
silver unit	£75	£145	£395
bronze unit	£65	£125	£495
bronze minim	£85	£175	£300
Anarevitos			
stater (unique)			—
Touto			
silver unit	£200	£450	£875
Verica			
silver unit	£200	£350	£695
bronze unit	£165	£300	£635
Sego			
stater	£525	£1000	£3250
quarter stater	£220	£500	£1275
silver unit	£150	£350	£675
silver minim	£80	£200	£425
bronze unit	£80	£165	£495
Amminus			
silver unit	£175	£325	£695
silver minim	£110	£215	£475
bronze unit	£85	£175	£535
Solidus			
silver unit	£535	£1100	£2350
silver minim	£535	£1100	£1575

Vosenos gold quarter stater

Verica gold stater

Sego Warrior gold stater

	F	VF	EF
REGINI & ATREBATES			
Commios			
stater	£595	£1575	£3000
silver unit	£80	£160	£345
silver minim	£65	£125	£295
Tincomarus			
stater	£465	£895	£2250
quarter stater	£150	£250	£475
silver unit	£75	£145	£300
silver minim	£65	£125	£200
Eppillus			
stater	£1000	£2500	£6000
quarter stater	£160	£245	£575
silver unit	£80	£165	£345
Verica			
stater	£275	£575	£1300
quarter stater	£155	£275	£435
silver unit	£55	£160	£275
silver minim	£50	£120	£245
Epaticcus			
stater	£1000	£2000	£4250
silver unit	£50	£100	£275
silver minim	£55	£120	£295
Caratacus			
stater (unique)			—
silver unit	£175	£320	£475
silver minim	£110	£220	£345
VECTUARII			
Crab			
silver unit	£165	£325	£695
silver minim	£120	£295	£435
ICENI			
Cani Duro			
silver unit	£115	£275	£575
Antedios			
stater	£425	£1000	£2500
silver unit	£40	£65	£195
silver half unit	£45	£100	£150
Ecen			
stater	£425	£1200	£2575
silver unit	£45	£85	£195
silver half unit	£50	£100	£175
Saenu			
silver unit	£65	£125	£300
Aesu			
silver unit	£65	£125	£300
Ale Scavo			
silver unit	£275	£500	£1275
Esuprasto			
silver unit	£425	£1000	£2000
CORIELTAUVI			
Cat			
silver unit	£400	£1100	£2200
silver half unit (unique)			—
VEPOCUNAVOS			
stater	£450	£1000	£2600
silver unit	£85	£150	£350
Esuprasu			
stater	£350	£675	£1375
silver unit	£175	£325	£575

Tincomarus gold stater

Norfolk Wolf gold stater

Ale Scavo silver unit

Vep CorF gold stater

	F	VF	EF
Aunt Cost			
stater	£275	£575	£1395
silver unit	£90	£195	£350
silver half unit	£90	£175	£325
Lat Ison			
stater	£1000	£2100	£4300
silver unit	£175	£425	£1175
silver half unit	£160	£300	£575
Dumnocoveros Tigirseno			
stater	£850	£2000	£3750
silver unit	£100	£195	£595
silver half unit	£100	£210	£625
Volisios Dumnocoveros			
stater	£350	£675	£1350
silver unit	£100	£185	£500
silver half unit	£100	£195	£495
Volisios Cartivellaunos			
stater	£1000	£2000	£4100
silver half unit	£300	£675	£1200
Volisios Dumnovellaunos			
stater	£320	£765	£1675
silver half unit	£150	£325	£675

Bodvoc Bold gold stater

DOBUNNI

	F	VF	EF
Bodvoc			
stater	£1000	£2250	£3250
quarter stater (unique)			—
silver unit	£200	£500	£895
Corio			
stater	£275	£560	£1550
quarter stater	£200	£350	£675
Comux			
stater	£285	£560	£1550
Catti			
stater	£285	£565	£1600
Inamn			
plated stater (unique)			—
silver unit (unique)			—
Anted			
stater	£350	£700	£1600
silver unit	£60	£125	£325
Eisu			
stater	£450	£750	£1600
silver unit	£75	£125	£335

Catti gold stater

TRINOVANTES

	F	VF	EF
Dubnovellaunos			
stater	£275	£475	£1350
quarter stater	£175	£350	£650
silver unit	£75	£150	£375
silver half unit	£100	£200	£475
bronze unit	£65	£140	£295

Dumno Tigir Seno gold stater

CATUVELLAUNI

	F	VF	EF
Addedomaros			
stater	£300	£450	£1300
quarter stater	£300	£550	£675
silver unit	£100	£200	£420
silver half unit	£100	£200	£475
bronze unit	£35	£95	£295

Addedomaros gold stater

	F	VF	EF
Tasciovanos			
stater	£250	£475	£2000
quarter stater	£165	£250	£500
silver unit	£85	£175	£395
bronze unit	£60	£135	£275
bronze half unit	£60	£135	£295
Andoco			
stater	£350	£575	£2000
quarter stater	£200	£420	£775
silver unit	£155	£400	£775
bronze unit	£85	£225	£365
Dias			
silver unit	£100	£200	£425
bronze unit	£50	£150	£425
Rues			
bronze unit	£50	£150	£425
Cat			
plated silver unit (unique)			—

Tasciovanos gold stater

CATUVELLAUNI & TRINOVANTES

	F	VF	EF
Cunobelinus			
stater	£250	£450	£2000
quarter stater	£150	£250	£495
silver unit	£85	£175	£495
bronze unit	£60	£145	£395
bronze half	£60	£145	£285
Trocc			
bronze unit	£50	£150	£550
Agr			
quarter stater	£125	£275	£895
silver unit	£100	£200	£525
bronze unit (only two)	(too rare to price)		
Dubn			
quarter stater (only three)	£1000	£3000	£7500

Cunobelinus gold stater

*Illustrations by courtesy of
Chris Rudd*

A SIMPLIFIED PRICE GUIDE TO
ANCIENT COINS USED IN BRITAIN

PART II

Roman Britain

The list below has been generously provided by coin dealer Mike Vosper. These prices are for the most common types unless otherwise noted. In most cases, especially with large bronze coins, the price for coins in extremely fine condition will be <u>much</u> higher than the price for the same coin in very fine condition as early bronze coins are seldom found in hoards and perfect, undamaged examples are rarely available.

The illustrations provided are a representative guide to assist with identification only.

REPUBLICAN COINAGE 280–41 BC

	FROM F	VF	EF
Republican			
Quadrigatus (or Didrachm) (Janus/Quadriga)	£150	£475	£2500
Victoriatus (Jupiter/Victory)	£45	£150	£600
+Denarius (Roma/Biga)	£25	£80	£550
+Denarius (other types)	£35	£100	£650
Denarius (Gallic warrior—L.Hostilius Saserna)	£400	£1150	£8000
Quinarius	£35	£85	£575
Cast Aes Grave, As	£400	£1250	—
Struck As/Semis/Litra	£60	£250	—
Struck Triens/Quadrands	£50	£175	—

IMPERATORIAL COINAGE 49–27 BC

Gnaeus Pompey Junior

Pompey the Great			
Denarius (Hd. of Pompilius/Prow)	£150	£550	£3250
Scipio			
Denarius (Jupiter/Elephant	£100	£350	£2000
Cato Uticensis			
Quinarius (Bacchus/Victory)	£45	£150	£1000
Gnaeus Pompey Junior			
Denarius (Roma/Hispania)	£110	£350	£2000
Sextus Pompey			
Denarius (his bust)	£275	£800	£5500
Denarius (other types)	£190	£600	£3850
As	£160	£600	—
Julius Caesar			
Aureus	£1250	£3500	£28,500
Denarius ("elephant" type)	£175	£500	£3000
Denarius (Ceasar portrait)	£475	£1500	£8750
Denarius (heads of godesses)	£150	£400	£2250

Julius Caesar

	FROM F	VF	EF
Brutus			
Aureus..	—	*Extremely rare*	
Denarius (his portrait/EID MAR)........	£25,000	*Extremely rare*	
Denarius (others)...............................	£150	£475	£3000
Cassius			
Denarius...	£125	£450	£2250
Ahenobarbus			
Denarius	£450	£1300	£7250
Mark Antony			
Denarius ("Galley" type)	£75	£280	£2250
Denarius (with portrait)	£100	£395	£2500
Denarius (other types)	£70	£300	£2300
Mark Antony & Lepidus			
AR quinarius	£75	£195	£1250
Mark Antony & Octavian			
AR denarius	£175	£650	£3250
Quninarius	£50	£175	£1100
Mark Antony & Lucius Antony			
AR denarius	£350	£950	£5000
Mark Antony & Octavia			
AR Cistophorus	£250	£685	£3750
Cleopatra VII & Mark Antony			
AR denarius	£1500	£4750	—
Fulvia			
AR quinarius	£125	£375	£2500
Octavian (later known as Augustus)			
Aureus	£1200	£4200	£30,000
Denarius	£150	£450	£2750
Quinarius (ASIA RECEPTA)	£50	£150	£1000
Octavian & Divos Julius Caesar			
AE sestertius	£275	£1575	—

Brutus

Mark Antony & Octavian

IMPERIAL COINAGE—Julio-Claudian Dynasty 27BC–AD 69

Augustus			
Aureus (Caius & Lucius Caesar)	£1500	£3850	£25,000
AR Cistophorus.................................	£200	£685	£3700
Denarius (Caius & Lucius Caesar)	£65	£185	£1250
Denarius (other types)	£65	£225	£1500
AR quinarius	£50	£175	£1000
Sestertius (large SC)	£135	£425	£2250
Dupondius or as (large SC)...............	£55	£170	£950
Quadrans	£20	£80	£350
Divus Augustus (struck under Tiberius)			
As	£70	£300	£1500
Augustus & Agrippa			
Dupondius (Crocodile rev)	£70	£250	£1500
Livia			
Sestertius or Dupondius	£200	£650	£5000
Gaius Caesar			
AR denarius	£375	£1500	£4700
Tiberius			
Aureus (Tribute penny)	£1000	£3600	£12,000
Denarius (Tribute penny)	£85	£245	£1200
Sestertius	£200	£650	£3850
Dupondius	£175	£585	£3250
As	£75	£250	£1250
Drusus			
Sestertius..	£275	£950	£5500
As (Large S C).................................	£75	£225	£1500
Caligula			
Denarius (rev. portrait)	£450	£1400	£7800
Sestertius (PIETAS & Temple)	£300	£2000	£10,000
As (VESTA)......................................	£100	£300	£1700

Mark Antony & Octavia

Augustus

Tiberius

Caligula

	FROM F	VF	EF
Agrippa (struck under Caligula)			
As......	£75	£200	£1450
Germanicus (struck under Caligula or Claudius)			
As (Large S C)	£75	£225	£1450
Agrippina Senior (struck under Caligula)			
Sestertius (Carpentum)......	£500	£1500	£10,500
Nero & Drusus (struck under Caligula)			
Dupondius (On horseback, galloping)	£200	£750	£5000
Claudius			
Aureus ("DE BRITANN" type)	£2000	£5500	£42,500
Denarius as above	£400	£1785	£11,000
Didrachm as above	£375	£1250	£7100
Denarius other types	£375	£1000	£7100
Sestertius	£175	£525	£4750
Dupondius	£60	£250	£1800
As	£45	£150	£1350
Quadrans	£20	£55	£325
Irregular British Sestertius......	£30	£100	£580
Irregular British As	£20	£80	£450
Claudius & Agrippina Junior or Nero			
Denarius	£450	£1450	£8500
Nero Cludius Drusus (struck under Claudius)			
Sestertius	£250	£895	£7150
Antonia (struck under Claudius)			
Dupondius	£150	£475	£3400
Britannicus			
Sestertius	£6500	£31,000	−
Nero			
Aureus	£1250	£3750	£20,500
Denarius	£100	£275	£2200
Sestertius	£135	£575	£4200
Sestertius (Port of Ostia)	£1800	£6500	£69,500
Dupondius	£85	£285	£1850
As	£50	£175	£1550
Semis......	£45	£150	£800
Quadrans	£25	£85	£450
Civil War			
Denarius	£200	£580	£3600
Galba			
Denarius	£125	£380	£2500
Sestertius	£170	£520	£3575
Dupondius	£180	£525	£3200
As	£110	£370	£2300
Otho			
Denarius	£200	£625	£4250
Vitellius			
Denarius	£100	£290	£2100
Sestertius	£1000	£2950	£22,000
Dupondius	£350	£1000	£6575
As	£195	£525	£3675

IMPERIAL COINAGE—Flavian Dynasty AD 69–96

Vespasian			
Aureus	£1000	£3500	£18,000
Denarius	£30	£100	£600
Denarius (IVDAEA)	£85	£250	£1550
Sestertius	£195	£625	£5250
Dupondius	£70	£220	£1800
As	£55	£210	£1600
Titus			
Aureus	£1000	£3500	£18,250
Denarius as Caesar	£40	£120	£950
Denarius as Augustus	£45	£140	£1050

Agrippina Senior

Claudius

Nero

Galba

Titus

	FROM F	VF	EF
Titus *continued*			
Sestertius	£150	£500	£4500
Dupondius	£50	£195	£1550
As	£45	£170	£1550
As (IVDAEA CAPTA)	£175	£550	£3750
Julia Titi			
Denarious	£200	£650	£3750
Domitian			
Aureus	£1250	£2850	£16,500
Cistophorus	£125	£450	£2750
Denarius as Caesar	£35	£95	£600
Denarius as Augustus	£25	£85	£485
Sestertius	£100	£350	£2150
Dupondius	£35	£150	£1600
As	£35	£115	£950
Ae Semis	£30	£95	£650
Ae Quadrands...................................	£25	£80	£400
Domitia			
Cistophorus	£250	£750	£4250

Domitian

IMPERIAL COINAGE—Adoptive Emperors AD 96–138

	FROM F	VF	EF
Nerva			
Aureus	£2250	£6750	£40,000
Denarius	£50	£150	£1000
Sestertius	£140	£550	£3850
Sestertius (Palm-tree)	£500	£1750	£2000
Dupondius	£70	£250	£1500
As	£65	£175	£1350
Trajan			
Aureus	£1100	£2850	£16,500
Denarius	£25	£65	£550
Denarius (Trajan's Column)	£40	£175	£1000
Sestertius	£65	£250	£1800
Sestertius (Dacian rev.)	£75	£275	£2000
Dupondius or as	£35	£100	£750
Ae Quadrands	£25	£70	£475
Plotina, Marciana or Matidia			
Denarius	£450	£1350	£5000
Hadrian			
Aureus	£1100	£3250	£18,500
Cistophourus	£125	£550	£2250
Denarius (Provinces)	£45	£150	£1000
Denarius other types	£25	£85	£650
Sestertius	£75	£250	£1750
Sestertius (RETITVTORI province types)	£150	£475	£3250
Sestertius (Britannia std)	£3000	£10,500	—
Dupondius or As	£35	£150	£850
As (Britannia std)	£225	£725	—
Ae Semiis or Quadrands	£30	£125	£600
Eygpt, Alexandrian Billon Tetradrachm	£30	£150	£850
Sabina			
Denarius	£30	£100	£650
Sestertius	£115	£385	£2700
As or Dupondius	£70	£225	£1500
Aelius Ceasar			
Denarius	£70	£225	£1500
Sestertius	£150	£550	£3200
As or Dupondius	£65	£125	£1650

Nerva

Trajan

Hadrian

	FROM F	VF	EF

IMPERIAL COINAGE—The Antonines AD 138–193

Antoninus Pius

Aureus	£825	£2200	£12,500
Denarius	£20	£55	£325
Sestertius Britannia seated	£500	£1500	£15,000
Sestertius other types	£40	£160	£1100
As - Britannia rev.	£65	£200	£1750
Dupondius or As other types	£25	£100	£500

Antoninus Pius

Antoninus Pius & Marcus Aurelius

Denarius (bust each side)	£30	£125	£675

Diva Faustina Senior

Denarius	£20	£50	£380
Sestertius..	£45	£155	£950
As or Dupondius	£25	£85	£550

Marcus Aurelius

Aureus...	£950	£2850	£16,500
Denarius as Caesar	£25	£70	£475
Denarius as Augustus	£20	£55	£385
Sestertius	£45	£185	£1500
As or Dupondius	£25	£80	£550

Marcus Aurelius

Faustina Junior

Denarius	£20	£70	£470
Sestertius	£40	£185	£1600
As or Dupondius	£30	£90	£650

Lucius Verus

Denarius	£25	£95	£550
Sestertius	£45	£200	£1600
As or Dupondius	£30	£105	£680

Lucilla

Denarius	£20	£70	£475
Sestertius	£65	£200	£1500
As or Dupondius	£30	£100	£680

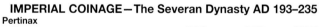

Faustina Junior

Commodus

Aureus...	£1250	£3500	£20,000
Denarius as Caesar	£30	£80	£575
Denarius as Augustus	£20	£55	£470
Sestertius	£45	£170	£1425
Sestertius (VICT BRIT)	£150	£525	£3800
As or Dupondius	£25	£90	£600

Crispina

Denarius	£25	£85	£550
Sestertius	£70	£250	£1600
As or Dupondius	£35	£125	£850

IMPERIAL COINAGE—The Severan Dynasty AD 193–235

Pertinax

Denarius..	£225	£750	£5000
Sestertius	£500	£2000	£15,500

Didius Julianus

Denarius..	£400	£1300	£10,000
Sestertius or Dupondius	£325	£1000	£9500

Lucius Verus

Manlia Scantilla or Didia Clara

Denarius	£400	£1300	£10,000

Pescennius Niger

Denarius	£275	£800	£5600

Clodius Albinus

Denarius as Caesar	£45	£150	£800
Denarius as Augustus	£85	£300	£1750
Sestertius	£275	£1000	£6300
As	£85	£265	£1600

Commodus

	FROM F	VF	EF
Septimius Severus			
Aureus	£1150	£3000	£18,000
Aureus (VICT BRIT)	£1350	£4500	£28,500
+Denarius (Mint of Rome)	£15	£55	£325
+Denarius (Mints of Emesa & Laodicea)	£20	£50	£350
Denarius (LEG XIIII)	£30	£125	£650
Denarius (VICT BRIT)	£25	£125	£600
Sestertius other types	£75	£275	£2000
Sestertius (VICT BRIT)	£350	£1000	£8500
Dupondius or as	£50	£175	£1500
Dupondius or As (VICT BRIT)	£125	£385	£2750
Julia Domna			
Denarius	£25	£50	£350
Sestertius	£75	£250	£1850
As or Dupondius	£50	£175	£1250
Caracalla			
Aureus (VICT BRIT)	£1500	£4250	£28,500
Denarius as Caesar	£15	£50	£375
Denarius as Augustus	£15	£45	£375
Denarius (VICT BRIT)	£30	£100	£650
Antoninianus	£25	£80	£550
Sestertius	£100	£325	£2250
Sestertius (VICT BRIT)	£300	£1000	£8250
Dupondius or As	£50	£175	£1150
Dupondius or As (VICT BRIT)	£100	£325	£2200
Plautilla			
Denarius	£25	£80	£650
Geta			
Denarius as Caesar	£15	£50	£380
Denarius as Augustus	£25	£75	£575
Denarius (VICT BRIT)	£30	£100	£725
Sestertius	£125	£375	£2750
Sestertius (VICT BRIT)	£250	£810	£5500
Dupondius or as	£75	£245	£1750
As (VICT BRIT)	£120	£365	£2750
Macrinus			
Antoninianus	£100	£325	£2000
Denarius	£45	£150	£1000
Sestertius	£175	£425	£3750
Diadumenian			
Denarius	£75	£225	£1250
Dupondius or As	£135	£425	£3500
Elagabalus			
Aureus	£1350	£4000	£22,500
Antoninianus	£20	£70	£550
Denarius	£15	£40	£350
Sestertius	£100	£350	£2150
Dupondius or As	£60	£185	£1275
Julia Paula			
Denarius	£30	£120	£725
Aquilla Severa			
Denarius	£55	£200	£1500
Julia Soaemias			
Denarius	£30	£80	£575
Dupondius or As	£65	£250	£1600
Julia Maesa			
Denarius	£15	£50	£365
Sestertius	£85	£275	£2250
Severus Alexander			
Aureus	£1150	£3000	£18,000
Denarius as Caesar	£65	£200	£1500
Denarius as Augustus	£25	£45	£350
Sestertius	£45	£120	£850
Dupondius or As	£35	£150	£750

Septimus Severus

Julia Domna

Geta

Macrinus

Elagabalus

Julia Maesa

	FROM F	VF	EF
Orbiana			
Denarius	£65	£225	£1750
As	£100	£350	£2250
Julia Mamaea			
Denarius	£20	£65	£400
Sestertius	£35	£125	£750

IMPERIAL COINAGE — Military Anarchy AD 235–270

	FROM F	VF	EF
Maximinus I			
Denarius	£15	£80	£375
Sestertius, Dupondius or As	£45	£150	£875
Diva Paula			
Denarius	£150	£450	£3000
Maximus Caesar			
Denarius	£70	£210	£1650
Sestertius	£65	£175	£1600
Gordian I & II, Africanus			
Denarius	£550	£1575	£7650
Sestertius	£550	£1850	£10,500
Balbinus & Pupienus			
Antoninanus	£90	£265	£1650
Denarius	£80	£275	£1850
Gordian III			
Antoninianus	£12	£30	£210
Denarius	£15	£40	£260
Sestertius or As	£25	£90	£595
Tranquillina			
Common Colonial	£30	£115	£735
Philip I			
Antoninianus "Animal":			
Lion, stag, antelope, wolf & twins ...	£25	£75	£485
Other Antoninianus	£15	£30	£250
Sestertius, Dupondius or As	£35	£100	£650
Otacilla Severa			
Antoninaius	£10	£30	£225
Antoninianus "Hipo"	£25	£85	£600
Sestertius	£25	£100	£575
Philip II			
Antoninianus	£15	£25	£225
Antoninianus "Goat"	£20	£75	£500
Sestertius, Dupondius or As	£35	£100	£675
Pacatian			
Antoninianus	£1500	£5000	—
Trajan Decius			
Antoninianus	£10	£35	£180
Antoninianus (DIVI series Augustus, Trajan etc)	£40	£135	£840
Double Sestertius	£275	£1250	£5500
Sestertius, Dupondius or As	£25	£100	£650
Herennius Etruscilla			
Antoninaius	£20	£50	£225
Sestertius, Dupondius or As	£30	£150	£850
Herennius Etruscus			
Antoninianus	£20	£75	£450
Sesterius, Dupondius or As	£55	£225	£1650
Hostilian			
Antoninianus as Caesar	£30	£150	£700
Antoninianus as Augustus	£70	£250	£1750
Trebonianus Gallus			
Antoninianus	£15	£45	£250
Sestertius or As	£30	£125	£700
Volusian			
Antoninianus	£15	£45	£325
Sestertius	£30	£120	£1250

Orbiana

Julia Mamaea

Diva Paula

Gordian III

Trajan Decius

Hostilian

87

	FROM F	VF	EF
Aemilian			
Antoninianus	£45	£175	£1000
Valerian I			
Antoninianus	£15	£35	£275
Sestertius & As................................	£50	£175	£1250
Diva Mariniana			
Antoninianus	£35	£150	£850
Gallienus			
Silver Antoninianus	£12	£45	£225
Ae Antoninianus	£10	£35	£185
Ae Antoninianus (Military bust).........	£12	£40	£250
Ae Antoninianus (Legionary)	£75	£235	—
Ae Sestertius	£45	£165	£1450
Ae Denarius	£50	£150	£1000
Saloninus			
Ae Antoninianus	£8	£25	£250
Valerian II			
Billon Antoninianus	£12	£45	£275
Saloninus			
Antoninianus	£15	£55	£2750
Macrianus & Quietus			
Billon Antoninianus	£45	£150	£1000
Regalianus or Dryantilla			
Billon Antoninianus	£1850	£7500	—
Postumus			
Silver Antoninianus	£10	£25	£225
Ae Antoninianus	£8	£25	£150
Radiated sestertius..........................	£50	£200	£1550
Laelianus			
Ae Antoninianus	£275	£875	£4000
Marius			
Ae Antoninianus	£45	£150	£850
Victorinus			
Ae Antoninianus	£8	£30	£200
Tetricus I & II			
Ae Antoninianus	£8	£30	£200
Claudius II Gothicus			
Ae Antoninianus	£8	£30	£225
Egypt, Alexandrian Billon tetradrachm	£8	£35	£225
DIVO Ae Antoninianus	£8	£35	£250
Quintillus			
Ae Antoninianus	£12	£45	£275

Postumus

Aurelian

Severina

IMPERIAL COINAGE — The Illyrian Emperors — AD 270–285

Aurelian			
Ae Antoninianus	£8	£50	£225
Ae Denarius	£20	£75	£550
Vabalathus & Aurelian			
Ae Antoninianus (bust both sides) ...	£20	£75	£500
Vabalathus			
Ae Antoninianus	£350	£1250	—
Severina			
Ae Antoninianus	£15	£55	£350
Ae As...	£35	£125	£700
Zenobia			
Eygpt, Alexandrian Billon Tetradrachm	£750	£3000	—
Tacitus			
Ae Antoninianus	£15	£35	£275
Florian			
Ae Antoninianus	£25	£100	£600

Tacitus

Florian

	FROM F	VF	EF
Probus			
Gold Aureus	£1500	£3750	£22,000
Ae Antoninianus	£10	£25	£225
Antoninianus (military or imp. Busts RIC G or H)	£10	£45	£275
Antoninianus			
(Other military or imp NOT BUSTS G or H)	£20	£75	£500
Antoninianus (VICTOR GERM rev.) ..	£12	£65	£250
Egypt, Alexandrian Billon tetradrachm	£8	£25	£150
Carus			
Ae Antoninianus	£15	£50	£350
Numerian			
Ae Antoninianus	£15	£45	£300
Carinus			
Ae Antoninianus	£12	£75	£275
Magna Urbica			
Ae Antoninianus	£100	£275	£2000
Julian of Pannonia			
Ae Antoninianus	£650	£2750	—

Carinus

Diocletian

IMPERIAL COINAGE—The Tetrarchy AD 285–307

	FROM F	VF	EF
Diocletian			
Gold Aureus	£1100	£3250	£18,750
AR Argenteus	£120	£275	£1750
Ae Antoninianus & Radiates	£10	£35	£275
Ae Follis (London Mint)	£15	£50	£375
As above with LON mint mark	£100	£350	£2000
Ae Follis (other mints)	£10	£35	£250
Ae Follis (Imperial bust)...................	£25	£85	£500
Maximianus			
AR Argenteus	£100	£325	£1650
Ae Follis (London mint)	£15	£45	£325
Ae Follis (other mints)	£10	£35	£225
Ae Follis (MONETA rev.)	£10	£50	£275
Carausius			
Aureus	£10,000	£30,000	—
Denarius	£400	£1500	£8500
Ae Antoninianus (PAX).....................	£25	£125	£600
As above but full silvering	£35	£150	£875
Legionary Antoninianus	£75	£250	£2250
Expectate Veni Antoninianus	£100	£325	—
In the name of Diocletian or Maximian	£35	£150	£1000
Allectus			
Aureus	£12,500	£35,000	—
Ae Antoninianus	£25	£100	£750
As above but full silvering	£45	£155	£1250
Quinarius	£25	£100	£850
Constantius I			
AR Argenteus	£20	£300	£1650
Ae Follis (London Mint)	£15	£50	£375
Ae Follis (other mints)	£10	£35	£250
Ae Follis (SALVS rev.)......................	£15	£55	£325
Ae 4 (Lion or Eagle)	£10	£35	£250
Galerius			
Ae Follis (London mint)	£15	£45	£275
Ae Follis (other mints)	£10	£35	£200
Galeria Valeria			
Ae Follis	£35	£100	£575
Severus II			
Ae Follis (London mint)	£35	£150	£725
Ae Follis (other mints)	£30	£125	£550
Ae Radiate......................................	£25	£55	£325
Ae Denarius	£25	£125	£550

Maximianus

Carausius

Severus II

	FROM F	VF	EF
Maximinus II			
Ae Follis (London mint)	£15	£50	£350
Ae Follis (other mints)	£8	£35	£175
Ae Radiate	£10	£45	£250
Maxentius			
Ae Follis	£10	£35	£250
Romulus			
Ae Follis	£50	£150	£1650
Licinius I			
Billon Argenteus	£50	£175	£1250
Ae Follis (London mint)	£12	£35	£200
Ae Follis (other mints)	£12	£35	£175
AE3	£8	£20	£150
Licinius II			
AE3	£10	£35	£200
Alexander or Martinian			
AE	£1550	£4750	—

Maximinus II

IMPERIAL COINAGE—Family of Constantine AD 307–350

	FROM F	VF	EF
Constantine I			
Billon Argenteus	£50	£175	£1250
Ae Follis (London mint)	£12	£35	£225
As above—helmeted bust	£15	£50	£325
Ae Follis (other mints) as Caesar ...	£15	£50	£375
Ae Follis (other mints) as Augustus	£8	£25	£150
AE3	£8	£25	£150
AE3 (London mint)	£12	£35	£225
AE3 (SARMATIA rev)	£12	£50	£275
Urbs Roma / Wolf & twins AE3/4	£8	£25	£155
Constantinopolis AE3/4	£8	£25	£145
Fausta & Helena			
AE3 (London mint)	£50	£175	£1250
AE3 (other mints)	£15	£75	£325
Theodora			
AE4	£10	£35	£250
Crispus			
AE3 (London mint)	£10	£35	£250
AE3	£10	£25	£150
Delmatius			
AE3/4	£15	£45	£275
Hanniballianus Rex			
AE4	£75	£250	£1500
Constantine II			
AE3 (London mint)	£10	£30	£225
AE3	£8	£30	£175
AE3/4	£8	£25	£125
Constans			
AE2 (centenionalis)	£10	£35	£250
AE3 (half centenionalis)	£8	£30	£200
AE4	£8	£25	£125
Constantius II			
Gold Solidus	£350	£900	£5250
Siliqua	£25	£100	£585
AE2 (or centenionalis)	£10	£35	£250
AE3 (or half centenionalis)	£8	£20	£150
AE3 (London mint)..........................	£15	£50	£325
AE3..	£8	£20	£100

Licinius II

Constantine I

Constantine II

IMPERIAL COINAGE—Late period to the collapse of the Empire AD 350 to end

	FROM F	VF	EF
Magnentius			
Gold Solidus....................................	£900	£3000	£15,000
Silver Siliqua	£275	£850	£5000
Double centenionalis	£45	£200	£1425
Centenionalis	£15	£55	£375

Magnentius

	FROM F	VF	EF
Decentius			
Double centenionalis	£75	£250	£1850
Centenionalis	£25	£75	£450
Vetranio			
AE2 (centenionalis)	£40	£150	£850
AE3 (half centenionalis)	£35	£125	£725
Nepotian			
AE2 (centenionalis)	£2000	£7250	—
Constantius Gallus			
AE2 (centenionalis)	£15	£45	£250
AE3 (half centenionalis)	£8	£30	£125
Julian II			
Siliqua	£30	£100	£625
AE1	£45	£150	£875
AE3 (helmeted bust)	£12	£35	£250
Anonymous, Serapis + Jupiter AE3	£200	£600	—
Jovian			
AE1	£65	£250	£1500
AE3	£15	£55	£250
Valentinian I			
Sold Solidus	£225	£650	£3000
Silver Milliarense	£175	£625	£4000
Siliqua	£25	£100	£600
AE3	£8	£25	£125
Valens			
Gold Solidus	£225	£600	£3000
Silver Milliarense	£200	£650	£4250
Siliqua	£25	£100	£625
AE3	£8	£25	£125
Procopius			
AE3	£45	£150	£900
Gratian			
Silver Milliarense	£175	£600	£2850
Siliqua	£25	£85	£550
AE3	£8	£45	£135
AE4	£8	£35	£125
Valentinian II			
Solidus	£225	£575	£3250
Siliqua	£25	£150	£600
AE2	£12	£35	£250
AE4	£5	£15	£100
Theodosius I			
Solidus	£250	£650	£3250
Siliqua	£30	£100	£675
AE2	£12	£50	£250
AE3	£10	£45	£250
Aelia Flaccilla			
AE2	£30	£125	£685
AE4	£15	£50	£375
Magnus Maximus			
Solidus (AVGOB)	£5450	£15,250	—
Solidus	£900	£3000	£16,750
Siliqua	£45	£150	£1000
Siliqua (AVGPS)	£750	£2500	—
AE2	£25	£75	£450
Flavius Victor			
Silver Sliqua	£150	£500	£2750
AE4	£30	£85	£500
Eugenius			
Silver Siliqua	£150	£550	£2750

Vetranio

Julian II

Jovian

Valentinian I

Valens

Theodosius I

	FROM F	VF	EF
Arcadius			
Gold Solidus..................................	£225	£600	£2850
Silver Siliqua.................................	£25	£125	£600
Silver Half-siliqua	£150	£500	£2850
AE2	£12	£50	£225
AE4	£5	£25	£100
Eudoxia			
AE3	£25	£85	£500
Honorius			
Gold Solidus	£225	£575	£2850
Silver Siliqua	£30	£125	£650
AE4	£8	£25	£125
Constantine III			
Silver Siliqua	£150	£550	£3000
Theodosius II			
Gold Solidus	£225	£550	£2850
Johannes			
AE4	£125	£500	—
Valentinian III			
Gold Soldius..................................	£225	£575	£2850
AE4	£25	£100	£500

Arcadius

Honorius

Theodosius II

Ae = bronze; AE 1, 2, 3, 4 = bronze coins in descending order of size.

Coin illustrations by courtesy of Classical Numismatic Group/Seaby Coins and Mike Vosper.

The outstanding EID MAR gold aureus of Brutus sold by Roma Numismatics Ltd in October 2020 for the world-record sum of £3.24 million (for the full story see COIN NEWS, December 2020). Image enlarged.

A SIMPLIFIED PRICE GUIDE TO

ENGLISH HAMMERED COINS

PART I

780-1485

INTRODUCTION

We have taken our starting point for English hammered coin prices from the middle Anglo-Saxon period. This time sees the country divided into separate kingdoms, and Viking divided areas and as well as the introduction of the silver "penny" as the standard unit of currency (and a few struck halfpennies). This is a complicated time in our history and that is reflected numismatically. We have therefore listed only the commonest or most frequently found pieces or rulers within their kingdoms. For many later rulers the price is for the more common non-portait issue.

PRICING

The prices given in the following pages are intended to be used as a "Pocket book guide" to the values of the most common coins within any denomination of any one reign. The price quoted is what a collector may expect to pay for such a piece in the condition indicated. For more detailed information we recommend the reader to one of the many specialist publications.

GRADING

The prices quoted are generally for three different grades of condition: Fine (F), Very Fine (VF) and Extremely Fine (EF). A "Fine" coin is assumed to be a fairly worn, circulated, piece but with all or most of the main features and lettering still clear. "Very Fine" is a middle grade with a small amount of wear and most details fairly clear. For this edition we have included the prices for coins in Extremely Fine condition where appropriate, although very few hammered coins actually turn up in this grade (i.e. nearly mint state with hardly any wear). In some instances the prices quoted are theoretically based and are only included to provide a guide. It is important to note that on all hammered coins the very nature of striking, i.e. individually, by hand, means hammered coinage is rarely a straight grade and when listed by a dealer the overall condition will often be qualified by terms such as: *weak in parts, struck off-centre, cracked or chipped flan, double struck,* etc. When applicable the price should be adjusted accordingly.

HISTORY

Below the heading for each monarch we have given a few historical notes as and when they apply to significant changes in the coinage.

KINGS OF KENT

	F	VF
CUTHRED (798–807)	£1000	£4000

(non portrait pieces may be not quite as highly priced)

ARCHBISHOPS OF CANTERBURY

WULFRED (805–832) £775 £3250

COELNOTH (833–870) £725 £2850

PLEGMUND (890–914) (non portrait) £700 £2850

KINGS OF MERCIA

OFFA (757–796) (non portrait) . £550 £1650

— — (portrait) £800 £3000

COENWULF (796–821) £400 £1300

BURGRED (852–874) £325 £750

KINGS OF EAST ANGLIA

EDMUND (855–870) £425 £1300

ST EDMUND (Danish E. Anglia 855–915)
(Many have crude lettering) £225 £500

VIKING ISSUES OF YORK

	F	VF
CNUT (READS CV N·NET·TI)	£200	£525

ST PETER COINAGE (905–915) £375   £1125

KINGS OF WESSEX (later all England)

ALFRED THE GREAT (871–99) £750   £2000

EDWARD THE ELDER (899–924) £275   £650

AETHELSTAN (924–39).....   £400   £1100

EADMUND (939–46)...........   £300   £750

EADRED (946–55).................   £300   £725

EADWIG (955–59).................   £750   £2200

EDGAR (First King of All England) (959–975)

	F	VF	EF
Edgar Penny, non portrait (2 line inscription)	£275	£600	—

EDWARD THE MARTYR (975–978)

	F	VF	EF
Edward, Penny, Portrait	£1600	£5350	—

AETHELRED II (978–1016)

	F	VF	EF
Aethelred II, Penny (1st hand type illustrated)	£225	£500	—
Penny, last small cross type	£175	£325	£800

CNUT (1016–35)

	F	VF	EF
Cnut, Penny (Quatrefoil type illustrated)	£180	£325	£725
Penny (short cross type)	£165	£300	£650

HAROLD I
(1035–40)

	F	VF	EF
Harold I, Penny (long cross type Illustrated)..	£325	£900	—

HARTHACANUTE
(1035–42)

	F	VF	EF
Harthacanute, Penny, English Mint (in his own name)	£1000	£3500	—
Harthacanute Penny (king's name given as "CNUT")..	£650	£1800	—
Harthacanute, Penny, Danish type........	£325	£850	—

Danish type

EDWARD THE CONFESSOR
(1042–66)

	F	VF	EF
Edward the Confessor, Penny (helmet type illustrated)..	£200	£450	£1350
Edward the Confessor, Penny, facing bust type	£170	£375	£1000

HAROLD II
(1066)

	F	VF	EF
Harold II, Penny..................................	£1300	£3500	—

WILLIAM I
(1066–87)

The Norman Conquest had very little immediate effect on the coinage of England. The Anglo-Saxon standard of minting silver pennies was very high and the practice of the moneyer putting his name and mint town on the reverse continued as before, except with William's portrait of course. It is worth noting here that non-realistic, stylised portraits were used until the reign of Henry VII.

There are eight major types of pennies of which the last, the PAXS type, is by far the commonest.

	F	VF	EF
William I, Penny (PAXS type illustrated).................................	£300	£650	—

WILLIAM II
(1087–1100)

Very little change from his father's reign except that five new types were issued, most of which were much more crudely designed than previous, all are scarce.

	F	VF	EF
William II, Penny (cross in quatrefoil type illustrated)...	£750	£2100	—

HENRY I
(1100–35)

There are fifteen different types of penny for this reign of which the last two are the most common. Most issues are of a very poor standard both in workmanship and metal, the prices reflect a poor quality of issue.

	F	VF	EF
Henry I, Penny type XV..............................	£150	£525	—
Henry I, Penny type XIV (illustrated)...........	£250	£825	—
Halfpenny	£2000	£6000	—

STEPHEN
(1135–54)

This is historically a very complicated time for the coinage, mainly due to civil war and a consequential lack of central control in the country which resulted in very poor quality and deliberately damaged pieces. Coins were struck not only in the name of Stephen and his main rival claimant Matilda rare, but also by their supporters. The commonest issue is the "Watford" type; so named, as are many issues, after the area in which a hoard was found.

	F	VF	EF
Stephen, Penny ("Watford" type illustrated)	£250	£900	—

(full flan pieces are worth considerably more)

HENRY II
(1154–89)

There were two distinct issues struck during this reign. The first, Cross and Crosslets or "Tealby" coinage (named after Tealby in Lincolnshire, where a large hoard was found), continued to be very poorly made and lasted 20 years. However, in 1180 the new and superior "Short Cross" issue commenced, being issued from only twelve major towns.

	F	VF	EF
Henry II, Penny, Tealby	£115	£375	—
Henry II, Penny, Short Cross	£60	£180	—

RICHARD I
(1189–99)

There were no major changes during this reign, in fact pennies continued to be struck with his father Henry's name throughout the reign. The coins struck under Richard tend to be rather crude in style.

	F	VF	EF
Richard I, Penny	£80	£235	—

JOHN
(1199–1216)

As with his brother before him, there were no major changes during the reign of King John, and pennies with his father's name were struck throughout the reign, although they tended to be somewhat neater in style than those struck during the reign of Richard I.

	F	VF
John, Penny.....................................	£50	£1640

HENRY III
(1216–72)

The coinage during Henry III's reign continued as before with the short cross issue. However, in 1247 a new long cross design was introduced to prevent clipping. This design was to last in one form or another for many centuries. Late in the reign saw a brief appearance of the 1st English gold coin.

	F	VF	EF
Henry III, Penny, Short Cross	£40	£115	£300
Henry III, Penny, Long Cross...................	£30	£70	£235

EDWARD I
(1272–1307)

After a few years of issuing similar pieces to his father, and in his farther's name in 1279 Edward I ordered a major re-coinage. This consisted of well-made pennies, halfpennies and farthings in relatively large quantities, and for a brief period a groat (four pence) was produced. These were often mounted and gilded, the price is for an undamaged piece. The pennies are amongst the most common of all hammered coins.

	F	VF	EF
Edward I (and Edward II)			
Groat (often damaged) see above ...	£2500	£7250	—
Penny......................................	£25	£70	£500
Halfpenny...............................	£25	£90	—
Farthing..................................	£25	£80	—

Edward I penny

EDWARD II
(1307–27)

	F	VF	EF
Edward II, long cross Pennies, Halfpennies and Farthings continued in very similar style to his father (Edward I)			
Pennies	£30	£85	–
Halfpennies	£60	£180	–
Farthings	£35	£125	–

EDWARD III
(1327–77)

This was a long reign which saw major changes in the coinage, the most significant being the introduction of a gold coinage (based on the Noble, valued at 6s 8d, and its fractions) and a regular issue of a large silver groat (and half groat). The provincial mints were limited to a few episcopal cities but coins of English type were also struck in the newly-acquired Calais Mint.

	F	VF	EF
Gold			
Noble	£900	£2850	£6500
Half Noble	£650	£1900	£4500
Quarter Noble	£350	£750	£1500
Silver			
Groat	£50	£165	£850
Half Groat	£30	£120	£550
Penny	£20	£85	£350
Half Penny	£20	£70	£275
Farthing	£35	£110	£325

Gold Noble

RICHARD II
(1377–99)

The denominations continued during this reign much as before. However, coins are quite scarce mainly due to the lack of bullion gold and silver going into the mints, mainly because of an inbalance with European weights and fineness.

	F	VF	EF
Gold			
Noble	£1400	£4500	–
Half Noble	£1450	£4700	–
Quarter Noble	£475	£1300	–
Silver			
Groat	£500	£1850	–
Half Groat	£225	£800	–
Penny	£70	£325	–
Half Penny	£30	£125	–
Farthing	£125	£500	–

Gold Noble

HENRY IV
(1399–1413)

Because of the continuing problems with the scarcity of gold and silver the coinage was reduced by weight in 1412, towards the end of the reign. All coins of this reign are quite scarce.

	F	VF
Gold		
Noble, Light coinage...................	£1750	£6250
Half Noble, Light coinage..........	£2350	£7750
Quarter Noble, Light coinage	£700	£2000
Silver		
Groat, Light coinage...................	£1500	£5750
Half Groat, Heavy coinage..........	£700	£2250
Penny..	£425	£1200
Half Penny	£250	£750
Farthing.....................................	£750	£2350

Noble

HENRY V
(1413–22)

Monetary reform introduced towards the end of his father's reign in 1412 improved the supply of bullion and hence coins of Henry V are far more common. All of the main denominations continued as before.

	F	VF	EF
Gold			
Noble £1300	£4250	£6750
Half Noble...........................£1000	£3000	—
Quarter Noble £425	£900	£1850
Silver			
Groat, class "C" £175	£575	—
Half Groat............................£110	£350	—
Penny...................................£45	£175	—
Half Penny............................£30	£115	—
Farthing...............................£350	£1100	—

Groat

HENRY VI
(1422–61 and again 1470–71)

Although there were no new denominations except for the Angel & Halfangel during the 2nd reign (see Edward IV below), Henry's first reign saw eleven different issues, each for a few years and distinguished by privy marks, i.e. annulets, pinecones, mascles, leaves etc.

HENRY VI *continued*

	F	VF	EF
Gold			
First reign—			
Noble, Annulet issue............. £1200	£3750	£6750	
Half Noble, Annulet issue........ £850	£2500	£5000	
Quarter Noble, Annulet issue... £375	£800	£1700	
2nd reign—			
Angel...................................... £2000	£5750	—	
Half Angel £4750	£13000	—	
Silver			
Groat, Annulet issue £60	£175	£425	
Half Groat, Annulet issue........... £30	£110	£375	
Penny... £30	£90	£350	
Half Penny, Annulet issue......... £25	£70	£185	
Farthing, Annulet issue............ £120	£400	—	

Noble

EDWARD IV
(1461–70 and again 1471–83)

The significant changes during these reigns were the replacement of the noble by the rose ryal (and revalued at 10 shillings) and the continuation of the angel at the old noble value. We also start to see mint-marks or initial marks appearing, usually at the top of the coin, they were used to denote the period of issue for dating purposes and often lasted for two to three years e.g. rose, lis, crown etc. Groats were issued at London, Bristol, Coventry, Norwich and York.

	F	VF	EF
Gold			
Noble and quarter noble (Heavy Coinage)		Very rare	
Ryal....................................... £1150	£3500	£6250	
"Flemish" copy of Ryal £800	£2400	—	
Half Ryal £800	£2300	£4750	
Quarter Ryal........................... £475	£1300	£2750	
Angel, 2nd reign.................... £1000	£3000	£4300	
Half Angel, 2nd reign £800	£2400	—	
Silver			
Groat....................................... £50	£150	£500	
Half Groat Canterbury £45	£140	£425	
Penny....................................... £35	£150	£350	
Half Penny £25	£100	—	
Farthing, Heavy coinage.......... £375	£1150	—	

Angel

RICHARD III
(1483–85)

The close of the Yorkist Plantagenet and Medieval period come together at this time. There are no new significant numismatic changes but most silver coins of Richard whilst not really rare, continue to be very popular and priced quite high. The smaller denominations are usually poor condition.

	F	VF	EF
Gold			
Angel...................................... £5500	£18500	—	
Half Angel £9000	£30000	—	
Silver			
Groat....................................... £800	£2250	—	
Half Groat £1350	£4500	—	
Penny....................................... £375	£1200	—	
Half Penny £350	£1000	—	
Farthing.................................. £1700	£4750	—	

Groat

PART II

Among the more significant features of the post-Renaissance period as it affected coinage is the introduction of realistic portraiture during the reign of Henry VII. We also have a much wider and varied number of new and revised denominations, for example eleven different gold denominations of Henry VIII and the same number of silver for Elizabeth I. Here we only mention the introduction or changes in the main denominations, giving a value for all of them, once again listing the commonest type.

HENRY VII
(1485–1509)

The gold sovereign of 20 shillings makes its first appearance in 1489 as does the testoon (later shilling) in about 1500. The silver penny was re-designed to a rather crude likeness of the sovereign, enthroned.

	F	VF	EF
Gold			
Sovereign	£25000	£90,000	—
Ryal	£32500	£135,000	—
Angel	£850	£2500	—
Half Angel	£750	£2200	—
Silver			
Testoon 1/-	£17500	£42,500	—
Groat, facing bust	£75	£225	£1000
Half Groat	£40	£150	£550
Penny, sovereign type	£40	£130	£375
Half Penny	£25	£80	—
Farthing	£500	£1500	—

Profile Groat

HENRY VIII
(1509–47)

After a long initial period of very little change in the coinage, in 1526 there were many, with an attempt to bring the gold/silver ratio in line with the continental currencies. Some gold coins only lasted a short time and are very rare. The crown (in gold) makes its first appearance. Towards the end of the reign we see large issues of debased silver coins (with a high copper content) bearing the well-known facing portrait of the ageing King. These tend to turn up in poor condition and include the shilling in greater numbers. Similar posthumous issues were minted during early reign of Edward VI.

Gold			
Sovereign, 3rd coinage	£6500	£24000	—
Half Sovereign	£1000	£3250	—
Angel	£900	£2650	£3650
Half Angel	£750	£2250	£3150
Quarter Angel	£850	£2500	—
George Noble	£10000	£37500	—
Half George Noble	£9000	£35000	—
Crown of the rose	£7000	£25000	—
Crown of the double rose	£850	£2650	—
Half Crown of the double rose	£650	£1850	—
Silver			
Testoon 1/-	£1100	£4350	—
Groat, 2nd coinage	£150	£375	£1350
Half Groat, 2nd coinage	£65	£185	£700
Penny	£40	£150	£425
Half Penny	£30	£130	—
Farthing	£300	£850	—

Gold Sovereign

EDWARD VI
(1547–53)

Some of the coins struck in the first few years of this short reign could really be called Henry VIII posthumous issues as there is continuity in both name and style from his father's last issue. However, overlapping this period are portrait issues of the boy King, particularly shillings (usually poor quality coins). This period also sees the first dated English coin (shown in Roman numerals) MDXLIX (1549). In 1551 however, a new coinage was introduced with a restored silver quality from the Crown (dated 1551) down to the new sixpence and threepence.

	F	VF	EF
Gold			
Sovereign (30s)	£7000	£22500	—
Half Sovereign (in own name)	£1900	£6750	—
Crown	£2150	£7600	—
Half Crown	£1650	£5500	—
Angel	£14000	£40000	—
Half Angel	—	£45000	—
Sovereign (20s)	£7500	£22000	—
Silver			
Crown	£1000	£3500	—
Half Crown	£700	£2000	—
Shilling (Fine coinage)	£150	£550	—
Sixpence (Fine coinage)	£160	£600	—
Groat	£750	£4500	—
Threepence	£225	£1250	—
Half Groat	£425	£1500	—
Penny	£65	£240	—
Half Penny	£325	£1300	—
Farthing	£1400	£4750	—

Crowned bust half sovereign

MARY
(1553–54)

The early coins of Mary's sole reign are limited and continue to use some of the same denominations as Edward, except that the gold ryal was reintroduced.

	F	VF
Gold		
Sovereign (30s)	£8750	£27000
Ryal	£33000	—
Angel	£2250	£6000
Half Angel	£6250	£17000
Silver		
Groat	£200	£700
Half Groat	£700	£2500
Penny	£650	£2250

Groat

PHILIP & MARY
(1554–58)

After a very short reign alone, Mary married Philip of Spain and they technically ruled jointly (although not for very long in practise) until her death. After her marriage we see both her and Philip on the shillings and sixpences with both full Spanish and then English titles alone.

	F	VF
Gold		
Angel	£6000	£20000
Half Angel	£14000	—
Silver		
Shilling	£450	£2000
Sixpence	£450	£1700
Groat	£225	£750
Half Groat	£525	£2000
Penny	£75	£250

Shilling

ELIZABETH I
(1558–1603)

As might be expected with a long reign there are a number of significant changes in the coinage which include several new denominations—so many in silver that every value from the shilling downwards was marked and dated to distinguish them. Early on we have old base Edward VI shillings countermarked to a new reduced value (not priced here). Also due to a lack of small change and the expense of making a miniscule farthing we have a new threehalfpence and threefarthings. Finally we see the beginnings of a milled (machine produced) coinage for a brief period from 1561–71.

	F	VF	EF
Gold			
Sovereign (30s)	£7500	£21000	—
Ryal (15s)	£23500	£70000	—
Angel	£1200	£3500	—
Half Angel	£1050	£3200	—
Quarter Angel	£1000	£3100	—
Pound (20s)	£3500	£12000	—
Half Pound	£1800	£5500	—
Crown	£1200	£3500	—
Half Crown	£1150	£3400	—
Silver			
Crown (mm l)	£1850	£5350	—
Half Crown (mm l)	£1000	£2900	—
Shilling	£100	£500	£1850
Sixpence	£70	£240	£1500
Groat	£75	£285	£850
Threepence	£50	£200	£600
Half Groat	£30	£100	£325
Threehalfpence	£50	£200	£450
Penny	£30	£100	£275
Threefarthings	£70	£270	£400
Half Penny	£40	£100	£165

Shilling

JAMES I
(1603–25)

Although the size of the gold coinage remains much the same as Elizabeth's reign, the name and weight or value of the denominations have several changes, i.e. Pound = Sovereign = Unite = Laurel. A new four shilling gold coin (thistle crown) was introduced. A number of the silver coins now have their value in Roman numerals on the coin. Relatively few angels were made from this period onwards and they are usually found pierced.

	F	VF	EF
Gold			
Sovereign (20s)	£3500	£14000	—
Unite	£750	£1900	£4000
Double crown/half unite	£525	£1500	£3000
Crown	£325	£775	£2000
Thistle Crown	£325	£850	£2000
Half Crown	£275	£550	—
Rose Ryal (30s)	£3650	£12500	—
Spur Ryal (15s)	£8250	£29250	—
Angel (pierced)	£675	£2000	—
Half Angel (Unpierced)	£3500	£10000	—
Laurel	£700	£1900	£4000
Half Laurel	£450	£1400	£3350
Quarter Laurel	£300	£750	£1850
Silver			
Crown	£800	£2100	—
Half Crown	£335	£875	—
Shilling	£90	£300	—
Sixpence	£70	£250	—
Half Groat	£25	£70	£150
Penny	£25	£60	£135
Half Penny	£15	£45	£135

Gold Unite,
second bust

Silver Halfcrown

CHARLES I
(1625–49)

This reign is probably the most difficult to simplify as there are so many different issues and whole books have been produced on this period alone. From the beginning of the King's reign and throughout the Civil War, a number of mints operated for varying lengths of time, producing both regular and irregular issues. The Tower mint was taken over by Parliament in 1642 but before this a small quantity of milled coinage was produced alongside the regular hammered issues. The Court then moved to Oxford from where, for the next three years, large quantities of gold and silver were struck (including rare triple unites and large silver pounds). The most prolific of the provincial mints were those situated at Aberystwyth, York, Oxford, Shrewsbury, Bristol, Exeter, Truro, Chester and Worcester as well as some smaller mints mainly situated in the West Country. Among the more interesting coins of the period are the pieces struck on unusually-shaped flans at Newark and Pontefract whilst those towns were under siege. As many of the coins struck during the Civil War were crudely struck on hastily gathered bullion and plate, they provide a fascinating area of study. The prices indicated below are the minimum for the commonest examples of each denomination irrespective of town of origin.

	F	VF	EF
Gold			
Triple Unite (£3) (Oxford)	£13000	£36000	—
Unite	£750	£2100	—
Double crown/Half unite	£475	£1350	—
Crown	£325	£800	—
Angel (pierced)	£700	£2250	—
Angel (unpierced)	£2400	£8750	—
Silver			
Pound (20 shillings—Oxford)	£3400	£9250	—
Half Pound (Shrewsbury)	£1400	£3650	—
Crown (Truro, Exeter)	£450	£1375	—
Half Crown	£70	£275	—
Shilling	£55	£180	£900
Sixpence	£50	£170	£800
Groat (Aberystwyth)	£80	£210	£575
Threepence (Aberystwyth)	£75	£200	£525
Half Groat	£20	£80	£225
Penny	£20	£70	£200
Half Penny	£15	£50	£80

Triple unite

Above: Newark siege shilling.

Oxford Halfcrown

THE COMMONWEALTH
(1649–60)

After the execution of Charles I, Parliament changed the design of the coinage. They are simple non- portrait pieces with an English legend.

	F	VF	EF
Gold			
Unite £2400	£5650	–
Double crown/Half unite...£1700	£5000	–
Crown £1400	£3850	–
Silver			
Crown £1400	£3150	£7500
Half Crown........................£375	£900	£3500
Shilling £300	£700	£2500
Sixpence...........................£225	£600	£2200
Half Groat £50	£150	£350
Penny................................£50	£150	£335
Halfpenny £40	£100	£190

Crown

CHARLES II
(1660–85)

Although milled coins had been produced for Oliver Cromwell in 1656–58, after the Restoration of the monarchy hammered coins continued to be produced until 1663, when the machinery was ready to manufacture large quantities of good milled pieces.

	F	VF	EF
Gold			
Unite (2nd issue)...............£2200	£6250	–
Double crown/Half unite...£1600	£4750	–
Crown (1st issue)..............£1850	£5400	–
Silver			
Half Crown (3rd issue) £250	£800	–
Shilling (3rd issue)..............£160	£650	–
Sixpence (3rd issue) £140	£500	–
Fourpence (3rd issue)...........£40	£150	£325
Threepence (3rd issue) £35	£140	£275
Twopence (3rd issue)............£20	£65	£175
Penny (3rd issue) £35	£100	£225

Halfcrown

A COMPREHENSIVE PRICE GUIDE
TO THE COINS OF

THE
UNITED KINGDOM
1656–2020
including

*England, Scotland,
Isle of Man,
Guernsey, Jersey, Alderney,
also Ireland*

When referring to this price guide one must bear a number of important points in mind. The points listed here have been taken into consideration during the preparation of this guide and we hope that the prices given will provide a true reflection of the market at the time of going to press. Nevertheless, the publishers can accept no liability for the accuracy of the prices quoted.

1. "As struck" examples with flaws will be worth less than the indicated price.
2. Any coin which is particularly outstanding, with an attractive natural toning or in superb state will command a much *higher* price than that shown.
3. These prices refer strictly to the British market, and do not reflect outside opinions.
4. Some prices given for coins not seen in recent years are estimates based on a knowledge of the market.
5. In the case of coins of high rarity, prices are not generally given.
6. In the listing, "—" indicates, where applicable, one of the following:
   a. Metal or bullion value only
   b. Not usually found in this grade
   c. Not collected in this condition
7. Proof coins are listed in FDC under the UNC column.
8. All prices are quoted in £ sterling, exclusive of VAT (where applicable).

FIFTY SHILLINGS

	F	VF	EF

OLIVER CROMWELL (1656–58)

	F	VF	EF
1656...	£30,000	£85,000	£220,000

Opinions differ as to whether the portrait coinage of Oliver Cromwell was ever meant for circulation but for the sake of completeness it has been decided to include it in this Yearbook. The fifty shillings gold coin is unique as it was only struck during Cromwell's time using the same dies that were used for the broad or 20 shillings coin but with a weight of approximately 2.5 times that of the broad.

FIVE GUINEAS

CHARLES II (1660–85)

	F	VF	EF
1668 First bust	£5500	£16000	£75000
1668 — Elephant below bust	£5500	£15000	£75000
1669 —	£5500	£15000	—
1669 — Elephant....................................	£5500	£15000	—
1670 —	£6000	£15000	£75000
1670 Proof...		Exceedingly Rare	
1671 —	£5500	£15000	£80000
1672 —	£5500	£14000	£75000
1673 —	£5500	£16000	£75000
1674 —	£6000	£17000	£80000
1675 —	£5500	£15000	£75000
1675 — Elephant....................................	£7000	£18000	—
1675 — Elephant & Castle below bust...	£6500	£17000	£85000
1676 —	£5500	£15000	£70000
1676 — Elephant & Castle	£6000	£18000	£80000
1677 —	£5500	£17000	£70000
1677/5 — Elephant.................................	£7000	£18000	£85000
1677 — Elephant & Castle	£6000	£17000	£75000
1678/7 — 8 over 7	£5500	£16000	£75000
1678/7 — Elephant & Castle	£6000	£17500	£85000
1678/7 Second Bust...............................	£5500	£15000	£70000
1679 —	£6000	£15000	£70000
1680 —	£6000	£15000	£70000
1680 — Elephant & Castle	£6500	£17000	£82500
1681 —	£5500	£15000	£75000
1681 — Elephant & Castle	£6500	£17000	£82000
1682 —	£5500	£15000	£75000
1682 — Elephant & Castle	£6500	£17000	£82000
1683 —	£5500	£15000	£70000
1683 — Elephant & Castle	£6500	£18000	£85000
1684 —	£5000	£18000	£70000
1684 — Elephant & Castle	£5500	£19000	£75000

Charles II

JAMES II (1685–88)

	F	VF	EF
1686...	£6000	£15000	£75000
1687...	£5000	£15000	£72000
1687 Elephant & Castle.........................	£6000	£16000	£75000
1688	£5000	£14000	£67500
1688 Elephant & Castle.........................	£6500	£20000	£85000

	F	VF	EF

WILLIAM AND MARY (1688–94)

	F	VF	EF
1691	£5000	£14000	£70000
1691 Elephant & Castle	£5000	£15000	£75000
1692	£5000	£14000	£70000
1692 Elephant & Castle	£5500	£17000	£75000
1693	£5000	£15000	£70000
1693 Elephant & Castle	£5500	£16000	£72000
1694	£5000	£15000	£60000
1694 Elephant & Castle	£6000	£16000	£72500

WILLIAM III (1694–1702)

	F	VF	EF
1699 First bust	£6000	£16500	£80000
1699 — Elephant & Castle	£7000	£18000	£90000
1700 —	£5750	£17000	£78000
1701 Second bust "fine work"	£5750	£18000	£75000

(1701 "fine work"—beware recent forgeries)

ANNE (1702–14)

Pre-Union with Scotland

	F	VF	EF
1703 VIGO below bust	£60000	£160000	£600000
1705	£8000	£24000	£90000
1706	£7000	£24000	£100000

Post-Union (different shields)

	F	VF	EF
1706	£5000	£18000	£75000
1709 Narrow shields	£5500	£18000	£78000
1711 Broader shields	£5500	£18000	£80000
1713 —	£6000	£17000	£78000
1714 —	£6000	£18000	£80000
1714/3	£6500	£19000	£82500

William & Mary

GEORGE I (1714–27)

	F	VF	EF
1716	£6500	£17000	£80000
1717	£6500	£18000	£80000
1720	£6500	£17000	£80000
1726	£6500	£17000	£75000

GEORGE II (1727–60)

	F	VF	EF
1729 Young head	£5000	£15000	£70000
1729 — E.I.C. below head	£4500	£15000	£70000
1731 —	£5000	£15000	£60000
1735 —	£5000	£15000	£75000
1738 —	£5000	£15000	£75000
1741	£5000	£14000	£60000
1741/38 41 over 38	£4750	£15000	£60000
1746 Old head, LIMA	£4750	£15000	£60000
1748 —	£4750	£15000	£55000
1753 —	£4750	£16000	£57500

GEORGE III (1760–1820)

	F	VF	EF
1770 Patterns	—	—	£375000
1773	—	—	£375000
1777	—	—	£375000

Anne

TWO GUINEAS

	F	VF	EF

CHARLES II (1660–85)

	F	VF	EF
1664 First bust	£2500	£6500	£22000
1664 — Elephant	£2400	£5500	£18000
1665 —		Extremely rare	
1669 —		Extremely rare	
1671 —	£3500	£8000	£35000
1673 First bust		Extremely rare	
1675 Second bust	£2500	£6000	£18000
1676 —	£2500	£6500	£24000
1676 — Elephant & Castle	£2500	£6500	£24000
1677 —	£2500	£6500	£22000
1677 — Elephant & Castle		Extremely rare	
1678/7 —	£2500	£6000	£20000
1678 — Elephant		Extremely rare	
1678 — Elephant & Castle	£2600	£6000	£28000
1679 —	£2600	£6000	£25000
1680 —	£2600	£5500	£26000
1681 —	£2600	£5000	£26000
1682 — Elephant & Castle	£2500	£6500	£27500
1683 —	£2500	£5000	£28000
1683 — Elephant & Castle	£2500	£6000	£30000
1684 —	£2500	£6000	£28000
1684 — Elephant & Castle	£2500	£6500	£35000

Charles II

JAMES II (1685–88)

	F	VF	EF
1687	£3000	£9000	£32000
1688/7	£3250	£8500	£33000

WILLIAM AND MARY (1688–94)

	F	VF	EF
1691 Elephant & Castle		Exceedingly rare	
1693	£2200	£7000	£24000
1693 Elephant & Castle	£2500	£7000	£27500
1694 — 4 over 3	£2200	£5500	£25000
1694/3 Elephant & Castle	£2400	£6000	£25000

James II

WILLIAM III (1694–1702)

	F	VF	EF
1701 "fine work"	£2500	£7500	£27500

ANNE (1702–14)

	F	VF	EF
1709 Post Union	£1800	£5000	£22000
1711	£1750	£5000	£20000
1713	£1750	£5000	£20000
1714/3	£1750	£5000	£23000

GEORGE I (1714–27)

	F	VF	EF
1717	£1750	£5500	£17000
1720	£1750	£5500	£17000
1720/17	£1850	£5500	£17000
1726	£1600	£5750	£18000

Anne

	F	VF	EF

GEORGE II (1727–60)

	F	VF	EF
1733 Proof only FDC		Extremely Rare	
1734 Young head 4 over 3	£2500	£6000	—
1735 —	£2500	£6000	£14000
1738 —	£950	£3000	£6500
1739 —	£950	£3000	£6000
1739 Intermediate head	£950	£3000	£8000
1740 —	£900	£2000	£8000
1748 Old head	£1100	£2300	£8000
1753 —	£1300	£3200	£9000

GEORGE III (1760–1820)

	F	VF	EF
1768 Patterns only	—	Extremely Rare	
1773 Patterns only	—	Extremely Rare	
1777 Patterns only	—	Extremely Rare	

George II

GUINEAS

CHARLES II (1660–85)

	F	VF	EF
1663 First bust	£3500	£12500	£50000
1663 — Elephant below	£4000	£12000	—
1663 Second bust	£3000	£9000	£40000
1664 Second bust	£3000	£8500	—
1664 — Elephant	£4000	£12000	£45000
1664 Third bust	£1000	£3000	£15000
1664 — Elephant	£1800	£5000	£18000
1665 —	£900	£3000	£14000
1665 — Elephant	£1800	£5000	£20000
1666 —	£900	£3000	£12000
1667 —	£900	£3000	£12000
1668 —	£850	£3000	£12000
1668 — Elephant		Extremely rare	
1669 —	£900	£3000	£14000
1670 —	£900	£3000	£13500
1671 —	£900	£3000	£13500
1672 —	£900	£3200	£15000
1672 Fourth bust	£850	£2750	£10000
1673 Third bust	£900	£3000	£15000
1673 Fourth bust	£700	£2500	£11000
1674 —	£700	£2500	£11000
1674 — Elephant & Castle		Extremely rare	
1675 —	£750	£2500	£10000
1675 — CRAOLVS Error		Extremely rare	
1675 — Elephant & Castle	£900	£3200	£14000
1676 —	£700	£2200	£9000
1676/4 — 6 over 4	£700	£2200	£9000
1676 — Elephant & Castle	£800	£3500	£15000
1677 —	£700	£2200	£9000
1677 — GRATIR Error		Extremely rare	
1677/5 — Elephant 7 over 5		Extremely rare	
1677 — Elephant & Castle	£800	£2800	£12000
1678 —	£750	£2000	£10000
1678 — Elephant		Extremely rare	
1678 — Elephant & Castle	£800	£3000	£13000

Charles II, third bust

Charles II, fourth bust, elephant & castle below

	F	VF	EF
1679 —	£800	£2200	£10000
1679 — Elephant & Castle	£900	£3300	£13000
1680 —	£800	£2200	£8500
1680 — Elephant & Castle	£900	£3500	£12500
1681 —	£800	£2500	£10000
1681 — Elephant & Castle	£900	£3500	£14000
1682 —	£800	£2750	£10000
1682 — Elephant & Castle	£900	£3800	£15000
1683 —	£700	£2200	£10000
1683 — Elephant & Castle	£850	£3500	£14000
1684 —	£700	£2500	£11000
1684 — Elephant & Castle	£900	£3750	£15000

James II, first bust, elephant & castle below

JAMES II (1685–88)

1685 First bust	£900	£3000	£12500
1685 — Elephant & Castle	£1000	£3200	£14000
1686 —	£800	£2750	£12000
1686 — Elephant & Castle		Extremely rare	
1686 Second bust	£800	£2500	£9000
1686 — Elephant & Castle	£900	£3500	£13000
1687 —	£800	£2300	£10000
1687 —Elephant & Castle	£900	£3500	£15000
1688 —	£800	£2400	£10000
1688 — Elephant & Castle	£850	£3200	£13000

James II, second bust

WILLIAM AND MARY (1688–94)

1689	£800	£2300	£10000
1689 Elephant & Castle	£850	£2500	£11000
1690	£800	£2700	£11000
1690 GVLIFLMVS	£800	£2700	£11000
1690 Elephant & Castle	£900	£3000	£13000
1691	£800	£2500	£10000
1691 Elephant & Castle	£800	£2500	£10000
1692	£800	£2500	£10000
1692 Elephant	£950	£3000	£11000
1692 Elephant & Castle	£850	£3000	£11000
1693	£800	£2750	£11000
1693 Elephant	£1100	£4000	£16000
1693 Elephant & Castle	£1000	£4000	£15000
1694	£900	£2800	£11000
1694/3	£900	£2800	£11000
1694 Elephant & Castle	£900	£3000	£11500
1694/3 Elephant & Castle	£900	£3000	£11500

(Please note there are several overstamp erros of this reign. Prices are similar to standard issues)

WILLIAM III (1694–1702)

1695 First bust	£700	£2500	£9000
1695 — Elephant & Castle	£1200	£5000	£15000
1696 —	£700	£2600	£9000
1696 — Elephant & Castle		Extremely rare	
1697 —	£750	£3000	£10000
1697 Second bust	£750	£2500	£9000
1697 — Elephant & Castle	£1500	£6000	—
1698 —	£700	£2500	£8000
1698 — Elephant & Castle	£1200	£4000	£12000
1699 —	£700	£2750	£10000
1699 — Elephant & Castle		Extremely rare	
1700 —	£750	£2500	£9000
1700 — Elephant & Castle	£1200	£5000	—
1701 —	£800	£2600	£8000
1701 — Elephant & Castle		Extremely rare	
1701 Third bust "fine work"	£1500	£5750	£17500

William III, second bust

	F	VF	EF

ANNE (1702–14)

	F	VF	EF
1702 (Pre-Union) First bust	£1200	£4000	£15000
1703 — VIGO below	£22000	£65000	£135000
1705 —	£1200	£4000	£13000
1706 —	£1200	£4000	£14000
1707 —	£1200	£4000	£14000
1707 — (Post-Union)	£800	£3000	£11000
1707 — Elephant & Castle	£1200	£5000	£15000
1707 Second bust	£700	£2800	£10000
1708 First bust	£750	£3000	£11000
1708 Second bust	£650	£2200	£7500
1708 — Elephant & Castle	£1000	£4000	£15000
1709 —	£800	£2000	£9000
1709 — Elephant & Castle	£900	£3500	£13000
1710 Third bust	£700	£1500	£5000
1711 —	£700	£1500	£5000
1712 —	£700	£1700	£6000
1713 —	£550	£1500	£4500
1714 —	£550	£1500	£4500
1714 GRΛTIΛ	£700	£1700	£5000

Anne, second bust

GEORGE I (1714–27)

	F	VF	EF
1714 First bust (Prince Elector)	£1800	£5000	£20000
1715 Second bust	£750	£1800	£5000
1715 Third bust	£500	£1500	£5200
1716 —	£600	£1500	£5500
1716 Fourth bust	£525	£1500	£5000
1717 —	£525	£1500	£5000
1718/7 — 8 over 7		Extremely rare	
1718 —		Extremely rare	
1719 —	£550	£1500	£5000
1720 —	£550	£1500	£4500
1721 —	£600	£1600	£5200
1721 — Elephant & Castle		Extremely rare	
1722 —	£550	£1600	£5000
1722 — Elephant & Castle		Extremely rare	
1723 —	£550	£1500	£5000
1723 Fifth bust	£550	£1500	£5000
1724 —	£550	£1500	£5000
1725 —	£550	£1500	£5000
1726 —	£525	£1500	£5000
1726 — Elephant & Castle	£2000	£7500	£25000
1727 —	£800	£2200	£6500

George I, third bust

GEORGE II (1727–60)

	F	VF	EF
1727 First young head, early large shield	£1000	£3000	£12000
1727 — Larger lettering, early small shield	£1000	£3200	£14000
1728 — —	£1100	£3500	£12500
1729 2nd young head E.I.C. below	£1100	£3500	£13000
1729 — Proof		Very Rare	
1730 —	£700	£1800	£6000
1731 —	£700	£2000	£7000
1731 — E.I.C. below	£1250	£4000	£15000
1732 —	£700	£2500	£8000
1732 — E.I.C. below	£900	£3000	£10000
1732 — Larger lettering obverse	£700	£1800	£7000
1732 — — E.I.C. below	£1200	£3000	£15000
1733 — —	£550	£1400	£4500
1734 — —	£550	£1400	£4500
1735 — —	£550	£1400	£4500
1736 — —	£550	£1500	£4500
1737 — —	£550	£1500	£4500

George II, 1759, old head, larger lettering

	F	VF	EF
1738 — —	£550	£1500	£4250
1739 Intermediate head	£500	£1400	£4000
1739 — E.I.C. below	£1100	£3000	£11000
1740 —	£650	£1500	£5000
1741/39 —	£800	£2400	£7000
1743 —	£800	£2400	£7000
1745 — Larger lettering obv. Older bust	£550	£1500	£5000
1745 — LIMA below	£2000	£7000	£22000
1746 — (GEORGIVS) Larger lettering obv.	£550	£1500	£4500
1747 Old head, large lettering	£500	£1300	£4000
1748 —	£500	£1300	£4200
1749 —	£500	£1400	£4200
1750 —	£500	£1300	£4200
1751 — small lettering	£450	£1200	£4200
1753 —	£450	£1200	£4200
1755 —	£450	£1300	£4200
1756 —	£450	£1200	£4200
1758 —	£450	£1200	£4200
1759 —	£450	£1200	£4200
1760 —	£450	£1200	£4000

George III first head

GEORGE III (1760–1820)

	F	VF	EF
1761 First head	£2200	£6000	£15000
1763 Second head	£1600	£4000	£12000
1764 —	£1400	£4000	£13000
1764 – No stop above bust	£2000	£5000	£13000
1765 Third head	£450	£800	£2000
1766 —	£450	£800	£2000
1767 —	£500	£1000	£2500
1768 —	£450	£800	£2000
1769 —	£450	£800	£2200
1770 —	£1350	£3000	£8000
1771 —	£450	£650	£1700
1772 —	£450	£650	£1700
1773 —	£450	£650	£1800
1774 Fourth head	£400	£650	£1250
1775 —	£425	£650	£1500
1776 —	£425	£675	£1400
1777 —	£425	£600	£1400
1778 —	£800	£1300	£3500
1779 —	£450	£725	£1250
1781 —	£400	£650	£1400
1782 —	£400	£650	£1400
1783 —	£375	£625	£1400
1784 —	£375	£625	£1300
1785 —	£375	£625	£1300
1786 —	£450	£700	£1350
1787 Fifth head, "Spade" reverse	£400	£575	£1150
1788 —	£400	£575	£1150
1789 —	£400	£575	£1200
1790 —	£425	£650	£1300
1791 —	£400	£600	£1200
1792 —	£400	£600	£1200
1793 —	£400	£650	£1250
1794 —	£400	£650	£1200
1795 —	£400	£650	£1200
1796 —	£400	£650	£1200
1797 —	£400	£650	£1200
1798 —	£400	£650	£1200
1799 —	£475	£800	£2000
1813 Sixth head, "Military" reverse	£1000	£2500	£7000

(Beware of counterfeits of this series—many dangerous copies exist)

Fourth head

Fifth head, Spade reverse

Sixth "Military" head

HALF GUINEAS

	F	VF	EF

CHARLES II (1660–85)

	F	VF	EF
1669 First bust	£500	£1700	£6000
1670 —	£500	£1700	£5500
1671 —	£550	£1800	£7000
1672 —	£550	£1700	£5500
1672 Second bust	£550	£1500	£5250
1673 —	£550	£1700	£5250
1674 —	£550	£1800	£6000
1675 —	£550	£1800	£6000
1676 —	£500	£1600	£5250
1676 — Elephant & Castle	£725	£3000	—
1677 —	£525	£1700	£5500
1677 — Elephant & Castle	£650	£2200	£8500
1678 —	£500	£1500	£5500
1678/7 —	£500	£1500	£5500
1678/7 — Elephant & Castle	£700	£2000	£8500
1679 —	£500	£1600	£5000
1680 —	£500	£2000	£6000
1680 — Elephant & Castle	£700	£2200	£8500
1681 —	£500	£1700	£6000
1682 —	£500	£1700	£5000
1682 — Elephant & Castle	£650	£2200	£9000
1683 —	£500	£1600	£5250
1683 — Elephant & Castle		Extremely rare	
1684 —	£500	£1500	£5000
1684 — Elephant & Castle	£700	£2200	£8500

Charles II, first bust

Charles II, second bust

JAMES II (1685–88)

	F	VF	EF
1686	£550	£1800	£6000
1686 Elephant & Castle	£900	£3750	£10000
1687	£550	£1800	£6000
1688	£525	£1850	£6000

WILLIAM AND MARY (1688–94)

	F	VF	EF
1689 First busts	£650	£2000	£5500
1690 Second busts	£600	£2000	£5500
1691 —	£625	£1800	£5750
1691 — Elephant & Castle	£700	£2400	£7000
1692 —	£700	£2000	£7000
1692 — Elephant		Extremely rare	
1692 — Elephant & Castle	£700	£2400	£7000
1693 —		Extremely rare	
1694 —	£600	£1800	£6000

William & Mary, first busts

WILLIAM III (1694–1702)

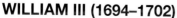

	F	VF	EF
1695	£450	£1300	£5000
1695 Elephant & Castle	£700	£2400	£7000
1696 —	£600	£1700	£6000
1697 Larger Harp rev.	£700	£2000	£7000
1698	£500	£1300	£4750
1698 Elephant & Castle	£700	£2000	£6500
1699		Extremely rare	
1700	£500	£1300	£5000
1701	£475	£1200	£5000

William III, elephant & castle below bust

	F	VF	EF

ANNE (1702–14)

	F	VF	EF
1702 (Pre-Union)	£1000	£3250	£12000
1703 VIGO below bust	£9000	£25000	£65000
1705	£900	£3000	£10000
1707 (Post-Union)	£450	£1100	£4500
1708	£425	£1200	£5000
1709	£450	£1100	£4250
1710	£400	£1000	£4250
1711	£400	£1000	£4250
1712	£425	£1100	£4250
1713	£400	£1000	£4200
1714	£400	£1000	£4200

Anne

GEORGE I (1714–27)

	F	VF	EF
1715 First bust	£750	£1600	£5500
1717 —	£400	£800	£4000
1718 —	£400	£800	£4000
1718/7 —	£400	£800	£4000
1719 —	£375	£750	£3750
1720 —	£400	£700	£4000
1721 —		Extremely rare	
1721 — Elephant & Castle		Extremely rare	
1722 —	£400	£900	£4000
1723 —	£500	£950	£4200
1724 —	£400	£1000	£4500
1725 Second bust	£425	£850	£3600
1726 —	£425	£850	£3800
1727 —	£425	£900	£4000

George I, second bust

GEORGE II (1727–60)

	F	VF	EF
1728 Young head	£600	£1500	£5000
1729 —	£550	£1400	£4500
1729 — E.I.C.	£700	£1700	£6000
1730 —	£450	£1000	£4000
1730 — E.I.C.	£800	£2200	—
1731 —	£350	£1000	£3500
1731 — E.I.C.		Extremely rare	
1732 —	£350	£1000	£3500
1732 — E.I.C.		Extremely rare	
1733 —		Unknown	
1734 —	£350	£900	£3500
1735 —		Unknown	
1736 —	£400	£900	£3500
1737 —	£400	£900	£4000
1738 —	£350	£900	£3500
1739 —	£350	£900	£3300
1739 — E.I.C.		Extremely rare	
1740 Intermediate head	£400	£1000	£3750
1743 —		Extremely rare	
1745 —	£375	£1000	£4000
1745 — LIMA	£1300	£4000	£13000
1746 —	£325	£800	£2750
1747 Old head	£375	£800	£3000
1748 —	£350	£750	£2750
1749 —	£375	£850	£3000
1750 —	£350	£750	£3000
1751 —	£325	£800	£2750
1752 —	£325	£800	£2750
1753 —	£325	£800	£2750
1755 —	£325	£700	£2600
1756 —	£350	£700	£2700
1758 —	£300	£750	£2750
1759 —	£300	£700	£2400
1759/8 —	£300	£650	£2800
1760 —	£300	£700	£2750

George II, young head

George II, old head

GEORGE III (1760–1820)

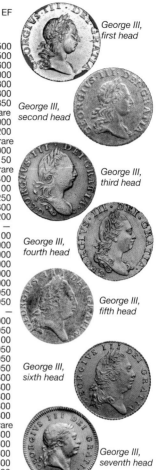

George III,
first head

George III,
second head

George III,
third head

George III,
fourth head

George III,
fifth head

George III,
sixth head

George III,
seventh head

	F	VF	EF
1762 First head	£700	£2000	£5500
1763 —	£800	£2500	£6500
1764 Second head	£275	£525	£1600
1765 —	£500	£1500	£4000
1766 —	£275	£600	£1800
1768 —	£275	£600	£1800
1769 —	£325	£600	£1850
1772 —		Extremely rare	
1773 —	£325	£700	£2000
1774 —	£350	£750	£2200
1774 Third head		Extremely rare	
1775 —	£1500	£4000	£11000
1775 Fourth head	£250	£450	£1150
1775 — Proof		Extremely rare	
1776 —	£275	£550	£1400
1777 —	£275	£550	£1100
1778 —	£275	£550	£1250
1779 —	£275	£550	£1300
1781 —	£275	£550	£1200
1783 —	£500	£1800	—
1784 —	£225	£500	£1100
1785 —	£225	£500	£1000
1786 —	£225	£500	£1000
1787 Fifth head, "Spade" rev.	£225	£375	£1000
1788 —	£225	£375	£1000
1789 —	£225	£375	£1000
1790 —	£225	£375	£950
1791 —	£225	£375	£950
1792 —	£1500	£4000	—
1793 —	£225	£475	£1000
1794 —	£225	£475	£950
1795 —	£225	£525	£1100
1796 —	£225	£475	£950
1797 —	£225	£475	£950
1798 —	£225	£475	£950
1800 —	£350	£1000	£2600
1801 Sixth head, Shield in Garter rev.	£225	£350	£800
1802 —	£225	£350	£800
1803 —	£225	£350	£800
1804 Seventh head	£225	£350	£800
1805 —		Extremely rare	
1806 —	£225	£400	£800
1808 —	£225	£400	£800
1899 —	£225	£400	£800
1810 —	£225	£400	£800
1811 —	£325	£600	£1500
1813 —	£325	£600	£1200

THIRD GUINEAS

DATE	F	VF	EF

GEORGE III (1760–1820)

	F	VF	EF
1797 First head, date in legend	£150	£275	£700
1798 — —	£150	£275	£700
1799 — —	£450	£1000	£2000
1800 — —	£160	£300	£800
1801 Date under crown	£170	£350	£775
1802 —	£170	£350	£775
1803 —	£170	£350	£750
1804 Second head	£140	£260	£700
1806 —	£140	£275	£650
1808 —	£140	£350	£725
1809 —	£140	£350	£700
1810 —	£140	£350	£725
1811 —	£525	£1300	£3000
1813 —	£300	£600	£1300

George III, date in legend

George III, date under crown

QUARTER GUINEAS

GEORGE I (1714–27)

	F	VF	EF
1718	£200	£350	£975

GEORGE III (1760–1820)

	F	VF	EF
1762	£250	£525	£900

George I

FIVE POUNDS

DATE	Mintage	F	VF	EF	UNC

GEORGE III (1760–1820)

1820 (pattern only)	—				Extremely rare

GEORGE IV (1820–30)

1826 proof only	—	—	—		£65,000

VICTORIA (1837–1901)

1839 Una & The Lion. Proof .   *

* In recent months the prices paid for Una & the Lion coins has risen astronomically. In August 2021 Hertiage Auctions sold an example for over $1 million.

1887	53,844	£1500	£2400	£3200	£4000
1887 Proof	797	—	—	—	£20,000
1887 S on ground on rev. (Sydney Mint)				Excessively rare	
1893	20,405	£2000	£2800	£5000	£8000
1893 Proof	773	—	—	—	£19,000

EDWARD VII (1902–10)

1902	34,910	£1500	£2000	£2750	£4000
1902 Matt proof	8,066	—	—	—	£3500

DATE	MINTAGE	F	VF	EF	UNC

GEORGE V (1911–36)
1911 Proof only   2,812   −   −   −   £9000

GEORGE VI (1937–52)
1937 Proof only   5,501   −   −   −   £8000

Later issues are listed in the Decimal section.

TWO POUNDS

GEORGE III (1760–1820)
1820 (pattern only)............   −   −   −   Extremely rare

GEORGE IV (1820–30)
1823 St George reverse.....   −   £800   £1100   £2500   £4500
1826 Proof only, shield reverse   −   −   −   Extremely rare

WILLIAM IV (1830–37)
1831 Proof only   225   −   −   −   £22500

VICTORIA (1837–1901)
1887...................................   91,345   £700   £1000   £1400   £2000
1887 Proof.......................   797   −   −   −   £3500
1887 S on ground of rev. (Sydney Mint)   Excessively rare
1893...................................   52,212   £800   £1100   £2000   £3000
1893 Proof........................   773   −   −   −   £6000

EDWARD VII (1902–10)
1902...................................   45,807   £650   £800   £1200   £2000
1902 Matt proof................   8,066   −   −   −   £1800

GEORGE V (1911–36)
1911 Proof only   2,812   −   −   −   £3000

GEORGE VI (1937–52)
1937 Proof only   5,501   −   −   −   £2750
Later issues are listed in the Decimal section.

CROMWELL GOLD

	F	VF	EF

OLIVER CROMWELL (1656–58)
1656 Fifty Shillings £30,000   £90,000   £220,000
1656 Twenty Shillings.............................   £7,000   £17,000   £40,000

SOVEREIGNS

DATE	MINTAGE	F	VF	EF	UNC

GEORGE III (1760–1820)

George III

DATE	MINTAGE	F	VF	EF	UNC
1817	3,235,239	£550	£900	£2000	£4500
1818	2,347,230	£700	£1200	£5000	£8500
1819	3,574		Exceedingly rare		
1820	931,994	£550	£850	£1800	£4000

GEORGE IV (1820–30)

1821 First bust, St George reverse	9,405,114	£500	£750	£1800	—
1821 — Proof	incl. above	—	—	—	£11000
1822 —	5,356,787	£450	£750	£2000	£3400
1823 —	616,770	£1000	£2750	£8000	—
1824 —	3,767,904	£500	£900	£2250	£4000
1825 —	4,200,343	£700	£2000	£6000	£9000
1825 Second bust, shield reverse	incl. above	£425	£700	£1750	£2600
1826 —	5,724,046	£425	£700	£1500	£2600
1826 — Proof	—	—	—	—	£9000
1827 —	2,266,629	£475	£750	£1750	£3500
1828 —	386,182	£6000	£15000	£30000	—
1829 —	2,444,652	£475	£800	£2500	£4000
1830 —	2,387,881	£475	£800	£2500	£4000

George IV, shield reverse

WILLIAM IV (1830–37)

1831	598,547	£600	£1000	£3250	£5000
1831 Proof, plain edge	—	—	—	—	£18,000
1832	3,737,065	£500	£900	£2500	£400
1833	1,225,269	£500	£900	£2500	£4000
1835	723,441	£500	£900	£2500	£4000
1836	1,714,349	£500	£900	£2000	£4000
1836 N. of Anno struck on shield	—	£6000	£11000	—	—
1837	1,172,984	£525	£950	£2000	£4500

William IV

Note—from the Victoria reign onwards, the prices of coins in lower grade are usually subject to the bullion price of gold.

VICTORIA (1837–1901)

Many of the gold coins struck at the colonial mints found their way into circulation in Britain, for the sake of completeness these coins are listed here. These can easily be identified by a tiny initial letter for the appropriate mint which can be found below the base of the reverse shield or, in the case of the St George reverse, below the bust on the obverse of the Young Head issues, or on the "ground" below the horse's hoof on the later issues.

YOUNG HEAD ISSUES

Shield reverse

(Note—Shield back sovereigns in Fine/VF condition, common dates, are normally traded as bullion + a percentage)

1838	2,718,694	£800	£1500	£4000	£8000
1839	503,695	£1100	£2750	£4000	£9500
1839 Proof, plain edge	—	—	—	—	£25000
1841	124,054	£5000	£9500	£22000	—
1842	4,865,375	£350	£400	£1000	£2000
1843	5,981,968	£350	£400	£1000	£2000
1843 "Narrow shield" variety	incl. above	£5000	£10000	—	—
1843 Roman I in date not 1841	—	£750	£1500	—	—
1844	3,000,445	£350	£400	£1000	£1800
1845	3,800,845	£350	£400	£1000	£1800
1846	3,802,947	£350	£400	£1000	£1800
1847	4,667,126	£350	£420	£1000	£1900

Victoria Young Head

DATE	MINTAGE	F	VF	EF	UNC
1848	2,246,701	£350	£420	£1000	£1900
1849	1,755,399	£350	£420	£1000	£1700
1850	1,402,039	£350	£420	£1000	£1700
1851	4,013,624	£350	£420	£750	£1700
1852	8,053,435	£350	£420	£850	£1700
1853	10,597,993	£350	£420	£750	£1750
1853 Proof	—	—	—	—	£22000
1854 Incuse WW	3,589,611	£350	£420	£750	£1750
1854 Surface raised WW	3,589,611	£350	£420	£750	£2000
1855	4,806,160	£350	£420	£750	£1750
1856	8,448,482	£350	£420	£750	£1750
1857	4,495,748	£350	£420	£750	£1750
1858	803,234	£350	£420	£750	£1750
1859	1,547,603	£350	£420	£750	£1750
1859 "Ansell" (additional line on lower part of hair ribbon)	—	£750	£1800	£9000	—
1860	2,555,958	£350	£400	£650	£1250
1861	7,624,736	£350	£400	£600	£1250
1862	7,836,413	£350	£400	£650	£1250
1863	5,921,669	£350	£400	£600	£1250
1863 Die No 827 on Truncation				Extremely rare	
1863 with Die number below shield	incl. above	£350	£400	£600	£1100
1864 —	8,656,352	£350	£400	£650	£1100
1865 —	1,450,238	£350	£400	£650	£1100
1866 —	4,047,288	£350	£400	£600	£1100
1868 —	1,653,384	£350	£400	£550	£1100
1869 —	6,441,322	£350	£400	£550	£1100
1870 —	2,189,960	£350	£400	£550	£1100
1871 —	8,767,250	£350	£400	£500	£1100
1872 —	8,767,250	£350	£400	£500	£1000
1872 no Die number	incl. above	£350	£400	£500	£1000
1873 with Die number	2,368,215	£350	£400	£600	£1000
1874 —	520,713	£2000	£4000	£12,000	—

M below reverse shield (Melbourne Mint)

1872	748,180	£350	£400	£500	£1250
1873	—			Extremely rare	
1874	1,373,298	£350	£400	£500	£1250
1879				Extremely rare	
1880	3,053,454	£700	£1650	£3000	£6000
1881	2,325,303	£350	£400	£450	£1600
1882	2,465,781	£350	£400	£450	£1150
1883	2,050,450	£350	£400	£600	£3200
1884	2,942,630	£350	£400	£450	£1000
1885	2,967,143	£350	£400	£450	£1000
1886	2,902,131	£1800	£4000	£6500	£8250
1887	1,916,424	£600	£1350	£3500	£5000

The die number appears between the wreath and the bottom rose, below the shield

The mint initial appears between the wreath and the bottom rose, below the shield, i.e. "S" indicates that the coin was struck at the Sydney Mint

S below reverse shield (Sydney Mint)

1871	2,814,000	£350	£400	£450	£1300
1872	1,815,000	£350	£400	£450	£1600
1873	1,478,000	£350	£400	£450	£1300
1875	2,122,000	£350	£400	£450	£1300
1877	1,590,000	£350	£400	£450	£1300
1878	1,259,000	£350	£400	£450	£1400
1879	1,366,000	£350	£400	£450	£1300
1880	1,459,000	£350	£400	£450	£1500
1881	1,360,000	£350	£400	£450	£1500
1882	1,298,000	£350	£400	£450	£1300
1883	1,108,000	£350	£400	£450	£1100
1884	1,595,000	£350	£400	£450	£1100
1885	1,486,000	£350	£400	£450	£1100
1886	1,667,000	£350	£400	£450	£1100
1887	1,000,000	£350	£400	£450	£1600

IMPORTANT NOTE: The prices quoted in this guide are set at August 2021 with the price of gold at £1,300 per ounce and silver £17.30 per ounce—market fluctuations can have a marked effect on the values of modern precious metal coins.

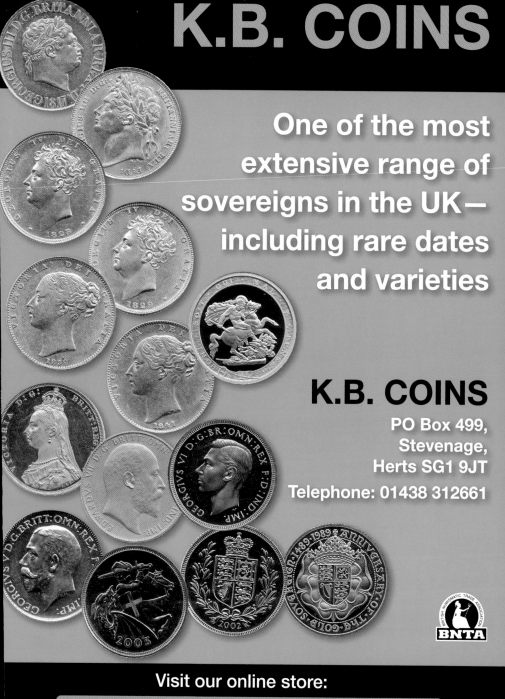

DATE	MINTAGE	F	VF	EF	UNC
St George & Dragon reverse					
1871	incl. above	£325	£330	£350	£550
1872	incl. above	£325	£330	£350	£550
1873	incl. above	£325	£330	£350	£550
1874	incl. above	£325	£330	£350	£550
1876	3,318,866	£325	£330	£350	£550
1878	1,091,275	£325	£330	£350	£550
1879	20,013	£600	£1500	£13,000	—
1880	3,650,080	£325	£330	£350	£550
1884	1,769,635	£325	£330	£350	£550
1885	717,723	£325	£330	£350	£550
M below bust on obverse (Melbourne Mint)					
1872	incl. above	£325	£500	£1150	£4200
1873	752,199	£325	£400	£450	£550
1874	incl. above	£325	£400	£450	£550
1875	incl. above	£325	£400	£450	£550
1876	2,124,445	£325	£400	£450	£550
1877	1,487,316	£325	£400	£450	£550
1878	2,171,457	£325	£400	£450	£550
1879	2,740,594	£325	£400	£450	£550
1880	incl. above	£325	£400	£450	£550
1881	incl. above	£325	£400	£450	£550
1882	incl. above	£325	£400	£450	£550
1883	incl. above	£325	£400	£450	£550
1884	incl. above	£325	£400	£450	£550
1885	incl. above	£325	£400	£450	£550
1886	incl. above	£325	£400	£450	£550
1887	incl. above	£325	£400	£450	£550
S below bust on obverse (Sydney Mint)					
1871	2,814,000	£325	£400	£450	£525
1872	incl. above	£325	£400	£450	£700
1873	incl. above	£325	£400	£450	£550
1874	1,899,000	£325	£400	£450	£550
1875	inc above	£325	£400	£450	£550
1876	1,613,000	£325	£400	£450	£550
1877	—				Unknown
1879	incl. above	£325	£400	£450	£550
1880	incl. above	£325	£400	£450	£550
1881	incl. above	£325	£400	£450	£550
1882	incl. above	£325	£400	£450	£550
1883	incl. above	£325	£400	£450	£550
1884	incl. above	£325	£400	£450	£550
1885	incl. above	£325	£400	£450	£550
1886	incl. above	£325	£400	£450	£550
1887	incl. above	£325	£400	£450	£550
JUBILEE HEAD ISSUES					
1887	1,111,280	£325	£400	£450	£550
1887 Proof	797	—	—	—	£3000
1888	2,717,424	£325	£400	£450	£550
1889	7,257,455	£325	£400	£450	£550
1890	6,529.887	£325	£400	£450	£550
1891	6,329,476	£325	£400	£450	£550
1892	7,104,720	£325	£400	£450	£550
M on ground on reverse (Melbourne Mint)					
1887	940,000	£325	£400	£450	£550
1888	2,830,612	£325	£400	£450	£550
1889	2,732,590	£325	£400	£450	£550
1890	2,473,537	£325	£400	£450	£550
1891	2,749,592	£325	£400	£450	£550
1892	3,488,750	£325	£400	£450	£550
1893	1,649,352	£325	£400	£450	£550

M below bust indicates Melbourne Mint

S below bust indicates Sydney Mint

Jubilee head type

"M" below the horse's hoof above the date indicates that the coin was struck at the Melbourne Mint

KNIGHTSBRIDGE COINS

EST. 1975

WANTED TO PURCHASE OR FOR AUCTION

UNA AND THE LION £5

GEORGE IV 1826 £5

VICTORIA 1887 PROOF £5

VICTORIA 1893 PROOF £5

DATE	MINTAGE	F	VF	EF	UNC
S on ground on reverse (Sydney Mint)					
1887	1,002,000	£325	£400	£1600	£2750
1888	2,187,000	£325	£400	£450	£550
1889	3,262,000	£325	£400	£450	£550
1890	2,808,000	£325	£400	£450	£550
1891	2,596,000	£325	£400	£450	£550
1892	2,837,000	£325	£400	£450	£550
1893	1,498,000	£325	£400	£450	£550

OLD HEAD ISSUES

1893	6,898,260	£325	£400	£450	£550
1893 Proof	773	—	—	—	£3250
1894	3,782,611	£325	£400	£450	£550
1895	2,285,317	£325	£400	£450	£550
1896	3,334,065	£325	£400	£450	£550
1898	4,361,347	£325	£400	£450	£550
1899	7,515,978	£325	£400	£450	£550
1900	10,846,741	£325	£400	£450	£550
1901	1,578,948	£325	£400	£450	£550
M on ground on reverse (Melbourne Mint)					
1893	1,914,000	£325	£400	£450	£550
1894	4,166,874	£325	£400	£450	£550
1895	4,165,869	£325	£400	£450	£550
1896	4,456,932	£325	£400	£450	£550
1897	5,130,565	£325	£400	£450	£550
1898	5,509,138	£325	£400	£450	£550
1899	5,579,157	£325	£400	£450	£550
1900	4,305,904	£325	£400	£450	£550
1901	3,987,701	£325	£400	£450	£550
P on ground on reverse (Perth Mint)					
1899	690,992	£325	£400	£500	£2500
1900	1,886,089	£325	£400	£450	£550
1901	2,889,333	£325	£400	£450	£550
S on ground on reverse (Sydney Mint)					
1893	1,346,000	£325	£400	£450	£550
1894	3,067,000	£325	£400	£450	£550
1895	2,758,000	£325	£400	£450	£550
1896	2,544,000	£325	£400	£450	£550
1897	2,532,000	£325	£400	£450	£550
1898	2,548,000	£325	£400	£450	£550
1899	3,259,000	£325	£400	£450	£550
1900	3,586,000	£325	£400	£450	£550
1901	3,012,000	£325	£400	£450	£550

Old head type

EDWARD VII (1902–10)

1902	4,737,796	£325	£400	£450	£550
1902 Matt proof	15,123	—	—	—	£700
1903	8,888,627	£325	£400	£450	£550
1904	10,041,369	£325	£400	£450	£550
1905	5,910,403	£325	£400	£450	£550
1906	10,466,981	£325	£400	£450	£550
1907	18,458,663	£325	£400	£450	£550
1908	11,729,006	£325	£400	£450	£550
1909	12,157,099	£325	£400	£450	£550
1910	22,379,624	£325	£400	£450	£550
C on ground on reverse (Ottawa Mint)					
1908 Satin finish Proof only	633		Extremely rare		
1909	16,300	£325	£400	£500	£800
1910	28,020	£325	£400	£500	£700

DATE	MINTAGE	F	VF	EF	UNC

M on ground on reverse (Melbourne Mint)

1902	4,267,157	£325	£400	£450	£550
1903	3,521,780	£325	£400	£450	£550
1904	3,743,897	£325	£400	£450	£550
1905	3,633,838	£325	£400	£450	£550
1906	3,657,853	£325	£400	£450	£550
1907	3,332,691	£325	£400	£450	£550
1908	3,080,148	£325	£400	£450	£550
1909	3,029,538	£325	£400	£450	£550
1910	3,054,547	£325	£400	£450	£550

P on ground on reverse (Perth Mint)

1902	3,289,122	£325	£400	£450	£550
1903	4,674,783	£325	£400	£450	£550
1904	4,506,756	£325	£400	£450	£550
1905	4,876,193	£325	£400	£450	£550
1906	4,829,817	£325	£400	£450	£550
1907	4,972,289	£325	£400	£450	£550
1908	4,875,617	£325	£400	£450	£550
1909	4,524,241	£325	£400	£450	£550
1910	4,690,625	£325	£400	£450	£550

S on ground on reverse (Sydney Mint)

1902	2,813,000	£325	£400	£450	£550
1902 Proof	incl. above			Extremely rare	
1903	2,806,000	£325	£400	£450	£550
1904	2,986,000	£325	£400	£450	£550
1905	2,778,000	£325	£400	£450	£550
1906	2,792,000	£325	£400	£450	£550
1907	2,539,000	£325	£400	£450	£550
1908	2,017,000	£325	£400	£450	£550
1909	2,057,000	£325	£400	£450	£550
1910	2,135,000	£325	£400	£450	£550

> **IMPORTANT NOTE:** The prices quoted in this guide are set at August 2021 with the price of gold at £1,300 per ounce and silver £17.30 per ounce — market fluctuations can have a marked effect on the values of modern precious metal coins.

GEORGE V (1911–36)

(Extra care should be exercised when purchasing as good quality forgeries exist of virtually all dates and mintmarks)

1911	30,044,105	£325	£400	£450	£550
1911 Proof	3,764	—	—	—	£1600
1912	30,317,921	£325	£400	£450	£550
1913	24,539,672	£325	£400	£450	£550
1914	11,501,117	£325	£400	£450	£550
1915	20,295,280	£325	£400	£450	£550
1916	1,554,120	£325	£400	£500	£750
1917	1,014,714	£1500	£5500	£20000	—
1925	4,406,431	£325	£400	£450	£550

C on ground on reverse (Ottawa Mint)

1911	256,946	£325	£400	£500	£750
1913	3,715	£325	£500	£1750	—
1914	14,891	£325	£450	£1500	—
1916	6,111			Extremely rare	
1917	58,845	£325	£400	£600	£850
1918	106,516	£325	£400	£500	£650
1919	135,889	£325	£400	£500	£650

I on ground on reverse (Bombay Mint)

1918	1,295,372	£325	£400	£450	—

M on ground on reverse (Melbourne Mint)

1911	2,851,451	£325	£400	£450	£550
1912	2,469,257	£325	£400	£450	£550
1913	2,323,180	£325	£400	£450	£550
1914	2,012,029	£325	£400	£450	£550
1915	1,637,839	£325	£400	£450	£550
1916	1,273,643	£325	£400	£450	£550
1917	934,469	£325	£400	£500	£750
1918	4,969,493	£325	£400	£450	£550
1919	514,257	£325	£400	£450	£550

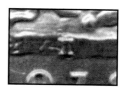

"I" on reverse ground for the Bombay Mint

133

DATE	MINTAGE	F	VF	EF	UNC
1920	530,266	£1350	£2500	£4000	£6500
1921	240,121	£4000	£7000	£8000	£24000
1922	608,306	£4000	£7000	£7000	£25000
1923	510,870	£325	£400	£500	£750
1924	278,140	£325	£400	£500	£750
1925	3,311,622	£325	£400	£450	£550
1926	211,107	£325	£400	£450	£550
1928	413,208	£500	£900	£1700	£4000
1929	436,719	£900	£1000	£1700	£5000
1930	77,547	£325	£400	£500	£800
1931	57,779	£325	£400	£750	£1000

P on ground on reverse (Perth Mint)

1911	4,373,165	£325	£400	£450	£550
1912	4,278,144	£325	£400	£450	£550
1913	4,635,287	£325	£400	£450	£550
1914	4,815,996	£325	£400	£450	£550
1915	4,373,596	£325	£400	£450	£550
1916	4,096,771	£325	£400	£450	£550
1917	4,110,286	£325	£400	£450	£550
1918	3,812,884	£325	£400	£450	£550
1919	2,995,216	£325	£400	£450	£550
1920	2,421,196	£325	£400	£450	£550
1921	2,134,360	£325	£400	£450	£550
1922	2,298,884	£325	£400	£450	£550
1923	2,124,154	£325	£400	£450	£550
1924	1,464,416	£325	£400	£450	£550
1925	1,837,901	£325	£400	£500	£650
1926	1,313,578	£500	£900	£1500	£4200
1927	1,383,544	£325	£400	£500	£750
1928	1,333,417	£325	£400	£450	£600
1929	1,606,625	£325	£400	£450	£550
1930	1,915,352	£325	£400	£500	£675
1931	1,173,568	£325	£400	£450	£550

S on ground on reverse (Sydney Mint)

1911	2,519,000	£325	£400	£450	£550
1912	2,227,000	£325	£400	£450	£550
1913	2,249,000	£325	£400	£450	£550
1914	1,774,000	£325	£400	£450	£550
1915	1,346,000	£325	£400	£450	£550
1916	1,242,000	£325	£400	£450	£550
1917	1,666,000	£325	£400	£450	£550
1918	3,716,000	£325	£400	£450	£550
1919	1,835,000	£325	£400	£450	£550 ⇨

Melbourne Mint (M on ground)

Perth Mint (P on ground)

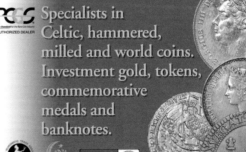

DATE	MINTAGE	F	VF	EF	UNC
1920	—		Excessively rare		
1921	839,000	£600	£900	£1750	£2750
1922	578,000		Extremely rare		
1923	416,000		Extremely rare		
1924	394,000	£600	£1100	£1500	£2750
1925	5,632,000	£325	£400	£450	£550
1926	1,031,050		Extremely rare		

SA on ground on reverse (Pretoria Mint)

1923	719	£800	£1850	£3500	£7500
1923 Proof	655		Extremely rare		
1924	3,184	—	£3000	£5000	—
1925	6,086,264	£325	£400	£450	£550
1926	11,107,611	£325	£400	£450	£550
1927	16,379,704	£325	£400	£450	£550
1928	18,235,057	£325	£400	£450	£550
1929	12,024,107	£325	£400	£450	£550
1930	10,027,756	£325	£400	£450	£550
1931	8,511,792	£325	£400	£450	£550
1932	1,066,680	£325	£400	£450	£550

Pretoria Mint (SA on ground)

GEORGE VI (1937–52)

1937 Proof only	5,501	—	—	£3750	£5500

ELIZABETH II (1952–)

Pre Decimal Issues

1957	2,072,000	£325	£400	£450	£550
1958	8,700,140	£325	£400	£450	£550
1959	1,358,228	£325	£400	£450	£550
1962	3,000,000	£325	£400	£450	£550
1963	7,400,000	£325	£400	£450	£550
1964	3,000,000	£325	£400	£450	£550
1965	3,800,000	£325	£400	£450	£550
1966	7,050,000	£325	£400	£450	£550
1967	5,000,000	£325	£400	£450	£550
1968	4,203,000	£325	£400	£450	£550

Later issues are included in the Decimal section.

HALF SOVEREIGNS

GEORGE III (1760–1820)

1817	2,080,197	£200	£370	£1000	£1800
1818	1,030,286	£220	£400	£1000	£1800
1820	35,043	£220	£400	£800	£1600

GEORGE IV (1820–30)

1821 First bust, ornate shield reverse	231,288	£600	£1600	£3750	£5000
1821 — Proof	unrecorded	—	—	—	£10000
1823 First bust, Plain shield rev.	224,280	£200	£280	£1000	£1800
1824 —	591,538	£200	£280	£850	£1600
1825 —	761,150	£200	£280	£750	£1250
1826 bare head, shield with full legend reverse	344,830	£200	£320	£1000	£1500
1826 — Proof	unrecorded	—	—	—	£5500
1827 —	492,014	£200	£340	£1000	£1700
1828 —	1,224,754	£200	£350	£800	£1500

DATE	MINTAGE	F	VF	EF	UNC

WILLIAM IV (1830–37)

1831 Proof only	unrecorded	–	–	–	£6000
1834	133,899	£300	£600	£1500	£2500
1835	772,554	£300	£600	£1000	£2200
1836	146,865	£250	£500	£1250	£2200
1836 obverse from 6d die	incl. above	£2500	£5000	£10000	–
1837	160,207	£275	£500	£1400	£2100

VICTORIA (1837–1901)

YOUNG HEAD ISSUES
Shield reverse

1838	273,341	£175	£250	£1000	£1800
1839 Proof only	1,230	–	–	–	£6500
1841	508,835	£200	£280	£1400	£3000
1842	2,223,352	£175	£250	£1000	£1600
1843	1,251,762	£175	£250	£1000	£1600
1844	1,127,007	£175	£250	£850	£1150
1845	887,526	£320	£800	£3000	£5000
1846	1,063,928	£175	£250	£850	£1300
1847	982,636	£175	£250	£750	£1200
1848	410,595	£175	£250	£850	£1300
1849	845,112	£175	£250	£750	£1200
1850	179,595	£240	£620	£2500	£3500
1851	773,573	£175	£250	£700	£1200
1852	1,377,671	£175	£250	£700	£1200
1853	2,708,796	£175	£250	£700	£1200
1853 Proof	unrecorded	–	–	–	£12500
1855	1,120,362	£175	£250	£700	£1200
1856	2,391,909	£175	£250	£700	£1200
1857	728,223	£175	£250	£700	£1200
1858	855,578	£175	£250	£700	£1200
1859	2,203,813	£175	£250	£700	£1200
1860	1,131,500	£175	£250	£700	£1200
1861	1,130,867	£175	£250	£700	£1200
1862	unrecorded	£750	£2000	£10000	–
1863	1,571,574	£175	£250	£700	£1100
1863 with Die number	incl. above	£175	£250	£800	£1100
1864 –	1,758,490	£175	£250	£650	£1100
1865 –	1,834,750	£175	£250	£650	£1100
1866 –	2,058,776	£175	£250	£650	£1100
1867 –	992,795	£175	£250	£650	£1100
1869 –	1,861,764	£175	£250	£650	£1100
1870 –	1,159,544	£175	£250	£650	£1100
1871 –	2,062,970	£175	£250	£650	£1100
1872 –	3,248,627	£175	£250	£650	£1100
1873 –	1,927,050	£175	£250	£650	£1100
1874 –	1,884,432	£175	£250	£650	£1100
1875 –	516,240	£175	£250	£650	£1100
1876 –	2,785,187	£175	£250	£650	£1100
1877 –	2,197,482	£175	£250	£650	£1100
1878 –	2,081,941	£175	£250	£650	£1100
1879 –	35,201	£175	£250	£650	£1100
1880 –	1,009,049	£175	£250	£650	£1100
1880 no Die number	incl. above	£175	£250	£900	£1300
1883 –	2,870,457	£175	£250	£600	£950
1884 –	1,113,756	£175	£250	£650	£1000
1885 –	4,468,871	£175	£250	£600	£1000

London Mint die number on reverse

M below shield (Melbourne Mint)

1873	165,034	£175	£250	£1000	–
1877	80,016	£175	£250	£2000	–
1881	42,009	£175	£330	£2000	–
1882	107,522	£175	£250	£700	–
1884	48,009	£175	£250	£1750	–
1885	11,003	£175	£330	£3750	–
1886	38,008	£175	£280	£6000	–
1887	64,013	£175	£630	£10000	£16,000

Melbourne Mint (M below shield)

Date	Mintage	F	VF	EF	UNC
S below shield (Sydney Mint)					
1871	180,000 (?)	£175	£250	£750	—
1872	356,000	£175	£250	£750	—
1875	unrecorded	£175	£250	£750	—
1879	94,000	£175	£250	£650	—
1880	80,000	£175	£250	£850	—
1881	62,000	£175	£280	£1000	—
1882	52,000		Extremely rare		
1883	220,000	£175	£250	£900	—
1886	82,000	£175	£250	£600	—
1887	134,000	£175	£250	£800	£4500

JUBILEE HEAD ISSUES

Date	Mintage	F	VF	EF	UNC
1887	871,770	£175	£250	£500	£750
1887 Proof	797	£175	£250	—	£2250
1890	2.266,023	£175	£250	£500	£750
1891	1,079,286	£175	£250	£300	£475
1892	13,680,486	£175	£250	£300	£475
1893	4,426,625	£175	£250	£300	£475
M below shield (Melbourne Mint)					
1887	incl. above	£175	£250	£400	£600
1893	110,024	£175	£250	£450	£750
S below shield (Sydney Mint)					
1887	incl. above	£175	£250	£300	£600
1889	64,000	£175	£280	£1500	—
1891	154,000	£175	£250	£1000	—

OLD HEAD ISSUES

Date	Mintage	F	VF	EF	UNC
1893	incl. above	£175	£250	£300	£450
1893 Proof	773	—	—	—	£2500
1894	3,794,591	£175	£250	£300	£450
1895	2,869,183	£175	£250	£300	£450
1896	2,946,605	£175	£250	£300	£450
1897	3,568,156	£175	£250	£300	£450
1898	2,868,527	£175	£250	£300	£450
1899	3,361,881	£175	£250	£300	£450
1900	4,307,372	£175	£250	£300	£450
1901	2,037,664	£175	£250	£300	£450
M on ground on reverse (Melbourne Mint)					
1893	unrecorded		Extremely rare		
1896	218,946	£175	£250	£450	—
1899	97,221	£175	£250	£550	—
1900	112,920	£175	£250	£600	—
P on ground on reverse (Perth Mint)					
1900	119,376	£175	£330	£550	—
S on ground on reverse (Sydney Mint)					
1893	250,000	£175	£250	£600	—
1897	unrecorded	£175	£250	£500	—
1900	260,00	£175	£250	£400	—

EDWARD VII (1902–10)

Date	Mintage	F	VF	EF	UNC
1902	4,244,457	£175	£250	£300	£450
1902 Matt proof	15,123	—	—	—	£600
1903	2,522,057	£175	£250	£300	£450
1904	1,717,440	£175	£250	£300	£450
1905	3,023,993	£175	£250	£300	£450
1906	4,245,437	£175	£250	£300	£450
1907	4,233,421	£175	£250	£350	£475
1908	3,996,992	£175	£250	£350	£475
1909	4,010,715	£175	£250	£350	£475
1910	5,023,881	£175	£250	£300	£450
M on ground on reverse (Melbourne Mint)					
1906	82,042	£175	£250	£750	£1100
1907	405,034	£175	£250	£300	£450
1908	incl. above	£175	£250	£300	£450
1909	186,094	£175	£250	£600	£750

DATE		F	VF	EF	UNC
P on ground on reverse (Perth Mint)					
1904	60,030	£175	£250	£1000	—
1908	24,668	£175	£250	£950	—
1909	44,022	£175	£250	£500	—
S on ground on reverse (Sydney Mint)					
1902	84,000	£175	£250	£300	£375
1902 Proof				Extremely rare	
1903	231,000	£175	£250	£300	£375
1906	308,000	£175	£250	£300	£375
1908	538,000	£175	£250	£300	£375
1910	474,000	£175	£250	£300	£375

GEORGE V (1911–36)

		F	VF	EF	UNC
1911	6,104,106	£175	£250	£300	£375
1911 Proof	3,764	—	—	—	£1100
1912	6,224,316	£175	£250	£300	£375
1913	6,094,290	£175	£250	£300	£375
1914	7,251,124	£175	£250	£300	£375
1915	2,042,747	£175	£250	£300	£375
M on ground on reverse (Melbourne Mint)					
1915	125,664	£175	£250	£300	£375
P on ground on reverse (Perth Mint)					
1911	130,373	£175	£250	£300	£375
1915	136,219	£175	£250	£300	£375
1918	unrecorded	£205	£600	£2000	£3750
1919	56,786				Rare
1920	53,208				Rare
S on ground on reverse (Sydney Mint)					
1911	252,000	£175	£250	£300	£375
1912	278,000	£175	£250	£300	£375
1914	322,000	£175	£250	£300	£375
1915	892,000	£175	£250	£300	£375
1916	448,000	£175	£250	£300	£375
SA on ground on reverse (Pretoria Mint)					
1923 Proof only	655	—	—	—	£1400
1925	946,615	£175	£250	£300	£375
1926	806,540	£175	£250	£300	£375

GEORGE VI (1937–52)

		F	VF	EF	UNC
1937 Proof only	5,501	—	—	—	£1000

Later issues are included in the Decimal section.

139

CROWNS

DATE	F	VF	EF	UNC

OLIVER CROMWELL

	F	VF	EF	UNC
1658 8 over 7 (always)	£2000	£4000	£8250	—
1658 Dutch Copy		Extremely rare		
1658 Patterns. In Various Metals		Extremely rare		

CHARLES II (1660–85)

	F	VF	EF	UNC
1662 First bust, rose (2 varieties)	£250	£900	£6000	—
1662 — no rose (2 varieties)	£250	£900	£6000	—
1663 —	£250	£900	£6000	—
1664 Second bust	£200	£900	£6000	—
1665 —	£1500	£5000	—	—
1666 —	£300	£1100	£6000	—
1666 — error RE.X for REX		Extremely rare		
1666 — Elephant below bust	£900	£3500	£20000	—
1667 —	£190	£600	£3000	—
1668/7 — 8 over 7	£200	£600	—	—
1668 —	£200	£600	£5000	—
1669/8 — 9 over 8	£350	£800	—	—
1669 —	£325	£1200	£6000	—
1670/69 — 70 over 69	£250	£1000	—	—
1670 —	£220	£750	£5000	—
1671	£220	£750	£4000	—
1671 Third bust	£220	£750	£4000	—
1672 —	£220	£600	£4000	—
1673 —	£220	£600	£4000	—
1674 —		Extremely rare		
1675 —	£800	£2750	—	—
1675/3 —	£700	£3000	—	—
1676 —	£180	£650	£4000	—
1677 —	£200	£650	£4250	—
1677/6 — 7 over 6	£200	£900	—	—
1678/7 —	£200	£900	—	—
1678/7 — 8 over 7	£275	£900	—	—
1679 —	£190	£750	£4000	—
1679 Fourth bust	£190	£750	£3750	—
1680 Third bust	£190	£1000	£4500	—
1680/79 — 80 over 79	£225	£850	—	—
1680 Fourth bust	£200	£800	£5500	—
1680/79 — 80 over 79	£240	£1100	—	—
1681 —	£200	£700	£4500	—
1681 — Elephant & Castle below bust	£5500	£15000	—	—
1682/1 —	£200	£800	£4000	—
1682 — edge error QVRRTO for QVARTO .	£400	—	—	—
1683 —	£400	£1150	£5500	—
1684 —	£400	£1300	—	—

JAMES II (1685–88)

	F	VF	EF	UNC
1686 First bust	£325	£1200	£7500	—
1686 — No stops on obv	£425	£1800	—	—
1687 Second bust	£300	£700	£5000	—
1688/7 — 8 over 7	£340	£900	—	—
1688 —	£280	£900	£5000	—

WILLIAM AND MARY (1688–94)

	F	VF	EF	UNC
1691	£750	£1800	£7500	—
1692	£750	£2000	£7000	—
1692 2 over upside down 2	£750	£2000	£7000	—

DATE	F	VF	EF	UNC

WILLIAM III (1694–1702)

	F	VF	EF	UNC
1695 First bust	£100	£370	£2500	—
1696 —	£100	£300	£2400	—
1696 — no stops on obv.	£225	£500	—	—
1996 — no stops obv./rev.	£250	£550	—	—
1696 — GEI for DEI	£750	£1800	—	—
1696 — Last 6 over 5	£200	£550	—	—
1696 Second bust				Unique
1696 Third bust	£100	£300	£2200	—
1697 —	£2800	£10000	£25000	—
1700 Third bust variety edge year DUODECIMO	£140	£550	£2500	—
1700 — edge year DUODECIMO TERTIO..	£140	£550	£2500	—

ANNE (1702–14)

	F	VF	EF	UNC
1703 First bust, VIGO	£350	£1400	£7500	—
1705 — Plumes in angles on rev.	£600	£2200	£8500	—
1706 — Roses & Plumes in angles on rev...	£275	£800	£3300	—
1707 — —	£275	£800	£3300	—
1707 Second bust, E below	£200	£700	£3200	—
1707 — Plain	£200	£700	£3200	—
1708 — E below	£200	£700	£3200	—
1708/7 — 8 over 7	£200	£800	—	—
1708 — Plain	£200	£700	£3300	—
1708 — — error BR for BRI			Extremely rare	
1708 — Plumes in angles on rev.	£200	£700	£3400	—
1713 Third bust, Roses & Plumes in angles on rev.	£220	£750	£4000	—

GEORGE I (1714–27)

	F	VF	EF	UNC
1716	£750	£1800	£6500	—
1718 8 over 6	£750	£1800	£6000	—
1720 20 over 18	£750	£1800	£6250	—
1723 SSC in angles on rev. (South Sea Co.)	£750	£1800	£6000	—
1726	£750	£2000	£7500	—

GEORGE II (1727–60)

	F	VF	EF	UNC
1732 Young head, Plain, Proof	—	—£22,000		
1732 — Roses & Plumes in angles on rev ..	£350	£850	£4000	—
1734 — —	£350	£850	£4000	—
1735 — —	£350	£850	£4000	—
1736 — —	£350	£850	£4000	—
1739 — Roses in angles on rev	£350	£600	£3750	—
1741 — —	£350	£600	£3750	—
1743 Old head, Roses in angles on rev	£350	£600	£2500	—
1746 — — LIMA below bust	£350	£600	£2500	—
1746 — Plain, Proof	—	—£18,000		
1750 — —	£500	£1400	£4500	—
1751 — —	£550	£1700	£5000	—

GEORGE III (1760–1820)

	F	VF	EF	UNC
Dollar with oval counterstamp	£175	£650	£1000	—
Dollar with octagonal counterstamp	£225	£700	£950	—
1804 Bank of England Dollar, Britannia rev.	£120	£275	£550	—
1818 LVIII	£50	£120	£450	£1100
1818 LIX	£50	£120	£450	£1100
1819 LIX	£50	£120	£450	£1100
1819 LIX 9 over 8	£55	£160	£600	—
1819 LIX no stops on edge	£65	£170	£425	£1200
1819 LX	£50	£140	£400	£1200
1820 LX	£45	£140	£400	£1150
1820 LX 20 over 19	£45	£220	£650	—

DATE	MINTAGE	F	VF	EF	UNC

GEORGE IV (1820–30)

1821 First bust, St George rev.

	MINTAGE	F	VF	EF	UNC
SECUNDO on edge	437,976	£50	£200	£700	£1800
1821 — — Proof..........................	—	—	—	£6000
1821 — — Proof TERTIO (error edge)........	—	—	—	£8000
1822 — — SECUNDO..................	124,929	£45	£200	£800	£1800
1822 — — TERTIO..................... Incl above		£45	£200	£800	£1800
1823 — — Proof only				Extremely rare	
1826 Second bust, shield rev, SEPTIMO					
Proof only...	—	—	—£20000		

WILLIAM IV (1830–37)

				UNC
1831 Proof only W.W. on truncation...........	—	—	£35000
1831 Proof only W. WYON on truncation....	—	—	£35000
1834 Proof only	—	—	—£50000

VICTORIA (1837–1901)

YOUNG HEAD ISSUES

	MINTAGE	F	VF	EF	UNC
1839 Proof only	—	—	—	—£27500
1844 Star stops on edge.............	94,248	£75	£350	£1500	£3300
1844 Cinquefoil stops on edge ...	incl. above	£75	£350	£1500	£3300
1845 Star stops on edge.............	159,192	£75	£350	£1500	£3300
1845 Cinquefoil stops on edge ...	incl. above	£75	£350	£1500	£3300
1847..	140,976	£90	£400	£1750	£5500

GOTHIC HEAD ISSUES (Proof only)

	MINTAGE	F	VF	EF	UNC
1847 mdcccxlvii UNDECIMO on edge	8,000	£1000	£1850	£3200	£6000
1847 — Plain edge.....................	—	—	—	—	£7250
1853 mdcccliii SEPTIMO on edge	460	—	—	—£30000	
1853 — Plain edge.....................	—	—	—	—Very rare	

JUBILEE HEAD ISSUES

	MINTAGE	F	VF	EF	UNC
1887	173,581	£24	£35	£75	£180
1887 Proof.................................	1,084	—	—	—	£2500
1888 Narrow date......................	131,899	£24	£35	£100	£325
1888 Wide date	incl above	£30	£75	£340	—
1889...	1,807,224	£24	£35	£75	£200
1890...	997,862	£24	£35	£85	£275
1891...	556,394	£24	£35	£85	£300
1892...	451,334	£24	£35	£90	£340

OLD HEAD ISSUES (Regnal date on edge in Roman numerals)

	MINTAGE	F	VF	EF	UNC
1893 LVI....................................	497,845	£25	£50	£160	£400
1893 LVII...................................	incl. above	£25	£50	£250	£475
1893 Proof.................................	1,312	—	—	—	£3400
1894 LVII...................................	144,906	£25	£50	£225	£550
1894 LVIII..................................	incl. above	£25	£50	£225	£550
1895 LVIII	252,862	£25	£50	£200	£550
1895 LIX	incl. above	£25	£50	£200	£550
1896 LIX	317,599	£25	£50	£200	£575
1896 LX	incl. above	£25	£50	£200	£550
1897 LX	262,118	£25	£50	£200	£550
1897 LXI....................................	incl. above	£25	£50	£200	£575
1898 LXI....................................	166,150	£25	£50	£200	£700
1898 LXII...................................	incl. above	£25	£50	£200	£550
1899 LXII...................................	166,300	£25	£50	£200	£550
1899 LXIII..................................	incl. above	£25	£50	£200	£550
1900 LXIII..................................	353,356	£25	£50	£200	£550
1900 LXIV	incl. above	£25	£50	£200	£550

Victoria, Jubilee head

143

DATE	MINTAGE	F	VF	EF	UNC

EDWARD VII (1901–10)

DATE	MINTAGE	F	VF	EF	UNC
1902	256,020	£85	£150	£240	£340
1902 "Matt Proof"	15,123	—	—	—	£330

GEORGE V (1910–36)

DATE	MINTAGE	F	VF	EF	UNC
1927 Proof only	15,030	—	£100	£170	£350
1928	9,034	£110	£170	£300	£500
1929	4,994	£110	£170	£300	£500
1930	4,847	£110	£170	£300	£550
1931	4,056	£110	£170	£300	£500
1932	2,395	£200	£400	£800	£1300
1933	7,132	£110	£175	£300	£550
1934	932	£800	£1600	£3500	£5500
1935 Jubilee issue. Incuse edge inscription	714,769	£15	£20	£30	£45
1935 — — error edge inscription	incl. above	—	—	—	£1500
1935 — Specimen in box	incl. above	—	—	—	£60
1935 — Proof	incl. above	—	—	—	£200
1935 — Proof. Raised edge inscription	2,500	—	—	£275	£600
1935 — — fine lettering	incl. above	—	—	—	£1000
1935 — — error edge inscription	incl. above	—	—	—	£1500
1935 — Gold proof	30	—	—	Extremely rare	
1936	2,473	£180	£350	£600	£1000

GEORGE VI (1936–52)

DATE	MINTAGE	F	VF	EF	UNC
1937 Coronation	418,699	£18	£24	£35	£55
1937 Proof	26,402	—	—	—	£70
1951 Festival of Britain, Proof-like	1,983,540	—	£3	£6	£8

ELIZABETH II (1952–)

Pre-Decimal issues (Five Shillings)

DATE	MINTAGE	F	VF	EF	UNC
1953	5,962,621	—	—	£3	£6
1953 Proof	40,000	—	—	—	£25
1960	1,024,038	—	—	£3	£6
1960 Polished dies	70,000	—	—	—	£9
1965 Churchill	19,640,000	—	—	—	£1

Later issues are listed in the Decimal section.

DOUBLE FLORINS

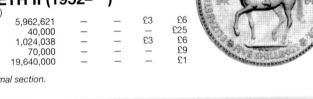

VICTORIA (1837–1901)

DATE	MINTAGE	F	VF	EF	UNC
1887 Roman I	483,347	£18	£34	£60	£135
1887 Roman I Proof	incl. above	—	—	—	£1000
1887 Arabic 1	incl. above	£18	£34	£60	£135
1887 Arabic 1 Proof	incl. above	—	—	—	£1000
1888	243,340	£18	£45	£90	£170
1888 Second I in VICTORIA an inverted 1	incl. above	£30	£60	£110	£400
1889	1,185,111	£20	£35	£65	£160
1889 inverted 1	incl. above	£30	£60	£110	£450
1890	782,146	£18	£45	£65	£160

Patterns were also produced in 1911, 1914 and 1950 and are all extremely rare.

HALFCROWNS

DATE	MINTAGE	F	VF	EF	UNC

OLIVER CROMWELL

1656				Extremely rare	
1658		£1750	£2750	£6250	—
1658 Proof in Gold				Extremely rare	

CHARLES II (1660–85)

	F	VF	EF	UNC
1663 First bust	£180	£700	£4000	—
1663 — no stops on obv.	£200	£800	—	—
1664 Second bust	£250	£1200	£5500	—
1666 Third bust	£900	—	—	—
1666 — Elephant	£900	£3500	—	—
1667/4 — 7 over 4			Extremely rare	
1668/4 — 8 over 4	£300	£1500	—	—
1669 —	£400	£1600	—	—
1669/4 — 9 over 4	£275	£1000	—	—
1670 —	£150	£600	£2750	—
1670 — MRG for MAG	£300	£1000	—	—
1671 —	£150	£600	£2600	—
1671/0 — 1 over 0	£160	£600	£3200	—
1672 — Third bust			Extremely rare	
1672 Fourth bust	£160	£550	£3000	—
1673 —	£160	£550	£2800	—
1673 — Plumes both sides			Extremely rare	
1673 — Plume below bust	£8000	£22,000	—	—
1674 —	£160	£700	—	—
1675 —	£150	£500	£2400	—
1676 —	£150	£500	£2400	—
1676 — inverted 1 in date	£150	£500	£2400	—
1677 —	£150	£500	£2100	—
1678 —	£220	£900	—	—
1679 — GRATTA error			Extremely rare	
1679 —	£160	£500	£2200	—
1680 —	£175	£750	—	—
1681/0 — 1 over 0	£300	—	—	—
1681 —	£200	£675	£3000	—
1681 — Elephant & Castle	£3750	£12000	—	—
1682 —	£170	£550	£3700	—
1683 —	£170	£550	£3500	—
1683 — Plume below bust			Extremely rare	
1684/3 — 4 over 3	£350	£1100	£5000	—

JAMES II (1685–88)

	F	VF	EF	UNC
1685 First bust	£230	£675	£4000	—
1686 —	£220	£650	£3700	—
1686/5 — 6 over 5	£250	£750	—	—
1686 — V over S	£225	£750	—	—
1687 —	£220	£675	£3500	—
1687/6 — 7 over 6	£300	£850	—	—
1687 Second bust	£200	£600	£3400	—
1688 —	£200	£600	£3200	—

WILLIAM AND MARY (1688–94)

	F	VF	EF	UNC
1689 First busts; first shield	£120	£350	£1800	—
1689 — — no pearls in crown	£120	£350	£1800	—
1689 — — FRA for FR	£170	£600	£2200	—
1689 — — No stop on obv	£120	£550	£2000	—
1689 — Second shield	£120	£400	£1800	—
1689 — — no pearls in crown	£130	£400	£1850	—
1690 — —	£180	£700	£3000	—
1690 — — error GRETIA for GRATIA	£600	£1600	£6000	—
1691 Second busts	£160	£500	£2350	—
1692 —	£160	£500	£2350	—

DATE	MINTAGE	F	VF	EF	UNC
1693 —		£170	£500	£2500	—
1693 — 3 over inverted 3		£220	£800	£3250	—

WILLIAM III (1694–1702)

DATE	F	VF	EF	UNC
1696 First bust, large shields, early harp	£80	£260	£1250	—
1696 — — — B (Bristol) below bust	£80	£270	£1400	—
1696 — — — C (Chester)	£90	£400	£1500	—
1696 — — — E (Exeter)	£120	£500	£1700	—
1696 — — — N (Norwich)	£100	£500	£1700	—
1696 — — — y (York)	£90	£400	£2200	—
1696 — — — — Scottish arms at date			Extremely rare	
1696 — — ordinary harp	£90	£325	£1700	—
1696 — — — C	£110	£500	£1600	
1696 — — — E	£100	£500	£1600	—
1696 — — — N	£170	£700	£2850	—
1696 — Small shields, ordinary harp	£70	£300	£1200	—
1696 — — — B	£100	£350	£1500	—
1696 — — — C	£100	£350	£1700	—
1696 — — — E	£120	£600	£2400	—
1696 — — — N	£110	£500	£2000	—
1696 — — — y	£100	£600	£2000	—
1696 Second bust			Only one known	
1697 First bust, large shields, ordinary harp	£80	£325	£1400	—
1697 — — — GRR for GRA			Extremely rare	
1697 — — — B	£90	£320	£1650	—
1697 — — — C	£90	£375	£1800	—
1697 — — — E	£100	£375	£1800	—
1697 — — — N	£100	£375	£1800	—
1697 — — — y	£90	£375	£1900	—
1698 — —	£100	£375	£1750	—
1698/7 — — 8 over 7			Extremely rare	
1699 — —	£160	£500	£3500	—
1699 — — Scottish arms at date			Extremely rare	
1700 — —	£140	£400	£2200	—
1701 — —	£150	£450	£2300	—
1701 — — No stops on rev	£160	£650	—	—
1701 — — Elephant & Castle below	Fair £2500			
1701 — — Plumes in angles on rev.	£275	£800	£4000	—

ANNE (1702–14)

DATE	F	VF	EF	UNC
1703 Plain (pre-Union)	£700	£2500	—	—
1703 VIGO below bust	£150	£500	£1800	—
1704 Plumes in angles on rev.	£200	£600	£2200	—
1705 —	£180	£700	£2200	—
1706 Roses & Plumes in angles on rev.	£100	£400	£1800	—
1707 —	£90	£325	£1400	—
1707 Plain (post-Union)	£90	£240	£1100	—
1707 E below bust	£90	£240	£1100	—
1707 — SEPTIMO edge			Extremely rare	
1708 Plain	£100	£280	£1250	—
1708 E below bust	£100	£280	£1400	—
1708 Plumes in angles on rev.	£110	£300	£1600	—
1709 Plain	£90	£300	£1200	—
1709 E below bust	£275	£1250	—	—
1710 Roses & Plumes in angles on rev.	£90	£370	£1450	—
1712 —	£90	£370	£1450	—
1713 Plain	£90	£370	£1450	—
1713 Roses & Plumes in angles on rev.	£90	£370	£1350	—
1714 —	£90	£370	£1350	—
1714/3 4 over 3	£125	£500	—	—

GEORGE I (1714–27)

DATE	F	VF	EF	UNC
1715 Roses & Plumes in angles on rev.	£475	£950	£3300	—
1715 Plain edge			Extremely rare	
1717 —	£475	£1000	£3500	—
1720 —	£470	£1000	£3500	—
1720/17 20 over 17	£450	£1000	£3400	—
1723 SSC in angles on rev.	£450	£1000	£3250	—
1726 Small Roses & Plumes in angles on rev..	£5000	£15,000	—	—

DATE	MINTAGE	F	VF	EF	UNC

GEORGE II (1727–60)

1731 Young head, Plain, proof only..................	—		—	£10000	—
1731 — Roses & Plumes in angles on rev........	£160	£450	£2000	—
1732 — —	£160	£450	£2000	—
1734 — —	£160	£450	£2100	—
1735 — —	£160	£450	£2100	—
1736 — —	£160	£450	£2000	—
1739 — Roses in angles on rev.	£150	£450	£1950	—
1741/39 — — 41 over 30	£160	£600	—	—
1741 — —	£150	£450	£1900	—
1743 Old head, Roses in angles on rev.	£85	£225	£1200	—
1745 — —	£85	£225	£1200	—
1745 — LIMA below bust.................................	£80	£200	£700	—
1746 — —	£80	£200	£700	—
1746/5 — — 6 over 5	£90	£275	£900	—
1746 — Plain, Proof	—	—	£6500	—
1750 — —	£225	£600	£2800	—
1751 — —	£250	£750	£3000	—

GEORGE III (1760–1820)

1816 "Bull head"	—	£28	£80	£275	£550
1817 —	8,092,656	£28	£80	£275	£550
1817 "Small head"......................	incl. above	£28	£80	£275	£525
1818 —	2,905,056	£28	£80	£275	£525
1819/8 — 9 over 8	incl. above			Extremely rare	
1819 —	4,790,016	£28	£80	£275	£550
1820 —	2,396,592	£50	£140	£500	£1000

GEORGE IV (1820–30)

1820 First bust, first reverse........	incl. above	£30	£80	£400	£750
1821 — —	1,435,104	£30	£80	£400	£750
1821 — — Proof..........................	incl. above		—	£4500	
1823 — —	2,003,760	£1300	£4250		
1823 — Second reverse.............	incl. above	£30	£80	£350	£675
1824 — —	465,696	£35	£90	£300	£750
1824 Second bust, third reverse .	incl. above			Extremely rare	
1825 — —	2,258,784	£30	£80	£200	£500
1826 — —	2,189,088	£30	£80	£200	£500
1826 — — Proof..........................	incl. above		—	£2500	
1828 — —	49,890	£110	£300	£850	£2500
1829 — —	508,464	£75	£175	£550	£1100

WILLIAM IV (1830–37)

1831 Plain edge............................	—			Extremely rare	
1831 Proof (W.W. in script & block)	—	—	—	—	£4000
1834 W.W. in block......................	993,168	£35	£85	£375	£1000
1834 W.W. in script.....................	incl. above	£35	£85	£375	£1000
1835...	281,952	£40	£100	£375	£1050
1836...	1,588,752	£35	£75	£375	£1000
1836/5 6 over 5	incl. above	£60	£125	£650	—
1837...	150,526	£50	£170	£750	£1600

VICTORIA (1837–1901)

YOUNG HEAD ISSUES

1839 (two varieties)	—	£1300	£4250	£11000	—
1839 Proof....................................	—	—	—	—	£6500
1840...	386,496	£60	£200	£800	£2200
1841...	42,768	£1000	£2000	£4500	£8000
1842...	486,288	£55	£150	£700	£1700
1843...	454,608	£150	£450	£1300	£4000
1844...	1,999,008	£50	£110	£550	£1750
1845...	2,231,856	£50	£110	£550	£1750
1846...	1,539,668	£55	£140	£600	£1800
1848 Plain 8.................................	367,488	£175	£450	£1650	£5000
1848/6	incl. above	£150	£400	£1250	£3500
1849...	261,360	£70	£160	£600	£2200
1849 Small date	incl. above	£90	£220	£850	£2400
1850...	484,613	£70	£240	£900	£2500
1853 Proof only	—	—	—	—	£7500

DATE	MINTAGE	F	VF	EF	UNC
1874	2,188,599	£25	£70	£340	£750
1875	1,113,483	£25	£70	£340	£700
1876	633,221	£30	£80	£340	£800
1876/5 6 over 5	incl. above	£35	£80	£280	£800
1876/6 6 over 6	incl. above	£75	£150	£450	—
1877	447,059	£25	£70	£250	£700
1878	1,466,323	£25	£70	£250	£700
1879	901,356	£35	£90	£300	£900
1880	1,346,350	£25	£70	£250	£650
1881	2,301,495	£25	£70	£250	£600
1882	808,227	£30	£75	£270	£650
1883	2,982,779	£25	£70	£250	£550
1884	1,569,175	£25	£70	£250	£550
1885	1,628,438	£25	£70	£250	£550
1886	891,767	£25	£70	£250	£550
1887	1,438,046	£25	£65	£275	£600
JUBILEE HEAD ISSUES					
1887	incl. above	£10	£16	£32	£80
1887 Proof	1,084	—	—	—	£675
1888	1,428,787	£12	£25	£60	£220
1889	4,811,954	£10	£20	£55	£175
1890	3,228,111	£12	£25	£80	£220
1891	2,284,632	£12	£25	£80	£220
1892	1,710,946	£12	£25	£80	£240
OLD HEAD ISSUES					
1893	1,792,600	£12	£25	£60	£120
1893 Proof	1,312	—	—	—	£1200
1894	1,524,960	£16	£40	£100	£275
1895	1,772,662	£14	£35	£80	£240
1896	2,148,505	£12	£22	£65	£220
1897	1,678,643	£12	£22	£65	£230
1898	1,870,055	£12	£22	£65	£230
1899	2,865,872	£12	£22	£65	£230
1900	4,479,128	£12	£22	£65	£230
1901	1,516,570	£12	£22	£65	£230

DATE	MINTAGE	F	VF	EF	UNC

EDWARD VII (1901–10)

DATE	MINTAGE	F	VF	EF	UNC
1902	1,316,008	£12	£30	£80	£170
1902 "Matt Proof"	15,123	—	—	—	£275
1903	274,840	£175	£550	£2200	£4500
1904	709,652	£60	£225	£500	£1500
1905	166,008	£500	£1400	£5000	£9000
1906	2,886,206	£12	£50	£200	£900
1907	3,693,930	£12	£50	£200	£900
1908	1,758,889	£20	£90	£400	£1400
1909	3,051,592	£12	£60	£350	£900
1910	2,557,685	£12	£45	£130	£500

GEORGE V (1910–36)

First issue

DATE	MINTAGE	F	VF	EF	UNC
1911	2,914,573	£15	£35	£80	£250
1911 Proof	6,007	—	—	—	£375
1912	4,700,789	£12	£25	£50	£200
1913	4,090,169	£12	£28	£75	£220
1914	18,333,003	£7	£12	£40	£70
1915	32,433,066	£7	£12	£35	£65
1916	29,530,020	£7	£12	£35	£65
1917	11,172,052	£8	£15	£45	£100
1918	29,079,592	£7	£12	£35	£70
1919	10,266,737	£7	£15	£45	£100

Second issue—debased silver

1920	17,982,077	£4	£8	£22	£70
1921	23,677,889	£4	£8	£30	£65
1922	16,396,724	£5	£9	£24	£70
1923	26,308,526	£6	£8	£20	£45
1924	5,866,294	£15	£35	£90	£230
1925	1,413,461	£30	£75	£300	£1000
1926	4,473,516	£12	£28	£50	£190

Third issue —Modified effigy

1926	incl. above	£6	£14	£40	£110
1927	6,837,872	£6	£12	£35	£75

Fourth issue—New shield reverse

1927 Proof	15,000	—	—	—	£100
1928	18,762,727	£5	£8	£20	£35
1929	17,632,636	£5	£8	£20	£35
1930	809,051	£15	£60	£325	£900
1931	11,264,468	£5	£8	£20	£35
1932	4,793,643	£6	£10	£25	£90
1933	10,311,494	£5	£8	£20	£40
1934	2,422,399	£7	£12	£65	£200
1935	7,022,216	£5	£8	£18	£30
1936	7,039,423	£5	£8	£18	£20

George V, fourth issue, new shield reverse

GEORGE VI (1936–52)

DATE	MINTAGE	F	VF	EF	UNC
1937	9,106,440	—	£6	£9	£14
1937 Proof	26,402	—	—	—	£25
1938	6,426,478	£5	£6	£15	£25
1939	15,478,635	£5	£6	£9	£12
1940	17,948,439	£5	£6	£9	£12
1941	15,773,984	£5	£6	£9	£12
1942	31,220,090	£5	£6	£9	£10
1943	15,462,875	£5	£6	£9	£10
1944	15,255,165	£5	£6	£9	£10
1945	19,849,242	£5	£6	£9	£10
1946	22,724,873	£5	£6	£9	£10

Cupro-nickel

1947	21,911,484	—	£1	£2	£4
1948	71,164,703	—	£1	£2	£4
1949	28,272,512	—	£1	£2	£6
1950	28,335,500	—	£1	£2	£6
1950 Proof	17,513	—	—	—	£35
1951	9,003,520	—	£1	£2	£6
1951 Proof	20,000	—	—	—	£10
1952			Only one known		

DATE	MINTAGE	F	VF	EF	UNC

ELIZABETH II (1952–)

DATE	MINTAGE	F	VF	EF	UNC
1953	4,333,214	–	–	£1	£3
1953 Proof	40,000	–	–	–	£8
1954	11,614,953	–	£1	£6	£40
1955	23,628,726	–	–	£1	£6
1956	33,934,909	–	–	£1	£6
1957	34,200,563	–	–	£1	£6
1958	15,745,668	–	£1	£6	£40
1959	9,028,844	–	£1	£9	£35
1960	19,929,191	–	–	£1	£3
1961	25,887,897	–	–	–	£2
1961 Polished dies	incl. above	–	–	£1	£2
1962	24,013,312	–	–	–	£1
1963	17,625,200	–	–	–	£1
1964	5,973,600	–	–	–	£2
1965	9,778,440	–	–	–	£1
1966	13,375,200	–	–	–	£1
1967	33,058,400	–	–	–	£1
1970 Proof	–	–	–	–	£8

FLORINS

VICTORIA (1837–1901)
YOUNG (CROWNED) HEAD ISSUES
"Godless" type (without D.G.– "Dei Gratia")

1848 "Godless" Pattern only plain edge	–		Very rare		
1848 "Godless" Pattern only milled edge	–		Extremely rare		
1849	413,820	£30	£75	£240	£500

(Beware of recent forgeries)

"Gothic" type i.e. date in Roman numerals in obverse legend

"brit." in legend. No die no.

1851 mdcccli Proof	1,540		Extremely rare		
1852 mdccclii	1,014,552	£30	£65	£280	£700
1853 mdcccliii	3,919,950	£30	£65	£280	£700
1853 — Proof	incl. above	–	–	–	£7000
1854 mdcccliv	550,413	£800	£2000	–	–
1855 mdccclv	831,017	£30	£75	£300	£850
1856 mdccclvi	2,201,760	£30	£75	£300	£850
1857 mdccclvii	1,671,120	£30	£70	£275	£900
1858 mdccclviii	2,239,380	£30	£70	£275	£875
1859 mdccclix	2,568,060	£30	£70	£275	£800
1860 mdccclx	1,475,100	£35	£90	£325	£1000
1862 mdccclxii	594,000	£300	£800	£1800	£4500
1862 plain edge Proof			Very rare		
1863 mdccclxiii	938,520	£1300	£2500	£6000	£13000
1863 plain edge Proof			Very rare		

"Godless" florin

"brit" in legend. Die no. below bust

1864 mdccclxiv	1,861,200	£30	£65	£325	£800
1864 Gothic Piedfort flan	incl. above		Extremely rare		
1865 mdccclxv	1,580,044	£40	£100	£400	£750
1866 mdccclxvi	914,760	£35	£90	£400	£750
1867 mdccclxvii	423,720	£50	£170	£500	£1200
1867 — only 42 arcs in border	incl. above		Extremely rare		

"britt" in legend. Die no. below bust

1868 mdccclxviii	896,940	£30	£80	£350	£850
1869 mdccclxix	297,000	£35	£100	£450	£1100
1870 mdccclxx	1,080,648	£30	£80	£350	£700
1871 mdccclxxi	3,425,605	£30	£80	£350	£675
1872 mdccclxxii	7,199,690	£30	£70	£270	£550
1873 mdccclxxiii	5,921,839	£30	£70	£270	£575
1874 mdccclxxiv	1,642,630	£30	£70	£270	£600
1874 — iv over iii in date	incl. above	£35	£80	£400	£800
1875 mdccclxxv	1,117,030	£35	£85	£275	£700
1876 mdccclxxvi	580,034	£50	£130	£500	£1100
1877 mdccclxxvii	682,292	£30	£70	£250	£600
1877 — 48 arcs in border no W.W.	incl. above	£30	£70	£240	£575

"Gothic" florin

DATE	MINTAGE	F	VF	EF	UNC
1877 — 42 arcs	incl. above	£30	£70	£240	£575
1877 — — no die number	incl. above			Extremely rare	
1878 mdccclxxviii with die number	1,786,680	£35	£70	£250	£600
1879 mdccclxxix no die no	1,512,247			Extremely rare	
1879 — 48 arcs in border............	incl. above	£30	£60	£300	£650
1879 — no die number...............	incl. above			Extremely rare	
1879 — 38 arcs, no W.W..	incl. above	£30	£60	£300	£650
1880 mdccclxxx Younger portrait	—			Extremely rare	
1880 — 34 arcs, Older portrait....	2,167,170	£30	£60	£250	£600
1881 mdccclxxxi — —	2,570,337	£28	£60	£250	£600
1881 — xxГi broken puncheon ...	incl. above	£35	£70	£250	£700
1883 mdccclxxxiii — —	3,555,667	£30	£70	£250	£650
1884 mdccclxxxiv — —	1,447,379	£30	£70	£250	£650
1885 mdccclxxxv — —	1,758,210	£30	£70	£250	£650
1886 mdccclxxxvi — —	591,773	£30	£70	£250	£650
1887 mdccclxxxvii — —	1,776,903	£50	£120	£325	£300
1887 — 46 arcs	incl. above	£50	£120	£350	£950

JUBILEE HEAD ISSUES

1887	incl. above	£8	£16	£35	£70
1887 Proof...............................	1,084	—	—	—	£550
1888	1,547,540	£8	£16	£45	£140
1889	2,973,561	£9	£20	£50	£150
1890	1,684,737	£10	£25	£100	£325
1891	836,438	£25	£80	£300	£600
1892	283,401	£40	£140	£400	£950

VICTORIA—OLD HEAD ISSUES

1893	1,666,103	£10	£20	£50	£125
1893 Proof...............................	1,312	—	—	—	£800
1894	1,952,842	£12	£30	£100	£300
1895	2,182,968	£12	£32	£100	£300
1896	2,944,416	£10	£30	£80	£220
1897	1,699,921	£10	£30	£80	£200
1898	3,061,343	£10	£30	£80	£200
1899	3,966,953	£10	£30	£80	£220
1900	5,528,630	£10	£30	£80	£200
1901	2,648,870	£10	£30	£80	£200

EDWARD VII (1901–10)

1902.....................................	2,189,575	£10	£22	£70	£140
1902 "Matt Proof"	15,123	—	—	—	£250
1903.....................................	1,995,298	£12	£35	£140	£600
1904.....................................	2,769,932	£15	£45	£160	£550
1905.....................................	1,187,596	£65	£200	£700	£1800
1906.....................................	6,910,128	£12	£40	£140	£600
1907.....................................	5,947,895	£12	£35	£140	£600
1908.....................................	3,280,010	£20	£55	£350	£900
1909.....................................	3,482,829	£15	£50	£250	£700
1910.....................................	5,650,713	£15	£40	£120	£350

GEORGE V (1910–36)

First issue

1911.....................................	5,951,284	£7	£12	£40	£100
1911 Proof...............................	6,007	—	—	—	£275
1912	8,571,731	£8	£18	£35	£140
1913.....................................	4,545,278	£10	£25	£50	£190
1914.....................................	21,252,701	£7	£18	£30	£80
1915.....................................	12,367,939	£7	£18	£30	£80
1916.....................................	21,064,337	£7	£18	£30	£80
1917.....................................	11,181,617	£7	£22	£40	£80
1918.....................................	29,211,792	£7	£18	£30	£100
1919.....................................	9,469,292	£9	£20	£45	£125

Second issue —debased silver

1920.....................................	15,387,833	£4	£12	£40	£90
1921.....................................	34,863,895	£4	£12	£40	£70
1922.....................................	23,861,044	£4	£12	£40	£70
1923.....................................	21,546,533	£4	£10	£30	£65
1924.....................................	4,582,372	£12	£35	£95	£275
1925.....................................	1,404,136	£30	£75	£300	£1000
1926.....................................	5,125,410	£10	£25	£60	£200

George V first type

DATE	MINTAGE	F	VF	EF	UNC
Fourth issue—*new reverse*					
1927 Proof only	101,497	—	—	—	£110
1928..	11,087,186	£4	£7	£15	£40
1929..	16,397,279	£4	£7	£18	£35
1930..	5,753,568	£4	£7	£22	£50
1931..	6,556,331	£4	£7	£20	£35
1932..	717,041	£15	£40	£300	£700
1933..	8,685,303	£4	£7	£18	£40
1935..	7,540,546	£4	£7	£15	£35
1936..	9,897,448	£4	£7	£15	£35

George V new reverse

GEORGE VI (1936–52)

1937..	13,006,781	£4	£5	£7	£12
1937 Proof....................................	26,402	—	—	—	£25
1938..	7,909,388	£6	£8	£15	£30
1939..	20,850,607	£4	£5	£8	£10
1940..	18,700,338	£4	£5	£7	£12
1941..	24,451,079	£4	£5	£7	£9
1942..	39,895,243	£4	£5	£7	£9
1943..	26,711,987	£4	£5	£7	£9
1944..	27,560,005	£4	£5	£7	£9
1945..	25,858,049	£4	£5	£7	£9
1946..	22,300,254	£4	£5	£7	£9
Cupro-nickel					
1947..	22,910,085	—	—	£1	£3
1948..	67,553,636	—	—	£1	£3
1949..	28,614,939	—	—	£1	£5
1950..	24,357,490	—	—	£2	£7
1950 Proof....................................	17,513	—	—	£1	£9
1951..	27,411,747	—	—	£2	£8
1951 Proof....................................	20,000	—	—	—	£9

ELIZABETH II (1952–   )

1953	11,958,710	—	—	—	£2
1953 Proof....................................	40,000	—	—	—	£7
1954..	13,085,422	—	—	£6	£45
1955..	25,887,253	—	—	£1	£3
1956..	47,824,500	—	—	£1	£3
1957..	33,071,282	—	—	£4	£25
1958..	9,564,580	—	—	£4	£45
1959..	14,080,319	—	—	£4	£35
1960..	13,831,782	—	—	£1	£4
1961..	37,735,315	—	—	£1	£2
1962..	35,147,903	—	—	£1	£2
1963..	26,471,000	—	—	£1	£2
1964..	16,539,000	—	—	£1	£2
1965..	48,163,000	—	—	—	£1.50
1966..	83,999,000	—	—	—	£1.50
1967..	39,718,000	—	—	—	£1.50
1970 Proof....................................	—	—	—	—	£8

SHILLINGS

OLIVER CROMWELL

1658	£1000	£2200	£4750	—
1658 Dutch Copy			Extremely rare	

CHARLES II (1660–85)

1663 First bust	£140	£600	£1800	—
1663 — GARTIA error.......................................			Extremely rare	
1663 — Irish & Scottish shields transposed	£300	£800	—	—
1666 — Elephant below bust	£650	£2400	£8500	—
1666 "Guinea" head, elephant	£3000	£6000	—	—
1666 Second bust			Extremely rare	
1668 —	£140	£400	£1850	—
1668/7 — 8 over 7..	£160	£600	—	—
1668 Second bust	£140	£450	£1800	—
1669/6 First bust variety..................................			Extremely rare	
1669..			Extremely rare	

DATE	F	VF	EF	UNC
1669 Second bust			Extremely rare	
1670 —	£150	£550	£2400	—
1671 —	£150	£550	£2400	—
1671 — Plume below, plume in centre rev.	£550	£1500	£5250	—
1672 —	£170	£600	£2400	—
1673 —	£170	£600	£2400	—
1673 — Plume below, plume in centre rev.	£600	£1500	£6250	—
1673/2 — 3 over 2	£200	£700	—	—
1674/3 — 4 over 3	£180	£600	—	—
1674 —	£180	£600	£2400	—
1674 — Plume below bust, plume in centre rev.	£550	£1800	£6000	—
1674 — Plume rev. only	£1000	£2700	£8000	—
1674 Third bust	£550	£2000	—	—
1675 Second bust	£220	£900	—	—
1675/4 — 5 over 4	£240	£850	—	—
1675 — Plume below bust, plume in centre rev.	£600	£1800	£6250	—
1675 Third bust	£350	£1400	—	—
1675/4 — 5 over 4	£300	£1200	—	—
1676 Second bust	£150	£600	£2000	—
1676/5 — 6 over 5	£160	£600	—	—
1676 — Plume below bust, plume in centre rev.	£600	£2000	£6200	—
1677 —	£150	£600	£2400	—
1677 — Plume below bust	£1200	£4000	£10000	—
1678 —	£170	£600	£2400	—
1678/7 — 8 over 7	£200	£800	—	—
1679 —	£150	£600	£2500	—
1679 — Plume below bust, plume in centre rev.	£550	£1700	£7000	—
1679 — Plume below bust	£1000	£3500	£7000	—
1679 — 9 over 7	£200	£700	—	—
1680 —			Extremely rare	
1680 — Plume below bust, plume in centre rev.	£1300	£4000	£8000	—
1680/79 — — 80 over 79	£1100	£3250	—	—
1681 —	£400	£1200	£3300	—
1681 — 1 over 0	£400	£1000	£3500	—
1681/0 Elephant & Castle below bust	£4000	£11000	—	—
1682/1 — 2 over 1	£1200	£3500	—	—
1683 —			Extremely rare	
1683 Fourth (Larger) bust	£250	£950	£3200	—
1684 —	£250	£950	£3200	—

JAMES II (1685–88)

	F	VF	EF	UNC
1685	£225	£600	£2750	—
1685 Plume in centre rev. rev			Extremely rare	
1685 No stops on rev.	£250	£700	—	—
1686	£240	£650	£2750	—
1686/5 6 over 5	£250	£700	£3000	—
1687	£250	£700	£3000	—
1687/6 7 over 6	£250	£650	£2800	—
1688	£270	£700	£2900	—
1688/7 last 8 over 7	£260	£675	£2800	—

WILLIAM & MARY (1688–94)

	F	VF	EF	UNC
1692	£200	£600	£2750	—
1692 inverted 1	£220	£650	£2850	—
1693	£180	£600	£2700	—
1690 9 over 0	£275	£700	£3000	—

WILLIAM III (1694–1702)

Provincially produced shillings carry privy marks or initials below the bust:
B: Bristol. C: Chester. E: Exeter. N: Norwich. Y or y: York.

	F	VF	EF	UNC
1695 First bust	£40	£120	£650	—
1696 —	£40	£100	£550	—
1696 — no stops on rev.	£60	£140	£800	—
1696 — MAB for MAG			Extremely rare	
1696 — 1669 error			Extremely rare	
1696 — 1669 various GVLELMVS errors			Extremely rare	
1696 — B below bust	£60	£180	£950	—
1696 — C	£70	£200	£1000	—
1696 — E	£75	£200	£1100	—

Charles II

James II

William & Mary

DATE	F	VF	EF	UNC
1696 — N	£80	£250	£1100	—
1696 — y	£70	£200	£1050	—
1696 — Y	£70	£200	£1050	—
1696 Second bust			Only one known	
1696 Third bust C below	£160	£500	£1600	—
1696 — Y			Extremely rare	
1697 First bust	£50	£110	£425	—
1697 — GRI for GRA error			Extremely rare	
1697 — Scottish & Irish shields transposed			Extremely rare	
1697 — Irish arms at date			Extremely rare	
1697 — no stops on rev	£80	£220	£900	—
1697 — GVLELMVS error			Extremely rare	
1697 — B	£90	£200	£1100	—
1697 — C	£80	£200	£1100	—
1697 — E	£90	£220	£1150	—
1697 — N	£75	£200	£1050	—
1697 — — no stops on obv			Extremely rare	
1697 — y	£80	£180	£1100	—
1697 — — arms of France & Ireland transposed			Extremely rare	
1697 — Y	£80	£180	£900	—
1697 Third bust	£50	£125	£550	—
1697 — B	£100	£225	£1100	—
1697 — C	£110	£220	£1100	—
1697 — — Fr.a error	£150	£500	—	—
1697 — — no stops on obv	£100	£325	—	—
1697 — — arms of Scotland at date			Extremely rare	
1697 — E	£85	£180	£1000	—
1697 — N	£100	£250	£1200	—
1697 — y	£90	£275	£1250	—
1697 Third bust variety	£65	£140	£600	—
1697 — B	£80	£200	£1250	—
1697 — C	£140	£800	—	—
1698 —	£110	£300	£1300	—
1698 — Plumes in angles of rev.	£275	£700	£2500	—
1698 Fourth bust "Flaming hair"	£200	£675	£2800	—
1698 Plain Edge Proof			Extremely rare	
1699 —	£180	£600	£2500	—
1699 Fifth bust	£120	£350	£1500	—
1699 — Plumes in angles on rev.	£220	£700	£2500	—
1699 — Roses in angles on rev.	£240	£900	£2700	—
1700 —	£70	£150	£650	—
1700 — Small round oo in date	£70	£150	£650	—
1700 — no stop after DEI	£60	£160	£700	—
1700 — Plume below bust	£3500	£11000	—	—
1701 — Plumes in angles on rev.	£200	£750	£2500	—

William III
First bust

William III
Fifth bust

ANNE (1702–14)

	F	VF	EF	UNC
1702 First bust (pre-Union with Scotland)	£100	£325	£1100	—
1702 — Plumes in angles on rev.	£120	£400	£1500	—
1702 — VIGO below bust	£100	£300	£1200	—
1702 — — colon before ANNA			Extremely rare	
1703 Second bust, VIGO below	£80	£260	£1000	—
1704 — Plain	£600	£2000	—	—
1704 — Plumes in angles on rev.	£100	£350	£1500	—
1705 — Plain	£150	£600	£2000	—
1705 — Plumes in angles on rev.	£100	£400	£1400	—
1705 — Roses & Plumes in angles on rev.	£120	£400	£1200	—
1707 — —	£110	£350	£1500	—
1707 Second bust (post-Union) E below bust	£80	£300	£1200	—
1707 — E* below bust	£90	£350	£1300	—
1707 Third bust, Plain	£35	£120	£600	—
1707 — Plumes in angles on rev.	£50	£180	£800	—
1707 — E below bust	£40	£100	£550	—
1707 2nd "E" bust Plain Edge Proof			Extremely rare	
1708 Second bust, E below	£100	£250	£1000	—
1708 — E* below bust	£120	£400	£1100	—
1708/7 — — 8 over 7			Extremely rare	

Anne, first bust, VIGO below

DATE	MINTAGE	F	VF	EF	UNC
1708 — Roses & Plumes in angles on rev.........		£100	£450	£800	—
1708 Third bust, Plain		£45	£140	£500	—
1708 — Plumes in angles on rev.		£80	£250	£800	—
1708 Third bust, E below bust		£80	£200	£750	—
1708/7 — — 8 over 7		£200	£450	—	—
1708 — Roses & Plumes in angles on rev.........		£80	£220	£750	—
1708 "Edinburgh" bust, E* below		£80	£220	£700	—
1709 Third bust, Plain		£50	£160	£500	—
1709 "Edinburgh" bust, E* below		£50	£170	£700	—
1710 Third bust, Roses & Plumes in angles......		£75	£180	£800	—
1710 Fourth bust, Roses & Plumes in angles ...		£80	£200	£850	—
1711 Third bust, Plain		£70	£160	£500	—
1711 Fourth bust, Plain		£30	£75	£250	—
1712 — Roses & Plumes in angles on rev.........		£70	£180	£700	—
1713 — —		£70	£180	£650	—
1713/2 — 3 over 2...		£90	£250	—	—
1714 — —		£70	£160	£500	—
1714/3 —		£120	£300	£1000	—

Anne, Fourth bust, roses and plumes reverse type

GEORGE I (1714–27)

	MINTAGE	F	VF	EF	UNC
1715 First bust, Roses & Plumes in angles on rev.		£80	£240	£1000	—
1716 — —		£150	£500	£2000	—
1717 — —		£120	£350	£1600	—
1718 — —		£75	£250	£900	—
1719 — —		£140	£600	£2350	—
1720 — —		£90	£250	£700	—
1720/18 — —		£150	£500	£1500	—
1720 — Plain		£50	£150	£600	—
1721 — Roses & Plumes in angles on rev.........		£130	£400	£2000	—
1721/0 — — 1 over 0		£100	£400	£1200	—
1721 — Plain		£200	£600	£1800	—
1721/19 — — 21 over 19		£125	£400	—	—
1721/18 21 over 18 error, Plumes & Roses.......		£500	£1800	—	—
1722 — Roses & Plumes in angles on rev.........		£100	£300	£1250	—
1723 — —		£120	£350	£1500	—
1723 — SSC rev., Arms of France at date		£100	£300	£900	—
1723 — SSC in angles on rev		£35	£110	£350	—
1723 Second bust, SSC in angles on rev..........		£50	£170	£600	—
1723 — Roses & Plumes in angles		£110	£350	£1300	—
1723 — WCC (Welsh Copper Co) below bust ..		£1000	£2500	£8000	—
1724 — Roses & Plumes in angles on rev.........		£110	£350	£1200	—
1724 — WCC below bust...................................		£1000	£2500	£8500	—
1725 — Roses & Plumes in angles on rev.........		£110	£300	£1200	—
1725 — — no stops on obv...............................		£120	£300	£1300	—
1725 — WCC below bust...................................		£1100	£2800	£9500	—
1726 — — Roses & Plumes		£700	£2500	£7500	—
1726 — WCC below bust...................................		£1200	£2750	£9500	—
1727 — —			Extremely rare		—
1727 — — no stops on obv...............................			Extremely rare		—

George I First bust with SSC in angles on reverse

George I Second bust, roses and plumes reverse type

GEORGE II (1727–60)

	MINTAGE	F	VF	EF	UNC
1727 Young head, Plumes in angles on rev.......		£100	£450	£2250	—
1727 — Roses & Plumes in angles on rev.........		£90	£300	£800	—
1728 — —		£100	£375	£900	—
1728 — Plain		£100	£300	£1000	—
1729 — Roses & Plumes in angles on rev.........		£100	£275	£900	—
1731 — —		£110	£300	£950	—
1731 — Plumes in angles on rev.		£150	£600	£1500	—
1732 — Roses & Plumes in angles on rev.........		£90	£300	£900	—
1734 — —		£70	£250	£800	—
1735 — —		£70	£250	£800	—
1736 — —		£70	£250	£750	—
1736/5 — — 6 over 5		£70	£250	£850	—
1737 — —		£65	£225	£700	—
1739 — Roses in angles on rev.		£55	£200	£550	—
1739/7 — — 9 over 7					Rare
1741 — —		£50	£200	£600	—
1741/39 — — 41 over 39					Rare
1743 Old head, Roses in angles on rev.............		£35	£130	£450	—
1745 — —		£35	£130	£450	—
1745 — — LIMA below bust		£35	£120	£500	—

George II Young head, roses and plumes reverse type

DATE	MINTAGE	F	VF	EF	UNC
1745/3 − − − 5 over 3		£60	£175	£600	−
1746 − − −		£60	£220	£750	−
1746/5 − − − 6 over 5		£100	£300	−	−
1746 − Plain, Proof		−	−	£4000	−
1747 − Roses in angles on rev.		£45	£130	£600	−
1750 − Plain		£45	£150	£600	−
1750/46 − − 50 over 46		£75	£170	£650	−
1751 − −		£140	£600	£1750	−
1758 − −		£25	£60	£175	−

George II Old head, plain reverse

GEORGE III (1760–1820)

	MINTAGE	F	VF	EF	UNC
1763 "Northumberland" bust (Beware of counterfeits)		£450	£800	£1600	−
First type,					
1787 rev. no semée of hearts in 4th shield		£25	£45	£110	−
1787 − No stop over head		£30	£50	£125	−
1787 − No stop at date		£50	£90	£160	−
1787 − No stops on obv		£400	£800	£2500	−
1787 rev. with semée of hearts in shield		£35	£65	£125	−
1798 "Dorrien Magens" bust £30,000+		−	−	−	−

NEW COINAGE—shield in garter reverse

	MINTAGE	F	VF	EF	UNC
1816	−	£12	£25	£75	£160
1817	3,031,360	£12	£35	£85	£180
1817 GEOE for GEOR	incl. above	£120	£250	£700	−
1818	1,342,440	£25	£45	£150	£425
1819	7,595,280	£15	£35	£100	£220
1819/8 9 over 8	incl. above	£20	£50	£160	−
1820	7,975,440	£15	£30	£100	£220

George III First type

George III New coinage Shield reverse type

GEORGE IV (1820–30)

	MINTAGE	F	VF	EF	UNC
1821 First bust, first reverse	2,463,120	£15	£50	£220	£600
1821 − − Proof	incl. above	−	−	−	£2000
1823 − Second reverse	693,000	£55	£95	£275	£700
1824 − −	4,158,000	£15	£50	£200	£450
1825 − −	2,459,160	£20	£55	£225	£650
1825/3 − − 5 over 3	incl. above	Extremely rare			
1825 Second bust, third reverse	incl. above	£10	£35	£100	£375
1825 − − Roman I	incl. above	Extremely rare			
1826 − −	6,351,840	£10	£30	£80	£225
1826 6 over 2		Does this exist?			
1826 − − Proof	incl. above	−	−	−	£1500
1827 − −	574,200	£40	£90	£300	£700
1829 − −	879,120	£30	£70	£250	£600

WILLIAM IV (1830–37)

	MINTAGE	F	VF	EF	UNC
1831Proof only, Plain Edge	−	−	−	−	£1800
1834	3,223,440	£15	£40	£225	£500
1835	1,449,360	£20	£60	£250	£550
1836	3,567,960	£18	£45	£190	£500
1837	478,160	£25	£80	£300	£700

George IV second bust type

VICTORIA (1837–1901)
YOUNG HEAD ISSUES
First head

	MINTAGE	F	VF	EF	UNC
1838 WW on truncation	1,956,240	£20	£50	£220	£500
1839 −	5,666,760	£30	£70	£250	£650
Second head					
1839 − Proof only, Plain Edge	incl. above	−	−	−	£2000
1839 no WW	incl. above	£20	£50	£180	£500
(Rare Proofs exist)					
1840	1,639,440	£20	£50	£200	£550
1841	875,160	£25	£60	£300	£600
1842	2,094,840	£20	£45	£200	£550
1843	1,465,200	£25	£60	£200	£600
1844	4,466,880	£15	£40	£160	£475
1845	4,082,760	£15	£40	£160	£475
1846	4,031,280	£15	£40	£160	£475

Victoria Second head type

DATE	MINTAGE	F	VF	EF	UNC
1848 last 8 of date over 6..........	1,041,480	£80	£200	£750	£1750
1849	845,480	£30	£75	£250	£700
1850	685,080	£800	£1800	£4500	£8000
1850/49	incl. above	£850	£1800	£5250	—
1851	470,071	£50	£120	£500	£1200
1852	1,306,574	£15	£35	£150	£400
1853	4,256,188	£15	£35	£150	£400
1853 Proof	incl. above	—	—	—	£3000
1854	552,414	£250	£650	£1800	£4500
1854/1 4 over 1	incl. above	£300	£900	—	—
1855	1,368,400	£12	£30	£140	£350
1856	3,168,000	£12	£30	£140	£350
1857	2,562,120	£12	£30	£140	£350
1857 error F:G with inverted G ...	incl. above	£220	£600	—	—
1858	3,108,600	£12	£30	£140	£350
1859	4,561,920	£12	£30	£140	£350
1860	1,671,120	£12	£35	£160	£450
1861	1,382,040	£15	£40	£180	£600
1862	954,360	£70	£180	£500	£1600
1863	859,320	£140	£400	£1000	£2400
1863/1 3 over 1			Extremely rare		

Die no. added above date up to 1879

Victoria Third head, with die no.

1864	4,518,360	£10	£30	£135	£300
1865	5,619,240	£10	£30	£135	£300
1866	4,984,600	£10	£30	£135	£300
1866 error BBITANNIAR	incl. above	£80	£300	£1000	—
1867	2,166,120	£15	£35	£140	£340

Third head—with die no

Victoria Fourth head, no die no.

1867	incl. above	£175	£500	—	—
1868	3,330,360	£12	£40	£125	£325
1869	736,560	£20	£55	£170	£450
1870	1,467,471	£15	£40	£120	£320
1871	4,910,010	£12	£40	£120	£300
1872	8,897,781	£12	£40	£120	£300
1873	6,489,598	£12	£40	£120	£300
1874	5,503,747	£15	£40	£130	£320
1875	4,353,983	£12	£40	£120	£300
1876	1,057,487	£18	£60	£170	£550
1877	2,989,703	£12	£40	£120	£320
1878	3,127,131	£12	£40	£120	£320
1879	3,611,507	£20	£70	£220	£600

Fourth head—no die no

1879 no Die no.	incl. above	£10	£28	£90	£225
1880	4,842,786	£10	£28	£90	£225
1881	5,255,332	£10	£28	£90	£225
1882	1,611,786	£25	£80	£200	£550
1883	7,281,450	£10	£28	£70	£200
1884	3,923,993	£10	£28	£70	£200
1885	3,336,526	£10	£28	£70	£200
1886	2,086,819	£10	£28	£70	£200
1887	4,034,133	£10	£28	£70	£200

JUBILEE HEAD ISSUES

Victoria Jubilee head

1887	incl. above	£4	£9	£18	£45
1887 Proof................................	1,084	—	—	—	£450
1888..	4,526,856	£6	£10	£25	£70
1889	7,039,628	£45	£100	£325	—
1889 Large bust (until 1892)........	incl. above	£6	£12	£50	£85
1890	8,794,042	£6	£12	£50	£85
1891	5,665,348	£6	£12	£50	£90
1892	4,591,622	£6	£12	£50	£120

OLD HEAD ISSUES

Victoria Old or Veiled head

1893..	7,039,074	£7	£14	£45	£100
1893 small lettering	incl. above	£7	£14	£45	£100
1893 Proof................................	1,312	—	—	—	£400
1894	5,953,152	£10	£28	£75	£200
1895	8,880,651	£9	£25	£60	£180
1896	9,264,551	£7	£15	£45	£110
1897	6,270,364	£7	£12	£45	£100
1898	9,768,703	£7	£12	£45	£100
1899	10,965,382	£7	£12	£45	£100
1900	10,937,590	£7	£12	£45	£110
1901..	3,426,294	£7	£12	£45	£100

EDWARD VII (1901–10)

DATE	MINTAGE	F	VF	EF	UNC
1902	7,809,481	£5	£15	£50	£90
1902 Proof matt	13,123	–	–	–	£175
1903	2,061,823	£10	£35	£160	£550
1904	2,040,161	£8	£35	£150	£525
1905	488,390	£110	£300	£1200	£3500
1906	10,791,025	£5	£12	£50	£140
1907	14,083,418	£5	£12	£50	£150
1908	3,806,969	£12	£30	£170	£600
1909	5,664,982	£9	£25	£125	£425
1910	26,547,236	£5	£10	£45	£100

GEORGE V (1910–36)

First issue

1911	20,065,901	£5	£9	£24	£60
1911 Proof	6,007	–	–	–	£160
1912	15,594,009	£6	£12	£28	£90
1913	9,011,509	£7	£20	£50	£150
1914	23,415,843	£4	£7	£30	£60
1915	39,279,024	£4	£7	£30	£60
1916	35,862,015	£4	£7	£30	£60
1917	22,202,608	£4	£7	£30	£70
1918	34,915,934	£4	£7	£30	£60
1919	10,823,824	£5	£8	£30	£70

Second issue – debased silver

1920	22,825,142	£2	£4	£25	£55
1921	22,648,763	£2	£4	£25	£55
1922	27,215,738	£2	£4	£25	£60
1923	14,575,243	£2	£4	£25	£55
1924	9,250,095	£7	£15	£60	£160
1925	5,418,764	£6	£10	£50	£140
1926	22,516,453	£3	£8	£30	£120

(Trial Proofs of 1923 and 1924 were struck in cupro nickel – both Rare)

George V First obverse

Third issue – Modified bust

1926 —	incl. above	£2	£4	£30	£60
1927 —	9,247,344	£2	£4	£30	£60

Fourth issue – new obverse: large lion and crown on rev., date in legend

1927	incl. above	£2	£4	£20	£45
1927 Proof	15,000	–	–	–	£70
1928	18,136,778	£2	£4	£15	£45
1929	19,343,006	£2	£4	£15	£45
1930	3,172,092	£2	£4	£20	£55
1931	6,993,926	£2	£4	£15	£45
1932	12,168,101	£2	£4	£15	£50
1933	11,511,624	£2	£4	£15	£40
1934	6,138,463	£2	£4	£18	£50
1935	9,183,462	–	£4	£12	£25
1936	11,910,613	–	£4	£12	£25

GEORGE VI (1936–52)

E = England rev. (lion standing on large crown). S = Scotland rev. (lion seated on small crown holding sword and mace)

George V Fourth issue, Second obverse

1937 E	8,359,122	–	£2	£4	£6
1937 E Proof	26,402	–	–	–	£25
1937 S	6,748,875	–	£2	£4	£6
1937 S Proof	26,402	–	–	–	£25
1938 E	4,833,436	–	£3	£10	£20
1938 S	4,797,852	–	£3	£10	£20
1939 E	11,052,677	–	£2	£4	£6
1939 S	10,263,892	–	£2	£4	£6
1940 E	11,099,126	–	–	£4	£7
1940 S	9,913,089	–	–	£4	£7
1941 E	11,391,883	–	–	£4	£6
1941 S	8,086,030	–	–	£4	£5
1942 E	17,453,643	–	–	£4	£5
1942 S	13,676,759	–	–	£4	£5

DATE	MINTAGE	F	VF	EF	UNC
1943 E	11,404,213	—	—	£4	£6
1943 S	9,824,214	—	—	£4	£5
1944 E	11,586,751	—	—	£4	£5
1944 S	10,990,167	—	—	£4	£5
1945 E	15,143,404	—	—	£4	£6
1945 S	15,106,270	—	—	£4	£5
1946 E	16,663,797	—	—	£4	£5
1946 S	16,381,501	—	—	£4	£5
Cupro-nickel					
1947 E	12,120,611	—	—	—	£2
1947 S	12,283,223	—	—	—	£2
1948 E	45,576,923	—	—	—	£2
1948 S	45,351,937	—	—	—	£2
1949 E	19,328,405	—	—	—	£5
1949 S	21,243,074	—	—	—	£5
1950 E	19,243,872	—	—	—	£5
1950 E Proof	17,513	—	—	—	£20
1950 S	14,299,601	—	—	—	£5
1950 S Proof	17,513	—	—	—	£20
1951 E	9,956,930	—	—	—	£5
1951 E Proof	20,000	—	—	—	£20
1951 S	10,961,174	—	—	—	£6
1951 S Proof	20,000	—	—	—	£20

English reverse

Scottish reverse

ELIZABETH II (1952–)

E = England rev. (shield with three lions). S = Scotland rev. (shield with one lion).

1953 E	41,942,894	—	—	—	£1
1953 E Proof	40,000	—	—	—	£4
1953 S	20,663,528	—	—	—	£1
1953 S Proof	40,000	—	—	—	£4
1954 E	30,262,032	—	—	—	£2
1954 S	26,771,735	—	—	—	£2
1955 E	45,259,908	—	—	—	£2
1955 S	27,950,906	—	—	—	£2
1956 E	44,907,008	—	—	—	£10
1956 S	42,853,639	—	—	—	£10
1957 E	42,774,217	—	—	—	£1
1957 S	17,959,988	—	—	—	£10
1958 E	14,392,305	—	—	—	£10
1958 S	40,822,557	—	—	—	£1
1959 E	19,442,778	—	—	—	£1
1959 S	1,012,988	£1	£3	£10	£70
1960 E	27,027,914	—	—	—	£1
1960 S	14,376,932	—	—	—	£1
1961 E	39,816,907	—	—	—	£1
1961 S	2,762,558	—	—	—	£3
1962 E	36,704,379	—	—	—	£1
1962 S	17,475,310	—	—	—	£1
1963 E	49,433,607	—	—	—	£1
1963 S	32,300,000	—	—	—	£1
1964 E	8,590,900	—	—	—	£1
1964 S	5,239,100	—	—	—	£1
1965 E	9,216,000	—	—	—	£1
1965 S	2,774,000	—	—	—	£2
1966 E	15,002,000	—	—	—	£1
1966 S	15,604,000	—	—	—	£1
1970 E Proof	—				£10
1970 S Proof	—				£10

English reverse

Scottish reverse

SIXPENCES

DATE		F	VF	EF	UNC

OLIVER CROMWELL
1658 Patterns by Thos. Simon & Tanner
Four varieties .... Extremely rare

CHARLES II (1660–85)

	F	VF	EF	UNC	
1674..................	£75	£300	£1000	—	
1675..................	£75	£300	£1100	—	
1675/4 5 over 4	£85	£300	£1100	—	
1676..................	£85	£300	£1000	—	
1676/5 6 over 5	£90	£300	£1000	—	
1677..................	£75	£300	£1000	—	
1678/7	£75	£300	£1100	—	
1679..................	£75	£300	£1000	—	
1680..................	£100	£500	£1300	—	Charles II
1681..................	£85	£300	£1100	—	
1682/1	£85	£300	£1100	—	
1682..................	£110	£350	£1350	—	
1683..................	£85	£300	£1000	—	
1684..................	£90	£300	£1000	—	

JAMES II (1685–88)

	F	VF	EF	UNC	
1686 Early shields	£150	£450	£1200	—	
1687 Ealy Shields	£160	£500	£1450	—	
1687/6 — 7 over 6...............................	£160	£500	£1300	—	
1687 Late shields	£160	£500	£1500	—	
1687/6 — 7 over 6	£160	£500	£1350	—	James II
1688 —...............................	£160	£500	£1450	—	

WILLIAM & MARY (1688–94)

	F	VF	EF	UNC
1693	£130	£450	£1250	—
1693 error inverted 3	£240	£500	£1550	—
1694..................	£130	£450	£1250	—

WILLIAM III (1694–1702)
Provincially produced sixpences carry privy marks or initials below the bust:
B: Bristol. C: Chester. E: Exeter. N: Norwich. Y or y: York.

	F	VF	EF	UNC	
1695 First bust, early harp in 4th shield on rev.	£35	£110	£420	—	William
1696 — —	£35	£110	£340	—	and Mary
1696 — — French arms at date		Extremely rare			
1696 — — Scottish arms at date		Extremely rare			
1696 — — DFI for DEI..............................		Extremely rare			
1696 — — No stops on obv.	£50	£150	£525	—	
1696 — — B..................	£40	£110	£450	—	
1696 — — — B over E		Extremely rare			
1696 — — C..................	£40	£100	£475	—	
1696 — — E..................	£50	£110	£475	—	
1696 — — N..................	£50	£100	£500	—	
1696 — — y..................	£50	£120	£575	—	
1696 — — Y..................	£50	£200	£600	—	
1696 — Later harp	£50	£175	£425	—	
1696 — — B..................	£70	£225	£650	—	
1696 — — no stops on obv	£80	£275	£575	—	Wiliam III
1696 — — C..................	£100	£400	£1000	—	
1696 — — N..................	£70	£325	—	—	
1696 Second bust	£300	£800	£2300	—	
1697 First bust, later harp	£30	£75	£300	—	
1697 — — Arms of France & Ireland transposed		Extremely rare			

DATE	MINTAGE	F	VF	EF	UNC
1697 — — B..		£55	£120	£475	—
1697 — — C..		£70	£200	£500	—
1697 — — — Irish shield at date			Extremely rare		
1697 — — E		£70	£200	£525	—
1697 — — — error GVLIEMVS.........................			Extremely rare		
1697 — — y..		£65	£140	£500	—
1697 — — Irish shield at date			Extremely rare		
1697 Second bust		£220	£550	£1800	—
1697 Third bust		£35	£75	£300	—
1697 — error GVLIEIMVS.................................			Extremely rare		
1697 — B		£55	£140	£500	—
1697 — — IRA for FRA			Extremely rare		
1697 — C		£80	£240	£575	—
1697 — E		£80	£240	£575	—
1697 — Y...		£60	£210	£575	—
1698 —		£60	£200	£550	—
1698 — Plumes in angles on rev.		£100	£250	£850	—
1699 —		£110	£275	£900	—
1699 — Plumes in angles on rev.		£80	£275	£950	—
1699 — Roses in angles on rev.		£75	£260	£875	—
1699 — — error GVLIELMVS			Extremely rare		
1700 —		£45	£110	£425	—
1700 — Plume below bust...............................		£2400	—	—	—
1701 —		£70	£175	£550	—

William III

ANNE (1702–14)

1703 VIGO below bust Before Union with Scotland	£40	£150	£500	—	
1705 Plain...		£60	£170	£550	—
1705 Plumes in angles on rev......................		£60	£175	£600	—
1705 Roses & Plumes in angles on rev.		£70	£180	£575	—
1707 Roses & Plumes in angles on rev.		£50	£160	£500	—
1707 (Post-Union), Plain...............................		£40	£90	£375	—
1707 E (Edinburgh) below bust		£40	£90	£350	—
1707 Plumes in angles on rev......................		£50	£140	£380	—
1708 Plain...		£45	£100	£400	—
1708 E below bust.......................................		£50	£100	£350	—
1708 E* below bust		£60	£140	£400	—
1708 "Edinburgh" bust E* below......................		£50	£140	£400	—
1708 Plumes in angles on rev......................		£60	£160	£550	—
1710 Roses & Plumes in angles on rev.		£40	£125	£500	—
1711 Plain...		£25	£70	£280	—

Queen Anne

GEORGE I (1714–27)

1717 Roses & Plumes in angles on rev.		£90	£300	£850	—
1717 Plain edge...			Extremely rare		
1720 —		£90	£300	£775	—
1723 SSC in angles on rev.		£30	£70	£220	—
1723 Larger lettering.....................................		£30	£70	£220	—
1726 Small Roses & Plumes in angles on rev. ..		£80	£240	£700	—

George I

GEORGE II (1727–60)

1728 Young head, Plain....................................		£70	£240	£525	—
1728 — Proof		—	—	£4000	—
1728 — Plumes in angles on rev.		£40	£140	£425	—
1728 — Roses & Plumes in angles on rev.........		£35	£125	£370	—
1731 — —		£40	£140	£400	—
1732 — —		£35	£130	£400	—
1734 — —		£40	£140	£400	—
1735 — —		£35	£140	£400	—
1735/4 5 over 4		£45	£150	£425	—
1736 — —		£45	£150	£425	—
1739 — Roses in angles on rev.		£30	£110	£350	—
1741 —		£30	£110	£340	—
1743 Old head, Roses in angles on rev.............		£25	£75	£250	—
1745 — —		£25	£75	£250	—
1745 — — 5 over 3		£30	£85	£275	—

George II, young head

DATE	MINTAGE	F	VF	EF	UNC
1745 — Plain, LIMA below bust........................		£30	£80	£275	—
1746 — —		£30	£80	£275	—
1746 — — Proof..		—	—	£1800	—
1750 — —		£35	£140	£350	—
1751 — —		£35	£150	£400	—
1757 — —		£18	£35	£95	—
1758 — —		£18	£35	£95	—

George II, old head

GEORGE III (1760–1820)

1787 rev. no semée of hearts on 4th shield		£15	£35	£80	£115
1787 rev. with semée of hearts.........................		£15	£35	£80	£115

NEW COINAGE

1816	—	£7	£15	£40	£110
1817	10,921,680	£7	£15	£40	£110
1818..	4,284,720	£10	£25	£80	£175
1819..	4,712,400	£8	£15	£40	£100
1819 very small 8 in date............	incl. above	£12	£22	£60	£140
1820..	1,488,960	£8	£15	£50	£125

George III

GEORGE IV (1820–30)

1821 First bust, first reverse	863,280	£12	£30	£120	£350
1821 error BBRITANNIAR............		£100	£300	£950	—
1821 — — Proof........................	incl. above	—	—	—	£1200
1824 — Second (garter) reverse..	633,600	£10	£30	£100	£325
1825 —	483,120	£12	£30	£100	£300
1826 — —	689,040	£40	£100	£250	£550
1826 Second bust, third (lion on crown) reverse	incl. above	£10	£30	£100	£220
1826 — — Proof........................	incl. above	—	—	—	£1100
1827 — —	166,320	£40	£110	£300	£700
1828 — —	15,840	£20	£50	£150	£350
1829 — —	403,290	£15	£45	£125	£350

George IV

WILLIAM IV (1830–37)

1831...................................	1,340,195	£15	£40	£125	£300
1831 Proof, milled edge	incl. above	—	—	—	£1000
1834....................................	5,892,480	£15	£40	£125	£300
1835....................................	1,552,320	£15	£40	£125	£300
1836....................................	1,987,920	£15	£45	£150	£350
1837....................................	506,880	£25	£50	£240	£550

William IV

VICTORIA (1837–1901)

YOUNG HEAD ISSUES
First head

1838..	1,607,760	£15	£40	£130	£350
1839	3,310,560	£15	£40	£130	£350
1839 Proof................................	incl. above	—	—	—	£1600
1840..	2,098,800	£15	£40	£130	£350
1841..	1,386,000	£18	£45	£150	£425
1842..	601,920	£15	£40	£130	£350
1843..	3,160,080	£15	£40	£130	£350
1844..	3,975,840	£15	£30	£140	£375
1844 Large 44 in date.................	incl. above	£18	£40	£130	£425
1845..	3,714,480	£15	£35	£100	£360
1846..	4,226,880	£15	£35	£100	£380
1847..	—	£1000	—	—	—
1848..	586,080	£50	£125	£375	£550
1848/6 final 8 over 6...................	incl. above	£50	£120	£400	—
1850..	498,960	£15	£40	£120	£425
1850/3 0 over 3	incl. above	£18	£40	£110	£400
1851..	2,288,107	£10	£30	£100	£400
1852..	904,586	£10	£30	£150	£380
1853..	3,837,930	£10	£30	£150	£380
1853 Proof................................	incl above	—	—	—	£1750

Victoria Young head

DATE	MINTAGE	F	VF	EF	UNC
1854..	840,116	£200	£600	£1200	3250
1855..	1,129,684	£10	£30	£120	£300
1855/3 last 5 over 3....................	incl. above	£15	£45	£140	£320
1856..	2,779,920	£10	£40	£120	£320
1857..	2,233,440	£10	£40	£120	£300
1858..	1,932,480	£10	£40	£120	£300
1859..	4,688,640	£10	£40	£120	£300
1859/8 9 over 8	incl. above	£12	£40	£120	£420
1860..	1,100,880	£10	£35	£120	£360
1862..	990,000	£100	£200	£600	£1800
1863..	491,040	£70	£150	£475	£1300
Die no. added above date from 1864 to 1879					
1864..	4,253,040	£10	£25	£110	£275
1865..	1,631,520	£10	£25	£100	£275
1866..	4,140,080	£10	£25	£100	£275
1866 no Die no.	incl. above			Extremely Rare	

Jubilee head, shield reverse

Second head

1867..	1,362,240	£10	£30	£120	£300
1868..	1,069,200	£10	£30	£110	£300
1869..	388,080	£10	£30	£110	£310
1870..	479,613	£10	£30	£110	£280
1871..	3,662,684	£8	£30	£75	£280
1871 no Die no.	incl. above	£8	£30	£75	£240
1872..	3,382,048	£8	£30	£75	£240
1873..	4,594,733	£8	£30	£75	£240
1874..	4,225,726	£8	£30	£90	£300
1875..	3,256,545	£8	£30	£75	£250
1876..	841,435	£8	£30	£75	£250
1877..	4,066,486	£8	£30	£75	£250
1877 no Die no	incl. above	£8	£30	£75	£250
1878..	2,624,525	£8	£30	£75	£280
1878/7 8 struck over 7 Error.......	incl. above	£45	£200	£750	—
1878 Dritanniar Error	incl. above	£125	£300	£1000	—
1879	3,326,313	£8	£25	£80	£250
1879 no Die no	incl. above	£8	£25	£80	£250
1880 no Die no	3,892,501	£8	£25	£75	£250

Jubilee head, wreath reverse

Third head

1880	incl above	£8	£20	£80	£200
1881..	6,239,447	£8	£20	£80	£200
1882..	759,809	£15	£50	£150	£475
1883..	4,986,558	£8	£20	£70	£175
1884..	3,422,565	£8	£20	£70	£175
1885..	4,652,771	£8	£20	£70	£175
1886..	2,728,249	£8	£20	£70	£170
1887..	3,675,607	£8	£20	£70	£170

JUBILEE HEAD ISSUES

1887 Shield reverse	incl. above	£6	£10	£15	£30
1887 — Proof	incl. above	—	—	—	£1200
1887 Six Pence in wreath reverse	incl. above	£6	£8	£18	£35
1888 —	4,197,698	£8	£12	£35	£60
1889 —	8,738,928	£8	£12	£35	£70
1890 —	9,386,955	£8	£12	£35	£70
1891 —	7,022,734	£8	£12	£35	£70
1892 —	6,245,746	£8	£12	£35	£80
1893 —	7,350,619	£800	£1500	£4000	—

OLD HEAD ISSUES

1893..	incl. above	£7	£12	£22	£50
1893 Proof.................................	1,312	—	—	—	£400
1894..	3,467,704	£8	£18	£55	£160
1895	7,024,631	£8	£18	£50	£125
1896..	6,651,699	£7	£15	£40	£80
1897..	5,031,498	£7	£15	£40	£80
1898..	5,914,100	£7	£15	£40	£80
1899..	7,996,80	£7	£15	£40	£75
1900..	8,984,354	£7	£15	£40	£75
1901..	5,108,757	£7	£15	£40	£75

Victoria Old Head

DATE	MINTAGE	F	VF	EF	UNC

EDWARD VII (1901–10)

DATE	MINTAGE	F	VF	EF	UNC
1902	6,367,378	£5	£10	£30	£60
1902 "Matt Proof"	15,123	—	—	—	£150
1903	5,410,096	£7	£20	£50	£170
1904	4,487,098	£15	£50	£175	£500
1905	4,235,556	£8	£20	£70	£220
1906	7,641,146	£7	£12	£40	£110
1907	8,733,673	£7	£12	£45	£120
1908	6,739,491	£10	£30	£110	£350
1909	6,584,017	£8	£18	£50	£175
1910	12,490,724	£5	£8	£25	£65

Edward VII

GEORGE V (1910–36)

First issue

DATE	MINTAGE	F	VF	EF	UNC
1911	9,155,310	£3	£7	£15	£40
1911 Proof	6,007	—	—	—	£150
1912	10,984,129	£3	£7	£20	£65
1913	7,499,833	£3	£8	£22	£80
1914	22,714,602	£3	£7	£10	£35
1915	15,694,597	£3	£7	£12	£45
1916	22,207,178	£3	£7	£10	£35
1917	7,725,475	£8	£25	£60	£150
1918	27,553,743	£3	£7	£12	£30
1919	13,375,447	£3	£7	£12	£40
1920	14,136,287	£3	£7	£10	£35

Second issue — debased silver

DATE	MINTAGE	F	VF	EF	UNC
1920	incl. above	£1	£3	£10	£40
1921	30,339,741	£1	£3	£10	£40
1922	16,878,890	£1	£3	£10	£30
1923	6,382,793	£4	£10	£45	£110
1924	17,444,218	£1	£5	£10	£35
1925	12,720,558	£1	£3	£10	£35
1925 Broad rim	incl. above	£1	£3	£10	£35
1926 —	21,809,621	£1	£3	£10	£35

George V first reverse

Third issue — Modified bust

DATE	MINTAGE	F	VF	EF	UNC
1926	incl. above	£1	£2	£10	£35
1927	8,924,873	—	£2	£10	£35

Fourth issue — New design (oakleaves)

DATE	MINTAGE	F	VF	EF	UNC
1927 Proof only	15,000	—	—	—	£60
1928	23,123,384	£1	£2	£8	£25
1929	28,319,326	£1	£2	£8	£25
1930	16,990,289	£1	£2	£8	£30
1931	16,873,268	£1	£2	£8	£30
1932	9,406,117	£1	£2	£8	£40
1933	22,185,083	£1	£2	£8	£25
1934	9,304,009	£1	£2	£12	£35
1935	13,995,621	£1	£2	£6	£15
1936	24,380,171	£1	£2	£6	£15

George V second reverse (fourth issue)

GEORGE VI (1936–52)

First type

DATE	MINTAGE	F	VF	EF	UNC
1937	22,302,524	—	—	£1	£5
1937 Proof	26,402	—	—	—	£15
1938	13,402,701	—	£2	£5	£18
1939	28,670,304	—	—	£1	£5
1940	20,875,196	—	—	£1	£5
1941	23,086,616	—	—	£1	£5
1942	44,942,785	—	—	£1	£4
1943	46,927,111	—	—	£1	£4
1944	36,952,600	—	—	£1	£4
1945	39,939,259	—	—	£1	£3
1946	43,466,407	—	—	£1	£3

George VI first reverse

Cupro-nickel

DATE	MINTAGE	F	VF	EF	UNC
1947	29,993,263	—	—	£1	£3
1948	88,323,540	—	—	£1	£3

Second type — new cypher on rev.

DATE	MINTAGE	F	VF	EF	UNC
1949	41,335,515	—	—	£1	£3
1950	32,741,955	—	—	£1	£3
1950 Proof	17,513	—	—	—	£7
1951	40,399,491	—	—	£1	£3

George VI second reverse

DATE	MINTAGE	F	VF	EF	UNC
1951 Proof..................................	20,000	—	—	—	£7
1952..	1,013,477	£7	£22	£50	£160

ELIZABETH II (1952–   )

1953..	70,323,876	—	—	—	£2
1953 Proof..................................	40,000	—	—	—	£4
1954..	105,241,150	—	—	—	£3
1955..	109,929,554	—	—	—	£1
1956..	109,841,555	—	—	—	£1
1957..	105,654,290	—	—	—	£1
1958..	123,518,527	—	—	—	£3
1959..	93,089,441	—	—	—	£1
1960..	103,283,346	—	—	—	£3
1961..	115,052,017	—	—	—	£3
1962..	166,483,637	—	—	—	25p
1963..	120,056,000	—	—	—	25p
1964..	152,336,000	—	—	—	25p
1965..	129,644,000	—	—	—	25p
1966..	175,676,000	—	—	—	25p
1967..	240,788,000	—	—	—	25p
1970 Proof..................................	—				£8

GROATS OR FOURPENCES

DATE	MINTAGE	F	VF	EF	UNC

The earlier fourpences are included in the Maundy oddments section as they are generally considered to have been issued for the Maundy ceremony.

WILLIAM IV (1831–37)

1836..	—	£8	£20	£45	£95
1837..	962,280	£8	£20	£45	£100

VICTORIA (1838–1901)

1837..	Extremely Rare Proofs or Patterns only				
1838..	2,150,280	£7	£15	£40	£90
1838 over last 8 on its side		£10	£20	£60	£135
1839..	1,461,240	£7	£16	£50	£110
1839 Proof..................................	incl. above				Rare
1840..	1,496,880	£7	£15	£50	£110
1840 Small 0 in date..................	incl. above	£7	£15	£50	£110
1841..	344,520	£7	£15	£50	£110
1842/1 2 over 1	incl. above	£7	£15	£50	£110
1842..	724,680	£7	£15	£45	£110
1843..	1,817640	£8	£18	£50	£130
1843 4 over 5.............................	incl. above	£7	£15	£50	£130
1844..	855,360	£7	£15	£50	£120
1845..	914,760	£7	£15	£50	£110
1846..	1,366,200	£7	£15	£50	£100
1847 7 over 6.............................	225,720	£15	£35	£125	—
1848..	712,800	£7	£15	£50	£100
1848/6 8 over 6	incl. above	£30	£110	—	—
1848/7 8 over 7	incl. above	£8	£20	£60	£110
1849..	380,160	£8	£16	£55	£110
1849/8 9 over 8	incl. above	£8	£20	£70	£140
1851..	594,000	£35	£80	£250	£450
1852..	31,300	£55	£130	£425	—
1853..	11,880	£80	£170	£600	—
1853 Proof Milled Rim.................	incl. above	—	—	—	£1300
1853 Plain edge Proof................				Extremely rare	
1854..	1,096,613	£7	£15	£40	£100
1855..	646,041	£7	£15	£40	£100
1855/3 Last 5 over 3	—	£12	£25	£75	£200
1857 Proofs only				Extremely rare	
1862 Proofs only				Extremely rare	
1888 Jubilee Head	—	£14	£28	£55	£125

THREEPENCES

DATE	MINTAGE	F	VF	EF	UNC

The earlier threepences are included in the Maundy oddments section.

WILLIAM IV (1830–37)

(issued for use in the West Indies)

1834		£12	£24	£100	£250
1835		£10	£20	£80	£230
1836		£10	£20	£85	£230
1837		£15	£32	£130	£300

Wiliam IV

VICTORIA (1837–1901)

1838 BRITANNIAB error			Extremely rare		
1838	—	£15	£30	£80	£250
1839	—	£15	£30	£90	£260
1840	—	£15	£30	£90	£260
1841	—	£18	£30	£100	£300
1842	—	£15	£28	£90	£270
1843	—	£15	£28	£70	£220
1843/34 43 over 34	—	£15	£28	£90	£250
1844	—	£16	£28	£90	£240
1845	1,319,208	£16	£28	£70	£235
1846	52,008	£25	£70	£275	£550
1847	4,488		Extremely rare		
1848	incl. above		Extremely rare		
1849	131,208	£12	£28	£80	£250
1850	954,888	£12	£25	£70	£225
1851	479,065	£12	£30	£70	£230
1851 reads 1551			Very rare		
1851 5 over 8	incl. above	£25	£50	£220	—
1852	4,488	£80	£220	£700	£1100
1853	36,168	£60	£140	£300	£700
1854	1,467,246	£8	£25	£75	£220
1855	383,350	£12	£30	£90	£260
1856	1,013,760	£10	£25	£90	£225
1857	1,758,240	£10	£25	£80	£250
1858	1,441,440	£10	£25	£70	£225
1858 BRITANNIAB error	incl. above		Extremely rare		
1858/6 final 8 over 6	incl. above	£15	£30	£200	—
1858/5 final 8 over 5	incl. above	£10	£30	£150	—
1859	3,579,840	£8	£20	£60	£200
1860	3,405,600	£12	£28	£75	£260
1861	3,294,720	£10	£25	£70	£200
1862	1,156,320	£10	£25	£70	£200
1863	950,400	£30	£70	£125	£350
1864	1,330,560	£7	£22	£50	£170
1865	1,742,400	£7	£22	£60	£190
1866	1,900,800	£7	£22	£60	£180
1867	712,800	£7	£22	£60	£180
1868	1,457,280	£7	£22	£60	£190
1868 RRITANNIAR error	incl. above		Extremely rare		
1869	—	£25	£175	£300	£650
1870	1,283,218	£6	£18	£60	£160
1871	999,633	£6	£18	£50	£140
1872	1,293,271	£5	£16	£50	£120
1873	4,055,550	£5	£16	£50	£120
1874	4,427,031	£5	£16	£50	£130
1875	3,306,500	£5	£16	£50	£120
1876	1,834,389	£5	£16	£50	£120
1877	2,622,393	£5	£16	£50	£120
1878	2,419,975	£6	£18	£55	£160
1879	3,140,265	£5	£16	£40	£110
1880	1,610,069	£5	£16	£40	£100
1881	3,248,265	£5	£16	£40	£95

Victoria Young head type

DATE	MINTAGE	F	VF	EF	UNC
1882	472,965	£8	£25	£70	£200
1883	4,369,971	£5	£10	£30	£65
1884	3,322,424	£5	£12	£35	£75
1885	5,183,653	£5	£12	£35	£80
1886	6,152,669	£5	£12	£30	£60
1887	2,780,761	£5	£12	£30	£65

Dates of 1838, 1839, 1840, 1841, 1842, 1843, 1844, 1847, 1848 and 1853 were issued for colonial use.

Victoria Jubilee head

JUBILEE HEAD ISSUES

1887	incl. above	£2	£4	£15	£30
1887 Proof	incl. above	—	—	—	£250
1888	518,199	£2	£5	£20	£45
1889	4,587,010	£2	£5	£20	£50
1890	4,465,834	£2	£5	£20	£50
1891	6,323,027	£2	£5	£20	£50
1892	2,578,226	£2	£5	£20	£55
1893	3,067,243	£20	£60	£180	£425

OLD HEAD ISSUES

1893	incl. above	£2	£5	£16	£35
1893 Proof	incl. above	—	—	—	£250
1894	1,608,603	£4	£7	£25	£70
1895	4,788,609	£2	£5	£22	£60
1896	4,598,442	£2	£5	£18	£40
1897	4,541,294	£2	£5	£18	£40
1898	4,567,177	£2	£5	£18	£40
1899	6,246,281	£2	£5	£18	£40
1900	10,644,480	£2	£5	£18	£40
1901	6,098,400	£2	£5	£15	£30

Victoria Old or Veiled head

EDWARD VII (1901–10)

1902	8,268,480	£2	£3	£10	£20
1902 "Matt Proof"	incl. above	—	—	—	£60
1903	5,227,200	£2	£5	£20	£55
1904	3,627,360	£4	£12	£50	£120
1905	3,548,160	£2	£5	£25	£65
1906	3,152,160	£3	£9	£40	£90
1907	4,831,200	£2	£4	£20	£60
1908	8,157,600	£2	£3	£20	£55
1909	4,055,040	£2	£4	£20	£60
1910	4,563,380	£2	£4	£18	£45

Edward VII

GEORGE V (1910–36)

First issue

1911	5,841,084	—	—	£3	£12
1911 Proof	incl. above	—	—	—	£70
1912	8,932,825	—	—	£3	£15
1913	7,143,242	—	—	£3	£15
1914	6,733,584	—	—	£3	£14
1915	5,450,617	—	—	£3	£16
1916	18,555,201	—	—	£3	£12
1917	21,662,490	—	—	£3	£12
1918	20,630,909	—	—	£3	£10
1919	16,845,687	—	—	£3	£10
1920	16,703,597	—	—	£3	£10

George V second issue

Second issue—debased silver

1920	incl. above	—	—	£3	£14
1921	8,749,301	—	—	£3	£14
1922	7,979,998	—	—	£3	£40
1925	3,731,859	—	—	£5	£28
1926	4,107,910	—	—	£7	£35

Third issue—Modified bust

1926	incl. above	—	—	£8	£25

George V, fourth issue oak leaves design reverse

Fourth issue—new design (oakleaves)

1927 Proof only	15,022	—	—	—	£120
1928	1,302,106	£4	£10	£30	£65
1930	1,319,412	£2	£4	£10	£40

DATE	MINTAGE	F	VF	EF	UNC
1931	6,251,936	–	–	£2	£7
1932	5,887,325	–	–	£2	£7
1933	5,578,541	–	–	£2	£7
1934	7,405,954	–	–	£2	£7
1935	7,027,654	–	–	£2	£7
1936	3,328,670	–	–	£2	£7

GEORGE VI (1936–52)

Silver

1937	8,148,156	–	–	£1	£5
1937 Proof	26,402	–	–	–	£20
1938	6,402,473	–	–	£1	£5
1939	1,355,860	–	–	£4	£15
1940	7,914,401	–	–	£1	£4
1941	7,979,411	–	–	£1	£4
1942	4,144,051	£2	£5	£12	£35
1943	1,397,220	£3	£8	£15	£40
1944	2,005,553	£10	£25	£50	£100
1945				Only one known	

George VI small silver 3d

1942, 1943, 1944, 1945 were for colonial issue only.

Nickel brass

1937	45,707,957	–	–	£1	£4
1937 Proof	26,402	–	–	–	£20
1938	14,532,332	–	–	£1	£25
1939	5,603,021	–	–	£5	£50
1940	12,636,018	–	–	£4	£35
1941	60,239,489	–	–	£1	£10
1942	103,214,400	–	–	£1	£10
1943	101,702,400	–	–	£1	£10
1944	69,760,000	–	–	£1	£12
1945	33,942,466	–	–	£5	£25
1946	620,734	£6	£25	£240	£900
1948	4,230,400	–	–	£7	£60
1949	464,000	£6	£28	£250	£950
1950	1,600,000	–	£2	£20	£140
1950 Proof	17,513	–	–	–	£25
1951	1,184,000	–	£4	£35	£170
1951 Proof	20,000	–	–	–	£25
1952	25,494,400	–	–	–	£12

*George VI "Thrift" design
of the nickel brass 3d*

ELIZABETH II (1952–)

1953	30,618,000	–	–	–	£1
1953 Proof	40,000	–	–	–	£12
1954	41,720,000	–	–	–	£5
1955	41,075,200	–	–	–	£5
1956	36,801,600	–	–	–	£6
1957	24,294,500	–	–	–	£6
1958	20,504,000	–	–	–	£9
1959	28,499,200	–	–	–	£6
1960	83,078,400	–	–	–	£2
1961	41,102,400	–	–	–	£1
1962	51,545,600	–	–	–	£1
1963	39,482,866	–	–	–	£1
1964	44,867,200	–	–	–	–
1965	27,160,000	–	–	–	–
1966	53,160,000	–	–	–	–
1967	151,780,800	–	–	–	–
1970 Proof	–				£6

TWO PENCES

DATE	F	VF	EF	UNC

GEORGE III (1760–1820)
1797 "Cartwheel" 722,972	£32	£85	£440	£1200
1797 Copper Proofs		Many types from £1000+		

VICTORIA (1837–1901)
For use in the Colonies
1838	£4	£10	£20	£45
1848...	£4	£12	£20	£50

Earlier issues of the small silver two pences are listed in the Maundy section.

THREE-HALFPENCES

WILLIAM IV (1830–37)
For use in the Colonies

1834	£6	£18	£40	£95
1835...	£10	£25	£75	£210
1835 over 4..	£6	£16	£40	£110
1836...	£8	£18	£50	£120
1837...	£15	£40	£120	£350

VICTORIA (1837–1901)
For use in the Colonies

1838	£6	£15	£35	£90
1839	£6	£15	£35	£90
1840...	£8	£20	£60	£150
1841...	£6	£15	£40	£90
1842...	£6	£18	£50	£110
1843...	£6	£15	£40	£85
1860...	£12	£30	£100	£225
1862...	£18	£40	£110	£275

PENNIES

The earlier small silver pennies are included in the Maundy oddments section.

GEORGE III (1760–1820)
Note: Mintage figures are from the on-line thesis, "Matthew Boulton and the Soho Mint— Copper to Customer", by Sue Tungate, Birmingham University, October 2011 (information supplied by Dennis Onions)

Soho Mint
1797 "Cartwheel" type, 10 laurel leaves	43,969,204 £25	£60	£320	£1000

Numerous proofs in different metals are known for this issue—all are rare.
1797 — 11 laurel leaves	incl. above £25	£60	£320	£1000
1806 (34mm)...............................	19,355,480 £7	£20	£85	£300
1807...	11,290,168 £7	£20	£85	£300
1808...	—			Unique

GEORGE IV (1820–30)
1825...	1,075,200 £18	£45	£260	£675
1826 (varieties)	5,913,600 £18	£45	£260	£675
1826 Proof...................................	— —	—	—	£1200
1827...	1,451,520 £300	£900	£4500	—

George III "Cartwheel" penny reverse. The obverse is as the two pence above.

DATE	MINTAGE	F	VF	EF	UNC

WILLIAM IV (1830–37)

DATE	MINTAGE	F	VF	EF	UNC
1831 (varieties)	806,400	£30	£75	£425	£1250
1831 Proof	—	—	—	—	£1500
1834	322,560	£32	£75	£425	£1350
1837	174,720	£70	£210	£800	£3000

VICTORIA (1837–1901)

YOUNG HEAD ISSUES

Copper

DATE	MINTAGE	F	VF	EF	UNC
1839 Proof	unrecorded	—	—	—	£3500
1841	913,920	£10	£50	£300	£875
1841 No colon after REG	incl. above	£8	£20	£175	£550
1843	483,840	£100	£350	£2000	£5000
1844	215,040	£12	£30	£200	£625
1844 Proofs exist	—			Extremely rare	
1845	322,560	£15	£35	£250	£800
1846	483,840	£15	£25	£220	£750
1846 FID: DEF colon spaced	incl. above	£15	£25	£220	£750
1846 FID:DEF colon close	incl. above	£16	£30	£220	£775
1847	430,080	£12	£25	£200	£620
1848	161,280	£12	£25	£175	£575
1848/7 final 8 over 7	incl. above	£9	£22	£160	£500
1848/6 final 8 over 6	incl. above	£20	£120	£525	—
1849	268,800	£225	£600	£2500	—
1851	268,800	£15	£45	£220	£800
1853	1,021,440	£7	£15	£100	£200
1853 Proof	—	—	—	—	£3500
1854	6,720,000	£8	£22	£120	£260
1854/3 4 over 3	incl. above	£15	£50	£200	—
1855	5,273,856	£8	£20	£100	£250
1856 Plain trident close colon DEF:	1,212,288	£110	£250	£1100	£3000
1856 Orn trident far colon DEF: ..	—	£120	£270	£1100	£3200
1856 Proofs exists	—			Extremely rare	
1857 Plain trident	752,640	£7	£18	£100	£330
1857 Ornamental trident	incl. above	£6	£18	£90	£340
1858/7 final 8 over 7	incl. above	£7	£18	£90	£350
1858/6 final 8 over 6	—	£40	£120	£550	—
1858/3 final 8 over 3	incl. above	£25	£90	£400	—
1858	1,599,040	£7	£16	£100	£360
1859	1,075,200	£10	£28	£180	£525
1860/59	32,256	£900	£2200	£4000	£7000

Note all are 60/59. All have a prominent die flan under Victoria's chin.

Victoria copper penny

Bronze

Prices of bronze Victoria Young "bun" head pennies are for the common types. There are many known varieties which are listed in detail in other more specialised publications. Prices for coins in mint with full lustre will be considerably higher.

DATE	MINTAGE	F	VF	EF	UNC
1860 Beaded border	5,053,440	£40	£100	£250	£1000
1860 Toothed border	incl. above	£10	£30	£80	£400
1860 — Piedfort flan	—			Extremely rare	
1861	36,449,280	£8	£15	£55	£375
1862	50,534,400	£8	£15	£55	£340
1862 8 over 6	incl. above			Extremely rare	
1863	28,062,720	£8	£15	£55	£320
1863 Die no below date	incl. above			Extremely rare	
1864 Plain 4	3,440,640	£30	£175	£700	£3500
1864 Crosslet 4	incl. above	£35	£185	£800	£3750
1865	8,601,600	£8	£20	£60	£400
1865/3 5 over 3	incl. above	£50	£160	£600	—
1866	9,999,360	£8	£25	£80	£500
1867	5,483,520	£8	£25	£100	£900
1868	1,182,720	£20	£80	£300	£2400
1869	2,580,480	£150	£500	£2000	£6000
1870	5,695,022	£18	£50	£200	£800
1871	1,290,318	£45	£150	£500	£2500
1872	8,494,572	£8	£25	£80	£325

Victoria Young or "Bun" head bronze penny

DATE	MINTAGE	F	VF	EF	UNC
1873............................	8,494,200	£8	£25	£80	£325
1874............................	5,621,865	£8	£25	£80	£325
1874 H.........................	6,666,240	£8	£25	£80	£380
1874 Later (older) bust	incl. above	£16	£48	£130	£575
1875............................	10,691,040	£8	£25	£75	£350
1875 H.........................	752,640	£35	£125	£900	£2500
1876 H.........................	11,074,560	£8	£15	£65	£370
1877............................	9,624,747	£8	£15	£65	£370
1878............................	2,764,470	£8	£15	£65	£370
1879............................	7,666,476	£6	£18	£60	£370
1880............................	3,000,831	£6	£18	£60	£360
1881............................	2,302,362	£8	£18	£60	£325
1881 H.........................	3,763,200	£12	£20	£65	£350
1882 H.........................	7,526,400	£8	£18	£60	£325
1882 no H.....................	—		Extremely Rare		
1883............................	6,237,438	£8	£18	£65	£275
1884............................	11,702,802	£8	£20	£65	£275
1885............................	7,145,862	£8	£18	£60	£275
1886............................	6,087,759	£8	£18	£60	£275
1887............................	5,315,085	£8	£18	£60	£275
1888............................	5,125,020	£8	£18	£65	£325
1889............................	12,559,737	£8	£18	£55	£375
1890............................	15,330,840	£8	£18	£55	£275
1891............................	17,885,961	£8	£15	£55	£275
1892............................	10,501,671	£10	£20	£100	£275
1893............................	8,161,737	£8	£15	£55	£275
1894............................	3,883,452	£15	£45	£160	£550

OLD HEAD ISSUES

1895 Trident 2mm from P(ENNY)	5,395,830	£20	£90	£300	£850
1895 Trident 1mm from P...........	incl. above	—	£2	£18	£75
1896............................	24,147,156	—	£2	£18	£65
1897............................	20,756,620	—	£2	£15	£60
1897 Raised dot after O of ONE (O·NE)	£150	£275	£900	—
1898............................	14,296,836	—	£3	£18	£65
1899............................	26,441,069	—	£3	£16	£60
1900............................	31,778,109	—	£3	£16	£45
1901............................	22,205,568	—	£3	£10	£30

EDWARD VII (1901–10)

1902............................	26,976,768	—	£1	£8	£30
1902 "Low tide" to sea line	incl. above	£4	£15	£60	£225
1903............................	21,415,296	—	£3	£15	£90
1904............................	12,913,152	—	£4	£25	£200
1905............................	17,783,808	—	£3	£15	£85
1906............................	37,989,504	—	£3	£15	£75
1907............................	47,322,240	—	£3	£15	£75
1908............................	31,506,048	—	£3	£18	£140
1909............................	19,617,024	—	£3	£20	£175
1910............................	29,549,184	—	£3	£15	£65

GEORGE V (1910–36)

1911............................	23,079,168	—	£3	£12	£65
1912............................	48,306,048	—	£3	£12	£60
1912 H.........................	16,800,000	—	£4	£40	£250
1913............................	65,497,812	—	£3	£15	£75
1914............................	50,820,997	—	£3	£18	£80
1915............................	47,310,807	—	£3	£20	£85
1916............................	86,411,165	—	£3	£15	£65
1917............................	107,905,436	—	£3	£15	£60
1918............................	84,227,372	—	£3	£12	£55
1918 H.........................	3,660,800	£1	£15	£150	£600
1918 KN........................	incl. above	£8	£80	£600	£2500
1919............................	113,761,090	—	£2	£15	£55
1919 H.........................	5,209,600	£1	£18	£250	£1000
1919 KN........................	incl. above	£15	£120	£800	£3200
1920............................	124,693,485	—	£2	£12	£30
1921............................	129,717,693	—	£2	£12	£40
1922............................	16,346,711	—	£3	£28	£160
1922 with reverse of 1927 (see article on p. 17)					Very rare
1926............................	4,498,519	—	£6	£25	£150
1926 Modified effigy..................	incl above	£25	£150	£800	£2700
1927............................	60,989,561	—	£2	£10	£45

DATE	MINTAGE	F	VF	EF	UNC
1928	50,178,00	—	£2	£10	£40
1929	49,132,800	—	£2	£10	£45
1930	29,097,600	—	£2	£20	£75
1931	19,843,200	—	£2	£10	£55
1932	8,277,600	—	£2	£15	£110
1933		Only 7 examples known			
1934	13,965,600	—	£2	£25	£110
1935	56,070,000	—	—	£2	£15
1936	154,296,000	—	—	£2	£12

GEORGE VI (1936–52)

1937	88,896,000	—	—	—	£4
1937 Proof	26,402	—	—	—	£15
1938	121,560,000	—	—	—	£6
1939	55,560,000	—	—	—	£15
1940	42,284,400	—	—	£8	£25
1944 Mint Dark	42,600,000	—	—	—	£8
1945 Mint Dark	79,531,200	—	—	—	£8
1946 Mint Dark	66,855,600	—	—	—	£8
1947	52,220,400	—	—	—	£5
1948	63,961,200	—	—	—	£5
1949	14,324,400	—	—	—	£8
1950	240,000	£8	£16	£30	£50
1950 Proof	17,513	—	—	—	£25
1951	120,000	£20	£28	£50	£75
1951 Proof	20,000	—	—	—	£40

ELIZABETH II (1952–)

1953	1,308,400	—	—	£2	£5
1953 Proof	40,000	—	—	—	£10
1954		Only one known			
1961	48,313,400	—	—	—	£2
1962	143,308,600	—	—	—	50p
1963	125,235,600	—	—	—	50p
1964	153,294,000	—	—	—	50p
1965	121,310,400	—	—	—	50p
1966	165,739,200	—	—	—	50p
1967	654,564,000	—	—	—	—
1970 Proof	—				£8

Later issues are included in the Decimal section.

HALFPENNIES

CHARLES II (1660–85)

1672	£70	£300	£1350	—
1672 CRAOLVS error		Extremely rare		
1673	£70	£300	£1350	—
1673 CRAOLVS error		Extremely rare		
1673 No rev. stop	£100	£600	—	—
1673 No stops on obv.		Extremely rare		
1675	£65	£500	£1500	—
1675 No stops on obv.	£80	£550	—	—
1675/3 5 over 3	£175	£650	—	—

JAMES II (1685–88)

1685 (tin)	£250	£750	£4000	—
1686 (tin)	£300	£750	£4200	—
1687 (tin)	£325	£800	£4000	—

WILLIAM & MARY (1688–94)

Tin

1689 Small draped busts, edge dated		Extremely rare		
1690 Large cuirassed busts, edge dated	£200	£750	£3500	—
1691 — date on edge and in exergue	£180	£700	£3200	—
1692 — —	£200	£750	£3400	—

Copper halfpenny of William & Mary

DATE	F	VF	EF	UNC

Copper

1694 Large cuirassed busts, date in exergue	£80	£300	£1300	—
1694 — — GVLIEMVS error		Extremely rare		
1694 — — MΛRIΛ error		Extremely rare		
1694 — — No stops on rev.		Extremely rare		

WILLIAM III (1694–1702)

	F	VF	EF	UNC
1695 First issue (date in exergue)....................	£50	£200	£1100	—
1695 — No stop after BRITANNIA on rev.		Extremely rare		
1696 —	£40	£180	£1000	—
1696 — TERTVS error		Extremely rare		
1697 —	£50	£180	£1000	—
1697 — No stop after TERTIVS on obv.	£55	£325	—	—
1698 —	£50	£200	£1000	—
1698 Second issue (date in legend)	£55	£200	—	—
1698 — No stop after date..............................	£50	£200	—	—
1699 —	£55	£220	£1100	—
1699 — No stop after date..............................	£250	—	—	—
1699 Third issue (date in exergue) (Britannia with right hand on knee).....................................	£40	£200	£900	—
1699 — No stop after date..............................		Extremely rare		
1699 — BRITΛNNIΛ error	£225	—	—	—
1699 — TERTVS error		Extremely rare		
1699 — No stop on rev....................................		Extremely rare		
1699 — No stops on obv.................................	£90	£375	—	—
1700 —	£50	£200	£1000	—
1700 — No stops on obv.................................	£100	£375	—	—
1700 — No stops after GVLIELMUS	£100	£375	—	—
1700 — BRITVANNIA error..............................		Extremely rare		
1700 — GVIELMS error..................................	£100	£350	—	—
1700 — GVLIEEMVS error...............................	£100	£350	—	—
1701 —	£50	£200	£950	—
1701 — BRITΛNNIΛ error	£80	£300	—	—
1701 — No stops on obv..................................		Extremely rare		
1701 — inverted As for Vs..............................	£90	£350	—	—

William III first issue

GEORGE I (1714–27)

	F	VF	EF	UNC
1717 "Dump" issue	£50	£250	£850	
1718 —	£40	£225	£8005	—
1719 "Dump" issue. Patterns...........................				Rare
1719 Second issue.......................................	£40	£200	£800	—
1720 —	£35	£160	£600	—
1721 —	£35	£150	£600	—
1721 — Stop after date..................................	£45	£160	—	—
1722 —	£35	£140	£650	—
1722 — inverted A for V on obv.		Extremely rare		
1723 —	£35	£160	£650	—
1723 — No stop on rev....................................	£110	£500	—	—
1724 —	£40	£160	£650	—

GEORGE II (1727–60)

	F	VF	EF	UNC
1729 Young head	£30	£100	£470	—
1729 — No stop on rev....................................	£30	£100	£470	—
1730 —	£22	£100	£475	—
1730 — GEOGIVS error..................................	£80	£250	£850	—
1730 — Stop after date..................................	£30	£130	£475	—
1730 — No stop after REX on obv.	£35	£160	£500	—
1731 —	£25	£120	£450	—
1731 — No rev. stop......................................	£28	£125	£450	—
1732 —	£25	£110	£450	—
1732 — No rev. stop......................................	£28	£140	£500	—
1733 —	£25	£100	£475	—
1734/3 — 4 over 3...	£35	£220	—	—
1734 — No stop on obv.	£35	£220	—	—

George I "Dump" type

DATE	MINTAGE	F	VF	EF	UNC
1735 —		£24	£90	£450	—
1736 —		£24	£90	£450	—
1737 —		£24	£95	£500	—
1738 —		£24	£90	£400	—
1739 —		£20	£70	£375	—
1740 Old head		£20	£75	£350	—
1742 —		£20	£75	£350	—
1742/0 — 2 over 0		£25	£150	£500	—
1743 —		£18	£75	£380	—
1744 —		£18	£75	£390	—
1745 —		£18	£75	£400	—
1746 —		£18	£75	£350	—
1747 —		£18	£75	£350	—
1748 —		£18	£75	£350	—
1749 —		£18	£75	£350	—
1750 —		£18	£75	£350	—
1751 —		£18	£75	£350	—
1752 —		£18	£75	£350	—
1753 —		£18	£75	£350	—
1754 —		£18	£75	£350	—

George II "Old" head

GEORGE III (1760–1820)

First type—Royal Mint

1770		£18	£50	£300	—
1770 No stop on rev.		£25	£70	£350	—
1771		£12	£50	£280	—
1771 No stop on rev.		£20	£65	£300	—
1772 Error GEORIVS		£80	£250	£850	
1772		£12	£50	£240	—
1772 No stop on rev		£20	£65	£280	—
1773		£10	£45	£280	—
1773 No stop after REX		£35	£100	£425	—
1773 No stop on rev.		£20	£70	£300	—
1774		£12	£40	£230	—
1775		£12	£40	£230	—

Second type—Soho Mint

1799	42,481,116	£5	£12	£55	£120

Third type

1806	87,993,526	£5	£12	£60	£110
1807	41,394,384	£5	£12	£60	£110

George III second type

GEORGE IV (1820–30)

1825	215,040	£12	£45	£190	£380
1826 (varieties)	9,031,630	£12	£45	£190	£380
1826 Proof	—	—	—	—	£750
1827	5,376,000	£12	£45	£160	£360

WILLIAM IV (1830–37)

1831	806,400	£12	£30	£130	£325
1831 Proof	—	—	—	—	£850
1834	537,600	£12	£30	£130	£325
1837	349,440	£12	£30	£130	£325

VICTORIA (1837–1901)

Copper

1838	456,960	£8	£20	£80	£320
1839 Proof	268,800	—	—	—	£950
1841	1,075,200	£6	£18	£70	£260
1843	967,680	£50	£100	£300	£1100
1844	1,075,200	£12	£40	£180	£400
1845	1,075,200	£250	£550	£2200	—
1846	860,160	£12	£25	£85	£280
1847	725,640	£12	£22	£85	£280

William IV

DATE	MINTAGE	F	VF	EF	UNC
1848.....................................	322,560	£12	£22	£80	£280
1848/7 final 8 OVER 7	incl. above	£15	£35	£110	£300
1851.....................................	215,040	£7	£18	£75	£270
1852.....................................	637,056	£10	£22	£80	£280
1853.....................................	1,559,040	£5	£10	£40	£120
1853/2 3 over 2	incl. above	£15	£30	£60	£250
1853 Proof..............................	—	—	—	—	£1300
1854.....................................	12,354,048	£5	£9	£40	£140
1855.....................................	1,455,837	£5	£9	£40	£140
1856.....................................	1,942,080	£12	£28	£90	£350
1857.....................................	1,820,720	£6	£18	£50	£160
1858.....................................	2,472,960	£5	£12	£50	£150
1858/7 final 8 over 7................	incl. above	£5	£12	£50	£150
1858/6 final 8 over 6................	incl. above	£5	£12	£50	£160
1859.....................................	1,290,240	£8	£25	£80	£275
1859/8 9 over 8	incl. above	£8	£25	£70	£300
1860.....................................	unrecorded	£1800	£3500	£7000	£12500

Bronze

1860 Beaded border	6,630,400	£3	£10	£50	£200
1860 Toothed border...............		£4	£12	£70	£300
1861.....................................	54,118,400	£4	£10	£40	£200
1862 Die letter A, B or C to left of lighthouse			Extremely rare		
1862.....................................	61,107,200	£3	£9	£40	£170
1863.....................................	15,948,800	£3	£9	£75	£160
1864.....................................	537,600	£3	£10	£50	£200
1865.....................................	8,064,000	£4	£18	£75	£300
1865/3 5 over 3	incl. above	£50	£120	£450	—
1866.....................................	2,508,800	£5	£15	£70	£270
1867.....................................	2,508,800	£5	£15	£60	£250
1868.....................................	3,046,400	£5	£15	£70	£300
1869.....................................	3,225,600	£30	£100	£400	£1750
1870.....................................	4,350,739	£5	£15	£60	£250
1871.....................................	1,075,280	£75	£100	£500	£1600
1872.....................................	4,659,410	£4	£10	£50	£220
1873.....................................	3,404,880	£4	£10	£50	£220
1874.....................................	1,347,655	£6	£25	£110	£320
1874 H..................................	5,017,600	£3	£10	£60	£270
1875.....................................	5,430,815	£3	£8	£60	£220
1875 H..................................	1,254,400	£5	£12	£60	£220
1876 H..................................	5,809,600	£5	£12	£70	£280
1877.....................................	5,209,505	£3	£10	£60	£200
1878.....................................	1,425,535	£6	£20	£100	£375
1878 Wide date		£100	£200	£550	—
1879.....................................	3,582,545	£3	£10	£40	£200
1880.....................................	2,423,465	£4	£12	£60	£210
1881.....................................	2,007,515	£4	£12	£50	£180
1881 H..................................	1,792,000	£3	£10	£50	£200
1882 H..................................	4,480,000	£3	£10	£50	£220
1883.....................................	3,000,725	£3	£12	£60	£250
1884.....................................	6,989,580	£3	£10	£45	£160
1885.....................................	8,600,574	£3	£10	£45	£160
1886.....................................	8,586,155	£3	£10	£45	£160
1887.....................................	10,701,305	£3	£10	£45	£160
1888.....................................	6,814,670	£3	£10	£45	£160
1889.....................................	7,748,234	£3	£10	£45	£160
1889/8 9 over 8	incl. above	£30	£60	£250	—
1890.....................................	11,254,235	£3	£10	£40	£120
1891.....................................	13,192,260	£3	£10	£35	£120
1892.....................................	2,478,335	£3	£10	£50	£150
1893.....................................	7,229,344	£3	£10	£35	£140
1894.....................................	1,767,635	£6	£14	£85	£330

Victoria copper halfpenny

Victoria bronze halfpenny

DATE	MINTAGE	F	VF	EF	UNC
OLD HEAD ISSUES					
1895	3,032,154	£2	£8	£25	£80
1896	9,142,500	£1	£4	£10	£55
1897	8,690,315	£1	£4	£10	£55
1898	8,595,180	£1	£5	£12	£65
1899	12,108,001	£1	£4	£10	£50
1900	13,805,190	£1	£4	£10	£40
1901	11,127,360	£1	£3	£8	£35

Victoria bronze Old head halfpenny

EDWARD VII (1901–10)

DATE	MINTAGE	F	VF	EF	UNC
1902	13,672,960	£2	£4	£8	£30
1902 "Low tide"	incl. above	£22	£90	£180	£450
1903	11,450,880	£2	£5	£20	£75
1904	8,131,200	£2	£6	£25	£100
1905	10,124,800	£2	£5	£20	£70
1906	16,849,280	£2	£5	£25	£85
1907	16,849,280	£2	£5	£20	£85
1908	16,620,800	£2	£5	£20	£85
1909	8,279,040	£2	£5	£20	£85
1910	10,769,920	£2	£5	£20	£55

GEORGE V (1910–36)

DATE	MINTAGE	F	VF	EF	UNC
1911	12,570,880	£1	£4	£15	£40
1912	21,185,920	£1	£3	£15	£35
1913	17,476,480	£1	£3	£15	£40
1914	20,289,111	£1	£3	£15	£40
1915	21,563,040	£2	£3	£20	£55
1916	39,386,143	£1	£2	£15	£40
1917	38,245,436	£1	£2	£15	£35
1918	22,321,072	£1	£2	£15	£35
1919	28,104,001	£1	£2	£15	£35
1920	35,146,793	£1	£2	£15	£40
1921	28,027,293	£1	£2	£15	£40
1922	10,734,964	£1	£4	£25	£45
1923	12,266,282	£1	£2	£15	£35
1924	13,971,038	£1	£2	£15	£30
1925	12,216,123	—	£2	£15	£30
1925 Modified effigy	incl. above	£4	£10	£50	£90
1926	6,172,306	—	£2	£10	£40
1927	15,589,622	—	£2	£10	£40
1928	20,935,200	—	£2	£8	£35
1929	25,680,000	—	£2	£8	£35
1930	12,532,800	—	£2	£8	£35
1931	16,137,600	—	£2	£8	£35
1932	14,448,000	—	£2	£8	£35
1933	10,560,000	—	£2	£8	£35
1934	7,704,000	—	£2	£12	£45
1935	12,180,000	—	£1	£6	£20
1936	23,008,800	—	£1	£5	£15

Edward VII

GEORGE VI (1936–52)

George V

DATE	MINTAGE	F	VF	EF	UNC
1937	24,504,000	—	—	£1	£5
1937 Proof	26,402	—	—	—	£20
1938	40,320,000	—	—	£1	£6
1939	28,924,800	—	—	£1	£5
1940	32,162,400	—	—	£2	£10
1941	45,120,000	—	—	£1	£8
1942	71,908,800	—	—	£1	£5
1943	76,200,000	—	—	£1	£5

DATE	MINTAGE	F	VF	EF	UNC
1944	81,840,000	—	—	£1	£5
1945	57,000,000	—	—	£1	£5
1946	22,725,600	—	—	£1	£6
1947	21,266,400	—	—	£1	£6
1948	26,947,200	—	—	£1	£4
1949	24,744,000	—	—	£1	£4
1950	24,153,600	—	—	£1	£5
1950 Proof	17,513	—	—	—	£18
1951	14,868,000	—	—	£1	£6
1951 Proof	20,000	—	—	—	£18
1952	33,784,000	—	—	£1	£4

ELIZABETH II (1952–)

George VI

1953	8,926,366	—	—	—	£1
1953 Proof	40,000	—	—	—	£4
1954	19,375,000	—	—	—	£3
1955	18,799,200	—	—	—	£3
1956	21,799,200	—	—	—	£3
1957	43,684,800	—	—	—	£1
1957 Calm sea	incl. above	—	—	£10	£30
1958	62,318,400	—	—	—	£1
1959	79,176,000	—	—	—	£1
1960	41,340,000	—	—	—	£1
1962	41,779,200	—	—	—	£1
1963	45,036,000	—	—	—	20p
1964	78,583,200	—	—	—	20p
1965	98,083,200	—	—	—	20p
1966	95,289,600	—	—	—	20p
1967	146,491,200	—	—	—	10p
1970 Proof	—				£5

Later issues are included in the Decimal section.

Elizabeth II

FARTHINGS

DATE		F	VF	EF	UNC

OLIVER CROMWELL

Undated (copper) Draped bust, shield rev. Variations — Extremely rare

CHARLES II (1660–85)

Copper

	F	VF	EF	UNC
1672	£45	£225	£800	—
1672 No stops on obv.	£70	£300	£900	
1673	£50	£250	£850	—
1673 CAROLA for CAROLO error	£150	£550	—	—
1673 No stops on obv.			Extremely rare	
1673 No stop on rev.			Extremely rare	
1674	£50	£270	£900	—
1675	£45	£240	£850	—
1675 No stop after CAROLVS			Extremely rare	
1679	£60	£300	£1000	—
1679 No stop on rev.	£70	£350	—	—
Tin				
1684 with date on edge	£250	£900	—	—
1685 —			Extremely rare	

Charles II copper issue

DATE	F	VF	EF	UNC

JAMES II (1685–88)

1684 (tin) Cuirassed bust		Extremely rare		
1685 (tin) —	£180	£700	£2800	—
1686 (tin) —	£190	£700	£2800	—
1687 (tin) —		Extremely rare		
1687 (tin) Draped bust	£250	£1000	—	—

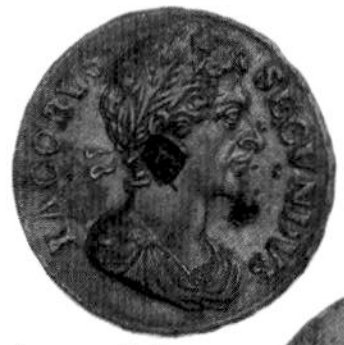

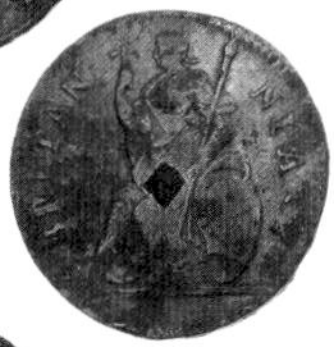

James II tin issue with central copper plug

WILLIAM & MARY (1688–94)

1689 (tin) Small draped busts	£300	£700	—	—
1689 (tin) — with edge date 1690		Extremely rare		
1690 (tin) Large cuirassed busts	£170	£650	£3000	—
1690 (tin) — with edge date 1689		Extremely rare		
1691 (tin) —	£200	£700	—	—
1692 (tin) —	£200	£700	£3000	—
1694 (copper) —	£70	£275	£1000	—
1694 No stop after MARIA		Extremely rare		
1694 No stop on obv.		Extremely rare		
1694 No stop on rev.		Extremely rare		
1694 Unbarred As in BRITANNIA		Extremely rare		

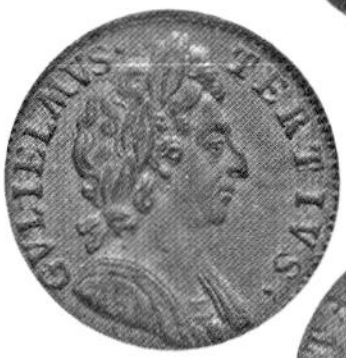

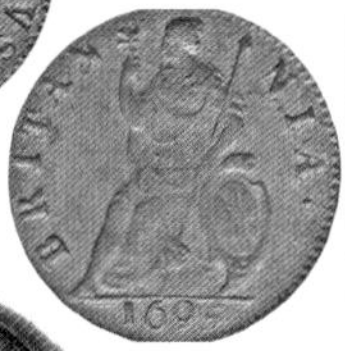

William III

WILLIAM III (1694–1702)

1695 First issue (date in exergue)	£45	£250	£900	—
1695 — GVLIELMV error		Extremely rare		
1696 —	£45	£225	£900	—
1697 —	£45	£225	£900	—
1697 — GVLIELMS error		Extremely rare		
1698 —	£220	£800	—	—
1698 Second issue (date in legend)	£50	£275	£950	—
1699 First issue	£40	£250	£900	—
1699 Second issue	£40	£240	£900	—
1699 — No stop after date	£50	£325	—	—
1700 First issue	£35	£150	£750	—
1700 — error RRITANNIA		Extremely rare		

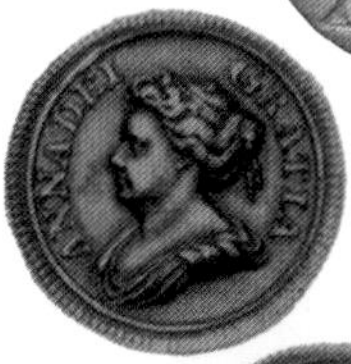

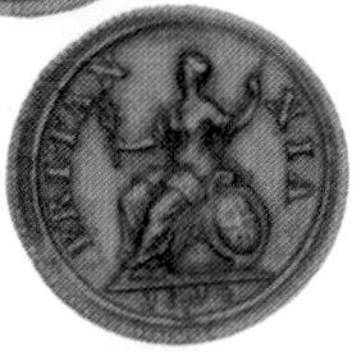

Queen Anne

ANNE (1702–14)

1714 pattern	£425	£700	£1500	—

GEORGE I (1714–27)

1717 First small "Dump" issue	£200	£650	£1250	—
1718 1 Known				—
1719 Second issue	£40	£175	£600	—
1719 — No stop on rev	£70	£375	—	—
1719 — No stops on obv	£70	£325	—	—
1720 —	£30	£160	£600	—
1721 —	£25	£160	£600	—
1721/0 — Last 1 over 0	£40	£170	—	—
1722 —	£35	£140	£550	—
1723 —	£35	£140	£570	—
1723 — R over sideways R in REX		Extremely rare		
1724 —	£35	£160	£575	—

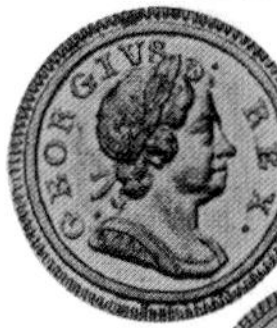

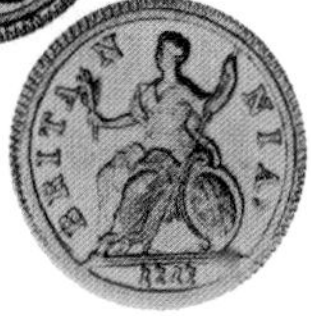

George I, first "Dump" type

GEORGE II (1727–60)

1730 Young head	£15	£60	£350	—
1731 —	£15	£60	£350	—
1732 —	£15	£75	£400	—
1733 —	£15	£80	£425	—
1734 —	£15	£65	£400	—
1734 — No stop on obv.	£30	£110	£450	—

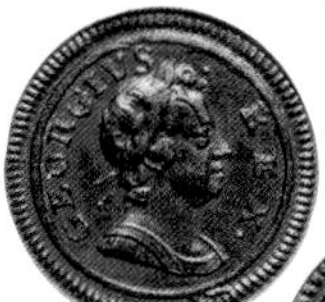

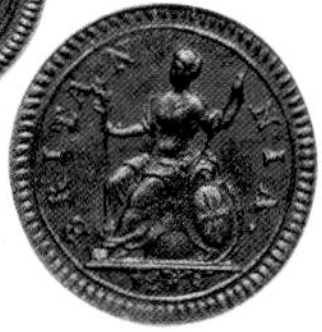

George I second type

179

DATE	MINTAGE	F	VF	EF	UNC
1735 —		£15	£70	£400	—
1735 — 3 over 5		£25	£110	£450	—
1736 —		£15	£60	£400	—
1737 —		£15	£60	£370	—
1739 —		£15	£60	£370	—
1741 Old Head		£15	£50	£350	—
1744 —		£15	£50	£350	—
1746 —		£15	£50	£330	—
1746 — V over LL in GEORGIVS				Extremely rare	
1749 —		£16	£65	£340	—
1750 —		£15	£55	£290	—
1754 —		£10	£30	£200	—
1754 — 4 over 0		£28	£120	£350	—

George II
Young head

GEORGE III (1760–1820)

	MINTAGE	F	VF	EF	UNC
1771 First (London) issue		£20	£65	£300	—
1773 —		£12	£40	£220	—
1773 — No stop on rev		£20	£60	£250	—
1773 — No stop after REX		£25	£80	£320	
1774 —		£12	£40	£220	—
1775 —		£12	£40	£220	—
1797 Second (Soho Mint) issue				Patterns only	
1799 Third (Soho Mint) issue	4,225,428	£2	£8	£40	£100
1806 Fourth (Soho Mint) issue	4,833,768	£2	£8	£40	£100
1807 —	1,075,200	£2	£8	£40	£100

George III, third (Soho Mint) issue

GEORGE IV (1820–30)

	MINTAGE	F	VF	EF	UNC
1821 First bust (laureate, draped), first reverse (date in exergue)...	2,688,000	£3	£10	£60	£130
1822 —	5,924,350	£3	£10	£60	£130
1823 —	2,365,440	£4	£10	£60	£130
1823 I for 1 in date	incl. above	£25	£75	£300	£600
1825 —	4,300.800	£4	£10	£60	£140
1826 —	6,666,240	£4	£10	£60	£130
1826 Second bust (couped, date below), second reverse (ornament in exergue)	incl. above	£4	£10	£60	£130
1826 — Proof	—	—	—	—	£750
1827 —	2,365,440	£4	£12	£60	£160
1828 —	2,365,440	£4	£12	£60	£160
1829 —	1,505,280	£4	£12	£60	£160
1830 —	2,365,440	£4	£12	£60	£160

George III, fourth (Soho Mint) issue

WILLIAM IV (1830–37)

	MINTAGE	F	VF	EF	UNC
1831	2,688,000	£5	£12	£45	£150
1831 Proof	—	—	—	—	£750
1834	1,935,360	£5	£12	£50	£160
1835	1.720,320	£5	£12	£50	£160
1836	1,290.240	£5	£12	£55	£160
1837	3.010,560	£5	£12	£55	£200

William IV

VICTORIA (1837–1901)

FIRST YOUNG HEAD (COPPER) ISSUES

	MINTAGE	F	VF	EF	UNC
1838	591,360	£5	£15	£50	£200
1839	4,300,800	£5	£15	£50	£200
1839 Proof	—	—	—	—	£900
1840	3,010,560	£4	£15	£40	£180
1841	1,720,320	£4	£15	£40	£190
1841 Proof				Extremely rare	
1842	1,290,240	£12	£40	£120	£400
1843	4,085,760	£5	£14	£40	£190

George IV

180

DATE	MINTAGE	F	VF	EF	UNC
1843 I for 1 in date		£90	£425	£900	—
1844..............................	430,080	£80	£220	£800	£2200
1845..............................	3,225,600	£6	£10	£50	£175
1846..............................	2,580,480	£7	£20	£55	£220
1847..............................	3,879,720	£5	£12	£50	£175
1848..............................	1,290,240	£5	£12	£50	£175
1849..............................	645,120	£50	£100	£350	£900
1850..............................	430,080	£5	£10	£40	£160
1851..............................	1,935,360	£8	£20	£80	£250
1851 D over sideways D in DEI ...	incl. above	£80	£110	£450	—
1852..............................	822,528	£10	£20	£80	£275
1853..............................	1,028,628	£4	£7	£30	£70
1853 Proof..............................	—	—	—	—	£1400
1854..............................	6,504,960	£4	£10	£35	£110
1855..............................	3,440,640	£4	£10	£35	£120
1856..............................	1,771,392	£10	£25	£80	£300
1856 R over E in VICTORIA........	incl. above	£20	£50	£250	—
1857..............................	1,075,200	£4	£10	£40	£100
1858..............................	1,720,320	£4	£10	£40	£100
1859..............................	1,290,240	£12	£25	£90	£350
1860..............................	unrecorded	£1600	£3750	£7000	—

Victoria Young Head first (copper) issue

SECOND YOUNG OR "BUN" HEAD (BRONZE) ISSUES

	MINTAGE	F	VF	EF	UNC
1860 Toothed border....................	2,867,200	£2	£5	£40	£120
1860 Beaded border	incl. above	£3	£7	£40	£130
1860 Toothed/Beaded border mule	incl. above			Extremely rare	
1861..............................	8,601,600	£2	£5	£35	£120
1862..............................	14,336,000	£1	£5	£35	£120
1862 Large 8 in date...................	incl. above			Extremely rare	
1863..............................	1,433,600	£45	£90	£300	£725
1864..............................	2,508,800	£1	£5	£30	£110
1865..............................	4,659,200	£1	£5	£30	£110
1865 5 over 2.............................	incl. above	£10	£20	£70	—
1866..............................	3,584,000	£1	£5	£25	£120
1867..............................	5,017,600	£1	£5	£25	£120
1868..............................	4,851,210	£1	£5	£25	£120
1869..............................	3,225,600	£2	£10	£50	£200
1872..............................	2,150,400	£1	£5	£25	£100
1873..............................	3,225,620	£1	£5	£25	£100
1874 H..............................	3,584,000	£1	£5	£25	£130
1874 H both Gs over sideways G	incl. above	£150	£350	£1000	—
1875..............................	712,760	£4	£12	£40	£150
1875 H..............................	6,092,800	£1	£5	£20	£85
1876 H..............................	1,175,200	£5	£18	£70	£240
1878..............................	4,008,540	£1	£4	£20	£80
1879..............................	3,977,180	£1	£4	£20	£80
1880..............................	1,842,710	£1	£4	£20	£80
1881..............................	3,494,670	£1	£4	£20	£80
1881 H..............................	1,792,000	£1	£4	£20	£80
1882 H..............................	1,792,000	£1	£5	£25	£100
1883..............................	1,128,680	£5	£20	£70	£170
1884..............................	5,782,000	£1	£4	£20	£50
1885..............................	5,442,308	£1	£4	£20	£50
1886..............................	7.707,790	£1	£4	£20	£50
1887..............................	1,340,800	£1	£4	£20	£50
1888..............................	1,887,250	£1	£4	£20	£50
1890..............................	2,133,070	£1	£4	£20	£50
1891..............................	4,959,690	£1	£4	£20	£50
1892..............................	887,240	£4	£15	£60	£170
1893..............................	3,904,320	£1	£4	£20	£45
1894..............................	2,396,770	£1	£4	£20	£45
1895..............................	2,852,852	£10	£30	£90	£300

Victoria Young Head second (bronze) issue

DATE	MINTAGE	F	VF	EF	UNC
OLD HEAD ISSUES					
1895 Bright finish	incl. above	£1	£2	£16	£40
1896 —	3,668,610	£1	£2	£16	£30
1897 —	4,579,800	£1	£2	£16	£30
1897 Dark finish	incl. above	£1	£2	£16	£30
1898 —	4,010,080	£1	£2	£16	£30
1899 —	3,864,616	£1	£2	£16	£30
1900 —	5,969,317	£1	£2	£16	£30
1901 —	8,016,460	£1	£2	£10	£28

Victoria
Old head

EDWARD VII (1901–10)

1902..	5,125,120	50p	£1	£10	£16
1903..	5,331,200	50p	£1	£12	£20
1904..	3,628,800	£2	£5	£20	£45
1905..	4,076,800	£1	£2	£12	£40
1906..	5,340,160	50p	£1	£12	£30
1907..	4,399,360	50p	£1	£10	£25
1908..	4,264,960	50p	£1	£10	£25
1909..	8,852,480	50p	£1	£10	£25
1910..	2,298,400	£5	£10	£30	£80

GEORGE V (1910–36)

1911..	5,196,800	50p	£1	£6	£14
1912..	7,669,760	50p	£1	£8	£14
1913..	4,184,320	50p	£1	£6	£14
1914..	6,126,988	50p	£1	£5	£14
1915..	7,129,255	50p	£1	£5	£16
1916..	10,993,325	50p	£1	£5	£14
1917..	21,434,844	25p	50p	£4	£10
1918..	19,362,818	25p	50p	£4	£10
1919..	15,089,425	25p	50p	£4	£10
1920..	11,480,536	25p	50p	£4	£8
1921..	9,469,097	25p	50p	£4	£8
1922..	9,956,983	25p	50p	£4	£8
1923..	8,034,457	25p	50p	£4	£8
1924..	8,733,414	25p	50p	£4	£8
1925..	12,634,697	25p	50p	£4	£8
1926 Modified effigy..................	9,792,397	25p	50p	£4	£8
1927	7,868,355	25p	50p	£4	£8
1928	11,625,600	25p	50p	£4	£8
1929	8,419,200	25p	50p	£4	£8
1930	4,195,200	25p	50p	£4	£8
1931	6,595,200	25p	50p	£4	£8
1932	9,292,800	25p	50p	£4	£8
1933	4,560,000	25p	50p	£4	£8
1934	3,052,800	25p	50p	£4	£8
1935..	2.227,200	£1	£3	£10	£25
1936	9,734,400	25p	50p	£3	£6

Edward VII

George V

GEORGE VI (1936–52)

1937..	8,131,200	—	—	50p	£1
1937 Proof.................................	26,402	—	—	—	£8
1938..	7,449,600	—	—	£1	£6
1939..	31,440,000	—	—	50p	£1
1940..	18,360,000	—	—	50p	£1
1941..	27,312,000	—	—	50p	£1
1942..	28,857,600	—	—	50p	£1
1943..	33,345,600	—	—	50p	£1
1944..	25,137,600	—	—	50p	£1
1945..	23,736,000	—	—	50p	£1

George VI

DATE	MINTAGE	F	VF	EF	UNC
1946	24,364,800	—	—	50p	£1
1947	14,745,600	—	—	50p	£1
1948	16,622,400	—	—	50p	£1
1949	8,424,000	—	—	50p	£1
1950	10,324,800	—	—	50p	£1
1950 Proof	17,513	—	—	50p	£8
1951	14,016,000	—	—	50p	£1
1951 Proof	20,000	—	—	50p	£8
1952	5,251,200	—	—	50p	£1

ELIZABETH II (1952–)

1953	6,131,037	—	—	—	£1
1953 Proof	40,000	—	—	—	£8
1954	6,566,400	—	—	—	£2
1955	5,779,200	—	—	—	£2
1956	1,996,800	—	£1	£2	£6

HALF FARTHINGS

DATE	MINTAGE	F	VF	EF	UNC

GEORGE IV (1820–30)

1828 (two different obverses) (issued for Ceylon)	7,680,000	£10	£22	£60	£225
1830 (large or small date) (issued for Ceylon)	8,766,320	£10	£22	£60	£220

WILLIAM IV (1830–37)

William IV

1837 (issued for Ceylon)	1,935,360	£25	£75	£200	£400

VICTORIA (1837–1901)

1839	2,042,880	£5	£10	£35	£100
1842	unrecorded	£4	£8	£30	£100
1843	3,440,640	£3	£6	£25	£70
1844	6,451,200	£3	£6	£15	£55
1844 E over N in REGINA	incl. above	£10	£45	£100	—
1847	3,010,560	£6	£12	£40	£120
1851	unrecorded	£6	£12	£40	£150
1851 5 over 0	unrecorded	£8	£20	£60	£180
1852	989,184	£6	£12	£45	£160
1853	955,224	£6	£15	£50	£175
1853 Proof	incl. above	—	—	—	£850
1854	677,376	£9	£30	£80	£220
1856	913,920	£9	£30	£80	£220
1868 Proof	unrecorded				Very Rare

Victoria

THIRD FARTHINGS

DATE	MINTAGE	F	VF	EF	UNC

GEORGE IV (1820–30)

1827 (issued for Malta)...............	unrecorded	£8	£20	£50	£125

WILLIAM IV (1830–37)

1835 (issued for Malta)...............	unrecorded	£8	£24	£55	£160

George IV

VICTORIA (1837–1901)

1844 (issued for Malta)...............	1,301,040	£15	£35	£110	£250
1844 RE for REG	incl. above	£30	£70	£275	—
1866...	576,000	£6	£15	£35	£75
1868...	144,000	£6	£15	£35	£70
1876...	162,000	£6	£15	£35	£90
1878...	288,000	£6	£15	£35	£80
1881...	144,000	£6	£15	£35	£80
1884...	144,000	£6	£15	£35	£80
1885...	288,000	£6	£15	£35	£80

EDWARD VII (1902–10)

1902 (issued for Malta)...............	288,000	£5	£10	£25	£45

Victoria

GEORGE V (1911–36)

1913 (issued for Malta)...............	288,000	£5	£10	£25	£45

QUARTER FARTHINGS

DATE	MINTAGE	F	VF	EF	UNC

VICTORIA (1837–1901)

1839 (issued for Ceylon).............	3,840,000	£50	£80	£150	£300
1851 (issued for Ceylon).............	2,215,680	£50	£80	£150	£300
1852 (issued for Ceylon).............	incl. above	£50	£80	£150	£300
1853 (issued for Ceylon).............	incl. above	£50	£80	£150	£320
1853 Proof..................................	—	—	—	—	£1500

EMERGENCY ISSUES

DATE	F	VF	EF	UNC

GEORGE III (1760–1820)

To alleviate the shortage of circulating coinage during the Napoleonic Wars the Bank of England firstly authorised the countermarking of other countries' coins, enabling them to pass as English currency. The coins, countermarked with punches depicting the head of George III, were mostly Spanish American 8 reales of Charles III. Although this had limited success it was later decided to completely overstrike the coins with a new English design on both sides — specimens that still show traces of the original host coin's date are avidly sought after by collectors. This overstriking continued for a number of years although all the known coins are dated 1804. Finally, in 1811 the Bank of England issued silver tokens which continued up to 1816 when a completely new regal coinage was introduced.

DOLLAR
Oval countermark of George III

	F	VF	EF	UNC
On "Pillar" type 8 reales	£200	£750	£1400	—
*On "Portrait" type.............	£200	£350	£1200	—

Octagonal countermark of George III

	F	VF	EF	UNC
On "Portrait" type..............	£200	£650	£1250	—

HALF DOLLAR
Oval countermark of George III

	F	VF	EF	UNC
On "Portrait" type 4 reales	£200	£450	£1100	—

FIVE SHILLINGS OR ONE DOLLAR
These coins were overstruck on Spanish-American coins

	F	VF	EF	UNC
1804..................................	£120	£300	£700	—

— With details of original coin still visible add from 10%.

BANK OF ENGLAND TOKENS

THREE SHILLINGS

	F	VF	EF	UNC
1811 Draped bust.............	£35	£70	£250	—
1812 —	£35	£70	£275	—
1812 Laureate bust	£35	£60	£175	—
1813 —	£35	£60	£175	—
1814 —	£35	£60	£175	—
1815 —	£35	£60	£175	—
1816 —	£250	£600	£1800	—

ONE SHILLING AND SIXPENCE

	F	VF	EF	UNC
1811 Draped bust.............	£20	£45	£100	£200
1812 —	£20	£45	£100	£200
1812 Laureate bust	£20	£45	£100	£200
1812 Proof in platinum				Unique
1813 —	£20	£40	£75	£200
1813 Proof in platinum				Unique
1814 —	£20	£35	£75	£200
1815 —	£20	£35	£75	£200
1816 —	£20	£35	£75	£200

NINEPENCE

1812 Pattern (three types)			from £3000	

MAUNDY SETS

DATE	F	VF	EF	UNC

Sets in contemporary dated boxes are usually worth a higher premium. For example approximately £30 can be added to sets from Victoria to George VI in contemporary undated boxes and above £40 for dated boxes.

GEORGE I (1714–27)

DATE	F	VF	EF	UNC
1723	£265	£450	£775	—
1727	£250	£435	£750	—

GEORGE II (1727–60)

DATE	F	VF	EF	UNC
1729	£200	£325	£675	—
1731	£200	£335	£675	—
1732	£195	£320	£660	—
1735	£195	£320	£660	—
1737	£190	£325	£640	—
1739	£190	£320	£625	—
1740	£175	£300	£585	—
1743	£300	£445	£840	—
1746	£170	£300	£565	—
1760	£185	£325	£605	—

CHARLES II (1660–85)

DATE	F	VF	EF	UNC
Undated	£240	£370	£825	—
1670	£225	£370	£800	—
1671	£260	£425	£850	—
1672	£240	£375	£750	—
1673	£225	£350	£720	—
1674	£225	£340	£735	—
1675	£220	£325	£715	—
1676	£230	£365	£755	—
1677	£195	£310	£690	—
1678	£290	£460	£830	—
1679	£225	£360	£775	—
1680	£225	£345	£730	—
1681	£250	£370	£775	—
1682	£230	£360	£725	—
1683	£230	£360	£750	—
1684	£250	£385	£775	—

GEORGE III (1760–1820)

DATE	F	VF	EF	UNC
1763	£170	£290	£465	—
1763 Proof	—			£19000
1766	£215	£350	£550	—
1772	£185	£300	£525	—
1780	£225	£350	£625	—
1784	£190	£320	£500	—
1786	£195	£310	£515	—
1792 Wire	£260	£450	£650	£875
1795	£115	£200	£325	£405
1800	£115	£200	£300	£375
New Coinage				
1817	£135	£250	£305	£475
1818	£135	£225	£290	£465
1820	£140	£250	£300	£455

JAMES II (1685–88)

DATE	F	VF	EF	UNC
1686	£235	£375	£750	—
1687	£235	£370	£750	—
1688	£260	£410	£775	—

GEORGE IV (1820–30)

DATE	F	VF	EF	UNC
1822	—	£160	£245	£450
1823	—	£155	£255	£425
1824	—	£160	£260	£425
1825	—	£150	£250	£400
1826	—	£145	£245	£400
1827	—	£145	£255	£405
1828	—	£150	£250	£415
1828 Proof	—	—	—	£3950
1829	—	£150	£250	£395
1830	—	£150	£240	£390

WILLIAM & MARY (1688–94)

DATE	F	VF	EF	UNC
1689	£825	£1250	£1850	—
1691	£650	£875	£1550	—
1692	£700	£925	£1650	—
1693	£625	£900	£1800	—
1694	£470	£735	£1300	—

WILLIAM IV (1830–37)

DATE	F	VF	EF	UNC
1831	—	£170	£280	£460
1831 Proof	—	—	—	£1700
1831 Proof Gold	—	—	—	£40000
1832	—	£195	£315	£480
1833	—	£170	£275	£425
1834	—	£175	£280	£450
1835	—	£160	£265	£415
1836	—	£175	£285	£440
1837	—	£190	£315	£475

WILLIAM III (1694–1702)

DATE	F	VF	EF	UNC
1698	£245	£480	£900	—
1699	£490	£675	£1575	—
1700	£265	£490	£925	—
1701	£245	£450	£875	—

ANNE (1702–14)

DATE	F	VF	EF	UNC
1703	£230	£440	£775	—
1705	£245	£450	£775	—
1706	£200	£375	£680	—
1708	£600	£1000	£1800	—
1709	£250	£475	£850	—
1710	£275	£485	£825	—
1713	£240	£435	£750	—

DATE	MINTAGE	EF	UNC
VICTORIA (1837–1901)			
YOUNG HEAD ISSUES			
1838	4,158	£250	£425
1838 Proof	unrecorded		£3400
1838 Proof Gold			£40000
1839	4,125	£300	£550
1839 Proof	unrecorded	£700	£1850
1840	4,125	£300	£445
1841	2,574	£395	£675
1842	4,125	£425	£615
1843	4,158	£260	£425
1844	4,158	£345	£565
1845	4,158	£225	£415
1846	4,158	£495	£775
1847	4,158	£575	£1025
1848	4,158	£525	£1025
1849	4,158	£365	£550
1850	4,158	£250	£425
1851	4,158	£305	£475
1852	4,158	£600	£1100
1853	4,158	£625	£1000
1853 Proof	unrecorded		£2000
1854	4,158	£260	£400
1855	4,158	£300	£475
1856	4,158	£235	£375
1857	4,158	£265	£420
1858	4,158	£240	£375
1859	4,158	£215	£325
1860	4,158	£240	£375
1861	4,158	£205	£385
1862	4,158	£245	£410
1863	4,158	£260	£425
1864	4,158	£240	£345
1865	4,158	£240	£355
1866	4,158	£225	£340
1867	4,158	£220	£345
1867 Proof	unrecorded	–	£3000
1868	4,158	£200	£315
1869	4,158	£240	£385
1870	4,458	£190	£290
1871	4,488	£185	£280
1871 Proof	unrecorded	–	£2800
1872	4,328	£180	£280
1873	4,162	£180	£270
1874	4,488	£185	£275
1875	4,154	£180	£265
1876	4,488	£190	£270
1877	4,488	£180	£265
1878	4,488	£185	£265
1878 Proof	unrecorded	–	£2600
1879	4,488	£190	£245
1879 Proof	unrecorded	–	£2850
1880	4,488	£185	£250
1881	4,488	£180	£250
1881 Proof	unrecorded	–	£2350
1882	4,146	£215	£285
1882 Proof	unrecorded	–	£2550
1883	4,488	£160	£225
1884	4,488	£160	£225
1885	4,488	£160	£225
1886	4,488	£165	£225
1887	4,488	£180	£265
JUBILEE HEAD ISSUES			
1888	4,488	£160	£230
1888 Proof	unrecorded	–	£2300

DATE	MINTAGE	EF	UNC
1889	4,488	£155	£240
1890	4,488	£160	£220
1891	4,488	£160	£220
1892	4,488	£170	£240
OLD HEAD ISSUES			
1893	8,976	£115	£185
1894	8,976	£130	£220
1895	8,976	£120	£190
1896	8,976	£120	£195
1897	8,976	£120	£190
1898	8,976	£120	£195
1899	8,976	£125	£200
1900	8,976	£110	£180
1901	8,976	£110	£180
EDWARD VII (1902–10)			
1902	8,976	£95	£175
1902 Matt proof	15,123	–	£200
1903	8,976	£100	£170
1904	8,976	£110	£180
1905	8,976	£110	£180
1906	8,800	£100	£170
1907	8,760	£100	£175
1908	8,769	£90	£165
1909	1,983	£175	£275
1910	1,440	£195	£285
GEORGE V (1911–36)			
1911	1,786	£150	£240
1911 Proof	6,007	–	£375
1912	1,246	£160	£260
1913	1,228	£155	£260
1914	982	£195	£280
1915	1,293	£165	£270
1916	1,128	£160	£250
1917	1,237	£160	£250
1918	1,375	£165	£260
1919	1,258	£160	£260
1920	1,399	£160	£250
1921	1,386	£160	£255
1922	1,373	£165	£260
1923	1,430	£165	£260
1924	1,515	£165	£260
1925	1,438	£150	£245
1926	1,504	£150	£245
1927	1,647	£155	£255
1928	1,642	£155	£260
1929	1,761	£160	£260
1930	1,724	£150	£240
1931	1,759	£150	£240
1932	1,835	£145	£250
1933	1,872	£140	£240
1934	1,887	£140	£240
1935	1,928	£155	£255
1936	1,323	£210	£310
GEORGE VI (1936–52)			
1937	1,325	£140	£175
1937 Proof	20,900	£140	£200
1938	1,275	£170	£255
1939	1,234	£175	£265
1940	1,277	£170	£255
1941	1,253	£180	£260
1942	1,231	£170	£255
1943	1,239	£175	£260
1944	1,259	£170	£260

DATE	MINTAGE	EF	UNC
1945	1,355	£170	£255
1946	1,365	£175	£255
1947	1,375	£180	£275
1948	1,385	£180	£280
1949	1,395	£185	£280
1950	1,405	£185	£285
1951	1,468	£190	£290
1952	1,012	£200	£305
1952 Proof (copper)			£16000

ELIZABETH II (1952–)

DATE AND PLACE OF ISSUE	MINTAGE	UNC
1953 St. Paul's Cathedral	1,025	£1000
1953 Proof in gold	unrecorded	Ex. rare
1953 Proof Matt		Very rare
1954 Westminster Abbey	1,020	£200
1955 Southwark Cathedral	1,036	£200
1955 Proof Matt		£3250
1956 Westminster Abbey	1,088	£205
1957 St. Albans Cathedral	1,094	£205
1958 Westminster Abbey	1,100	£205
1959 St. George's Chapel, Windsor	1,106	£205
1960 Westminster Abbey	1,112	£205
1961 Rochester Cathedral	1,118	£205
1962 Westminster Abbey	1,125	£200
1963 Chelmsford Cathedral	1,131	£200
1964 Westminster Abbey	1,137	£200
1965 Canterbury Cathedral	1,143	£200
1966 Westminster Abbey	1,206	£205
1967 Durham Cathedral	986	£220
1968 Westminster Abbey	964	£235
1969 Selby Cathedral	1,002	£220
1970 Westminster Abbey	980	£225
1971 Tewkesbury Abbey	1,018	£215
1972 York Minster	1,026	£220
1973 Westminster Abbey	1,004	£215
1974 Salisbury Cathedral	1,042	£215
1975 Peterborough Cathedral	1,050	£215
1976 Hereford Cathedral	1,158	£220
1977 Westminster Abbey	1,138	£230
1978 Carlisle Cathedral	1,178	£215
1979 Winchester Cathedral	1,188	£215
1980 Worcester Cathedral	1,198	£215
1981 Westminster Abbey	1,178	£215

DATE AND PLACE OF ISSUE	MINTAGE	UNC
1982 St David's Cathedral	1,218	£220
1983 Exeter Cathedral	1,228	£215
1984 Southwell Minster	1,238	£215
1985 Ripon Cathedral	1,248	£215
1986 Chichester Cathedral	1,378	£225
1987 Ely Cathedral	1,390	£225
1988 Lichfield Cathedral	1,402	£220
1989 Birmingham Cathedral	1,353	£220
1990 Newcastle Cathedral	1,523	£220
1991 Westminster Abbey	1,384	£220
1992 Chester Cathedral	1,424	£225
1993 Wells Cathedral	1,440	£225
1994 Truro Cathedral	1,433	£225
1995 Coventry Cathedral	1,466	£225
1996 Norwich Cathedral	1,629	£230
1997 Birmingham Cathedral	1,786	£230
1998 Portsmouth Cathedral	1,654	£230
1999 Bristol Cathedral	1,676	£230
2000 Lincoln Cathedral	1,686	£220
2000 Silver Proof	13,180	£195
2001 Westminster Abbey	1,132	£250
2002 Canterbury Cathedral	1,681	£215
2002 Gold Proof	2,002	£2250
2003 Gloucester Cathedral	1,608	£235
2004 Liverpool Cathedral	1,613	£240
2005 Wakefield Cathedral	1,685	£240
2006 Guildford Cathedral	1,937	£240
2006 Silver Proof	6,394	£195
2007 Manchester Cathedral	1,822	£280
2008 St Patrick's Cathedral (Armagh)	1,833	£685
2009 St. Edmundsbury Cathedral	1,602	£600
2010 Derby Cathedral	1,617	£550
2011 Westminster Abbey	1,734	£500
2012 York Minster	1,633	£600
2013 Christ Church Cathedral Oxford	1,627	£640
2014 Blackburn Cathedral	1,693	£725
2015 Sheffield Cathedral	1,721	£650
2016 St. George's Chapel, Windsor	1,940	£625
2017 Leicester Cathedral	1,919	£700
2018 St. George's Chapel, Windsor	1,993	£725
2019 St. George's Chapel, Windsor	1,997	£750
2020 Service cancelled. Recipients received the coins in the post	2,010	£800
2021 Service cancelled. Recipients received the coins in the post	1,995	£800

Despite the decimalisation of the coinage in 1971, in keeping with ancient tradition the Royal Maundy sets are still made up of four silver coins (4p, 3p, 2p and 1p). The designs for the reverse of the coins are a crowned numeral in a wreath of oak leaves—basically the same design that has been used for Maundy coins since George IV.

MAUNDY ODDMENTS
SINGLE COINS

DATE	F	VF	EF

FOUR PENCE
CHARLES II (1660–85)

It is nowadays considered that the early small denomination silver coins 4d–1d were originally struck for the Maundy ceremony although undoubtedly many subsequently circulated as small change—therefore they are listed here under "Maundy silver single coins".

DATE	F	VF	EF
Undated	£70	£125	£195
1670	£70	£140	£235
1671	£100	£190	£285
1672/1	£80	£120	£185
1673	£75	£120	£180
1674	£70	£115	£175
1674 7 over 6	£75	£130	£205
1675	£60	£110	£165
1675/4	£70	£115	£190
1676	£65	£100	£190
1676 7 over 6	£80	£125	£205
1677	£55	£95	£160
1678	£55	£95	£160
1678 8 over 6	£60	£100	£165
1678 8 over 7	£65	£115	£175
1679	£55	£85	£150
1680	£55	£95	£160
1681	£55	£110	£170
1681 B over R in HIB	£65	£125	£200
1682	£60	£90	£180
1682/1	£70	£100	£195
1683	£60	£90	£180
1684	£70	£120	£200
1684 4 over 3	£85	£130	£215

Charles II

JAMES II (1685–88)

	F	VF	EF
1686	£70	£120	£205
1686 Date over crown	£80	£125	£225
1687	£65	£110	£185
1687 7 over 6	£80	£115	£190
1687 8 over 7	£75	£115	£200
1688	£85	£125	£220
1688 1 over 8	£100	£145	£230
1688/7	£85	£130	£225

WILLIAM & MARY (1688–94)

	F	VF	EF
1689	£70	£125	£195
1689 GV below bust	£75	£130	£210
1689 GVLEELMVS	£140	£260	£335
1690	£75	£130	£220
1690 6 over 5	£95	£135	£230
1691	£90	£135	£235
1691 1 over 0	£90	£150	£230
1692	£130	£185	£285
1692 MAR·IA	£215	£310	£400
1692 2 over 1	£130	£160	£260
1693	£125	£240	£360
1693 3 over 2	£140	£255	£385
1694	£90	£145	£225
1694 small lettering	£95	£155	£230

William & Mary

WILLIAM III (1694–1702)

	F	VF	EF
1697—Reported	—	—	—
1698	£80	£145	£225
1699	£70	£125	£210
1700	£90	£155	£250
1701	£85	£140	£235
1702	£80	£130	£225

Queen Anne

DATE	F	VF	EF	UNC

ANNE (1702–14)

DATE	F	VF	EF	UNC
1703	£85	£135	£225	—
1704	£65	£115	£185	—
1705	£140	£210	£295	—
1706	£75	£120	£185	—
1708	£80	£130	£210	—
1709	£80	£125	£205	—
1710	£60	£110	£165	—
1713	£80	£125	£195	—

GEORGE I (1714–27)

DATE	F	VF	EF	UNC
1717	£75	£125	£190	—
1721	£75	£125	£185	—
1723	£90	£145	£220	—
1727	£90	£140	£230	—

George I

GEORGE II (1727–60)

DATE	F	VF	EF	UNC
1729	£75	£120	£180	—
1731	£65	£115	£170	—
1732	£65	£110	£170	—
1735	£60	£100	£165	—
1737	£70	£115	£170	—
1739	£60	£105	£160	—
1740	£55	£95	£145	—
1743	£135	£195	£310	—
1743 3 over 0	£145	£220	£330	
1746	£55	£85	£140	—
1760	£65	£115	£160	—

George II

GEORGE III (1760–1820)

DATE	F	VF	EF	UNC
1763 Young head	£55	£95	£145	—
1763 Proof	—	—	Extremely rare	
1765	£450	£750	£1100	—
1766	£65	£110	£150	—
1770	£165	£260	£375	—
1772	£80	£130	£200	—
1776	£65	£120	£170	—
1780	£50	£95	£135	—
1784	£50	£95	£130	—
1786	£70	£120	£170	—
1792 Older head, Thin 4	£100	£170	£235	£325
1795	—	£55	£100	£140
1800	—	£50	£90	£130
1817 New coinage	—	£60	£95	£145
1818	—	£60	£90	£140
1820	—	£55	£90	£145

George III

GEORGE IV (1820–30)

DATE	F	VF	EF	UNC
1822	—	—	£90	£160
1823	—	—	£80	£150
1824	—	—	£75	£150
1826	—	—	£70	£135
1827	—	—	£70	£145
1828	—	—	£75	£135
1829	—	—	£70	£130
1830	—	—	£75	£130

George IV

WILLIAM IV (1830–37)

DATE	F	VF	EF	UNC
1831–37	—	—	£80	£155
1831 Proof	—	—	£300	£475

VICTORIA (1837–1901)

DATE	F	VF	EF	UNC
1838 Proof	—	—	—	£925
1839 Proof	—	—	—	£525
1853 Proof	—	—	—	£700
1838–87 (Young Head)	—	—	£40	£60

Victoria

DATE	F	VF	EF	UNC
1841	−	−	£45	£75
1888–92 (Jubilee Head)	−	−	£35	£55
1893–1901 (Old Head)	−	−	£30	£50

EDWARD VII (1901–10)

	F	VF	EF	UNC
1902–08	−	−	£30	£45
1902 Proof	−	−	£35	£50
1909 & 1910	−	−	£60	£90

GEORGE V (1910–36)

	F	VF	EF	UNC
1911–36	−	−	£45	£65
1911 Proof	−	−	£55	£75

GEORGE VI (1936–52)

	F	VF	EF	UNC
1937–52	−	−	£50	£70
1937 Proof	−	−	£40	£60

ELIZABETH II (1952–)

	F	VF	EF	UNC
1953	−	−	£200	£260
1954–85	−	−	£45	£75
1986–2007	−	−	£60	£85
2002 in Gold Proof	−	−	£500	£750
2008	−	−	−	£190
2009	−	−	−	£180
2010	−	−	−	£160
2011	−	−	−	£145
2012	−	−	−	£160
2013	−	−	−	£165
2014	−	−	−	£200
2015	−	−	−	£165
2016	−	−	−	£170
2017	−	−	−	£200
2018	−	−	−	£210
2019	−	−	−	£210
2020	−	−	−	£220
2021	−	−	−	£225

Elizabeth II

THREEPENCE
CHARLES II (1660–85)

	F	VF	EF	UNC
Undated	£65	£115	£200	−
1670	£75	£120	£185	−
1671	£65	£120	£175	−
1671 GRVTIA	£80	£150	£245	−
1672	£80	£130	£195	−
1673	£70	£100	£175	−
1674	£70	£110	£175	−
1675	£70	£110	£180	−
1676	£75	£120	£220	−
1676 6 over 5	£85	£135	£235	−
1676 ERA for FRA	£110	£160	£250	−
1677	£65	£90	£165	−
1678	£55	£85	£135	−
1679	£50	£80	£135	−
1679 O/A in CAROLVS	£120	£170	£265	−
1680	£65	£100	£175	−
1681	£70	£110	£190	−
1682/1	£65	£110	£175	−
1682	£65	£115	£175	−
1683	£60	£105	£170	−
1684	£60	£105	£175	−
1684/3	£75	£115	£180	−

Charles II

James II

JAMES II (1685–88)

	F	VF	EF	UNC
1685	£80	£120	£200	−
1685 Struck on fourpence flan	£140	£220	£325	−
1686	£80	£110	£175	−
1687	£80	£110	£170	−
1687 7 over 6	£85	£115	£175	−
1688	£80	£130	£215	−
1688 8 over 7	£85	£135	£225	−

William & Mary

DATE	F	VF	EF	UNC

WILLIAM & MARY (1688–94)

DATE	F	VF	EF	UNC
1689	£75	£120	£190	—
1689 No stop on reverse	£80	£130	£200	—
1689 LMV over MVS (obverse)	£120	£160	£240	—
1690	£85	£130	£195	—
1690 9 over 6	£90	£140	£215	—
1690 6 over 5	£85	£135	£210	—
1691 First bust	£390	£590	£850	—
1691 Second bust	£250	£375	£525	—
1692	£115	£165	£265	—
1692 G below bust	£105	£165	£270	—
1692 GV below bust	£105	£160	£270	—
1692 GVL below bust	£105	£160	£275	—
1693	£145	£215	£300	—
1693 3 over 2	£150	£240	£310	—
1694	£90	£115	£200	—
1694 MARIΛ	£135	£180	£265	—
1694 GV below bust	£100	£135	£210	—
1694 GVL below bust	£100	£140	£220	—

William III

WILLIAM III (1694–1702)

DATE	F	VF	EF	UNC
1698	£80	£140	£225	—
1699	£70	£125	£195	—
1700	£80	£140	£220	—
1701 Small lettering	£80	£130	£215	—
1701 GBA instead of GRA	£90	£150	£225	—
1701 Large lettering	£90	£140	£210	—

ANNE (1702–14)

DATE	F	VF	EF	UNC
1703	£80	£120	£205	—
1703 7 of date above crown	£90	£150	£225	—
1704	£65	£95	£170	—
1705	£85	£135	£215	—
1706	£65	£100	£170	—
1707	£60	£100	£155	—
1708	£70	£120	£185	—
1708 8 over 7	£70	£110	£190	—
1709	£70	£140	£195	—
1710	£55	£105	£150	—
1713	£75	£130	£185	—

Queen Anne

GEORGE I (1714–27)

DATE	F	VF	EF	UNC
1717	£70	£110	£170	—
1721	£70	£110	£170	—
1723	£80	£135	£200	—
1727	£75	£130	£195	—

George I

GEORGE II (1727–60)

DATE	F	VF	EF	UNC
1729	£60	£100	£150	—
1731	£60	£100	£155	—
1731 Small lettering	£70	£115	£175	—
1732	£55	£100	£155	—
1732 Stop over head	£65	£110	£170	—
1735	£70	£110	£175	—
1737	£60	£100	£165	—
1739	£65	£100	£175	—
1740	£55	£95	£145	—
1743 Small and large lettering	£65	£95	£160	—
1743 Stop over head	£65	£95	£165	—
1746	£45	£80	£135	—
1746 6 over 3	£55	£85	£150	—
1760	£60	£90	£155	—

George II

GEORGE III (1760–1820)

DATE	F	VF	EF	UNC
1762	£30	£50	£70	—
1763	£30	£50	£75	—
1763 Proof	—	—	Extremely rare	

DATE	F	VF	EF	UNC
1765	£375	£525	£825	—
1766	£70	£110	£185	—
1770	£85	£130	£210	—
1772	£55	£85	£120	—
1780	£55	£85	£125	—
1784	£80	£115	£195	—
1786	£80	£110	£190	—
1792	£105	£150	£240	£340
1795	—	£40	£80	£120
1800	—	£45	£85	£130
1817	—	£55	£95	£165
1818	—	£55	£95	£165
1820	—	£55	£95	£165

GEORGE IV (1820–30)

1822	—	—	£85	£165
1823	—	—	£75	£155
1824	—	—	£75	£165
1825–30	—	—	£75	£155

WILLIAM IV (1830–37)

1831 Proof	—	—	£375	£625
1831	—	—	£110	£175
1832	—	—	£120	£215
1833–1836	—	—	£80	£170
1837	—	—	£105	£195

VICTORIA (1837–1901)

1838	—	—	£120	£225
1838 Proof	—	—	—	£1650
1839	—	—	£225	£400
1839 Proof	—	—	—	£575
1840	—	—	£160	£275
1841	—	—	£315	£550
1842	—	—	£290	£455
1843	—	—	£130	£235
1844	—	—	£215	£365
1845	—	—	£85	£165
1846	—	—	£415	£725
1847	—	—	£475	£850
1848	—	—	£450	£825
1849	—	—	£215	£350
1850	—	—	£115	£225
1851	—	—	£175	£325
1852	—	—	£475	£850
1853	—	—	£475	£850
1853 Proof	—	—	—	£1000
1854	—	—	£155	£300
1855	—	—	£180	£365
1856	—	—	£100	£220
1857	—	—	£150	£285
1858	—	—	£120	£235
1859	—	—	£100	£195
1860	—	—	£135	£250
1861	—	—	£140	£245
1862	—	—	£155	£275
1863	—	—	£190	£305
1864	—	—	£135	£245
1865	—	—	£135	£260
1866	—	—	£125	£250
1867	—	—	£125	£235
1868	—	—	£115	£215
1869	—	—	£170	£290
1870	—	—	£105	£195
1871	—	—	£100	£185
1872	—	—	£95	£180
1873	—	—	£90	£170
1874	—	—	£90	£185

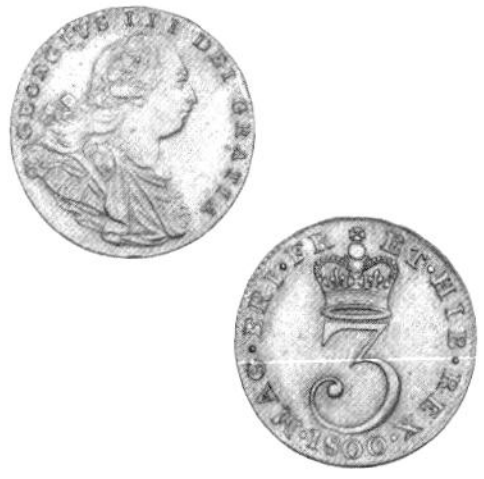

George III

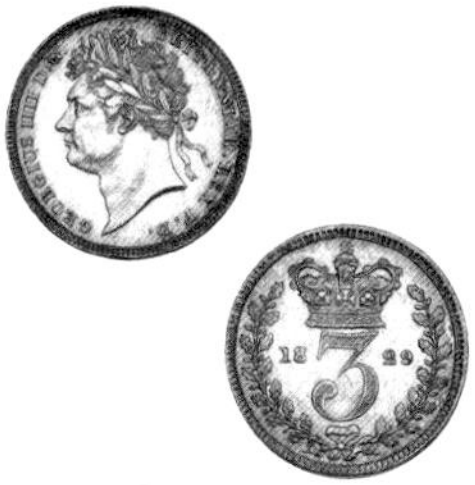

George IV

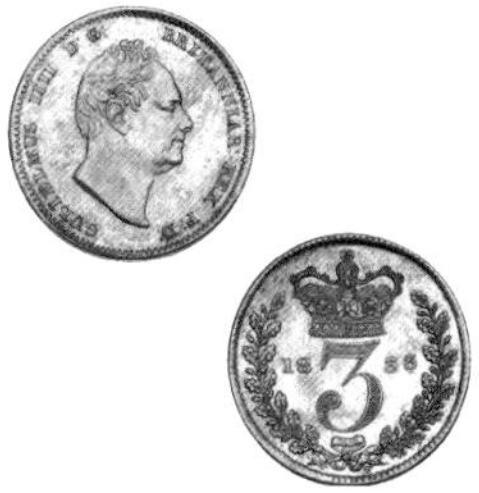

William IV

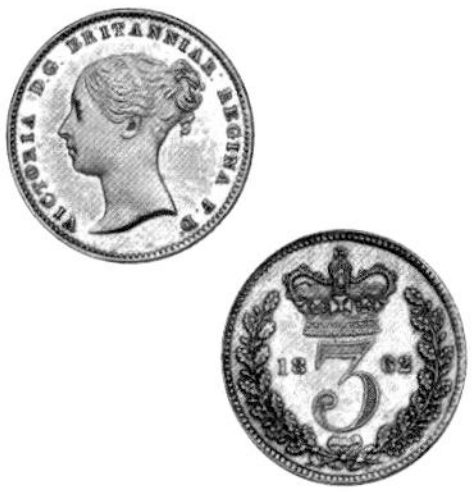

Victoria

DATE	F	VF	EF	UNC
1875....................................	—	—	£85	£175
1876....................................	—	—	£85	£175
1877....................................	—	—	£80	£170
1878....................................	—	—	£85	£175
1879....................................	—	—	£85	£170
1880....................................	—	—	£80	£160
1881....................................	—	—	£80	£160
1882....................................	—	—	£145	£230
1883....................................	—	—	£75	£155
1884....................................	—	—	£75	£155
1885....................................	—	—	£70	£140
1886....................................	—	—	£70	£135
1887....................................	—	—	£80	£170
1888–1892 (Jubilee Head)......	—	—	£60	£115
1893–1901 (Old Head)...........	—	—	£45	£70

Edward VII

EDWARD VII (1901–10)

	F	VF	EF	UNC
1902....................................	—	—	£30	£50
1902 Proof............................	—	—	—	£55
1903....................................	—	—	£40	£80
1904....................................	—	—	£55	£100
1905....................................	—	—	£55	£90
1906....................................	—	—	£45	£85
1907....................................	—	—	£45	£85
1908....................................	—	—	£40	£75
1909....................................	—	—	£75	£130
1910....................................	—	—	£85	£145

George V

GEORGE V (1910–36)

	F	VF	EF	UNC
1911–34................................	—	—	£60	£85
1911 Proof............................	—	—	—	£110
1935....................................	—	—	£70	£110
1936....................................	—	—	£75	£135

GEORGE VI (1936–52)

	F	VF	EF	UNC
1937–52................................	—	—	£55	£85
1937 Proof............................	—	—	—	£70

ELIZABETH II (1952–)

	F	VF	EF	UNC
1953....................................	—	—	£200	£305
1954–85................................	—	—	£45	£75
1986–2007............................	—	—	£55	£80
2002 In gold (proof)	—	—	—	£615
2008....................................	—	—	—	£155
2009....................................	—	—	—	£145
2010....................................	—	—	—	£150
2011....................................	—	—	—	£130
2012....................................	—	—	—	£140
2013....................................	—	—	—	£140
2014....................................	—	—	—	£165
2015....................................	—	—	—	£155
2016....................................	—	—	—	£150
2017....................................	—	—	—	£170
2018....................................	—	—	—	£180
2019....................................	—	—	—	£190
2020....................................	—	—	—	£200
2021....................................	—	—	—	£210

Elizabeth

TWOPENCE
CHARLES II (1660–85)

	F	VF	EF	UNC
Undated................................	£60	£95	£155	—
1668....................................	£65	£100	£170	—
1670....................................	£50	£80	£150	—
1671....................................	£50	£90	£150	—
1672....................................	£50	£90	£150	—
1672/1	£65	£110	£160	—
1673....................................	£50	£85	£155	—
1674....................................	£55	£95	£150	—

Charles II

DATE	F	VF	EF	UNC
1675	£50	£90	£140	—
1676	£55	£95	£155	—
1677	£45	£85	£135	—
1678	£35	£75	£130	—
1679	£40	£70	£125	—
1679 HIB over FRA	£45	£90	£140	—
1680	£50	£85	£135	—
1680 over 79	£45	£80	£130	—
1681	£55	£80	£135	—
1682	£65	£90	£165	—
1682/1 ERA for FRA	£80	£125	£225	—
1683	£60	£100	£160	—
1683 over 2	£60	£110	£180	—
1684	£55	£95	£155	—

James II

JAMES II (1685–88)

	F	VF	EF	UNC
1686	£60	£100	£160	—
1686 reads IACOBVS	£90	£135	£230	—
1687	£65	£100	£165	—
1687 ERA for FRA	£80	£130	£225	—
1688	£55	£85	£155	—
1688/7	£65	£90	£170	—

WILLIAM & MARY (1688–94)

	F	VF	EF	UNC
1689	£65	£105	£180	—
1691	£60	£95	£150	—
1692	£80	£135	£205	—
1693	£75	£120	£195	—
1693 GV below bust	£85	£125	£195	—
1693/2	£70	£110	£180	—
1694	£55	£90	£150	—
1694 MARLA error	£90	£140	£250	—
1694 GVLI under bust	£70	£110	£195	—
1694 GVL under bust	£65	£110	£190	—
1694/3	£65	£115	£200	—

William & Mary

WILLIAM III (1694–1702)

	F	VF	EF	UNC
1698	£70	£120	£185	—
1699	£55	£95	£150	—
1700	£75	£120	£190	—
1701	£70	£115	£175	—

William III

ANNE (1702–14)

	F	VF	EF	UNC
1703	£70	£110	£190	—
1704	£50	£80	£135	—
1704 No stops on obverse	£60	£90	£170	—
1705	£65	£105	£165	—
1706	£80	£130	£195	—
1707	£50	£85	£150	—
1708	£75	£105	£180	—
1709	£85	£140	£225	—
1710	£50	£80	£115	—
1713	£75	£120	£200	—

Queen Anne

GEORGE I (1714–27)

	F	VF	EF	UNC
1717	£50	£85	£135	—
1721	£50	£90	£130	—
1723	£70	£105	£170	—
1726	£55	£85	£135	—
1727	£65	£95	£155	—

GEORGE II (1727–60)

	F	VF	EF	UNC
1729	£45	£90	£125	—
1731	£45	£85	£125	—
1732	£45	£85	£120	—
1735	£50	£80	£120	—

George II

DATE	F	VF	EF	UNC
1737.....................................	£45	£85	£120	—
1739.....................................	£45	£80	£120	—
1740.....................................	£45	£75	£115	—
1743.....................................	£35	£70	£110	—
1743/0	£45	£80	£115	—
1746.....................................	£35	£70	£95	—
1756.....................................	£35	£65	£95	—
1759.....................................	£35	£70	£95	—
1760.....................................	£50	£75	£100	—

GEORGE III (1760–1820)

	F	VF	EF	UNC
1763.....................................	£45	£70	£95	—
1763 Proof............................			Extremely rare	
1765.....................................	£375	£500	£675	—
1766.....................................	£45	£75	£95	—
1772.....................................	£40	£70	£95	—
1772 second 7 over 6............	£40	£80	£105	—
1780.....................................	£40	£70	£95	—
1784.....................................	£40	£70	£90	—
1786.....................................	£50	£80	£95	—
1792.....................................	—	£90	£135	£200
1795.....................................	—	£35	£60	£85
1800.....................................	—	£35	£70	£85
1817.....................................	—	£40	£70	£90
1818.....................................	—	£40	£70	£90
1820.....................................	—	£45	£80	£100

GEORGE IV (1820–30)

	F	VF	EF	UNC
1822–30..................................	—	—	£40	£70
1825 TRITANNIAR	—	—	£65	£125

WILLIAM IV (1830–37)

	F	VF	EF	UNC
1831–37..................................	—	—	£45	£80
1831 Proof.............................	—	—	£135	£250

VICTORIA (1837–1901)

	F	VF	EF	UNC
1838–87 (Young Head)	—	—	£30	£55
1859 BEITANNIAR.................	—	—	£80	£135
1861 6 over 1........................	—	—	£40	£80
1888–92 (Jubilee Head).........	—	—	£35	£55
1893–1901 (Old Head............	—	—	£30	£45
1838 Proof.............................	—	—	—	£475
1839 Proof.............................	—	—	—	£300
1853 Proof.............................	—	—	—	£325

EDWARD VII (1901–10)

	F	VF	EF	UNC
1902–08..................................	—	—	£25	£35
1902 Proof.............................	—	—	£30	£50
1909.....................................	—	—	£45	£80
1910.....................................	—	—	£50	£90

GEORGE V (1910–36)

	F	VF	EF	UNC
1911–34..................................	—	—	£35	£60
1911 Proof.............................	—	—	£40	£70
1935.....................................	—	—	£40	£65
1936.....................................	—	—	£50	£75

GEORGE VI (1936–52)

	F	VF	EF	UNC
1937–47	—	—	£40	£65
1937 Proof.............................	—	—	£35	£60
1948–52	—	—	£45	£70

George III

George IV

William IV

Victoria

DATE	F	VF	EF	UNC

ELIZABETH II (1952–   )

DATE	F	VF	EF	UNC
1953	—	—	£140	£215
1954–85	—	—	£40	£55
1986–2007	—	—	£40	£70
2002 Gold Proof	—	—	—	£425
2008	—	—	—	£125
2009	—	—	—	£115
2010	—	—	—	£110
2011	—	—	—	£85
2012	—	—	—	£115
2013	—	—	—	£120
2014	—	—	—	£140
2015	—	—	—	£115
2016	—	—	—	£135
2017	—	—	—	£170
2018	—	—	—	£170
2019	—	—	—	£175
2020	—	—	—	£185
2021	—	—	—	£175

Elizabeth

PENNY
CHARLES II (1660–85)

DATE	F	VF	EF	UNC
Undated	£80	£120	£200	—
1670	£75	£115	£180	—
1671	£75	£115	£175	—
1672/1	£70	£115	£175	—
1673	£70	£115	£170	—
1674	£70	£115	£175	—
1674 Ɔratia (error)	£105	£160	£250	—
1675	£70	£115	£170	—
1675 Ɔratia (error)	£105	£165	£260	—
1676	£85	£120	£190	—
1676 Ɔratia (error)	£115	£170	£275	—
1677	£60	£100	£165	—
1677 Ɔratia (error)	£95	£135	£230	—
1678	£150	£255	£365	—
1678 Ɔratia (error)	£175	£280	£380	—
1679	£85	£125	£210	—
1680	£85	£120	£200	—
1680 on 2d flan	£130	£250	£300	—
1681	£110	£155	£230	—
1682	£75	£125	£195	—
1682 ERA for FRA	£90	£150	£245	—
1683	£85	£120	£195	—
1683/1	£85	£150	£225	—
1684	£130	£230	£290	—
1684/3	£135	£235	£300	—

Charles II

JAMES II (1685–88)

DATE	F	VF	EF	UNC
1685	£75	£115	£180	—
1686	£80	£115	£180	—
1687	£80	£125	£185	—
1687 7 over 6	£90	£135	£195	—
1687/8	£85	£130	£190	—
1688	£65	£110	£170	—
1688/7	£75	£115	£190	—

James II

WILLIAM & MARY (1688–94)

DATE	F	VF	EF	UNC
1689	£450	£675	£950	—
1689 MΛRIΛ	£470	£685	£925	—
1689 GVIELMVS (Error)	£450	£700	£950	—
1690	£85	£150	£235	—
1691	£85	£155	£230	—
1691/0	£85	£160	£250	—

William & Mary

197

DATE	F	VF	EF	UNC
1692....................................	£240	£350	£525	—
1692/1	£250	£355	£550	—
1693....................................	£115	£180	£270	—
1694....................................	£80	£135	£230	—
1694 HI for HIB.....................	£125	£180	£275	—
1694 No stops on obverse	£100	£155	£240	—

William III

WILLIAM III (1694–1702)

	F	VF	EF	UNC
1698....................................	£90	£150	£200	—
1698 HI. BREX (Error)............	£110	£165	£270	—
1698 IRA for FRA..................	£100	£160	£210	—
1699....................................	£270	£410	£550	—
1700....................................	£95	£160	£225	—
1701....................................	£90	£140	£210	—

ANNE (1702–14)

Anne

	F	VF	EF	UNC
1703....................................	£85	£130	£195	—
1705....................................	£75	£115	£180	—
1706....................................	£70	£95	£165	—
1708....................................	£425	£550	£775	—
1709....................................	£60	£95	£150	—
1710....................................	£140	£210	£305	—
1713/0	£85	£130	£190	—

GEORGE I (1714–27)

George I

	F	VF	EF	UNC
1716....................................	£45	£90	£115	—
1718....................................	£45	£90	£115	—
1720....................................	£50	£95	£125	—
1720 HIPEX (Error)................	£75	£120	£205	—
1723....................................	£75	£125	£180	—
1725....................................	£50	£85	£130	—
1726....................................	£50	£85	£125	—
1727....................................	£70	£120	£170	—

GEORGE II (1727–60)

	F	VF	EF	UNC
1729....................................	£45	£85	£125	—
1731....................................	£50	£85	£125	—
1732....................................	£50	£80	£120	—
1735....................................	£40	£70	£100	—
1737....................................	£40	£70	£105	—
1739....................................	£40	£70	£100	—
1740....................................	£45	£70	£100	—
1743....................................	£40	£65	£95	—
1746....................................	£45	£80	£115	—
1746/3	£50	£80	£120	—
1750....................................	£30	£55	£85	—
1752....................................	£30	£55	£85	—
1752/0	£35	£60	£90	—
1753....................................	£30	£55	£85	—
1754....................................	£30	£55	£85	—
1755....................................	£30	£55	£85	—
1756....................................	£30	£55	£80	—
1757....................................	£30	£55	£80	—
1757 No colon after Gratia	£45	£75	£90	—
1758....................................	£30	£60	£85	—
1759....................................	£35	£60	£80	—
1760....................................	£40	£75	£95	—

GEORGE III (1760–1820)

George III

	F	VF	EF	UNC
1763....................................	£50	£75	£110	—
1763 Proof............................	—	—	Extremely rare	
1766....................................	£40	£70	£90	—
1770....................................	£60	£90	£120	—
1772....................................	£40	£70	£85	—
1780....................................	£110	£160	£220	—

DATE	F	VF	EF	UNC
1781	£35	£60	£85	—
1784	£45	£65	£90	—
1786	£40	£60	£90	—
1792	£40	£70	£105	£140
1795	—	£25	£50	£70
1800	—	£25	£45	£70
1817	—	£30	£45	£70
1818	—	£30	£45	£70
1820	—	£35	£50	£75

George IV

GEORGE IV (1820–30)

	F	VF	EF	UNC
1822–30	—	—	£35	£60

William IV

WILLIAM IV (1830–37)

	F	VF	EF	UNC
1831–37	—	—	£45	£65
1831 Proof	—	—	£170	£250

VICTORIA (1837–1901)

	F	VF	EF	UNC
1838–87 (Young Head)	—	—	£30	£45
1888–92 (Jubilee Head)	—	—	£30	£40
1893–1901 (Old Head)	—	—	£25	£30
1838 Proof	—	—	—	£265
1839 Proof	—	—	—	£185
1853 Proof	—	—	—	£225

Victoria

EDWARD VII (1901–10)

	F	VF	EF	UNC
1902–08	—	—	£20	£30
1902 Proof	—	—	£25	£35
1909	—	—	£40	£75
1910	—	—	£55	£90

Edward VII

GEORGE V (1910–36)

	F	VF	EF	UNC
1911–14	—	—	£45	£75
1911 Proof	—	—	£45	£90
1915	—	—	£50	£85
1916–19	—	—	£45	£80
1920	—	—	£45	£80
1921–28	—	—	£45	£75
1929	—	—	£45	£80
1930–34	—	—	£40	£75
1935	—	—	£45	£80
1936	—	—	£55	£85

George V

GEORGE VI (1936–52)

	F	VF	EF	UNC
1937–40	—	—	£50	£75
1937 Proof	—	—	£45	£80
1941	—	—	£55	£85
1942–47	—	—	£50	£85
1948–52	—	—	£60	£90

ELIZABETH II (1952–)

	F	VF	EF	UNC
1953	—	—	£300	£425
1965–85	—	—	£45	£75
1986–2007	—	—	£50	£80
2002 Proof in gold	—	—	—	£450
2008	—	—	—	£145
2009	—	—	—	£140
2010	—	—	—	£120
2011	—	—	—	£105
2012	—	—	—	£130
2013	—	—	—	£125
2014	—	—	—	£135
2015	—	—	—	£110
2016	—	—	—	£135
2017	—	—	—	£150
2018	—	—	—	£155
2019	—	—	—	£160
2020	—	—	—	£170
2021	—	—	—	£180

Elizabeth II

DECIMAL COINAGE

Since the introduction of the Decimal system in the UK, many coins have been issued for circulation purposes in vast quantities. In addition, from 1982 sets of coins to non-proof standard, and including examples of each denomination found in circulation, have been issued each year. For 1982 and 1983 they were to "circulation" standard and described as "Uncirculated". Individual coins from these sets are annotated "Unc" on the lists that follow. From 1984 to the present day they were described as "Brilliant Uncirculated" (BU on the lists), and from around 1986 these coins are generally distinguishable from coins intended for circulation. They were from then produced by the Proof Coin Division of the Royal Mint (rather than by the Coin Production Room which produces circulation-standard coins). For completeness however, we have included the annotations Unc and BU back to 1982, the start year for these sets.

It is emphasised that the abbreviations Unc and BU in the left-hand columns adjacent to the date refer to an advertising description or to an engineering production standard, not the preservation condition or grade of the coin concerned. Where no such annotation appears adjacent to the date, the coin is circulation-standard for issue as such.

We have included the "mintage" figures for circulation coins down to Half Penny where known. The figure given for the 1997 Two Pounds, is considerably less than the actual quantity struck, because many were scrapped before issue due to failing an electrical conductivity test. Where a coin is available in uncirculated grade at, or just above, face value no price has been quoted. NOTE: *For many of the later issues, especially the latest issue precious metal coins, the price quoted is the issue price.*

Base metal Proof issues of circulation coinage (£2 or £1 to one or half penny) of the decimal series were only issued, as with Unc or BU, as part of Year Sets, but many of these sets have been broken down into individual coins, hence the appearance of the latter on the market.

The lists do not attempt to give details of die varieties, except where there was an obvious intention to change the appearance of a coin, e.g. 1992 20p.

2008 saw new reverses and modified obverses for all circulation denominations from the One Pound to the One Penny. All seven denominations were put into circulation dated 2008, all with both the old and the new reverses.

The circulation standard mintage figures have mainly been kindly supplied by courtesy of the Head of Historical Services and the Department of UK Circulation Coin Sales, both at the Royal Mint.

KILO COINS
(gold and silver)

The UK's first-ever Kilo coins were struck to commemorate the 2012 Olympic Games in 0.999 fine gold and 0.999 fine silver. These and subsequent issues are listed in detail below, and all were struck to proof standard and to similar metallic standards. They are also listed under their relevant "series" where appropriate. In addition some issues were struck in 2, 5 or 10 kilos but these are not specifically listed here.

DATE	FACE VALUE	AUTHORISED ISSUE QTY.	NO. ISSUED	ISSUE PRICE
2012 Olympic Gold;				
obverse: 1998 Ian Rank-Broadley's Royal Portrait				
reverse: Sir Anthony Caro's "Individual Endeavour" £1,000		60	20	£100,000
2012 Olympic Silver;				
obverse: 1998 Rank-Broadley Royal Portrait				
reverse: Tom Phillip's "Team Endeavour" £500		2,912	910	£3,000
2012 Diamond Jubilee Gold;				
obverse: Queen in Garter Robes (Rank-Broadley)				
reverse: Royal Arms (Buckingham Palace Gates) £1,000		21	21	£60,000
2012 Diamond Jubilee Silver;				
obverse: Queen in Garter Robes (Rank-Broadley)				
reverse: Royal Arms (Buckingham Palace Gates) £500		1,250	206	£2,600
2013 Coronation Anniversary Gold;				
obverse: 1998 Rank-Broadley Royal Portrait				
reverse: John Bergdahl's Coronation Regalia £1,000		27	13	£50,000
2013 Coronation Anniversary Silver;				
obverse: 1998 Rank-Broadley Royal Portrait				
reverse: John Bergdahl's Coronation Regalia £500		400	301	£2,600
2013 Royal Christening Gold;				
obverse: 1998 Rank-Broadley Royal Portrait				
reverse: John Bergdahl's Lily Font £1,000		22	19	£48,000
2013 Royal Christening Silver;				
obverse: 1998 Rank-Broadley Royal Portrait				
reverse: John Bergdahl's Lily Font £500		500	194	£2,600
2014 First World War Outbreak Gold;				
obverse: 1998 Rank-Broadley Royal Portrait				
reverse: Sandle's Hostile Environment.. £1,000		25	10	£45,000
2014 First World War Outbreak Silver;				
obverse: 1998 Rank-Broadley Royal Portrait				
reverse: Sandle's Hostile Environment £500		430	165	£2,000
2015 50th Anniversary of Death of Sir Winston Churchill Gold;				
obverse: 1998 Rank-Broadley Royal Portrait				
reverse: Millner's image of Churchill... £1,000		15	9	£45,000
2015 50th Anniversary of Death of Sir Winston Churchill Silver;				
obverse: 1998 Rank-Broadley Royal Portrait				
reverse: Milner's image of Churchill £500		170	117	£2,000
2015 The Longest Reign Gold;				
obverse: Butler Royal Portrait				
reverse: Stephen Taylor Queen's Portraits £1,000		15	15	£42,500
2016 The Longest Reign Silver;				
obverse: Butler Royal Portrait				
reverse: Stephen Taylor Queen's Portraits £500		320	278	£2,000
2016 Year of the Monkey Gold;				
obverse: Clark Royal Portrait				
reverse: Wuon-Gean Ho's Rhesus monkey £1,000		8	—	£42,500
2016 Year of the Monkey Silver;				
obverse: Butler Royal Portrait				
everse: Wuon-Gean Ho's Rhesus monkey....................................... £500		88	—	£2,000
2016 Queen's 90th Birthday Gold;				
obverse: Clark Royal Portrait				
reverse: Christopher Hobbs Floral design..................................... £1,000		25	15	—
2016 Queen's 90th Birthday Silver;				
obverse: Clark Royal Portrait				
reverse: Christopher Hobbs Floral design.. £500		450	447	£2,000

DATE	FACE VALUE	AUTHORISED ISSUE QTY.	NO. ISSUED	ISSUE PRICE
2017 The Queen's Sapphire Accession Jubilee Silver; obverse: Clark Royal Portrait reverse: Gregory Cameron's design of Crowned Coat of Arms....... £500		300	225	£2,050
2017 Lunar Year of the Rooster Gold; obverse: Clark Royal Portrait reverse: Wuon-Gean Ho's Rooster.. £1,000		8	8	£42,500
2017 Lunar Year of the Rooster Silver; obverse: Clark Royal Portrait reverse: Wuon-Gean Ho's Rooster.. £500		68	—	£2,050
2017 Platinum Wedding Gold; obverse: Etienne Millner Double Royal Portrait reverse: Heraldic shields by John Bergdahl £1,000		31	15	£49,950
2017 Platinum Wedding Silver; obverse: Etienne Millner Double Royal Portrait reverse: Heraldic shields by John Bergdahl £500		550	—	£2,025
2018 Anniversary of the Armistice Gold; obverse: Clark Royal Portrait reverse: Kneeling soldier by Paul Day £1,000		10	—	£49,995
2018 Anniversary of the Armistice Silver; obverse: Clark Royal Portrait reverse: Kneeling soldier by Paul Day £500		100	—	£2,025
2018 Lunar Year of the Dog Gold; obverse: Clark Royal Portrait reverse: Wuon-Gean Ho's Dog... £1,000		8	—	£42,500
2018 Lunar Year of the Dog Silver; obverse: Clark Royal Portrait reverse: Wuon-Gean Ho's Dog.. £500		108	—	£2,025
2018 Britannia Silver; obverse: Clark Royal Portrait reverse: David Lawrence Stylised bust of Britannia £500		250	—	£2,025
2018 Sapphire Coronation Jubilee Gold; obverse: Jody Clark Royal Portrait reverse: Dominique Evans The Queen in the Royal Coach........... £1,000		15	—	£49,950
2018 Sapphire Coronation Jubilee Silver; obverse: Jody Clark Royal Portrait reverse: Dominique Evans The Queen in the Royal Coach............. £500		250	—	£2,025

2015
50th Anniversary
of Death of
Sir Winston
Churchill
Silver

2021 Lunar—
Year of the Ox

2017
Platinum
Wedding
Gold

2021
White
Greyhound
of
Richmond

Illustrations on this page are not shown to scale.

DATE	FACE VALUE	AUTHORISED ISSUE QTY.	NO. ISSUED	ISSUE. PRICE
2019 Britannia Silver;				
obverse: Clark Royal Portrait				
reverse: David Lawrence's portrait of Britannia beside a lion £500		115	—	£2,025
2019 Queen Victoria Silver;				
obverse: Clark Royal Portrait				
reverse: William Wyon portrait of Queen Victoria and Prince Albert £500		125	—	£2,025
2019 Lunar Year of the Pig Gold;				
obverse: Clark Royal Portrait				
reverse: Harry Brockway's Pig... £1000		8	—	—
2019 Lunar Year of the Pig Silver;				
obverse: Clark Royal Portrait				
reverse: Harry Brockway's Pig... £500		38	—	£2,025
2019 The Falcon of the Plantagenets Gold;				
obverse: Clark Royal Portrait				
reverse: by Jody Clark... £1000		10	—	£59,995
2019 The Falcon of the Plantagenets Silver;				
obverse: Clark Royal Portrait				
reverse: by Jody Clark... £500		125	—	£2,050
2019 The Yale of Beaufort Gold;				
obverse: Clark Royal Portrait				
reverse: by Jody Clark... £1000		13	—	—
2019 The Yale of Beaufort Silver;				
obverse: Clark Royal Portrait				
reverse: by Jody Clark... £500		120	—	£2,025
2019 Great Engraver Series: Una & the Lion Silver (also in 2 and 5 kilos);				
obverse: Clark Royal Portrait				
reverse: William Wyon's Una.. £5000		12	—	£59,995
2020 White Lion of Mortimer Gold;				
obverse: Clark Royal Portrait				
reverse: by Jody Clark... £1000		10	—	£59,995
2020 White Lion of Mortimer Silver;				
obverse: Clark Royal Portrait				
reverse: by Jody Clark... £500		90	—	£2,025
2020 White Horse of Hanover Gold;				
obverse: Clark Royal Portrait				
reverse: by Jody Clark... £1000		13	—	£57,750
2020 White Horse of Hanover Silver;				
obverse: Clark Royal Portrait				
reverse: by Jody Clark... £500		115	—	£2,050
2020 Lunar Year of the Rat Gold;				
obverse: Clark Royal Portrait				
reverse: P. J. Lynch's Rat.. £1000		8	—	£59,995
2020 Lunar Year of the Rat Silver;				
obverse: Clark Royal Portrait				
reverse: P. J. Lynch's Rat.. £500		28	—	£2,050
2021 Lunar Year of the Ox Gold,				
obverse: Jody Clark				
reverse: Harry Brockway £1000		10	—	£63,865
2021 Lunar Year of the Ox Silver,				
obverse: Jody Clark				
reverse: Harry Brockway £500		38	—	£2,050
2021 White Greyhound of Richmond Gold,				
obverse: Jody Clark				
reverse: Jody Clark £1000		10	—	£63,865
2021 White Greyhound of Richmond Silver;				
obverse: Jody Clark				
reverse: Jody Clark £500		80	—	£2,050

As the issuing of one kilo coins as part of a collection or series of coins has become a more regular occurrence for the Royal Mint, see Precious Metal Bullion and Collector Coins (Series) for a more in-depth listing of the latest bullion coin releases.

FIVE-OUNCE COINS
(gold and silver)

Appearing for the first time in 2012 were Five-Ounce coins, minted in the same metals and standards as the Kilo Coins. The Five-Ounce Britannia coins, both gold (50mm) and silver (65mm) proofs, which appeared first in 2013 are listed in the Britannia section.

DATE	FACE VALUE	AUTHORISED ISSUE QTY.	NO ISSUED	ISSUE PRICE
2012 Olympic Gold; obverse: 1998 Rank-Broadley Royal Portrait reverse: Pegasus (C. Le Brun) £10		500	193	£11,500
2012 Olympic Silver; obverse: 1998 Rank-Broadley Royal Portrait reverse: Pegasus (C. Le Brun) £10		7,500	5,056	£525
2012 Diamond Jubilee Gold; obverse: Queen in Garter Robes (Rank-Broadley) reverse: Queen seated (facing).....................................£10		250	140	£9,500
2012 Diamond Jubilee Silver; obverse: Queen in Garter Robes (Rank-Broadley) reverse: Queen seated (facing).....................................£10		1,952	1,933	£450
2013 Coronation Anniversary Gold; obverse: 1998 Rank-Broadley Royal Portrait reverse: Regalia in Westminster Abbey (J. Olliffe) £10		129	74	£9,500
2013 Coronation Anniversary Silver; obverse: 1998 Rank-Broadley Royal Portrait reverse: Regalia in Westminster Abbey (J. Olliffe) £10		1,953	1,604	£450
2013 Royal Christening Gold; obverse: 1998 Rank-Broadley Royal Portrait reverse: Bergdahl's Lily Font £10		150	48	£8,200
2013 Royal Christening Silver; obverse: 1998 Rank-Broadley Royal Portrait reverse: Bergdahl's Lily Font £10		1,660	912	£450
2014 First World War Outbreak Gold; obverse: 1998 Rank-Broadley Royal Portrait reverse: Bergdahl's Britannia...£10		110	36	£7,500
2014 First World War Outbreak Silver; obverse: 1998 Rank-Broadley Royal Portrait reverse: Bergdahl's Britannia...£10		1,300	606	£395

DATE	FACE VALUE	AUTHORISED ISSUE QTY.	NO. ISSUED	ISSUE PRICE
2014 Lunar Year of the Horse Gold; obverse: 1998 Rank-Broadley Royal Portrait reverse: Wuon-Gean Ho's Horse................................£500	—	—	£7,500	
2014 Lunar Year of the Horse Silver; obverse: 1998 Rank-Broadley Royal Portrait reverse: Wuon-Gean Ho's Horse................................£10	799	799	£395	
2015 Year of the Sheep Gold; obverse: 1998 Rank-Broadley Royal Portrait reverse: Wuon-Gean Ho's Swaledale Sheep £500	38	26	£7,500	
2015 Year of the Sheep Silver; obverse: 1998 Rank-Broadley Royal Portrait reverse: Wuon-Gean Ho's Swaledale Sheep £10	1,088	331	£395	
2015 50th Anniversary of Death of Sir Winston Churchill Gold; obverse: Clark Royal Portrait reverse: Millner's image of Churchill.............................£10	60	58	£7,500	
2015 50th Anniversary of Death of Sir Winston Churchill Silver; obverse: Clark Royal Portrait reverse: Millner's image of Churchill.............................£10	500	855 (?)	£450	
2015 First World War Gold; obverse: Clark Royal Portrait reverse: James Butler Devastation of War £500	50	17	£6,950	
2015 First World War Silver; obverse: Clark Royal Portrait reverse: James Butler Devastation of War £10	500	355	£395	
2015 The Longest Reign Gold; obverse: Butler Royal Portrait reverse: Stephen Taylor Queen's Portraits £500	180	180	£6,950	
2015 The Longest Reign Silver; obverse: Butler Royal Portrait reverse: Stephen Taylor Queen's Portraits £10	1,500	1499	£395	
2015 Christening of Princess Charlotte; obverse: Clark Royal Portrait reverse: John Bergdahl Baroque design £10	500	500	£400	
2016 Year of the Monkey Gold; obverse: Clark Royal Portrait reverse: Wuon-Gean Ho's Rhesus monkey £500	38	—	£7,500	
2016 Year of the Monkey Silver; obverse: Butler Royal Portrait reverse: Wuon-Gean Ho's Rhesus monkey £10	588	—	£395	
2016 Queen's 90th Birthday Gold; obverse: Clark Royal Portrait reverse: Christopher Hobbs Floral design..................................£500	170	170	£7,500	
2016 Queen's 90th Birthday Silver; obverse: Clark Royal Portrait reverse: Christopher Hobbs Floral design..................................£10	1,750	1727	£395	
2016 First World War Gold; obverse: Clark Royal Portrait reverse: David Lawrence Four Soldiers walking £500	30	—	£7,500	
2016 First World War Silver; obverse: Clark Royal Portrait reverse: David Lawrence Four Soldiers walking £10	500	—	£395	
2016 2016 Shakespeare Gold; obverse: Clark Royal Portrait; reverse: Tom Phillips Shakespeare Portrait £500	—	50	—	
2016 Shakespeare Silver; obverse: Clark Royal Portrait; reverse: Tom Phillips Shakespeare Portrait £10	750	343	£395	
2017 Lunar Year of the Rooster Gold; obverse: Clark Royal Portrait reverse: Wuon-Gean Ho's Rooster...£500	38	35	£8,250	
2017 Lunar Year of the Rooster Gold; obverse: Clark Royal Portrait reverse: Wuon-Gean Ho's Rooster...£10	388	369	£415	
2017 The Queen's Sapphire Jubilee Gold; obverse: Clark Royal Portrait reverse: Gregory Cameron's Crowned Coat of Arms.................£500	110	110	£8,250	

DATE	FACE VALUE	AUTHORISED ISSUE QTY.	NO. ISSUED	ISSUE PRICE
2017 The Queen's Sapphire Jubilee Silver; obverse: Clark Royal Portrait reverse: Gregory Cameron's Crowned Coat of Arms....................£10		1,500	1,445	£415
2017 First World War Gold; obverse: Clark Royal Portrait reverse: Philip Jackson Soldier £500		50	—	£8,250
2017 First World War Silver; obverse: Clark Royal Portrait reverse: Philip Jackson Soldier £10		450	—	£415
2017 Royal Platinum Wedding Gold; obverse: Royal Portraits by Etienne Millner reverse: John Bergdahl Heraldic design.......................................£500		450	86	£415
2018 Lunar Year of the Dog Gold; obverse: Clark Royal Portrait reverse: Wuon-Gean Ho's Dog...£500		58	—	£8,565
2018 Lunar Year of the Dog Silver; obverse: Clark Royal Portrait reverse: Wuon-Gean Ho's Dog...£10		388	—	£420
2018 Four Generations of Royalty Gold; obverse: Clark Royal Portrait reverse: Timothy Noad Initials of the Royal succession.............£500		100	—	£8,565
2018 Four Generations of Royalty Silver; obverse: Clark Royal Portrait reverse: Timothy Noad Initials of the Royal succession...............£10		1,000	—	£420
2018 Sapphire Coronation Gold; obverse: Clark Royal Portrait reverse: Dominique Evans Queen in Coronation Coach £500		85	—	£8,565
2018 Sapphire Coronation Silver; obverse: Clark Royal Portrait reverse: Dominique Evans Queen in Coronation Coach £10		1,050	—	£420
2018 Anniversary of the Armistice Gold; obverse: Clark Royal Portrait reverse: Paul Day Lone Soldier £500		50	—	£8,565
2018 Anniversary of the Armistice Silver; obverse: Clark Royal Portrait reverse: Paul Day Lone Soldier £10		525	—	£420
2019 Queen Victoria Gold; obverse: Clark Royal Portrait reverse: W. Wyon's portrait of Queen Victoria and Prince Albert £500		70	—	£8,645
2019 Queen Victoria Silver; obverse: Clark Royal Portrait reverse: W. Wyon's portrait of Queen Victoria and Prince Albert £10		800	—	£420
2019 The Tower of London Gold; obverse: Clark Royal Portrait reverse: Glyn Davis Yeoman Warder £500		45	—	£8,645
2019 The Tower of London Silver; obverse: Clark Royal Portrait reverse: Glyn Davis Yeoman Warder £10		585	—	£420
2019 The Tower of London Gold; obverse: Clark Royal Portrait reverse: Glyn Davis Ceremony of the Keys £500		45	—	£8,645
2019 The Tower of London Silver; obverse: Clark Royal Portrait reverse: Glyn Davis Ceremony of the Keys £10		585	—	£420
2019 The Falcon of the Plantagenets Gold; obverse: Clark Royal Portrait reverse: Clark's Falcon £500		85	—	£8,645
2019 The Falcon of the Plantagenets Silver; obverse: Clark Royal Portrait reverse: Clark's Falcon £10		550	—	£420
2019 The Tower of London Gold; obverse: Clark Royal Portrait reverse: Glyn Davis Crown Jewels £500		45	—	£8,645
2019 The Tower of London Silver; obverse: Clark Royal Portrait reverse: Glyn Davis Crown Jewels £10		585	—	£420

207

DATE	FACE VALUE	AUTHORISED ISSUE QTY.	NO. ISSUED	ISSUE PRICE
2019 Lunar Year of the Pig Gold; obverse: Clark Royal Portrait reverse: Harry Brockway's Pig	£500	38	—	£8,645
2019 Lunar Year of the Pig Silver; obverse: Clark Royal Portrait reverse: Harry Brockway's Pig	£10	288	—	£420
2019 The Tower of London Gold; obverse: Clark Royal Portrait reverse: Glyn Davies Legend of the Ravens	£500	45	—	£8,645
2019 The Tower of London Silver; obverse: Clark Royal Portrait reverse: Glyn Davies Legend of the Ravens	£10	585	—	£420
2019 The Yale of Beaufort Gold; obverse: Clark Royal Portrait reverse: by Clark	£500	70	—	£8,645
2019 The Yale of Beaufort Silver; obverse: Clark Royal Portrait reverse: by Clark	£10	335	—	£420
2019 Great Engraver Series: Una & the Lion Gold; obverse: Clark Royal Portrait reverse: William Wyon	£500	65	—	£9,995
2020 White Lion of Mortimer Gold; obverse: Clark Royal Portrait reverse: by Clark	£500	55	—	£9,995
2020 White Lion of Mortimer Silver; obverse: Clark Royal Portrait reverse: by Clark	£10	250	—	£420
2020 White Horse of Hanover Gold; obverse: Clark Royal Portrait reverse: by Clark	£500	69	—	£9,595
2020 White Horse of Hanover Silver; obverse: Clark Royal Portrait reverse: by Clark	£10	315	—	£420
2020 Lunar Year of the Rat Gold; obverse: Clark Royal Portrait reverse: P. J. Lynch	£500	28	—	£9,995
2020 Lunar Year of the Rat Silver; obverse: Clark Royal Portrait reverse: P. J. Lynch	£10	188	—	£420
2021 Lunar Year of the Ox Gold; obverse: Jody Clark reverse: Harry Brockway	£500	38	—	£10,605
2021 Lunar Year of the Ox Silver; obverse: Jody Clark reverse: Harry Brockway	£10	198	—	£420

FIVE POUNDS (Sovereign series)

This series is all minted in gold, and, except where stated, have the Pistrucci St George and Dragon reverse. BU coins up to 2001 bear a U in a circle. From 2009 the initials B.P. in the exergue are replaced by PISTRUCCI in small letters on the left. From 2014 the denomination is called the "Five-Sovereign" piece by the Royal Mint in their marketing publications.

> **NOTE: The prices quoted in this guide are set at August 2021 with the price of gold at £1,300 per ounce and silver £17.30 per ounce—market fluctuations will have a marked effect on the values of modern precious metal coins. Many of the prices given for recent gold coins are the Royal Mint issue price.**

DATE	Mintage	UNC
1980 Proof	10,000	£2000
1981 Proof	5,400	£2000
1982 Proof	2,500	£2000
1984 BU	15,104	£1750
1984 Proof	8,000	£2000
1985 New portrait BU	13,626	£1750
1985 — Proof	6,130	£2000
1986 BU	7,723	£1500
1987 Uncouped portrait BU	5,694	£1750
1988 BU	3,315	£1750
1989 500th Anniversary of the Sovereign. Enthroned portrayal obverse and Crowned shield reverse BU	2,937	£2000
1989 — Proof	5,000	£2000
1990 Reverts to couped portrait BU	1,226	£1750
1990 Proof	1,721	£2000
1991 BU	976	£1750
1991 Proof	1,336	£2000
1992 BU	797	£1750
1992 Proof	1,165	£2000
1993 BU	906	£1750
1993 Proof	1,078	£2000
1994 BU	1,000	£1750
1994 Proof	918	£2000
1995 BU	1,000	£1750
1995 Proof	1,250	£2000
1996 BU	901	£1750
1996 Proof	742	£2000
1997 BU	802	£1750
1997 Proof	860	£2000
1998 New portrait BU	825	£1750
1998 Proof	789	£2000
1999 BU	970	£1750
1999 Proof	1,000	£2000
2000 ("Bullion")	10,000	£1750
2000 BU	994	£1750
2000 Proof	3,000	£2000
2001 BU	1,000	£1750
2001 Proof	3,500	£2000
2002 Shield rev. ("Bullion")	—	£1750
2002 BU	—	£1750
2002 Proof	3,000	£2000
2003 BU	812	£1750
2003 Proof	—	£2000
2004 BU	1,000	£1750
2004 Proof	—	£2000
2005 Noad's heraldic St George and Dragon BU	936	£1750
2005 — Proof	—	£2200
2006 BU	731	£1750
2006 Proof	—	£2000
2007 BU	768	£1750
2007 Proof	—	£2000
2008 BU	750	£1750
2008 Proof	—	£2000
2009 BU	1,000	£1750
2009 Proof	—	£2000
2010 BU	1,000	£1750
2010 Proof	—	£2000

Pistrucci's famous rendering of St George and the Dragon which appears on all except special commemorative five pound coins.

The obverse of the 1989 500th Anniversary of the original Sovereign coin portrays HM the Queen enthroned.

DATE	Mintage	UNC
2011 BU	657	£1750
2011 Proof	—	£2000
2012 Day's St George and Dragon BU	496	£1750
2012 — Proof	—	£1850
2013 BU	262	£1750
2013 Proof	—	£2000
2014 BU	645	£1750
2014 Proof	—	£2000
2015 Proof	—	£2000
2015 Jody Clark Portrait BU	609	£2000
2015 — Proof	—	£1750
2016 BU	498	£1750
2016 James Butler Portrait Proof	575	£2250
2017 200th Anniversary of the Sovereign (Clark portrait) BU ...	992	£2000
2017 — Proof	750	£2250
2018 BU	1,500	£1750
2018 Proof	850	£2000
2019 BU Matt finish	550	£2000
2020 200th Anniversary of death of George III		
With GR cypher privy mark	—	£2250
2021 BU	£350	£2420

2017 200th Anniversary reverse design as the original issue.

FIVE POUNDS (Crown series)

This series commenced in 1990 when the "Crown" was declared legal tender at £5, instead of 25p as all previous issues continued to be. Mintage is in cupro-nickel unless otherwise stated. BU includes those in individual presentation folders, and those in sets sold with stamp covers and/or banknotes.

DATE	Mintage	UNC
1990 Queen Mother's 90th Birthday.	2,761,431	£6
1990 — BU	48,477	£10
1990 — Silver Proof	56,800	£40
1990 — Gold Proof	2,500	£2000
1993 Coronation 40th Anniversary	1,834,655	£6
1993 — BU	—	£10
1993 — Proof	—	£15
1993 — Silver Proof	58,877	£45
1993 — Gold Proof	2,500	£2000
1996 HM the Queen's 70th Birthday	2,396,100	£6
1996 — BU	—	£10
1996 — Proof	—	£15
1996 — Silver Proof	39,336	£45
1996 — Gold Proof	2,127	£2000
1997 Royal Golden Wedding	1,733,000	£8
1997 — BU	—	£10
1997 — — with £5 note	5,000	£75
1997 — Proof	—	£20
1997 — Silver Proof	33,689	£45
1997 — Gold Proof	2,750	£2000
1998 Prince of Wales 50th Birthday	1,407,300	£9
1998 — BU	—	£12
1998 — Proof	—	£20
1998 — Silver Proof	13,379	£50
1998 — Gold Proof	—	£2500
1999 Princess of Wales Memorial.	1,600,000	£10
1999 — BU	—	£14
1999 — Proof	—	£20
1999 — Silver Proof	49,545	£60
1999 — Gold Proof	7,500	£3000
1999 Millennium	3,796,300	£8
1999 — BU	—	£12
1999 — Proof	—	£20
1999 — Silver Proof	49,057	£45

DATE	Mintage	UNC
1999 — Gold Proof	2,500	£2000
2000 —	3,147,092*	£12
2000 — BU	—	£20
2000 — — with special Millennium Dome mintmark	—	£35
2000 — Proof	—	£25
2000 — Silver Proof with gold highlight	14,255	£50
2000 — Gold Proof	2,500	£2000
2000 Queen Mother's 100th Birthday	—	£8
2000 — BU	—	£12
2000 — Silver Proof	31,316	£48
2000 — — Piedfort	14,850	£65
2000 — Gold Proof	3,000	£2000
2001 Victorian Era	851,491	£10
2001 — BU	—	£12
2001 — Proof	—	£20
2001 — Silver Proof	19,216	£50
2001 — — with frosted relief	596	£150
2001 — Gold Proof	3,000	£2000
2001 — — with frosted relief	733	£2750
2002 Golden Jubilee	3,469,243*	£8
2002 — BU	—	£12
2002 — Proof	—	£20
2002 — Silver Proof	54,012	£45
2002 — Gold Proof	5,502	£2000
2002 Queen Mother Memorial	incl. above*	£9
2002 — BU	—	£12
2002 — Silver Proof	16,117	£45
2002 — Gold Proof	3,000	£2000
2003 Coronation Jubilee	1,307,147	£10
2003 — BU	100,481	£13
2003 — Proof	—	£20
2003 — Silver Proof	28,758	£45
2003 — Gold Proof	1,896	£2000
2004 Entente Cordiale Centenary	1,205,594	£10
2004 — Proof Reverse Frosting	6,065	£15
2004 — Silver Proof	11,295	£50
2004 — — Piedfort	2,500	£125
2004 — Gold Proof	926	£2000
2004 — Platinum Proof Piedfort	501	£4250
2005 Trafalgar Bicentenary	1,075 516*	£12
2005 — BU	—	£14
2005 — Proof	—	£25
2005 — Silver Proof	21,448	£50
2005 — — Piedfort	2,818	£75
2005 — Gold Proof	1,805	£2000
2005 Bicentenary of the Death of Nelson	incl. above*	£12
2005 — BU	—	£14
2005 — Proof	—	£25
2005 — Silver Proof	12,852	£50
2005 — — Piedfort	2,818	£80
2005 — Gold Proof	1,760	£2000
2005 — Platinum Proof Piedfort	200	£4000
2006 Queen's 80th Birthday	52,267	£10
2006 — BU	—	£14
2006 — Proof	—	£20
2006 — Silver Proof	20,790	£50
2006 — — Piedfort, selective gold plating on reverse	5,000	£85
2006 — Gold Proof	2,750	£2000
2006 — Platinum Proof Piedfort	250	£4000
2007 Queen's Diamond Wedding	30,561	£10
2007 — BU	—	£15
2007 — Proof	—	£20
2007 — Silver Proof	15,186	£50
2007 — — Piedfort	2,000	£80
2007 — Gold Proof	2,380	£2000
2007 — Platinum Proof Piedfort	250	£4000
2008 Prince of Wales 60th Birthday	14,088	£12
2008 — BU	54,746	£15
2008 — Proof	—	£20

DATE	Mintage	UNC
2008 — Silver Proof	6,264	£55
2008 — — Piedfort	1,088	£90
2008 — Gold Proof	867	£2000
2008 Elizabeth I 450th Anniversary of Accession	20,047	£12
2008 — BU	26,700	£15
2008 — Proof	—	£20
2008 — Silver Proof	9,216	£50
2008 — — Piedfort	1,602	£90
2008 — Gold Proof	1,500	£2000
2008 — Platinum Proof Piedfort	125	£4000
2009 500th Anniversary of Henry VIII Accession	30,000	£12
2009 — BU	69,119	£15
2009 — Proof	—	£25
2009 — Silver Proof	10,419	£50
2009 — — Piedfort	3,580	£90
2009 — Gold Proof	1,130	£2000
2009 — Platinum Proof Piedfort	100	£4250
2009 Olympic Countdown (3 years) BU	184,921	£12
2009 — Silver Proof	26,645	£55
2009 — — Piedfort	4,874	£90
2009 — Gold Proof	1,860	£2000
2009 Olympic Celebration of Britain "The Mind" series (incl. green logo):		
Stonehenge Silver Proof	—	£60
Palace of Westminster/Big Ben Silver Proof	—	£60
— Cu Ni Proof	—	£20
Angel of the North Silver Proof	—	£60
Flying Scotsman Silver Proof	—	£60
Globe Theatre Silver Proof	—	£60
Sir Isaac Newton Silver Proof	—	£60
2010 350th Anniversary of the Restoration of the Monarchy	15,000	£15
2010 — BU	30,247	£20
2010 — Proof	—	£25
2010 — Silver Proof	6,518	£50
2010 — — Piedfort	4,435	£120
2010 — Gold Proof	1,182	£2000
2010 — Platinum Proof Piedfort	—	£4000
2010 Olympic Countdown (2 years) BU	153,080	£12
2010 — Silver Proof	20,159	£55
2010 — — Piedfort	2,197	£150
2010 — Gold Proof	1,562	£2000
2010 Olympic Celebration of Britain, "The Body" series (incl. red logo):		
Coastline of Britain (Rhossili Bay) Silver Proof	—	£65
Giants Causeway Silver Proof	—	£65
River Thames Silver Proof	—	£65
British Fauna (Barn Owl) Silver Proof	—	£65
British Flora (Oak Leaves and Acorn) Silver Proof	—	£65
Weather Vane Silver Proof	—	£65
2010 Olympic Celebration of Britain "The Spirit" series (incl. blue logo):		
Churchill Silver Proof	—	£75
— CuNi Proof	—	£20
Spirit of London (Kind Hearts etc.) Silver Proof	—	£75
— CuNi Proof	—	£20
Humour Silver Proof	—	£75
Unity (Floral emblems of Britain) Silver Proof	—	£75
Music Silver Proof	—	£75
Anti-slavery Silver Proof	—	£75
2011 90th Birthday of the Duke of Edinburgh BU	18,730	£12
2011 — Proof	—	£15
2011 — Silver Proof	4,599	£75
2011 — — Piedfort	2,659	£125
2011 — Gold Proof	636	£2000
2011 — Platinum Proof Piedfort	—	£7500
2011 Royal Wedding of William and Catherine BU	250,000	£15
2011 — Silver Proof	26,069	£60
2011 — Gold-plated Silver Proof	7,451	£80
2011 — Silver Proof Piedfort	2,991	£100
2011 — Gold Proof	2,066	£2000
2011 — Platinum Proof Piedfort	—	£5500

DATE	Mintage	UNC
2011 Olympic Countdown (1 year) BU	163,235	£12
2011 — Silver Proof	25,877	£55
2011 — — Piedfort	4,000	£100
2011 — Gold Proof	1,300	£2000
2012 Diamond Jubilee BU	484,775	£15
2012 — Proof	—	£25
2012 — Silver Proof	16,370	£65
2012 — — Piedfort	3,187	£100
2012 — Gold-plated silver proof	12,112	£85
2012 — Gold proof	1,025	£2000
2012 — Platinum Piedfort Proof	20	£5500
2012 Olympic Countdown (Games Time) BU	52,261	£13
2012 — Silver Proof	12,670	£65
2012 — — Piedfort	2,324	£120
2012 — Gold proof	1,007	£2000
2012 Official Olympic BU	315,983	£15
2012 — Silver Proof	20,810	£70
2012 — — Piedfort	5,946	£125
2012 — Gold-plated silver proof	12,112	£85
2012 — Gold proof	1,045	£2000
2012 Official Paralympic BU	—	£15
2012 — Silver Proof	—	£70
2012 — — Piedfort	—	£125
2012 — Gold proof	—	£2000
2013 60th Anniversary of the Queen's Coronation BU	57,262	£15
2013 — Proof	—	£35
2013 — Silver Proof	4,050	£80
2013 — — Piedfort	2,626	£125
2013 — Gold-plated silver proof	2,547	£100
2013 — Gold proof	418	£2000
2013 — Platinum Piedfort Proof	106	£7500
2013 Queen's Portraits, 4 coins each with one of the four portraits, paired with James Butler's Royal Arms. Issued only as sets of 4 in precious metals (see under Proof and Specimen Set section)	—	—
2013 Royal Birth of Prince George (St George & Dragon), Silver Proof	7,460	£150
2013 Christening of Prince George BU	56,014	£15
2013 — Silver Proof	7,264	£80
2013 — — Piedfort	2,251	£160
2013 — Gold Proof	486	£2000
2013 — Platinum Proof Piedfort	38	£7500
2014 300th Anniversary of the death of Queen Anne BU	12,181	£15
2014 — Proof	—	£35
2014 — Silver Proof	2,212	£80
2014 — — Piedfort	636	£160
2014 — Gold-plated Silver Proof	627	£100
2014 — Gold Proof	253	£2000
2014 First Birthday of Prince George Silver Proof	7,451	£85
2014 100th Anniversary of the First World War Outbreak, issued only as set of 6 coins (see under Proof and Specimen Sets)	—	—
2014 Portrait of Britain, issued only as set of 4 coins, with trichromatic colour-printing (see under Proof and Specimen Sets section)	—	—
2015 50th Anniversary of death of Sir Winston Churchill BU	—	£15
2015 — Silver Proof	4,238	£80
2015 — — Piedfort	1,800	£160
2015 — Gold Proof	325	£2000
2015 — Platinum Proof Piedfort	90	£5000
2015 200th Anniversary of the Battle of Waterloo, BU	24,554	£15
2015 — Silver Proof	2,523	£80
2015 — — Piedfort	896	£160
2015 — Gold Proof	273	£2000
2015 First World War 100th Anniversary, continued, issued only as set of 6 coins	807	—
New Portrait		
2015 2nd Birthday of Prince George, Silver Proof	4,009	£85

DATE	Mintage	UNC
2015 Birth of Princess Charlotte, BU	—	£15
2015 — Silver Proof	—	£80
2015 — Gold Proof	500	£2000
2015 Christening of Princess Charlotte, Silver Proof	4,842	£2000
2015 — Gold Proof	350	£80
2015 The Longest Reign, BU	48,848	£15
2015 — Silver Proof	10,249	£80
2015 — — Piedfort	3,171	£175
2015 — Gold Proof	899	£2000
2015 — Platinum Proof Piedfort	88	£5000
2016 Queen's 90th Birthday, BU	74,195	£15
2016 — Proof	—	£25
2016 — Silver Proof	8,947	£80
2016 — — Piedfort	3,099	£160
2016 — Gold Proof	906	£2000
2016 — Platinum Proof Piedfort	81	£4500
2016 Portraits of Britain, issued only as set of 4 coins, with trichromatic colour-printing (see under Proof and Specimen Sets section)	1,098	—
2016 First World War Centenary, continued, issued only as a set of 6 Silver Proof coins	1,916	—
2016 Battle of the Somme, Silver Proof	3,678	£85
2017 Portraits of Britain, issued only as set of 4 coins, with trichromatic colour-printing (see under Proof and Specimen Sets section)	1,500	—
2017 1000th Anniversary of Coronation of King Canute, BU	26,567	£15
2017 — Proof	—	£30
2017 — Silver Proof	2,925	£85
2017 — — Piedfort	1,069	£175
2017 — Gold Proof	150	£2000
2017 Prince Philip, Celebrating a Life of Service, BU	29,097	£15
2017 — Silver Proof	2,574	£85
2017 — — Piedfort	1,250	£155
2017 — Gold Proof	299	£2000
2017 Remembrance Day Poppy	—	£15
2017 — Silver Proof	5,000	£100
2017 — — Piedfort	1,500	£200
2017 First World War Centenary, continued, issued only as set of 6 Silver Proof coins	1,917	—
2017 House of Windsor Centenary, BU	—	£15
2017 — — in pack for Engagement of Prince Harry	5,000	£20
2017 — Proof	—	£30
2017 — Silver Proof	13,000	£85
2017 — — Piedfort	5,500	£185
2017 — Gold Proof	884	£2000
2017 Christmas Tree BU	—	£13
2018 Her Majesty's Sapphire Jubilee, BU	—	£15
2018 — Proof	—	£30
2018 — Silver Proof	8,260	£85
2018 — — Piedfort	2,471	£155
2018 — Gold Proof	648	£2000
2018 70th Birthday of the Prince of Wales BU	—	£15
2018 — Silver Proof	3,500	£85
2018 — — Piedfort	1,000	£155
2018 — Gold Proof	50	£2,500
2018 — Platinum Proof	525	£650
2018 — Platinum Proof Piedfort	70	£5,500
2018 Prince George's 5th Birthday	—	£15
2018 — Proof	—	£18
2018 — Silver Proof	—	£85
2018 — — Piedfort	—	£165
2018 — Gold Proof	650	£2000
2018 Four generations of the Royal Family	—	£15
2018 — Proof	—	£20
2018 — Silver Proof	5,000	£100
2018 — — Piedfort	2,000	£175
2018 — Gold Proof	500	£2000
2018 250 years of the Royal Academy	—	£15
2018 — Silver Proof	2,750	£100

2017 Portrait of Britain, issued only as set of 4 coins, with trichromatic colour-printing.

DATE	Mintage	UNC
2018 Royal Wedding of Prince Harry	12,000	£20
2018 — Proof	—	£25
2018 — Silver Proof	15,000	£100
2018 — — Piedfort	2,220	£175
2018 — Gold Proof	500	£2000
2018 Portraits of Britain, issued only as set of 4 coins, with trichromatic colour-printing (see under Proof and Specimen Sets section)	2,016	—
2018 Stories of War set of six coins (see under Proof and Specimen Sets section)	—	—
2019 The Ceremony of the Keys BU	—	£15
2019 — Silver Proof	4,000	£85
2019 — — Piedfort	1,160	£175
2019 — Gold	385	£2000
2019 The Tower of London 4 coin set BU	—	£85
2019 — Silver Proof	4,000	£350
2019 — — Piedfort	1,160	£650
2019 — Gold	385	£8000
2019 200th Anniversary of the Birth of Queen Victoria BU	—	£15
2019 — Silver Proof	7,500	£85
2019 — — Piedfort	2,750	£175
2019 — Gold Proof	725	£2000
2019 Pride of England BU	—	£13
2019 Centenary of Remembrance BU	—	£17
2019 — Silver Proof	3,240	£100
2019 — — Piedfort	775	£185
2019 — Gold	240	£2500
2020 The Tower of London series—The White Tower BU	—	£13
2020 — Silver Proof	2,500	£85
2020 — — Piedfort	450	£175
2020 — Gold Proof	125	£2500
2020 Reign of George III BU	—	£15
2020 — Silver Proof	2,500	£85
2020 — — Piedfort	550	£175
2020 — Gold Proof	250	£2500
2020 250th Anniversary of William Wordsworth BU	—	£15
2020 — Silver Proof	3,000	£85
2020 — Gold Proof	300	£2500
2020 Tower of London Collection—the Royal Menagerie BU	—	£15
2020 — Silver Proof	1,510	£85
2020 — — Piedfort	410	£175
2020 — Gold Proof	135	£2500
2020 Remembrance Day BU	—	£15
2020 — Silver Proof	1920	£85
2020 — — Piedfort	700	£185
2020 75th Anniversary of the end of World War II BU	—	£15
2020 — Silver Proof	2575	£85
2020 — — Piedfort	565	£175
2020 — Gold Proof	225	£2500
2020 150th Anniversary of the British Red Cross BU	—	£18
2020 — Silver Proof	4000	£850
2020 — — Piedfort	1150	£175
2020 — Gold Proof	250	£2500
2021 Alfred the Great BU	—	£13
2021 — Silver Proof	2,250	£90
2021 — — Piedfort	900	£167.50
2021 — Gold Proof	160	£2590

**See also under "The Queen's Beasts",
"Music Legends" and other series as appropriate.**

DOUBLE SOVEREIGN

As with the Sovereign series Five Pound coins, those listed under this heading bear the Pistrucci St George and Dragon reverse, except where otherwise stated, and are minted in gold. They are, and always have been, legal tender at £2, and have a diameter indentical to that of the base metal Two Pound coins listed further below under a different heading. The denomination does not appear on Double Sovereigns. Most were originally issued as part of Royal Mint sets.

DATE	Mintage	UNC
1980 Proof	10,000	£750
1982 Proof	2,500	£750
1983 Proof	12,500	£750
1985 New Portrait Proof	5,849	£750
1987 Proof	14,301	£750
1988 Proof	12,743	£750
1989 500th Anniversary of the Sovereign. Enthroned portrayal obverse and Crowned shield reverse Proof	2,000	£1200
1990 Proof	4,374	£750
1991 Proof	3,108	£750
1992 Proof	2,608	£750
1993 Proof	2,155	£750
1996 Proof	3,167	£750
1998 New Portrait Proof	4,500	£750
2000 Proof	2,250	£750
2002 Shield reverse Proof	8,000	£750
2003 Proof	2,250	£750
2004 Proof	2,500	£750
2005 Noad's heraldic St George and Dragon reverse Proof	—	£800
2006 Proof	—	£750
2007 Proof	—	£750
2008 Proof	—	£750
2009 Proof	—	£750
2010 Proof	2,750	£750
2011 Proof	2,950	£750
2012 Day's stylised St George and Dragon reverse, BU	60	£1000
2012 − Proof	1,945	£1200
2013 BU	—	£800
2013 Proof	1,895	£800
2014 BU	1,300	£750
2014 Proof	—	£800
2015 Proof	1,100	£700
2015 New Portrait by Jody Clark Proof	1,100	£900
2016 Butler Portrait Proof	925	£900
2017 200th Anniv. of the Sovereign design as 1817 issue	1,200	£1000
2018 Proof	1,600	£1200
2020 BU	—	£850
2020 200th Anniversary of death of George III With GR cypher privy mark Proof	1,100	£1200

Standard reverse

Reverse by Timothy Noad

Reverse by Paul Day

IMPORTANT NOTE:
The prices quoted in this guide are set at August 2021 with the price of gold at £1,300 per ounce and silver £17.30 per ounce—market fluctuations can have a marked effect on the values of modern precious metal coins.
Note: most of the prices given for recent gold issues are the
Royal Mint issue price

TWO POUNDS

This series commenced in 1986 with nickel-brass commemorative coins, with their associated base metal and precious metal BU and proof coins. From 1997 (actually issued in 1998) a thinner bi-metal version commenced with a reverse theme of the advance of technology, and from this date the coin was specifically intended to circulate. This is true also for the parallel issues of anniversary and commemorative Two Pound issues in 1999 and onwards. All have their BU and proof versions, as listed below.

In the case of Gold Proofs, a few have Certificates of Authenticity and/or green boxes of issue describing the coin as a Double Sovereign. All Gold Proofs since 1997 are of bi-metallic gold except for 2001 (red gold with the inner circle coated in yellow gold) and 2002 (Technology issue, uncoated red gold). After 2008 all RM boxes were black for all denominations.

A new definitive design was introduced during 2015 incorporating the Jody Clark portrait and Britannia by Antony Dufort but to date the mintage each year has been relatively low.

NOTE: The counterfeiting of circulation £2 coins has been around for several years but 2015 saw several proof-like base metal designs. Five types are known at present: 2011 (Mary Rose) and 2015 (all four designs).

First bi-metal
standard reverse

DATE	Mintage	UNC
1986 Commonwealth Games	8,212,184	£5
1986 — BU	—	£8
1986 — Proof	59,779	£15
1986 — Silver BU	—	£35
1986 — — Proof	—	£45
1986 — Gold Proof	—	£750
1989 Tercentenary of Bill of Rights.	4,392,825	£10
1989 — BU (issued in folder with Claim of Right)	—	£25
1989 — BU folder	—	£8
1989 — Proof	—	£15
1989 — Silver Proof	—	£35
1989 — — Piedfort	—	£60
1989 Tercentenary of Claim of Right (issued in Scotland)	381,400	£25
1989 — BU (see above)	—	£30
1989 — Proof	—	£35
1989 — Silver Proof	—	£45
1989 — — Piedfort	—	£65
1994 Tercentenary of the Bank of England	1,443,116	£8
1994 — BU	—	£10
1994 — Proof	—	£30
1994 — Silver Proof	27,957	£35
1994 — — Piedfort	9,569	£65
1994 — Gold Proof	—	£750
1994 — — with Double Sovereign obverse (no denomination) —		£1000
1995 50th Anniversary of End of WWII.	4,394,566	£8
1995 — BU	—	£10
1995 — Proof	—	£12
1995 — Silver Proof	35,751	£35
1995 — — Piedfort	—	£65
1995 — Gold Proof	—	£750
1995 50th Anniversary of The United Nations	1,668,575	£8
1995 — BU	—	£10
1995 — Proof	—	£12
1995 — Silver Proof	—	£40
1995 — — Piedfort	—	£65
1995 — Gold Proof	—	£750
1996 European Football Championships.	5,195,350	£8
1996 — BU	—	£10
1996 — Proof	—	£12
1996 — Silver Proof	25,163	£40
1996 — — Piedfort	7,634	£65
1996 — Gold Proof	—	£750
1997 Technology Standard rev. **First Bi-metallic issue**	13,734,625	£5
1997 — BU	—	£8
1997 — Proof	—	£12
1997 — Silver Proof	29,910	£35
1997 — — Piedfort	16,000	£65
1997 — Gold Proof (red (outer) and yellow (inner) 22ct)	—	£750

DATE	Mintage	UNC
1998 *New Portrait by Ian Rank-Broadley*	—	£4
1998 BU	91,110,375	£8
1998 Proof	—	£12
1998 Silver Proof	19,978	£35
1998 — — Piedfort	7,646	£60
1999 Technology Standard rev.	33,719,000	£4
1999 Rugby World Cup	4,933,000	£6
1999 — BU	—	£10
1999 — Silver Proof (gold plated ring)	9,665	£45
1999 — — — Piedfort (Hologram)	10,000	£85
1999 — Gold Proof	—	£750
2000 Technology Standard rev.	25,770,000	£4
2000 — BU	—	£6
2000 — Proof	—	£10
2000 — Silver Proof	—	£40
2001 Technology Standard rev.	34,984,750	£4
2001 — BU	—	£5
2001 — Proof	—	£10
2001 Marconi	4,558,000	£5
2001 — BU	—	£8
2001 — Proof	—	£10
2001 — Silver Proof (gold plated ring)	11,488	£40
2001 — — — Reverse Frosting (issued in set with Canada $5)	—	£65
2001 — — — Piedfort	6,759	£65
2001 — Gold Proof	—	£750
2002 Technology Standard rev.	13,024,750	£4
2002 — BU	—	£6
2002 — Proof	—	£10
2002 — Gold Proof (red 22ct)	—	£750
2002 Commonwealth Games, Scotland	771,750	£15
2002 — Wales	558,500	£15
2002 — Northern Ireland	485,500	£30
2002 — England	650,500	£15
2002 — BU (issued in set of 4)	—	£60
2002 — Proof (issued in set of 4)	—	£75
2002 — Silver Proof (issued in set of 4)	—	£250
2002 — — — Piedfort (painted) (issued in set of 4)	—	£350
2002 — Gold Proof (issued in set of 4)	—	£2500
2003 Technology Standard rev.	17,531,250	£4
2003 — BU	—	£8
2003 — Proof	—	£12
2003 DNA Double Helix	4,299,000	£5
2003 — BU	41,568	£8
2003 — Proof	—	£10
2003 — Silver Proof (Gold-plated ring)	11,204	£40
2003 — — — Piedfort	8,728	£65
2003 — Gold Proof	3,237	£750
2004 Technology Standard rev.	11,981,500	£4
2004 — BU	—	£6
2004 — Proof	—	£12
2004 Trevithick Steam Locomotive	5,004,500	£5
2004 — BU	56,871	£8
2004 — Proof	—	£10
2004 — Silver BU	1,923	£25
2004 — — Proof (Gold-plated ring)	10,233	£45
2004 — — — Piedfort	5,303	£65
2004 — Gold Proof	1,500	£750
2005 Technology Standard rev.	3,837,250	£4
2005 — BU	—	£6
2005 — Proof	—	£8
2005 Gunpowder Plot	5,140,500	£5
2005 — BU	—	£8
2005 — Proof	—	£10
2005 — Silver Proof	4,394	£40
2005 — — — Piedfort	4,585	£65
2005 — Gold Proof	914	£750

DATE	Mintage	UNC
2005 End of World War II	10,191,000	£5
2005 — BU	—	£8
2005 — Silver Proof	21,734	£40
2005 — — — Piedfort	4,798	£65
2005 — Gold Proof	2,924	£750
2006 Technology Standard rev.	16,715,000	£4
2006 — Proof	—	£6
2006 Brunel, The Man (Portrait)	7,928,250	£5
2006 — BU	—	£6
2006 — Proof	—	£10
2006 — Silver Proof	7,251	£40
2006 — — — Piedfort	3,199	£65
2006 — Gold Proof	1,071	£750
2006 Brunel, His Achievements (Paddington Station)	7,452,250	£5
2006 — BU	—	£6
2006 — Proof	—	£10
2006 — Silver Proof	5,375	£40
2006 — — — Piedfort	3,018	£65
2006 — Gold Proof	746	£750
2007 Technology Standard rev.	10,270,000	£4
2007 — Proof	—	£8
2007 Tercentenary of the Act of Union	7,545,000	£5
2007 BU	—	£6
2007 — Proof	—	£8
2007 — Silver Proof	8,310	£45
2007 — — — Piedfort	4,000	£65
2007 — Gold Proof	750	£750
2007 Bicentenary of the Abolition of the Slave Trade	8,445,000	£6
2007 — BU	—	£8
2007 — Proof	—	£10
2007 — Silver Proof	7,095	£45
2007 — — — Piedfort	3,990	£65
2007 — Gold Proof	1,000	£750
2008 Technology Standard rev.	15,346,000	£4
2008 — BU	—	£6
2008 — Proof	—	£12
2008 Centenary of 4th Olympiad, London	910,000	£8
2008 — BU	—	£12
2008 — Proof	—	£15
2008 — Silver Proof	6,841	£45
2008 — — — Piedfort	1,619	£70
2008 — Gold Proof	1,908	£750
2008 Olympic Games Handover Ceremony	853,000	£8
2008 — BU	47,765	£10
2008 — Silver Proof	30,000	£45
2008 — — — Piedfort	3,000	£75
2008 — Gold Proof	3,250	£750
2009 Technology Standard rev.	8,775,000	£4
2009 — BU	—	£5
2009 — Proof	—	£10
2009 — Silver Proof	—	£45
2009 250th Anniversary of birth of Robert Burns	3,253,000	£5
2009 — BU	120,223	£8
2009 — Proof	—	£12
2009 — Silver Proof	9,188	£45
2009 — — — Piedfort	3,500	£70
2009 — Gold Proof	1,000	£750
2009 200th Anniversary of birth of Charles Darwin	3,903,000	£5
2009 — BU	119,713	£8
2009 — Proof	—	£12
2009 — Silver Proof	9,357	£45
2009 — — — Piedfort	3,282	£70
2009 — Gold Proof	1,000	£750
2010 Technology Standard rev.	6,890,000	£4
2010 — BU	—	£8
2010 — Proof	—	£12

DATE	Mintage	UNC
2010 — Silver Proof	—	£40
2010 Florence Nightingale 150 Years of Nursing	6,175,000	£5
2010 — BU..	73,160	£10
2010 — Proof	—	£12
2010 — Silver Proof	5,117	£50
2010 – — - Piedfort...	2,770	£75
2010 — Gold Proof..	472	£750
2011 Technology Standard rev.	24,375,000	£4
2011 — BU	—	£5
2011 — Proof	—	£12
2011 — Silver Proof	—	£35
2011 500th Anniversary of the Mary Rose	1,040,000	£10
2011 — BU..	53,013	£12
2011 — Proof	—	£15
2011 — Silver Proof	6,618	£50
2011 — — Piedfort	2,680	£75
2011 — Gold Proof..	692	£750
2011 400th Anniversary of the King James Bible	975,000	£9
2011 — BU..	56,268	£10
2011 — Proof	—	£15
2011 — Silver Proof	4,494	£45
2011 — — — Piedfort	2,394	£75
2011 — Gold Proof..	355	£750
2012 Technology Standard rev.	3,900,000	£4
2012 — BU..	—	£6
2012 — Proof	—	£12
2012 — Silver Proof	—	£30
2012 — Gold Proof..	—	£750
2012 200th Anniversary of birth of Charles Dickens ...	8,190,000	£5
2012 — BU..	15,035	£11
2012 — Proof	—	£12
2012 — Silver Proof	2,631	£45
2012 — — — Piedfort	1,279	£75
2012 — Gold Proof..	202	£750
2012 Olympic Handover to Rio	845,000	£8
2012 — BU..	28,356	£20
2012 Proof	—	£25
2012 — Silver Proof	3,781	£85
2012 — — — Piedfort	2,000	£120
2012 — Gold Proof..	771	£750
2013 Technology Standard rev.	15,860,250	£4
2013 — BU..	—	£6
2013 — Proof	—	£12
2013 — Silver Proof	—	£65
2013 — Gold Proof..	—	£750
2013 150th Anniversary of the London Underground, Roundel design	1,560,000	£6
2013 — BU..	11,647	£12
2013 — Proof	—	£18
2013 — Silver Proof	3,389	£50
2013 — — — Piedfort	162	£100
2013 — Gold Proof..	132	£750
2013 150th Anniversary of the London Underground, Train design..	1,690,000	£6
2013 — BU..	11,647	£12
2013 — Proof	—	£18
2013 — Silver Proof	4,246	£50
2013 — — — Piedfort	186	£100
2013 — Gold Proof..	140	£750
2013 350th Anniversary of the Guinea	2,990,000	£5
2013 — BU..	10,340	£12
2013 — Proof	—	£18
2013 — Silver Proof	1,640	£50
2013 — — — Piedfort	969	£100
2013 — Gold Proof..	284	£750

DATE	Mintage	UNC	
2014 Technology Standard rev.	18,200,000	£4	
2014 — BU	—	£10	
2014 — Proof	—	£25	
2014 — Silver Proof	—	£55	
2014 100th Anniversary of First World War Outbreak	5,720,000	£4	
2014 — BU	40,557	£10	
2014 — Proof	—	£20	
2014 — Silver Proof	4,983	£50	
2014 — — Piedfort	2,496	£100	
2014 — Gold Proof	—	£750	
2014 500th Anniversary of Trinity House	3,705,000	£5	
2014 — BU	10,521	£12	
2014 — Proof	—	£20	
2014 — Silver Proof	1,285	£50	
2014 — — Piedfort	652	£100	
2014 — Gold Proof	204	£750	
2015 Technology Standard rev.	35,360,058	£4	
2015 — BU	39,009	£10	
2015 — Proof	3,930	£20	
2015 — Silver Proof	1,512	£50	
2015 — Gold Proof	406	£750	
2015 Anniversary of First World War—Royal Navy	650,000	£9	
2015 — BU	39,009	£10	
2015 — Proof	—	£20	
2015 — Silver Proof	3,030	£50	
2015 — — Piedfort	1,512	£100	
2015 — Gold Proof	406	£750	
2015 800th Anniversary of Magna Carta	1,495,000	£10	*Britannia standard reverse*
2015 — BU	32,818	£15	
2015 — Proof	—	£20	
2015 — Silver Proof	2,995	£50	
2015 — — Piedfort	1,988	£100	
2015 — Gold Proof	399	£750	

New Portrait by Jody Clark

	Mintage	UNC	
2015 — Silver Proof	—	£50	
2015 — — Piedfort	—	£100	
2015 — Gold Proof	—	£750	
2015 Britannia—**the new standard reverse design**	650,000	£8	
2015 — BU	—	£10	
2015 — Proof	—	£20	
2015 — Silver Proof	—	£50	
2015 — Gold Proof	—	£750	
2015 — Platinum Proof	—	£900	
2016 Britannia Standard rev.	2,925,000	£5	
2016 — BU	—	£10	
2016 — Proof	—	£20	
2016 — Silver Proof	—	£50	
2016 400th Anniversary Shakespeare's death, Comedies	4,355,000	£4	
2016 — — BU	—	£10	
2016 — — Proof	—	£20	
2016 — — Silver Proof	951	£50	
2016 — — — Piedfort	533	£125	
2016 — — Gold Proof	152	£750	
2016 — Tragedies	5,695,000	£4	
2016 — — BU	—	£10	
2016 — — Proof	—	£20	
2016 — — Silver Proof	1,004	£50	
2016 — — — Piedfort	679	£125	
2016 — — Gold Proof	209	£750	
2016 — Histories	4,615,000	£4	
2016 — — BU	—	£10	
2016 — — Proof	—	£20	
2016 — — Silver Proof	965	£50	

DATE	Mintage	UNC
2016 — — — — Piedfort..	624	£125
2016 — — Gold Proof...	156	£750
2016 350th Anniversary of Great Fire of London	5,135,000	£4
2016 — BU..	23,215	£10
2016 — Proof	—	£20
2016 — Silver Proof	1,649	£50
2016 — — Piedfort...	1,356	£125
2016 — Gold Proof..	259	£750
2016 Anniversary of First World War—Army	9,550,000	£4
2016 — BU..	19,066	£10
2016 — Proof	—	£20
2016 — Silver Proof	1,703	£50
2016 — — Piedfort...	931	£125
2016 — Gold Proof..	279	£750

2017 Britannia Standard rev. BU..............................	—	£10
2017 — Proof	—	£20
2017 — Silver Proof	—	£50
2017 — Gold Proof..	—	£750
2017 Anniversary of First World War—Aviation BU.....	55,840	£12
2017 — Proof	—	£20
2017 — Silver Proof	7,000	£75
2017 — — Piedfort...	1,528	£125
2017 — Gold Proof..	634	£750
2017 Jane Austen BU...	54,729	£12
2017 — Proof	—	£20
2017 — Silver Proof	7,498	£75
2017 — — Piedfort...	2,125	£125
2017 — Gold Proof..	884	£800

2018 Britannia Standard rev.	—	£5
2018 —BU..	—	£10
2018 — Proof	—	£20
2018 — Silver Proof	—	£50
2018 — Gold Proof..	—	£750
2018 Bicentenary of Mary Shelley's "Frankenstein" BU	—	£15
2018 — Proof	—	£25
2018 — Silver Proof	—	£50
2018 — Gold Proof..	—	£750
2018 Journey to Armistice BU	—	£12
2018 — Proof	—	£20
2018 — Silver Proof	5,000	£50
2018 — — Piedfort...	2,500	£125
2018 — Gold Proof..	750	£750
2018 Centenary of the RAF BU.................................	—	£15
2018 — Proof	—	£25
2018 — Silver Proof	7,500	£50
2018 — — Piedfort...	3,000	£125
2018 — Gold Proof..	1,000	£750

2018 250th Anniversary of Captain Cook's "Voyage of Discovery"—I BU...	—	£15
2018 — Proof	—	£25
2018 — Silver Proof	4,795	£50
2018 — — Piedfort...	4,000	£125
2018 —Gold Proof...	340	£750
2019 Britannia Standard rev.	—	£5
2019 — BU...	—	£10
2019 — Proof	—	£20
2019 — Silver Proof	—	£50
2019 — Gold Proof..	—	£750
2019 D-Day: 75th Anniversary BU	—	£10
2019 — Proof	—	£25
2019 — Silver Proof	8,750	£75
2019 — — Piedfort...	3,010	£125
2019 — Gold Proof..	750	£850
2019 Captain Cook II BU..	—	£15
2019 — Proof	—	£25
2019 — Silver Proof	5,000	£85

DATE	Mintage	UNC
2019 — — — Piedfort	4,000	£125
2019 — Gold Proof	350	£850
2019 Samuel Pepys BU	—	£10
2019 — Proof	—	£25
2019 — Silver Proof	3,500	£85
2019 — — Piedfort	2,019	£125
2019 — Gold Proof	350	£850
2019 260th Anniversary of Wedgwood BU	—	£10
2019 — Proof	—	£25
2019 — Silver Proof	4,500	£100
2019 — — Piedfort	2,250	£125
2019 — Gold Proof	350	£850
2020 Britannia Standard rev.	—	£5
2020 — BU	—	£10
2020 — Proof	—	£20
2020 — Silver Proof	—	£85
2020 — Gold Proof	—	£850
2020 Captain Cook III BU	—	£10
2020 — Proof	—	£25
2020 — Silver Proof	4,795	£85
2019 — — Piedfort	2,250	£125
2020 — Gold Proof	340	£1000
2020 VE Day Anniversary	—	£5
2020 — BU	—	£10
2020 — Proof	—	£25
2020 — Silver Proof	—	£85
2020 — — — Piedfort	—	£150
2020 — Gold Proof	—	£850
2020 100 years of Agatha Christie	—	£5
2020 — BU	—	£10
2020 — Proof	—	£25
2020 — Silver Proof	—	£85
2020 — — — Piedfort	—	£150
2020 — Gold Proof	—	£850
2020 Anniversary of the sailing of the "Mayflower"	—	£5
2020 — BU	—	£10
2020 — Proof	—	£25
2020 — Silver Proof	—	£85
2020 — — — Piedfort	—	£150
2020 — Gold Proof	—	£1155
2021 Celebrating the life and work of H. G. Wells	—	£5
2021 — BU	—	£10
2021 — Proof	—	£25
2021 — Silver Proof	3135	£72.50
2021 — — Piedfort	985	£117.50
2021 — Gold Proof	330	£1095
2021 250th Anniversary of the birth of Sir. Walter Scott	—	£5
2021 — BU	—	£10
2021 — Proof	—	£25
2021 — Silver Proof	1771	£72.50
2021 — — Piedfort	771	£117.50
2021— Gold Proof	175	£1095

Note: The silver editions are silver centres with silver outers plated with gold.
The gold issues are 22ct yellow gold centres with 22ct red gold outers.

SOVEREIGN

All are minted in gold, bear the Pistrucci St George and Dragon reverse except where stated, and are legal tender at one pound. From 2009 there is no streamer behind St George's Helmet in the Pistrucci design.

DATE	Mintage	UNC
1974..	5,002,566	£325
1976..	4,150,000	£325
1976 Brilliant Proof...	—	£10000
1978..	6,550,000	£325
1979..	9,100,000	£325
1979 Proof..	50,000	£325
1980..	5,100,000	£325
1980 Proof..	91,200	£375
1981..	5,000,000	£325
1981 Proof..	32,960	£375
1982..	2,950,000	£325
1982 Proof..	22,500	£375
1983 Proof	21,250	£375
1984 Proof	19,975	£375
1985 **New portrait** Proof	17,242	£450
1986 Proof	17,579	£375
1987 Proof	22,479	£375
1988 Proof..	18,862	£375
1989 500th Anniversary of the Sovereign—Details as Five Pounds (Sov. Series). Proof	23,471	£1250
1990 Proof	8,425	£450
1991 Proof	7,201	£450
1992 Proof	6,854	£450
1993 Proof	6,090	£450
1994 Proof	7,165	£450
1995 Proof	9,500	£450
1996 Proof	9,110	£450
1997 Proof	9,177	£450
1998 **New Portrait** Proof	11,349	£550
1999 Proof	11,903	£450
2000 (first Unc issue since 1982)	129,069	£375
2000 Proof	12,159	£550
2001..	49,462	£325
2001 Proof..	10,000	£500
2002 Golden Jubilee Shield Rev. ("bullion")...............	74,263	£375
2002 Proof..	20,500	£750
2003 ("bullion")...	43,208	£350
2003 Proof..	12,433	£500
2004 ("bullion")...	30,688	£350
2004 Proof..	10,175	£450
2005 Timothy Noad's heraldic St George and Dragon	75,542	£550
2005 — Proof	12,500	£750
2006 ("bullion")...	—	£350
2006 Proof..	9,195	£500
2007 ("bullion")...	75,000	£325
2007 Proof..	8,199	£500
2008 ("bullion")...	35,000	£350
2008 Proof..	12,500	£475
2009 ("bullion")...	75,000	£350
2009 Proof..	9,770	£475
2010 ("bullion")...	243,986	£325
2010 Proof..	8,828	£525
2011 ("bullion")...	250,000	£350
2011 Proof..	15,000	£425

Standard reverse

500th Anniversary reverse

Golden Jubilee Shield reverse

Noad modern reverse

DATE	Mintage	UNC
2012 Paul Day's St George and Dragon BU "bullion".	250,000	£500
2012 — Proof	5,501	£1250
2013 BU ("bullion")	2,695	£350
2013 Proof	8,243	£475
2013 With "I" mintmark, minted by MMTC-PAMP, Haryana, India,		
under Licence from, and supervision of, the Royal Mint	—	£450
2014 BU ("bullion"	15,000	£350
2014 Proof)	9,725	£500
2014 BU ("bullion") with "I" mintmark	—	£450
2015 BU ("bullion")	10,000	£350
2015 Proof	4,456	£475
2015 **New Portrait** by Jody Clark BU	10,000	£400
2015— Proof	7,494	£475
2016 BU ("bullion")	1,251	£350
2016 Queen's 90th Birthday, Butler portrait. Proof	7,995	£575
2017 200th Anniversary of the Sovereign. Original		
1817 "Garter" design. Proof-like	13,500	£575
2017 — Piedfort	3,750	£1500
2017 BU with 200 Privy mark	—	£500
2017 Royal Platinum Wedding Strike on the day (no		
privy mark)	1,793	£850
2017 BU ("bullion")	—	£350
2018 BU ("bullion")	—	£350
2018 Proof	10,500	£500
2018 — Piedfort	2,675	£1200
2019 BU Matt finish	20,500	£475
2019 Proof	9,500	£550
2020 BU ("bullion")	—	£350
2020 200th Anniversary of death of George III		
With GR cypher privy mark	9,845	£650
2020 Matt finish, plain edge	—	£750
2021 BU ("bullion")	—	£350
2021 Proof with 95 in crown privy mark	9,850	£600

For coins struck on the day of a special event see the table overleaf.

Note that coins struck on the actual day of the event are always accompanied by a certificate of authenticity from the Royal Mint. With many of these "Strike on the day" coins this is the only means of identification as they do not all carry special privy marks. Only those with these privy marks are listed here.

Day's stylised reverse

200th Anniversary reverse

2020 Withdrawal from the EU

2020 Anniversary of VE Day

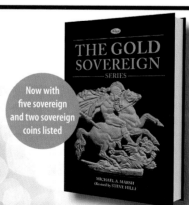

SOVEREIGNS STRUCK ON THE DAY

To commemorate certain special occasions the Royal Mint strike a limited number of sovereigns on the day of the event. Listed below are the events so marked and the quantities issued. Some are only identified by a special certificate issued with the coin, but the later issues are marked with a special privy mark appropriate to the occasion. The first strike on the day was to mark the Diamond Jubilee of Her Majesty the Queen on June 2, 2012, followed by the 60th anniversary of the Coronation the following year. Since then various occasions have been celebrated and this has generated a great deal of interest among collectors, with the generally low quantities struck reflected in their values if kept in their original box accompanied by the certificate.

Date	Occasion struck	Quantity	Type	Privy mark
June 2, 2012	Diamond Jubilee of Her Majesty the Queen	1,990	BU	—
June 2, 2013	60th anniversary of the Coronation	900	BU	—
July 22, 2013	Birth of Prince George	2,013	BU	—
July 22, 2014	First birthday of Prince George	398	BU	—
May 2, 2015	Birth of Princess Charlotte	743	BU	—
July 22, 2015	Second birthday of Prince George	301	BU (Jody Clark obv.)	—
June 11, 2016	90th birthday of Her Majesty the Queen	499	BU	—
June 2, 2017	65th anniversary of the accession of Her Majesty the Queen	739	BU	—
July 1, 2017	200th anniversary of the issue of the 1817 sovereign	1,793	BU, plain edge	—
November 20, 2017	Platinum Wedding of Her Majesty the Queen and Prince Philip	745	BU	—
June 2, 2018	65th anniversary of the Coronation	323	BU, plain edge	65
July 22, 2018	5th birthday of Prince George	457	BU, plain edge	—
May 24, 2019	200th anniversary of birth of Queen Victoria	Limit 650	Matt, plain edge	VR
August 26, 2019	200th anniversary of birth of Prince Albert	Limit 650	Matt, plain edge	VA
January 31, 2020	"Brexit" Day	Limit 1,500	Matt, plain edge	Crowned portcullis
May 8, 2020	75th anniversary of VE Day	Limit 750	Matt, plain edge	VE75
August 15, 2020	75th anniversary of the End of WWII	Limit 750	Matt, plain edge	VJ75
April 21, 2021*	The 95th birthday of Her Majesty the Queen	Limit 1,295	Matt, plain edge	95 in Crown

* Owing to the death of HRH Prince Philip this occasion was postponed until June 12, Her Majesty's official birthday.

In addition to the above, the Royal Mint have also adopted the policy of striking other denominations on appropriate dates and these are offered as "Strike on the Day" coins. It has been decided that these are outside of the scope of this publication and are therefore not recorded. For more information visit the Royal Mint website at www.royalmint.com

---

IMPORTANT NOTE:
The prices quoted in this guide are set at August 2021 with the price of gold at £1,300 per ounce and silver £17.30 per ounce—market fluctuations can have a marked effect on the values of modern precious metal coins.

HALF SOVEREIGN

Legal Tender at 50 pence, otherwise the notes for the Sovereign apply. From 2009 the exergue in the Pistrucci design is larger in area, and the initials B.P. are absent. From 2011, however, the initials were restored.

DATE	Mintage	UNC
1980 Proof only	86,700	£225
1982	2,500,000	£175
1982 Proof	21,590	£220
1983 Proof	19,710	£220
1984 Proof	19,505	£220
1985 New portrait Proof	15,800	£220
1986 Proof	17,075	£220
1987 Proof	20,687	£220
1988 Proof	18,266	£220
1989 500th Anniversary of the Sovereign—details as Five Pounds (Sov. Series) Proof	21,824	£550
1990 Proof	7,889	£225
1991 Proof	6,076	£225
1992 Proof	5,915	£225
1993 Proof	4,651	£225
1994 Proof	7,167	£225
1995 Proof	7,500	£225
1996 New Portrait Proof	7,340	£225
1997 Proof	9,177	£225
1998 Proof	7,496	£225
1999 Proof	9,403	£225
2000	146,822	£175
2000 Proof	9,708	£200
2001	98,763	£175
2001 Proof	7,500	£200
2002 Golden Jubilee Shield reverse ("bullion")	61,347	£175
2002 Proof	—	£200
2003 ("bullion")	47,805	£175
2003 Proof	—	£200
2004 ("bullion")	32,479	£175
2004 Proof	—	£200
2005 Timothy Noad's heraldic St George and Dragon	—	£275
2005 — Proof	—	£300
2006 ("bullion")	—	£175
2006 Proof	—	£200
2006 ("bullion")	—	£175
2007 Proof	—	£200
2008 ("bullion")	—	£175
2008 Proof	—	£200
2009 ("bullion")	—	£175
2009 Proof	—	£200
2010 ("bullion")	16,485	£175
2010 Proof	—	£200
2011 ("bullion")	—	£175
2011 Proof	—	£200
2012 Paul Day's stylised reverse. Diamond Jubilee BU	—	£175
2012 — Proof	—	£225
2013 BU "bullion"	—	£175
2013 Proof	—	£200
2014 BU "bullion"	—	£175
2014 Proof	—	£225
2014 BU "bullion" with "I" mintmark	—	£200
2015 BU "bullion"	500	£175
2015 Proof	1,704	£300
2015 New Jody Clark portrait. Proof	—	£300
2016 BU "bullion"	472	£175
2016 Queen's 90th Birthday, Butler portrait. Proof	1,995	£300

Standard reverse

500th Anniversary reverse

Golden Jubilee Shield reverse

Timothy Noad's Heraldic reverse

Paul Day's Diamond Jubilee reverse

227

DATE	Mintage	UNC
2017 200th Anniversary of the Sovereign. Original 1817 "Garter" design. Proof-like..............................	1,817	£350
2017 With 200 Privy mark	—	£500
2018 BU "bullion"..	—	£175
2018 Proof with 65 privy mark	2,500	£225
2019 BU Matt finish..	4,620	£225
2019 Proof..	—	£250
2020 200th Anniversary of death of George III With GR cypher privy mark.....................................	3,910	£280
2021 Proof with 95 privy mark	3,260	£315

200th Anniversary reverse

QUARTER SOVEREIGN

Minted in 22ct gold, this denomination was introduced in 2009 in the same style as the rest of the sovereign series.

DATE	Mintage	UNC
2009 ("bullion")..	50,000	£100
2009 Proof..	13,495	£150
2010 ("bullion")..	250,000	£100
2010 Proof..	6,007	£150
2011 ("bullion")..	50,000	£100
2011 Proof..	7,764	£150
2012 Paul Day's stylised reverse Diamond Jubilee.....	137	£175
2012 — Proof...	7,579	£200
2013 ("bullion")..	—	£100
2013 Proof..	1,729	£150
2014 ("bullion")..	—	£100
2014 Proof..	1,696	£150
2015 ("bullion")..	4,600	£125
2015 Proof..	1,808	£145
2015 Jody Clark portrait Proof	550	£155
2016 Butler portrait Proof...	1,727	£220
2017 200th Anniversary Proof....................................	5,100	£200
2018 ("bullion")..	—	£125
2018 Proof with 65 privy mark	—	£175
2019 BU Matt finish..	1,750	£165
2019 Proof...	—	£200
2020 200th Anniversary of death of George III With GR cypher privy mark, proof	—	£200
2021 Proof with 95 privy mark	1,700	£200

ONE POUND

Introduced into circulation in 1983 to replace the £1 note, the original, £1 coins are minted in nickel-brass unless otherwise stated. The reverse changed yearly until 2008, and until 2008 the Royal Arms was the "definitive" version. 2008 also saw the introduction of the Matthew Dent Uncrowned Shield of the Royal Arms, a new "definitive", and this reverse appeared in 2008 and every year until 2017. A Capital Cities Series of two coins each year for two years commenced in 2010. From 2013 a further 4-coin series over two years was issued, portraying two floral emblems associated with each of the four countries making up the United Kingdom. Collectors and others should be aware of the many different counterfeit £1 coin versions that circulated up until 2017, a high proportion of which do not have matching obverses and reverses although many do. These original £1 coins have now been withdrawn from circulation. A 12-sided bi-metallic coin replaced the round £1 coin in 2017 which incorporates several security features to help defeat the counterfeiters.

DATE	Mintage	UNC
1983 Royal Arms	443,053,510	£3
1983 — BU	1,134,000	£5
1983 — Proof	107,800	£8
1983 — Silver Proof	50,000	£35
1983 — — Piedfort	10,000	£85
1984 Scottish Thistle	146,256,501	£3
1984 — BU	199,430	£6
1984 — Proof	106,520	£8
1984 — Silver Proof	44,855	£35
1984 — — Piedfort	15,000	£75
1985 **New portrait.** Welsh Leek	228,430,749	£3
1985 — BU	213,679	£5
1985 — Proof	102,015	£6
1985 — Silver Proof	50,000	£38
1985 — — Piedfort	15,000	£75
1986 Northern Ireland Flax	10,409,501	£3
1986 — BU	—	£6
1986 — Proof	—	£7
1986 — Silver Proof	37,958	£38
1986 — — Piedfort	15,000	£75
1987 English Oak	39,298,502	£3
1987 — BU	—	£5
1987 — Proof	—	£8
1987 — Silver Proof	50,000	£38
1987 — — Piedfort	15,000	£75
1988 Crowned Shield Of The Royal Arms	7,118,825	£5
1988 — BU	—	£7
1988 — Proof	—	£8
1988 — Silver Proof	50,000	£38
1988 — — Piedfort	10,000	£75
1989 Scottish Thistle	70,580,501	£4
1989 — BU	—	£6
1989 — Proof	—	£9
1989 — Silver Proof	22,275	£38
1989 — — Piedfort	10,000	£75
1990 Welsh Leek	—	£4
1990 — BU	97,269,302	£6
1990 — Proof	—	£7
1990 — Silver Proof	23,277	£38
1991 Northern Ireland Flax	38,443,575	£3
1991 — BU	—	£6
1991 — Proof	—	£9
1991 — Silver Proof	22,922	£38

1983, 1993, 1998, 2003
EDGE: **DECUS ET TUTAMEN**

1984, 1989
NEMO ME IMPUNE LACESSIT

1985, 1990
PLEIDIOL WYF I'M GWLAD

1986, 1991
DECUS ET TUTAMEN

1987, 1992
DECUS ET TUTAMEN

DATE	Mintage	UNC
1992 English Oak	36,320,487	£3
1992 — BU	—	£6
1992 — Proof	—	£7
1992 — Silver Proof	13,065	£38
1993 Royal Arms	114,744,500	£3
1993 — BU	—	£6
1993 — Proof	—	£7
1993 — Silver Proof	16,526	£35
1993 — — Piedfort	12,500	£55
1994 Scottish Lion	29,752,525	£4
1994 — BU	—	£6
1994 — Proof	—	£8
1994 — Silver Proof	25,000	£35
1994 — — Piedfort	11,722	£55
1995 Welsh Dragon	34,503,501	£3
1995 — BU	—	£6
1995 — — (Welsh)	—	£7
1995 — Proof	—	£10
1995 — Silver Proof	27,445	£35
1995 — — Piedfort	8,458	£65
1996 Northern Ireland Celtic Cross	89,886,000	£4
1996 — BU	—	£6
1996 — Proof	—	£7
1996 — Silver Proof	25,000	£35
1996 — — Piedfort	10,000	£55
1997 English Lions	57,117,450	£4
1997 — BU	—	£6
1997 — Proof	—	£7
1997 — Silver Proof	20,137	£35
1997 — — Piedfort	10,000	£55
1998 **New portrait.** Royal Arms. BU	—	£15
1998 — Proof	—	£20
1998 — Silver Proof	13,863	£35
1998 — — Piedfort	7,894	£50
1999 Scottish Lion. BU	—	£15
1999 — Proof	—	£20
1999 — Silver Proof	16,328	£35
1999 — — Reverse Frosting	—	£45
1999 — — Piedfort	9,975	£60
2000 Welsh Dragon	109,496,500	£3
2000 — BU	—	£6
2000 — Proof	—	£8
2000 — Silver Proof	15,913	£35
2000 — — Reverse Frosting	—	£45
2000 — — Piedfort	9,994	£55
2001 Northern Ireland Celtic Cross.	63,968,065	£3
2001 — BU	58,093,731	£6
2001 — Proof	—	£8
2001 — Silver Proof	11,697	£35
2001 — — Reverse Frosting	—	£45
2001 — — Piedfort	8,464	£50
2002 English Lions	77,818,000	£3
2002 — BU	—	£5
2002 — Proof	—	£8
2002 — Silver Proof	17,693	£35
2002 — — Reverse Frosting	—	£45
2002 — — Piedfort	6,599	£50
2002 — Gold Proof	—	£450
2003 Royal Arms	61,596,500	£4
2003 — BU	23,760	£6
2003 — Proof	—	£10
2003 — Silver Proof	15,830	£35
2003 — — Piedfort	9,871	£50

1988
DECUS ET TUTAMEN

1994, 1999
NEMO ME IMPUNE LACESSIT

1995, 2000
PLEIDIOL WYF I'M GWLAD

1996, 2001
DECUS ET TUTAMEN

1997, 2002
DECUS ET TUTAMEN

2004
PATTERNED EDGE

DATE	Mintage	UNC
2004 Forth Railway Bridge	39,162,000	£4
2004 — BU	24,014	£6
2004 — Proof	—	£10
2004 — Silver Proof	11,470	£35
2004 — — — Piedfort	7,013	£50
2004 — Gold Proof	—	£450
2005 Menai Bridge	99,429,500	£4
2005 — BU	—	£6
2005 — Proof	—	£10
2005 — Silver Proof	8,371	£35
2005 — — — Piedfort	6,007	£55
2005 — Gold Proof	—	£450
2006 Egyptian Arch	38,938,000	£4
2006 — BU	—	£6
2006 — Proof	—	£10
2006 — Silver Proof	14,765	£35
2006 — — — Piedfort	5,129	£50
2006 — Gold Proof	—	£450
2007 Gateshead Millennium Bridge	26,180,160	£4
2007 — BU	—	£6
2007 — Proof	—	£10
2007 — Silver Proof	10,110	£40
2007 — — — Piedfort	5,739	£50
2007 — Gold Proof	—	£450
2008 Royal Arms	3,910,000	£3
2008 — BU	18,336	£6
2008 — Proof	—	£8
2008 — Silver Proof	8,441	£35
2008 — Gold Proof	674	£450
2008 — Platinum Proof	—	£500
2008 A series of 14 different reverses, the 25th Anniversary of the modern £1 coin, Silver Proof with selected gold highlighting on the reverses. the latter being all those used since 1983, the coins being with appropriate edge lettering	—	£450
2008 The same as above, Gold Proof (the 2008 Royal Arms being already listed above)	150	£6250
2008 **New Rev.,** Shield of the Royal Arms, no border beads on Obv.	29,518,000	£3
2008 BU	—	£5
2008 Proof	—	£6
2008 Silver Proof	5,000	£35
2008 Silver Proof Piedfort	2,456	£65
2008 Gold Proof	860	£475
2008 Platinum Proof	—	£600
2009	7,820,000	£2
2009 BU	130,644	£5
2009 Proof	—	£6
2009 Silver Proof	8,508	£38
2009 Gold Proof	540	£600
2010	38,505,000	£2
2010 BU	—	£5
2010 Proof	—	£6
2010 Silver BU	—	£30
2010 — Proof	—	£45
2010 City Series (London)	2,635,000	£3
2010 — BU	66,313	£7
2010 — Proof	—	£9
2010 — Silver Proof	7,693	£45
2010 — — Piedfort	3,682	£65
2010 — Gold Proof	950	£500
2010 City Series (Belfast)	6,205,000	£3
2010 — BU	64,461	£7

2005
PATTERNED EDGE

2006
PATTERNED EDGE

2007
PATTERNED EDGE

2008 (proof sets—silver and gold)
DECUS ET TUTAMEN

2008, 2009, 2010, 2011
DECUS ET TUTAMEN

2011
**Y DDRAIG GOCH
DDYRY CYCHWYN**

DATE	Mintage	UNC
2010 — Proof	—	£9
2010 — Silver Proof	5,805	£45
2010 — — — Piedfort	3,503	£65
2010 — Gold Proof	585	£500
2011	25,415,000	£3
2011 BU	—	£4
2011 Proof	—	£8
2011 Silver BU (in 21st and 18th Birthday cards)	—	£45
2011 — Proof	—	£55
2011 City Series (Cardiff)	1,615,000	£5
2011 — BU	47,933	£7
2011 — Proof	—	£9
2011 — Silver Proof	5,553	£40
2011 — — — Piedfort	1,615	£60
2011 — Gold Proof	524	£500
2011 City Series (Edinburgh)	935,000	£6
2011 — BU	47,896	£7
2011 — Proof	—	£9
2011 — Silver Proof	4,973	£45
2011 — — — Piedfort	2,696	£60
2011 — Gold Proof	499	£500
2012	35,700,030	£3
2012 BU	—	£5
2012 Proof	—	£8
2012 Silver BU (in Silver Baby Gift)	—	£75
2012 Silver Proof	—	£50
2012 — with selective gold plating	—	£55
2012 Gold Proof	—	£500
2013	13,090,500	£3
2013 BU	—	£6
2013 Proof	—	£8
2013 Silver BU	—	£60
2013 Silver Proof	—	£45
2013 Gold Proof	—	£500
2013 Floral Series (England)	5,270,000	£2
2013 — BU	6112	£6
2013 — Proof	—	£10
2013 — Silver Proof	3,334	£45
2013 — — — Piedfort	1,071	£65
2013 — Gold Proof	284	£750
2013 Floral Series (Wales)	5,270,000	£2
2013 — BU	6112	£6
2013 — Proof	—	£10
2013 — Silver Proof	3,094	£45
2013 — — — Piedfort	860	£60
2013 — Gold Proof	274	£750
2013 Royal Coat of Arms (Sewell), Gold Proof	—	£550
2013 Crowned Royal Arms (Gorringe), Gold Proof	—	£550

(The above two coins are part of a set of three, along with the 2013 gold proof, with definitive reverse with Uncrowned Royal Arms (Dent)).

2014	79,305,200	£3
2014 BU	—	£6
2014 Proof	—	£10
2014 Silver BU	—	£50
2014 Silver Proof	—	£55
2014 Floral Series (Scotland)	5,185,000	£2
2014 — BU	3,832	£6
2014 — Proof	—	£10
2014 — Silver Proof	1,540	£45
2014 — — — Piedfort	—	£65
2014 — Gold Proof	154	£850

2011
NISI DOMINUS FRUSTRA

2013 Wales £1 Floral gold proof.

Most £1 coins are also available in precious metals.

2014 Scotland £1 Floral gold proof.

2015

DATE	Mintage	UNC
2014 Floral Series (Northern Ireland)	5,780,000	£2
2014 — BU	—	£6
2014 — Proof	—	£10
2014 — Silver Proof	1,502	£45
2014 — — Piedfort	788	£65
2014 — Gold Proof	166	£850
2015	29,580,000	£3
2015 BU	—	£6
2015 Proof	—	£10
2015 Silver Proof	—	£50
2015 Gold Proof	—	£550
2015 Platinum Proof	—	—
2015 *New Portrait* BU	62,495,640	£3
2015 Proof	—	£10
2015 Silver Proof	7,500	£50
2015 Gold Proof	500	£550
2015 Heraldic Royal Arms	—	£3
2015 — BU	—	£6
2015 — Silver Proof	3,500	£50
2015 — — Piedfort	2,000	£100
2015 — Gold Proof	500	£550
2016 BU	—	£20
2016 Proof	—	£25
2016 Silver Proof	—	£50
2016 The Last Round Pound		
2016 — BU	96,089	£15
2016 — Proof	—	£20
2016 — Silver Proof	7,491	£55
2016 — — Piedfort	2,943	£150
2016 — Gold Proof	499	£650
12-sided coin Nations of the Crown design		
2016	648,936,536	£3
2016 BU	—	£15
2016 BU cross crosslet mm in folder with Last Round £1	10,000	£75
2017	749,616,200	£3
2017 BU	—	£10
2017 Proof	—	£12
2017 Silver Proof	26,000	£100
2017 Silver Proof Piedfort	4,500	£250
2017 Gold Proof	2,008	£650
2017 Platinum Proof	232	£750
2018 BU	—	£10
2018 Proof	—	£12
2018 Silver Proof	—	£100
2018 Silver Proof Piedfort	—	£250
2018 Gold Proof	—	£650
2018 Platinum Proof	250	£750
2019 BU	—	£12
2019 Proof	—	£15
2019 Silver Proof	—	£100
2019 Silver Proof Piedfort	—	£250
2019 Gold Proof	—	£650
2020 BU	—	£12
2020 Proof	—	£15
2020 Silver Proof	—	£100
2020 Silver Proof Piedfort	—	£250
2020 Gold Proof	—	£650
2021 BU	—	£12
2021 Proof	—	£15
2021 Silver Proof	—	£100
2021 Gold Proof	—	£650

2016 The last round pound

12-sided issue with Jody Clark portrait obverse and the reverse designed by 15-year-old David Pearce

FIFTY PENCE

Introduced as legal tender for 10 shillings to replace the banknote of that value prior to decimalisation, coins of the original size are no longer legal tender. Unless otherwise stated, i.e. for commemoratives, the reverse design is of Britannia. The reverse legend of NEW PENCE became FIFTY PENCE from 1982.

The description of "Unc" has been used against some 50 pence pieces dated 2009 and 2011 (for Olympic and Paralympic sports) to distinguish them from coins minted to circulation standard and BU standard, being a standard between the latter two. The uncirculated standard coins have a more even rim than the circulation standard examples, particularly observable on the obverse.

Since the surge of interest in collecting 50p coins prices have increased. The following values are for uncirculated coins. Any found in change will of course have been circulated and will not command such a high premium but the rarer ones will still be worth more than face value.

DATE	Mintage	UNC
1969	188,400,000	£2
1970	19,461,500	£3
1971 Proof	—	£8
1972 Proof	—	£7
1973 Accession to EEC	89,775,000	£3
1973 — Proof	—	£8
1973 — Silver Proof Piedfort	About 24	£3250
1974 Proof	—	£7
1975 Proof	—	£8
1976	43,746,500	£2
1976 Proof	—	£7
1977	49,536,000	£2
1977 Proof	—	£6
1978	72,005,000	£2
1978 Proof	—	£6
1979	58,680,000	£2
1979 Proof	—	£6
1980	89,086,000	£2
1980 Proof	—	£6
1981	74,002,000	£2
1981 Proof	—	£8
1982	51,312,000	£3
1982 Unc	—	£6
1982 Proof	—	£8
1983	62,824,000	£2
1983 Unc	—	£6
1983 Proof	—	£8
1984 BU (only issued in Year Sets)	158,820	£5
1984 Proof	—	£12
1985 *New portrait*	682,103	£2
1985 BU (only issued in Year Sets)	—	£5
1985 Proof	—	£6
1986 BU (only issued in Year Sets)	—	£5
1986 Proof	—	£12
1987 BU (only issued in Year Sets)	—	£4
1987 Proof	—	£12
1988 BU (only issued in Year Sets)	—	£4
1988 Proof	—	£12
1989 BU (only issued in Year Sets)	—	£4
1989 Proof	—	£12
1990 BU (only issued in Year Sets)	—	£4
1990 Proof	—	£12
1991 BU (only issued in Year Sets)	—	£5
1991 Proof	—	£12
1992 BU (only issued in Year Sets)	—	£7

Presidency of the EC Council 1992.

1994

Accession to the EEC 1973.

DATE	Mintage	UNC
1992 Proof	—	£12
1992 Presidency of EC Council and EC accession 20th anniversary (includes 1993 date)	109,000	£60
1992 — BU	—	£75
1992 — Proof	—	£85
1992 — Silver Proof	26,890	£100
1992 — — — Piedfort	10,993	£140
1992 — Gold Proof	—	£550
1993 BU (only issued in Year Sets)	—	£5
1993 Proof	—	£12
1994 50th Anniversary of the Normandy Landings	6,705,520	£3
1994 — BU (also in presentation folder)	—	£8
1994 — Proof	—	£15
1994 — Silver Proof	40,000	£35
1994 — — — Piedfort	10,000	£60
1994 — Gold Proof	—	£500
1995 BU (only issued in Year Sets)	—	£8
1995 Proof	—	£12
1996 BU (only issued in Year Sets)	—	£8
1996 Proof	—	£12
1996 Silver Proof	—	£25
1997 BU	—	£8
1997 Proof	—	£10
1997 Silver Proof	—	£25
1997 *New reduced size*	456,364,100	£2
1997 BU	—	£5
1997 Proof	—	£6
1997 Silver Proof	—	£25
1997 — — Piedfort	—	£35
1998 *New portrait*	64,306,500	£2
1998 BU	—	£5
1998 Proof	—	£8
1998 Presidency and 25th anniversary of EU entry	5,043,000	£3
1998 — BU	—	£5
1998 — Proof	—	£8
1998 — Silver Proof	8,859	£30
1998 — — — Piedfort	8,440	£45
1998 — Gold Proof	—	£500
1998 50th Anniversary of the National Health Service	5,001,000	£3
1998 — BU	—	£5
1998 — Silver Proof	9,032	£30
1998 — — — Piedfort	5,117	£45
1998 — Gold Proof	—	£500
1999	24,905,000	£2
1999 BU	—	£5
1999 Proof	—	£10
2000	27,915,500	£2
2000 BU	—	£5
2000 Proof	—	£7
2000 150th Anniversary of Public Libraries	11,263,000	£2
2000 — BU	—	£6
2000 — Proof	—	£9
2000 — Silver Proof	7,634	£30
2000 — — — Piedfort	5,721	£45
2000 — Gold proof	—	£500
2001	84,998,500	£2
2001 BU	—	£5
2001 Proof	—	£7
2002	23,907,500	£2
2002 BU	—	£5
2002 Proof	—	£7
2002 Gold Proof	—	£475
2003	23,583,000	£2
2003 BU	—	£5
2003 Proof	—	£6
2003 Suffragette	3,124,030	£6
2003 — BU	9582	£7
2003 — Proof	—	£10
2003 — Silver Proof	6,267	£30

1998 EU Presidency

1998 NHS

2000 Public Libraries

2003 Suffragettes

DATE	Mintage	UNC
2003 — — — Piedfort	6,795	£45
2003 — Gold Proof	942	£450
2004	35,315,500	£2
2004 BU	—	£5
2004 Proof	—	£8
2004 Roger Bannister	9,032,500	£3
2004 — BU	10,371	£6
2004 — Proof	—	£8
2004 — Silver Proof	4,924	£30
2004 — — — Piedfort	4,054	£45
2004 — Gold Proof	644	£450
2005	25,363,500	£2
2005 BU	—	£6
2005 Proof	—	£8
2005 Samuel Johnson	17,649,000	£3
2005 — BU	—	£5
2005 — Proof	—	£8
2005 — Silver Proof	4,029	£30
2005 — — — Piedfort	3,808	£45
2005 — Gold Proof	—	£450
2006	24,567,000	£2
2006 Proof	—	£8
2006 Silver Proof	—	£30
2006 Victoria Cross, The Award	12,087,000	£3
2006 — BU	—	£5
2006 — Proof	—	£8
2006 — Silver Proof	6,310	£30
2006 — — — — Piedfort	3,532	£50
2006 — Gold Proof	866	£450
2006 Victoria Cross, Heroic Acts	10,000,500	£3
2006 — BU	—	£5
2006 — Proof	—	£8
2006 — Silver Proof	6,872	£30
2006 — — — — Piedfort	3,415	£50
2006 — Gold Proof	804	£450
2007	11,200,000	£2
2007 BU	—	£6
2007 Proof	—	£8
2007 Centenary of Scout Movement	7,710,750	£3
2007 — BU	—	£8
2007 — Proof	—	£12
2007 — Silver Proof	10,895	£30
2007 — — — Piedfort	1,555	£65
2007 — Gold Proof	1,250	£450
2008	3,500,000	£2
2008 — BU	—	£5
2008 — Proof	—	£6
2008 — Silver Proof	—	£25
2008 — Gold Proof	—	£450
2008 — Platinum Proof	—	£1550
2008 **New Shield Rev.** Obv. rotated by approx. 26⁰	22,747,000	£5
2008 BU	—	£6
2008 Proof	—	£8
2008 Silver Proof	—	£25
2008 Silver Proof Piedfort	—	£45
2008 Gold Proof	—	£450
2008 Platinum Proof	—	£1550

2004 Roger Bannister

2005 Samuel Johnson

2006 Victoria Cross—the Award

2006 Victoria Cross—Heroic Acts

2007 Centenary of Scouting

The **"Shield" design which replaced Britannia on the reverse of the circulating 50 pence coin was introduced in 2008 and continues in use as the standard reverse each year in addition to the many commemorative issues available.**

2008 Shield design

DATE	Mintage	UNC
2009 BU	—	£10
2009 Proof	—	£15
2009 Silver Proof	—	£25
2009 250th Anniversary of Kew Gardens	210,000	£150
2009 — BU	128,364	£175
2009 — Proof	—	£200
2009 — Silver Proof	7,575	£250
2009 — — — Piedfort	2,967	£300
2009 — Gold Proof	629	£750
2009 Olympic and Paralympic Sports (Track & Field Athletics) Unc (Blue Peter Pack)	19,751	£125
2009 16 different reverses from the past marking the 40th Anniversary of the 50p coin. Proof	1,039	£350
2009 — Silver Proof	1,163	£650
2009 — Gold Proof	70	£8250
2009 — — — Piedfort	40	£22,000
2010 BU	—	£12
2010 Proof	—	£25
2010 Silver Proof	—	£35
2010 100 years of Girl Guiding UK	7,410,090	£3
2010 — BU	99,075	£7
2010 — Proof	—	£20
2010 — Silver Proof	5,271	£35
2010 — — — Piedfort	2,879	£55
2010 — Gold Proof	355	£575
2011 BU	—	£10
2011 Proof	—	£20
2011 Silver Proof	—	£50
2011 50th Anniversary of the WWF	3,400,000	£4
2011 — BU	67,299	£6
2011 — Proof	—	£25
2011 — Silver Proof	24,870	£45
2011 — — — Piedfort	2,244	£65
2011 — Gold Proof	243	£675
2011 Olympic & Paralympic Sports Issues:		
Aquatics Unc, head clear of lines	2,179,000	£4
— Head with lines BU (as illustrated below)	—	£850
— Head clear of lines. BU	—	£5
— Silver BU	30,000	£25
Archery Unc	3,345,000	£3
— BU	—	£4
— Silver BU	30,000	£25
Athletics Unc	2,224,000	£3
— BU	—	£4
— Silver BU	30,000	£25
Badminton Unc	2,133,000	£3
— BU	—	£4
— Silver BU	30,000	£25
Basketball Unc	1,748,000	£3
— BU	—	£4
— Silver BU	30,000	£25
Boccia Unc	2,166,000	£3
— BU	—	£4
— Silver BU	30,000	£25
Boxing Unc	2,148,000	£3
— BU	—	£4
— Silver BU	30,000	£25

2009 Kew Gardens

2010 100 years of Guiding

2011 WWF Anniversary

Archery
by Piotr Powaga

Aquatics—the rare error coin
by Jonathan Olliffe

Badminton
by Emma Kelly

Basketball
by Sarah Payne

Athletics
by Florence Jackson

Boccia
by Justin Chung

Boxing
by Shane Abery

Canoeing
by Timothy Lees

Cycling
by Theo Crutchley-Mack

Equestrian
by Thomas Babbage

Fencing
by Ruth Summerfield

Football
by Neil Wolfson

Goalball
by Jonathan Wren

Gymnastics
by Jonathan Olliffe

Handball
by Natasha Ratcliffe

Hockey
by Robert Evans

Judo
by David Cornell

Modern Pentathlon
by Daniel Brittain

Rowing
by Davey Podmore

Sailing
by Bruce Rushin

Shooting
by Pravin Dewdhory

Table Tennis
by Alan Linsdell

Taekwando
by David Gibbons

Tennis
by Tracy Baines

Triathlon
by Sarah Harvey

DATE	Mintage	UNC
Canoeing Unc	2,166,000	£3
— BU	—	£4
— Silver BU	30,000	£25
Cycling Unc	2,090,000	£3
— BU	—	£4
— Silver BU	30,000	£25
Equestrian Unc	2,142,000	£3
— BU	—	£4
— Silver BU	30,000	£25
Fencing Unc	2,115,000	£3
— BU	—	£4
— Silver BU	30,000	£25
Football Unc	1,125,000	£10
— BU	—	£15
— Silver BU	30,000	£35
Goalball Unc	1,615,000	£8
— BU	—	£10
— Silver BU	30,000	£25
Gymnastics Unc	1,720,000	£3
— BU	—	£4
— Silver BU	30,000	£25
Handball Unc	1,676,000	£8
— BU	—	£10
— Silver BU	30,000	£30
Hockey Unc	1,773,000	£3
— BU	—	£4
— Silver BU	30,000	£25
Judo Unc	1,161,000	£10
— BU	—	£5
— Silver BU	30,000	£35
Modern Pentathlon Unc	1,689,000	£3
— BU	—	£4
— Silver BU	30,000	£25
Rowing Unc	1,717,000	£3
— BU	—	£4
— Silver BU	30,000	£25
Sailing Unc	1,749,000	£3
— BU	—	£4
— Silver BU	30,000	£25
Shooting Unc	1,656,000	£3
— BU	—	£4
— Silver BU	30,000	£25
Table Tennis Unc	1,737,000	£3
— BU	—	£4
— Silver BU	30,000	£25
Taekwondo Unc	1,664,000	£3
— BU	—	£4
— Silver BU	30,000	£25
Tennis Unc	1,454,000	£8
— BU	—	£10
— Silver BU	30,000	£25
Triathlon Unc	1,163,000	£10
— BU	—	£15
— Silver BU	30,000	£30
Volleyball Unc	2,133,000	£3
— BU	—	£4
— Silver BU	30,000	£25
Weightlifting Unc	1,879,000	£3
— BU	—	£4
— Silver BU	30,000	£25
Wheelchair Rugby Unc	1,765,000	£3
— BU	—	£4
— Silver BU	30,000	£25
Wrestling Unc	1,129,000	£10
— BU	—	£15
— Silver BU	30,000	£35

Volleyball
by Daniela Boothman

Weight Lifting
by Rob Shakespeare

Wheelchair Rugby
by Natasha Ratcliffe

Wrestling
by Roderick Enriquez

Note—Each of the artists of the 29 Olympic sports above was presented with a gold proof coin with their own design. The Track & Field Athletics design coin was dated 2009, the Cycling was dated 2010, and the remaining issues 2011.

DATE	Mintage	UNC
2012	32,300,030	£2
2012 BU	—	£5
2012 Proof	—	£10
2012 Silver Proof with selective gold plating	—	£50
2012 Gold Proof	—	£500
2012 Olympic Gold Proof Piedfort. *The 11 Olympic sports in which the United Kingdom Team GB achieved a Gold Medal was celebrated with an issue limit of only 27 Piedfort coins for each sport, some in sets, some as individual coins (see under Proof and Specimen sets)*	27	—
2013	10,301,000	£2
2013 BU	—	£5
2013 Proof	—	£10
2013 Silver Proof	2,013	£55
2013 Gold Proof	198	£450
2013 100th anniversary of Birth of Christopher Ironside	7,000,000	£8
2013 — BU	4,403	£10
2013 — Proof	—	£15
2013 — Silver Proof	1,823	£50
2013 — — — Piedfort	816	£90
2013 — Gold Proof	198	£450
2013 Centenary of the Birth of Benjamin Britten	5,300,000	£8
2013 — BU	—	£10
2013 — Silver Proof	717	£55
2013 — — — Piedfort	515	£90
2013 — Gold Proof	70	£475
2014	49,001,000	£2
2014 BU	—	£5
2014 Proof	—	£12
2014 Silver Proof	—	£55
2014 XX Commonwealth Games	6,502,918	£8
2014 — BU	14,581	£10
2014 — Proof	—	£15
2014 — Silver Proof	2,610	£45
2014 — — — Piedfort	792	£100
2014 — Gold Proof	—	£450
2015	20,101,000	£2
2015 BU	—	£5
2015 Proof	—	£10
2015 Silver Proof	—	£30
2015 Gold Proof	—	£450
2015 Platinum Proof	—	—
2015 Battle of Britain 75th Anniversary BU (no denomination)	35,199	£5
2015 — Proof	—	£15
2015 — Silver Proof	2,839	£30
2015 — — — Piedfort	1,422	£80
2015 — Gold Proof	389	£450

New Portrait by Jody Clark

2015 Battle of Britain 75th Anniversary (with denomination) UNC	5,900,000	£3
2015 Standard Shield rev.	—	£2
2015 BU	—	£5
2015 Proof	—	£12
2015 Silver Proof	—	£30
2015 Gold Proof	—	£450
2015 Platinum Proof	—	—
2016 BU	—	£4
2016 Proof	—	£12
2016 Silver Proof	—	£35
2016 Battle of Hastings 950th Anniversary	6,700,000	£3
2016 — BU	21,718	£5
2016 — Proof	—	£10
2016 — Silver Proof	2,338	£35
2016 — — — Piedfort	1,469	£155
2016 — Gold Proof	237	£450
2016 Beatrix Potter 150th Anniversary	6,900,000	£4
2016 — BU	61,658	£5
2016 — Proof	—	£10
2016 — Silver Proof	7,471	£35
2016 — — — Piedfort	2,486	£250
2016 — Gold Proof	732	£550

2013 Christopher Ironside

2013 Benjamin Britten

2015 Battle of Britain

2016 Beatrix Potter

DATE	Mintage	UNC
2016 Beatrix Potter: Peter Rabbit	9,600,000	£4
2016 — BU...	93,851	£15
2016 — Silver Proof with coloured highlights	15,245	£50
2016 Beatrix Potter: Jemima Puddle-Duck...................	2,100,000	£16
2016 — BU...	54,929	£20
2016 — Silver Proof with coloured highlights	15,171	£75
2016 Beatrix Potter: Mrs. Tiggy-Winkle	8,800,000	£4
2016 — BU...	47,597	£10
2016 — Silver Proof with coloured highlights	15,243	£50
2016 Beatrix Potter: Squirrel Nutkin...........................	5,000,000	£4
2016 — BU...	45,884	£10
2016 — Silver Proof with coloured highlights	15,143	£50
2016 Team GB for Olympics	6,400,000	£3
2016 — BU...	34,162	£10
2016 — Silver Proof	4,456	£25
2016 — — Piedfort	1,246	£150
2016 — Gold Proof...	302	£450
2017 BU	—	£5
2017 Proof...	—	£12
2017 Silver Proof..	—	£30
2017 375th anniversary of Sir Isaac Newton's birth......	1,801,500	£5
2017 — BU...	54,057	£10
2017 — Proof..	—	£15
2017 — Silver Proof	3,875	£50
2017 — — Piedfort	1,935	£95
2017 — Gold Proof...	282	£775
2017 Beatrix Potter: Peter Rabbit	19,900,000	£4
2017 — BU...	221,866	£12
2017 — — Silver Proof with coloured highlights...........	40,000	£55
2017 — — Gold Proof...	425	£1000
2017 Beatrix Potter: Mr. Jeremy Fisher.......................	9,900,000	£4
2017 — BU...	165,618	£8
2017 — Silver Proof with coloured highlights	40,000	£50
2017 Beatrix Potter: Tom Kitten	9,500,000	£4
2017 — BU...	159,302	£8
2017 — Silver Proof with coloured highlights	34,140	£50
2017 Beatrix Potter: Benjamin Bunny	25,000,000	£4
2017 — BU...	—	£8
2017 — Silver Proof with coloured highlights	35,821	£50
2018 BU	—	£5
2018 Proof...	—	£12
2018 Silver Proof..	—	£30

2016 Peter Rabbit

2016 Team GB

2017 Isaac Newton

The four 2017 Beatrix Potter 50p commemoratives in silver with colour

DATE	Mintage	UNC
2018 375th anniversary of Sir Isaac Newton's birth (see above: 2018 only available from the Royal Mint Experience)		£75
2018 Anniversary of the Representation of the People Act	9,000,000	£3
2018 Beatrix Potter: Peter Rabbit	1,400,000	£5
2018 — BU	—	£5
2018 — Silver Proof with coloured highlights	—	£55
2018 — Gold Proof	450	£1000
2018 Beatrix Potter: Flopsy Bunny	1,400,000	£4
2018 —BU	—	£5
2018 —Silver Proof with coloured highlights	—	£55
2018 Beatrix Potter: The Tailor of Gloucester	3,900,000	£5
2018 — BU	—	£6
2018 —Silver Proof with coloured highlights	—	£55
2018 Beatrix Potter: Mrs Tittlemouse	1,700,000	£5
2018 — BU	—	£6
2018 — Silver Proof with coloured highlights	—	£55
2018 Paddington Bear at Paddington Station	5,001,000	£5
2018 — BU	—	£10
2018 .... — Silver Proof with coloured highlights	75,000	£60
2018 — Gold Proof	1,250	£780
2018 Paddington Bear at Buckingham Palace	5,901,000	£5
2018 — BU	—	£10
2018 — Silver Proof with coloured highlights	75,000	£60
2018 — Gold Proof	1,250	£780
2018 The Snowman BU	—	£10
2018 — Silver Proof	15,000	£60
2018 — Gold Proof	400	£775
2019 BU	—	£5
2019 Proof	—	£12
2019 Silver Proof	—	£30
2019 Stephen Hawking BU	—	£10
2019 — Silver Proof	7,000	£55
2019 — — Piedfort	2,500	£95
2019 — Gold Proof	400	£795
2019 Sherlock Holmes BU	—	£10
2019 — Silver Proof	7,500	£55
2019 — — Piedfort	3,500	£95
2019 — Gold Proof	600	£795
2019 The Gruffalo BU	—	£10
2019 — Silver Proof	30,000	£65
2019 — Gold Proof	600	£795
2019 Peter Rabbit BU	—	£10
2019 — Silver Proof	30,000	£65
2019 — Gold Proof	500	£795
2019 Paddington Bear at the Tower of London	—	£3
2019 — BU	—	£10
2019 — Silver Proof with coloured highlights	25,000	£65
2019 — Gold Proof	600	£980
2019 Paddington Bear at St. Paul's	—	£3
2019 — BU	—	£10
2019 — Silver Proof with coloured highlights	25,000	£65
2019 — Gold Proof	600	£980
2019 50 years of the 50p BU	—	£10
2019 — Silver Proof Piedfort	1,969	£95
2019 — Silver Proof	3,500	£55
2019 — Gold Proof	300	£980
2019 20th Anniversary of the Gruffalo BU	—	£10
2019 — Silver Proof	25,000	£65
2019 — Gold (Red) Proof	600	£980
2019 The Snowman II BU	—	£10
2019 — Silver Proof	25,000	£65
2019 — Gold (Red) Proof	600	£980
2019 Wallace & Gromit BU	—	£10
2019 — Silver Proof	25,000	£65
2019 — Gold (Red) Proof	630	£980
2020 BU	—	£5
2020 Proof	—	£12
2020 Silver Proof	—	£30
2020 Withdrawal from the EU (Brexit) BU	—	£10
2020 — BU (EEC 1973 + EU Withdrawal, 2-coin set)	5,000	£30
2020 — Silver Proof	47,000	£60
2020 — Gold (Red) Proof	1,500	£945

2018 Flopsy Bunny

Paddington at the Tower of London

2018 The Snowman

2019 Stephen Hawking

2019 Sherlock Holmes

Note: the prices given for recently-issued gold coins are the Royal Mint issue prices.

DATE	Mintage	UNC
2020 Team GB BU	—	£5
2020 — Proof	—	£12
2020 — Silver Proof	—	£55
2020 Rosalind Franklin BU	—	£10
2020 — Proof	—	£15
2020 — Silver Proof	—	£55
2020 — Silver Proof Piedfort	—	£99
2020 — Gold (Red) Proof	250	£1075
2020 Dinosauria (Megalosaurus) BU	—	£10
2020 — BU (coloured coin)	50,000	£20
2020 — Silver Proof	3,000	£65
2020 — — Proof (coloured coin)	7,000	£75
2020 — Gold Proof	350	£945
2020 Dinosauria (Iguanodon) BU	—	£10
2020 — BU (coloured coin)	50,000	£20
2020 — Silver Proof	14,500	£65
2020 — — Proof (coloured coin)	7,000	£75
2020 — Gold Proof	500	£1020
2020 Dinosauria (Hylaeosaurus) BU	—	£10
2020 — BU (coloured coin)	50,000	£20
2020 — Silver Proof	14,500	£65
2020 — — Proof (coloured coin)	7,000	£75
2020 — Gold Proof	500	£1020
2020 Winnie the Pooh—Christopher Robin BU	—	£10
2020 — BU (coloured coin)	45,000	£20
2020 — Silver Proof	18,000	£67.50
2020 — Gold Proof	525	£1,125
2020 — Winnie the Pooh BU	—	£10
2020 — BU (coloured coin)	45,000	£20
2020 — Silver Proof (coloured coin)	18,000	£67.50
2020 — Gold Proof	525	£1,125
2020 — Piglet BU	—	£10
2020 — BU (coloured coin)	45,000	£20
2020 — Silver Proof	18,000	£67.50
2020 — Gold Proof	525	£1,125
2020 The Snowman BU	—	£10
2020 — BU (coloured coin)	15,000	£20
2020 — Silver Proof	7,000	£67.50
2020 — Gold Proof	275	£1,125
2020 Diversity Built Britain		
2020 — BU	—	£10
2020 — Silver Proof	25,000	£57.50
2020 — — Piedfort	2,500	£100
2020 — Gold Proof	950	£1,125
2020 — — Piedfort	200	£2,225
2020 Peter Rabbit BU	—	£10
2020 — Silver Proof	15,000	£65
2020 — Gold Proof	500	£945
2021 50th Anniversay of Decimal Day BU	—	£10
2021 — Silver Proof	6,000	£57.50
2021 — — Piedfort	2,500	£100.00
2021 — Gold Proof (coin struck on the day)	700	£1,250
2021 — —	450	£1,100
2021 — — Piedfort	200	£2,175
2021 Mary Anning Collection—Temnodantesaurus BU	—	£10
2021 — BU (coloured coin)	50,000	£20
2021 — Silver Proof	3,000	£62.50
2021 — — (coloured coin)	7,000	£67.50
2021 — Gold Proof	250	£1,100
2021 John Logie Baird BU	—	£10
2021 — Silver Proof	5,010	£57.50
2021 — — Piedfort	2,200	£100
2021 — Gold Proof	405	£1,005
2021 Olympic Games Team 2020 (GB) BU	—	£10
2021 — BU (coloured coin)	12,021	£20
2021 — Silver Proof (coloured coin)	5,510	£67.50
2021. — — Piedfort	1,510	£105
2021 — Gold Proof	260	£1,00

2020
Dinosauria—Iguanodon

TWENTY-FIVE PENCE (CROWN)

This series is a continuation of the pre-decimal series, there having been four crowns to the pound. The coins below have a legal tender face value of 25p to this day, and are minted in cupro-nickel except where stated otherwise.

DATE	Mintage	UNC
1972 Royal Silver Wedding	7,452,100	£2
1972 — Proof	150,000	£8
1972 — Silver Proof	100,000	£36
1977 Silver Jubilee	37,061,160	£2
1977 — in Presentation folder	Incl. above	£3
1977 — Proof	193,000	£8
1977 — Silver Proof	377,000	£32
1980 Queen Mother 80th Birthday	9,306,000	£2
1980 — in Presentation folder	Incl. above	£3
1980 — Silver Proof	83,670	£32
1981 Royal Wedding	26,773,600	£2
1981 — in Presentation folder	Incl. above	£3
1981 — Silver Proof	218,140	£32

TWENTY PENCE

The series commenced in 1982, some 11 years after the introduction of decimal coinage. Its presence from introduction date meant that there was no requirement for ten pence circulation-standard coins until the latter's size was reduced in 1992. Its alloy is uniquely 84% copper and 16% nickel, unlike the 75/25 of the fifty pence.

DATE	Mintage	UNC	DATE	Mintage	UNC
1982	740,815,000	£2	1992	Est. approx. 29,705,000	£4
1982 Proof	—	£7	1992 — BU	—	£5
1982 Silver Proof Piedfort	—	£35	1992 — Proof	—	£8
1983	158,463,000	£3	1993	123,123,750	£1
1983 Proof	—	£6	1993 BU	—	£3
1984	65,350,000	£1	1993 Proof	—	£6
1984 BU	—	£3	1994	67,131,250	£1
1984 Proof	—	£7	1994 BU	—	£3
New portrait			1994 Proof	—	£5
1985	74,273,699	£2	1995	102,005,000	£1
1985 BU	—	£4	1995 BU	—	£3
1985 Proof	—	£6	1995 Proof	—	£5
1986 BU	—	£5	1996	83,163,750	£2
1986 Proof	—	£7	1996 BU	—	£3
1987	137,450,000	£1	1996 Proof	—	£5
1987 BU	—	£3	1996 Silver Proof	—	£30
1987 Proof	—	£6	1997	89,518,750	£2
1988	38,038,344	£1	1997 BU	—	£3
1988 BU	—	£3	1997 Proof	—	£5
1988 Proof	—	£5	*New portrait*		
1989	132,013,890	£1	1998	76,965,000	£2
1989 BU	—	£3	1998 BU	—	£4
1989 Proof	—	£6	1998 Proof	—	£5
1990	88,097,500	£1	1999	73,478,750	£2
1990 BU	—	£3	1999 BU	—	£3
1990 Proof	—	£6	1999 Proof	—	£5
1991	35,901,250	£1	2000	136,428,750	£2
1991 BU	—	£4	2000 BU	—	£3
1991 Proof	—	£8	2000 Proof	—	£5
1992	Est. approx. 1,500,000	£4	2000 Silver Proof	—	£30
1992 BU	—	£5	2001	148,122,500	£2
Enhanced effigy			2001 BU	—	£3

DATE	Mintage	UNC
2001 Proof	—	£5
2002	93,360,000	£2
2002 BU	—	£3
2002 Proof	—	£5
2002 Gold Proof	—	£350
2003	153,383,750	£2
2003 BU	—	£4
2003 Proof	—	£6
2004	120,212,500	£2
2004 BU	—	£4
2004 Proof	—	£6
2005	124,488,750	£2
2005 BU	—	£4
2005 Proof	—	£6
2006	114,800,000	£2
2006 BU	—	£6
2006 Proof	—	£7
2006 Silver Proof	—	£25
2007	117,075,000	£2
2007 BU	—	£4
2007 Proof	—	£6
2008	11,900,000	£2
2008 BU	—	£4
2008 Proof	—	£7
2008 Silver Proof	—	£25
2008 Gold Proof	—	£350
2008 Platinum Proof	—	£750
New Reverse, date on Obverse		
2008	115,022,000	£2
2008 Mule—paired with old Obv. (thus no date) Est. approx. 120,000 (?)		£100
2008 BU	—	£3
2008 Proof	—	£6
2008 Silver Proof	—	£25
2008 — — Piedfort	—	£30
2008 Gold Proof	—	£350
2008 Platinum Proof	—	£750
2009	121,625,300	£2
2009 BU	—	£5
2009 Proof	—	£7
2009 Silver Proof	—	£25
2010	112,875,500	£2
2010 BU	—	£5
2010 Proof	—	£7
2010 Silver Proof	—	£25
2011	191,625,000	£2
2011 BU	—	£5

DATE	Mintage	UNC
2011 Proof	—	£8
2011 Silver Proof	—	£25
2012	69,650,030	£2
2012 BU	—	£5
2012 Proof	—	£8
2012 Silver Proof (issued in set with Victorian 4 Shilling piece)	—	£30
2012 — — with selective gold plating	—	£35
2012 Gold Proof	—	£350
2013	66,325,000	£2
2013 BU	—	£5
2013 Proof	—	£10
2013 Silver Proof	—	£25
2013 Gold Proof	—	£350
2014	173,775,000	£2
2014 BU	—	£5
2014 Proof	—	£10
2014 Silver Proof	—	£25
2015	63,175,000	£3
2015 BU	—	£5
2015 Proof	—	£10
2015 Silver Proof	—	£25
2015 Gold Proof	—	£350
2015 Platinum Proof	—	—
New Portrait		
2015	131,250,000	£3
2015 BU	—	£5
2015 Proof	—	£5
2015 Silver Proof	—	£30
2015 Gold Proof	—	£350
2015 Platinum Proof	—	—
2016	212,625,000	£3
2016 BU	—	£5
2016 Proof	—	£10
2016 Silver Proof	—	£25
2017 BU	—	£5
2017 Proof	—	£10
2017 Silver Proof	—	£25
2018 BU	—	£5
2018 Proof	—	£10
2018 Silver Proof	—	£25
2019 BU	—	£5
2019 Proof	—	£10
2019 Silver Proof	—	£25
2020 BU	—	£5
2020 Proof	—	£10
2020 Silver Proof	—	£25

TEN PENCE

The series commenced before decimalisation with the legend NEW PENCE, this changed to TEN PENCE from 1982. These "florin-sized" coins up to 1992 are no longer legal tender. Cupro-nickel was replaced by nickel-plated steel from 2011.

DATE	Mintage	UNC
1968	336,143,250	£3
1969	314,008,000	£4
1970	133,571,000	£3
1971	63,205,000	£3
1971 Proof	—	£4
1972 Proof only	—	£5
1973	152,174,000	£3
1973 Proof	—	£4
1974	92,741,000	£3
1974 Proof	—	£4
1975	181,559,000	£3
1975 Proof	—	£4
1976	228,220,000	£3
1976 Proof	—	£4
1977	59,323,000	£6
1977 Proof	—	£8
1978 Proof	—	£6
1979	115,457,000	£2
1979 Proof	—	£4
1980	88,650,000	£3
1980 Proof	—	£4
1981	3,487,000	£8
1981 Proof	—	£15
1982 BU	—	£4
1982 Proof	—	£6
1983 BU	—	£3
1983 Proof	—	£4
1984 BU	—	£4
1984 Proof	—	£6
New portrait		
1985 BU	—	£5
1985 Proof	—	£7
1986 BU	—	£4
1986 Proof	—	£6
1987 BU	—	£4
1987 Proof	—	£7
1988 BU	—	£5
1988 Proof	—	£7
1989 BU	—	£6
1989 Proof	—	£9
1990 BU	—	£6
1990 Proof	—	£9
1991 BU	—	£6
1991 Proof	—	£9
1992 BU	—	£5
1992 Proof	—	£7
1992 Silver Proof	—	£25
Size reduced (24.5mm).		
1992	1,413,455,170	£3
1992 BU	—	£4
1992 Proof	—	£5
1992 Silver Proof	—	£25
1992 — — Piedfort	14,167	£45
1993 BU	—	£2
1993 Proof	—	£7
1994 BU	—	£2
1994 Proof	—	£7

DATE	Mintage	UNC
1995	43,259,000	£1
1995 BU	—	£5
1995 Proof	—	£7
1996	118,738,000	£2
1996 BU	—	£4
1996 Proof	—	£7
1996 Silver Proof	—	£25
1997	99,196,000	£2
1997 BU	—	£4
1997 Proof	—	£4
New portrait		
1998 BU	—	£8
1998 Proof	—	£10
1999 BU	—	£4
1999 Proof	—	£11
2000	134,733,000	£1
2000 BU	—	£4
2000 Proof	—	£7
2000 Silver Proof	—	£25
2001	129,281,000	£1
2001 BU	—	£3
2001 Proof	—	£4
2002	80,934,000	£2
2002 BU	—	£3
2002 Proof	—	£5
2002 Gold Proof	—	£400
2003	88,118,000	£2
2003 BU	—	£3
2003 Proof	—	£5
2004	99,602,000	£1
2004 BU	—	£3
2004 Proof	—	£5
2005	69,604,000	£1
2005 BU	—	£2
2005 Proof	—	£4
2006	118,803,000	£1
2006 BU	—	£3
2006 Proof	—	£7
2006 Silver Proof	—	£25
2007	72,720,000	£1
2007 BU	—	£4
2007 Proof	—	£7
2008	9,720,000	£2
2008 BU	—	£5
2008 Proof	—	£8
2008 Silver Proof	—	£25
2008 Gold Proof	—	£400
2008 Platinum Proof	—	£450
New Reverse, no border beads on Obverse		
2008	71,447,000	£1
2008 BU	—	£4
2008 Proof	—	£5
2008 Silver Proof	—	£25
2008 — — Piedfort	—	£45
2008 Gold Proof	—	£400
2008 Platinum Proof	—	£450
2009	84,360,000	£1

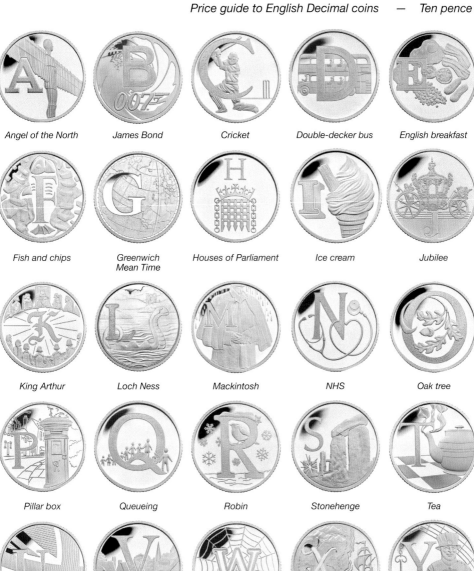

Angel of the North	James Bond	Cricket	Double-decker bus	English breakfast
Fish and chips	Greenwich Mean Time	Houses of Parliament	Ice cream	Jubilee
King Arthur	Loch Ness	Mackintosh	NHS	Oak tree
Pillar box	Queueing	Robin	Stonehenge	Tea
Union Flag	Village	World Wide Web	X marks the spot	Yeoman warder

Zebra crossing

In 2018 a special series was introduced for the 10p denomination. There are 26 coins, each depicting a letter of the alphabet as shown above.

247

DATE	Mintage	UNC
2009 BU	—	£3
2009 Proof	—	£5
2009 Silver Proof	—	£30
2010	96,600,500	£1
2010 BU	—	£5
2010 Proof	—	£7
2010 Silver Proof	—	£30
Nickel-plated steel		
2011	59,603,850	£1
2011 — BU	—	£5
2011 — Proof	—	£10
2011 Silver Proof	—	£30
2012	11,600,030	£1
2012 BU	—	£5
2012 Proof	—	£10
2012 Silver proof with selective gold plating	—	£35
2012 Gold Proof	—	£400
2013	320,200,750	£1
2013 BU	—	£5
2013 Proof	—	£10
2013 Silver Proof	—	£30
2013 Gold Proof	—	£400
2014	490,202,020	£1
2014 BU	—	£5
2014 Proof	—	£12
2014 Silver Proof	—	£30
2015	119,000,000	£1
2015 BU	—	£4
2015 Proof	—	£5
2015 Silver Proof	—	£30
2015 Gold Proof	—	£400
2015 Platinum Proof	—	—

DATE	Mintage	UNC
New portrait		
2015	91,900,000	£1
2015 BU	—	£5
2015 Proof	—	£6
2015 Silver Proof	—	£30
2015 Gold Proof	—	£400
2016	135,380,000	£1
2016 BU	—	£4
2016 Proof	—	£6
2016 Silver Proof	—	£30
2017	32,300,000	£1
2017 BU	—	£4
2017 Proof	—	£5
2017 Silver Proof	—	£30
2018 BU	—	£1
2018 Proof	—	£4
2018 Silver Proof	—	£30
2018 Alphabet series (26 different letters)	220,000 of each coin	£2 each
2018 — Silver Proof	—	£35 each
2019 BU	—	£1
2019 Proof	—	£6
2019 Silver Proof	—	£35
2019 Alphabet series (26 different letters)	—	£2 each
2019 — Silver Proof	—	£35 each
2020 BU	—	£1
2020 Proof	—	£6
2020 Silver Proof	—	£35
2021 BU	—	£1
2021 Proof	—	£6
2021 Silver Proof	—	£35

SIX PENCE

This new denomination has been struck, as part of the Royal Mint's gifting range (originally priced at £30). They are of Sterling silver to BU standard, and of diameter 19.41mm. Being similar in size to the pre-decimal 6d (or latterly 2 1/2p) they have also been marketed as part of coin sets along with old sixpences. A recent check (2020) of the Royal Mint's gifting range shows that a two coin set to celebrate the Platinum Wedding Anniversary of HM the Queen and HRH Prince Philip with a 1947 sixpence and a 2017 sixpence is still available to purchase.

The Platinum Wedding Anniversary two-coin set featuring a 1947 sixpence and a 2017 sixpence.

FIVE PENCE

This series commenced simultaneously with the Ten Pence (qv). They were the same size and weight as their predecessor, the shilling, and such coins up to 1990 are no longer legal tender. As with the Ten Pence, cupro-nickel was replaced by nickel-plated steel from 2011.

DATE	Mintage	UNC	DATE	Mintage	UNC
1968	98,868,250	£3	1992 BU	—	£3
1969	120,270,000	£3	1992 Proof	—	£7
1970	225,948,525	£3	1993 BU	—	£3
1971	81,783,475	£3	1993 Proof	—	£5
1971 Proof	—	£3	1994	93,602,000	£1
1972 Proof	—	£7	1994 BU	—	£5
1973 Proof	—	£8	1994 Proof	—	£7
1974 Proof	—	£8	1995	183,384,000	£1
1975	141,539,000	£3	1995 BU	—	£5
1975 Proof	—	£6	1995 Proof	—	£7
1976 Proof	—	£7	1996	302,902,000	£1
1977	24,308,000	£8	1996 BU	—	£4
1977 Proof	—	£9	1996 Proof	—	£7
1978	61,094,000	£4	1996 Silver proof	—	£25
1978 Proof	—	£4	1997	236,596,000	£1
1979	155,456,000	£4	1997 BU	—	£4
1979 Proof	—	£4	1997 Proof	—	£7
1980	220,566,000	£3	*New portrait*		
1980 Proof	—	£4	1998	217,376,000	£1
1981 Proof	—	£7	1998 BU	—	£4
1982 BU Legend changed to FIVE PENCE.	—	£7	1998 Proof	—	£7
1982 Proof	—	£9	1999	195,490,000	£1
1983 BU	—	£5	1999 BU	—	£4
1983 Proof	—	£6	1999 Proof	—	£7
1984 BU	—	£4	2000	388,512,000	£1
1984 Proof	—	£6	2000 BU	—	£4
New Portrait.			2000 Proof	—	£7
1985 BU	—	£2	2000 Silver Proof	—	£25
1985 Proof	—	£7	2001	337,930,000	£1
1986 BU	—	£2	2001 BU	—	£3
1986 Proof	—	£7	2001 Proof	—	£5
1987	48,220,000	£1	2002	219,258,000	£1
1987 BU	—	£3	2002 BU	—	£3
1987 Proof	—	£5	2002 Proof	—	£5
1988	120,744,610	£1	2002 Gold Proof	—	£250
1988 BU	—	£3	2003	333,230,000	£1
1988 Proof	—	£5	2003 BU	—	£3
1989	101,406,000	£1	2003 Proof	—	£5
1989 BU	—	£4	2004	271,810,000	£1
1989 Proof	—	£5	2004 BU	—	£3
1990 BU	—	£2	2004 Proof	—	£5
1990 Proof	—	£5	2005	236,212,000	£1
1990 Silver Proof	—	£15	2005 BU	—	£3
Size reduced (18mm)			2005 Proof	—	£5
1990	1,634,976,005	£2	2006	317,697,000	£1
1990 BU	—	£3	2006 BU	—	£3
1990 Proof	—	£4	2006 Proof	—	£7
1990 Silver Proof	—	£20	2006 Silver Proof	—	£25
1990 — — Piedfort	—	£35	2007	246,720,000	£1
1991	724,979000	£1	2007 BU	—	£5
1991 BU	—	£3	2007 Proof	—	£7
1991 Proof	—	£5	2008	92,880,000	£1
1992	453,173,500	£1	2008 BU	—	£3

DATE	Mintage	UNC
2008 Proof	—	£5
2008 Silver Proof	—	£25
2008 Gold Proof	—	£225
2008 Platinum Proof	—	£300
New Reverse, no border beads on Obverse		
2008	155,172,000	£1
2008 BU	—	£4
2008 Proof	—	£5
2008 Silver Proof	—	£20
2008 — — Piedfort	—	£35
2008 Gold Proof	—	£225
2008 Platinum Proof	—	£300
2009	132,960,300	£1
2009 BU	—	£6
2009 Proof	—	£7
2009 Silver Proof	—	£15
2010	296,245,500	£1
2010 BU	—	£4
2010 Proof	—	£5
2010 Silver Proof	—	£15
2011 Nickel-plated steel	50,400,000	£1
2011 — BU	—	£4
2011 — Proof	—	£6
2011 Silver Proof	—	£15
2012	339,802,350	£1
2012 BU	—	£5
2012 Proof	—	£8
2012 Silver Proof with selective gold plating	—	£15
2012 Gold Proof	—	£225
2013	318,800,750	£1
2013 BU	—	£5
2013 Proof	—	£8
2013 Silver Proof	—	£25

DATE	Mintage	UNC
2013 Gold Proof	—	£250
2014	885,004,520	£1
2014 BU	—	£5
2014 Proof	—	£8
2014 Silver Proof	—	£20
New Portrait		
2015	536,600,000	£2
2015 BU	—	£4
2015 Proof	—	£6
2015 Silver Proof	—	£20
2015 Gold Proof	—	£275
2016	308,200,000	£2
2016 BU	—	£4
2016 Proof	—	£6
2016 Silver Proof	—	£20
2017	220,515,000	—
2017 BU	—	£4
2017 Proof	—	£6
2017 Silver Proof	—	£25
2017 Gold Proof	—	£275
2018 BU	—	£5
2018 Proof	—	£6
2018 Silver Proof	—	£25
2019 BU	—	£4
2019 Proof	—	£6
2019 Silver Proof	—	£25
2020 BU	—	£4
2020 Proof	—	£6
2020 Silver Proof	—	£25
2021 BU	—	£4
2021 Proof	—	£6
2021 Silver Proof	—	£25

TWO PENCE

Dated from 1971, and legal tender from Decimal Day that year, early examples are found in the blue Specimen decimal set wallets of 1968. They were minted in bronze up to 1991, and mainly in copper-plated steel from 1992. However details of where this rule does not totally apply (1992, 1996, 1998–2000 and 2002, 2006, 2008 and 2009) are given below. As with other denominations, "NEW" was replaced by "TWO" from 1982. Note that some years the 2p is only issued in the Year Sets

DATE	Mintage	UNC
1971	1,454,856,250	£2
1971 Proof	—	£3
1972 Proof	—	£6
1973 Proof	—	£8
1974 Proof	—	£8
1975	Est. approx. 273,145,000	£2
1975 Proof	—	£4
1976	Est. approx. 53,779,000	£2
1976 Proof	—	£4
1977	109,281,000	£2
1977 Proof	—	£4
1978	189,658,000	£3
1978 Proof	—	£4
1979	260,200,000	£2
1979 Proof	—	£4
1980	408,527,000	£1
1980 Proof	—	£2

DATE	Mintage	UNC
1981	353,191,000	£4
1981 Proof	—	£4
Legend changed to TWO PENCE		
1982	205,000	£4
1982 Proof	—	£5
1983	631,000	£2
1983 Error NEW instead of TWO	—	£1250
1983 Proof	—	£4
1984	158,820	£2
1984 Proof	—	£4
New portrait		
1985	107,113,000	£2
1985 BU	—	£2
1985 Proof	—	£4
1986	168,967,500	£1
1986 BU	—	£2
1986 Proof	—	£4

DATE	Mintage	UNC
1987	218,100,750	£1
1987 BU	—	£2
1987 Proof	—	£4
1988	419,889,000	£1
1988 BU	—	£2
1988 Proof	—	£4
1989	359,226,000	£1
1989 BU	—	£2
1989 Proof	—	£4
1990	204,499,700	£1
1990 BU	—	£2
1990 Proof	—	£3
1991	86,625,250	£1
1991 BU	—	£2
1991 Proof	—	£5
1992 Copper plated steel	102,247,000	£1
1992 Bronze BU	—	£2
1992 — Proof	—	£5
1993	235,674,000	£1
1993 BU	—	£2
1993 Proof	—	£3
1994	531,628,000	£1
1994 BU	—	£2
1994 Proof	—	£5
1995	124,482,000	£1
1995 BU	—	£2
1995 Proof	—	£5
1996	296,278,000	£1
1996 BU	—	£2
1996 Proof	—	£5
1996 Silver Proof	—	£25
1997	496,116,000	£1
1997 BU	—	£2
1997 Proof	—	£5
New Portrait		
1998	Est. approx. 120,243,000	£1
1998 BU	—	£2
1998 Proof	—	£4
1998 Bronze	Est. approx. 93,587,000	£1
1999	353,816,000	£1
1999 Bronze BU	—	£2
1999 — Proof	—	£4
2000	536,659,000	£1
2000 BU	—	£3
2000 Proof	—	£5
2000 Silver Proof	—	£25
2001	551,880,000	£1
2001 BU	—	£2
2001 Proof	—	£4
2002	168,556,000	£1
2002 BU	—	£3
2002 Proof	—	£4
2002 Gold Proof	—	£500
2003	260,225,000	£1
2003 BU	—	£2
2003 Proof	—	£4
2004	356,396,000	£1
2004 BU	—	£2
2004 Proof	—	£4
2005	280,396,000	£1
2005 BU	—	£2
2005 Proof	—	£3
2006	170,637,000	£1
2006 BU	—	£3
2006 Proof	—	£4
2006 Silver Proof	—	£25
2007	254,500,000	£2
2007 BU	—	£3

DATE	Mintage	UNC
2007 Proof	—	£5
2008	10,600,000	£2
2008 BU	—	£3
2008 Proof	—	£5
2008 Silver Proof	—	£25
2008 Gold Proof	—	£500
2008 Platinum Proof	—	£600
New Rev., no border beads on Obv.		
2008	241,679,000	£2
2008 — BU	—	£3
2008 — Proof	—	£5
2008 — Silver Proof	—	£20
2008 — Silver Proof Piedfort	—	£45
2008 — Gold Proof	—	£500
2008 — Platinum Proof	—	£600
2009	150,500,500	£2
2009 BU	—	£3
2009 Proof	—	£5
2009 Silver Proof	—	£25
2010	99,600,000	£2
2010 BU	—	£3
2010 Proof	—	£6
2010 Silver Proof	—	£25
2011	144,300,000	£2
2011 BU	—	£3
2011 Proof	—	£6
2011 Silver Proof	—	£25
2012	67,800,000	£2
2012 BU	—	£3
2012 Proof	—	£8
2012 Silver Proof with selective gold plating	—	£45
2012 Gold Proof	—	£550
2013	40,600,000	£2
2013 BU	—	£3
2013 Proof	—	£8
2013 Silver Proof	—	£25
2013 Gold Proof	—	£450
2014	247,600,020	£2
2014 BU	—	£3
2014 Proof	—	£8
2014 Silver Proof	—	£45
New Portrait		
2015	139,200,000	£2
2015 BU	—	£3
2015 Proof	—	£5
2015 Silver Proof	—	£25
2015 Gold Proof	—	£450
2015 Platinum Proof	—	£500
2016	185,200,000	£2
2016 BU	—	£3
2016 Proof	—	£5
2016 Silver Proof	—	£25
2017	16,600,000	£2
2017 BU	—	£3
2017 Proof	—	£5
2017 Silver Proof	—	£25
2018 BU	—	£5
2018 Proof	—	£8
2018 Silver Proof	—	£30
2019 BU	—	£5
2019 Proof	—	£8
2019 Silver Proof	—	£25
2020 BU	—	£5
2020 Proof	—	£8
2020 Silver Proof	—	£25
2021 BU	—	£5
2021 Proof	—	£8
2021 Silver Proof	—	£25

ONE PENNY

The history of this coin is very similar to that of the Two Pence coin (qv) except that all 1998 examples were of copper-plated steel.

DATE	Mintage	UNC
1971	1,521,666,250	£1
1971 Proof	—	£2
1972 Proof	—	£5
1973	280,196,000	£2
1973 Proof	—	£5
1974	330,892,000	£2
1974 Proof	—	£3
1975	221,604,000	£2
1975 Proof	—	£4
1976	300,160,000	£2
1976 Proof	—	£3
1977	285,430,000	£2
1977 Proof	—	£3
1978	292,770,000	£3
1978 Proof	—	£3
1979	459,000,000	£3
1979 Proof	—	£3
1980	416,304,000	£2
1980 Proof	—	£3
1981	301,800,000	£2
1981 Proof	—	£3
Legend changed to ONE PENNY		
1982	100,292,000	£1
1982 Unc	—	£2
1982 Proof	—	£3
1983	243,002,000	£1
1983 Unc	—	£2
1983 Proof	—	£4
1984	154,759,625	£1
1984 BU	—	£2
1984 Proof	—	£3
New portrait		
1985	200,605,245	£1
1985 BU	—	£2
1985 Proof	—	£3
1986	369,989,130	£1
1986 BU	—	£2
1986 Proof	—	£3
1987	4999,946,000	£1
1987 BU	—	£2
1987 Proof	—	£3
1988	793,492,000	£1
1988 BU	—	£2
1988 Proof	—	£3
1989	658,142,000	£1
1989 BU	—	£2
1989 Proof	—	£3
1990	529,047,500	£2
1990 BU	—	£3
1990 Proof	—	£4
1991	206,457,000	£1
1991 BU	—	£2
1991 Proof	—	£4
1992 Copper-plated steel	253,867,000	£3

DATE	Mintage	UNC
1992 Bronze BU	—	£6
1992 — Proof	—	£4
1993	602,590,000	£1
1993 BU	—	£2
1993 Proof	—	£5
1994	843,834,000	£1
1994 BU	—	£2
1994 Proof	—	£5
1995	303,314,000	£1
1995 BU	—	£3
1995 Proof	—	£5
1996	723,840,060	£1
1996 BU	—	£2
1996 Proof	—	£5
1996 Silver Proof	—	£28
1997	396,874,000	£1
1997 BU	—	£2
1997 Proof	—	£4
New portrait		
1998	739,770,000	£1
1998 — BU	—	£3
1998 Proof	—	£4
1999	891,392,000	£2
1999 Bronze BU	—	£4
1999 Bronze Proof	—	£8
2000	1,060,420,000	£1
2000 BU	—	£2
2000 Proof	—	£4
2000 Silver Proof	—	£25
2001	928,698,000	£1
2001 BU	—	£2
2001 Proof	—	£4
2002	601,446,000	£1
2002 BU	—	£2
2002 Proof	—	£4
2002 Gold Proof	—	£200
2003	539,436,000	£1
2003 BU	—	£2
2003 Proof	—	£3
2004	739,764,000	£1
2004 BU	—	£2
2004 Proof	—	£4
2005	536,318,000	£1
2005 BU	—	£2
2005 Proof	—	£3
2006	524,605,000	£1
2006 BU	—	£2
2006 Proof	—	£4
2006 Silver Proof	—	£15
2007	548,002,000	£1
2007 BU	—	£4
2007 Proof	—	£7
2008	180,600,000	£1
2008 BU	—	£3
2008 Proof	—	£5

DATE	Mintage	UNC
2008 Silver Proof	—	£15
2008 Gold Proof	—	£200
2008 Platinum Proof	—	£250
New Rev, no border beads		
2008	507,952,000	£1
2008 — BU	—	£2
2008 — Proof	—	£3
2008 — Silver Proof	—	£15
2008 Silver Proof Piedfort	—	£25
2008 Gold Proof	—	£200
2008 Platinum Proof		£250
2009	556,412,800	£1
2009 BU	—	£3
2009 Proof	—	£4
2009 Silver BU, in "Lucky Baby Gift Pack"	—	£15
2009 — Proof	—	£15
2010	609,603,000	£1
2010 BU	—	£3
2010 Proof	—	£4
2010 Silver BU, in "Lucky Baby Gift Card"	9,701	£15
2010 — Proof	—	£15
2011	431,004,000	£1
2011 BU	—	£2
2011 Proof	—	£3
2011 Silver BU in "Lucky Baby Pack"	—	£20
2011 – Proof	—	£15
2012	227,201,000	£1
2012 BU	—	£2
2012 Proof	—	£4
2012 Silver BU (three different packagings)	—	£15
2012 Silver Proof with selective gold plating	—	£18
2012 Gold Proof	—	£250
2013	260,900,000	£1
2013 BU	—	£2
2013 Proof	—	£5
2013 Silver BU	—	£25
2013 — Proof	—	£30
2013 Gold Proof	—	£250
2014	464,801,520	£1
2014 BU	—	£2
2014 Proof	—	£5
2014 Silver BU	—	£20

DATE	Mintage	UNC
2014 Silver Proof	—	£25
2015	154,600,000	£1
2015 BU	—	£2
2015 Proof	—	£5
2015 Silver BU	—	£20
2015 — Proof	—	£25
2015 Gold Proof	—	£250
2015 Platinum Proof	—	—
New Portrait		
2015	418,201,016	£2
2015 BU	—	£3
2015 Proof	—	£6
2015 Silver Proof	—	£25
2015 Gold Proof	—	£250
2015 Platinum Proof	—	—
2016	371,002,000	£1
2016 BU	—	£2
2016 Proof	—	£5
2016 Silver BU	2,842	£20
2016 Silver Proof	—	£25
2017	240,999,600	£1
2017 BU	—	£2
2017 Proof	—	£5
2017 Silver BU	—	£20
2017 Silver Proof	—	£25
2018 BU	—	£2
2018 Proof	—	£5
2018 Silver BU	—	£20
2018 Silver Proof	—	£25
2019		£2
2019 BU	—	£5
2019 Proof	—	£8
2019 Silver BU	—	£20
2019 Silver Proof	—	£25
2020 BU	—	£5
2020 Proof	—	£8
2020 Silver BU	—	£20
2020 Silver Proof	—	£25
20211 BU	—	£5
2021 Proof	—	£8
2021 Silver BU	—	£20
2021 Silver Proof	—	£25

HALF PENNY

No longer legal tender, its history tracks that of the Two Pence and One Penny.

	Mintage	UNC
1971	1,394,188,250	£2
1971 Proof	—	£3
1972 Proof	—	£20
1973	365,680,000	£2
1973 Proof	—	£3
1974	365,448,000	£2
1974 Proof	—	£3
1975	197,600,000	£2
1975 Proof	—	£3
1976	412,172,000	£2
1976 Proof	—	£3
1977	66,368,000	£1
1977 Proof	—	£3
1978	59,532,000	£1
1978 Proof	—	£4
1979	219,1322,000	£2

	Mintage	UNC
1979 Proof	—	£4
1980	202,788,000	£2
1980 Proof	—	£3
1981	46,748,000	£2
1981 Proof	—	£4
Legend changed to HALF PENNY		
1982	190,752,000	50p
1982 Unc	—	£2
1982 Proof	—	£3
1983	7,600,000	50p
1983 Unc	—	£1
1983 Proof	—	£4
1984	40,000	£4
1984 BU	—	£5
1984 Proof	—	£6

THE BRITANNIA SERIES

In addition to the large Britannia coin issues already listed, the series has grown to include many denominations and strikes in silver, gold and platinum. The coins are essentially bullion pieces and their values are usually related to the current price of precious metals, although the increasing popularity of the series in recent years has seen examples changing hands for figures well in excess of their bullion values, this is so especially with proof and other special strikes or the occasional mule or error. To ascertain the value of a piece it is usually only necessary to check with the prevailing price of precious metals. Hopefully this guide will give an indication of the recent market prices

SILVER

The silver Britannia series commenced in 1997, and, as with the Gold Britannia series, sets of the coins are listed in the "Proof and Specimen Sets" section. Coins contain one Troy ounce of fine silver (£2) alloyed to Britannia standard, i.e. 95.8 per cent fine silver, or fractions of one ounce as follows: half ounce (£1), quarter ounce (50 pence) and one tenth of an ounce (20 pence). Reverses change annually, all four coins of any particular date being of the same design. The reverses by Philip Nathan appear as follows: 1997 Chariot, 1998 Standing Britannia, 1999 Chariot, 2000 Standing Britannia, 2001 Una and the Lion, 2002 Standing Britannia, 2003 Britannia's Helmeted Head, 2004 Standing Britannia, 2005 Britannia Seated, 2006 Standing Britannia, 2009 Chariot.

The 2007 design is by Christopher Le Brun, and features a seated Britannia with Lion at her feet. The 2008 is by John Bergdahl, and features a standing Britannia facing left.

Two pounds Britannia coins to BU or "bullion" standard have been issued as individual coins for each year from 1998 onwards. 2010 features Suzie Zamit's Britannia with a portrait with a Corinthian style helmet.

The 2011 coins feature a seated Britannia and Union Flag, as described in the Britannia gold series below.

2012 saw the 15th anniversary of the Silver Series, but the reverse chosen was that of the Standing Britannia by Philip Nathan, which also marked the 25th Gold series. In addition, there is a 9-coin proof set of Half-Ounce silver coins dated 2012 featuring each of the Reverses used in the past, a 25th Anniversary collection. The story of the 2013 silver Britannia coins closely parallels that of the gold coins. The silver one-twentieth of an ounce has the logical face value of 10 pence.

The 2014 Silver Britannias closely follow the pattern of the three designs of 2014 Gold. This included the introduction of the silver one-fortieth of an ounce, with a face value of 5 pence. The Nathan Britannia has crenellated borders on both the obverse and the reverse, while the Year of the Horse has plain borders on both. Examples exist, however, of both One ounce silver bullion coins having the Other's obverse, thus producing two error coins, or "mules". 2014 also saw the SS *Gairsoppa* Quarter-ounce silver Britannia bullion coin with the edge inscription SS GAIRSOPPA. These coins have the Nathan Britannia reverse, and are struck from metal recovered from the vessel which was sunk by enemy action in 1941.

Both 2013 and 2014 one-ounce BU bullion Nathan Britannia coins exist with snakes or horses (respectively) on a plain edge. These were the result of a contract between the Royal Mint and the bullion dealers A-mark of Santa Monica, California, and commemorate Chinese Lunar years. In 2015 Designer Jody Clark scored a first when his portrayal of Britannia was used on the £50 coin which also carried his new portrait of the Queen.

GOLD

In 1987 the gold Britannia £100 coin was introduced. It contained one Troy ounce of fine gold, alloyed to 22 carat, and this has continued to the present day. At the same time, and also continuing, gold coins of face value £50, £25 and £10 appeared, containing a half ounce, quarter ounce and one tenth of an ounce of fine gold respectively. From 1987 to 1989 the alloy was of copper (Red Gold), whereas from 1990 to the present day the alloy has been of silver and copper (yellow gold).

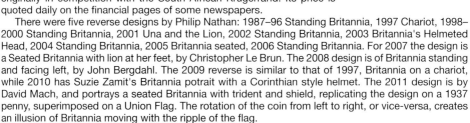

Proof sets of these coins are listed in the "Proof and Specimen Sets" section. In addition, non-proof coins have been minted, it is believed for each of the four coins for every year. The one ounce £100 Britannia is primarily issued as a bullion coin in the non-proof standard, originally in competition with the South African Krugerrand. Its price is quoted daily on the financial pages of some newspapers.

There were five reverse designs by Philip Nathan: 1987–96 Standing Britannia, 1997 Chariot, 1998–2000 Standing Britannia, 2001 Una and the Lion, 2002 Standing Britannia, 2003 Britannia's Helmeted Head, 2004 Standing Britannia, 2005 Britannia seated, 2006 Standing Britannia. For 2007 the design is a Seated Britannia with lion at her feet, by Christopher Le Brun. The 2008 design is of Britannia standing and facing left, by John Bergdahl. The 2009 reverse is similar to that of 1997, Britannia on a chariot, while 2010 has Suzie Zamit's Britannia potrait with a Corinthian style helmet. The 2011 design is by David Mach, and portrays a seated Britannia with trident and shield, replicating the design on a 1937 penny, superimposed on a Union Flag. The rotation of the coin from left to right, or vice-versa, creates an illusion of Britannia moving with the ripple of the flag.

In general the proof coins have reverse features frosted. The proofs with Standing Britannia and Una and the Lion reverses include P NATHAN on the reverse, whereas the equivalent bullion coins have NATHAN. The other three reverses have PN on both proofs and bullion coins.

2012 was the 25th anniversary of the Gold Britannia coin series, and the reverse design chosen was that of the 1987 coins, standing Britannia, by Philip Nathan. This was repeated in 2013, but only for Brilliant Uncirculated "Bullion" coins. A separate new series was introduced for Proof coins, a seated Britannia with an owl was featured, the artist being Robert Hunt. The range of Britannia Proofs was increased from 4 to 6, with the addition of a Five-ounce coin (qv) and a one-twentieth of an ounce, curiously denominated at One Pound and with a diameter of 12mm, just larger than a Maundy One Penny. All 2013 Gold Britannias are minted in 0.999 Au alloy.

2014 and 2015 each saw three Reverse designs. The Nathan outstretched arm of Britannia continued as the bullion coin. The series by new artists were of a standing Britannia facing left with lion (2014) by Jody Clark, and a "head and shoulders" Britannia holding the trident on her right shoulder, by Antony Dufont, the latter coin included the Clark portrayal of the Queen on the obverse.

The 2016 series Reverse was designed by Suzie Zamit and depicts Britannia as the Warrior Queen. The 2017 series celebrating the 30th anniversary of the gold Britannia used a design by Louis Tamlin which depicts a helmeted outline of Britain .

A further new denomination appeared in 2014, the gold one-fortieth of an ounce, diameter 8mm and face value 50 pence.

In 2018 David Lawrence chose to portray a beautiful head and shoulders of Britannia wearing a Corinthian helmet, returning to her classical roots. However, for 2019 David once again had her standing in a warlike pose with a lion at her feet and pointing her trident towards the sun. As David Lawrence himself explained: "My initial thoughts were influenced by the great engravers of the past. Their work has classical grace and gravitas I was keen to recreate . . . The end result is an Anglicised version of ancient Rome."

On the following pages we have collated all the known information on the Britannia series and give the current market price you should expect to pay. However, for the later issues, many of which are still available from the Royal Mint, we have given the original issue price.

The Britannia was initially introduced as a bullion coin and changed hands at the prevailing rate, but today they are also collected for their numismatic interest and as such many of them can reach a value much higher than their intrinsic worth, so it is well worth checking before buying or selling coins of the series.

"Set only" indicates that the coin so listed was originally only available as part of a set and the prices are not given individually. BV indicates that the coin currently changes hands at the prevailing price of bullion gold or silver.

Note: whilst all British legal tender gold coins are VAT free, silver bullion coinage attracts VAT at the prevailing rate.

STANDING BRITANNIA
Obverse by Raphael Maklouf
Reverse by Philip Nathan

Date	Metal	Face value	Weight	No. struck	Value
1987	Gold Proof	£10.00	1/10oz	3,500	£225
1987	Gold Bullion	£10.00	1/10oz	Unlimited	BV
1987	Gold Proof	£25.00	1/4oz	3,500	£485
1987	Gold Bullion	£25.00	1/4oz	Unlimited	BV
1987	Gold Proof	£50.00	1/2oz	2,486	£800
1987	Gold Bullion	£50.00	1/2oz	Unlimited	BV
1987	Gold Proof	£100.00	1oz	2,485	£1650
1987	Gold Bullion	£100.00	1oz	Unlimited	BV
1987	Gold Proof Set	£25 and £10		11,100	£750
1987	Gold Proof Set	£100, £50, £25 and £10		10,000	£3750
1988	Gold Proof	£10.00	1/10oz	2,694	£225
1988	Gold Bullion	£10.00	1/10oz	Unlimited	BV
1988	Gold Proof	£25.00	1/4oz	Set only	—
1988	Gold Bullion	£25.00	1/4oz	Unlimited	BV
1988	Gold Proof	£50.00	1/2oz	Set only	—
1988	Gold Bullion	£50.00	1/2oz	Unlimited	BV
1988	Gold Proof	£100.00	1oz	Set only	—
1988	Gold Bullion	£100.00	1oz	Unlimited	BV
1988	Gold Proof Set	£25 and £10		894	£750
1988	Gold Proof Set	£100, £50, £25 and £10		3,505	£3750
1989	Gold Proof	£10.00	1/10oz	1,609	£225
1989	Gold Bullion	£10.00	1/10oz	Unlimited	BV
1989	Gold Proof	£25.00	1/4oz	Set only	—
1989	Gold Bullion	£25.00	1/4oz	Unlimited	BV
1989	Gold Proof	£50.00	1/2oz	Set only	—
1989	Gold Bullion	£50.00	1/2oz	Unlimited	BV
1989	Gold Proof	£100.00	1oz	Set only	—
1989	Gold Bullion	£100.00	1oz	Unlimited	BV
1989	Gold Proof Set	£25 and £10		451	£750
1989	Gold Proof Set	£100, £50, £25 and £10		2,268	£3750
1990	Gold Proof	£10.00	1/10oz	1,571	£225
1990	Gold Bullion	£10.00	1/10oz	Unlimited	BV
1990	Gold Proof	£25.00	1/4oz	Set only	—
1990	Gold Bullion	£25.00	1/4oz	Unlimited	BV
1990	Gold Proof	£50.00	1/2oz	Set only	—
1990	Gold Bullion	£50.00	1/2oz	Unlimited	BV
1990	Gold Proof	£100.00	1oz	Set only	—
1990	Gold Bullion	£100.00	1oz	Unlimited	BV
1990	Gold Proof Set	£100, £50, £25 and £10		527	£3750
1991	Gold Proof	£10.00	1/10oz	(954)	£225
1991	Gold Bullion	£10.00	1/10oz	Unlimited	BV

1987 Gold Proof 1 ounce

Date	Metal	Face value	Weight	No. struck	Value
1991	Gold Proof	£25.00	1/4oz	Set only	—
1991	Gold Bullion	£25.00	1/4oz	Unlimited	BV
1991	Gold Proof	£50.00	1/2oz	Set only	—
1991	Gold Bullion	£50.00	1/2oz	Unlimited	BV
1991	Gold Proof	£100.00	1oz	Set only	—
1991	Gold Bullion	£100.00	1oz	Unlimited	BV
1991	Gold Proof Set	£100, £50, £25 and £10		509	£3750
1992	Gold Proof	£10.00	1/10oz	1,000	£225
1992	Gold Bullion	£10.00	1/10oz	Unlimited	BV
1992	Gold Proof	£25.00	1/4oz	Set only	—
1992	Gold Bullion	£25.00	1/4oz	Unlimited	BV
1992	Gold Proof	£50.00	1/2oz	Set only	—
1992	Gold Bullion	£50.00	1/2oz	Unlimited	BV
1992	Gold Proof	£100.00	1oz	Set only	—
1992	Gold Bullion	£100.00	1oz	Unlimited	BV
1992	Gold Proof Set	£100, £50, £25 and £10		500	£3800
1993	Gold Proof	£10.00	1/10oz	997	£225
1993	Gold Bullion	£10.00	1/10oz	Unlimited	BV
1993	Gold Proof	£25.00	1/4oz	Set only	—
1993	Gold Bullion	£25.00	1/4oz	Unlimited	BV
1993	Gold Proof	£50.00	1/2oz	Set only	—
1993	Gold Bullion	£50.00	1/2oz	Unlimited	BV
1993	Gold Proof	£100.00	1oz	Set only	—
1993	Gold Bullion	£100.00	1oz	Unlimited	BV
1993	Gold Proof Set	£100, £50, £25 and £10		462	£3750
1994	Gold Proof	£10.00	1/10oz	994	£225
1994	Gold Bullion	£10.00	1/10oz	Unlimited	BV
1994	Gold Proof	£25.00	1/4oz	Set only	—
1994	Gold Bullion	£25.00	1/4oz	Unlimited	BV
1994	Gold Proof	£50.00	1/2oz	Set only	—
1994	Gold Bullion	£50.00	1/2oz	Unlimited	BV
1994	Gold Proof	£100.00	1oz	Set only	—
1994	Gold Bullion	£100.00	1oz	Unlimited	BV
1994	Gold Proof Set	£100, £50, £25 and £10		435	£3800
1995	Gold Proof	£10.00	1/10oz	1,500	£225
1995	Gold Bullion	£10.00	1/10oz	Unlimited	BV
1995	Gold Proof	£25.00	1/4oz	Set only	—
1995	Gold Bullion	£25.00	1/4oz	Unlimited	BV
1995	Gold Proof	£50.00	1/2oz	Set only	—
1995	Gold Bullion	£50.00	1/2oz	Unlimited	BV
1995	Gold Proof	£100.00	1oz	Set only	—
1995	Gold Bullion	£100.00	1oz	Unlimited	BV
1995	Gold Proof Set	£100, £50, £25 and £10		500	£3800
1996	Gold Proof	£10.00	1/10oz	2,379	£250
1996	Gold Bullion	£10.00	1/10oz	Unlimited	BV
1996	Gold Proof	£25.00	1/4oz	Set only	—
1996	Gold Bullion	£25.00	1/4oz	Unlimited	BV
1996	Gold Proof	£50.00	1/2oz	Set only	—
1996	Gold Bullion	£50.00	1/2oz	Unlimited	BV
1996	Gold Proof	£100.00	1oz	Set only	—
1996	Gold Bullion	£100.00	1oz	Unlimited	BV
1996	Gold Proof Set	£100, £50, £25 and £10		483	£3800

BRITANNIA IN CHARIOT
Obverse by **Raphael Maklouf**
Reverse by **Philip Nathan**

1997	Silver Proof	20 pence	1/10oz	8,686	£20
1997	Silver Proof	50 pence	1/4oz	Set only	—

Date	Metal	Face value	Weight	No. struck	Value
1997	Silver Proof	£1.00	1/2oz .... Set only		—
1997	Silver Proof	£2.00	1oz 4,173		£75
1997	Silver Bullion	£2.00	1oz .... 100,000"		BV
1997	Silver Proof Set	£2, £1, 50p and 20p 11,832			£225
1997	Gold Proof	£10.00	1/10oz 1,821		£225
1997	Gold Bullion	£10.00	1/10oz .... Unlimited		BV
1997	Gold Proof	£25.00	1/4oz 923		£485
1997	Gold Bullion	£25.00	1/4oz .... Unlimited		BV
1997	Gold Proof	£50.00	1/2oz .... Set only		—
1997	Gold Bullion	£50.00	1/2oz .... Unlimited		BV
1997	Gold Proof	£100.00	1oz 164		£1650
1997	Gold Bullion	£100.00	1oz .... Unlimited		BV
1997	Gold Proof Set	£100, £50, £25 and £10 892			£3750

STANDING BRITANNIA
Obverse by Ian Rank-Broadley
Reverse by Philip Nathan

Date	Metal	Face value	Weight	No. struck	Value
1998	Silver Proof	20 pence	1/10oz 2,724		£20
1998	Silver Proof	50 pence	1/4oz .... Set only		—
1998	Silver Proof	£1.00	1/2oz .... Set only		—
1998	Silver Proof	£2.00	1oz .... Set only		—
1998	Silver Bullion	£2.00	1oz 88,909		BV
1998	Silver Proof Set	£2, £1, 50p and 20p 2,500			£225
1998	Gold Proof	£10.00	1/10oz 392		£225
1998	Gold Bullion	£10.00	1/10oz .... Unlimited		BV
1998	Gold Proof	£25.00	1/4oz 560		£475
1998	Gold Bullion	£25.00	1/4oz .... Unlimited		BV
1998	Gold Proof	£50.00	1/2oz .... Set only		—
1998	Gold Bullion	£50.00	1/2oz .... Unlimited		BV
1998	Gold Proof	£100.00	1oz .... Set only		—
1998	Gold Bullion	£100.00	1oz .... Unlimited		BV
1998	Gold Proof Set	£100, £50, £25 and £10 750			£3800

BRITANNIA IN CHARIOT (SILVER) / STANDING (GOLD)
Obverse by Ian Rank-Broadley
Reverse by Philip Nathan

Date	Metal	Face value	Weight	No. struck	Value
1999	Silver Bullion	£2.00	1oz 69,394		BV
1999	Gold Proof	£10.00	1/10oz 1,058		£225
1999	Gold Bullion	£10.00	1/10oz .... Unlimited		BV
1999	Gold Proof	£25.00	1/4oz 1,000		£485
1999	Gold Bullion	£25.00	1/4oz .... Unlimited		BV
1999	Gold Proof	£50.00	1/2oz .... Set only		—
1999	Gold Bullion	£50.00	1/2oz .... Unlimited		BV
1999	Gold Proof	£100.00	1oz .... Set only		—
1999	Gold Bullion	£100.00	1oz .... Unlimited		BV
1999	Gold Proof Set	£100, £50, £25 and £10 740			£3800

STANDING BRITANNIA
Obverse by Ian Rank-Broadley
Reverse by Philip Nathan

Date	Metal	Face value	Weight	No. struck	Value
2000	Silver Bullion	£2.00	1oz 81,301		BV
2000	Gold Proof	£10.00	1/10oz 3,250		£225
2000	Gold Bullion	£10.00	1/10oz .... Unlimited		BV
2000	Gold Proof	£25.00	1/4oz 1,250		£485
2000	Gold Bullion	£25.00	1/4oz .... Unlimited		BV
2000	Gold Proof	£50.00	1/2oz .... Set only		—
2000	Gold Bullion	£50.00	1/2oz .... Unlimited		BV
2000	Gold Proof	£100.00	1oz .... Set only		—
2000	Gold Bullion	£100.00	1oz .... Unlimited		BV
2000	Gold Proof Set	£100, £50, £25 and £10 750			£3750

Date	Metal	Face value	Weight	No. struck	Value

UNA AND THE LION
Obverse by Ian Rank-Broadley
Reverse by Philip Nathan

Date	Metal	Face value	Weight	No. struck	Value
2001	Silver Proof	20 pence	1/10oz	10,000	£10
2001	Silver Proof	50 pence	1/4oz	Set only	—
2001	Silver Proof	£1.00	1/2oz	Set only	—
2001	Silver Proof	£2.00	1oz	10,000	£75
2001	Silver Bullion	£2.00	1oz	44,816	BV
2001	Silver Proof Set	"£2, £1, 50p and 20p"		Unknown	£225
2001	Gold Proof	£10.00	1/10oz	1,100	£225
2001	Gold Bullion	£10.00	1/10oz	Unlimited	BV
2001	Gold Proof	£25.00	1/4oz	500	£485
2001	Gold Bullion	£25.00	1/4oz	Unlimited	BV
2001	Gold Proof	£50.00	1/2oz	Set only	—
2001	Gold Bullion	£50.00	1/2oz	Unlimited	BV
2001	Gold Proof	£100.00	1oz	Set only	—
2001	Gold Bullion	£100.00	1oz	Unlimited	BV
2001	Gold Proof Set	£100, £50, £25 and £10		1,000	£3750

STANDING BRITANNIA
Obverse by Ian Rank-Broadley
Reverse by Philip Nathan

Date	Metal	Face value	Weight	No. struck	Value
2002	Silver Bullion	£2.00	1oz	36,543	BV
2002	Gold Proof	£10.00	1/10oz	2,500"	£225
2002	Gold Bullion	£10.00	1/10oz	Unlimited	BV
2002	Gold Proof	£25.00	1/4oz	1,750	£485
2002	Gold Bullion	£25.00	1/4oz	Unlimited	BV
2002	Gold Proof	£50.00	1/2oz	Set only	—
2002	Gold Bullion	£50.00	1/2oz	Unlimited	BV
2002	Gold Proof	£100.00	1oz	Set only	—
2002	Gold Bullion	£100.00	1oz	Unlimited	BV
2002	Gold Proof Set	£100, £50, £25 and £10		945	£3750

BRITANNIA'S HELMETED HEAD
Obverse by Ian Rank-Broadley
Reverse by Philip Nathan

Date	Metal	Face value	Weight	No. struck	Value
2003	Silver Proof	20 pence	1/10oz	1,179	£20
2003	Silver Proof	50 pence	1/4oz	Set only	—
2003	Silver Proof	£1.00	1/2oz	Set only	—
2003	Silver Proof	£2.00	1oz	2,016	£65
2003	Silver Bullion	£2.00	1oz	73,271	BV
2003	Silver Proof Set	£2, £1, 50p and 20p		3,669	£225
2003	Gold Proof	£10.00	1/10oz	1,382	£225
2003	Gold Bullion	£10.00	1/10oz	Unlimited	BV
2003	Gold Proof	£25.00	1/4oz	609	£485
2003	Gold Bullion	£25.00	1/4oz	Unlimited	BV
2003	Gold Proof	£50.00	1/2oz	Set only	—
2003	Gold Bullion	£50.00	1/2oz	Unlimited	BV
2003	Gold Proof	£100.00	1oz	Set only	—
2003	Gold Bullion	£100.00	1oz	Unlimited	BV
2003	Gold Proof Set	£50, £25 and £10		825	£1650
2003	Gold Proof Set	£100, £50, £25 and £10		1,250	£3750

STANDING BRITANNIA
Obverse by Ian Rank-Broadley
Reverse by Philip Nathan

Date	Metal	Face value	Weight	No. struck	Value
2004	Silver Proof	£2.00	1oz	2,174	£65
2004	Silver Bullion	£2.00	1oz	57,000	BV
2004	Gold Proof	£10.00	1/10oz	929	£225
2004	Gold Bullion	£10.00	1/10oz	Unlimited	BV
2004	Gold Proof	£25.00	1/4oz	750	£485
2004	Gold Bullion	£25.00	1/4oz	Unlimited	BV

Date	Metal	Face value	Weight		No. struck	Value
2004	Gold Proof	£50.00	1/2oz	Set only		—
2004	Gold Bullion	£50.00	1/2oz	Unlimited		BV
2004	Gold Proof	£100.00	1oz	Set only		—
2004	Gold Bullion	£100.00	1oz	Unlimited		BV
2004	Gold Proof Set	£50, £25 and £10			223	£1750
2004	Gold Proof Set	£100, £50, £25 and £10			973	£3750

BRTANNIA SEATED
Obverse by Ian Rank-Broadley
Reverse by Philip Nathan

2005	Silver Proof	20 pence	1/10oz	913		£20
2005	Silver Proof	50 pence	1/4oz	Set only		—
2005	Silver Proof	£1.00	1/2oz	Set only		—
2005	Silver Proof	£2.00	1oz	1,539		£65
2005	Silver Bullion	£2.00	1oz	57,000		BV
2005	Silver Proof Set	£2, £1, 50p and 20p		2,360		£250
2005	Gold Proof	£10.00	1/10oz	1,225		£225
2005	Gold Bullion	£10.00	1/10oz	Unlimited		BV
2005	Gold Proof	£25.00	1/4oz	750		£500
2005	Gold Bullion	£25.00	1/4oz	Unlimited		BV
2005	Gold Proof	£50.00	1/2oz	Set only		—
2005	Gold Bullion	£50.00	1/2oz	Unlimited		BV
2005	Gold Proof	£100.00	1oz	Set only		—
2005	Gold Bullion	£100.00	1oz	Unlimited		BV
2005	Gold Proof Set	£50, £25 and £10		417		£1750
2005	Gold Proof Set	£100, £50, £25 and £10		1,439		£3750

STANDING BRITANNIA
Obverse by Ian Rank-Broadley
Reverse by Philip Nathan

2006	Silver Proof	20 pence	1/10oz	Set only		—
2006	Silver Proof	50 pence	1/4oz	Set only		—
2006	Silver Proof	£1.00	1/2oz	Set only		—
2006	Silver Proof	£2.00	1oz	2,529		£65
2006	Silver Bullion	£2.00	1oz	50,300		BV
2006	Silver Proof "Silhouette" Set of five designs					
		5 x £2	1oz	3,000		£450
2006	Silver Proof Set	£2, £1, 50p and 20p		2,500		£225
2006	Gold Proof	£10.00	1/10oz	700		£250
2006	Gold Bullion	£10.00	1/10oz	Unlimited		BV
2006	Gold Proof	£25.00	1/4oz	728		£500
2006	Gold Bullion	£25.00	1/4oz	Unlimited		BV
2006	Gold Proof	£50.00	1/2oz	Set only		—
2006	Gold Bullion	£50.00	1/2oz	Unlimited		BV
2006	Gold Proof	£100.00	1oz	Set only		—
2006	Gold Bullion	£100.00	1oz	Unlimited		BV
2006	Gold Proof Set	£100, £50, £25 and £10		1,163		£3750
2006	Gold Proof Set of Five Designs					
		5 x £25	1/4oz	250		£2750

BRITANNIA SEATED LION AT FEET
Obverse by Ian Rank-Broadley
Reverse by Christopher le Brun

2007	Silver Proof	20 pence	1/10oz	901		£20
2007	Silver Proof	50 pence	1/4oz	Set only		—
2007	Silver Proof	£1.00	1/2oz	Set only		—
2007	Silver Proof	£2.00	1oz	2,500		£75
2007	Silver Bullion	£2.00	1oz	94,000		BV
2007	Silver Proof Set (20th Anniversary) 6 Satin Finish Reverses					
		6 x £1		2,000		£275
2007	Silver Proof Set	£2, £1, 50p and 20p		2,500		£225
2007	Gold Proof	£10.00	1/10oz	893		£250

Date	Metal	Face value	Weight	No. struck	Value
2007	Gold Bullion	£10.00	1/10oz............................Unlimited		BV
2007	Gold Proof	£25.00	1/4oz....................................1,000		£485
2007	Gold Bullion	£25.00	1/4oz.............................Unlimited		BV
2007	Gold Proof	£50.00	1/2oz.............................Set only		—
2007	Gold Bullion	£50.00	1/2oz.............................Unlimited		BV
2007	Gold Proof	£100.00	1oz...................................Set only		—
2007	Gold Bullion	£100.00	1oz................................Unlimited		BV
2007	Gold Proof Set	£100, £50, £25 and £10	250		£3750
2007	Platinum Proof	£10	1/10oz...................................691		£190
2007	Platinum Proof	£25	1/4oz....................................210		£390
2007	Platinum Proof	£50	1/2oz.............................Set only		—
2007	Platinum Proof	£100	1oz...................................Set only		—
2007	Platinum Proof Set £100, £50, £25 and £10		250		£2750

STANDING BRITANNIA ON WAVES
Obverse by Ian Rank-Broadley
Reverse by John Bergdahl

Date	Metal	Face value	Weight	No. struck	Value
2008	Silver Proof*	20 pence	1/10oz.................................2,500		£20
2008	Silver Proof*	50 pence	1/4oz.............................Set only		—
2008	Silver Proof*	£1.00	1/2oz.............................Set only		—
2008	Silver Proof*	£2.00	1oz.......................................2,500		£75
2008	Silver Bullion	£2.00	1oz...................................100,000		BV
2008	Silver Proof Set £2, 50p and 20p		2,500		£225
2008	Gold Proof	£10.00	1/10oz....................................748		£250
2008	Gold Bullion	£10.00	1/10oz............................Unlimited		BV
2008	Gold Proof	£25.00	1/4oz....................................1,000		£485
2008	Gold Bullion	£25.00	1/4oz.............................Unlimited		BV
2008	Gold Proof	£50.00	1/2oz.............................Set only		—
2008	Gold Bullion	£50.00	1/2oz.............................Unlimited		BV
2008	Gold Proof	£100.00	1oz...................................Set only		—
2008	Gold Bullion	£100.00	1oz................................Unlimited		BV
2008	Gold Proof Set	£100, £50, £25 and £10	1,250		£3750
2008	Platinum Proof	£10	1/10oz...................................268		£190
2008	Platinum Proof	£25	1/4oz....................................100		£390
2008	Platinum Proof	£50	1/2oz.............................Set only		—
2008	Platinum Proof	£100	1oz...................................Set only		—
2008	Platinum Proof Set £100, £50, £25 and £10		150		£2750

*Satin finish

BRITANNIA IN CHARIOT
Obverse by Ian Rank-Broadley
Reverse by Philip Nathan

Date	Metal	Face value	Weight	No. struck	Value
2009	Silver Proof	20 pence	1/10oz.................................2,500		£18
2009	Silver Proof	50 pence	1/4oz.................................2,500		£25
2009	Silver Proof	£1.00	1/2oz.................................2,500		£35
2009	Silver Proof	£2.00	1oz.......................................6,784		£75
2009	Silver Bullion	£2.00	1oz...................................100,000		BV
2009	Silver Proof Set £2, £1, 50p and 20p		2,500		£225
2009	Gold Proof	£10.00	1/10oz.................................1,546		£225
2009	Gold Bullion	£10.00	1/10oz............................Unlimited		BV
2009	Gold Proof	£25.00	1/4oz....................................1,567		£485
2009	Gold Bullion	£25.00	1/4oz.............................Unlimited		BV
2009	Gold Proof	£50.00	1/2oz......................................797		£800
2009	Gold Bullion	£50.00	1/2oz.............................Unlimited		BV
2009	Gold Proof	£100.00	1oz...797		£1650
2009	Gold Bullion	£100.00	1oz................................Unlimited		BV
2009	Gold Proof Set	£100, £50, £25 and £10	797		£3800

Date	Metal	Face value	Weight	No. struck	Value

BRITANNIA WEARING A CORINTHIAN HELMET
Obverse by Ian Rank-Broadley
Reverse by Suzie Zamit

Date	Metal	Face value	Weight	No. struck	Value
2010	Silver Proof	20 pence	1/10oz	4,486	£12
2010	Silver Proof	50 pence	1/4oz	3,497	£20
2010	Silver Proof	£1.00	1/2oz	3,497	£35
2010	Silver Proof	£2.00	1oz	6,539	£75
2010	Silver Bullion	£2.00	1oz	126,367	BV
2010	Silver Proof Set £2, £1, 50p and 20p			3,500	£225
2010	Gold Proof	£10.00	1/10oz	2,102	£225
2010	Gold Bullion	£10.00	1/10oz	3,530	BV
2010	Gold Proof	£25.00	1/4oz	1,670	£485
2010	Gold Bullion	£25.00	1/4oz	1,501	BV
2010	Gold Proof	£50.00	1/2oz	1,053	£800
2010	Gold Bullion	£50.00	1/2oz	1,301	BV
2010	Gold Proof	£100.00	1oz	867	£1650
2010	Gold Bullion	£100.00	1oz	13,860	BV
2010	Gold Proof Set First Strike £100, £50, £25 and £10			500	£4000
2010	Gold Proof Set £100, £50, £25 and £10			1,250	£3850

"PENNY" BRITANNIA SUPERIMPOSED ON A UNION FLAG
Obverse by Ian Rank-Broadley
Reverse by David Mach

Date	Metal	Face value	Weight	No. struck	Value
2011	Silver Proof	20 pence	1/10oz	2,483	£12
2011	Silver Proof	50 pence	1/4oz	2,483	£20
2011	Silver Proof	£1.00	1/2oz	2,483	£35
2011	Silver Proof	£2.00	1oz	4,973	£75
2011	Silver Bullion	£2.00	1oz	269,282	BV
2011	Silver Proof Set £2, £1, 50p , 20p and 10 pence			3,500	£250
2011	Gold Proof	£10.00	1/10oz	3,511	£225
2011	Gold Proof	£25.00	1/4oz	698	£500
2011	Gold Bullion	£25.00	1/4oz	Unlimited	BV
2011	Gold Proof	£50.00	1/2oz	847	£800
2011	Gold Bullion	£50.00	1/2oz	Unlimited	BV
2011	Gold Proof	£100.00	1oz	5,735	£1650
2011	Gold Bullion	£100.00	1oz	Unlimited	BV
2011	Gold Proof Set £50, £25 and £10			250	£1750
2011	Gold Proof Set £100, £50, £25 and £10			1,000	£3850

STANDING BRITANNIA
Obverse by Ian Rank-Broadley
Reverse by Philip Nathan

Date	Metal	Face value	Weight	No. struck	Value
2012	Silver Proof	20 pence	1/10oz	Set only	—
2012	Silver Proof	50 pence	1/4oz	Set only	—
2012	Silver Proof	£1.00	1/2oz	Set only	—
2012	Silver Proof	£2.00	1oz	5,550	£75
2012	Silver Bullion	£2.00	1oz	351,372	BV
2012	Silver BU	£2.00	1oz	Unknown	BV
2012	Silver Proof Set £2, £1, 50p and 20p			2,595	£225
2012	Silver Proof Set 9 Reverse Portraits		9 x £1.00	1,656	£500
2012	Gold Proof	£10.00	1/10oz	1,249	£225
2012	Gold Proof	£25.00	1/4oz	316	£500
2012	Gold Bullion	£25.00	1/4oz	Unlimited	BV
2012	Gold Proof	£50.00	1/2oz	Set only	—
2012	Gold Bullion	£50.00	1/2oz	Unlimited	BV
2012	Gold Proof	£100.00	1oz	Set only	—
2012	Gold Bullion	£100.00	1oz	Unlimited	BV
2012	Gold Proof Set £50, £25 and £10			99	£1750
2012	Gold Proof Set First Strike £100, £50, £25 and £10			200	£4000
2012	Gold Proof Set £100, £50, £25 and £10			352	£3750
2012	Gold Proof Set 9 Reverse Portraits		9 x £50	25	£8000

Date	Metal	Face value	Weight	No. struck	Value

BRITANNIA SEATED WITH OWL
Obverse by Ian Rank-Broadley
Reverse by Jody Clark

Date	Metal	Face value	Weight	No. struck	Value
2013	Silver Proof	10 pence	1/20oz	Set only	—
2013	Silver Proof	20 pence	1/10oz	Set only	—
2013	Silver Proof	50 pence	1/4oz	Set only	—
2013	Silver BU (SS *Gairsoppa*) Nathan Reverse	50 pence	1/4oz	584,946	£50
2013	Silver Proof	£1.00	1/2oz	Set only	—
2013	Silver Proof	£2.00	1oz	3,468	£300
2013	Silver Bullion (Nathan Reverse)	£2.00	1oz	Unlimited	BV
2013	Silver Bullion (Year of the Snake Privy Mark)	£2.00	1oz	Unlimited	£40
2013	Silver BU	£2.00	1oz	2,387	£24
2013	Silver Proof	£10.00	5oz	4,054	£450
2013	Silver Proof Set £2, £1, 50p , 20p and 10 pence			3,087	£250
2013	Gold Proof	£1.00	1/20oz	2,496	£150
2013	Gold Proof	£10.00	1/10oz	1,150	£250
2013	Gold Proof	£25.00	1/4oz	Set only	—
2013	Gold Bullion (Nathan Reverse)	£25.00	1/4oz	Unlimited	BV
2013	Gold Proof	£50.00	1/2oz	Set only	—
2013	Gold Bullion (Nathan Reverse)	£50.00	1/2oz	Unlimited	BV
2013	Gold Proof	£100.00	1oz	Set only	—
2013	Gold Bullion (Nathan Reverse)	£100.00	1oz	Unlimited	BV
2013	Gold Proof	£500.00	5oz	61	£8250
2013	Gold Proof Set £50, £25 and £10			136	£1750
2013	Gold Proof Set (Premium) £50, £25 and £10			90	£2000
2013	Gold Proof Set £100, £50, £25 and £10			261	£4000

STANDING BRITANNIA WITH GLOBE
Obverse by Ian Rank-Broadley
Reverse by Jody Clark

Date	Metal	Face value	Weight	No. struck	Value
2014	Silver Proof	5 pence	1/40oz	Set only	—
2014	Silver Proof	10 pence	1/20oz	Set only	—
2014	Silver Proof	20 pence	1/10oz	Set only	—
2014	Silver Proof	50 pence	1/4oz	Set only	—
2014	Silver Bullion (SS *Gairsoppa*) Nathan Reverse	50 pence	1/4oz	19,214	£25
2014	Silver Proof	£1.00	1/2oz	Set only	—
2014	Silver Proof	£2.00	1oz	2,981	£75
2014	Silver Proof Gilded Britannia 24k Gold	£2.00	1oz	5,000	£85
2014	Silver Bullion (Nathan Reverse)	£2.00	1oz	623,741	BV
2014	Silver Bullion (Year of the Horse Privy Mark)	£2.00	1oz	Unlimited	£40
2014	Silver Bullion Year of the Horse Obverse Mule	£2.00	1oz	Unknown	—
2014	Silver BU	£2.00	1oz	1,493	£25
2014	Silver Proof	£10.00	5oz	1,348	£400
2014	Silver Proof Set 20p, 10p and 5 pence			998	£45
2014	Silver Proof Set £2, £1, 50p , 20p and 10 pence			550	£250
2014	Silver Proof Set £2, £1, 50p , 20p, 10p and 5 pence			1,735	£300
2014	Gold Proof	50 pence	1/40oz	5,521	£70
2014	Gold Proof	£1.00	1/20oz	993	£150
2014	Gold Proof	£10.00	1/10oz	Set only	—
2014	Gold Bullion (Nathan Reverse)	£10.00	1/10oz	Unlimited	BV

Date	Metal	Face value	Weight	No. struck	Value

2014 Gold Proof   £25.00   1/4oz.............................Set only   —
2014 Gold Bullion (Nathan Reverse)
                      £25.00   1/4oz...........................Unlimited   BV
2014 Gold Proof   £50.00   1/2oz.............................Set only   —
2014 Gold Bullion (Nathan Reverse)
                      £50.00   1/2oz...........................Unlimited   BV
2014 Gold Proof   £100.00   1oz................................Set only   —
2014 Gold Bullion (Nathan Reverse)
                      £100.00   1oz...............................Unlimited   BV
2014 Gold Proof   £500.00   5oz..75   £8000
2014 Gold Proof Set   £50, £25 and £10 140   £1750
2014 Gold Proof Set (Premium) £50, £25 and £10 98   £2000
2014 Gold Proof Set   £100, £50, £25, £10 and £1....................150   £4500
2014 Gold Proof Set (Premium)
                      £100, £50, £25, £10, £1 and 50 pence.... 225   £5000

BRITANNIA WITH TRIDENT
Obverse by Ian Rank-Broadley
Reverse by Antony Dufort

2015 Silver Proof   5 pence   1/40oz................................8,000   £12
2015 Silver Proof   10 pence 1/20oz............................Set only   —
2015 Silver Proof   20 pence 1/10oz............................Set only   —
2015 Silver Proof   50 pence 1/4oz..............................Set only   —
2015 Silver Proof   £1.00   1/2oz..............................Set only   —
2015 Silver Proof   £2.00   1oz....................................2,990   £60
2015 Silver Proof First Release
                         £2.00   1oz....................................1,250   £85
2015 Silver Proof Gilded Britannia 24k Gold
                         £2.00   1oz....................................5,000   £80
2015 Silver Bullion (Nathan Reverse)
                         £2.00   1oz...............................2,780,529   BV
2015 Silver Bullion (Year of the Sheep Privy Mark)
                         £2.00   1oz....................................1,000   £40
2015 Silver BU   £2.00   1oz....................................2,870   £25
2015 Silver Proof   £10.00   5oz.......................................495   £395
2015 Silver Proof First Release
                         £10.00   5oz.......................................500   £420
2015 Silver Proof   £50.00   31g....................................78,644   £60
2015 Silver Proof Set $2, £1, 50p, 20p, 10p and 5 pence...... 1,009   £250
2015 Silver Proof Set First Release.................................
                         £2, £1, 50p , 20p and 10 pence..............550   £250
2015 Gold Proof   50 pence 1/40oz................................3,075   £50
2015 Gold Proof   £1.00   1/20oz............................Set only   —
2015 Gold Proof   £10.00   1/10oz............................Set only   —
2015 Gold Bullion (Nathan Reverse)
                         £10.00   1/10oz...........................Unlimited   BV
2015 Gold Proof   £25.00   1/4oz..............................Set only   —
2015 Gold Bullion (Nathan Reverse)
                         £25.00   1/4oz............................Unlimited   BV
2015 Gold Proof   £50.00   1/2oz..............................Set only   —
2015 Gold Bullion (Nathan Reverse)
                         £50.00   1/2oz............................Unlimited   BV
2015 Gold Proof   £100.00   1oz................................Set only   —
2014 Gold Bullion (Nathan Reverse)
                         £100.00   1oz...............................Unlimited   BV
2015 Gold Proof   £500.00   5oz..50   £8000
2015 Gold Proof First Release
                         £500.00   5oz..10   £8500
2015 Gold Proof Set   £50, £25 and £10 176   £1750
2015 Gold Proof Set (Premium) £50, £25 and £10 99   £1950
2015 Gold Proof Set   £100, £50, £25, £10 and £1....................96   £4500
2015 Gold Proof Set   £100, £50, £25, £10, £1 and 50 pence.... 138   £5000

Date	Metal	Face value	Weight	No. struck	Value

BRITANNIA AS WARRIOR QUEEN
Obverse by Jody Clark
Reverse by Suzie Zamit

2016	Silver Proof	5 pence	1/40oz.............................Set only	—
2016	Silver Proof	10 pence	1/20oz.............................Set only	—
2016	Silver Proof	20 pence	1/10oz.............................Set only	—
2016	Silver Proof	50 pence	1/4oz...............................Set only	—
2016	Silver Proof	£1.00	1/2oz...............................Set only	—
2016	Silver Proof	£2.00	1oz.....................................4,137	£75

2016 Silver Proof First Release
£2.00   1oz..416   £85

2016 Silver Bullion (Nathan Reverse)
£2.00   1oz................................Unlimited   BV

2016 Silver Bullion (Year of the Monkey Privy Mark)
£2.00   1oz.....................................1,000   £26

2016	Silver BU	£2.00	1oz.....................................2,901	£24
2016	Silver BU	£2.00	1oz in Capsule....................1,000	£25
2016	Silver Proof	£10.00	5oz.......................................533	£395

2016 Silver Proof First Release
£10.00   5oz..25   £420

2016 Silver Proof 1oz Suzie Zamit and 1oz Nathan Reverse.....500   £75
2016 Silver Proof Set £2, £1, 50p , 20p, 10p and 5 pence......1,050   £215
2016 Silver Proof Set Ultra Cameo Slabbed
£2, £1, 50p , 20p and 10 pence...............250   £400

2016	Gold Proof	50 pence	1/40oz.................................1,447	£70
2016	Gold Proof	£1.00	1/20oz.............................Set only	—
2016	Gold Proof	£10.00	1/10oz.............................Set only	—
2016	Gold Proof	£25.00	1/4oz.....................................729	£500

2016 Gold Proof First Release
£25.00   1/4oz....................................100   £550

2016	Gold Proof	£50.00	1/2oz...............................Set only	—
2016	Gold Proof	£100.00	1oz...................................Set only	—

2016 Gold Bullion (Nathan Reverse)
£100.00   1oz................................Unlimited   BV

2016 Gold Proof   £500.00   5oz...54   £8000

2016 Gold Proof First Release
£500.00   5oz..10   £8000

2016 Gold Proof Set   £50, £25 and £10 69   £...
2016 Gold Proof Set   £100, £50, £25, £10, £1 and 50 pence....174   £5430

HELMETED OUTLINE OF BRITAIN
Obverse by Jody Clark
Reverse by Louis Tamlyn

2017	Silver Proof	5 pence	1/40oz.............................Set only	—
2017	Silver Proof	10 pence	1/20oz.............................Set only	—
2017	Silver Proof	20 pence	1/10oz.............................Set only	—
2017	Silver Proof	50 pence	1/4oz...............................Set only	—
2017	Silver Proof	£1.00	1/2oz...............................Set only	—
2017	Silver BU	£2.00	1oz.....................................3,977	£24
2017	Silver Proof	£2.00	1oz.....................................5,225	£80

2017 Silver Bullion (Nathan Reverse)
£2.00   1oz................................Unlimited   BV

2017 Silver Bullion (30th Anniversary Trident Privy Mark)
£2.00   1oz................................120,000   BV

2017 Silver Bullion (Year of the Rooster Privy Mark)
£2.00   1oz................................Unlimited   £26

2017	Silver Proof	£10.00	5oz.......................................656	£415
2017	Silver Proof	£250.00	20oz.....................................103	£450

2017 Silver Proof Set £2, £1, 50p , 20p, 10p and 5 pence......1,347   £250

2017	Gold Proof	50 pence	1/40oz...................................871	£70
2017	Gold Proof	£1.00	1/20oz.............................Set only	—
2017	Gold Proof	£10.00	1/10oz.............................Set only	—

Date	Metal	Face value	Weight	No. struck	Value

2017 Gold bullion (Nathan Reverse)
£10.00 1/10oz.............................Set only —
2017 Gold Proof £25.00 1/4oz.....................................687 £500
2017 Gold Bullion (Nathan Reverse)
£25.00 1/4oz.............................Set only —
2017 Gold Proof £50.00 1/2oz.............................Set only —
2017 Gold Bullion (Nathan Reverse)
£50.00 1/2oz.............................Unlimited BV
2017 Gold Proof £100.00 1oz...............................Set only —
2017 Gold Bullion (Nathan Reverse)
£100.00 1oz................................Unlimited BV
2017 Gold Bullion (30th Anniversary Trident Privy Mark)
£100.00 1oz.................................7,030 BV
2017 Gold Proof £500.00 5oz...98 £8250
2017 Gold Proof (30th Anniversary Trident Privy Mark)
£500.00 30oz...................................6 —
2017 Gold Proof Set £50, £25 and £10...................................143 £1750
017 Gold Proof Set £100, £50, £25, £10 and £1.....................62 £4500
2017 Gold Proof Set £100, £50, £25, £10, £1 and 50 pence....176 £5000
2017 Platinum Bullion (Nathan Reverse)
£10 1/10oz............................Unlimited BV
2017 Platinum Proof £25.00 1/4oz.....................................538 £525
2017 Platinum Bullion (Nathan Reverse)
£25.00 1/4oz.............................Unlimited BV
2017 Platinum Bullion (Nathan Reverse)
£100.00 1oz................................Unlimited BV

BRITANNIA FACING RIGHT WEARING A CORINTHIAN HELMET
Obverse **by Jody Clark**
Reverse **by David Lawrence**

2018 Silver Proof 5 pence 1/40oz............................Set only —
2018 Silver Proof 10 pence 1/20oz............................Set only —
2018 Silver Proof 20 pence 1/10oz............................Set only —
2018 Silver Proof 50 pence 1/4oz.............................Set only —
2018 Silver Proof £1.00 1/2oz.................................Set only —
2018 Silver Proof £2.00 1oz.................................5,100 £85
2018 Silver Bullion (Nathan Reverse)
£2.00 1oz...............................Unlimited BV
2018 Silver Bullion (Year of the Dog Privy Mark)
£2 1oz...............................Unlimited £26
2018 Silver Bullion "Oriental Border" (Nathan Reverse)
£2.00 1oz.............................100,000 BV
2018 BU £2.00 1oz.....................................7,000 BV
2018 Silver Proof £10.00 5oz..650 £420
2018 Silver Proof £500.00 1kg...150 £2050
2018 Silver Proof Set £2, £1, 50p , 20p, 10p and 5 pence......1,350 £300
2018 Gold Proof 50 pence 1/40oz............................Set only —
2018 Gold Proof £1.00 1/20oz............................Set only —
2018 Gold Proof £10.00 1/10oz............................Set only —
2018 Gold bullion (Nathan Reverse)
£10.00 1/10oz..........................Unlimited BV
2018 Gold Proof £25.00 1/4oz.....................................1,080 £595
2018 Gold Bullion (Nathan Reverse)
£25.00 1/4oz.............................Unlimited BV
2018 Gold Proof £50.00 1/2oz.............................Set only —
2018 Gold Bullion (Nathan Reverse)
£50.00 1/2oz.............................Set only —
2018 Gold Bullion (Nathan Reverse)
£100.00 1oz................................Unlimited BV
2018 Gold bullion "Oriental Border" (Nathan Reverse)
£100.00 1oz.................................5,000 BV
2018 Gold Proof £500.00 5oz...90 £9995

2018	Gold Proof Set	£100, £50, £25, £10, £1 and 50 pence....	220	£4400	
2018	Gold Proof Set	£50, £25 and £10	170	£1945	
2018	Platinum Bullion (Nathan Reverse)				
		£100.00	1oz	5,000	BV
2018	Platinum Proof	£25.00	1/4oz	600	£525
2018	Platinum Bullion (Nathan Reverse)				
		£25.00	1/4oz	Unlimited	BV
2018	Platinum Bullion (Nathan Reverse)				
		£10	1/10oz	Unlimited	BV

STANDING BRITANNIA IN WARLIKE POSE
Obverse by Jody Clar
Reverse by David Lawrence

2019	Silver Proof	5 pence	1/40oz	Set only	—
2019	Silver Proof	10 pence	1/20oz	Set only	—
2019	Silver Proof	20 pence	1/10oz	Set only	—
2019	Silver Proof	50 pence	1/4oz	Set only	—
2019	Silver Proof	£1.00	1/2oz	Set only	—
2019	Silver Proof	£2.00	1oz	5,200	£75
2019	Silver Proof Coin and Print Set				
		£2.00	1oz	200 each frame colour	£245
2019	Silver Bullion 'Oriental Border' (Nathan Reverse)				
		£2.00	1oz	Unlimited	BV
2019	Silver Bullion (Nathan Reverse)				
		£2.00	1oz	Unlimited	BV
2019	Silver Bullion (Year of the Pig Privy Mark)				
		£2.00	1oz	Unknown	£26
2019	BU (Year of the Pig Privy Mark)				
		£2.00	1oz	Unknown	
2019	Silver BU	£2.00	1oz	10,000	£55
2019	Silver BU	£10.00	5oz	250	£420
2019	Silver Proof	£500.00	1kg	85	£2050
2019	Silver Proof Set	£2, £1, 50p , 20p, 10p and 5 pence	950	£250	
2019	Gold Proof	50 pence	1/40oz	Set only	—
2019	Gold Proof	£1.00	1/20oz	Set only	—
2019	Gold Proof	£10.00	1/10oz	Set only	—
2019	Gold bullion (Nathan Reverse)				
		£10.00	1/10oz	Unlimited	BV
2019	Gold Proof	£25.00	1/4oz	645	£555
2019	Gold Bullion (Nathan Reverse)				
		£25.00	1/4oz	Unlimited	BV
2019	Gold Proof	£50.00	1/2oz	Set only	—
2019	Gold Bullion (Nathan Reverse)				
		£50.00	1/2oz	Unlimited	BV
2019	Gold Bullion (Nathan Reverse)				
		£100.00	1oz	Unlimited	BV
2019	Gold bullion "Oriental Border" (Nathan Reverse)				
		£100.00	1oz	Unlimited	BV
2019	Gold Proof	£200.00	2oz	100	£4395
2019	Gold Proof	£500.00	5oz	57	£9995
2019	Gold Proof Set	£100, £50, £25, £10, £1 and 50 pence....	150	£3895	
2019	Gold Proof Set	£50, £25 and £10	130	£1945	
2019	Platinum Bullion (Nathan Reverse)				
		£10	1/10oz	Unlimited	BV
2019	Platinum Proof	£25.00	1/4oz	240	£525
2019	Platinum Bullion (Nathan Reverse)				
		£100.00	1oz	Unlimited	BV

STANDING BRITANNIA WITH UNION FLAG BACKGROUND
Obverse **by Jody Clark**
Reverse **by James Tottle**

2020 Silver Proof	5 pence	1/40oz	Set only	—
2020 Silver Proof	10 pence	1/20oz	Set only	—
2020 Silver Proof	20 pence	1/10oz	Set only	—
2020 Silver Proof	50 pence	1/4oz	Set only	—
2020 Silver Proof	£1.00	1/2oz	Set only	—
2020 Silver Proof	£2.00	1oz	3,000	£85
2020 Silver Proof Coin and Print Set				
	£2.00	1oz	100	£245
2020 Silver Bullion (Nathan Reverse)				
	£2.00	1oz	Unlimited	BV
2020 Silver Bullion (Year of the Rat Privy Mark)				
	£2.00	1oz	Unlimited	£26
2020 Silver Proof Set: 1 x frosted reverse, 1 x standard				
	2 x £2	1oz	700	£170
2020 BU	£2.00	1oz	3,000	£55
2020 Silver Proof	£10.00	5oz	250	£420
2020 Silver Proof	£500.00	1kg	30	£2050
2020 Silver Proof Set £2, £1, 50p , 20p, 10p and 5 pence			1,000	£205
2020 Gold Proof	50 pence	1/40oz	Set only	—
2020 Gold Proof	£1.00	1/20oz	Set only	—
2020 Gold Proof	£10.00	1/10oz	Set only	—
2020 Gold bullion (Nathan Reverse)				
	£10.00	1/10oz	Unlimited	BV
2020 Gold Proof	£25.00	1/4oz	700	£500
2020 Gold Bullion (Nathan Reverse)				
	£25.00	1/4oz	Unlimited	BV
2020 Gold Proof	£50.00	1/2oz	Set only	—
2020 Gold Bullion (Nathan Reverse)				
	£50.00	1/2oz	Set only	—
2020 Gold Proof	£100.00	1oz	Coin and print set 25	£2600
2020 Gold Bullion (Nathan Reverse)				
	£100.00	1oz	Unlimited	BV
2020 Gold bullion "Oriental Border" (Nathan Reverse)				
	£100.00	1oz	Unlimited	BV
2020 Gold Proof	£200.00	2oz	150	£4395
2020 Gold Proof Set £100, £50, £25, £10, £1 and 50 pence			150	£4165
2020 Gold Proof Set £50, £25 and £10			130	£1840
2020 Gold Proof Coin and Print Set				
	£100	1oz	25	£2600
2020 Gold Proof	£500	5oz	50	£10,605
2020 Platinum Bullion (Nathan Reverse)				
	£10	1/10oz	Unlimited	BV
2020 Platinum Proof	£25.00	1/4oz	160	£525
2020 Platinum Bullion (Nathan Reverse)				
	£25.00	1/4oz	Unlimited	BV
2020 Platinum Bullion (Nathan Reverse)				
	£100.00	1oz	Unlimited	BV

Most of the later prices given above are the original Royal Mint issue prices as very few of the coins have come onto the market.

BRITANNIA SEATED WITH LION AND BRITANNIA IN PROFILE FOR PREMIUM EXCLUSIVE COINS
Obverse by Jody Clark
Reverse by P.J. Lynch

2021	Silver Proof	5 pence	1/40oz	Set only	—
2021	Silver Proof	10 pence	1/20oz	Set only	—
2021	Silver Proof	20 pence	1/10oz	Set only	—
2021	Silver Proof	50 pence	1/4oz	Set only	—
2021	Silver Proof	£1.00	1/2oz	Set only	—
2021	Silver Proof Britannia Seated with Lion	£2.00	1oz	2,900	£95
2021	Silver Bullion (Nathan Reverse)	£2.00	1oz	Unlimited	BV
2021	Silver Proof set Britannia Seated with Lion - 1 x frosted reverse, 1 x standard	2 x £2	1oz	500	£185
2021	Premium Exclusive (Britannia in Profile) BU	£2.00	1oz	7,500 (7,510 struck)	£62.50
	Silver Proof (Britannia seated with Lion)	£2.00	1oz	4860	£92.50
2021	Silver Proof Premium Exclusive (Britannia in Profile)	£5.00	2oz	550 (560 struck)	£195
2021	Silver Proof (Britannia seated with Lion)	£10.00	5oz	285	£455
2021	Premium Exclusive' Britannia in Profile Silver Proof	£500.00	1kg	40 (50 Struck)	£2,445
2021	Silver Proof (Britannia seated with Lion)	£1000.00	2kg	110	£4,890
2021	Silver Proof Set (Britannia seated with Lion)	£2, £1, 50p , 20p, 10p and 5 pence		1,100	£235
2021	Gold Proof	50 pence	1/40oz	Set only	—
2021	Gold Proof	£1.00	1/20oz	Set only	—
2021	Gold Proof	£10.00	1/10oz	Set only	—
2021	Gold bullion (Nathan Reverse)	£10.00	1/10oz	Unlimited	BV
2021	Gold Proof Set (Britannia seated with Lion)	£25.00	1/4oz	775 (1060 minted)	£650
2021	Gold Bullion (Nathan Reverse)	£25.00	1/4oz	Unlimited	BV
2021	Gold Proof	£50.00	1/2oz	Set only	—
2021	Gold Bullion (Nathan Reverse)	£50.00	1/2oz	Set only	BV
2021	Gold Bullion (Nathan Reverse)	£100.00	1oz	Unlimited	BV
2021	Gold Proof (Britannia seated with Lion)	£200.00	2oz	103	£8,190
			Sold price at LondonCoin Auctions		
2021	Gold Proof Premium Exclusive (Britannia in Profile)	£200.00	2oz	220 (230 struck)	£4,650
2021	Gold Proof (Britannia seated with Lion)	£500.00	5oz	83	£10,820
2021	Gold Proof Premium (Britannia in Profile)	£1000.00	1kg	5 (6 struck)	£70,275
2021	Gold Proof Premium Exclusive (Britannia in Profile)	£100, £50, £25, £10, £1 and 50 pence		150	£4,485
2021	Gold Proof Set (Briannia seated with Lion)	£50, £25 and £10		115	£1,985
2021	Platinum Bullion (Nathan Reverse)	£10	1/10oz	Unlimited	BV
2021	Platinum Proof (Britannia seated with Lion)	£25.00	1/4oz	150	£550
2021	Platinum Bullion (Nathan Reverse)	£100.00	1oz	Unlimited	BV

PRECIOUS METAL BULLION AND COLLECTOR COINS (SERIES)

The Shengxiào Lunar Collection

The Shengxiào Collection of Lunar Coins by designer Wuon-Gean Ho was begun for the Year of the Horse in 2014 bringing the Royal Mint in line with most other major mints of the world. The Shengxiào series ended in 2018 but the Lunar series continues to be issued each year. We list them separately here, however, the larger denominatiions have also been listed under their respective headings.

Date	Weight Face value/	Auth. issue qty	No. Issued	Issue price
2014 YEAR OF THE HORSE				
Silver bullion	1 ounce /£2	—	—	BV
Silver Proof	1 ounce/£2	8,888	—	£85
Silver Proof	5 ounces/£10	1,488	—	£450
Gold BU	One-tenth ounce/£10	2,888	1,779	£225
Gold bullion	1 ounce/£100	—	—	BV
Gold Proof	1 ounce/£100	888	811	£1950
2015 YEAR OF THE SHEEP				
Silver bullion	1 ounce /£2	—	—	BV
Silver Proof	1 ounce/£2	9,888	4,463	£85
Silver Proof with gold plating	1 ounce/£2	4,888	1,358	£120
Silver Proof	5 ounces/£10	1,088	—	£395
Gold BU	One-tenth ounce/£10	2,888	922	£225
Gold bullion	1 ounce/£100	—	—	BV
Gold Proof	1 ounce/£100	888	548	£1950
Gold Proof	5 ounces/£500	38	—	£7500
2016 YEAR OF THE MONKEY				
Silver bullion	1 ounce /£2	—	—	BV
Silver Proof	1 ounce/£2	8,888	—	£85
Silver Proof	5 ounces/£10	588	—	£395
Silver Proof	1 kilo/£500	88	—	£2000
Gold BU	One-tenth ounce/£10	1,888	—	£175
Gold bullion	1 ounce/£100	—	—	BV
Gold Proof	1 ounce/£100	888	—	£1495
Gold Proof	5 ounces/£500	38	—	£7500
Gold Proof	1 kilo/£1,000	8	—	£42,500
2017 YEAR OF THE ROOSTER				
Silver bullion	1 ounce /£2	—	—	BV
Silver Proof	1 ounce/£2	3,888	3,846	£85
Silver Proof	5 ounces/£10	388	369	£415
Silver Proof	1 kilo/£500	88	—	£2050
Gold BU	One-tenth ounce/£10	2,088	980	£205
Gold bullion	1 ounce/£100	—	—	BV
Gold Proof	1 ounce/£100	688	—	£1780
Gold Proof	5 ounces/£500	38	35	£8250
Gold Proof	1 kilo/£1,000	8	8	£49,995
2018 YEAR OF THE DOG				
Silver bullion	1 ounce /£2	—	—	BV
Silver Proof	1 ounce/£2	5,088	—	£85
Silver Proof	5 ounces/£10	388	—	£415
Silver Proof	1 kilo/£500	108	—	£2050
Gold BU	One-tenth ounce/£10	1,088	—	£175
Gold bullion	1 ounce/£100	—	—	BV
Gold Proof	1 ounce/£100	888	—	£1795

The Lunar series, *continued*

From 2019 the Royal Mint has invited various artists to create the reverses for the Lunar serties as noted in each section below.

Date	Weight/ Face value	Auth. issue qty	No. Issued	Issue price
2019 LUNAR YEAR OF THE PIG				
Obverse: Jody Clark Royal portrait				
Reverse: by Harry Brockway				
Silver bullion............................ 1 ounce /£2		—	—	BV
Silver Proof .... 1 ounce/£2		3,888	—	£85
Silver Proof ....5 ounces/£10		288	—	£420
Silver Proof ....1 kilo/£500		38	—	£2025
Gold BU .... One-tenth ounce/£10		1,088	—	£210
Gold bullion............................ 1 ounce/£100		—	—	BV
Gold Proof............................. 1 ounce/£100		888	—	£1880
Gold Proof............................5 ounces/£500		38	—	£8645
Gold Proof................................1 kilo/£1,000		8	—	—

2020 LUNAR YEAR OF THE RAT;				
Obverse: Jody Clark Royal portrait				
Reverse: by P. J. Lynch				
Silver bullion............................ 1 ounce /£2		—	—	BV
Silver Proof .... 1 ounce/£2		2,588	—	£85
Silver Proof ....5 ounces/£10		188	—	£420
Silver Proof ....1 kilo/£500		28	—	£2050
Gold BU .... One-tenth ounce/£10		1,088	—	£210
Gold Proof...................... Quarter ounce/£25		388	—	£530
Gold bullion............................ 1 ounce/£100		—	—	BV
Gold Proof............................. 1 ounce/£100		888	—	£2100
Gold Proof............................5 ounces/£500		28	—	£9995
Gold Proof................................1 kilo/£1,000		8	—	£59,995

2021 LUNAR YEAR OF THE OX;				
Obverse: Jody Clark				
Reverse: Harry Brockway				
Silver bullion .... 1 ounce /£2		—	—	BV
Silver Proof .... 1 ounce/£2		3998	—	£85
Silver Proof ....5 ounces/£10		198	—	£420
Silver Proof ....1 kilo/£500		38	—	£2050
Gold Proof .... Quarter ounce/£25		398	—	£585
Gold Proof .... 1 ounce/£100		898	—	£2,320
Gold Proof ....5 ounces/£500		38	—	£10,605
Gold Proof ....1 kilo/£1,000		10	—	£63,865

A number of countries strike coins to mark the new lunar year with many appearing in rather creative ways such as the Year of the Ox Silver 1,000 togrog along with the more traditional, coin-shaped reverse of 1,000 togrog gold issue from Mongolia. (Images courtesy Coin Invest Trust.)

The Queen's Beasts

In 2016 a new series of coins was introduced by the Royal Mint entitled "The Queen's Beasts". These are intended as a homage to Her Majesty becoming Britain's longest reigning monarch and each coin in the series represents one of the heraldic animals sculpted by James Woodford, RA, for the Coronation ceremony held in Westminster Abbey in 1953. The 6-foot tall sculptures each symbolised the various strands of royal ancestry and were inspired by the King's Beasts of Henry VIII that still line the bridge at Hampton Court .So far six beasts have been chosen as the subjects of the reverse designs of the series: the Lion (bullion and collector), the Griffin (bullion only), the Dragon (bullion and collector), the Unicorn (bullion and collector), the Bull (bullion and collector) and the Falcon (collector coin only). The coins all carry the effigy of Her Majesty the Queen by Jody Clark on the obverse with the heraldic beasts, by the same designer, appearing on the reverse. The coins have been struck in a variety of metals and in different sizes with the bullion issues and the collector coins actually bearing slightly different designs, even though the "beast" is the same". To make it simple for collectors to follow the series we list them below, showing the issue price, rather than under their various denominations.

Date	Weight Face value/	Auth. issue qty	No. Issued	Issue price
THE LION OF ENGLAND				
2016 Silver bullion	2 ounces/£5	—		BV
2016 Gold bullion	1 ounce/£100	—		BV
2017 Cu-Ni BU	£5	—	31,838	£13
2017 Silver Proof	1 ounce/£2	8,500	8,376	£85
2017 Silver Proof	5 ounces/£10	2,500	674	£415
2017 Silver bullion	10 ounces/£10	—	684	BV
2017 Silver Proof	1 kilo/£500	350	117	£2050
2017 Gold Proof	Quarter ounce/£25	2,500	2,492	£475
2017 Gold Proof	1 ounce/£100	1,000	591	£1780
2017 Gold Proof	5 ounces/£500	125	100	£8250
2017 Gold proof	1 kilo/£1,000	—	13	£49,995
2017 Platinum bullion	1 ounce/£100	—	—	BV
THE GRIFFIN OF EDWARD III				
2017 Silver bullion	2 ounces/£5	—	—	BV
2017 Gold bullion	Quarter ounce/£25	—	—	BV
2017 Gold bullion	1 ounce/£100	—	—	BV
THE RED DRAGON OF WALES				
2017 Silver bullion	2 ounces/£5	—	—	BV
2017 Gold bullion	Quarter ounce/£25	—	—	BV
2017 Gold bullion	1 ounce/£100	—	—	BV
2018 Gold Proof	1 kilo/£1000	—	—	£49,995
2018 Silver Proof	1 kilo/£500	—	—	£2025
THE UNICORN OF SCOTLAND				
2017 Cu-Ni BU	£5	—	31,978	£13
2017 Silver Proof	1 ounce/£2	6,250	5,952	£85
2017 Silver Proof	5 ounces/£10	750	458	£415
2017 Silver Proof	10 ounces/£10	850	—	£795
2017 Silver Proof	1 kilo/£500	225	—	£2050
2017 Gold Proof	Quarter ounce/£25	1,500	1,499	£475
2017 Gold Proof	1 ounce/£100	500	418	£475
2017 Gold Proof	5 ounces/£500	–	75	£475
2017 Gold Proof	1 kilo/£1,000	—	8	£475
THE BLACK BULL OF CLARENCE				
2018 Cu-Ni BU	£5	—	—	£13
2018 Silver Proof	1 ounce/£2	6,000	—	£85
2018 Silver Proof	5 ounces/£10	700	—	£420
2018 Silver Proof	10 ounces/£10	600	—	£795
2018 Silver Proof	1 kilo/£500	150	—	£2025
2018 Gold Proof	1 ounce/£100	500	—	£1850
2018 Gold Proof	5 ounces/£500	85	—	£8565

Date	Weight Face value/	Auth. issue qty	No. Issued	Issue price
THE YALE OF BEAUFORT				
2019 Cu-Ni BU	£5	—	—	£13
2019 Silver Proof	1 ounce/£2	5,500	—	BV
2019 Silver Proof	5 ounces/£10	400	—	£420
2019 Silver Proof	10 ounces/£10	240	—	£795
2019 Silver Proof	1 kilo/£500	120	—	£2025
2019 Gold Proof	1/4 ounce/£25	1,250	—	BV
2019 Gold Proof	1 ounce/£100	400	—	BV
2019 Gold Proof	5 ounces/£500	70	—	£8645
2019 Gold Proof	1 kilo/£1000	13	—	£59,995
FALCON OF THE PLANTAGENETS				
2019 Cu-Ni BU	£5	—	—	£13
2019 Silver Proof	1 ounce/£2	5,510	—	BV
2019 — Proof	5 ounces/£10	400	—	£420
2019 — Proof	10 ounces/£10	350	—	£795
2019 — Proof	1 kilo/£500	100	—	£2050
2019 Gold Proof	1/4 ounce/£25	1250	—	BV
2019 — Proof	1 ounce/£100	400	—	BV
2019 — Proof	5 ounces/£500	75	—	£9995
2019 — Proof	1 kilo/£1000	10	—	£59,995
WHITE LION OF MORTIMER				
2020 Cu-Ni BU	£5	—	—	£13
2020 Silver Proof	1 ounce/£2	4,250	—	BV
2020 — Proof	5 ounces/£10	250	—	£420
2020 — Proof	10 ounces/£10	200	—	£795
2020 — Proof	1 kilo/£500	90	—	£2025
2020 Gold Proof	1/4 ounce/£25	1,000	—	BV
2020 — Proof	1 ounce/£100	390	—	BV
2020 — Proof	5 ounces/£500	55	—	£9995
2020 — Proof	1 kilo/£1000	10	—	—
WHITE HORSE OF HANOVER				
2020 Cu-Ni BU	£5	—	—	£13
2020 Silver Proof	1 ounce/£2	4,310	—	£85
2020 — Proof	5 ounces/£10	315	—	£420
2020 — Proof	10 ounces/£10	235	—	£795
2020 — Proof	1 kilo/£500	115	—	£2050
2020 Gold Proof	1/4 ounce/£25	1,000	—	£510
2020 — Proof	1 ounce/£100	435	—	£2020
2020 — Proof	5 ounces/£500	69	—	£9595
2020 — Proof	1 kilo/£1000	13	—	£57,750
WHITE GREYHOUND OF RICHMOND				
2021 Cu-Ni BU	£5	—	—	£13
2021 Silver Proof	1 ounce/£2	3,960		£85
2021 — Proof	5 ounces/£10	370		£420
2021 — Proof	10 ounces/£10	195		£795
2021 — Proof	1 kilo/£500	80		£2,025
2021 Gold Proof	1/4 ounce/£25	1,010		£585
2021 — Proof	1 ounce/£100	425		£2,320
2021 — Proof	5 ounces/£500	69		£10,605
2021 — Proof	1 kilo/£1000	10		£63,865
GRIFFIN OF EDWARD III				
2021 Cu-Ni BU	£5	—		£13
2021 Silver Proof	1 ounce/£2	4,400		£92.50
2021 — Proof	5 ounces/£10	290		£455
2021 — Proof	10 ounces/£10	140		£865
2021 — Proof	1 kilo/£500	70		£2,270
2021 Gold Proof	1/4 ounce/£25	1,240		£605
2021 — Proof	1 ounce/£100	500		£2,370
2021 — Proof	5 ounces/£500	115		£10,820
2021 — Proof	1 kilo/£1000	10		£65,275

THE QUEEN'S BEASTS 2021—COMPLETER COIN

2021 Cu-Ni BU £5	—	—	£13
2021 Silver Proof ....1kilo/£500	—	—	£714.44
2021 Gold Proof ....1 ounce/£100		—	£1372.29
2021 Gold Proof .... 1 kilo/£1000	16		£63,865

The above coin was issued in 2021 depicting all 10 designs from the Queen's Beasts series. A so called "completer coin" to round up this popular collection.

The Valiant

The Valiant series of silver bullion-related coins portraying St George slaying the Dragon by artist Etienne Millner was introduced in 2018 with an attractive 10 ounce silver piece with the weight shown in the field. In 2019 the design was modified to give the weight in the legend around the circumference of the reverse. The obverse carries the effigy of Her Majesty the Queen by Jody Clark.

Date Face value/	Weight	Auth. issue qty	Issue price
2018 silver ....10 ounces		—	£191.58
2019 silver .... 1 ounce		100,000	£19.76
2019 silver ....10 ounces		—	£198.60
2020 silver .... 1 ounce		100,000	£25.19
2020 silver ....10 ounces		—	£250.76
2021 silver ....10 ounces		—	£256.00
2021 silver .... 1 ounce		100,000	£25.49

The information contained in this section is as supplied and is correct at the time of going to press (August 2021) but the quantities struck and the issue prices can be subject to change by the Royal Mint. To keep up to date on the new releases visit www.royalmint.com and www.royalmintbullion.com or check in COIN NEWS magazine every month.

ABBREVIATIONS COMMONLY USED TO DENOTE METALLIC COMPOSITION	
Cu	Copper
Cu/Steel	Copper plated steel
Ag/Cu	Silver plated copper
Ae	Bronze
Cu-Ni	Cupro-nickel
Ni-Ag	Nickel silver (note—does not contain silver)
Brass/Cu-Ni	Brass outer, cupro-nickel inner
Ni-Brass	Nickel-brass
Ag	Silver
Au/Ag	Gold plated silver
Au	Gold
Pl	Platinum

The Royal Arms

Another bullion coin aimed at the investor, The Royal Arms series in gold and silver was introduced in 2019. The coins carry the Royal Arms as depicted by Eric Sewell in 1983 but reinterpreted in this design by Timothy Noad. The common obverse carries the effigy of Her Majesty the Queen by Jody Clark.

These coins are available in one ounce gold, one ounce platinum, 10 ounce silver and one ounce silver. As they are intended as bullion investment coins rather than for the collector market the prices asked for them will vary according to the prevailing metal markets.

> In addition to their various investor coins, the Royal Mint regularly introduces other series of interest in various metals and weights. All can be found on the Mint's website which gives full details and issue prices

Great Engravers series

This new series commemorates the work of the great designers of the past. The first issue released in November 2019 celebrates the skill of William Wyon, his original Una and the Lion design has been skilfully remastered using modern technology by Royal Mint engraver Gordon Summers. In addition to those listed below, just one example was struck as a 5 kilo coin. The obverse carries the effigy of Her Majesty the Queen by Jody Clark.

Date	Weight Face value/	Auth. issue qty	Issue price
UNA & THE LION			
2019 Silver Proof .... 2 ounces/£5		2980	£180
2019 Gold Proof .... 2 ounces/£200		205	£3995
2019 — Proof .... 5 ounces/£500		65	£9995
2019 — Proof ....1 kilo/£1000		7	£59,995
2019 — Proof ....2 kilos/£2000		4	£119,950
THE THREE GRACES			
2020 Silver Proof .... 2 ounces/£5		3500	£185
2020 Gold Proof .... 2 ounces/£200		325	£4995
2020 — Proof .... 5 ounces/£500		150	£11,995
2020 — Proof ....1 kilo/£1000		20	£74,000

The James Bond Collection

Released to coincide with the 25th James Bond movie "No Time to Die" in 2020, the commemorative coin collection offered three coins in several editions from BU to precious metal including just one 7 kilo coin, a first for the Royal Mint. Precious metal gold and silver bars were also available. Designers of the reverse images were Matt Dent, Christian Davies and Laura Clancy. The common obverse carries the effigy of Her Majesty the Queen by Jody Clark.

Date	Weight Face value/	Auth. issue qty	Issue price
CORE RANGE—ASTON MARTIN			
2020 BU £5		—	£13
2020 Silver Proof .... 1/2 ounce/£1		15017	£65
2020 — Proof .... 1 ounce/£2		8517	£87.50
2020 Gold Proof .... 1/4 ounce/£25		1067	£517
2020 — Proof .... 1 ounce/£100		360	£2070
INSPIRED INNOVATION RANGE—SUBMARINE CAR			
2020 Silver Proof .... 2 ounce/£5		2017	£235
2020 Gold Proof .... 2 ounce/£200		260	£3,985
SPECIAL ISSUE RANGE—JAMES BOND'S JACKET AND TIE			
2020 Silver Proof .... 5 ounce/£10		700	£485
2020 Gold Proof .... 5 ounce/£500		64	£9,895
2020 — Proof ....1 kilo coin/£1,000		20	£59,750
2020 — Proof ....2 kilo coin/£2,000		10	£129,990
2020 — Proof ....7 kilo coin/£7,000		1	POA

The 50th anniversary of the Mr Men Collection

This delightful series of coins marked the 50th anniversary of the creation of these much-loved characters commencing with Mr Tickle who was created by Roger Hargreaves in 1971. The Mr Men, and later Little Miss, characters were featured in over 90 books, translated into 17 different languages. In 1988, the role of illustrating Mr Men and Little Miss characters was taken over by Adam Hargreaves, Roger's son. Adam provided the reverse designs for the Royal Mint 50th anniversary series. The common obverse carries the effigy of Her Majesty the Queen by Jody Clark.

Date	Weight Face value/	Auth. issue qty	Issue price
50TH ANNIVERSARY OF MR MEN—LITTLE MISS SUNSHINE			
2021 BU £5		—	£13
2021 — (coloured coin) £5		15,000	£22.50
2021 Silver Proof .... 1/2 ounce/£1		9,000	£65
2021 — Proof .... 1 ounce/£2		6,500	£97.50
2021 Gold Proof .... 1/4 ounce/£25		750	£595
2021 — Proof .... 1 ounce/£100		275	£2315
50TH ANNIVERSARY OF MR MEN—MR HAPPY			
2021 BU £5		—	£13
2021 — (coloured coin) £5		15,000	£22.50
2021 Silver Proof .... 1/2 ounce/£1		9,000	£65
2021 — Proof .... 1 ounce/£2		6,500	£97.50
2021 Gold Proof .... 1/4 ounce/£25		750	£650
2021 — Proof .... 1 ounce/£100		275	£2440

The 50th anniversary of the Mr Men Collection cont/

50TH ANNIVERSARY OF MR MEN—MR STRONG AND LITTLE MISS GIGGLES

2021 BU £5	—	£13
2021 — (coloured coin) £5	15,000	£22.50
2021 Silver Proof .... 1/2 ounce/£1	9,000	£65
2021 — Proof .... 1 ounce/£2	6,500	£97.50
2021 Gold Proof .... 1/4 ounce/£25	750	£650
2021 — Proof .... 1 ounce/£100	275	£2440

The Alice Collection

Two-coin set to mark 160 years since the publication by Lewis Carroll of **Alice's Adventures in Wonderland** and the later **Through the Looking Glass**. Issued as part of the Treasury of Tales and in partnership with the Victoria & Albert Museum, the designs depict the exquisite Sir John Tenniel's illustrations as used in the first editions of both books. Reverse design by Ffion Gwillim. The common obverse carries the effigy of Her Majesty the Queen by Jody Clark.

ALICE'S ADVENTURES IN WONDERLAND

2021 BU £5	—	£13
2021 — Coloured Coin £5	1,500	£20
2021 Silver Proof .... 1/2 ounce /£1	5,510	£65
2021 — — Coloured Coin .... 1 ounce /£2	3,510	£100
2021 Gold Proof .... 1/4 ounce/£25	510	£650
2021 — — .... 1 ounce/£100	160	£2440

THROUGH THE LOOKING GLASS

2021 BU £5	—	£13
2021 — Coloured Coin £5	1,500	£20
2021 Silver Proof .... 1/2 ounce /£1	5,510	£65
2021 — — Coloured Coin .... 1 ounce /£2	3,510	£100
2021 Gold Proof .... 1/4 ounce/£25	510	£650
2021 — — .... 1 ounce/£100	160	£2440

The latest collection of coins from the Royal Mint are often available in a variety of collector-pack versions.

Myths and Legends Series 2021

Taking their inspiration from UK myths and legends, this latest issue from the Royal Mint's bullion series explores the story of Robin Hood, the gallant hero who famously stole from the rich to give to the poor. The series reverse designs are by Jody Clark as is the obverse image of Her Majesty the Queen. Issues thus far are a 999.9 gold one ounce coin and a one ounce silver edition.

ROBIN HOOD

2021 Silver Proof .... 1 ounce/£2	—	£25
2021 Gold Proof .... 1 ounce/£100	—	£1,406

MAID MARIAN

2021 Silver Proof .... 1 ounce/£2	—	£25
2021 Gold Proof .... 1 ounce/£100	—	£1,406

The Music Legends Collection

This series is intended to celebrate famous bands and musicians. The first issue is dedicated to Queen and all four members of the band are named with edge lettering on the silver editions. The subsequent issues carry images synonymous with their subject. The common obverse carries the effigy of Her Majesty the Queen by Jody Clark.

Date	Weight Face value/	Auth. issue qty	Issue price

MUSIC LEGENDS COLLECTION—QUEEN
The BU £5 coin comes in a special illustrated pack with one of four designs

2020 BU (with pack design 1)	£5	—	£13
2020 BU (with pack design 2)	£5	25,000	£15
2020 BU (with pack design 3)	£5	25,000	£15
2020 BU (with pack design 4)	£5	25,000	£15
2020 Silver Proof	half ounce/£1	20,000	£60
2020 — Proof	1 ounce/£2	10,000	£90
2020 Gold Proof	quarter ounce/£25	1,350	£510
2020 — Proof	1 ounce/£100	350	£2020

MUSIC LEGENDS COLLECTION—ELTON JOHN
The BU £5 coin comes in a special illustrated pack with one of four designs

2020 BU (with pack design 1)	£5	—	£13
2020 BU (with pack design 2)	£5	15,000	£15
2020 BU (with pack design 3)	£5	15,000	£15
2020 BU (with pack design 4)	£5	15,000	£15
2020 Silver Proof	half ounce/£1	15,000	£60
2020 — Proof	1 ounce/£2	10,000	£95
2020 — Proof	2 ounces/£5	500	£95
2020 — Proof	5 ounces/£10	425	£95
2020 Gold Proof	quarter ounce/£25	1,150	£585
2020 — Proof	1 ounce/£100	300	£2320
2020 — Proof	2 ounces/£200	50	£4555
2020 — Proof	5 ounces/£500	50	£2320
2020 — Proof	1 kilo/£100	4	£68,865

MUSIC LEGENDS COLLECTION—DAVID BOWIE
The BU £5 coin comes in a special illustrated pack with one of four designs

2020 BU (with pack design 1)	£5	—	£13
2020 BU (with pack design 2)	£5	15,000	£15
2020 BU (with pack design 3)	£5	15,000	£15
2020 BU (with pack design 4)	£5	15,000	£15
2020 Silver Proof	half ounce/£1	13,500	£65
2020 — Proof	1 ounce/£2	8,100	£97.50
2020 — Proof	2 ounces/£5	550	£195
2020 — Proof	5 ounces/£10	500	£520
2020 Gold Proof	quarter ounce/£25	1,400	£615
2020 — Proof	1 ounce/£100	400	£2425
2020 — Proof	2 ounces/£200	100	£4760
2020 — Proof	5 ounces/£500	60	£11,815
2020 — Proof	1 kilo/£100	11	£72,195

MUSIC LEGENDS COLLECTION—THE WHO
The BU £5 coin comes in a special illustrated pack with one of four designs

2021 BU	£5	—	£13
2021 — Coloured coin	£5	10,000	£22.50
2021 Silver Proof	half ounce/£1	10,010	£65
2021 — Proof	1 ounce/£2	8110	£97.50
2021 — Proof	2 ounces/£5	550	£195
2021 — Proof	5 ounces/£10	500	£520
2021 Gold Proof	quarter ounce/£25	1,010	£595
2021 — Proof	1 ounce/£100	360	£2315
2021 — Proof	2 ounces/£200	150	£4530
2021 — Proof	5 ounces/£500	64	£11,225
2021 — Proof	1 kilo/£1000	12	£68,380

In addition to the above, other series, such as the "Tower of London", the "Portrait of Britain", etc. will be found under specific denominations or in the Proof and Specimen sets section.

With an interesting programme of issues intended to promote coin collecting, the Royal Mint produced a series of coins which were offered to the public at face value. The first issue was made in 2013 and was a £20 coin. The series was extended in 2015 to include a £100. In the same year the £50 silver coin in the Britannia series was offered as part of this programme. The issues are listed below.

HUNDRED POUNDS

Following on from the late 2013 introduction of the Twenty Pounds (see below) a "Hundred Pounds for £100" appeared, again a 0.999 Fine Silver coin, of two ounces weight, in early 2015.

DATE	Auth. issue qty	No. Issued	Issue price
2015 Big Ben, BU	50,000	49,147	£100
2015 Buckingham Palace, BU	50,000	47,851	£100
2016 Trafalgar Square	—	14,878	£100

FIFTY POUNDS

A new denomination introduced in 2015, with the slogan "Fifty Pounds for £50". A double first for Jody Clark, minted in 99.99 silver, diameter 34mm.

DATE	Auth. issue qty	No. Issued	Issue price
2015 Britannia BU	100,000	78,644	£50
2016 Shakespeare BU	—	14,948	£60

TWENTY POUNDS

Another new denomination was added in late 2013. Marketed by the Royal Mint under the slogan "Twenty Pounds for £20", it is a 27mm diameter 0.999 Fine silver coin.

DATE	Auth. issue qty	No. Issued	Issue price
2013 Pistrucci St George & Dragon BU	250,000		£24
2014 Centenary of the outbreak of the WWI	—	141,751	£24
2015 Sir Winston Churchill	—	132,142	£20
2015 The Longest Reigning Monarch, New Portrait	—	149,408	£20
2016 The 90th Birthday of Her Majesty the Queen	—	116,354	£20
2016 The Welsh Dragon	—	—	£25
2016 Christmas Nativity	—	29,929	£30
2017 Platinum Wedding Anniversary	70,000	24,223	£25

> NOTE: The prices quoted in this guide were set at August 2021 with the price of gold around £1,300 per ounce and silver £17.30 per ounce—market fluctuations will have a marked effect on the values of modern precious metal coins. However, the prices quoted here for the *recently issued* sets are the original Royal Mint retail prices.

PROOF AND SPECIMEN SETS

The following listings are an attempt to include all officially marketed products from the Royal Mint of two coins or more, but excluding those which included non-UK coins. It is appreciated that not all have been advertised as new to the public, but it is assumed that at some time they have been, or will be, available. In a few cases, therefore, the prices may be conjectural but are, nevertheless, attempts at listing realistic values, in some instances based on an original retail price. In the case of Elizabeth II sets, if no metal is stated in the listing, the coins in the sets are of the same metal as the circulation coin equivalent. In addition to the above we have excluded historical gold coin sets, such as sets of sovereigns from different mints, where the dates of the coins vary from one set to another.

DATE	FDC
GEORGE IV	
1826 £5–farthing (11 coins)	From £50,000
WILLIAM IV	
1831 Coronation £2–farthing (14 coins)	From £40,000
VICTORIA	
1839 "Una and the Lion" £5–farthing (15 coins)	— *
1853 Sovereign–quarter farthing, including "Gothic"crown (16 coins)	From £85,000
1887 Golden Jubilee £5–3d (11 coins)	From £35,000
1887 Golden Jubilee Crown–3d (7 coins)	From £6500
1893 £5–3d (10 coins)	From £35,000
1893 Crown–3d (6 coins)	From £5500
EDWARD VII	
1902 Coronation £5–Maundy penny, matt proofs (13 coins)	From £8500
1902 Coronation Sovereign–Maundy penny, matt proofs (11 coins)	From £4500
GEORGE V	
1911 Coronation £5–Maundy penny (12 coins)	From £8000
1911 Sovereign–Maundy penny (10 coins)	From £3500
1911 Coronation Halfcrown–Maundy penny (8 coins)	From £2000
1927 New types Crown–3d (6 coins)	From £1000
GEORGE VI	
1937 Coronation £5–half sovereign (4 coins)	£8500
1937 Coronation Crown–farthing including Maundy money (15 coins)	£550
1950 Mid-century Halfcrown–farthing (9 coins)	£200
1951 Festival of Britain, Crown–farthing (10 coins)	£250
ELIZABETH II	
1953 Proof Coronation Crown–farthing (10 coins)	£125
1953 Currency (plastic) set halfcrown–farthing (9 coins)	£15
1968 Specimen decimal set 10p, 5p and 1971-dated bronze in blue wallet (5 coins)	£5
1970 Proof Last £sd coins (issued from 1972) Halfcrown–halfpenny (8 coins)	£20
1971 Proof (issued 1973) 50p–half penny (6 coins)	£20
1972 Proof (issued 1976) 50p–half penny (7 coins including Silver Wedding crown)	£25
1973 Proof (issued 1976) 50p–half penny (6 coins)	£16
1974 Proof (issued 1976) 50p–half penny (6 coins)	£20

* In recent months prices for individual Una and the Lion coins have reached astronomical proportions. In August 2021 an example was sold at Heritage Auctions in the USA for over $1 million therefore it is impossible to list a price.

DATE	FDC
1975 Proof (issued 1976) 50p–half penny (6 coins)	£20
1976 Proof 50p–half penny (6 coins)	£18
1977 Proof 50p–half penny (7 coins including Silver Jubilee crown)	£22
1978 Proof 50p–half penny (6 coins)	£16
1979 Proof 50p–half penny (6 coins)	£18
1980 Proof gold sovereign series (4 coins)	£3500
1980 — 50p–half penny (6 coins)	£16
1981 Proof £5, sovereign, Royal Wedding Silver crown, 50p–half penny (9 coins)	£2500
1981 — 50p–half penny (6 coins)	£18
1982 Proof gold sovereign series (4 coins)	£2500
1982 — 50p–half penny (7 coins)	£20
1982 Uncirculated 50p–half penny (7 coins)	£15
1983 Proof gold double-sovereign to half sovereign (3 coins)	£1350
1983 — £1–half penny (8 coins) (includes H. J. Heinz sets)	£25
1983 Uncirculated £1–half penny (8 coins) (includes Benson & Hedges and Martini sets)	£30
1983 — — (8 coins) (only Benson & Hedges and Martini sets) with "2 NEW PENCE" legend	£1350
1983 — 50p–half penny (7 coins) (H. J. Heinz sets)	£16
1983 — — (7 coins) (H. J. Heinz set) with "2 NEW PENCE" legend	£1250
1984 Proof gold five pounds, sovereign and half-sovereigns (3 coins)	£2500
1984 — £1 (Scottish rev.)–half penny (8 coins)	£20
1984 BU £1 (Scottish rev.)–half penny (8 coins)	£16
1985 New portrait proof gold sovereign series (4 coins)	£4000
1985 Proof £1–1p in de luxe case (7 coins)	£25
1985 — in standard case	£20
1985 BU £1–1p (7 coins) in folder	£15
1986 Proof gold Commonwealth Games £2, sovereign and half sovereign (3 coins)	£1500
1986 — Commonwealth Games £2–1p, de luxe case (8 coins)	£30
1986 — — in standard case (8 coins)	£25
1986 BU £2–1p in folder (8 coins)	£20
1987 Proof gold double- to half sovereign (3 coins)	£1500
1987 — £1–1p in de luxe case (7 coins)	£35
1987 — £1–1p in standard case (7 coins)	£25
1987 BU £1–1p in folder (7 coins)	£20
1988 Proof gold double- to half sovereign (3 coins)	£1500
1988 — £1–1p in de luxe case (7 coins)	£35
1988 — £1–1p in standard case (7 coins)	£30
1988 BU £1–1p in folder (7 coins) (includes Bradford & Bingley sets)	£18
1989 Proof gold 500th anniversary of the sovereign series set (4 coins)	£4000
1989 — — — double- to half sovereign (3 coins)	£2250
1989 — Silver Bill of Rights £2, Claim of Right £2 (2 coins)	£65
1989 — — Piedfort as above (2 coins)	£125
1989 BU £2 in folder (2 coins)	£25
1989 Proof £2 (both)–1p in de luxe case (9 coins)	£35
1989 — in standard case (9 coins)	£30
1989 BU £1–1p in folder (7 coins)	£25
1990 Proof gold sovereign series set (4 coins)	£2750
1990— — double- to half sovereign (3 coins)	£1250
1990 — silver 5p, 2 sizes (2 coins)	£28
1990 — £1–1p in de luxe case (8 coins)	£35
1990 — £1–1p standard case (8 coins)	£30
1990 BU £1–1p in folder (8 coins)	£20
1991 Proof gold sovereign series set (4 coins)	£3500
1991 — — double- to half sovereign (3 coins)	£1500
1991 — £1–1p in de luxe case (7 coins)	£35
1991 — £1–1p in standard case (7 coins)	£28
1991 BU £1–1p in folder (7 coins)	£18
1992 Proof gold Britannia set (4 coins)	£2500
1992 — — sovereign series set (4 coins)	£3000
1992 — — double- to half sovereign (3 coins)	£1500
1992 — £1–1p including two each 50p and 10p in de luxe case (9 coins)	£75
1992 — £1–1p as above in standard case (9 coins)	£65
1992 BU £1–1p as above in folder (9 coins)	£60
1992 — with Enhanced Effigy on obverse of 20p	£60

DATE
FDC

1992 Proof silver 10p, two sizes (2 coins)..£25
1993 Proof gold sovereign series set (4 coins plus silver Pistrucci medal)...£3500
1993 — — double- to half sovereign (3 coins)..£1500
1993 — Coronation anniversary £5–1p in de luxe case (8 coins) £38
1993 — — in standard case (8 coins) £35
1993 BU £1–1p including 1992 EU 50p (8 coins)..£65
1994 Proof gold sovereign series set (4 coins)...£3500
1994 — — £2 to half sovereign (3 coins) £1500
1994 — Bank of England Tercentenary £2–1p in de luxe case (8 coins) £38
1994 — — in standard case (8 coins) £35
1994 BU £1–1p in folder (7 coins)..£18
1994 Proof gold 1992 and 1994 50p (2 coins)...£450
1994 — "Family silver" set £2–50p (3 coins)...£65
1995 Proof gold sovereign series (4 coins) £3000
1995 — — £2 to half sovereign (3 coins) £1500
1995 — 50th Anniversary of WWII £2–1p in de luxe case (8 coins) £40
1995 — — as above in standard case (8 coins)..£35
1995 BU as above in folder (8 coins) £16
1995 Proof "Family Silver" set £2 (two) and £1 (3 coins) £90
1996 Proof gold sovereign series set (4 coins)...£3000
1996 — — double- to half sovereign (3 coins) £1500
1996 — Royal 70th Birthday £5–1p in de luxe case (9 coins)...£50
1996 — — as above in standard case (9 coins) £45
1996 BU Football £2–1p in folder (8 coins) £20
1996 Proof gold Britannia £10 and half-sovereign (2 coins) £750
1996 — — sovereign and silver £1 (2 coins)..£250
1996 — — "Family silver" set £5–£1 (3 coins) £100
1996 — silver 25th Anniversary of Decimal currency £1–1p (7 coins) £150
1996 Circulation and BU 25th Anniversary of Decimalisation 2s 6d–halfpenny (misc.) and £1–1p in folder (14 coins)...............£25
1997 Proof gold sovereign series set (4 coins)...£3000
1997 — — — £2 to half sovereign (3 coins)..£1500
1997 — Golden Wedding £5–1p in red leather case £45
1997 — — as above in standard case (10 coins) £35
1997 BU £2 to 1p in folder (9 coins)..£25
1997 Proof silver 50p set, two sizes (2 coins) £45
1997/1998 Proof silver £2 set, both designs (2 coins)..£70
1998 Proof gold sovereign series set (4 coins)..£3500
1998 — — double- to half sovereign (3 coins) £1500
1998 Prince of Wales £5–1p (10 coins) in red leather case...£45
1998 — as above in standard case (10 coins) £38
1998 BU £2–1p in folder (9 coins)...£16
1998 Proof silver European/NHS 50p set (2 coins)..£60
1998 BU Britannia/EU 50p set (2 coins)..£8
1999 Proof gold Sovereign series set (4 coins)..£3500
1999 — — £2 to half sovereign (3 coins) £1500
1999 Princess Diana £5–1p in red leather case (9 coins)...£65
1999 — as above in standard case (9 coins) £45
1999 BU £2–1p (8 coins) in folder £20
1999 Proof "Family Silver" set. Both £5, £2 and £1 (4 coins) £150
1999/2000 Reverse frosted proof set, two x £1 (2 coins) £75
2000 Proof gold Sovereign series set (4 coins)...£3500
2000 — — double- to half sovereign (3 coins) £1500
2000 Millennium £5–1p in de luxe case (10 coins) £50
2000 — — as above in standard case (10 coins)...£45
2000 — Silver set Millennium £5 to 1p plus Maundy (13 coins) £225
2000 BU £2–1p set in folder (9 coins)...£20
2000 Millennium "Time Capsule" BU £5 to 1p (9 coins) £30
2001 Proof gold Sovereign series set (4 coins)...£3500
2001 — — £2–half sovereign (3 coins) £1500
2001 — Victoria £5–1p in Executive case (10 coins)..£100
2001 — — as above in red leather case (10 coins) £75
2001 — — as above in "Gift" case (10 coins) £48
2001 — — as above in standard case (10 coins) £40

DATE	FDC
2001 BU £2–1p in folder (9 coins)	£20
2002 Proof gold Sovereign series set, all Shield rev. (4 coins)	£3500
2002 — — — double- to half sovereign (3 coins)	£1500
2002 — — Golden Jubilee set £5–1p plus Maundy (13 coins)	£4500
2002 — Golden Jubilee £5–1p in Executive case (9 coins)	£75
2002 — — as above in red leather de luxe case (9 coins)	£50
2002 — — as above in "Gift" case (9 coins)	£42
2002 — — as above in standard case (9 coins)	£40
2002 BU £2–1p (8 coins) in folder	£16
2002 Proof Gold Commonwealth Games £2 set (4 coins)	£2500
2002 — Silver Piedfort Commonwealth Games £2 set (4 coins)	£250
2002 — — Commonwealth Games £2 set (4 coins)	£125
2002 — Commonwealth Games £2 set (4 coins)	£30
2002 BU Commonwealth Games £2 set (4 coins) in folder	£25
2003 Proof gold Sovereign series set (4 coins)	£3500
2003 — — — series £2–half sovereign (3 coins)	£1500
2003 — — — type set (one of each £2 reverse) (4 coins)	£85
2003 — £5 to 1p, two of each £2 and 50p in Executive case (11 coins)	£80
2003 — — as above in red leather case (11 coins)	£55
2003 — — as above in standard case (11 coins)	£48
2003 BU £2 (two)–1p in folder (10 coins)	£22
2003 Proof silver Piedfort set. DNA £2, £1 and Suffragette 50p (3 coins)	£150
2003 Proof "Family Silver" set £5, Britannia and DNA £2, £1 and Suffragette 50p (5 coins)	£175
2003 Circ & BU "God Save the Queen" Coronation anniversary set 5s/0d to farthing (1953) and £5 to 1p (2003) in folder (19 coins)	£55
2003 Circulation or bullion "Royal Sovereign" collection, example of each Elizabeth II date (21 coins)	£4000
2004 Proof gold Sovereign series set (4 coins)	£3500
2004 — — — Series £2-half sovereign (3 coins)	£1500
2004 (Issue date) Royal Portrait gold sovereign set, all proof except the first: Gillick, Machin, Maklouf and Rank-Broadley sovereigns, and the 2nd, 3rd and 4th of above half-sovereigns, various dates (7 coins)	£3500
2004 Proof "Family Silver" set £5, Britannia and Trevithick £2, £1 and Bannister 50p (5 coins)	£200
2004 — Silver Piedfort set, Trevithick £2, £1 and Bannister 50p (3 coins)	£200
2004 — £2 to 1p, two each of £2 and 50p in Executive case (10 coins)	£125
2004 — — as above in red leather case (10 coins)	£45
2004 — — as above in standard case (10 coins)	£40
2004 BU £2 to 1p in folder (10 coins)	£22
2004 — "New Coinage" set, Trevithick £2, £1 and Bannister 50p (3 coins)	£10
2004 BU "Season's Greetings" £2 to 1p and Royal Mint Christmas medal in folder (8 coins)	£18
2005 Proof Gold Sovereign series set (4 coins)	£3500
2005 — — — series, double to half sovereign (3 coins)	£1500
2005 — Gold Trafalgar and Nelson £5 crowns (2 coins)	£4000
2005 — Silver, as above (2 coins)	£85
2005 — — Piedfort, as above (2 coins)	£150
2005 — Silver Piedfort set, Gunpowder Plot and World War II £2, £1 and Johnson 50p (4 coins)	£200
2005 — £5 to 1p, two of each of £5, £2 and 50p in Executive case (12 coins)	£80
2005 — — as above in red leather case (12 coins)	£60
2005 — — as above in standard case (12 coins)	£45
2005 BU Trafalgar and Nelson £5 crowns in pack (2 coins)	£35
2005 — £2 (two) to 1p in folder (10 coins)	£25
2005 — "New Coinage" set, Gunpowder Plot £2, £1 and Johnson 50p (3 coins)	£10
2005 — "Merry Xmas" £2 to 1p and Royal Mint Christmas medal in folder (8 coins)	£20
2006 Proof Gold Sovereign Series set (4 coins)	£3500
2006 — — — series, double to half sovereign (3 coins)	£1500
2006 — Silver Brunel £2 coin set (2 coins)	£75
2006 — — Piedfort Brunel £2 coin set (2 coins)	£125
2006 — Gold Brunel £2 coin set (2 coins)	£950
2006 — Silver VC 50p coin set (2 coins)	£75
2006 — Silver Piedfort VC 50p coin set (2 coins)	£115
2006 — Gold VC 50p coin set (2 coins)	£1750
2006 — Silver proof set, £5 to 1p plus Maundy coins (13 coins)	£325
2006 — — — Piedfort collection £5, with trumpets enhanced with 23 carat gold, both Brunel £2, £1, both VC 50p (6 coins)	£450

DATE   FDC

2006 — £5 to 1p, three of each £2 and 50p in Executive case (13 coins)..£80
2006 — as above in red leather case (13 coins) £55
2006 — as above in standard case (13 coins) £45
2006 BU £2 (two), £1, 50p (two) and to 1p in folder (10 coins)..£18
2006 Proof Brunel £2 in folder (2 coins)..£15
2006 — VC 50p in folder (2 coins)...£15
2006 — Gold Half-Sovereign set dated 2005 Noad and 2006 Pistrucci St George and the Dragon (2 coins).......£350
2007 — — Sovereign Series set (4 coins) £3500
2007 — — — series, double to half sovereign (3 coins) £1500
2007 — — Sovereign and half-sovereign (2 coins) £475
2007 — "Family Silver" set, Britannia, £5 crown, Union and Slavery £2, Gateshead £1
       and Scouting 50p (6 coins)..£250
2007 Proof Silver Piedfort Collection, as "Family Silver" above but excluding a Britannia (5 coins)....................£300
2007 — Silver £1 Bridge series coins, dated 2004 to 2007 (4 coins)..£135
2007 — Silver Proof Piedfort £1 Bridge Series, dated 2004 to 2007 (4 coins) £275
2007 — Gold £1 Bridge series coins, dated as above (4 coins) £2500
2007 — £5 to 1p, three £2 and two 50p in Executive case (12 coins)..£85
2007 — as above, Deluxe in red leather case (12 coins) £65
2007 — as above, in standard case (12 coins) £50
2007 BU £2 (two) to 1p (9 coins)...£18
2007 50th Anniversary Sovereign set, 1957 circulation standard and 2007 Proof (2 coins)................£750
2008 Proof Gold Sovereign series set (4 coins) £3500
2008 — — — double to half-sovereign (3 coins) £1500
2008 — — Sovereign and half-sovereign (2 coins) £750
2008 — "Family silver" set, 2x £5, Britannia £2, Olympiad £2 and Royal Arms £1 (5 coins)...............£250
2008 — Silver Piedfort Collection, 2x £5, Olympiad £2 and Shield of Royal Arms £1 (4 coins)..........£325
2008 — 2 x £5, 2 x £2, £1 to 1p in Executive case (11 coins) £85
2008 — as above, Deluxe in black leather case (11 coins) £55
2008 — as above, in standard back case (11 coins) £60
2008 BU 2 x £2, Royal Arms £1 to 1p (9 coins) £20
2008 — "Emblems of Britain" ("old" Revs) Royal Arms £1 to 1p (7 coins) £15
2008 — "Royal Shield of Arms" ("new" Revs) Shield of Royal Arms £1 to 1p (7 coins) £15
2008 — Above two sets housed in one sleeve £28
2008 Proof Base Metal "Royal Shield of Arms" set, £1 to 1p (7 coins)..£40
2008 — Silver "Emblems of Britain" set, £1 to 1p (7 coins)..£160
2008 — — "Royal Shield of Arms" set, £1 to 1p (7 coins)..£160
2008 — — Above two sets in one black case £325
2008 — Gold "Emblems of Britain" set, £1 to 1p (7 coins) £3550
2008 — — "Royal Shield of Arms" set, £1 to 1p (7 coins) £3550
2008 — — Above two sets in one oak-veneer case £7000
2008 — Platinum "Emblems of Britain" set, £1 to 1p (7 coins) £8500
2008 — — "Royal Shield of Arms" set, £1 to 1p (7 coins) £8500
2008 — — Above two sets in one walnut veneer case...£15,750
2008 — Silver Piedfort "Royal Shield of Arms" set, £1 to 1p (7 coins) £325
2008 — Gold set of 14 £1 coins, one of each Rev used since 1983,
       all dated 2008 (25th anniversary)   (14 coins) £9500
2008 — Silver with gold Rev highlighting as above (14 coins)..£500
2008 — 2 x £2, Royal Arms £1 to 1p (9 coins) Christmas Coin Sets,
       two different outer sleeves, Father Christmas or Three Wise men...£20
2009 Proof Gold Sovereign series set (5 coins) £3500
2009 — — — double to half-sovereign (3 coins) £1500
2009 — — sovereign and half-sovereign (2 coins)..£550
2009 — "Family Silver" set, Henry VIII £5, Britannia £2, Darwin and Burns £2,
       £1 and Kew 50p (6 coins)...£250
2009 — Silver Piedfort collection, Henry VIII £5, Darwin and Burns £2
       and Kew Gardens 50p (4 coins)..£375
2009 — Silver Set, £5 to 1p (12 coins)..£275
2009 — Base metal Executive set, £5 to 1p (12 coins)..£80
2009 — — — Deluxe set, £5 to 1p (12 coins) £55
2009 — — — Standard set, £5 to 1p (12 coins) £45
2009 BU Base metal set, £2 to 1p (11 coins)..£22
2009 — — —, £1 to 1p "Royal Shield of Arms" set (7 coins) £12
2009 — — —, £2 to 1p (8 coins) £15

DATE	FDC
2009 Proof set of 50p coins as detailed in FIFTY PENCE section, CuNi (16 coins)	£350
2009 — Silver (16 coins)	£650
2009 — Gold (16 coins)	£8250
2009 — Gold Piedfort (16 coins)	£22,000
2009 "Mind" set of £5 coins, silver (6 coins)	£350
2010 Proof Gold Olympic Series "Faster", £100 and £25 (2), (3 coins)	£2500
2010 — — Sovereign series set (5 coins)	£2750
2010 — — — double to half (3 coins)	£1250
2010 — — — sovereign to quarter (3 coins)	£575
2010 — "Silver Celebration" set, Restoration £5, Nightingale £2, London and Belfast £1 and Girlguiding 50p (5 coins)	£185
2010 Silver Piedfort set, coins as in "Silver Celebration" set (5 coins)	£350
2010 — Silver Collection, £5 to 1p (13 coins)	£300
2010 — Base Metal Executive Set, £5 to 1p (13 coins)	£80
2010 — — Deluxe set	£50
2010 — — Standard set	£40
2010 BU — Capital Cities £1 (2 coins)	£15
2010 — — Set, £2 to 1p (12 coins)	£35
2010 — — Definitive pack, £2 to 1p (8 coins)	£20
2010 Proof "Body" Collection of £5 coins, silver (6 coins)	£350
2010 Proof "Spirit" Collection of £5 coins, silver (6 coins)	£300
2011 Proof Gold Sovereign set (5 coins)	£3500
2011 — — double to half (3 coins)	£1500
2011 — — sovereign to quarter (3 coins)	£750
2011 — Olympic gold "Higher" set (3 coins)	£2750
2011 — — — "Faster" (2010) and "Higher" set (6 coins) in 9-coin case	£6000
2011 — Silver Collection, £5 to 1p (14 coins)	£400
2011 — — Celebration set, Duke of Edinburgh £5, Mary Rose and King James bible Cardiff and Edinburgh £1 and WWF 50p (6 coins)	£250
2011 — — — Piedfort, as above (6 coins)	£395
2011 Executive Proof Base metal set (14 coins)	£85
2011 De-luxe Proof Base metal set (14 coins)	£50
2011 Standard Proof Base metal set (14 coins)	£40
2011 BU set including £2, £1 and 50p commemoratives (13 coins)	£26
2011 BU set of Definitives (8 coins)	£25
2012 Proof Gold Sovereign set (5 coins)	£4000
2012 — — Double to Half (3 coins)	£1650
2012 — — Sovereign to Quarter (3 coins)	£825
2012 BU Sovereign set Double to Half (3 coins)	£1550
2012 Proof Olympic gold Stronger set (3 coins)	£3500
2012 — — — 2x £25 (2 coins)	£1200
2010, 2011, 2012 Proof Olympic gold complete set (9 coins)	£10,500
2009, 2010, 2011, 2012 Complete Countdown sets:	
Gold Proof (4 coins)	£11,500
Silver Proof Piedport (4 coins)	£850
Silver Proof (4 coins)	£325
CuNi BU (4 coins)	£45
2012 Proof Gold set, Diamond Jubilee £5, Dickens & Technology £2, £1 to 1p (10 coins)	£8500
2012 — Silver set, as above with Selective Gold plating on £1 to 1p coins (10 coins)	£490
2012 — set (Premium) (10 coins)	£100
2012 — set (Collector) (10 coins)	£55
2012 BU set, include Diamond Jubilee £5 (10 coins)	£40
2012 — set, Technology £2 to 1p (8 coins)	£21
2012 Proof Gold, Diamond Jubilee £5 and Double Sovereign (2 coins)	£3200
2012 — Olympic and Paralympic £5 (2 coins)	£5500
2012 — Gold Piedfort 50p set, one each of the coins of Olympic sports in which Team GB gained gold medals (11 coins)	£25,000
2013 Proof Gold Sovereign set (5 coins)	£4000
2013 — — Double to Half (3 coins)	£1650
2013 — — One to Quarter (3 coins)	£825
2013 — Gold £5 Portraits set (4 coins)	£9500
2013 — Silver Portraits set (4 coins) (1,465)	£400

DATE   FDC

2013 — Silver Piedfort Portraits set (4 coins) (697)..£800
2013 — Gold set, £5 Coronation anniversary to 1p (15 coins) £12,500
2013 — Gold set of both London Underground £2 (2 coins) £2000
2013 — Silver Piedfort set, as above (2 coins)..£200
2013 — Silver set, as above (2 coins) £100
2013 BU set, as above (2 coins)...£20
2013 — Gold set, 30th anniversary of the One Pound coin, reverses from 1983 (Sewell), 1988 (Gorringe)
    and 2013 (Dent). (3 coins) £3600
2013 — Silver, as above (3 coins) £150
2013 BU Sovereign set, Double to Half (3 coins), struck June 2, 2013 ....£1550
2013 Proof Silver annual set, £5 Coronation anniv to 1p (15 coins) £600
2013 — — Piedfort commemorative set (7 coins) £650
2013 — "Premium" set (15 coins plus a "Latent Image" item)......................................£150
2013 — "Collector" set (15 coins) £110
2013 — Commemorative set (7 coins) £65
2013 BU annual set (15 coins)..£50
2013 — Definitive Set (8 coins) £25
2014 Proof Gold Britannia (Clark) set £100 to 50p (6 coins) £2600
2014 — — — £50 to £10 (3 coins) £1175
2014 — — — £25 to £1 (3 coins) £595
2014 — Silver Britannia (Clark) set £2 to 5p (6 coins) £200
2014 — — — 20p to 5p (3 coins) £45
2014 — Sovereign set (5 coins)..£3300
2014 — — Double to half (3 coins) £1300
2014 — — One to quarter (3 coins)..£625
2014 — Gold Commemorative set, £5 Queen Anne, 2 x £2, 2 x £1, 50p (6 coins)......£5500
2014 — Silver Piedfort set, as above (6 coins) £570
2014 — — set as above (6 coins) £295
2014 — — all major coins of 2014 (14 coins)..£560
2014 — Premium set (14 coins and a premium medal) £155
2014 — Collector set (14 coins) £110
2014 — Commemorative set (6 coins) £65
2014 BU Annual set (14 coins) £50
2014 — Definitive set (8 coins) £25
2014 — Floral £1 set, Scotland and Northern Ireland (2 coins) £18
2014 Proof Silver Outbreak of First World War set of £5 (6 coins)...............................£450
2014 — Gold set as above (6 coins) ....—
2014 — Silver Portrait of Britain £5 Silver collection (4 coins) £36
2015 Proof Gold Sovereign set, Rank-Broadley portrait (5 coins) £2700
2015 — — Double to half, Rank-Broadley portrait (3 coins) £1300
2015 — — One to quarter, Rank-Broadley portrait (3 coins) £625
2015 — Gold Commemorative set, 2 x £5, 2 x £2, 2 x £1, 50p, Rank-Broadley portrait (5 coins) £5500
2015 — Silver Piedfort set, as above (5 coins) £570
2015 — — set as above (5 coins) £295
2015 — Base metal set as above (5 coins) £65
2015 — Platinum definitive set £2 to 1p, Rank-Broadley portrait plus £2 to 1p Clark portrait (16 coins) £12,500
2015 — Gold ditto £7600
2015 — Silver ditto...£480
2015 — Base metal ditto £120
2015 BU definitive set as per Platinum set above (16 coins) £50
The above four entries are also available as 8-coin sets with either the Rank-Broadley ("Final Edition") or the Clark
("First Edition") portrait. These are issued at half the prices quoted above.
2015 Proof Silver set of definitive and commemorative coins, Rank-Broadley portrait (13 coins) £560
2015 — Premium set as above (13 coins and a Premium medal)...................................£155
2015 Collector set as above (13 coins and medal) £110
2015 Proof Double to half sovereign, Clark portrait (3 coins) £1200
2015 — Silver commemorative set, Anniversary of First World War (6 coins) £450
2015 Portrait of Britain Silver Proof Collection (4x£5 with colour) £310
2016 Proof Gold Sovereign set, Butler Portrait (5 coins) £2700
2016 — — Double to half, Butler Portrait (3 coins)...£1200
2016— — One to quarter, Butler Portrait (3 coins)..£625
2016 — Gold Commemorative set, £5, 5x £2, £1, 50p (8 coins) £6100

DATE	FDC
2016 — Silver Piedfort set, as above (8 coins)	£595
2016 — — set as above (8 coins)	£395
2016 — Base metal set as above (8 coins)	£95
2016 — silver set, commemoratives and definitives (16 coins)	£595
2016 — Base metal set as above, Premium plus Medal (16 coins)	£195
2016 — — Collector set (16 coins)	£145
2016 Portrait of Britain Silver Proof Collection (4x£5 with colour)	£310
2016 BU Annual set including commemoratives (16 coins)	£55
2016 — Definitive set (8 coins)	£30
2016 Proof Silver set of £5 coins, Anniversary of First World War (6 coins)	£450
2016 Beatrix Potter 150th Anniversary 50p coin set (5 coins)	£75
2017 BU Annual "Premium" set (13 coins & premium medal)	£195
2017 BU Annual set (13 coins as above)	£55
2017 — Definitive set (8 coins)	£30
2017 Proof Annual "Collector" set (13 coins & medal)	£145
2017 — Commemorative set (5 coins), 2x£5, 2x£2, 50p	£95
2017 — Silver Piedfort Commemorative set (coins as above)	£595
2017 — Silver Commemorative set (coins as above)	£350
2017 — Silver set (13 coins £5–1p)	£625
2017 — Silver Portrait of Britain Collection (4x£5 with colour)	£310
2017 — Silver Outbreak of First World War set of £5 (6 coins)	£450
2018 BU Annual set (13 coins)	£55
2018 — Definitive set (8 coins)	£30
2018 Proof Annual set (13 coins)	£155
2018 — "Premium" set (13 coins & premium medal)	£210
2018 — Portrait of Britain Silver Proof Collection (4x£5 with colour)	£310
2018 — Centenary of World War I Silver Proof set of £5 (6 coins)	£465
2018 — — Gold (6 coins)	£11,100
2018 — — Silver Piedfort set (5 coins)	£555
2018 Silver set (5 commemorative and 8 circulating coins)	£610
2018 Commemorative coin set (5 coins)	£95
2019 BU Annual set (13 coins)	£55
2019 — Annual definitive set (8 coins)	£30
2019 Proof Annual coin set with Medal (13 coins £5–1p)	£210
2019 — Silver set (13 coins £5–1p)	£610
2019 — Gold Proof commemorative set (5 coins £5–50p)	£6300
2019 — Silver Proof Piedfort commemorative set (5 coins)	£550
2019 — Sovereign Proof set (5 coins)	£4200
2019 — "Premium" Sovereign Proof set (3 coins)	£1695
2019 — Sovereign Proof set (3 coins)	£890
2019 — Paddington Bear Silver Proof set (2 coins)	£65
2019 BU Paddington Bear BU set (2 coins)	£10

2019 Proof set Celebrating 50 Years of the 50 pence (3 types):

    i. *British Military and Culture Set* (10 coins): New 50 Pence, Girl Guides, Kew Gardens, Roger Bannister, Scouting, Battle of Hastings, Battle of Britain, D-Day, Victoria Cross 150th Anniversary, Victoria Cross Heroic Acts, BU £76.50

    ii. *British Military Set* (5 coins): Battle of Hastings, Battle of Britain, D-Day, Victoria Cross 150th Anniversary, Victoria Cross Heroic Acts, BU £45

    iii. *British Culture Set* (5 coins): New 50 Pence, Girl Guides, Kew Gardens, Roger Bannister, Scouting, BU.....£45

2019 — — Proof (3,500)	£90
2019 — — Silver Proof (1,969)	£225
2019 — — Gold Proof (75)	£3825

2020 Monumental Coin Designs (5 coins) including Team GB 50p, 75th Anniversary of VE Day £2, 400th Anniversary of the Mayflower £2, Centenary of Agatha Christie £2, 200th Anniversary since the reign of George III £5 .... —

2020 BU Annual coin set, 1p–£2 plus the 5 above (13 coins)	£55
2020 — Definitive coin set, 1p–£2 (8 current circulating coinage designs only)	£30
2020 Proof Annual coin set (13 coins) (7000)	£155
2020 — Premium set (13 coins) (2500)	£210
2020 — Silver set (13 coins) (500)	£610
2020 — Silver Piedfort set (5 coins, 50p–£5) (300)	£550
2020 — Gold Proof Sovereign series (5 coins) (75)	£6150

DATE

FDC

2021 BU Annual coin set £2–1p (8 coins) £30
2021 — including coins from the 5-piece coin set below (13 coins) £55
2021 Proof Annual coin set (13 coins) (7000) £155
2021 — Premium Proof set (13 coins) (2500) £210
2021 — Silver Proof set (13 coins) (550) £640
2021 — Gold Proof Sovereign series set (5 coins, £5–quarter sovereign) £4785
2021 — — (4 coins, £2–quarter sovereign) £2050
2021 — — (3 coins, Sovereign–quarter sovereign) £1015
2021 — — Special commemorative Sovereign set comprising George V 1926, EII 1957 and a "Struck on the Day"
2021 (3 coins) (100) £1995
2021 Five piece coin set comprising: 50th Anniversary of Decimal Day 2021 UK 50p, Celebrating the life and work
of John Logie Baird 2021 UK 50p, Celebrating the life and work of H. G. Wells 2021UK £2, 250th Anniversary of
the birth of Sir Walter Scott 2021 UK £2. The 95th Birthday of Her Majesty the Queen 2021 UK £5. Silver Proof
Piedfort (5 coins) (300) £587.50
2021 — — Gold Proof (95) £7100
2021 10 piece coin set comprising: The Lion of England, The Unicorn of Scotland, The Red Dragon of Wales, The
Black Bull of Clarence, The Falcon of Plantagenets, The Yale of Beaufort, The White Lion of Mortimer, The
White Horse of Hanover, The Greyhound of Richmond, The Griffin of Edward III. Silver Proof 1/4 ounce/50p
(1250) £360
2021 — — Silver Proof 2 ounce/£5 (300) £1835
2021 — — Gold Proof 1/4 ounce/£25 (250) £5840

*In addition to the above the Royal Mint produce the BU sets detailed above in Wedding and in Baby gift packs each
year. Also various patterns and sets have been made available from time to time. These include the following:*

1999 (dated 1994) Bi-metal £2, plus three unprocessed or part-processed elements .... —
2003 Set of patterns of £1 coins with "Bridges" designs, in gold, hall-marked on edges (4 coins) .... —
2003 — Silver £1 as above (4 coins) £150
2004 — Gold £1 featuring heraldic animal heads, hall-marked on edge (4 coins) £1000
2004 — Silver £1 featuring heraldic animal heads, hall-marked on edge (4 coins) £150
The Centenary of the Burial of the Unknown Warrior Historic coin set comprising: Remembrance Day 2020 UK Silver
Proof £5 Coin, George VI Half Penny, George V Farthing, Sixpence, Shilling, Florin, Half Crown, Penny, Three-
pence (100) £280

IMPORTANT NOTE:

In this section the prices quoted were set at August 2021 with the price of gold at around £1,300
per ounce and silver £17.30 per ounce. As the market for precious metals is notoriously volatile and
unpredictable any price fluctuations have a marked effect on the values of modern precious metal
coins, therefore it is important to seek professional advice when requiring a valuation for any of the
precious metal sets listed. *The prices quoted here are for guidance only whereas the prices quoted
for the recently issued sets are the original Royal Mint retail prices.*

SCOTLAND

The coins illustrated are pennies representative of the reign, unless otherwise stated.

	F	VF

DAVID I (1124–53)
Berwick, Carlisle, Edinburgh and Roxburgh Mints

	F	VF
Penny in the name of David	£3000	£10500
Cut Halfpenny		Extremely rare
Penny in name of Stephen	£1000	£4000

David I

HENRY (1136–52)
Bamborough, Carlisle and Corbridge Mints for the Earl of Huntingdon and Northumberland

	F	VF
Penny	£1500	£6250
Cut Halfpenny		Extremely rare

MALCOLM IV (1153–65)
Berwick and Roxburgh Mints

Penny (5 different types)		Extremely rare

Henry

WILLIAM THE LION (1165–1214)
Berwick, Edinburgh, Dun (Dunbar?), Perth and Roxburgh Mints

		F	VF
Penny – cross pattee early issue	from	£2500	£7000
Penny – pellet & crescent	from	£225	£600
Penny – short cross & stars – mint & moneyer	from	£160	£450
Penny – short cross & stars HVE WALTER & var	from	£100	£295

William the Lion

ALEXANDER II (1214–49)
Berwick and Roxburgh Mints

		F	VF
Penny – in the name of William the Lion	from	£400	£1200
Penny – in own name	from	£600	£1750

Alexander II

ALEXANDER III (1249–86)
FIRST COINAGE (1250–80)
Pennies struck at the Mints at

		F	VF
Aberdeen	from	£140	£390
Ayr	from	£200	£660
Berwick	from	£75	£195
Dun (Dumfries / Dunfermline? / Dundee?)	from	£160	£480
Edinburgh	from	£140	£360
Forfar	from	£275	£900
Fres (Dumfries)	from	£275	£780
Glasgow	from	£275	£780
Inverness	from	£260	£695
Kinghorn	from	£275	£900
Lanark	from	£245	£750
Montrose	from	£530	£1320
Perth	from	£100	£290
Roxburgh	from	£110	£340
St Andrews	from	£275	£795
Stirling	from	£190	£630

SECOND COINAGE (1280–86)

		F	VF
Penny		£85	£210
Halfpenny		£100	£325
Farthing		£275	£825

Alexander III First Coinage

Alexander III Second Coinage

F   VF

JOHN BALIOL (1292–1306)

FIRST COINAGE *(Rough Surface issue)*

		F	VF
Penny	from	£150	£425
Halfpenny	from	£400	Ex. rare
Penny – St. Andrews	from	£175	£475
Halfpenny – St. Andrews	from	£800	Ex. rare

SECOND COINAGE *(Smooth Surface issue)*

Penny	from	£200	£475
Halfpenny	from	£150	£425
Farthing		Extremely rare	
Penny – St. Andrews	from	£350	£950
Halfpenny – St. Andrews		Extremely rare	

John Baliol

ROBERT BRUCE (1306–29)

Berwick Mint

Penny	from	£700	£1750
Halfpenny	from	£500	£1250
Farthing	from	£850	£2250

Robert Bruce

DAVID II (1329–71)

Aberdeen and Edinburgh Mints

Noble		Extremely Rare	
Groat (Edinburgh)	from	£125	£325
Groat (Aberdeen)	from	£750	£2100
Halfgroat (Edinburgh)	from	£100	£275
Halfgroat (Aberdeen)	from	£525	£1500
Penny 1st Coinage 2nd Issue	from	£65	£195
Penny 2nd Coinage (Edinburgh)	from	£100	£275
Penny 2nd Coinage (Aberdeen)	from	£450	£1100
Halfpenny	from	£250	£725
Farthing	from	£350	£950

David II

ROBERT II (1371–90)

Dundee, Edinburgh and Perth Mints

Groat	from	£100	£300
Halfgroat	from	£135	£425
Penny	from	£85	£215
Halfpenny	from	£125	£350

Robert II

ROBERT III (1390–1406)

Aberdeen, Dumbarton, Edinburgh, Perth Mints

Lion or crown	from	£1750	£5750
Demy lion or halfcrown	from	£1500	£5250
Groat	from	£135	£325
Halfgroat	from	£175	£350
Penny	from	£250	£725
Halfpenny	from	£275	£850

JAMES I (1406–37)

Aberdeen, Edinburgh, Inverness, Linlithgow, Perth, Stirling Mints

Demy	from	£1150	£3250
Half demy	from	£900	£3000
Groat Edinburgh	from	£195	£525
Groat Other Mints	from	£325	£1050
Penny	from	£250	£650
Halfpenny		Extremely rare	

Robert III Lion

	F	VF

JAMES II (1437–60)

Aberdeen, Edinburgh, Linlithgow, Perth, Roxburgh, Stirling Mints

		F	VF
Demy	from	£1150	£3250
Lion	from	£1250	£4500
Half lion		Extremely rare	
Early groats (fleur-de-lis) Edinburgh	from	£195	£600
Early groats (fleur-de-lis) Other Mints		Extremely rare	
Later groats (crown) Edinburgh	from	£300	£950
Later groats (crown) Other Mints	from	£600	£1950
Later Halfgroats (crown) Edinburgh	from	£650	£1975
Later Halfgroats (crown) Other Mints		Extremely rare	
Penny (billon)	from	£250	£650

JAMES III (1460–88)

Aberdeen, Berwick and Edinburgh Mints

		F	VF
Rider		£2250	£8000
Half rider		£2000	£6500
Quarter rider		£3000	£9000
Unicorn		£3000	£9000
Groat (facing bust) Edinburgh	from	£250	£750
Groat (facing bust) Berwick	from	£650	£2100
Groat (thistle & mullet) Edinburgh		£300	£900
Groat (threequarter bust) Edinburgh	from	£550	£1500
Groat (threequarter bust) Aberdeen	from	£750	£2250
Halfgroat	from	£500	£1550
Penny (silver)	from	£325	£950
Plack (billon)	from	£175	£450
Half plack	from	£195	£525
Penny (billon)	from	£150	£425
Farthing (copper)		£200	£650
Penny – ecclesiastical issue	from	£90	£225
Farthing – ecclesiastical issue	from	£125	£350

James III Groat, Berwick Mint

JAMES IV (1488–1513)

Edinburgh Mint

		F	VF
Unicorn		£1500	£4250
Half unicorn		£1500	£4250
Lion or crown		Extremely rare	
Half lion		Extremely rare	
Groat	from	£750	£1800
Halfgroat	from	£700	£2250
Penny (silver)	from	£150	£400
Plack		£40	£100
Half plack		Extremely rare	
Penny (billon)	from	£40	£120

James IV Unicorn

JAMES V (1513–42)

Edinburgh Mint

		F	VF
Unicorn		£2050	£7500
Half Unicorn		Extremely rare	
Crown		£1350	£4250
Ducat or Bonnet piece	from	£2000	£8500
Two-thirds ducat		£2500	£6500
One-third ducat		£3500	£9500
Groat	from	£375	£1250
One-third groat	from	£275	£775
Plack	from	£50	£125
Bawbee	from	£75	£185
Half bawbee	from	£140	£325
Quarter bawbee		Extremely rare	

James V Ducat or Bonnet Piece

F   VF

MARY (1542–67)
Edinburgh and Stirling Mints
FIRST PERIOD (1542–58)

	F	VF
Crown	£1750	£6500
Twenty shillings	Extremely rare	
Lion (Forty-four shillings)	£2000	£8500
Half lion (Twenty-two shillings)	£1750	£6500
Ryals (Three pounds)	£5000	£17500
Half ryal	£4500	£12500
Portrait testoon	£5000	£14500
Non-portrait testoon .... from	£450	£950
Half testoon .... from	£275	£900
Bawbee .... from	£85	£225
Half bawbee .... from	£125	£325
Bawbee - Stirling	£175	£475
Penny (facing bust) .... from	£325	£900
Penny (no bust) .... from	£225	£650
Lion .... from	£50	£145
Plack .... from	£85	£225

SECOND PERIOD (Francis and Mary, 1558–60)

	F	VF
Ducat (Sixty shillings)	Extremely rare	
Non-portrait testoon .... from	£375	£1000
Half testoon .... from	£375	£1000
12 penny groat .... from	£80	£225
Lion .... from	£55	£135

Mary Lion or Forty-Four Shillings

THIRD PERIOD (Widowhood, 1560–65)

	F	VF
Portrait testoon	£4500	£11500
Half testoon.	£3000	£8500

FOURTH PERIOD (Henry and Mary, 1565–67)

	F	VF
Portrait ryal.	£45000	£125000
Non-portrait ryal .... from	£750	£1750
Two-third ryal .... from	£650	£1550
One-third ryal .... from	£850	£2500

FIFTH PERIOD (Second widowhood, 1567)

	F	VF
Non-portrait ryal .... from	£750	£1750
Two thirds ryal .... from	£475	£1350
One-third ryal .... from	£650	£1550

JAMES VI (1567–1603)
(Before accession to the English throne)
FIRST COINAGE (1567–71)

	F	VF
Ryal .... from	£400	£1100
Two-thirds ryal .... from	£300	£950
One-third ryal .... from	£350	£1000

SECOND COINAGE (1571–80)

	F	VF
Twenty pounds	£25,000	£75,000
Noble (or half merk) .... from	£125	£300
Half noble (or quarter merk) .... from	£125	£300
Two merks or Thistle dollar .... from	£2000	£6500
Merk .... from	£3000	£8500

THIRD COINAGE (1580–81)

	F	VF
Ducat	£5000	£14500
Sixteen shillings	£2500	£7250

*James VI Fourth coinage
Ten Shillings*

	F	VF
Eight shillings	£1950	£5750
Four shillings	£4000	£9500
Two shillings		Extremely rare

FOURTH COINAGE (1582–88)

	F	VF
Lion noble	£5500	£15000
Two-third lion noble	£4750	£13500
One-third lion noble		Extremely rare
Forty shillings	£5000	£14500
Thirty shillings	£800	£2500
Twenty shillings	£425	£1500
Ten shillings	£425	£1500

FIFTH COINAGE (1588)

	F	VF
Thistle noble	£2150	£7500

James VI Seventh Coinage Rider

SIXTH COINAGE (1591–93)

		F	VF
"Hat" piece		£4000	£10000
"Balance" half merk	from	£300	£895
"Balance" quarter merk		£725	£2000

SEVENTH COINAGE (1594–1601)

		F	VF
Rider		£1250	£3500
Half rider		£1200	£3500
Ten shillings	from	£160	£500
Five shillings	from	£125	£400
Thirty pence	from	£225	£625
Twelve pence	from	£130	£375

EIGHTH COINAGE (1601–04)

		F	VF
Sword and sceptre piece	from	£750	£2100
Half sword and sceptre piece	from	£425	£1250
Thistle-merk	from	£110	£350
Half thistle-merk	from	£65	£175
Quarter thistle-merk	from	£55	£135
Eighth thistle-merk	from	£50	£110

James VI Seventh Coinage 10 Shillings

BILLON AND COPPER ISSUES

		F	VF
Eightpenny groat	from	£45	£125
Fourpenny groat	from	£350	£1000
Twopenny plack	from	£130	£375
Hardhead	from	£30	£85
Twopence	from	£80	£230
Penny plack	from	£160	£750
Penny	from	£500	£1250

JAMES VI (1603–25)
(After accession to the English throne)

		F	VF
Unit	from	£950	£2500
Double crown	from	£1100	£3250
British crown	from	£550	£1550
Halfcrown	from	£750	£2150
Thistle crown	from	£650	£2050
Sixty shillings	from	£375	£1350
Thirty shillings	from	£195	£550
Twelve shillings	from	£175	£575
Six shillings	from	£575	Ex. rare
Two shillings	from	£35	£100
One shilling	from	£125	£350
Copper twopence	from	£25	£70
Copper penny	from	£85	£250

James VI after accession thirty shillings

	F	VF

CHARLES I (1625–49)

FIRST COINAGE (1625–36)

	F	VF
Unit	£1250	£3500
Double crown	£1000	£3150
British crown	Extremely rare	
Sixty shillings	£800	£2750
Thirty shillings	£175	£575
Twelve shillings	£175	£575
Six shillings .... from	£350	£1000
Two shillings	£45	£110
One shilling	£150	£495

SECOND COINAGE (1636)

	F	VF
Half merk	£120	£300
Forty penny piece	£75	£210
Twenty penny piece	£70	£200

*Charles I Third Coinage
Sixty Shillings*

THIRD COINAGE (1637–42)

		F	VF
Unit	from	£1600	£5750
Half unit	from	£1000	£3500
British crown	from	£600	£1750
British half crown	from	£525	£1500
Sixty shillings		£875	£3250
Thirty shillings	from	£150	£475
Twelve shillings	from	£150	£550
Six shillings	from	£100	£325
Half merk	from	£120	£395
Forty pence	from	£55	£185
Twenty pence	from	£30	£85

FOURTH COINAGE (1642)

	F	VF
Three shillings thistle	£60	£150
Two shillings large II	£40	£110
Two shillings small II	£60	£155
Two shillings no value	£80	£225

*Charles I Fourth Coinage
Two Shillings*

COPPER ISSUES

(1629 Issue)

	F	VF
Twopence (triple thistle	£25	£70
Penny	£175	£500

(1632-39 Issue)

		F	VF
Twopence (Stirling turner	from	£25	£70

(1642-50 ISSUE)

	F	VF
Twopence (CR crowned	£20	£55

CHARLES II (1660–85)

FIRST COINAGE

Four merks

	F	VF
1664 Thistle above bust	£1250	£4000
1664 Thistle below bust	£2500	£7250
1665	Extremely rare	
1670 .... varieties from	£1550	£6950
1673	£1550	£6950
1674 F below bust .... varieties from	£1250	£4000
1675	£950	£2750

Two merks

	F	VF
1664 Thistle above bust	£1000	£2500

Charles II two merks

	F	VF
1664 Thistle below bust	£2500	£7250
1670	£1200	£3000
1673	£750	£1950
1673 F below bust	£1350	£3250
1674	£1200	£3000
1674 F below bust	£1200	£3000
1675	£750	£1950

Merk

	F	VF
1664 .... varieties from	£250	£715
1665	£275	£780
1666	£325	£950
1668	£325	Ex. rare
1669 .... varieties from	£100	£275
1670	£145	£375
1671	£110	£300
1672 .... varieties from	£100	£275
1673 .... varieties from	£110	£300
1674	£250	£715
1674 F below bust	£225	£650
1675 F below bust	£200	£550
1675	£210	£585

Charles II Dollar

Half merk

	F	VF
1664	£275	£725
1665 .... varieties from	£325	£600
1666 .... varieties from	£300	£750
1667	£325	£600
1668	£150	£400
1669 .... varieties from	£105	£325
1670 .... varieties from	£150	£400
1671 .... varieties from	£105	£285
1672	£150	£400
1673	£175	£475
1675 F below bust	£175	£575
1675	£195	£550

SECOND COINAGE
Dollar

	F	VF
1676	£750	£2000
1679	£650	£1650
1680	£750	£1650
1681	£550	£1325
1682	£475	£1250

Charles II Sixteenth Dollar

Half Dollar

	F	VF
1675	£650	£1500
1676	£750	£1950
1681	£400	£1100

Quarter Dollar

	F	VF
1675	£195	£550
1676 .... varieties from	£100	£295
1677 .... varieties from	£145	£400
1678	£165	£450
1679	£185	£500
1680	£135	£325
1681	£105	£275
1682 .... varieties from	£145	£400

Eighth Dollar

	F	VF
1676 .... varieties from	£85	£210

Charles II Bawbee

	F	VF
1677..	£125	£300
1678/7	£195	£495
1679..	£300	Ext. rare
1680.. varieties from	£150	£345
1682.. varieties from	£225	£495

Sixteenth Dollar

1677..	£85	£210
1678/7 .... varieties from	£120	£320
1679/7	£135	£360
1680.. varieties from	£135	£360
1681..	£75	£175

Copper Issues

Twopence CR crowned .... varieties from	£25	£70
Bawbees 1677-79 .... varieties from	£65	£195
Turners 1677-79 .... varieties from	£45	£125

JAMES VII (1685–89)

Sixty shillings

1688 proof only .... varieties from	—	£3250

Forty shillings

1687.. varieties from	£400	£950
1688.. varieties from	£400	£950

Ten shillings

1687..	£165	£525
1688.. varieties from	£250	£700

James VII ten shillings

WILLIAM & MARY (1689–94)

Sixty shillings

1691..	£475	£1750
1692..	£775	£2100

Forty shillings

1689.. varieties from	£295	£850
1690.. varieties from	£185	£525
1691.. varieties from	£195	£550
1692.. varieties from	£225	£600
1693.. varieties from	£195	£550
1694.. varieties from	£225	£775

Twenty shillings

1693..	£500	£1650
1694..	Extremely rare	

William & Mary ten shillings

Ten shillings

1689..	Extremely rare	
1690.. varieties from	£295	£750
1691.. varieties from	£195	£600
1692.. varieties from	£195	£600
1694.. varieties from	£250	£700

Five shillings

1691..	£200	£575
1694.. varieties from	£120	£350

Copper Issues

Bawbees 1691–94........................... varieties from	£100	£275
Bodle (Turners) 1691–94................. varieties from	£55	£180

	F	VF

WILLIAM II (1694–1702)

Pistole £3000 £7500
Half pistole £3750 £8500

Forty shillings
1695.. varieties from £225 £650
1696.. £250 £625
1697.. £300 £650
1698.. £250 £595
1699.. £375 £750
1700.. Extremely rare

Twenty shillings
1695.. £200 £625
1696.. £200 £625
1697.. varieties from £250 £700
1698.. varieties from £175 £650
1699.. £225 £625

William II ten shillings

Ten shillings
1695.. £150 £375
1696.. £150 £375
1697.. varieties from £150 £375
1698.. varieties from £150 £375
1699.. £295 £750

Five shillings
1695.. £70 £195
1696.. £65 £180
1697.. varieties from £75 £225
1699.. £95 £275
1700.. £85 £230
1701.. £125 £350
1702.. £125 £350

Copper Issues
Bawbee 1695–97................................... varieties from £85 £325
Bodle (Turners) 1695–97....................... varieties from £50 £150

Anne five shillings

ANNE (1702–14)

Pre -Union 1702–7 **(For POST-UNION 1707–1** See listing in the English section)
Ten shillings
1705.. £175 £450
1706.. varieties from £225 £650

Five shillings
1705.. varieties from £85 £225
1706.. £85 £225

JAMES VIII (The Old Pretender) (1688–1766)

A number of Guineas and Crowns in various metals were struck in 1828 using original dies prepared by Norbert Roettiers, all bearing the date 1716. These coins are extremely rare and are keenly sought after.

Guinea
1716 Gold Old Bust Right Type 1 .... Generally EF+ £12000
1716 Silver Old Bust Right Type 1 .... Generally EF+ £1250
1716 Silver Young Bust Left Type .... Generally EF+ £1750

Crown
1716.. Generally EF+ £2500

*Our grateful thanks go to David Stuart of ABC Coins & Tokens for updating this
Scottish section of the Yearbook*

ISLE OF MAN

HIBERNO-MANX PENNY

Recent research has established that a Mint did exist in the Isle of Man and evidence suggests that silver pennies were minted on the Island from c.1025. Resulting from finds in various locations on the Island, it had been suggested that Hiberno-Manx pennies were coined at a mint located in the northern area, perhaps Maughold. However, the mint was more likely to have been in the fortress on St. Patrick's Isle at Peel in the west of the Island. They have been found in hoards from Park Llewellyn (Maughold), West Nappin (Jurby), Kirk Andreas and at Kirk Michael. The dies for these Hiberno-Manx silver pennies may have originally come from a moneyer called Færemin in Dublin.

Hiberno-Manx silver penny, c.1025

JOHN MURREY'S PENNIES OF 1668

The first Manx tokens to become 'official' legal tender in the Isle of Man are attributed to John Murrey's Pennies of 1668. British coins circulated alongside these tokens, together with much extraneous coinage. At this time there was a severe shortage of pennies and halfpennies. An Act of Tynwald dated 24th June 1679 proclaimed that "...no copper or brass money called Butchers' halfpence, Patrick's halfpence and copper farthings, or any of that nature, shall pass in the Island from the first day of January next." The Act also stated that only the King's (Charles II) farthings and halfpence, and the brass money called Ino Murrey's pence was to pass as currency. Consequently, the Act had the effect of making John Murrey's brass tokens legal tender pennies. The Isle of Man thus had its own distinctive legal currency for the first time. John Murrey was a merchant of Douglas and lived at Ronaldsway near Castletown. Two distinct types of his penny have been recorded and both are rare.

The two known types of John Murrey's penny of 1668

Murrey's coins remained in circulation as legal tender until the 1710 Coinage Act of Tynwald. This Act authorised the new coinage of James Stanley, Earl of Derby, and declared all coins previously circulating to be illegal. When this Act was promulgated, it is believed that a descendant of John Murrey redeemed nearly all the "murreys" then in circulation and destroyed them.

The new Stanley coinage was cast at Castle Rushen in Castletown and dated 1709. The penny and halfpenny were proclaimed legal currency on 24th June 1710.

DATE	F	VF	EF	UNC
PENNY (Copper except where stated)				
"Derby" coinage				
1709 Cast	£55	£185	£350	—
1709 Silver cast Proof	—	—	—	£2000
1709 Brass	£50	£175	£350	—
1733 "Quocunque"	£40	£75	£275	£450
1733 "Ouocunoue"	£45	£85	£300	£750
1733 Bath metal "Quocunque"	£30	£75	£300	—
1733 Silver Proof	—	—	—	£850
1733 Bronze Proof	—	—	—	£500
1733 Proof	—	—	—	£675

Cast penny.

DATE	F	VF	EF	UNC
1733 Cap frosted.......................................	£35	£75	£300	£500
1733 Brass, cap frosted	£40	£75	£325	£650
1733 Silver Proof cap frosted.....................	—	—	—	£650
1733 Bronze annulets instead of pellets	£50	£100	£400	£500
"Atholl" coinage				
1758..	£30	£50	£250	£450
1758 — Proof	—	—	—	£650
1758 — Silver Proof	—	—	—	£1000
Regal coinage				
1786 Engrailed edge	£35	£65	£275	£450
1786 Engrailed edge Proof	—	—	—	£600
1786 Plain edge Proof	—	—	—	£1000
1786 Pellet below bust	£35	£65	£275	£550
1798..	£35	£65	£250	£500
1798 Proof..	—	—	—	£450
1798 Bronze Proof......................................	—	—	—	£450
1798 Copper-gilt Proof...............................	—	—	—	£2000
1798 Silver Proof	—	—	—	£2500
1813	£40	£75	£300	£500
1813 Proof..	—	—	—	£650
1813 Bronze Proof......................................	—	—	—	£650
1813 Copper-gilt Proof...............................	—	—	—	£2500
1839	£35	£75	£200	£450
1839 Proof..	—	—	—	£500

"Derby" coinage.

HALF PENCE (Copper except where stated)

"Derby" coinage

	F	VF	EF	UNC
1709 Cast	£50	£125	£250	—
1709 Brass	£55	£185	£500	—
1723 Silver	£725	£1250	£3500	—
1723 Copper	£300	£600	£1750	£2500
1733 Copper	£35	£55	£225	£450
1733 Bronze	£35	£55	£225	£450
1733 Silver Proof plain cap	—	—	—	£700
1733 Silver Proof frosted cap	—	—	—	—
1733 Bronze Proof......................................	—	—	—	£500
1733 Bath metal plain cap..........................	£40	£50	£215	—
1733 Bath metal frosted cap	£40	£50	£215	—

Regal coinage.

"Atholl" coinage

	F	VF	EF	UNC
1758	£40	£50	£215	£450
1758 — Proof	—	—	—	£800
Regal coinage				
1786 Engrailed edge	£30	£45	£120	£350
1786 Proof engrailed edge	—	—	—	£450
1786 Plain edge...	£40	£65	£250	£350
1786 Proof plain edge	—	—	—	£650
1786 Bronze Proof......................................	—	—	—	£450
1798..	£35	£45	£150	£350
1798 Proof..	—	—	—	£450
1798 Bronze Proof......................................	—	—	—	£400
1798 Copper-gilt Proof...............................	—	—	—	£1500
1798 Silver Proof	—	—	—	£1500
1813	£30	£45	£150	£300
1813 Proof..	—	—	—	£375
1813 Bronze Proof......................................	—	—	—	£350
1813 Copper-gilt Proof...............................	—	—	—	£1250
1839	£30	£45	£150	£300
1839 Bronze Proof......................................	—	—	—	£450

FARTHING
Regal coinage

	F	VF	EF	UNC
1839 Copper	£30	£45	£150	£300
1839 Bronze Proof	—	—	—	£450
1839 Copper-gilt Proof	—	—	—	£2500

"Atholl" coinage.

MANX DECIMAL COINS FROM 1971

This section lists the circulating coins issued by the Isle of Man Government Treasury. The Royal Mint produced the initial issue in 1971 which satisfied the needs of the Island until 1975. In 1972, 73 and 74 the Pobjoy Mint sent to the Government 1,000 samples of each denomination of the current series in anticipation of securing future contracts for the minting of Manx coins. Pobjoy won the contract in 1975 and minted all Isle of Man coins up to and including 2016. One exception was the 1972 Royal Silver Wedding crown which was minted by the Royal Canadian Mint in Ottawa. In 1975 the Manx Government released the Pobjoy samples into circulation with the 1975 coins. In 2016 the Tower Mint in London won the contract for minting Manx coins from 2017.

From 1979 Pobjoy introduced die marks on their coins in the form of small Celtic letters in the form AA, AB, AC, etc. Alternative letter(s) were used for diamond finish and precious metal coins. 'PM' mint marks also appear on most Pobjoy minted coins. The positions of die marks and mint marks can randomly appear on both obverse and reverse. There are many variations on practically all denominations and are outside the scope of this yearbook.

Where known, minting figures are shown in the lists but from about 1986 Pobjoy did not release minting quantities. On the Christmas 50p coins where the 'Minting Limit' is quoted the actual quantities produced were far less, usually up to 5,000 coins for circulation in the Isle of Man.

In some years when no coins were required for circulation, the only source for certain denominations of that year was from uncirculated sets. Unsold sets were often broken up by the Treasury and the coins put into circulation. Coins bearing those dates are, therefore, scarce.

Sculptors of Queen's Profile used on Manx Coins

1971-1984	Arnold Machin
1985-1997	Raphael Maklouf (full bust on Crowns)
1998-2016	Ian Rank-Broadley (full bust on Crowns)
2017-	Jody Clark (full bust version)

Privy and Provenance Marks

Privy marks can be found on a number of Manx circulating coins. A stylised Triskeles was used on coins dated 1979 to commemorate the Millennium of Tynwald - The Manx Parliament. Some coins dated 1982 bore a baby crib to commemorate the birth of Prince William. In 1985 the Manx Year of Sport logo was incorporated into the designs of circulating coins.

Provenance marks may be found on some £1 coins dated 1980 and 1981 minted at the Daily Mail Ideal Home Exhibition in London (D.M.I.H.E.) and minted at the Daily Mail Ideal Home Exhibition in Birmingham (D.M.I.H.E./N.). Also Belfast Ideal Home Exhibition (I.I.H.E.) on the 1981 £1 and £5 coins minted at this location. In 1980 a number of £1 coins bore the T.T. (Tourist Trophy motorcycle races) provenance mark.

A few two pounds (£2) and five pounds (£5) coins dated 1991 bore the privy mark 'RAOB'. Both are scarce

Precious Metals Coins

Many coins have been produced in various precious metals such as silver, gold, platinum and palladium.

Coins not intended for Circulation

Fractional coins, odd denominations and unusual shapes have all featured and a few examples are listed at the end of this section, however, details of these coins are outside the scope of this yearbook.

DATE	Mintage	UNC

HALF PENNY

Metal: Bronze
Size: 17mm diameter

1971 Cushag (Ragwort)	495,000	£2
1972	1,000	£25
1973	1,000	£25
1974	1,000	£25
1975	705,610	£1
1976 Herring on Map of Island	335,554	£1
1977	887,803	£1
1978	120,225	£2
1979	251,152	£2
1980 Stylised Norse Herring	117,665	£2
1981	169,772	£2
1981 Herring on Map - World Food Day	10,000	£3
1982 Stylised Norse Herring	17,385	£2
1983	24,576	£2
1984 Fuchsia	39,009	£2
1985	25,000	£3

Cushag   *Herring on Map of Island*

Stylised Norse Herring   *Fuchsia*

Half pennies are no longer legal tender in the Isle of Man

PENNY

Metal: Bronze up to 1995 then Bronze Plated Steel
Size: 20mm diameter

1971 Ring Chain Pattern	100,000	£2
1972	1,000	£25
1973	1,000	£25
1974	1,000	£25
1975	826,032	£1
1976 Loughtan Sheep on Map of Island	823,572	£1
1977	479,751	£1
1978	850,415	£1
1979	1,096,285	£1
1980 Tailless Manx Cat	593,401	£1
1981	224,126	£2
1982	324,440	£2
1983	447,820	£1
1984 Cormorant on Shield	406,858	£1
1985	25,000	£2
1986		£2
1987		£2
1988 Metalwork Lathe & Cog		£1
1989		£1
1990		£1
1991		£1
1992		£1
1993		£1
1994		£1
1995		£1
1996 Rugby Ball & Goal Posts		£1
1997		£1
1998		£1
1999		£1
2000 St. Michael's Chapel, Langness		£1
2001		£1
2002		£1
2003		£1
2004 Santon War Memorial		£1
2005		£1
2006		£1
2007		£1

Ring Chain Pattern   *Loughtan Sheep on map*

Tailless Manx Cat   *Cormororant on Shield*

Metalwork Lathe & Cog   *Rugby Ball & Goal Posts*

St. Michael's Chapel   *Santon War Memorial*

DATE	Mintage	UNC
2008		£1
2009		£1
2010		£1
2011		£1
2012		£1
2013		£1
2014		£1
2015		£1
2016		£1

Pennies are no longer minted for circulation in the Isle of Man.

Cast of Falcons

TWO PENCE
Metal: Bronze up to 1995 then Bronze Plated Steel
Size: 26mm diameter

1971	Cast of Falcons	100,000	£3
1972		1,000	£30
1973		1,000	£30
1974		1,000	£30
1975		683,549	£1
1976	Manx Shearwater	875,146	£1
1977		458,089	£1
1978		620,695	£1
1979		602,593	£1
1980	Chough & Hiberno-Norse Bronze	569,993	£1
1981		172,170	£2
1982		236,376	£1
1983		371,735	£1
1984	Peregrine Falcon on Shield	178,296	£1
1985		25,000	£2
1986			£2
1987			£2
1988	Ancient Manx Crafts		£1
1989			£1
1990			£1
1991			£1
1992			£1
1993			£1
1994			£1
1995			£1
1996	Racing Pedal Cyclists		£1
1997			£1
1998			£1
1999			£1
2000	Manx Fishermens Evening Hymn		£1
2001			£1
2002			£1
2003			£1
2004	Albert Tower, Ramsey		£1
2005			£1
2006			£1
2007			£1
2008			£1
2009			£1
2010			£1
2011			£1
2012			£1
2013			£1
2014			£1
2015			£1
2016			£1

Two Pence coins are no longer minted for circulation in the Isle of Man.

Peregrine Falcon on Shield

Ancient Manx Crafts

Manx Fishermens Evening Hymn

Albert Tower, Ramsey

DATE		Mintage	UNC

FIVE PENCE

Metal: Cupro Nickel to 2016 then Nickel Plated Steel
Size: 23,5mm diameter up to 1989 then 18mm diameter from 1990

Year	Description	Mintage	UNC
1971	Tower of Refuge	100,000	£3
1972		1,000	£30
1973		1,000	£30
1974		1,000	£30
1975		1,017,103	£1
1976	Laxey Wheel on Map of Island	677,404	£1
1977		201,306	£2
1978		677,031	£1
1979		271,526	£2
1980	Loughtan Ram on Norse Brooch	403,296	£1
1981		67,289	£3
1982		405,381	£1
1983		137,365	£2
1984	Cushag & a la Bouche Shield	313,994	£1
1985		25,000	£3
1986			£2
1987			£2
1988	Windsurfer		£3
1989			£3
1990	Windsurfer (small diameter)		£1
1991			£1
1992			£1
1993			£1
1994	Golf Ball & Crossed Clubs		£3
1995			£3
1996	Golfer in Action		£2
1997			£2
1998			£2
1999			£2
2000	Gaut's Cross		£1
2001			£1
2002			£1
2003			£1
2004	Tower of Refuge, Douglas		£1
2005			£1
2006			£1
2007			£1
2008			£1
2009			£1
2010			£1
2011			£1
2012			£10
2013			£1
2014			£1
2015			£1
2016			£1
2017	Manx Shearwater in Flight	460,000	£1
2018		20,000	£2
2019		2,000	£5
2020		2,000	£5

Tower of Refuge

Laxey Wheel

Loughtan Ram

Golf Ball & Clubs

Gaut's Cross

Tower of Refuge

DATE   Mintage   UNC

TEN PENCE

Metal: Cupro Nickel to 2016 then Nickel Plated Steel
Size: 28mm diameter up to 1992 then 24,5mm diameter from 1992

Date	Description	Mintage	UNC
1971	Triskeles (Three Legs oF Mann)	100,000	£3
1972		1,000	£30
1973		1,000	£30
1974		1,000	£30
1975		1,454,265	£1
1976	Triskeles on Map of Island	1,412,309	£1
1977		483,550	£1
1978		103,383	£2
1979		276,554	£2
1980	Peregrine Falcon	90,657	£3
1981		760,086	£1
1982		378,912	£2
1983		98,797	£3
1984	Loughtan Ram on Shield	289,789	£2
1985		25,000	£3
1986			£2
1987			£2
1988	Portcullis on Map of World		£3
1989			£3
1990			£3
1991			£20
1992			£15
1992	Triskeles (small diameter)		£1
1993			£10
1994			£10
1995			£10
1996	Sailing Boat		£5
1997			£5
1998			£3
1999			£5
2000	St. German's Cathedral, Peel		£2
2001			£2
2002			£2
2003			£2
2004	Chicken Rock Lighthouse		£2
2005			£2
2006			£2
2007			£2
2008			£2
2009			£2
2010			£2
2011			£2
2012			£15
2013			£2
2014			£2
2015			£2
2016			£2
2017	Manx Tailless Cat	220,000	£1
2018		20,000	£2
2019		720,000	£1
2020		500,000	£1

Triskeles

Peregrine Falcon

Portcullis on Map

Triskeles

*Chicken Rock
Lighthouse*

A comprehensive listing of all the coins and tokens produced for the Isle of Man, together with a detailed history and all recorded variations including die marks, can be found in the book *Coins of the Isle of Man* by Mike J. Southall. ISBN 9 780995 738720 third edition.

DATE   Mintage   UNC

TWENTY PENCE

Metal: Cupro Nickel
Wider border with incuse lettering from 1993

Date	Description	Mintage	UNC
1982	Viking Arms & Armour	824,892	£2
1983		115,610	£2
1984	Three Herrings on Shield	141,393	£2
1985		25,000	£3
1986			£3
1987			£3
1988	Combine Harvester		£3
1989			£2
1990			£2
1991			£2
1992			£2
1993			£3
1994			£2
1995			£3
1996	Rally Racing Car		£2
1997			£2
1998			£2
1999			£2
2000	Manx Bible at Rushen Abbey		£2
2001			£3
2002			£2
2003			£3
2004	Castle Rushen 1597 Clock		£2
2005			£2
2006			£2
2007			£2
2008			£2
2009			£2
2010			£2
2011			£2
2012			£15
2013			£2
2014			£2
2015			£2
2016			£2
2017	Sailing Viking Longship	281,250	£1
2018		262,500	£1
2019		937,500	£2
2020		625,000	£2

Viking Arms

Three Herrings

Combine Harvester

Castle Rushen 1597 Clock

TOURIST TROPHY (TT) FIFTY PENCE

Metal: Cupro Nickel
Size: 30mm diameter up to 1997 then 27,3mm diameter from 1997

Date	Description	Mintage	UNC
1981	Joey Dunlop	30,000	£15
1982	Mick Grant	30,000	£15
1983	Ron Haslam	30,000	£15
1984	Mick Boddice	30,000	£15
1999	Leslie Graham	4,500	£35
2004	Tourist Trophy (TT)	3,000	£50
2007	Dave Molyneux and Sidecar	3,500	£30
2007	Tourist Trophy (TT)	3,500	£30
2009	John McGuinness	3,500	£40
2010	Suzuki Team Rider		£30
2011	Yamaha Motorcycle		£20
2012	Mark Cavendish Cyclist		£40
2012	Dave Knight Enduro Motorcyclist		£30
2014	John McGuinness Twenty TT Wins		£25
2015	TT Legends, TT Winners, Duke etc.		£15
2016	TT Legends, TT Winners, Dunlop etc.		£15

Joey Dunlop, TT Champion

Geoff Duke, etc. TT Legends

Regular circulating coins issued in 1996 to 1999 inclusive depict TT motorcyclist Phil McCallen. They were not part of the 50p series commemorating TT riders and events.

DATE   Mintage   UNC

FIFTY PENCE

Metal: Cupro Nickel
Size: 30mm diameter up to 1997 then 27,3mm diameter from 1997

Date	Description	Mintage	UNC
1971	Viking Longship	100,000	£3
1972		1,000	£30
1973		1,000	£30
1974		1,000	£30
1975		121,817	£1
1976	Viking Longship on Map	116,242	£1
1977		131,784	£1
1978		76,203	£2
1979		164,316	£1
1979	Odin's Raven Longship	100,000	£3
1979	Odin's Raven, Royal Visit (edge)	50,000	£4
1980	Odin's Raven, New York (edge)	20,000	£6
1980	Stylised Viking Longship	203,138	£1
1981		332,940	£1
1982		118,166	£2
1983		162,524	£2
1984	Viking Longship on Shield	282,567	£2
1985		25,000	£3
1986			£3
1987			£3
1988	Triskelion on Computer Screen		£5
1989			£10
1990			£15
1991			£30
1992			£30
1993			£30
1994			£40
1994	Tynwald Legislative Centenary	2,500	£20
1995	Triskelion on Computer Screen		£50
1996	TT Motorcycle Racing, Phil McCallen	6,000	£150
1997			£200
1997	As above but small 27,3mm diameter		£2
1998			£15
1999			£15
2000	Calf of Man Crucifixion Stone		£2
2001			£2
2002			£2
2003			£2
2004	Milner's Tower, Bradda Head		£2
2005			£2
2006			£2
2007			£2
2008			£2
2009			£2
2010			£2
2011			£2
2012			£25
2012	Queen's Diamond Jubilee		£10
2013	Milner's Tower, Bradda Head		£2
2014			£2
2015			£2
2016			£2
2017	Manx Loughton Sheep	325,000	£1
2018		200,000	£2
2019		937,500	£1
2020		375,000	£1

Viking Longship

*Viking Longship
on Shield*

*TT Motorcycle Racing
Phil McCallen*

*Calf of Man
Crucifixion Stone*

*Miner's Tower
Bradda Head*

DATE		Mintage	UNC

CHRISTMAS FIFTY PENCE

Metal: Cupro Nickel
Size: 30mm diameter up to 1997 then 27,3mm diameter from 1997

1980	Steam Packet's Mona's Isle	30,000	£20
1981	Manx Nikki Fishing Boat	30,000	£10
1982	Carol Singers at Castletown	30,000	£25
1983	Model T Ford Car	30,000	£25
1984	Steam Engine No.1 Sutherland	50,000	£25
1985	De Haviland Rapide Aircraft	30,000	£25
1986	Douglas Corporation Horse Tram	30,000	£25
1987	Douglas Vosper Thorneycroft Bus	30,000	£25
1988	Motorcycle & Sidecar at Cregneash	30,000	£40
1989	Laxey Tram Station	50,000	£20
1990	Steam Packet's Lady of Mann	30,000	£30
1991	Nativity Scene	30,000	£30
1992	Manks Mercury Newspaper	30,000	£100
1993	St. Georges Stained Glass Window	30,000	£70
1994	Hunting the Wren	30,000	£120
1995	Snowball scene on S.M.R.	30,000	£115
1996	Choir Boys at Lonan Old Church	30,000	£80
1997	Thomas Edward Brown, Manx Poet	30,000	£50
1998	Victorian Manx Family Scene	30,000	£40
1999	Decorating Christmas Tree	30,000	£80
2000	Manx Bible at Rushen Abbey	30,000	£80
2001	Victorian Fluted Pillar Box	30,000	£50
2002	Charles Dickens Christmas Carol	30,000	£50
2003	The Snowman and James	10,000	£260
2004	The Great Laxey Wheel	30,000	£40
2005	12 Days of Christmas, Pear Tree	30,000	£120
2006	12 Days of Christmas, Turtle Doves	30,000	£100
2007	12 Days of Christmas, French Hens	30,000	£60
2008	12 Days of Christmas, Calling Birds	30,000	£50
2008	The Snowman and James	30,000	£310
2009	12 Days of Christmas, Gold Rings	30,000	£50
2010	12 Days of Christmas, Geese	30,000	£50
2011	Santa with Sack and Parcel	30,000	£50
2012	Christmas Angel	30,000	£35
2013	Christmas Stocking	30,000	£35
2014	Snowman and Snowdog	30,000	£35
2015	No issue	—	—
2016	Christmas Pudding	30,000	£15

Numbers of Christmas 50p coins circulated in the Isle of Man are usually around 5,000 and sometimes much less. The Christmas theme after 2016 was continued by the Tower Mint with £5 and £2 coins.

ONE POUND

Metal: Virenium to 1995. Nickel-Brass from 1996
Size: 22mm diameter x 1,5mm thick to 1982. 3mm thick from 1983 -

1978	Triskeles on Map of Isle of Man	323,071	£3
1979		67,687	£5
1979	As above, X-oars Prov. Mark	1,000	£50
1980		78,288	£8
1980	As above, D.M.I.H.E. Prov. Mark	100,000	£15
1980	As above, D.M.I.H.E./N Prov. Mk.		£20
1980	As above, T.T. Prov. Mark		£10
1981		12,590	£8
1981	As above, I.I.H.E. Prov. Mark		£75
1982			£50
1982	As above, Baby Crib Prov. Mark		£25

1980 Mona's Isle Paddle Steamer

1984 Steam Engine No.1 Sutherland

1997 T. E. Brown Manx Poet

2003 The Snowman and James

Triskeles on Map

DATE		Mintage	UNC
1983	Town Arms—Peel	19,619	£5
1984	Town Arms—Castletown	25,000	£15
1985	Town Arms—Ramsey	25,000	£15
1986	Town Arms—Douglas		£20
1987	Viking on Horseback		£8
1988	Cellnet Telephone		£3
1989			£4
1990			£4
1991			£4
1992			£4
1993			£4
1994			£4
1995			£4
1996	Douglas Corporation Centenary		£8
1996	Cricket Stumps, Bat and Ball		£5
1997			£5
1998			£5
1999			£5
2000	Triskeles with Millennium Bells		£4
2001			£4
2002			£4
2003			£4
2004	Tynwald Hill and St.Johns Church		£3
2005			£3
2006			£3
2007			£3
2008			£3
2009			£3
2010			£3
2011			£3
2012			£3
2013			£3
2014			£3
2015			£3
2016			£3
2017	Manx Shearwater in Flight	460,000	£2
2018		20,000	£3
2019		2,000	£5
2020		2,000	£5

Town Arms
Ramsey

Cellnet
Telephone

Triskeles with
Milennium Bells

Tynwald Hill and
St. John's Church

The Isle of Man has retained the round pound but the UK dodecagonal coin is often seen alongside in circulation.

TWO POUNDS

Metal:Virenium up to 1997. Bi-metal Nickel-Brass / Cupro-Nickel 1997
Size: 28,4mm diameter

1986	Tower of Refuge (Metal: Virenium)		£15
1987			£15
1988	Manx Airlines BAe 146-100 Jet		£15
1989	Manx Airship Dirigible		£400
1990	Manx Airlines BAe 146-100 Jet		£15
1991			£15
1992			£20
1993			£20
1993	Nigel Mansell Formula 1		£30
1994	Nigel Mansell PPG Indi Car		£25
1995	Royal British Legion VE / VJ Day		£25
1996	E-Type Jaguar Racing (Virenium)		£25
1997			£25
1997	E-Type Jaguar Racing (Bi-Metal)		£5
1998			£5
1999			£10
2000	Thorwald's Cross, Andreas Church		£15

Manx Airlines BAe 145-100
Jet

DATE		Mintage	UNC
2001	....		£15
2002	....		£15
2003	....		£15
2004	Round Tower Peel Castle		£10
2005	....		£10
2006	....		£10
2007	....		£10
2008	....		£10
2009	....		£10
2010	....		£10
2011	....		£10
2011	Commonwealth Games, Tosha the Cat............		£120
2012	Round Tower Peel Castle		£30
2013	....		£10
2014	....		£10
2015	....		£10
2016	....		£20
2017	Tower of Refuge..	300,000	£4
2018	....	20,000	£8
2019	....	176,000	£4
2020	....	156,000	£4

E-Type Jaguar Racing Virenium version

E-Type Jaguar Racing Bi-metal version

FIVE POUNDS

Metal: Virenium up to 2016. Alpaca (nickel silver) from 2017
Size: 36mm diameter up to 2016. 32mm diameter from 2017

1981	Triskeles on Map of Isle of Man....................	22,414	£10
1982	....	1,075	£30
1983	....		1,473
£25			
1984			—
1984	Knight on Horseback....................................	2,068	£25
1985	25,000		£20
1986	....		£25
1987	....		£25
1988	Peel Inshore Fishing Boat............................		£25
1989	....		£25
1990	....		£25
1991	....		£25
1992	....		£25
1993	....		£25
1993	Nigel Mansell, Formula 1		£35
1994	Nigel Mansell, PPG Indi Car		£30
1995	50 Years, End of World War II.......................		£30
1996	Footballers Euro96		£30
1997	Footballers..		£25
1997	Royal Golden Wedding Anniv.		£30
1998	Prince Charles 50th Birthday........................		£30
1998	Footballers..		£25
1999	....		£25
1999	175th Anniversary of RLNI............................		£30
2000	St. Patrick's Hymn		£25
2001	....		£30
2002	....		£30
2003	....		£30
2004	The Great Laxey Wheel		£30
2005	....		£30
2006	....		£50
2007	....		£30
2008	....		£30
2009	....		£50
2010	....		£50

Knight on Horseback

Peel Inshore Fishing Boat

St. Patrick's Hymn

311

DATE	Mintage	UNC
2011		£50
2012		£70
2013		£50
2014		£50
2015		£30
2016		£40
2017 Manx Triskele Symbol	20,000	£15
2018	20,000	£25
2019	1,000	£35
2020	1,000	£35

The Great Laxey Wheel

ISLE OF MAN CROWNS

Isle of Man crowns minted from 1970 to 2016 have a face value of twenty five pence (25p) or five shillings (5/- 1970 pre-decimal issue). Manx Crowns were revalued at five pounds (£5) by the Isle of Man Government from 2017.

Crowns listed in this section are standard size coins 38.61mm diameter made of cupro-nickel (CuNi) and have a nominal value of 25p. Howsever, the supply and demand for these coins is very erratic according to the retail source, therefore it has been decided not to price them.

Many of these Crowns were also struck from precious metals such as Silver (Ag), Gold (Au), Platinum (Pt) and Palladium (Pd). There are also many odd-shaped Crowns and part Crowns issued in CuNi and various precious metals. Multiple Crown values also exist. These coins to detail individually are outside the scope of this Year Book but a selection is illustrated after this list.

A comprehensive listing of all the coins and tokens produced for the Isle of Man, together with a detailed history and all recorded variations including die marks, can be found in the book *Coins of the Isle of Man* by Mike J. Southall. ISBN 9 780995 738720 third edition.

DATE

1970 Manx Cat
1972 Royal Silver Wedding
1974 Centenary of Churchill's birth
1975 Manx Cat
1976 Bi-Centenary of American Independence
1976 Centenary of the Horse Drawn Tram
1977 Silver Jubilee
1977 Silver Jubilee Appeal
1978 25th Anniversary of the Coronation
1979 300th Anniversary of Manx Coinage
1979 Millennium of Tynwald (5 coins)
1980 22nd Olympics (3 coins)
1980 80th Birthday of Queen Mother
1980 Derby Bicentennial
1980 Winter Olympics—Lake Placid
1981 Duke of Edinburgh Award Scheme (4 coins)
1981 Prince of Wales' Wedding (2 coins)
1981 Year of Disabled (4 coins)
1982 12th World Cup—Spain (4 coins)
1982 Maritime Heritage (4 coins)
1983 Manned Flight (4 coins)
1984 23rd Olympics (4 coins)
1984 Commonwealth Parliamentary Conference (4 coins)
1984 Quincentenary of College of Arms (4 coins)
1985 Queen Mother (6 coins)
1986 13th World Cup—Mexico (6 coins)
1986 Prince Andrew Wedding (2 coins)
1987 200th Anniversary of the United States Constitution
1987 America's Cup Races (5 coins)
1988 Australia Bicentennial (6 coins)

DATE

1988 Bicentenary of Steam Navigation (6 coins)
1988 Manx Cat
1989 Queen Elizabeth II & Prince Philip Royal Visit
1989 Bicentenary of the Mutiny on the Bounty (4 coins)
1989 Bicentenary of Washington's Inauguration (4 coins)
1989 Persian Cat
1989 Royal Visit
1989 13th World Cup Mexico (2 coins)
1990 150th Anniversary of the Penny Black
1990 25th Anniversary of Churchill's Death (2 coins)
1990 Alley Cat
1990 Queen Mother's 90th Birthday
1990 World Cup—Italy (4 coins)
1991 1992 America's Cup
1991 Centenary of the American Numismatic Association
1991 Norwegian Forest Cat
1991 10th Anniversary of Prince of Wales' Wedding (2 coins)
1992 1992 America's Cup
1992 Discovery of America (4 coins)
1992 Siamese Cat
1993 Maine Coon Cat
1993 Preserve Planet Earth—Dinosaurs (2 coins)
1994 Japanese Bobtail Cat
1994 Normandy Landings (8 coins)
1994 Preserve Planet Earth—Endangered Animals (3 coins)
1994 Preserve Planet Earth—Mammoth
1994 World Football Cup (6 coins)
1994 Year of the Dog
1994 D-Day Normandy Landings (8 coins)
1994 Man in Flight—Series i (8 coins)
1995 Aircraft of World War II (19 coins)
1995 America's Cup
1995 Famous World Inventions—Series i (12 coins)
1995 Man in Flight—Series ii (8 coins)
1995 Preserve Planet Earth—Egret and Otter
1995 Queen Mother's 95th Birthday
1995 Turkish Cat
1995 Year of the Pig
1996 70th Birthday of HM the Queen
1996 Burmese Cat
1996 European Football Championships (8 coins)
1996 Explorers (2 coins)
1996 Famous World Inventions—Series ii (6 coins)
1996 Football Championships Winner
1996 King Arthur & the Knights of the Round Table (5 coins)
1996 Olympic Games (6 coins)
1996 Preserve Planet Earth—Killer Whale and Razorbill (2 coins)
1996 Robert Burns (4 coins)
1996 The Flower Fairies—Series i (4 coins)
1996 Year of the Rat
1997 10th Anniversary of the "Cats on Coins" series (silver only)
1997 Royal Golden Wedding
1997 90th Anniversary of the TT Races (4 coins)
1997 Explorers—Eriksson and Nansen (2 coins)
1997 Long-haired Smoke Cat
1997 Royal Golden Wedding (2 coins)
1997 The Flower Fairies—Series ii (4 coins)
1997 Year of the Ox
1998 The Millennium (4 coins)
1998 125th Anniversary of Steam Railway (8 coins)
1998 18th Winter Olympics, Nagano (4 coins)
1998 Birman Cat
1998 Explorers—Vasco da Gama and Marco Polo (2 coins)
1998 FIFA World Cup (4 coins)
1998 International Year of the Oceans (4 coins)
1998 The Flower Fairies—Series iii (4 coins)
1998 The Millennium (16 coins issued over 3 years)
1998 Year of the Tiger
1999 The Millennium (4 coins)

DATE

1999 27th Olympics in Sydney (5 coins)
1999 Rugby World Cup (6 coins)
1999 The Millennium (4 coins)
1999 Titanium Millennium crown
1999 Wedding of HRH Prince Edward and Sophie Rhys-Jones
1999 Year of the Rabbit
2000 The Millennium (4 coins)
2000 Millennium Intertwined MM (Issued to every Manx school child)
2000 18th Birthday of HRH Prince William
2000 60th Anniversary of the Battle of Britain
2000 BT Global Challenge
2000 Explorers, Francisco Piarro and Wilem Brents (2 coins)
2000 Life and times of the Queen Mother (4 coins)
2000 Millennium—own a piece of time
2000 Queen Mother's 100th Birthday
2000 Scottish Fold cat
2000 Year of the Dragon

2001 75th Birthday of HM the Queen
2001 Explorers, Martin Frobisher and Roald Amundsen (2 coins)
2001 Harry Potter (6 coins)
2001 Joey Dunlop
2001 Life and times of the Queen Mother (2 coins)
2001 The Somali cat
2001 Year of the Snake
2002 A Tribute to Diana Princess of Wales—5 years on
2002 Introduction of the Euro
2002 The Bengal Cat
2002 The Queen's Golden Jubilee—i (1 coin)
2002 The Queen's Golden Jubilee—ii (4 coins)
2002 The XIX Winter Olympiad, Salt Lake City (2 coins)
2002 World Cup 2002 in Japan/Korea (4 coins)
2002 Year of the Horse

2003 Golden Coronation Jubilee
2003 XII Olympic Games 2004 (4 coins)
2003 Anniversary of the "Star of India"
2003 Lord of the Rings (5 coins)
2003 Prince William's 21st Birthday
2003 The Balinese Cat
2003 Year of the Goat
2004 Year of the Monkey
2004 100 Years of Powered Flight (2 coins)
2004 Olympics (4 coins)
2004 Ten New EU Entries
2004 Harry Potter—Prisoner of Azkaban
2004 Queen Mary 2—World's Largest Passenger Liner
2004 D-Day Re-enactment—Parachute Jump
2004 Football, Euro 2004 (2 coins)
2004 Lord of the Rings—Return of the King
2004 Tonkinese Cats
2004 Battle of Trafalgar
2004 60th Anniversary of D-Day (6 coins)

2005 60th Anniversary of Peace (coins as 2004 D-Day) (6 coins)
2005 60th Anniversary of Victory in Europe
2005 Bicentenary of the Battle of Trafalgar (6 coins)
2005 175th Anniversary of Isle of Man Steam Packet (2 coins)
2005 400th Anniversary of the Gunpowder Plot (2 coins)
2005 Bicentenary of Hans Christian Andersen
2005 Harry Potter and the Goblet of Fire (4 coins)
2005 Italy and the Isle of Man TT races (2 coins)
2005 Manx Hero Lt. John Quilliam (2 coins)
2005 The Himalayan Cat with kittens
2005 Bicentenary of the Battle of Trafalgar (6 coins)
2006 150th Anniversary of the Victoria Cross (2 coins)
2006 30th Anniversary of the first Translantic Flight
2006 80th Birthday of Her Majesty the Queen (4 coins)
2006 The Battles that Changed the World—Part II (6 coins)
2006 Transatlantic Flight (2 coins)
2006 Exotic Short Hair Cat
2006 World Cup FIFA 2006

DATE

2006 Queen's Beasts
2006 Fairy Tales (2 coins)
2006 Aircraft of World War II—Spitfire
2006 The Battles that Changed the World—Part I (6 coins)
2007 The Tales of Peter Rabbit
2007 Fairy Tales (3 coins)
2007 The Centenary of the Scouting
2007 The Centenary of the TT races (5 coins)
2007 The Graceful Swan
2007 The Ragdoll Cat
2007 The Royal Diamond Wedding Anniversary (4 coins)
2008 50th Anniversary of Paddington Bear
2008 Burmilla Cat
2008 Prince Charles 60th Birthday
2008 The Adorable Snowman
2008 The Return of Tutankhamun (2 coins)
2008 UEFA European Football Championships
2008 Year of Planet Earth
2008 Olympics China (6 coins)
2009 40th Anniversary of the 1st Concorde Test Flight
2009 Fifa World Cup South Africa 2010
2009 The Chinchilla Cat
2009 Winter Olympics (2 coins)
2009 500th Anniversary of Henry VIII (2 coins)
2009 BeeGees—Freedom of Douglas
2009 Fall of the Berlin Wall
2009 40th Anniversary of the First Man on the Moon
2009 Olympics 2012 (6 coins)
2010 Olympics 2012 (6 coins)
2010 Vancouver Olympics 2010 (2 coins)
2010 Buckingham Palace
2010 Abyssinian Cat and her Kitten
2011 A Lifetime of Service—Queen Elizabeth II and Prince Philip
2011 Buckingham Palace
2011 Royal Wedding of HRH Prince William and Catherine Middleton
2011 The Turkish Angora Cat
2011 TT Mountain Course 100 years
2011 Year of the Rabbit
2012 Life of Queen Elizabeth II (2 coins)
2012 Centenary of RMS *Titanic* (2 coins)
2012 European Football Championships (4 coins)
2012 Juno Moneta Coin
2012 Manx Cat Coin
2012 Olympics (6 coins).
2012 River Thames Diamond Jubilee Pageant
2013 Anniversary of Queen Victoria and Queen Elizabeth II Coronations
2013 Kermode Bear
2013 60th Anniversary of Coronation
2013 Siberian Cat
2013 St. Patrick Commemorative
2013 Winter Olympic (4 coins)
2014 Centenary of WWI (2 coins). Coloured Silver Proof.
2014 200th Anniversary of Matthew Flinders
2014 70th Anniversary of D-Day (3 coins)
2014 Snowman and Snow Dog Crown (£5)
2014 Snowshoe Cat
201 Snow Dog
2014 Winter Olympic Games (4 Coin Collection)
2015 175th Anniversary of the Penny Black Stamp (issued in a pack)
2015 200th Anniversary of the Battle of Waterloo—Napoleon
2015 200th Anniversary of the Battle of Waterloo—Wellington
2015 75th Anniversary of the Battle of Britain (search lights in yellow)
2015 Her Majesty the Queen Elizabeth II Longest reigning Monarch
2015 Paddington Bear
2015 Selkirk Rex Cat
2015 Sir Winston Churchill
2016 90th Birthday Queen Elizabeth II
2016 Tobacco Brown Cat

Tower Mint has produced commemorative
crowns from 2017 with a nominal value of £5.

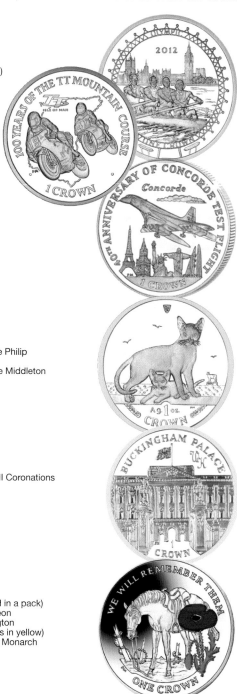

CROWNS FROM THE TOWER MINT

Crowns listed in this section are standard size coins 38.61mm diameter made of cupro-nickel (CuNi) and have a nominal value of £5.Some of these Crowns were also struck from precious metals such as Silver (Ag) and/or Gold (Au) and a few issues were minted piedfort.

2017 Duke of Edinburgh 70 Years of Service
2017 Platinum Wedding Anniversary
2017 Viking Scenes (*CuNi Antique silver plate finish*) (5 coins)
2017 Centenary of the House of Windsor (*CuNi gold plated*)
2017 Sapphire Wedding of Her Majesty and Prince Philip
2018 60th Anniversary of Queen Elizabeth II Coronation
2019 Centenary of the First Man on the Moon
2019 200th Anniversary of the Birth of Queen Victoria (3 coins)

Other Crowns Minted only in Precious Metals:
2018 World War I Armistice Centenary (poppies in red and black) *Ag*
2018 Birth of Prince Louis Arthur Charles. *Ag*
2020 Manx Wildlife Series Part I. *Ag, Au*

Coins with High Denominations have also been minted:
2017 £10 King Canute (*Ag with antique finish*)
2018 £10 WWI Armistice Centenary (poppies in red and black) *Ag*
2019 £10 50th Anniversary of the Moon Landing *Ag*
2018 £50 World War I Armistice Centenary (poppies in red) *Ag*
2019 £100 Age of the Vikings (*Ag with antique finish*)

*60th Anniversary of
Queen Elizabeth II Coronation*

*Viking Scenes (CuNi Antique
silver plate finish) (5 coins)*

*Centenary of the House of
Windsor (CuNi gold plated)*

*Centenary of the First Man
on the Moon*

ODD SIZE AND IRREGULAR SHAPED CROWNS

Many odd shaped Crowns have been produced by the Pobjoy Mint and a representative selection is illustrated here. A variety of metals, from cupro-nickel, silver, gold, platinum and palladium have been used in the minting of these coins. Parts and multiples of a Crown struck in precious metals also exist. Denominations that exist for some Crown issues are 1/64 Crown, 1/32 Crown, 1/25 Crown, 1/20 Crown, 1/10 Crown, 1/5 Crown, 1/4 Crown, 1/2 Crown, 2 Crowns, 5 Crowns, 10 Crowns, 13 Crowns, 32 Crowns, 64 Crowns, 100 Crowns and 130 Crowns. Coins illustrated here are not to scale.

NOTABLE MANX FIRSTS

Golden Jubilee of Queen Elizabeth II 2002 3kg .9999 fine silver

2010 750th Anniv. of Mongol ruler Kublai Khan

1978 World's First £1 Coin

2012 Queen's Diamond Jubilee. ½ Crown silver

2009 Terracotta Army - 1/5 Crown

1990 First Black Coin Penny Black Anniversary

1 crown

2008 Tutankhamun's Death Mask ½ Crown. Fine 999.9 gold.

Commemorating the 2008 - 09 Tutankhamun Exhibition in London

1999 First White Gold Coins 1/25, 1/10, 1/5 and 1/2 Platina

Tower Mint Crown (£5)

2019 Manannan - First King of Mann. 99.9% Silver Crown.

2002 First Spinning Coin Currency Converter

COINS OF OTHER DENOMINATIONS

SOVEREIGNS, PARTS & MULTIPLES

Isle of Man sovereigns, multiples and parts were minted in gold in certain years between the years 1965 and 1993. Sovereigns were of standard imperial size, contained between 91.6% and 99.9% gold and depicted a Viking in armour on horseback.

The 1965 gold coins (Five, One and Half Sovereign) to mark the bicentenary of the Act of Revestment are 98% (23.5ct). They were also minted in 91.7% (22ct) gold.

Sovereigns in 99.99 gold were again minted from 2019 by the Tower Mint in London.

The "ace value"of a sovereign is one pound sterling (£1) but its intrinsic or bullion value is much greater owing to the value of its metal content.

ANGELS, PARTS & MULTIPLES

In addition to the Sovereign, bullion coinage has been issued in several different denominations, viz. Angels and Nobles. Bullion coins are legal tender and their face value is equal to the current market or bullion value of the metal content in the coins.

The Angel was launched in the Isle of Man for legal tender status purposes on 13th March 1985. However, a token issue of the 1oz gold Angels dated 1984 were struck by the Pobjoy Mint and sent to the United States for 'test marketing' ahead of the official release by the Isle of Man Treasury.

Pobjoy Mint produced Angels until 2016 when Tower Mint continued the series in 2017.

The reverse of the Angel coin depicts the Archangel Michael slaying the Dragon. The series of Christmas 1/20 Angels have been struck in fine gold and others in 22ct. gold and many also exist as proof coins.

NOBLES, PARTS & MULTIPLES

The first Manx 1 Noble coin was issued in 1983 followed by the 1/10 Noble in 1984. The latter was known then as a 'Noblette'. Pobjoy Mint produced Nobles periodically until 2016 when the Tower Mint continued the series in 2017.

The reverse of the Noble coin depicts the Viking Ship 'Thusly' in full sail. Nobles have been struck in fine gold and others in gold and platinum. Proof coins exist for some issues.

A full listing of crowns, with their multiples and parts and a full listing of Angel and Noble coins, with their multiples and parts, can be found in the book *Coins of the Isle of Man* by Mike J. Southall. ISBN 9 780995 738720 third edition.

TOWER MINT CIRCULATING COIN DESIGNS

No Isle of Man **One Penny** or **Two Pence** coins have been produced by the Tower Mint. All 1p and 2p coins from 1971 to 2016 inclusive remain legal tender on the island and circulate with their UK equivalents.

Jody Clark's portrait of Her Majesty the Queen was adopted for use on coins of the Commonwealth countries, including the Isle of Man, and this effigy was first used by the Tower Mint from 2017 for Manx coins. These coins from the Tower Mint are included in the general list of Manx Decimal Coins from 1971.

The **five pence** (5p) design depicts the Manx Shearwater, a medium-sized sea bird of the family *Procellaridae*. It is an amber-listed species of particular conservation concern in the Isle of Man. It is found around the cliffs on the east coast and on the Calf of Man.

The **ten pence** (10p) design depicts the famous Manx tailless cat with its most distinguishing characteristics of its elongated hind legs and rounded head. Manx cats are best known as being entirely tailless and are affectionately called a "rumpy", but some have a small stub of a tail and they are known as a "stumpy".

The **twenty pence** (20p) design depicts a typical sailing Viking longship. The Isle of Man has a significant Viking heritage, particularly with the Viking longship *Odin's Raven*, a replica of which is in the House of Mannan at Peel.

The **fifty pence** (50p) design shows the famous breed of Manx Loaghtan sheep native to the Isle of Man. The sheep, which has dark brown wool, is depicted full-face with its characteristic four horns.

The **one pound** (£1) design depicts a Pergrine Falcon and a Raven. The Isle of Man was granted a coat-of-arms by Queen Elizabeth II in 1966 in which the two birds are shown. They are both symbolically associated with the island.

The **two pounds** (£2) design depicts the Tower of Refuge, an important landmark built on Conister Rock in Douglas Bay. It was built in 1832 by Sir William Hilary, founder of the Royal National Lifeboat Institution, who lived at Fort Anne overlooking Douglas Bay.

The **five pounds** (£5) design depicts the famous Triskelion or Triskele, symbol of the Isle of Man. It is based on the Manx coat-of-arms, dating back to the 13th century. The three legs are known in Manx as "ny tree cassyn".

The Tower Mint produces commemorative coins for general circulation at appropriate intervals. In addition, coins are also minted in various precious metals. Bullion coins in precious metals have also been minted.

COMMEMORATIVE CIRCULATING COINS FROM THE TOWER MINT

Quantities shown as "No. Minted" are for coins circulated in the Isle of Man

DATE		No. Minted	UNC

FIFTY PENCE

2017	150th Anniversary of House of Keys	33,000	£3
2018	Platinum Wedding Queen & Prince Philip (8 coins)	each design 2,500	£30
2018	Sapphire Coronation of Her Majesty QEII (5 coins)	each design 2,500	£25
2018	Centenary of World War I Armistice, Plain	25,000	£3
2018	Centenary of World War I Armistice, Coloured	15,000	£10
	Coloured coins were given to all school pupils.		
2019	ICC Cricket World Cup (5 coins)	each design 12,000	£20
2019	Peter Pan, Part I (6 coins)	each design 25,000	£20
2020	75th Anniversary of VE Day—Individual letters spelling "VICTORY" on 7 coin designs.	25,000	£25
2020	Rupert Bear (5 coins)	each design 25,000	£30
2020	Peter Pan, Part 2 (6 coins)	each design 25,000	£30
2021	Alice in Wonderland (5 Coins)	each design 10,000	£20
2021	HM Queen 95th Birthday (6 coins)	each design 10,000	£20

TWO POUNDS

2018	Prince Harry & Meghan Markle Wedding	2,500	£5
2018	Mike Hailwood, TT 40 Years	15,000	£5
2018	Mike Hailwood, TT 60 Years	15,000	£5
2018	Christmas, Hunt the Wren	10,000	£6
2019	D-Day, King George VI	2,500	£8
2019	D-Day, Winston Spencer Churchill	2,500	£8
2019	D-Day, Field Marshall Montgomery	2,500	£8
2019	Steve Hislop's 120mph TT Lap	15,000	£5
2019	Steve Hislop's 11 TT Wins	12,500	£5
2019	Father Christmas	12,500	£6
2020	Operation Dynamo. 80th Anniversary (2 coins)	each design 3,000	£15
2020	Dickens Christmas (3 coins)	each design 3,500	£15
2020	Mayflower 400th Anniversary	each design 3,500	£10

FIVE POUNDS

2017	110 Years of the Tourist Trophy	20,000	£20
2017	Christmas - Dove of Peace	10,000	£25

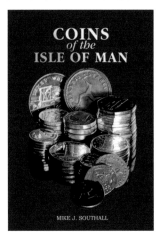

COINS *of the* **ISLE OF MAN**

MIKE J. SOUTHALL

Coins of the Isle of Man by Mike J. Southall, MBE

This book contains a comprehensive history of coins used in the Isle of Man and a definitive study of Manx decimal coins that have been in circulation since 1971. Adding further interest, the die marks, mint marks, provenance marks, etc. found on the 1979-2016 Manx decimal coins are also included. A section listing the non-circulating, precious metal and bullion coins follows that of the circulating coins.

After John Murrey's first legal penny token of 1668, the first official Manx coins, halfpennies and pennies, were issued by the Lord of Mann, James Stanley 10th Earl of Derby. They were made legal tender by an Act of Tynwald on 24th June 1710. Manx coins, and a variety of tokens, were circulating on the Island until 1839. Thereafter British coins became the only legal currency until decimalisation in 1971.

This updated third edition book makes compelling reading and is a most useful and comprehensive reference work for anyone with the slightest interest in the coins of the Isle of Man.

ISBN 9 780995 738720 from Lily Publications Limited, PO Box 33, Ramsey, Isle of Man. IM99 4LP £29.95 plus postage.

GUERNSEY

DATE	F	VF	EF	UNC

TEN SHILLINGS

1966	—	£5	£10	£15
1966 Proof	—	—	—	£35

THREEPENCE

1956	£1	£4	£8	£10
1956 Proof	—	—	—	£15
1959	£1	£4	£8	£15
1966 Proof	—	—	—	£15

EIGHT DOUBLES

1834	£10	£15	£65	£250
1858 5 berries	£6	£10	£50	£150
1858 4 berries	£6	£10	£55	£175
1864 1 stalk	£6	£10	£40	£75
1864 3 stalks	£6	£10	£45	£85
1868	£6	£10	£30	£75
1874	£4	£6	£20	£55
1885H	£4	£6	£20	£50
1889H	£3	£4	£20	£45
1893H small date	£3	£4	£20	£45
1893H large date	£3	£4	£20	£50
1902H	£3	£4	£20	£45
1903H	£3	£4	£20	£45
1910	£3	£4	£20	£45
1911H	£3	£4	£20	£50
1914H	£1	£3	£10	£35
1918H	£1	£3	£8	£25
1920H	£1	£3	£8	£25
1934H	£1	£3	£10	£35
1934H Proof	—	—	—	£275
1938H	£1	£3	£10	£25
1945H	£1	£2	£8	£15
1947H	£1	£2	£8	£15
1949H	—	£2	£10	£18
1956	—	£1	£7	£15
1956	—	£1	£5	£15
1959	—	£1	£5	£15
1966 Proof	—	—	—	£35

FOUR DOUBLES

1830	£4	£10	£55	£165
1830 Mule with obv. St Helena 1/2d	—	£850	—	—
1858	£6	£15	£55	£150
1864 Single stalk	£2	£6	£20	£65
1864 3 stalks	£2	£6	£25	£75
1868	£3	£7	£22	£75
1874	£2	£6	£22	£75
1885H	£2	£6	£20	£45
1889H	£2	£3	£15	£35
1893H	£2	£3	£15	£35
1902H	£2	£3	£10	£30
1903H	£2	£3	£13	£30
1906H	£2	£3	£10	£25
1908H	£2	£3	£10	£25
1910H	£2	£3	£10	£25
1911H	£2	£3	£8	£25
1914H	£2	£3	£15	£50
1918H	£2	£3	£12	£35
1920H	£2	£3	£10	£35
1945H	£2	£3	£10	£35
1949H	£2	£3	£12	£35
1956	£1	£2	£8	£15
1966 Proof	—	—	—	£25

DATE	F	VF	EF	UNC
TWO DOUBLES				
1858..	£6	£10	£50	£265
1868 Single stick	£6	£12	£55	£265
1868 3 stalks	£7	£15	£85	£275
1874..	£4	£12	£75	£175
1885H..	£3	£6	£20	£35
1889H..	£3	£5	£20	£35
1899H..	£3	£5	£25	£50
1902H..	£3	£5	£20	£35
1903H..	£3	£5	£20	£35
1906H..	£3	£5	£20	£35
1908H..	£3	£5	£20	£35
1911H..	£3	£5	£25	£45
1914H..	£3	£5	£25	£45
1917H..	£7	£25	£95	£275
1918H..	£3	£5	£15	£35
1920H..	£3	£5	£15	£35
1929H..	£2	£5	£12	£30
ONE DOUBLE				
1830..	£3	£5	£25	£55
1868..	£4	£12	£55	£165
1868/30	£5	£7	£30	£85
1885H..	£2	£5	£15	£35
1889H..	£1	£3	£8	£25
1893H..	£1	£3	£8	£25
1899H..	£1	£3	£8	£25
1902..	£1	£3	£8	£25
1903H..	£1	£3	£8	£25
1911H..	£1	£4	£10	£35
1911 (new shield)	£1	£3	£8	£25
1914H..	£1	£4	£10	£25
1929H..	£1	£3	£6	£25
1933H..	£1	£3	£6	£25
1938H..	£1	£3	£6	£25

DECIMAL COINAGE

Ordinary circulating coinage from 1986 onwards is usually available in uncirculated condition at a small premium above face value thus it is not listed here. The coins listed are cupro-nickel unless otherwise stated. The coins listed are cupro-nickel unless otherwise stated.

UNC

ONE HUNDRED POUNDS

	UNC
1994 50th Anniversary of Normandy Landings. Gold proof....................	£1650
1995 Anniversary of the Liberation. Gold proof	£1650

FIFTY POUNDS

1994 50th Anniversary of Normandy Landings. Gold proof....................	£1250
1995 Anniversary of the Liberation. Gold proof	£1250
1998 Queen Elizabeth and Queen Mother Gold proof	£1250
1999 Queen Elizabeth and Queen Mother Gold	£1250
2004 Anniversary of D-Day. Gold	£1250
2013 70th Anniversary of the Dambuster Raid. Silver proof 10oz	£350
2015 Magna Carta 800th anniversary. Silver proof 10oz	£350
2016 Her Majesty the Queen's 90th Birthday. Gold Proof	£13,000

TWENTY-FIVE POUNDS (x22mm gold)

1994 50th Anniversary of Normandy Landings. Gold	£400
1994 — Gold proof...	£450
1995 Anniversary of the Liberation. Gold proof	£450
1995 Queen Mothers 95th Birthday. Gold..	£400
1996 European Football Championships. Gold proof............................	£450
1997 Royal Golden Wedding. Gold proof	£450
1998 Royal Air Force. Gold proof...	£450
2000 Queen Mother 100th Birthday. Gold proof....................................	£450
2001 Queen Victoria centennial Gold proof	£450
2001 Queen Victoria Gold proof..	£450

In recent years a number of companies have been involved in marketing the coins of the Channel Islands. As a consequence many special limited edition commemorative coins have been issued in a wide variety of sizes, metals and finishes. These are very numerous with some issues being produced in very small numbers and many are omitted from our listings. These issues are generally outside of the scope of this catalogue.

DATE	UNC
2001 HM the Queen's 75th Birthday. Gold proof	£450
2002 Princess Diana memorial. Gold proof	£450
2002 Duke of Wellington. Gold proof	£450
2002 Golden Jubilee. Gold proof	£450
2002 Queen Mother. Gold proof	£450
2003 Golden Jubilee. Gold proof	£450
2003 Golden Hind. Gold proof	£450
2004 Anniversary of D-Day. Gold proof	£450
2004 Age of Steam—Truro. Gold proof	£450
2004 Age of Steam—Mallard. Gold proof	£450
2004 HMS Invincible. Gold proof	£450
2005 HMS Ark Royal. Gold proof	£450
2006 FIFA World Cup. Gold proof	£450

TEN POUNDS

1994 50th Anniversary of Normandy Landings. Gold proof	£350
1995 Anniversary of the Liberation. Gold proof	£350
1997 Royal Golden wedding. 5oz Silver proof	£250
2000 Century of Monarchy. 5oz Silver proof	£250
2000 Guernsey Gold proof "Nugget"	£350
2001 19th Century Monarchy. Silver proof	£150
2002 18th Century Monarchy. Silver proof	£150
2003 1700 Years of Monarchy. Silver proof	£150
2004 16th Century Monarchy. Silver proof	£150
2004 Anniversary of D-Day. Silver proof	£150
2004 150th anniversary of the Crimean War. 5oz Gold proof	£8000
2005 Return of the Islanders. Silver proof	£50
2005 — 5oz Gold proof	£8000
2005 Anniversary of Trafalgar. 5oz Gold proof	£8000
2005 End of World War II. Silver proof	£25
2005 — 5oz Gold proof	£8000
2005 — 5oz Platinum proof	£8250
2009 Anniversary of Moon Landing. Silver proof	£75
2009 — 5oz Gold proof	£8000
2012 Diamond Jubilee. 5oz Silver proof	£250
2013 Coronation Jubilee. 5oz Silver proof	£250
2015 Reflections of the Reign 5oz gold proof	£8000
2017 Sapphire Jubilee. 5oz Silver proof	£450
2017 The House of Windsor. 5oz Silver proof	£450
2018 RAF Centenary 5oz Silver proof	£450
2019 200th Anniversary of Queen Victoria birth. 5oz Silver Proof, Gold detail	£550

FIVE POUNDS

1995 Queen Mother's 95th birthday	£25
1995 — Silver proof	£55
1995 — Small size Gold	£350
1996 HM the Queen's 70th birthday	£20
1996 — Silver proof	£55
1996 European Football Championships	£15
1996 — Silver proof	£25
1997 Royal Golden Wedding	£15
1997 — Silver proof	£25
1997 — Small size Gold. BU	£350
1997 Castles of the British Isles—Castle Cornet, Guernsey	£15
1997 — Silver proof	£25
1997 Castles of the British Isles—Caernarfon Castle. Silver proof	£30
1997 Castles of the British Isles—Leeds Castle. Silver proof	£30
1998 Royal Air Force.	£15
1998 Royal Air Force. Silver proof	£30
1999 Millennium. Brass	£15
1999 — Silver proof	£25
1999 Wedding of HRH Prince Edward and Sophie Rhys-Jones	£15
1999 — Silver proof	£25
1999 Queen Mother	£25
1999 — Silver proof	£80
1999 Winston Churchill	£15
1999 — 1oz Gold	£1800

DATE	UNC
2000 Queen Mother's 100th Birthday	£10
2000 — Silver proof	£85
2000 — Small size Gold proof	£375
2000 Centuries of the British Monarchy	£45
2000 — Silver proof	£85
2000 — Small size Gold proof	£375
2001 The Reign of Queen Victoria	£20
2001 — proof	£60
2001 — Silver proof	£60
2001 — Gold proof	£400
2001 HM the Queen's 75th Birthday	£15
2001 — Silver proof	£25
2001 — Small size Gold proof	£3750
2001 19th Century Monarchy	£20
2001 — Silver proof	£25
2001 — Small size Gold proof	£375
2002 Golden Jubilee (two types)	£15
2002 — Silver proof	£25
2002 Princess Diana Memorial	£15
2002 — proof	£35
2002 — Gold proof	£1500
2002 Century of Monarchy	£15
2002 — Silver proof	£35
2002 — Small size Gold proof	£350
2002 Queen Mother Memoriam	£15
2002 — proof	£20
2002 — Silver proof	£35
2002 — Small size Gold proof	£350
2002 — Large size Gold proof	£1500
2003 Duke of Wellington	£15
2003 — Silver proof	£25
2003 — Small size Gold proof	£350
2003 — Large size Gold proof	£1500
2003 Prince William	£20
2003 — Silver proof	£35
2003 — Gold proof	£1500
2003 Golden Hind	£20
2003 17th Century Monarchy	£20
2003 History of the Royal Navy, Nelson	£20
2003 — Nelson with coloured flag proof	£25
2004 — Invincible. Silver proof	£30
2004 16th Century monarchs	£15
2004 History of the Railways, Mallard	£12
2004 — City of Truro	£15
2004 — The Boat Train	£12
2004 — The Train Spotter	£15
2004 History of the Royal Navy, Henry VIII	£15
2004 — Invincible	£15
2004 Anniversary of D-Day	£12
2004 — Silver proof	£25
2004 — Gold proof	£1500
2004 Anniversary of the Crimean War. Plain	£12
2004 — with colour	£15
2004 — Silver proof	£25
2004 — Gold proof with colour	£1500
2005 200th Anniversary of the Battle of Trafalgar	£20
2005 60th Anniversary of the Liberation of the Channel Islands	£20
2005 End of World War II. Silver proof	£25
2005 — Gold proof	£1500
2005 Anniversary of Liberation. Gold proof	£1500
2006 Royal 80th Birthday. Silver proof	£25
2006 FIFA World Cup. Silver proof	£25
2006 Great Britons—Sir Winston Churchill Silver. Issued as part of set	£60
2006 80th Birthday of Her Majesty the Queen	£20
2007 History of the Royal Navy—Henry VIII, The Golden Hind (2 coins). ea.	£65
2007 Royal Diamond Wedding	£20
2008 90th Anniversary of the RAF (10 designs in silver proof)............ ea.	£35

Note: Many of these issues have also been produced in different metals and finishes to those listed here.

DATE   UNC

2009 British Warships (6 designs in silver proof) .... ea.	£35
2009 Anniversary of Apollo Moon landings. Cu-ni..................................	£5
2009 – Silver proof...	£35
2010 Charles II Unite. Gold proof	£1750
2010 Florence Nightingale. Gold proof	£1750
2010 Battle of Britain 70th anniversary. Silver and coloured	£55
2011 350th Anniversary of the Crown Jewels. Silver proof......................	£95
2011 90th Anniversary of the British Legion (Gold-plated copper)...........	£45
2011 – Silver proof...	£95
2011 40th Anniversary of decimalisation proof.................................	£20
2011 Anniversary of the sinking of the *Titanic*	£20
2011 – Silver proof...	£55
2011 30th Birthday of Duke of Cambridge.......................................	£20
2011 – Silver proof...	£55
2011 Wedding of Prince William and Kate Middleton............................	£25
2011 – Silver proof...	£55
2011 400th Anniversary of the King James Bible	£25

2012 Diamond Jubilee £5..	£25
2012 – Gold proof..	£1750
2012 Tribute to the British Army. Gold proof.....................................	£2000
2013 70th Anniversary of the Dambuster Raid.	£20
2013 – Silver proof...	£65
2013 – Gold proof..	£2000
2013 Coronation Jubilee	£25
2013 – Silver proof...	£55
2013 – Gold proof..	£2000
2013 200th Guinea Anniversary	£25
2013 – Silver proof...	£55
2013 – Gold proof..	£2000
2014 Centenary of the First World War. Silver proof	£85
2014 – 5oz Silver proof..	£450
2014 – Gold proof..	£2500
2015 VE Day 70th Anniversary	£15
2015 Magna Carta 800th anniversary	£15
2016 90th Birthday of HM the Queen BU	£15

2016 – Silver Proof	£75
2016 Battle of the Somme...	£12
2016 Battle of Hastings Anniversary	£15
2017 Sapphire Jubilee. Silver plated..	£10
2017 Prince Philip Years of Service (only available in 3-coin set)	£20
2017 70th Royal Wedding Anniversary Silver proof	£75
2018 Centenary of WWI	£15
2018 – Silver proof	£75
2018 Prince Harry Royal Wedding Silver proof	£75
2018 65th Coronation Jubilee Silver proof.......................................	£75
2018 Prince of Wales 70th Birthday. Cu-Ni with gold ink	£25
2018 – Silver Proof	£85
2018 – 5oz Silver Proof..	£500
2019 The King's Speech Outbreak of WWII 80th anniversary Silver proof	£85
2019 – Silver Proof 5oz..	£495
2019 75th Anniversary of D-Day. Cu-Ni with gold ink..........................	£25
2019 – Coloured BU	£15
2019 Remembrance Poppy..	£5

2020 Battle of Britain 80th Anniversary. BU	£12
2020 – Gold Plated Proof..	£40
2020 – 3 coin sets. Silver Proof..	£270
2020 VE Day..	£12
2020 75th Anniversary of the Liberation of the CI...............................	£12
2020 –date stamped pair..	£40
2020 Florence Nightingale Bicentenary	£25
2020 – Silver Proof	£85
2020 – 5oz Silver Proof..	£495
2020 – Gold Proof...	£2750
2021 Queen Elizabeth II 95th Birthday BU..	–
2021 – Silver Proof	–
2021 50 years of Decimalisation	–
2021 – Silver Proof with selected gold plating	–

DATE   UNC

TWO POUNDS
1985 40th anniversary of Liberation £10
1985 — Proof £30
1985 — Silver proof... £55
1986 Commonwealth Games, in plastic case................................... £12
1986 — in special folder.. £12
1986 — .500 Silver £45
1986 — .925 Silver proof... £55
1987 900th Anniv. of death of William the Conqueror, in folder £15
1987 — Silver proof... £55
1987 — Gold proof.. £1500
1988 William II, in presentation folder £15
1988 — Silver proof... £55
1989 Henry I, in presentation folder £15
1989 — Silver proof... £55
1989 Royal Visit.. £15
1989 — Silver proof... £55
1990 Queen Mother's 90th birthday... £15
1990 — Silver proof... £55
1991 Henry II, in presentation folder £15
1991 — Silver proof... £55
1993 40th Anniversary of the Coronation.. £15
1993 — Silver proof... £60
1994 Anniversary of the Normandy Landings £15
1994 — Silver proof... £55
1995 50th Anniversary of Liberation £154
1995 — Silver proof... £55
1995 — Silver Piedfort proof.. £100
1997 Conserving Nature i... £12
1997 — Silver proof... £55
1997 Bimetallic Latent image.. £8
1997 — proof £10
1998 Conserving Nature ii.. £10
1998 Bimetallic Latent image.. £6
2003 — £6
2006 — £8
2011 Prince Philip's 90th Birthday (conjoined portraits) £6
2011 — Silver proof... £50
2011 40th Anniversary of Decimalisation £12
2012 Diamond Jubilee Proof... £20
2012 "8 Doubles" modern variant.. —

ONE POUND
1981 .... £10
1981 Gold proof £350
1981 Gold piedfort £650
1983 New specification, new reverse.. £10
1985 New design (in folder).. £10
1995 Queen Mother's 95th Birthday. Silver proof £50
1996 Queen's 70th Birthday. Silver proof.. £55
1997 Royal Golden Wedding. Silver BU.. £20
1997 — Silver proof... £55
1997 Castles of the British Isles—Tower of London. Silver proof only ... £35
1998 Royal Air Force. Silver proof... £45
1999 Wedding of Prince Edward. Silver proof £55
1999 Queen Mother. Silver proof... £55
1999 Winston Churchill. Silver proof.. £55
2000 Millennium. Silver proof (Gold plated) £65
2000 Queen Mother's 100th Birthday. Silver proof £45
2001 .... £2
2001 HM the Queen's 75th Birthday. Silver proof £45
2002 William of Normandy. Silver £20
2003 .... £2
2006... £2
2015 Magna Carta 800th anniversary. Gold proof £500
2018 HRH Prince Charles 70th Birthday. Gold proof £500

DATE	UNC
2018 RAF Centenary	£15
2018 — Gold Proof	£500

FIFTY PENCE (initially 7-sided, some issues round)

1969 Ducal cap reverse	£4
1970	£6
1971 proof	£9
1981	£4
1982	£4
1985 New flower design	£4
2000 60th Anniversary of the Battle of Britain.	£4
2000 — Silver proof	£55
2000 — Silver piedfort	£55
2000 — Gold proof	£375
2003	£2
2003 Coronation Jubilee (four types)	£2
2003 — Proof	£4
2006	£2
2008	£2
2012 The Diamond Jubilee (coloured portrait)	£10
2012 — Cu-Ni Fine Gold-Plated	£5
2013 60th Anniversary of Coronation (two different designs: Queen in State Coach and Queen in White Dress), Gold clad steel ... ea.	£5
2013 The RAF 617 Squadron Gold-plated copper	£15
2013 The RAF No. 1 Squadron Gold-plated copper	£15
2013 The Red Arrows. Gold-plated copper	£15
2013 Battle of Britain Memorial Flight. Gold-plated copper	£15
2013 50th Anniversary of the Flying Scotsman's retirement in 1963	£25
2014 New Queen Elizabeth II	£45
2015 Queen Elizabeth II—Reflections of a Reign, Cu-Ni	£5
2016 90th Birthday of Queen Elizabeth II (two round crown-size coloured coins) ... ea.	£5
2016 Churchill Tank. Gold-plated copper	£10
2016 Centenary of the WWI Tank. Gold-plated copper	£10
2017 The Spitfire. Silver-plated copper	£12
2017 Sapphire Jubilee, Cu-Ni	£10
2017 Prince George's Birthday. Gold-plated	£75
2017 70th Anniversary Royal Wedding. Gold-plated Copper	£40
2018 RAF Centenary. Gold-plated	£45
2019 Concorde 50th Anniversary	£10
2019 — — set (3 designs: Runway, Take Off, Flight) ... ea.	£25
2019 — — (paired with a Jersey 50p)	£12
2019 — SIlver Proof	£125
2019 50th Anniversary of the 50p (paired with Jersey). BU x 2	£20
2019 — — SIlver Proof	£125
2019 — Moon Landings. Coloured Titanium 3-coin set	£150
2019 — — Orange Titanium	£50
2019 — — Green Titanium	£50
2019 — — Blue Titanium	£50
2019 Pantomime 5 coin set. BU	£30
2019 — Silver, coloured Proof set	£325
2020 75th Anniversary of the Liberation of the CI. 2 coins. BU	£12
2020 — Date stamped BU x 2 coins	£40
2020 — Cu-Ni Proof x 2 coins	£60
2020 Offical RAF Battle of Britain Spitfire. Copper with 24ct gold plating	£40
2020 Christmas Carol 5-coin set	£30
2020 — Silver Proof coloured 5-coin set	£250
2021 Mr Benn 5-coin set	—
2021 — Silver Proof coloured 5-coin set	—

Note: in addition to the coins listed here, there are many others produced for Guernsey, often in tandem with the other Channel Islands. Regretfully information on many of these issues is difficult or impossible to obtain, thus they are omitted from this guide.Ordinary circulating coinage from 1986 onwards is usually available in uncirculated condition at a small premium above face value thus it is not listed here.

JERSEY

DATE	F	VF	EF	UNC

FIVE SHILLINGS

	F	VF	EF	UNC
1966	—	£3	£7	£15
1966 Proof	—	£3	£9	£25

ONE QUARTER OF A SHILLING

	F	VF	EF	UNC
1957	—	£2	£5	£10
1960 Proof	—	—	£5	£15
1964	—	—	£4	£10
1966	—	—	£4	£10

ONE TWELFTH OF A SHILLING

	F	VF	EF	UNC
1877H	£2	£3	£20	£65
1877H Proof in nickel	—	—	—	£1275
1877 Proof only	—	—	—	£500
1877 Proof in nickel	—	—	—	£1275
1881	£3	£3	£15	£60
1888	£2	£3	£15	£50
1894	£2	£3	£20	£50
1909	£2	£3	£15	£50
1911	£2	£3	£10	£30
1913	£2	£3	£10	£30
1923 Spade shield	£2	£3	£12	£45
1923 Square shield	£2	£3	£10	£30
1926	£2	£3	£12	£45
1931	£2	£3	£8	£15
1933	£2	£3	£8	£15
1935	£2	£3	£8	£15
1937	£2	£3	£8	£15
1946	£2	£3	£8	£15
1947	—	£3	£8	£15
"1945" GVI	—	—	£2	£10
"1945" QE2	—	—	£2	£8
1957	—	—	£2	£7
1960 1660–1960 300th anniversary	—	—	£3	£10
1960 Mule	—	—	—	£200
1964	—	£2	£3	£10
1966 "1066–1966"	—	—	£1	£8

ONE THIRTEENTH OF A SHILLING

	F	VF	EF	UNC
1841	£4	£8	£40	£200
1844	£4	£9	£40	£200
1851	£5	£12	£60	£250
1858	£4	£9	£45	£200
1861	£5	£13	£60	£175
1865 Proof only	—	—	—	£750
1866 with LCW	£2	£5	£95	£150
1866 without LCW Proof only	—	—	—	£450
1870	£4	£8	£40	£125
1871	£4	£8	£42	£125

ONE TWENTY-FOURTH OF A SHILLING

	F	VF	EF	UNC
1877H	£3	£4	£15	£60
1877 Proof only	—	—	—	£300
1888	£3	£4	£15	£45
1894	£3	£4	£15	£45
1909	£3	£4	£15	£45
1911	£2	£3	£10	£45

DATE	F	VF	EF	UNC
1913	£2	£3	£10	£45
1923 Spade shield	£2	£3	£10	£35
1923 Square shield	£2	£3	£8	£35
1926	£2	£3	£10	£25
1931	£2	£3	£10	£25
1933	£2	£3	£10	£25
1935	£2	£3	£10	£25
1937	£1	£2	£6	£20
1946	£1	£2	£6	£20
1947	£1	£2	£6	£20

ONE TWENTY-SIXTH OF A SHILLING

	F	VF	EF	UNC
1841	£4	£7	£30	£100
1844	£4	£7	£25	£100
1851	£3	£6	£25	£100
1858	£4	£11	£50	£200
1861	£3	£6	£25	£65
1866	£3	£6	£30	£85
1870	£3	£6	£20	£55
1871	£3	£6	£20	£55

ONE FORTY-EIGHTH OF A SHILLING

	F	VF	EF	UNC
1877H	£6	£12	£60	£150
1877 Proof only	–	–	–	£450

ONE FIFTY-SECOND OF A SHILLING

	F	VF	EF	UNC
1841	£9	£25	£60	£200
1861 Proof only	–	–	–	£650

DECIMAL COINAGE

Ordinary circulating coinage from 1986 onwards is usually available in uncirculated condition at a small premium above face value thus it is not listed here.

ONE HUNDRED POUNDS

1990 50th Anniversary of the Battle of Britain. Gold Proof.	£2000
1995 50th Anniversary of Liberation. Gold proof	£2000
2020 75th Anniversary VE Day. 1kg of silver gold-plated proof	£2500

FIFTY POUNDS

1972 Silver Wedding. Gold proof	£1000
1990 50th Anniversary of the Battle of Britain. Gold proof	£1000
1995 50th Anniversary of Liberation. Gold proof	£1000
2003 Golden Jubilee. Silver Proof (100mm)	£650
2013 RMS Titanic Centenary. 10oz Silver proof	£600

TWENTY-FIVE POUNDS

1972 25th Royal Wedding anniversary. Gold	£450
1972 – Gold proof	£500
1990 50th Anniversary of Battle of Britain. Gold proof	£450
1995 50th Anniversary of Liberation. Gold proof	£450
2002 Princess Diana memorial. Gold proof	£450
2002 Queen Mother. Gold proof	£450
2002 Golden Jubilee. Gold proof	£450
2002 Duke of Wellington. Gold proof	£450
2003 Golden Jubilee. Gold proof	£450
2003 History of the Royal Navy. Naval Commanders	£450
2003 – Francis Drake	£450
2003 – Sovereign of the Seas	£450
2004 60th Anniversary of D-Day. Gold proof	£450
2004 Charge of the Light Brigade. Gold proof	£450
2004 HMS Victory. Gold proof	£450
2004 John Fisher 1841–1920 Gold proof	£450
2004 The Coronation Scot. Gold proof	£450
2004 The Flying Scotsman. Gold proof	£450

Since the introduction of decimal coinage a number of companies have been involved in marketing the coins of the Channel Islands. As a consequence many special limited edition commemorative coins have been issued in a wide variety of sizes, metals and finishes. These are very numerous with some issues being produced in very small numbers and many are omitted from our listings. These issues are generally outside of the scope of this catalogue.

DATE	UNC
2004 Golden Arrow. Gold proof	£350
2004 Rocket and Evening Star. Gold proof	£350
2005 Andrew Cunningham. Gold proof	£350
2005 HMS Conqueror. Gold Proof	£350
2005 200th Anniversary of Nelson. Gold proof	£350
2009 500th Anniversary of Accession. Gold proof	£350

TWENTY POUNDS

1972 Royal Wedding. The Ormer. Gold	£350
1972 — Gold proof	£450

TEN POUNDS (65mm unless stated o/wise)

1972 25th Royal Wedding anniversary. Small gold	£275
1972 — Gold proof	£350
1990 50th Anniversary of the Battle of Britain. Gold proof	£350
1995 50th Anniversary of Liberation. Gold proof	£350
2003 Coronation Anniversary. Gold/silver proof	£375
2004 150th anniversary of the Crimean War. Gold proof	£6000
2005 Trafalgar. Gold proof	£5000
2005 End of World War II. Silver proof	£25
2007 Diamond Wedding. Platinum proof	£280
2008 History of RAF. Silver proof	£25
2011 Royal Wedding of HRH Prince William & Catherine Middleton, silver (65mm)	£395
2012 Poppy. 5oz Silver Proof	£375
2013 Flying Scotsman. 5oz Silver proof	£375
2014 First World War Centenary 5oz Silver proof	£450
2017 Masterpiece Poppy. 5oz Silver proof	£400
2017 Battle of Britain Memorial Flight. 5oz Silver proof	£400
2018 Prince George's 5th Birthday 5oz Silver proof	£400
2018 Coronation Anniversary. 5oz Silver proof	£400
2018 Prince George's 5th birthday 5oz Silver proof	£425
2019 Remembrance Poppy. Gold proof 5oz (20 struck)	£12,000
2019 Remembrance Poppy. 5oz Silver Proof	£550
2019 50th Anniversary of Concord 5oz Silver Proof	£495
2020 Battle of Britain 80th Anniversary 5oz Silver Proof	£495

(Enlarged)

FIVE POUNDS (38mm unless stated o/wise)

1972 Gold proof (2.62g)	£125
1990 50th Anniversary of the Battle of Britain. Silver Proof (5 ounces)	£250
1997 Royal Golden Wedding	£10
1997 — Silver proof	£25
2000 Millennium. Silver proof	£35
2002 Princess Diana memorial	£12
2002 — Silver proof	£30
2002 — Gold proof (38mm)(38mm)	£1250
2002 Royal Golden Jubilee	£25
2003 Golden Jubilee	£20
2003 — Silver proof	£55
2003 — Gold proof	£1250
2003 Prince William 21st Birthday	£15
2003 — Silver Proof	£55
2003 —Gold proof	£1250
2003 Naval Commanders	£15
2003 — Silver proof	£55
2003 — Gold proof	£1250
2003 Francis Drake	£15
2003 — Silver proof	£55
2003 — Gold proof	£1250
2003 Sovereign of the Seas	£15
2003 — Silver proof	£55
2003 — Gold proof	£1250
2004 60th Anniversary of 'D' Day	£15
2004 — Silver proof	£55
2004 — Gold proof	£1250

(Enlarge

DATE   UNC

2004 Charge of the Light Brigade	£15
2004 — Silver proof	£50
2004 — Gold proof	£1250
2004 HMS Victory	£15
2004 — Silver proof	£55
2004 — Gold proof	£1250
2004 John Fisher 1841–1920	£15
2004 — Silver proof	£55
2004 — Gold proof	£1250
2004 The Coronation Scot	£15
2004 — Silver proof	£55
2004 — Gold proof	£1250
2004 The Flying Scotsman	£15
2004 — Silver proof	£55
2004 — Silver/Gold proof	£500
2004 — Gold proof	£1250
2004 Golden Arrow	£15
2004 — Silver proof	£55
2004 — Gold proof	£1250

2005 Driver and Fireman	£15
2005 — Silver proof	£45
2005 — Gold proof	£1250
2005 Box Tunnel and King Loco	£15
2005 — Silver Proof	£45
2005 — Gold Proof	£1250
2005 Rocket and Evening Star	£15
2005 — Silver proof	£45
2005 — Silver/Gold proof	£500
2005 — Gold proof	£1250
2005 200th Anniversary of the Battle of Trafalgar	£30
2005 Andrew Cunningham	£20
2005 — Silver proof	£65
2005 — Gold proof	£1250
2005 HMS Conqueror	£15
2005 — Silver proof	£20
2005 — Gold proof	£1250
2005 Battle of Trafalgar	£15
2005 — Silver proof	£45
2005 — Gold proof (9mm)	£500
2005 — Gold proof (38.6mm)	£1750
2005 Returning Evacuees	£15
2005 — Silver proof	£45
2005 — Gold proof	£1250
2005 Searchlights and Big Ben	£15
2005 — Silver proof	£45
2005 — Gold proof	£1250

2006 60th Anniversary of the Liberation of the Channel Islands	£30
2006 80th Birthday of Her Majesty the Queen (3-coin set)	—
2006 Sir Winston Churchill	£15
2006 — Silver proof	£45
2006 — Gold proof	£1250
2006 Charles Darwin	£15
2006 — Silver proof	£45
2006 — Gold proof	£1250
2006 Bobby Moore	£20
2006 — Silver Proof	£55
2006 — Gold Proof	£1250
2006 Florence Nightingale	£20
2006 — Silver proof	£55
2006 — Gold proof	£1250
2006 Queen Mother	£20
2006 — Silver proof	£55
2006 — Gold proof	£1250
2006 Henry VIII	£15
2006 — Silver proof	£55
2006 — Gold proof	£1250

DATE	UNC
2006 Princess Diana	£20
2006 — Silver Proof	£60
2006 — Gold Proof	£1250
2006 Sir Christopher Wren	£15
2006 — Silver proof	£55
2006 — Gold proof	£1250
2006 HM the Queen's 80th Birthday—Streamers	£15
2006 — Silver proof	£60
2006 — Gold proof	£1250
2006 HM the Queen's 80th Birthday—Trooping colour	£25
2006 — Proof	£60
2006 — Silver proof	£1250
2006 — Silver/Gold proof	£750
2006 — Gold proof	£1250
2006 HM the Queen's 80th Birthday—Wembley Stadium	£20
2006 — Silver proof	£55
2006 — Gold proof	£1250
2006 Guy Gibson	£15
2006 — Silver proof	£55
2006 — Gold proof	£1250
2006 Eric James Nicholson	£15
2006 — Silver proof	£55
2006 — Gold proof	£1250
2006 Hook, Chard and Bromhead	£15
2006 — Silver proof	£55
2006 — Gold proof	£1250
2006 1st Lancs Fusiliers	£15
2006 — Silver proof	£55
2006 — Gold proof	£1250
2006 Noel Chavasse	£15
2006 — Silver proof	£55
2006 — Gold proof	£1250
2006 David Mackay	£15
2006 — Silver proof	£55
2006 — Gold proof	£1250
2006 Coronation Scot. Silver proof	£60
2006 Flying Scotsman. Silver proof	£60
2006 Fireman and Driver. Silver proof	£60
2006 Box Tunnel. Silver proof	£60
2007 Diamond Wedding balcony scene waving	£15
2007 — Silver proof	£60
2007 Diamond Wedding cake	£15
2007 — Silver proof	£60
2007 Diamond Wedding balcony scene waving	£15
2007 —Silver proof	£60
2007 Diamond Wedding HM the Queen and Prince Philip	£20
2007 — Silver proof	£60
2007 Diamond Wedding arrival at Abbey	£20
2007 — Silver proof	£55
2007 — Gold proof	£1250
2008 George & Dragon	£20
2008 Dambusters, Wallis, Chadwick, Gibson	£15
2008 — Silver/Copper proof	£30
2008 — Silver proof	£55
2008 Frank Whittle	£15
2008 — Silver proof	£55
2008 — Gold proof	£1250
2008 R. J. Mitchell	£15
2008 — Silver proof	£55
2008 — Gold proof	£1250
2008 Maj. Gen. Sir Hugh Trenchard	£15
2008 — Silver proof	£55
2008 — Gold proof	£1250
2008 Bomber Command	£15
2008 — Silver proof	£55
2008 — Gold proof	£1250

DATE	UNC
2008 Coastal Command	£20
2008 — Silver proof	£60
2008 — Gold proof	£1250
2008 Fighter Command	£20
2008 — Silver proof	£60
2008 — Gold proof	£1250
2008 Battle of Britain	£20
2008 — Silver proof	£75
2008 — Gold proof	£1250
2008 RBL Poppy	£20
2008 — Silver proof	£60
2008 — Gold proof	£1250
2008 Flying Legends	£15
2008 — Silver proof	£55
2008 — Gold proof	£1250
2009 George & Dragon. Silver proof	£50
2009 Great Battles Series (8 coins). Silver proof. each.	£25
2009 Capt. Cook and *Endeavour.* Silver proof	£55
2009 500th Anniversary of Accession of Henry VIII. Silver proof	£55
2010 Battle of Britain heroes (3 coins available). Silver proof. each.	£50
2011 Landmark birthdays of HM the Queen & Prince Philip	£15
2011 90th Anniversary of the British Legion (poppy-shaped)	£40
2011 — Silver proof	£95
2011 — 5oz silver	£500
2011 — Gold proof	£2500
2011 30th Birthday of the Duke of Cambridge. Silver proof	£50
2011 Wedding of Prince William and Kate Middleton. Silver proof	£50
2011 — Gold proof	£2000
2011 Spirit of the Nation (4 coins). Silver proof, each	£50
2012 HM the Queen's Diamond Jubilee. Gold proof	£2000
2012 Poppy. Silver Proof	£65
2012 — Gold Proof	£2000
2012 RMS *Titanic* Centenary. Cu-Ni Gold plated	£15
2012 — Silver Proof	£65
2013 Coronation Jubilee. Silver proof	£65
2013 — Gold Proof	£2000
2013 The Flying Scotsman. Silver proof	£65
2013 350th Guinea Anniversary. Silver proof	£55
2013 — Gold Proof	£2000
2013 Poppy Coin. Silver proof	£95
2014 70th Anniversary of D-Day. Silver proof	£85
2014 — Gold Proof	£2500
2014 Remembrance Day (two designs), Cu-Ni	£10
2014 — Silver	£50
2014 — Gold proof	£2000
2014 The Red Arrows 50th Display Season. Silver proof	£95
2014 William Shakespeare—450th Birthday. Silver proof	£80
2015 Remembrance day "Lest we forget", Cu-Ni	£10
2015 50th Anniversary of Winston Churchill's death, Cu-Ni	£10
2015 The Longest Reign, Cu-Ni	£10
2015 200th Anniversary of the Battle of Waterloo, Cu-Ni	£10
2015 Red Arrows, Cu-Ni	£10
2016 90th Birthday of Queen Elizabeth II	£10
2016 Remembrance Day, Cu-Ni	£10
2017 Royal 70th Wedding Anniversary. Cu-Ni	£10
2017 Prince Philip 70 Years of Service. Cu-Ni	£12
2017 — Silver proof	£75
2017 Remembrance Day. Cu-Ni	£12
2017 — Cu-Ni Gold plated	£25
2017 — Silver proof	£85
2018 Prince George's 5th Birthday. Silver proof	£75
2018 Coronation 65th Anniversary. Cu-Ni	£10
2018 — Silver proof	£75
2018 Remembrance Day. Cu-Ni	£12
2018 — Cu-Ni Gold plated	£20
2018 — Silver proof	£75
2018 — Gold proof	£2000

DATE	UNC
2018 Dove of Peace. Cu-Ni	£12
2018 RAF 100. Cu-Ni	£15
2018 — Silver proof	£85
2019 Remembrance Poppy Gold Proof	£3250
2019 — Silver Proof	£90
2019 —Cu-Ni	£5
2019 Concorde's first supersonic flight comm. Silver Proof	£85
2019 50th Anniversary of Moon Landing. Silver with Black Proof finish	£125
2020 Captain Cook's Voyage of Discovery. Silver Proof	£90
2020 Battle of Britain 80th Anniversary. Silver Proof. 3-coin set	£270
2021 Queen Elizabeth II 95th Birthday BU	—
2021 — Silver Proof	—
2021 50 years of Decimalisation	—
2021 — Silver Proof with selected gold plating	—

TWO POUNDS FIFTY PENCE

1972 Royal Silver Wedding	£25
1972 — Silver proof	£35

TWO POUNDS

(note all modern Proof coins have frosted relief)

1972 Royal Silver Wedding. Silver	£25
1972 — Silver proof	£35
1981 Royal Wedding, nickel silver (crown size)	£5
1981 — in presentation pack	£8
1981 — Silver proof	£20
1981 — Gold proof	£550
1985 40th Anniversary of Liberation (crown size)	£5
1985 — in presentation pack	£12
1985 — Silver proof	£20
1985 — Gold proof	£1250
1986 Commonwealth Games	£6
1986 — in presentation case	£8
1986 — .500 silver	£12
1986 — .925 silver proof	£20
1987 World Wildlife Fund 25th Anniversary	£80
1987 — Silver proof	£25
1989 Royal Visit	£15
1989 — Silver proof	£25
1990 Queen Mother's 90th Birthday	£15
1990 — Silver proof	£25
1990 — Gold proof	£750
1990 50th Anniversary of the Battle of Britain, silver proof	£30
1993 40th Anniversary of the Coronation	£15
1993 — Silver proof	£20
1993— Gold proof	£750
1995 50th Anniversary of Liberation	£15
1995 — Silver Proof	£25
1995 — — Piedfort	£75
1996 HM the Queen's 70th Birthday	£15
1996 — Silver proof	£25
1997 Bi-metal	£5
1997 — Silver proof	£50
1997 — new portrait	£5
1998 —	£5
2003 —	£5
2005 —	£5
2006 —	£5
2007 —	£5
2011 Prince Philip's 90th Birthday	£12
2012 HM the Queen's Diamond Jubilee. Gold proof	£1500
2019 Red Arrows	£10
2020 Battle of Britain 80th Anniversary 3-coin set.	£45

DATE	UNC
2020 150th Anniversary of Sandringham House..	£12
2020 150th Anniversary of death of Charles Dickens 5-coin set	£50
2020 — Silver Proof with coloured highlights	£250
2021 150th Anniversary of the RFU 5 coin set.......................................	—
2021 —Silver Proof 5-coin set	—
2021 Her Majesty the Queen's 95th Birthday 12-coin set	—

ONE POUND

1972 Royal Silver Wedding	£15
1972 — Silver proof...	£20
1981...	£15
1981 Silver proof	£15
1981 Gold proof	£550
1983 New designs and specifications on presentation card (St Helier).....	£5
1983 — Silver proof...	£20
1983 — Gold proof..	£650
1984 Presentation wallet (St Saviour)..	£20
1984 — Silver proof...	£45
1984 — Gold proof..	£650
1984 Presentation wallet (St Brelade)	£20
1984 — Silver proof...	£45
1984 — Gold proof..	£650
1985 Presentation wallet (St Clement)	£25
1985 — Silver proof...	£45
1985 — Gold proof..	£600
1985 Presentation wallet (St Lawrence)....................................	£25
1985 — Silver proof...	£40
1985 — Gold proof..	£650
1986 Presentation wallet (St Peter)	£15
1986 — Silver proof...	£35
1986 — Gold proof..	£650
1986 Presentation wallet (Grouville)	£20
1986 — Silver proof...	£40
1986 — Gold proof..	£650
1987 Presentation wallet (St Martin)...	£20
1987 — Silver proof...	£40
1987 — Gold proof..	£650
1987 Presentation wallet (St Ouen)..	£18
1987 — Silver proof...	£40
1987 — Gold proof..	£650
1988 Presentation wallet (Trinity)..	£20
1988 — Silver proof...	£40
1988 — Gold proof..	£650
1988 Presentation wallet (St John)...	£15
1988 — Silver proof...	£40
1988 — Gold proof..	£650
1989 Presentation wallet (St Mary)...	£15
1989 — Silver proof...	£40
1989 — Gold proof..	£650
1991 Ship Building in Jersey Series	
1991 "Tickler". Nickel-brass	£5
1991 — Silver proof...	£25
1991 — Gold proof Piedfort	£750
1991 "Percy Douglas". Nickel-brass..	£5
1991 — Silver proof	£25
1991 — Gold proof Piedfort	£750
1992 "The Hebe". Nickel-brass...	£5
1992 — Silver proof...	£25
1992 — Gold proof Piedfort	£750
1992 "Coat of Arms". Nickel-brass	£5
1992 — Silver proof	£25
1992 — Gold proof Piedfort	£750

DATE	UNC
1993 "The Gemini". Nickel-brass	£5
1993 — Silver proof	£25
1993 — Gold proof Piedfort	£750
1993 "The Century". Nickel-brass	£5
1993 — Silver proof	£25
1993 — Gold proof Piedfort	£750
1994 "Resolute". Nickel-brass	£5
1994— Silver proof	£25
1994 — Gold proof Piedfort	£750

Coat of Arms design

| |
---|---
1997 | £5
1998 | £5
2003 | £5
2005 | £5
2006 | £5
2007 Diana Commemoration. Gold proof | £650
2012 Diamond Jubilee. Gold proof | £650
2013 Coronation Jubilee. Gold proof | £750
2018 WWI Armistice. Gold Proof | £700

FIFTY PENCE (initially 7-sided, some issues round)

| |
---|---
1969 | £10
1972 Royal Silver Wedding | £12
1972 — Silver proof | £35
1980 | £2
1980 Proof | £8
1981 | £2
1981 Proof | £8
1983 Grosnez Castle | £12
1983 — Silver proof | £35
1984 | £2
1985 40th Anniversary of Liberation | £3
1986 | £3
1986 | £3
1987 | £3
1988 | £3
1989 | £3
1990 | £3
1992 | £3
1994 | £5
1997 | £4
1997 Smaller size | £3
1998 | £3
2003 | £5
2003 Coronation Anniversary (4 types) .... ea. | £15
2003 — 4 types. Silver proof .... ea. | £4
2005 | £4
2006 | £5
2009 | £15
2011 Diamond Jubilee (full colour reverse, gold-plated) | £25
2013 Coronation Jubilee | £15
2014 Lord Kitchener. Gold plated steel | £25
2015 Battle of Britain. Gold plated steel | £25
2016 Battle of Hastings, Halley's Comet. Silver | £25
2016 Bayeux Tapestry. Silver | £25
2016 Battle of the Somme. Gold plated steel | £25
2018 RAF Centenary. Gold plated brass | £22
2019 50th Anniversary of the 50p. Silver proof | £45
2019 — BU | £15
2020 75th Anniversary of VE Day. Gold plated steel proof | £40
2020 75th Anniversary of the Liberation of Channel Islands (2 BU coins) . ea.£12
2020 — date stamped (2 BU coins) .... ea.£40
2020 — Proof (2 coins) .... ea.£25

DATE	UNC
2021 Centenary of the Royal British Legion	£10
2021 —Silver with coloured poppy	£50

TWENTY-FIVE PENCE
1977 Royal Jubilee	£3
1977 — Silver proof	£20

TWENTY PENCE
1982 Corbiere Lighthouse (cased)	£8
1982 — Silver proof piedfort	£35
1983 — Obv. with date, rev. no date on rocks	£5
1983 — — Silver proof	£15
1984 to date	£1 ea.

SOVEREIGN—Gold sovereign size
1999 The Millennium. King William on Throne. Gold	£400
1999 — Gold proof	£475

TEN PENCE
1968 Arms	£1
1975 Arms	£1
1979 (dated 1975 on thick flan)	£5
1980 —	£1
1980 — Proof	£5
1981 -	£1
1981 — Proof	£5
1983 L'Hermitage	£1
1983 — Silver proof	£12
1984 to date	£1 ea.

Other denominations are generally available at face value or a small premium above. However, one penny denomination coins are struck in precious metals each year to commemorate special occasions.

Note: in addition to the coins listed here, there are many others produced for Jersey, often in tandem with the other Channel Islands. Regretfully information on many of these issues is difficult or impossible to obtain, thus they are omitted from this guide. Ordinary circulating coinage from 1986 onwards is usually available in uncirculated condition at a small premium above face value thus it is not listed here.

ALDERNEY

DATE	UNC

ONE THOUSAND POUNDS
2003 Concorde. Gold proof... —
2004 D-Day Anniversary. Gold proof................................... —
2005 Prince Harry's 21st Birthday. Gold proof....................... —
2011 Wedding of Prince William and Catherine Middleton. Gold proof..... —

ONE HUNDRED POUNDS
1994 50th Anniversary of D-Day Landings. Gold proof .... —
2003 Prince Wiliam. Gold proof (100mm) .... —
2005 Trafalgar Anniversary. Gold proof (100mm)..................... —

FIFTY POUNDS
1994 50th Anniversary of D–Day Landing. Gold proof............................ £500
2002 Royal Golden Jubilee. Silver proof (100mm) £850
2003 Anniversary of Coronation (4 types). Silver proof (100mm).......... ea. £750
2003 Prince William. Silver proof (100mm).. £750
2004 Anniversary of D-Day. Silver proof (100mm) £750
2005 200th Anniversary of the Battle of Trafalgar. Silver proof (100mm) ... £750

TWENTY FIVE POUNDS
1993 40th Anniversary of Coronation. Gold proof.................................... £350
1994 50th Anniversary of D-Day Landings. Gold proof £350
1997 Royal Golden Wedding. Gold proof £350
1997 — Silver proof... £40
1999 Winston Churcill. Gold proof £350
2000 Queen Mother. Gold proof.. £375
2000 60th Anniversary of the Battle of Britain. Gold proof £400
2001 Royal Birthday. Gold proof £350
2002 Golden Jubilee. Gold proof £350
2002 Princess Diana. Gold proof £350
2002 Duke of Wellington. Gold proof.. £350
2003 Prince William. Gold proof.. £300
2003 HMS Mary Rose. Gold proof.. £350
2004 D-Day Anniversary. Gold proof... £400
2004 The Rocket. Gold proof £350
2004 Merchant Navy Class Locomotive. Gold proof £350
2005 Battle of Saints Passage. Gold proof £350
2006 World Cup 2006 (4 Coins). Gold ea.. £400

TEN POUNDS
1994 50th Anniversary of D–Day Landing. Gold proof............................. £250
2003 Concorde. Silver proof (65mm) £300
2005 60th Anniversary of the Liberation of the Channel Islands (65mm)... £250
2007 80th Birthday of Her Majesty the Queen (65mm)............................ £180
2008 Concorde. Silver proof £180
2008 90th Anniversary of the end of WWI. Silver Proof £180
2009 50th Anniversary of the Mini—Silver with colour............................ £180
2012 Prince William's 30th Birthday .... —

FIVE POUNDS
1995 Queen Mother £15
1995 — Silver proof... £50
1995 — Silver piedfort... £155
1995 — Gold proof... £1250
1996 HM the Queen's 70th Birthday £20
1996 — Silver proof... £60
1996 — Silver piedfort... £150
1996 — Gold proof... £1250

DATE	UNC
1999 Eclipse of the Sun	£25
1999 — Silver proof with colour centre	£55
1999 Winston Churchill. Gold proof	£1750
2000 60th Anniversary of the Battle of Britain	£25
2000 — Silver proof	£55
2000 Queen Mother. 100th Birthday. Silver proof	£50
2000 Millennium. Silver proof	£35
2001 HM Queen's 75th Birthday.	£15
2001 — Silver proof	£45
2002 Golden Jubilee. Silver proof	£50
2002 50 Years of Reign.	£15
2002 —Silver proof	£50
2002 Diana memorial	£15
2002 — Silver proof	£45
2002 — Gold proof	£1250
2002 Duke of Wellington	£20
2002 — Silver proof	£50
2002 — Gold proof	£1250
2003 Prince William	£20
2003 — Silver proof	£50
2003 — Gold proof	£1250
2003 Mary Rose	£20
2003 — Silver proof	£120
2003 Alfred the Great. Silver proof	£150
2003 —Gold proof	£1250
2003 Last Flight of Concorde	£25
2003 — Silver proof	£150
2003 — Gold proof	£1250
2004 Anniversary of D-Day	£20
2004 — Silver proof	£75
2004 — Gold proof	£1250
2004 Florence Nightingale	320
2004 — Silver proof	£45
2004 150th Anniversary of the Crimean War	£20
2004 — Silver proof	£45
2004 — Gold proof	£1250
2004 The Rocket	£20
2004 — Silver proof	£45
2004 — Gold proof	£1250
2004 Royal Scot	£20
2004 — Silver proof	£45
2004 Merchant Navy Class Locomotive	£20
2004 — Silver proof	£45
2005 End of WWII. Silver proof	£45
2005 — Gold proof	£1250
2005 200th Anniversary of the Battle of Trafalgar	£16
2005 — Silver proof	£50
2005 History of the Royal Navy. John Woodward. Silver proof	£30
2005 Anniversary of Liberation. Gold proof	£1250
2005 Anniversary of the Battle of Saints Passage	£15
2005 — Silver proof	£45
2005 HMS Revenge 1591	£15
2005 — Silver proof	£45
2005 Prince Harry's 21st Birthday. Gold proof	£1250
2006 80th Birthday of Her Majesty the Queen (3-coin set) ea	£20
2006 Gold plated portraits of Her Majesty the Queen	—
2006 80th Birthday of Her Majesty the Queen (3-coin set) ea	£16
2007 History of the Royal Navy—*Mary Rose* (2 coins) ea	£16
2007 150th Anniversary of the Victoria Cross (18 coin set). Silver proof	£250
2007 Monarchs of England (12 coin set). Gold plated	£150
2008 90th Anniversary of the end of WWI (3 coins). Gold proof	£2750
2008 Classic British Motorcars (18 coin set). Silver proof.	£250
2008 Concorde. Gold proof	£1250

DATE	UNC
2009 50th Anniversary of the Mini (4 coins). Silver proof ea.	£50
2011 Royal Engagement gold proof	£1250
2011 — Gold plated silver proof	£150
2011 — Silver proof	£55
2011 — Cupro Nickel	£15
2011 John Lennon Silver proof	£55
2011 Battle of Britain 70th Anniversary silver proof	£55
2012 RMS *Titanic*	£15
2012 Remembrance Day (Re-issued 2013)	£25
2014 70th Anniversary of D-Day	£15
2014 — Silver proof	£25
2014 — Gold proof	£1250
2014 Destiny to Dynasty. Silver proof	£25
2014 300th Anniversary of the Coronation of King George I	£20
2014 — Silver proof	£25
2014 — Gold proof	£1500
2014 Centenary of the birth of poet Dylan Thomas	£15
2014 — Silver proof	£45
2014 — Gold proof	£1500
2014 Remembrance Day "Remember the Fallen"	—
2015 Churchill Quotations (4-coin set)	£40
2015 — Silver proof (4-coin set)	£250
2015 70th Anniversary of VE Day	£15
2015 — Silver proof	£45
2015 — Silver proof piedfort	£75
2015 150th Anniversary of the Salvation Army	£10
2015 — Silver proof	£45
2015 Remembrance Day	£10
2015 — Silver	£45
2015 — — piedfort	£85
2016 The FIFA World Cup	£15
2016 — Silver proof	£45
2016 — Gold proof	£1250
2016 Remembrance Day	£15
2016 — Silver Proof	£35
2016 — — piedfort	£85
2017 Remembrance Day	£17
2017 — Silver Proof	£90
2017 — Silver Piedfort	£170
2019 The Puffin	£12
2019 — Silver proof	£35
2019 Una and the Lion	£12
2019 — Silver proof	£35
2019 — Gold proof	£2000
2019 Anniversary of the Moon Landing	£25
2019 — Silver proof	£35
2019 — Gold proof	£2000
2019 Concorde	£25
2019 — Silver proof	£35
2019 —Gold proof	£2000
2020 Remembrance day	£15
2020 — Silver proof	£35
2020 — Gold proof	£2000
2020 Sir Winston Churchill"s speech	£15
2020 — Silver proof	£35

TWO POUNDS

1989 Royal Visit	£12
1989 — Silver proof	£25
1989 — Silver piedfort	£45
1989 — Gold proof	£1200
1990 Queen Mother's 90th Birthday	£12
1990 — Silver proof	£25

DATE UNC

1990 — Silver piedfort	£45
1990 — Gold proof	£1200
1992 40th Anniversary of Accession	£15
1992 — Silver proof	£35
1992 — Silver piedfort	£50
1992 — Gold proof	£1200
1993 40th Anniversary of Coronation	£15
1993 — Silver proof	£35
1993 — Silver piedfort	£50
1994 50th Anniversary of D-Day Landings	£15
1994 — Silver proof	£35
1994 — Silver piedfort	£50
1995 50th Anniversary of Return of Islanders	£15
1995 — Silver proof	£35
1995 — Silver piedfort	£50
1995 — Gold proof	£1250
1997 WWF Puffin	£18
1997 — Silver proof	£35
1997 Royal Golden Wedding	£20
1997 — Silver proof	£50
1999 Eclipse of the Sun. Silver	£20
1999 — Silver proof	£50
1999 — Gold proof	£1250
2000 Millennium. Silver proof	£50

ONE POUND

1993 40th Anniversary of Coronation Silver proof	£50
1995 50th Anniversary of VE Day Silver proof	£45
1995 — Gold proof	£500
2005 Nelson	£100
2008 Concorde. Gold proof	£375
2009 50th Anniversary of the Mini. Gold proof	£475
2020 Dunkirk	£10
2020 — Silver proof	£30
2020 — Gold proof	£650

In recent years a number of companies have been involved in marketing the coins of the Channel Islands. As a consequence many special limited edition commemorative coins have been issued in a wide variety of sizes, metals and finishes. These are very numerous with some issues being produced in very small numbers and many are omitted from our listings. These issues are generally outside of the scope of this catalogue.

We are indebted to Westminster Collections and Changechecker.com for supplying a number of images for this section.

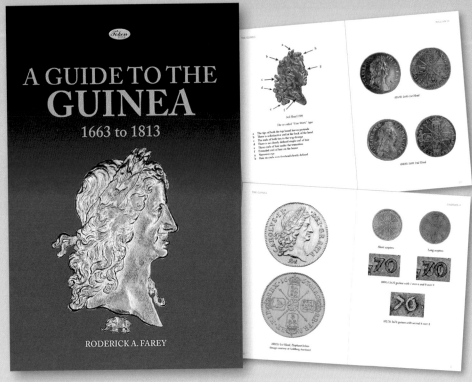

IRELAND

As in the English hammered section (q.v.) the prices given here are for the most common coins in the series. For a more specialised listing the reader is referred to Coincraft's *Standard Catalogue of Scotland, Ireland, Channel Islands & Isle of Man*, or other specialised publications. Collectors should be aware that with most of the coins of the Irish series there are many varieties struck at different mints. The coins listed are all silver unless mentioned otherwise. Another important factor to consider when collecting early Irish coins is that few examples exist in high grades.

	F	VF

HIBERNO-NORSE ISSUES (995–1155)
Penny, imitating English silver pennies,
many various types £300   £650

JOHN, Lord of Ireland (1185–99)
Halfpenny, profile .... Extremely rare
Halfpenny, facing £200   £550
Farthing £500   £1850

Hiberno-Norse phase II example.

JOHN de COURCY, Lord of Ulster (1177–1205)
Halfpenny .... Extremely rare
Farthing £750   £3750

JOHN as King of England and Lord of Ireland (c. 1199–1216)
Penny £75   £450
Halfpenny £175   £5000
Farthing £650   £2500

John Lord of Ireland penny.

HENRY III (1216–72)
Penny £150   £575

EDWARD I (1272–1307)
Penny £75   £220
Halfpenny £75   £175
Farthing £150   £450

No Irish coins were struck for Edward II (1307–27).

Henry III penny.

EDWARD III (1327–77)
Halfpenny .... Extremely rare

No Irish coins were struck for Richard II (1377–99), Henry IV (1399–1413) or Henry V (1413–22).

HENRY VI (1422–61)
Penny .... Extremely rare   *Edward I penny.*

	F	VF

EDWARD IV (1461–83)

	F	VF
"Anonymous crown" groat	£700	£13500
— penny	£1200	—
"Titled crown" groat	£1600	—
— halfgroat		Extremely rare
— penny		Extremely rare
Cross on rose/Sun groat	£1850	—
Bust/Rose on sun double groat	£2250	£7500
— groat	£2250	—
— halfgroat		Extremely rare
— penny		Extremely rare
Bust/Cross & pellets groat—First issue	£150	£585
— halfgroat	£650	£1700
— penny	£100	£375
— halfpenny		Extremely rare
— Second (light) issue	£150	£550
— halfgroat	£650	£1700
— penny	£100	
£250— halfpenny		Extremely rare
Bust/Rose on cross groat	£570	£1500
— penny	£80	£250
Billon/Copper issues		
Small crown/Cross farthing (1460–61)	£1700	—
— half farthing ("Patrick")	£1100	—
Large crown/Cross farthing (1462)		Extremely rare
Patricius/Salvator farthing (1463–65)	£350	£2000
— half farthing		Extremely rare
Shield/Rose on sun farthing	£250	£1000

Edward IV groat. "Anonymous crown" issue.

Edward IV penny struck in Dublin.

RICHARD III (1483–85)

	F	VF
Bust/Rose on cross groat	£1100	£4000
— halfgroat		Unique
— penny		Unique
Bust/Cross and pellets penny	£100	£3500
Shield/Three-crowns groat	£650	£3000

HENRY VII (1485–1509)

	F	VF
Early issues (1483–90)		
Shield/Three crowns groat	£170	£550
— halfgroat	£250	£565
— penny	£650	£2600
— halfpenny		Extremely rare
Later issues (1488–90)		
Shield/Three crowns groat	£150	£475
— halfgroat	£200	£600
— penny	£500	£1400
Facing bust groat (1496–1505)	£200	£500
— halfgroat	£1100	—
— penny	£1000	—

Richard III bust/rose on cross groat.

LAMBERT SIMNEL (as EDWARD VI, Pretender, 1487)

	F	VF
Shield/Three crowns groat	£1300	£4750

Henry VII groat.

	F	VF

HENRY VIII (1509–47)

"Harp" groat	£150	£4000
— halfgroat	£500	£2600

The "Harp" coins have crowned initials either side of the reverse harp, e.g. HR (Henricus Rex), HA (Henry and Anne Boleyn), HI (Henry and Jane Seymour), HK (Henry and Katherine Howard).

Posthumous (Portrait) issues

Sixpence	£185	£575
Threepence	£160	£575
Threehalfpence	£500	£1800
Threefarthings	£650	£2200

Henry VIII Posthumous portrait issues threepence.

EDWARD VI (1547–53)

Shilling (base silver) 1552 (MDLII)	£1100	£3750
Brass contemporary copy	£110	£400

MARY (1553–54)

Shilling 1553 (MDLIII)	£1000	£3500
Shilling 1554 (MDLIIII)		Extremely rare
Groat		Extremely rare
Halfgroat		Extremely rare
Penny		Extremely rare

PHILIP & MARY (1554–58)

Shilling	£350	£1500
Groat	£150	£475
Penny		Extremely rare

ELIZABETH I (1558–1603)

Base silver portrait coinage

Shilling	£500	£1750
Groat	£250	£800

Philip & Mary shilling

Fine silver, portrait coinage (1561)

Shilling	£300	£1200
Groat	£350	£1200

Third (base silver) shield coinage

Shilling	£250	£800
Sixpence	£200	£575

Copper

Threepence	£275	£750
Penny	£75	£250
Halfpenny	£150	£350

JAMES I (1603–25)

Shilling	£125	£500
Sixpence	£125	£475

Coins struck under Royal Licence from 1613

"Harrington" farthing (small size)	£75	£285
"Harrington" farthing (large size)	£75	£250
"Lennox" farthing	£75	£265

Elizabeth I "fine" shilling of 1561.

CHARLES I (1625–49)

During the reign of Charles I and the Great Rebellion many coins were struck under unusual circumstances, making the series a difficult but fascinating area for study. Many of the "coins" were simply made from odd-shaped pieces of plate struck with the weight or value.

	F	VF
Coins struck under Royal Licence from 1625		
"Richmond" farthing	£60	£250
"Maltravers" farthing	£50	£250
"Rose" farthing	£50	£265

Siege money of the Irish Rebellion, 1642–49

"Inchiquin" Money (1642)

	F	VF
Crown	£2500	£6500
Halfcrown	£2000	£5500
Shilling		Extremely rare
Ninepence		Extremely rare
Sixpence		Extremely rare
Groat		Extremely rare

"Dublin" Money (1643)

	F	VF
Crown	£1000	£3750
Halfcrown	£600	£2600

"Ormonde" Money (1643–44)

	F	VF
Crown	£575	£1600
Halfcrown	£375	£1275
Shilling	£150	£475
Sixpence	£150	£475
Groat	£120	£425
Threepence	£120	£350
Twopence	£500	£1600

Charles I "Ormonde" crown.

"Ormonde" gold coinage (1646)

Double pistole. 2 known (both in museums)		Extremely rare
Pistole. 10 known (only 1 in private ownership		Extremely rare

"Ormonde" Money (1649)

	F	VF
Crown		Extremely rare
Halfcrown	£1300	£4000

Dublin Money 1649

	F	VF
Crown	£3000	£8000
Halfcrown	£2200	£5500

Issues of the Confederated Catholics

Kilkenny issues (1642–43)

	F	VF
Halfpenny	£350	£1000
Farthing	£450	£1200

Rebel Money (1643–44)

	F	VF
Crown	£2600	£5750
Halfcrown	£2000	£5750

"Blacksmith's" Money (16??)

A rare Charles I "Rebel" halfcrown.

	F	VF
Imitation of English Tower halfcrown.....	£750	£3200

Local Town issues of "Cities of Refuge"

Bandon
Farthing (copper) .... Extremely rare

Cork
Shilling .... Extremely rare
Sixpence... £775 £1500
Halfpenny (copper) .... Extremely rare
Farthing (copper) .... £635 —

Kinsale
Farthing (copper) .... £425 —

Youghal
Farthing (copper) £500 £2250

CHARLES II (1660–85)

Halfpenny of Charles I.

	Fair	F	VF	EF
"Armstrong" coinage				
Farthing (1660–61)...............................	£75	£250	—	—
"St Patrick's" coinage				
Halfpenny	£235	£475	—	—
Farthing	£85	£200	£500	£1750
Legg's Regal coinage				
Halfpennies				
1680 large lettering...............................	£35	£100	£325	—
1681 large lettering...............................	—	£200	£695	—
1681 small lettering			Extremely rare	
1682 small lettering	—	£200	£675	—
1683 small lettering	£35	£45	£465	
1684 small lettering	£50	£125	£675	—

JAMES II (1685–88)

REGAL COINAGE

Halfpennies

1685...	£35	£85	£320	£750
1686...	£35	£65	£200	£625
1687...			Extremely rare	
1688...	£45	£125	£300	£1400

"St Patrick" farthing of Charles II.

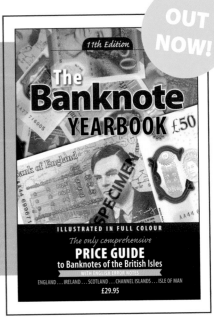

	Fair	F	VF	EF

EMERGENCY COINAGE

GUN MONEY
Most of these coins were struck in gun metal but a few rare specimens are also known struck in gold and in silver

Crowns
1690 (many varieties)......................from   £45   £65   £650   —

Large halfcrowns
Dated July 1689–May 1690
....from   £35   £65   £225   —

Small halfcrowns
Dated April–October1690
....from   £35   £65   £250   —

Large shillings
Dated from July 1689–April 1690
....from   £35   £75   £125   £525

Small shillings
Dated from April–September 1690
....from   £30   £35   £125   £450

"Gun Money" crown.

Sixpences
Dated from June 1689–October 1690
....from   £35   £60   £300   —

PEWTER MONEY (1689–90)

	Fair	F	VF	EF
Crown..	£700	£1200	£3200	—
Groat...		Extremely rare		
Penny large bust...................................	£230	£675	—	—
— small bust	£165	£485	£1500	—
Halfpenny large bust	£130	£345	£800	—
— small bust	£110	£245	£700	—

LIMERICK MONEY (1690–91)

	Fair	F	VF	EF
Halfpenny, reversed N in HIBERNIA......	£35	£75	£275	—
Farthing, reversed N in HIBERNIA........	£35	£75	£275	—
— normal N	£45	£135	£335	—

WILLIAM & MARY (1689–94)

Halfpennies

	Fair	F	VF	EF
1692..	£15	£50	£100	£695
1693..	£15	£50	£85	£675
1694..	£25	£75	£135	£750

William & Mary half-penny of 1693.

WILLIAM III (1694–1702)

	Fair	F	VF	EF
1696 Halfpenny draped bust................	£35	£85	£275	—
1696 — crude undraped bust	£45	£275	£900	—

DATE	F	VF	EF	UNC

No Irish coins were struck during the reign of Queen Anne (1706–11).

GEORGE I (1714–27)

Farthings

	F	VF	EF	UNC
1722 D.G. REX Harp to left (Pattern)	£650	£1600	£2400	—
1723 D.G. REX Harp to right	£120	£225	£525	—
1723 DEI GRATIA REX Harp to right	£35	£65	£265	£650
1723 — Silver Proof	—	—	—	£2500
1724 DEI GRATIA REX Harp to right	£60	£150	£365	£875

Halfpennies

	F	VF	EF	UNC
1722 Holding Harp left	£55	£130	£395	£1100
1722 Holding Harp right	£45	£120	£350	£800
1723/2 Harp right	£50	£150	£350	£800
1723 Harp right	£30	£65	£200	£565
1723 Silver Proof	—	—	—	£3575
1723 Obv. Rs altered from Bs	£35	£100	£295	—
1723 No stop after date	£25	£80	£295	£565
1724 Rev. legend divided	£40	£100	£300	—
1724 Rev. legend continuous	£40	£110	£395	—

GEORGE II (1727–60)

Farthings

	F	VF	EF	UNC
1737	£35	£60	£185	£500
1737 Proof	—	—	—	£525
1737 Silver Proof	—	—	—	£1300
1738	£35	£65	£165	£485
1744	£35	£65	£165	£485
1760	£30	£50	£100	£385

Halfpenny of George II

Halfpennies

	F	VF	EF	UNC
1736	£25	£60	£225	£675
1736 Proof	—	—	—	£685
1736 Silver Proof	—	—	—	£1400
1737	£25	£50	£225	—
1738	£30	£60	£225	—
1741	£30	£60	£225	—
1742	£30	£60	£225	—
1743	£30	£60	£200	—
1744/3	£30	£60	£200	—
1744	£30	£60	£375	—
1746	£30	£60	£250	—
1747	£30	£60	£225	—
1748	£30	£60	£225	—
1749	£30	£60	£225	—
1750	£35	£60	£225	—
1751	£30	£60	£225	—
1752	£30	£60	£225	—
1753	£30	£60	£250	—
1755	£30	£110	£350	—
*1760	£30	£75	£250	—

GEORGE III (1760–1820)

All copper unless otherwise stated

Pennies

	F	VF	EF	UNC
1805	£20	£40	£185	£500
1805 Proof	—	—	—	£625
1805 in Bronze Proof	—	—	—	£600
1805 in Copper Gilt Proof	—	—	—	£600
1805 in Silver Proof (restrike)	—	—	—	£3500

George III proof penny 1805

DATE	F	VF	EF	UNC

Halfpennies

1766	£30	£55	£165	—
1769	£30	£55	£165	—
1769 Longer bust	£40	£75	£250	£675
1774 Pattern only Proof	—	—	—	£2000
1775	£30	£55	£200	£475
1775 Proof	—	—	—	£675
1776	£55	£140	£400	—
1781	£45	£60	£175	£465
1782	£45	£60	£175	£465
1805	£18	£45	£120	£465
1805 Copper Proof	—	—	—	£465
1805 in Bronze	—	—	—	£320
1805 in Gilt Copper	—	—	—	£475
1805 in Silver (restrike)	—	—	—	£1850

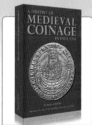

Farthings

1806	£20	£35	£100	£200
1806 Copper Proof	—	—	—	£375
1806 Bronzed Copper Proof	—	—	—	£265
1806 Copper Gilt Proof	—	—	—	£350
1806 Silver Proof (restrike)	—	—	—	£1250

One of the scarcer dates, a 1776 George III halfpenny.

GEORGE IV (1820–30)

Pennies

1822	£20	£40	£195	£450
1822 Proof	—	—	—	£595
1823	£12	£25	£150	£410

DATE	F	VF	EF	UNC
1823 Proof....................................	—	—	—	£625
Halfpennies				
1822..	£20	£40	£125	£400
1822 Proof.....................................	—	—	—	£650
1823..	£20	£40	£125	£400
1823 Proof.....................................	—	—	—	£695

NB Prooflike Uncirculated Pennies and Halfpennies of 1822/23 are often mis-described as Proofs. The true Proofs are rare. Some are on heavier, thicker flans.

Farthings				
1822 (Pattern) Proof	—	—	—	£1875

TOKEN ISSUES BY THE BANK OF IRELAND

Five Pence in Silver				
1805..	£30	£45	£75	£375
1806..	£30	£65	£150	£410
1806/5	£60	£145	£450	£1475

Ten Pence in Silver				
1805..	£20	£35	£95	£275
1806..	£20	£65	£150	£295
1813..	£20	£35	£95	£335
1813 Proof.....................................	—	—	—	£475

Thirty Pence in Silver				
1808..	£45	£100	£250	£675

1804 six shillings.

Six Shillings				
1804 in Silver................................	£100	£250	£465	£1875
1804 Proof.....................................	—	—	—	£1800
1804 in Copper (restrike)................	—	—	—	£800
1804 Copper Gilt	—	—	—	£1850
1804 in Gilt Silver	—	—	—	£3100

In this series fully struck specimens, with sharp hair curls, etc., are worth appreciably more than the prices quoted.

IRISH FREE STATE/EIRE

DATE	F	VF	EF	UNC
TEN SHILLINGS				
1966 Easter Rising	—	£12	£18	£25
1966 Cased Proof	—	—	—	£45
1966 Special double case	—	—	—	£95
HALF CROWNS				
Silver				
1928	£7	£12	£45	£100
1928 Proof	—	—	—	£125
1930	£12	£35	£175	£575
1931	£12	£35	£175	£545
1933	£12	£25	£175	£575
1934	£20	£12	£55	£275
1937	£60	£200	£650	£1900
Modified obverse: Eire				
1938				Unique
1939	£7	£17	£30	£85
1939 Proof	—	—	—	£650
1940	£8	£18	£35	£95
1941	£7	£17	£35	£95
1942	£7	£20	£35	£90
1943	£85	£300	£995	£3450
Cupro-nickel				
1951	£2	£3	£20	£75
1951 Proof	—	—	—	£525
1954	£2	£3	£15	£95
1954 Proof	—	—	—	£525
1955	£2	£3	£15	£45
1955	—	—	—	£600
1959	£2	£3	£12	£50
1961	£2	£3	£25	£60
1961 Obv as 1928, rev. as 1951	£30	£75	£325	£850
1962	£2	£3	£6	£35
1963	£2	£3	£6	£35
1964	£2	£3	£6	£35
1966	£2	£3	£6	£35
1967	£2	£3	£6	£35

	F	VF	EF	UNC
FLORINS				
Silver				
1928	£5	£8	£25	£65
1928 Proof	—	—	—	£85
1930	£5	£20	£150	£475
1930 Proof				Unique
1931	£5	£20	£175	£475
1933	£5	£18	£140	£475
1934	£15	£125	£275	£775
1934 Proof	—	—	—	£3000
1935	£5	£18	£65	£200
1937	£6	£25	£140	£425
Modified obverse: Eire				
1939	£3	£6	£35	£85
1939 Proof	—	—	—	£685
1940	£5	£6	£30	£85
1941	£5	£6	£35	£85
1941 Proof	—	—	—	£875
1942	£7	£15	£30	£85
1943	£3000	£6000	£10000	£22500

Beware of fake 1943 florins.

DATE	F	VF	EF	UNC
Cupro-nickel				
1951..	60p	£2	£15	£50
1951 Proof...	—	—	—	£495
1954..	60p	£2	£10	£50
1954 Proof...	—	—	—	£400
1955..	—	£2	£6	£50
1955 Proof...	—	—	—	£565
1959..	40p	£2	£6	£45
1961..	60p	£3	£15	£55
1962..	40p	£2	£6	£30
1963..	30p	£2	£6	£30
1964..	30p	£2	£6	£30
1965..	30p	£2	£6	£30
1966..	30p	£2	£6	£30
1968..	30p	£2	£6	£30

SHILLINGS
Silver

	F	VF	EF	UNC
1928..	£5	£10	£25	£60
1928 Proof...	—	—	—	£75
1930..	£6	£25	£100	£465
1930 Proof...	—	—	—	£875
1931..	£3	£17	£95	£475
1933..	£3	£17	£95	£460
1935..	£3	£13	£50	£160
1937..	£10	£75	£250	£1300
1939..	£3	£6	£25	£80
1939 Proof...	—	—	—	£775
1940..	£3	£6	£17	£60
1941..	£3	£5	£17	£60
1942..	£3	£5	£12	£55
Cupro-nickel				
1951..	£1	£2	£6	£25
1951 Proof...	—	—	—	£450
1954..	£1	£2	£6	£25
1954 Proof...	—	—	—	£500
1955..	£1	£2	£6	£25
1959..	£1	£2	£6	£35
1962..	50p	£2	£5	£22
1963..	50p	£2	£5	£15
1964..	50p	£2	£5	£15
1966..	50p	£2	£5	£15
1968..	50p	£2	£5	£15

SIXPENCES
Nickel

	F	VF	EF	UNC
1928..	£1	£6	£25	£65
1928 Proof...	—	—	—	£65
1934..	£1	£3	£18	£100
1935..	£1	£3	£25	£130
Modified obverse: Eire				
1939..	£1	£2	£10	£65
1939 Proof...	—	—	—	£675
1940..	£1	£2	£6	£65
Cupro-nickel				
1942..	£1	£2	£9	£65
1945	£3	£12	£35	£100
1946..	£5	£10	£100	£410
1947..	£2	£2	£25	£95
1948..	£1	£3	£15	£75
1949..	£1	£2	£10	£50
1950..	£2	£3	£25	£100
1952..	£1	£2	£5	£25

DATE	F	VF	EF	UNC
1953	£1	£2	£5	£35
1953 Proof	–	–	–	£125
1955	£1	£2	£4	£30
1956	£1	£2	£3	£30
1956 Proof	–	–	–	£175
1958	£4	£6	£12	£75
1958 Proof	–	–	–	£395
1959	50p	60p	£3	£25
1960	50p	60p	£2	£25
1961	–	£2	£3	£25
1962	£2	£6	£35	£80
1963	£2	£3	£6	£20
1964	£2	£3	£6	£15
1966	£2	£3	£6	£15
1967	£2	£3	£6	£12
1968	£2	£3	£6	£12
1969	£5	£8	£10	£30

THREEPENCES
Nickel

	F	VF	EF	UNC
1928	£2	£3	£10	£45
1928 Proof	–	–	–	£45
1933	£3	£13	£75	£385
1934	£1	£3	£15	£85

Modified obverse: Eire

	F	VF	EF	UNC
1935	£2	£4	£30	£235
1939	£3	£7	£60	£385
1939 Proof	–	–	–	£1200
1940	£2	£3	£13	£75

Cupro-nickel

	F	VF	EF	UNC
1942	–	£2	£6	£65
1942 Proof	–	–	–	£525
1943	£2	£3	£15	£80
1946	£2	£5	£10	£55
1946 Proof	–	–	–	£525
1948	£2	£3	£25	£85
1949	–	£2	£6	£45
1950	–	£2	£6	£35
1950 Proof	–	–	–	£555
1953	–	£2	£4	£20
1956	–	£2	£3	£15
1961	–	60p	£2	£5
1962	–	60p	£2	£12
1963	–	60p	£2	£12
1964	–	60p	£2	£5
1965	–	60p	£2	£5
1966	–	60p	£2	£5
1967	–	60p	£2	£5
1968	–	–	£2	£5

PENNIES

	F	VF	EF	UNC
1928	£2	£3	£12	£55
1928 Proof	–	–	–	£65
1931	£2	£4	£35	£125
1931 Proof	–	–	–	£1000
1933	£2	£5	£50	£275
1935	£1	£2	£25	£85
1937	£1	£2	£35	£135
1937 Proof	–	–	–	£1100

Modified obverse: Eire

	F	VF	EF	UNC
1938		Only two known		
1940	£10	£50	£175	£765
1941	£1	£2	£10	£35
1942	–	£2	£5	£25

DATE	F	VF	EF	UNC
1943	—	£2	£6	£45
1946	—	£2	£4	£20
1948	—	£2	£4	£20
1949	—	£2	£4	£20
1949 Proof	—	—	—	£500
1950	—	£2	£6	£40
1952	—	£2	£4	£15
1962	—	£2	£4	£15
1962 Proof	—	—	—	£200
1963	—	—	£2	£20
1963 Proof	—	—	—	£200
1964	—	—	£2	£10
1964 Proof	—	—	—	£500
1965	—	—	£1	£5
1966	—	—	£1	£5
1967	—	—	£1	£5
1968	—	—	£1	£5
1968 Proof	—	—	—	£300

HALFPENNIES

	F	VF	EF	UNC
1928	£2	£3	£15	£45
1928 Proof	—	—	—	£45
1933	£6	£20	£100	£520
1935	£5	£10	£50	£235
1937	£5	£10	£25	£75

Modified obverse: Eire

	F	VF	EF	UNC
1939	£5	£10	£50	£200
1939 Proof	—	—	—	£900
1940	£2	£4	£50	£195
1941	£1	£2	£6	£25
1942	£1	£2	£6	£25
1943	£1	£2	£8	£35
1946	£2	£5	£20	£100
1949	£1	£2	£6	£25
1953	—	£2	£3	£12
1953 Proof	—	—	—	£500
1964	—	—	£1	£5
1965	—	—	£1	£6
1966	—	—	£1	£4
1967	—	—	£1	£4

FARTHINGS

	F	VF	EF	UNC
1928	£3	£4	£15	£32
1928 Proof	—	—	—	£45
1930	£3	£4	£10	£32
1931	£4	£6	£15	£35
1931 Proof	—	—	—	£875
1932	£4	£6	£18	£45
1933	£3	£4	£12	£32
1935	£4	£6	£18	£35
1936	£4	£6	£18	£35
1937	£4	£6	£18	£35

Modified obverse: Eire

	F	VF	EF	UNC
1939	£3	£4	£10	£20
1939 Proof	—	—	—	£675
1940	£4	£5	£10	£25
1941	£3	£4	£6	£12
1943	£3	£4	£6	£12
1944	£3	£4	£6	£12
1946	£3	£4	£6	£12
1949	£4	£6	£8	£25
1949 Proof	—	—	—	£475
1953	£3	£4	£5	£12
1953 Proof	—	—	—	£345
1959	£3	£4	£5	£12
1966	£3	£4	£5	£12

For the 1928–50 copper issues it is worth noting that UNC means UNC with some lustre. BU examples with full lustre are extremely elusive and are worth much more than the quoted prices.

IRISH DECIMAL COINAGE

DATE	MINTAGE	BU	DATE	MINTAGE	BU
HALF PENCE			1995	55,500,000	£5
1971	100,500,000	£5	1996	69,300,000	£2
1975	10,500,000	£6	1998	33,700,000	£2
1976	5,500,000	£6	2000	Unknown	£2
1978	20,300,000	£5			
1980	20,600,000	£4	**FIVE PENCE**		
1982	9,700,000	£4			
1985	2,800,000	Rare			
1986. Only issued in the 1986 set	19,750,000	£135			

ONE PENNY

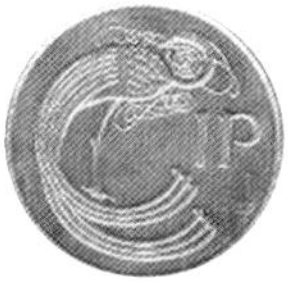

			1969 Toned	5,000,000	£8
			1970	10,000,000	£5
1971	100,500,000	£5	1971	8,000,000	£8
1974	10,000,000	£12	1974	7,000,000	£10
1975	10,000,000	£18	1975	10,000,000	£10
1976	38,200,000	£5	1976	20,600,000	£5
1978	25,700,000	£8	1978	28,500,000	£5
1979	21,800,000	£12	1980	22,200,000	£5
1980	86,700,000	£3	1982	24,400,000	£4
1982	54,200,000	£5	1985	4,200,000	£8
1985	19,200,000	£8	1986	15,300,000	£5
1986	36,600,000	£5	1990	7,500,000	£8
1988	56,800,000	£5	Size reduced to 18.4mm		
1990	65,100,000	£5	1992	74,500,000	£5
1992	25,600,000	£6	1993	89,100,000	£5
1993	10,000,000	£8	1994	31,100,000	£5
1994	45,800,000	£5	1995	12,000,000	£5
1995	70,800,000	£3	1996	14,700,000	£2
1996	190,100,000	£1	1998	158,500,000	£2
1998	40,700,000	£1	2000	Unknown	£1
2000	Unknown	£1			

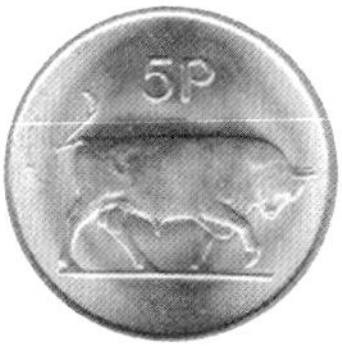

TWO PENCE

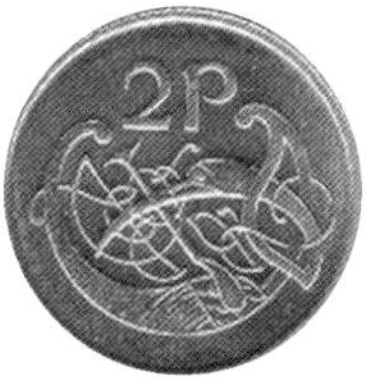

TEN PENCE

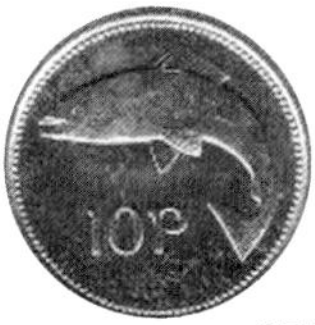

			1969	27,000,000	£12
			1971	4,000,000	£15
			1973	2,500,000	£16
1971	75,500,000	£5	1974	7,500,000	£12
1975	20,000,000	£10	1975	15,000,000	£12
1976	5400,000	£15	1976	9,400,000	£12
1978	12,000,000	£12	1978	30,900,000	£10
1979	32,400,000	£8	1980	44,600,000	£8
1980	59,800,000	£6	1982	7,400,000	£10
1982	30,400,000	£5	1985	4,100,000	£12
1985	14,500,000	£6	1986. Only issued in the 1986 set	11,280	£285
1986	23,900,000	£6	Size reduced to 22mm		
1988	35,900,000	£5	1992	2 known	—
1990	34,300,000	£5	1993	80,100,000	£5
1992	10,200,000	£10	1994	58,500,000	£5

DATE	MINTAGE	BU		DATE	MINTAGE	BU

1995	16,100,000	£5
1996	18,400,000	£3
1997	10,000,000	£4
1998	10,000,000	£4
1999	24,500,000	£3
2000	Unknown	£3

TWENTY PENCE

1985. Only 600 minted and 556 melted down, only 3 known	Extremely rare	
1986	50,400,000	£8
1988	20,700,000	£6
1992	14,800,000	£5
1994	11,100,000	£5
1995	18,200,000	£5
1996	29,300,000	£5
1998	25,000,000	£3
1999	11,000,000	£3
2000	Unknown	£2

FIFTY PENCE

1970	9,000,000	£8
1971	650,000	£7
1974	1,000,000	£55
1975	2,000,000	£55
1976	3,000,000	£45
1977	4,800,000	£55
1978	4,500,000	£45
1979	4,000,000	£45
1981	6,000,000	£25
1982	2,000,000	£25
1983	7,000,000	£25
1986 Only issued in the 1986 set	10,000	£325
1988	7,000,000	£5
1988 Dublin Millennium	5,000,000	£5
1988 — Proof	50,000	£35
1996	6,000,000	£7
1997	6,000,000	£7
1998	13,800,000	£5
1999	7,000,000	£4
2000	Unknown	£4

ONE POUND

1990	42,300,000	£5
1990 Proof	50,000	£25
1994	14,900,000	£5
1995	9,200,000	£5
1995 UN silver proof in case of issue	2,850	£175
1996	9,200,000	£5
1998	22,960,000	£4
1999	10,000,000	£5
2000	4,000,000	£5

2000 Millennium	5,000,000	£8
2000 – Silver Proof Piedfort	90,000	£45

OFFICIAL COIN SETS ISSUED BY THE CENTRAL BANK

1971 Specimen set in green wallet. 6 coins	£25
1975 6 coin set	£65
1978 6 coin set	£65
1978 6 coin set. Black cover, scarce	£75
1982 6 coin set. Black cover	£75
1986 Specimen set in card folder 1/2p to 50p, 7 coins. Very scarce. Most sets have glue problems	£650
1996 7 coin set	£60
1998 7 coin set	£50
2000 Millennium set. Last decimal set	£135
2000 — With 1999 instead of the 2000 £1 coin	£285

Dublin Millennium 50p

OFFICIAL AND SEMI-OFFICIAL COMMEMORATIVE MEDALS

It is probably a strong love of history, rather than the strict disciplines of coin collecting that make collectors turn to commemorative medals. The link between the two is intertwined, and it is to be hoped that collectors will be encouraged to venture into the wider world of medallions, encouraged by this brief guide, originally supplied by Daniel Fearon (author of the *Catalogue of British Commemorative Medals)* and kindly updated again this year by Charles Riley.

James I Coronation, 1603

DATE	VF	EF
JAMES I		
1603 Coronation (possibly by C. Anthony), 29mm, Silver	£1200	£1950
QUEEN ANNE		
1603 Coronation, 29mm, AR	£800	£1500
CHARLES I		
1626 Coronation (by N. Briot), 30mm, Silver	£650	£1000
1633 Scottish Coronation (by N. Briot), 28mm, Silver	£450	£795
1649 Memorial (by J. Roettier). Struck after the Restoration, 50mm, Bronze	£90	£175
CROMWELL		
1653 Lord Protector (by T. Simon), 38mm, Silver	£700	£1700
— Cast examples	£350	£600
CHARLES II		
1651 Scottish Coronation, in exile (from design by Sir J. Balfour), 32mm, Silver	£2000	£4000
CHARLES II		
1661 Coronation (by T. Simon), 29mm		
— Gold	£2500	£5000
— Silver	£350	£550
1685 Death (by N. Roettier), 39mm, Bronze	£150	£325

Charles II Coronation, 1661

DATE	VF	EF

JAMES II
1685 Coronation (by J. Roettier), 34mm
— Gold £2000 £3600
— Silver £400 £700

MARY
1685 Coronation (by J. Roettier), 34mm
— Gold £2000 £4000
— Silver £400 £650

WILLIAM & MARY
1689 Coronation (by J. Roettier), 32mm
— Gold £1750 £3000
— Silver £350 £550
1689 Coronation, "Perseus" (by G. Bower),
  38mm, Gold £1750 £3000

MARY
1694 Death (by N. Roettier), 39mm, Bronze........ £95 £245

WILLIAM III
1697 "The State of Britain" (by J. Croker), 69mm,
  Silver.. £850 £1500

ANNE
1702 Accession, "Entirely English" (by J. Croker), 34mm
— Gold .... £1750 £3000   *Queen Anne, 1702–1713.*
— Silver £150 £225
1702 Coronation (by J. Croker), 36mm
— Gold £2000 £3500
— Silver £225 £300
1707 Union with Scotland (by J. Croker, rev. by S. Bull), 34mm
— Gold £1750 £3000
— Silver £200 £300
1713 Peace of Utrecht (by J. Croker—issued in gold to Members
of Parliament), 34mm
— Gold £850 £1500
— Silver £150 £250

GEORGE I
1714 Coronation (by J. Croker), 34mm
— Gold £1500 £2000
— Silver £250 £350
1727 Death (by J. Dassier), 31mm, Silver £150 £275

GEORGE II
1727 Coronation (by J. Croker), 34mm
— Gold £1500 £3200
— Silver £125 £225

QUEEN CAROLINE
1727 Coronation (by J. Croker), 34mm
— Gold .... £1750 £3000   *George I Coronation, 1714.*
— Silver £185 £375
1732 The Royal Family (by J. Croker), 70mm
— Silver.. £1500 £3000
— Bronze.. £400 £700

361

DATE	VF	EF

GEORGE III
1761 Coronation (by L. Natter), 34mm
— Gold	£2750	£4250
— Silver	£350	£550
— Bronze	£150	£250

QUEEN CHARLOTTE
1761 Coronation (by L. Natter), 34mm
— Gold	£1850	£3500
— Silver	£375	£600
— Bronze	£150	£295
1810 Golden Jubilee, "Frogmore", 48mm, Silver	£130	£275
— Bronze	£95	£175

GEORGE IV
1821 Coronation (by B. Pistrucci), 35mm
— Gold	£1600	£2500
— Silver	£200	£325
— Bronze	£95	£150

WILLIAM IV
1831 Coronation (by W. Wyon; rev.shows
Queen Adelaide), 33mm
— Gold	£1250	£2500
— Silver	£175	£325
— Bronze	£95	£150

QUEEN VICTORIA
1838 Coronation (by B. Pistrucci), 37mm
— Gold	£1500	£2500
— Silver	£185	£320
— Bronze	£60	£120

George III, Coronation, 1761

Queen Victoria Coronation, 1838

Queen Victoria Diamond Jubilee 1897

DATE	VF	EF
1887 Golden Jubilee (by J. E. Boehm, rev. by Lord Leighton)		
— Gold, 58mm	£3950	£4500
— Silver, 78mm	£250	£500
— Bronze, 78mm	£95	£180
1897 Diamond Jubilee (by G. de Saulles),		
— Gold, 56mm	£3750	£4500
— Silver, 56mm	£95	£125
— Bronze, 56mm	£35	£60
— Gold, 25mm	£750	£950
— Silver, 25mm	£20	£35

EDWARD VII

1902 Coronation (August 9) (by G. W. de Saulles)

	VF	EF
— Gold, 56mm	£3950	£4500
— Silver, 56mm	£95	£150
— Bronze, 56mm	£30	£55
— Gold, 31mm	£750	£950
— Silver, 31mm	£20	£30

Some rare examples of the official medal show the date as June 26, the original date set for the Coronation which was postponed because the King developed appendicitis.

George V Silver Jubilee, 1935

GEORGE V

1911 Coronation (by B. Mackennal)

	VF	EF
— Gold, 51mm	£3950	£4500
— Silver, 51mm	£95	£250
— Bronze, 51mm	£30	£65
— Gold, 31mm	£750	£950
— Silver, 31mm	£20	£35

1935 Silver Jubilee (by P. Metcalfe)

	VF	EF
— Gold, 58mm	£3950	£4500
— Silver, 58mm	£100	£150
— Gold, 32mm	£750	£950
— Silver, 32mm	£20	£30

PRINCE EDWARD

1911 Investiture as Prince of Wales (by W. Goscombe John)

	VF	EF
— Gold, 31mm	£1500	£2500
— Silver, 31mm	£50	£85

Edward, Prince of Wales, 1911

EDWARD VIII

1936 Abdication (by L. E. Pinches), 35mm

	VF	EF
— Gold	£1500	£2000
— Silver	£45	£65
— Bronze	£20	£35

GEORGE VI

1937 Coronation (by P. Metcalfe)

	VF	EF
— Gold, 58mm	£5250	£5750
— Silver, 58mm	£65	£95
— Gold, 32mm	£1000	£1250
— Silver, 32mm	£25	£35
— Bronze, 32mm	£12	£15

Edward VIII, Abdication, 1936.

DATE	VF	EF

ELIZABETH II
1953 Coronation (by Spink & Son)—illustrated
— Gold, 57mm £3950 £4500
— Silver, 57mm £65 £125
— Bronze, 57mm £35 £65
— Gold, 32mm £750 £950
— Silver, 32mm £25 £35
— Bronze, 32mm £12 £15
1977 Silver Jubilee (by A. Machin)
— Silver, 57mm .... — £70
— Silver, 44mm .... — £40

*The gold medals are priced for 18ct—they can also be found as 22ct and 9ct, and prices should be adjusted accordingly.

PRINCE CHARLES
1969 Investiture as Prince of Wales (by M. Rizello)
— Silver, 57mm .... — £75
— Bronze gilt, 57mm............................ — £40
— Silver, 45mm .... — £50
— Gold, 32mm .... — £750
— Silver, 32mm .... — £35
— Bronze, 32mm .... — £10

QUEEN ELIZABETH THE QUEEN MOTHER
1980 80th Birthday (by L. Durbin)
— Silver, 57mm .... — £65
— Silver, 38mm .... — £38
— Bronze, 38mm .... — £25

N.B.—Official Medals usually command a premium when still in their original case of issue.

Prince Charles, Prince of Wales 1969.

The Royal Mint Museum contains a charming group of medallic portraits of seven of the children of Queen Victoria and Prince Albert. They appear to have been made in 1850 and therefore do not include the two children who were born after that date. The skilfully-executed portraits are the work of Leonard Wyon, a member of the extremely talented family of engravers whose name is so well known to numismatists. The son of William Wyon, he was actually born in the Royal Mint in 1826. These particular portraits were not commissioned by the Mint and little is known about the circumstances in which they were prepared, but for some reason the dies have survived in the Royal Mint Museum, along with single-sided bronze impressions roughly the size of a half-crown.

Images and information courtesy of Dr Kevin Clancy, The Royal Mint.

Directory
section

O N the following pages will be found the most useful names and addresses needed by the coin collector.

At the time of going to press with this edition of the YEARBOOK the information is correct, as far as we have been able to ascertain. However, people move and establishments change, so it is always advisable to make contact with the person or organisation listed before travelling any distance, to ensure that the journey is not wasted.

Should any of the information in this section not be correct we would very much appreciate being advised in good time for the preparation of the next edition of the COIN YEARBOOK.

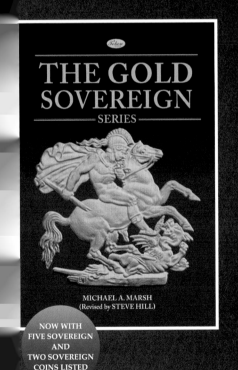

BRITISH NUMISMATIC TRADE ASSOCIATION

DEALER MEMBERS BY COUNTY

LONDON AREA
*ArtAncient Ltd - www.artancient.com
ATS Bullion Ltd - www.atsbullion.com
Beaver Coin Room - janjlis@yahoo.com
Ion Blyth - www.jonblyth.com
Bonhams 1793 Ltd - www.bonhams.com
Classical Numismatic Group LLC -
www.cngcoins.com
Philip Cohen Numismatics -
www.coinheritage.co.uk
André de Clermont -
www.declermont.com
Dix Noonan Webb - www.dnw.co.uk
Christopher Eimer -
www.christophereimer.co.uk
Heritage Auctions UK - www.ha.com
Knightsbridge Coins -
info@knightsbridgecoins.com
C.J. Martin (Coins) Ltd -
www.antiquities.co.uk
Morton & Eden Ltd -
www.mortonandeden.com
Numismatica Ars Classica -
www.arsclassicacoins.com
Pax Romana - www.paxromana.auction
Physical Gold Ltd -
www.physicalgold.co.uk
Simmons Gallery -
www.simmonsgallery.co.uk
Sovereign Rarities Ltd - www.sovr.co.uk
Spink & Son Ltd - www.spink.com
St James's Auctions - www.sjauctions.com
The Coin Cabinet Ltd -
www.thecoincabinet.co.uk
The London Coin Company Ltd -
www.thelondoncoincompany.com

BERKSHIRE
Douglas Saville Numismatic Books -
www.douglassaville.com

BUCKINGHAMSHIRE
Charles Riley - www.charlesriley.co.uk

CAMBRIDGESHIRE
Den Of Antiquity International Ltd -
www.denofantiquity.co.uk
Cambridgeshire Coins -
www.cambridgshirecoins.com

CHESHIRE
Colin Cooke - www.colincooke.com

CORNWALL
Richard W. Jeffery - richard@trebehor.co.uk

DEVON
Glenn S. Ogden - www.glennogdencoins.com

DORSET
*Dorset Coin Co Ltd -
www.dorsetcoincompany.co.uk
Timothy Medhurst Coins & Antiquities -
www.timothymedhurst.co.uk

ESSEX
*Time Line - www.time-lines.co.uk

GLOUCESTERSHIRE
Silbury Coins Ltd - www.silburycoins.com

HAMPSHIRE
Asprey Coins - www.apreycoins.co.uk
Studio Coins - www.studiocoins.net
Victory Coins - vcpompey@yahoo.co.uk
Wessex Coins - www.wessexcoins.co.uk
West Essex Coin Investment - 01425-656459

HERTFORDSHIRE
DRG Coins and Antiquities -
www.drgcoinsandantiquities.com
KB Coins - www.kbcoins.com
Whitmore Coins, Tokens and Medallions -
john@whitmorectm.com

KENT
*London Coins Ltd - www.londoncoins.co.uk
*Peter Morris - www.petermorris.co.uk

LEICESTERSHIRE
Hall's Hammered Coins -
www.hallshammeredcoins.com

MERSEYSIDE
*Merseyside Collectors Centre -
www.mccentre.co.uk

MONMOUTHSHIRE
Anthony M. Halse -
www.coinsandtokens.com

NORFOLK
*BucksCoins - www. buckscoins.com
Roderick Richardson -
www.roderickrichardson.com
Chris Rudd - www.celticcoins.com

NOTTINGHAMSHIRE
History in Coins - www.historyincoins.com

OXFORDSHIRE
Richard Gladdle - Gladdle@plumpudding.org

SHROPSHIRE
M. Veissid - m.veissid@btinternet.com

STAFFORDSHIRE
*English Coin Company -
www.englishcoincompany.com

SUFFOLK
* Lockdale Coins Ltd - www.lockdales.com
Simon Monks - www.simonmonks.co.uk

SURREY
*M.J. Hughes - www.gbgoldcoins.co.uk
Mark Rasmussen Numismatist - www.rascoins.com

SUSSEX
John Newman Coins -
www.johnnewmancoins.com

TYNE AND WEAR
*Corbitts Ltd - www.corbitts.com

WARWICKSHIRE
Brittonum Ltd - www.brittonum.com
* Peter Viola - 07770897707
* Warwick & Warwick Ltd -
www.warwickandwarwick.com

WEST MIDLANDS
*Atkinsons Coins and Bullion -
www.atkinsonsbullion.com
*Birmingham Coins - 0121 707 2808
David Craddock -
davidcraddock373@btinternet.com
Paul Davis Birmingham Ltd -
pjdavis79@btinternet.com

WILTSHIRE
*Gold-Traders (UK) Ltd -
https://britanniacoincompany.com
Hammered British Coins -
www.hammeredbritishcoins.com

YORKSHIRE
AMR Coins - www.amrcoins.com
Keith Chapman - www.anglosaxoncoins.com
Paul Clayton -
paulnormanclayton@googlemail.com
Paul Davies Ltd - paul@pauldaviesltd.co.uk
*Paul Dawson York Ltd -
pauldawsonyork@hotmail.co.uk

SCOTLAND
Paul Menzies Ltd - www.paulmenziesltd.com
*Scotmint Ltd - www.scotmint.com

WALES
Lloyd Bennett - www.coinsofbritain.com
Colin Rumney - pru@rumneyp.fsnet.co.uk

WWW.BNTA.NET

*Retail premises

Museums
and libaries

Listed below are the Museums and Libraries in the UK which have coins or items of numismatic interest on display or available to the general public.

A

• Kings Museum, University of Aberdeen, Old Aberdeen Town House, **Aberdeen**, AB9 1AS. Tel: 01224 274 330.

• Curtis Museum (1855), High Street, **Alton**, Hants, GU34 1BA. Tel: 0142082802. *General collection of British coins.*

• Ashburton Museum, The Bullring, **Ashburton**, Devon, TQ13 7DT. *Ancient British and Roman antiquities including local coin finds.*

• Ashwell Village Museum (1930), Swan Street, **Ashwell**, Baldock, Herts, SG7 5NY. Tel: 01462 742 956 *Roman coins from local finds, local trade tokens, Anglo-Gallic coins and jetons.*

• Buckinghamshire County Museum (1862), Church Street, **Aylesbury**, Bucks, HP20 2QP. Tel: 01296 331 441. *Roman and medieval English coins found locally, 17th/18th century Buckinghamshire tokens, commemorative medals.*

B

• Banbury Museum, Castle Quay Shopping Center, Spiceball Park Road, **Banbury**, Oxon, OX16 2PQ. Tel: 01295 236165. *Wrexlin Hoard of Roman coins.*

• Museum of Barnstaple and North Devon (1931). **The Square, Barnstaple, EX23 8LN.** Tel: 01271 346 747. *General coin and medal collection, including local finds. Medals of the Royal Devonshire Yeomanry.*

• Roman Baths Museum, Abbey Church Yard, Stall St, **Bath**, Avon, BA1 1LZ. Tel: 01225 477 785. *Comprehensive collection of Roman coins from local finds.*

• Bagshaw Museum and Art Gallery (1911), Wilton Park, **Batley**, West Yorkshire, WF17 0AS. Tel: 01924 324 765. *Roman, Scottish, Irish, English hammered, British and foreign coins, local traders' tokens, political medalets, campaign medals and decorations.*

• The Higgins Art Gallery and Museum (1961), Castle Lane, **Bedford**, MK40 3XD. Tel: 01234 718 618. *Collections of the Bedford Library and Scientific Institute, the Beds Archaeological Society and Bedford Modern School (Pritchard Memorial) Museum.*

• Ulster Museum (1928), Botanic Gardens, **Belfast**, BT9 5AB. Tel: 028 9044 0000 *Irish, English and British coins and commemorative medals.*

• Berwick Museum and Art Gallery (1867), The Clock Block, Berwick Barracks, Parade, **Berwick**, TD15 1DQG. Tel: 01289 309538. *Roman, Scottish and medievial coins.*

• Treasure House and Art Gallery (1910), Champney Road, **Beverley**, Humberside, HU17 8HE. Tel: 01482 393939. *Beverley trade tokens, Roman, English, British and foreign coins.*

• Bignor Roman Villa (1811), **Bignor**, nr Pulborough, West Sussex, RH20 1PH. Tel: 01798 869 259. *Roman coins found locally.*

• City Museum and Art Gallery (1861), Chamberlain Square, **Birmingham**, B3 3DH. Tel: 0121 348 8000. *Coins, medals and tokens - special emphasis on the products of the Soho, Heaton, Birmingham and Watt mints.*

• Blackburn Museum, Museum Street, **Blackburn**, Lancs, BB1 7AJ. Tel: 01254 667 130. *Incorporates the Hart (5,000 Greek, Roman and early English) and Hornby (500 English coins) collections, as well as the museum's own collection of British and Commonwealth coins.*

• Bognor Regis Museum, 25 – 27 West Street, **Bognor Regis**, West Sussex, PO21 1XA. Tel: 01243 865 636 *Roman, English and British coins and trade tokens.*

• Bolton Museum and Art Gallery,(1893), Le Mans Crescent, **Bolton**, Lancashire, BL1 1SE. **Tel: 01204 332211**

• Roman Town and Museum (1949) Front Street, Aldborough, **Boroughbridge**, N. Yorks, YO51 9ES. Tel: 01423 322 768. *Roman coins.*

• The Museum (1929),Boston Guildhall, South Street, **Boston**, Lincs, PE21 6HT. Tel: 01205 365 954. *Small collection of English coins.*

• Natural Science Society Museum (1903), 39 Christchurch Road, **Bournemouth**, Dorset, BH1 3NS. Tel: 01202 553 525. *Greek, Roman and English hammered coins (including the Hengistbury Hoard), local trade tokens.*

• Bolling Hall Museum (1915), Bowling Hall Road, **Bradford**, West Yorkshire, BD4 7LP. Tel: 01274 431 826. *Some 2,000 coins and tokens, mostly 18th–20th centuries.*

• Bridport Museum (1932), 25 South Street, **Bridport**, Dorset DT6 3RJ. Tel: 01308 458 703. *Roman coins, mainly from excavations at Claudian Fort.*

• Bristol Museum and Art Gallery (1820), Queen's Road, **Bristol**, BS8 1RL. Tel: 0117 922 3571. *Ancient British, Roman (mainly from local hoards), English hammered coins, especially from the Bristol mint, and several hundred local trade tokens.*

• Buxton Museum and Art Gallery (1891), Terrace Road, **Buxton**, Derbyshire, SK17 6DA. Tel: 01629 533 540. *English and British coins, tokens and commemorative medals. Numismatic library.*

C

• Segontium Fort Museum (1928), Beddgelert Road, **Caernarfon**, Gwynedd, LL55 2LN. Tel: 0300 025 6000. *Roman coins and artifacts excavated from the fort.*

• Fitzwilliam Museum (1816), Trumpington Street, **Cambridge**, CB2 1RB. Tel: 01223 332 900. *Ancient, English, medieval European, oriental coins, medals, plaques, seals and cameos.*

• National Museum & Galleries of Wales, Cathays Park, **Cardiff**, CF10 3NP. Tel: 0300 111 2 333. *Greek, Celtic, Roman and British coins and tokens with the emphasis on Welsh interest. Also military, civilian and comm. medals.*

• Guildhall Museum (1979), 31-33 Fisher Street, **Carlisle**, Cumbria, CA3 8JE. Tel: 01228 618 718. *General collection of coins and medals.*

• Tullie House (1877), Castle Street, **Carlisle**, Cumbria, CA3 8TP. Tel: 01228 618 718. *Roman, medieval and later coins from local finds, including medieval counterfeiter's coin-moulds.*

• Gough's Caves Museum (1934), The Cliffs, **Cheddar**, Somerset, BS27 3QF. Tel: 01934 742 343. *Roman coins.*

• Chelmsford Museum (1835), Oaklands Park, Moulsham Street, **Chelmsford**, Essex, CM2 9AQ. Tel: 01245 605 700. *Ancient British, Roman, medieval and later coins mainly from local finds, local medals.*

• Chepstow Museum, Bridge Street, Chepstow, (1949), **Chepstow**, Gwent, NP15 5EZ. Tel: 01291 625 981. *Local coins and trade tokens.*

• Grosvenor Museum (1886), 27 Grosvenor Street, **Chester**, CH1 2DD. Tel**:** 01244 972 197. *Roman coins from the fortress site, Anglo-Saxon, English medieval and post-medieval coins of the Chester and Rhuddlan mints, trade tokens, English and British milled coins.*

• Public Library (1879), New Beetwell Street, **Chesterfield**, Derbyshire, S40 1QN. Tel: 01629 533 400. *Roman coins from local finds, Derbyshire trade tokens, medals, seals and railway passes. Numismatic library and publications.*

• Red House Museum (1919), Quay Road, **Christchurch**, Dorset. Tel: 01202 482 860. *Coins of archaeological significance from Hampshire and Dorset, notably the South Hants Hoard, ancient British, Armorican, Gallo-Belgic, Celtic and Roman coins, local trade tokens and medals.*

• Corinium Museum (1856), Park Street, **Cirencester**, Glos.Tel:01285 655 611. *Roman coins.*

• Colchester and Essex Museum (1860), The Castle, **Colchester**, Essex. Tel: 01206 282 931. *Ancient British and Roman coins from local finds, medieval coins (especially the Colchester Hoard), later English coins and Essex trade tokens, commemorative medals.*

D

• Public Library, Museum and Art Gallery (1921), Crown Street, **Darlington**, Co Durham DL1 1ND. Tel: 01325 462 034. *Coins, medals and tokens.*

• Borough Museum (1908), 18 - 20 Market Street, **Dartford**, Kent, DA1 1EU. Tel: 01322 224 739. *Roman, medieval and later English hammered coins, trade tokens and commemorative medals.*

• Dartmouth Museum (1953), The Butterwalk, **Dartmouth**, Devon TQ6 9PZ. Tel: 01803 832 923. *Coins and medals of a historical and maritime nature.*

• Museum and Art Gallery (1878), The Strand, **Derby**, DE1 1BS. Tel:01332 641 901. *Roman coins, English silver and copper regal coins, Derbyshire tradesmen's tokens, British campaign medals and decorations of the Derbyshire Yeomanry and the 9/12 Royal Lancers.*

• Museum and Art Gallery (1909), Chequer Road, **Doncaster**, South Yorkshire, DN1 2AE. Tel: 01302 734 293. *General collection of English and foreign silver and bronze coins. Representative collection of Roman imperial silver and bronze coins, including a number from local hoards. English trade tokens, principally of local issues, medals.*

• Dorset County Museum (1846), High West Street, **Dorchester**, Dorset, DT1 1XA. Tel: 01305 262 735. *British, Roman, medieval and later coins of local interest.*

• Dumfries Museum (1835), The Observatory, Rotchell Road, **Dumfries** Tel: 01387 253 374. *Greek, Roman, Anglo-Saxon, medieval English and Scottish coins, especially from local hoards. Numismatic library.*

• The McManus Dundee's Art Galleries and Museums (1873), Albert Square, **Dundee**, DD1 1DA. Tel:01382 307 200. *Coins and medals of local interest.*

• The Cathedral Treasury (995 AD), The College, **Durham**, DH1 3EH. Tel: 0191 338 7178. *Greek and Roman coins bequeathed by Canon Sir George Wheeler (1724), Renaissance to modern medals, medieval English coins, especially those struck at the Durham ecclesiastical mint.*

• Durham Heritage Centre, St Mary le Bow, North Bailey, **Durham**, DH1 3ET. Tel: 0191 384 5589. *Roman, medieval and later coins, mainly from local finds.*

E

• National Museum of Scotland (1781), Chambers Street, **Edinburgh**, EH1 1JF. Tel: 0300 123 6789. *Roman, Anglo-Saxon, Englsh and Scottish coins, trade tokens, commemorative medals and communion tokens. Numismatic library. Publications.*

• Royal Albert Memorial Museum (1868), Queen Street, **Exeter**, EX4 3RX. Tel: 01392 265 858. *Roman and medieval. Coins of the Exeter Mint.*

G

• Hunterian Museum (1807), Gilbert Scott Building, University Of Glasgow, University Avenue, **Glasgow**, G12 8QQ. Tel: 0141 330 4221. *Greek, Roman, Byzantine, Scottish, English and Irish coins, Papal and other European medals, Indian and Oriental coins, trade and communion tokens.*

• Kelvingrove Art Gallery and Museum (1888), Argyle Street, **Glasgow.** Tel: 0141 276 9599. *General collection of coins, trade tokens, communion tokens, commemorative and military medals.*

• Riverside Museum (1974), 100 Pointhouse Place **Glasgow**, G3 8RS. Tel: 0141 287 2720. *Transport tokens and passes, commemorative medals, badges and insignia of railway companies and shipping lines.*

• City Museum and Art Gallery (1859), Brunswick Road, **Gloucester.** Tel: 01452 396 131. *Ancient British, Roman, Anglo-Saxon (from local finds), early medieval (from local mints), Gloucestershire trade tokens.*

• Guernsey Museum and Art Gallery, St Peter Port, **Guernsey.** Tel: 01481 726 518. *Armorican, Roman, medieval and later coins, including the coins, medals, tokens and paper money of Guernsey.*

• Guildford Museum (1898), Castle Hill, **Guildford**, Surrey, GU1 3SX. Tel: 01483 444 751. *Roman and medieval coins and later medals.*

H

• Gray Museum and Art Gallery, Church Square, Clarence Road, **Hartlepool**, Cleveland. Tel: 01429 523 438. *General collection, including coins from local finds.*

• Public Museum and Art Gallery (1890), John's Place, Bohemia Road , **Hastings**, East Sussex. Tel: 01424 451 052 *General collection of English coins, collection of Anglo-Saxon coins from Sussex mints.*

• City Museum (1874), Broad Street, **Hereford** HR4 9AU. Tel: 01432 260692

• Hertford Museum (1902), 18 Bull Plain, **Hertford.** Tel: 01992 582 686. *British, Roman, medieval and later English coins and medals.*

• Honiton and Allhallows Public Museum (1946), High Street, **Honiton**, Devon. Tel:01404 44966. *Small general collection, including coins from local finds.*

• Museum and Art Gallery (1891), 19 New Church Road, **Hove**. Tel:0300 029 0200. *English coins, Sussex trade tokens and hop tallies, campaign medals, orders and decorations, comm. medals.*

• Tolson Memorial Museum (1920), Ravensknowle Park, **Huddersfield**, West Yorkshire. Tel: 01484 223 240. *Representative collection of British coins and tokens, Roman and medieval coins, mainly from local finds.*

• Hull and East Riding Museum (1928), 36 High Street, **Hull.** Tel: 01482 300 300. *Celtic, Roman and medieval coins and artifacts from local finds. Some later coins including tradesmen's tokens.*

I

• The Manx Museum, Douglas, **Isle of Man.** Tel: 01624 648 000. *Roman, Celtic, Hiberno-Norse, Viking, medieval English and Scottish coins, mainly from local finds, Manx traders' tokens from the 17th to 19th centuries, Manx coins from 1709 to the present day.*

J

• Jersey Museum, Weighbridge, St Helier, **Jersey** Tel: 01534 633 300. *Armorican, Gallo-Belgic, Roman, medieval English and French coins, coins, paper money and tokens of Jersey.*

K

• Cliffe Castle Museum, Spring Gardens Lane, **Keighley** West Yorkshire. Tel: 01535 618 231. *Roman coins found locally.*

• Dick Institute Museum and Art Gallery (1893), Elmbank Avenue, **Kilmarnock**, Ayrshire. Tel: 01563 554 300. *General collection of coins and medals, and the Hunter-Selkirk collection of communion tokens.*

L

• City Museum (1923), Old Town Hall, Market Square, **Lancaster.** Tel: 01524 64637. *Roman, Anglo-Saxon, medieval English coins, provincial trade tokens, medals of the King's Own Royal Lancashire Regiment.*

• City Museum (1820), Millenium Square, **Leeds**, West Yorkshire. Tel: 0113 378 5001. *Greek, Roman, Anglo-Saxon, English medieval, Scottish, Irish, British, Commonwealth and foreign coins. Several Roman and Saxon hoards. The Backhouse collection of Yorkshire banknotes, the Thornton collection of Yorkshire tokens, British and foreign commemorative medals.*

• New Walk Museum (1849), 53 New Walk, **Leicester**. Tel: 0116 225 4900. *Roman, medieval and later coins, mainly from local finds, tokens, commemorative medals, campaign medals and decorations.*

• Pennington Hall Museum and Art Gallery, **Leigh**, Lancashire. *Roman and British coins and medals.*

• City Library, Art Gallery and Museum (1859), The Friary, **Lichfield**, Staffs. Email: info@lichfieldheritage. org.uk. *Roman, medieval and later English coins, Staffordshire trade tokens and commemorative medals.*

• World Museum(1851), William Brown Street, **Liverpool**, L3 8EN. Tel: 0151 478 4393. *General collection of Roman, medievaland later British coins, tokens.*

• Bank of England Museum, Bartholomew Lane, **London**. Tel: 020 3461 5545. *Exhibits relating to gold bullion, coins, tokens and medals, the design and manufacture of banknotes, and a comprehensive collection of bank notes dating from the 17th century to the present day.*

• British Museum(1752), HSBC Coin Gallery, Great Russell Street, **London**, WC1. Tel: 020 7323 8000. *Almost a million coins, medals, tokens and badges of all period from Lydia, 7th century BC to the present time. Extensive library of books and periodicals.*

• British Numismatic Society (1903), Warburg Institute, Woburn Square, **London**, WC1. *Library containing over 5,000 volumes, including sale catalogues, periodicals and pamphlets. Open to members only.*

• Gunnersbury Park Museum (1927), Acton, **London**, W3. Tel: 0203 9610280

• Horniman Museum and Library (1890), 100 London Road, Forest Hill, **London**, SE23 3PQ Tel: 020 8699 1872. *General collection, primitive currency, some tokens.*

• Imperial War Museum, Lambeth Road, **London**, SE1 6HZ. Tel: 020 7416 5000. *Emergency coinage of two world wars, occupation and invasion money, extensive collection of German Notgeld, commemorative, propaganda and military medals, badges and insignia.*

• Sir John Soane's Museum (1833), 13 Lincoln's Inn Fields, **London**, WC2. Tel: 020 7405 2107. *Napoleonic medals and medallic series of the late 18th and early 19th centuries.*

• National Maritime Museum, Romney Road, Greenwich, **London**, SE10. Tel: 020 8858 4422. *Commemorative medals with a nautical or maritime theme, naval medals and decorations.*

• Victoria and Albert Museum (1852), Cromwell Road, South Kensington, **London**, SW7 2RL. Tel: 020 7942 2000. *Byzantine gold and medieval Hispano-Mauresque coins (Department of Metalwork), large collection of Renaissance and later medals (Department of Architecture and Sculpture). Numismatic books.*

• Ludlow Museum (1833). The Assembly Rooms. Castle Square, **Ludlow**. Tel: 01584 878 697. *Roman and medieval coins from local finds.*

• Luton Museum and Art Gallery (1927), Wardown House, Old Bedford Road, **Luton**, Beds. Tel: 01582 546722. *Coins, tokens and medals.*

M

• Museum and Art Gallery (1858), St Faiths Street, **Maidstone**, Kent. Tel: 01622 602838. *Ancient British, Roman, Anglo-Saxon and medieval coins found in Kent, modern British coins, Kent trade tokens, banknotes, hop tallies and tokens, primitive currency, collections of Kent Numismatic Society.*

• The Manchester Museum (1868), The University, **Manchester**. Tel: 0161 275 2648. *Very fine collections of Greek and Roman coins, comprehensive collections of English, European and Oriental coins, over 30,000 in all.*

• Margate Museum (1923), Market Place, Margate Old Town, **Margate**, Kent. Tel: 01843 231 213. *Small collection of coins, including Roman from local finds.*

• Montrose Museum and Art Gallery (1836). Panmure Place, **Montrose**, Angus, DD10 8HF. Tel: 01674 907447. *Scottish and British coins.*

N

• Newark-on-Trent Museum (1912), 14 Appletongate, **Newark**, Notts. Tel 01636 655765 *Siege pieces, trade tokens and coins from local finds and hoards.*

• West Berkshire Museum, The Wharf, **Newbury**, Berkshire. Tel: 01635 519562. *Ancient British, Roman and medieval coins and artifacts, later coins and tokens.*

• Great North Museum, Hancock Barras Bridge, **Newcastle-upon-Tyne.** Tel: 0191 208 6765. *Ancient coins.*

O

• Heberden Coin Room, Ashmolean Museum (1683), **Oxford**. Tel: 01865 278058. *Extensive collections of all periods, notably Greek, Roman, English and Oriental coins, Renaissance portrait and later medals, tokens and paper money. Large library. Numerous publications.*

P

• Peterborough Museum (1881), Priestgate, **Peterborough**, Cambs. Tel: 01733 864 663. *Roman (mainly from local hoards and finds), Anglo-Saxon, medieval English, British and modern European coins, English and British commemorative medals and tokens.*

• City Museum and Art Gallery (1897), Drake Circus, **Plymouth**, Devon. **Closed for redevelopment.**

• Waterfront Museum, 4 High Street, **Poole**, BH15 1BW. Tel: 01202 262 600. *General collection of British and foreign coins, medals and tokens (view by appointment).*

• Portsmouth Museum (1972), Museum Road, Old **Portsmouth**, PO1 2LJ. Tel: 023 9283 4779. *Roman, medieval and later coins mainly from local finds and archaeological excavation, British coins, trade tokens of Hampshire, commemorative medals.*

• Harris Museum and Art Gallery (1893), Market Square, **Preston**, PR1 2PP. Tel: 01772 258 248. *English and British coins, tokens and medals.*

R

• The Museum of Reading (1883), Blagrave Street, **Reading**, RG1 1QH. Tel: 0118 937 3400. *British, Roman and medieval English coins, many from local finds, tradesmen's tokens and commemorative medals.*

• Rochdale Pioneers Museum (1905), 31 Toad Lane, **Rochdale**, OL12 ONU. Tel: 01706 524 920. *Roman and medieval coins from local finds, Rochdale trade tokens, miscellaneous British and foreign coins and medals.*

• Clifton Park Museum (1893), Clifton Park, **Rotherham**, S65 2AA. Tel: 01709 336 633. *Collection includes Roman coins from Templeborough Forts, medieval English coins from local hoards and a general collection of British coins.*

S

• Saffron Walden Museum (1832) (1939), Museum Street, **Saffron** Walden, CB10 1JL. Tel: 01799 510 333. *Ancient British, Roman, medieval and later coins, mainly from local finds and archaeological excavation, trade tokens and commemorative medals.*

• Verulamium Museum, St Michael's, **St Albans**, Herts . Tel: 01727 751 810. *Coins and artifacts excavated from the Roman town.*

• Salisbury and South Wiltshire Museum (1861), The Kings House 65 The Close, **Salisbury**, Wilts. Tel: 01722 332 151. *Collection of coins minted or found locally, including finds of Iron Age, Roman, Saxon and medieval coins, as well as 18th and 19th century tradesmen's tokens.*

• Richborough Castle Museum (1930), **Sandwich**, Kent. Tel: 0304 612013. *Roman coins of 1st–5th centuries from excavations of the Richborough site.*

• Rotunda Museum (1829), Vernon Road, **Scarborough**, YO11 2PS. Tel: 01723 353 665. Collection of *over 4,000 Roman coins, 1,500 English and 600 coins from local finds, siege pieces and trade.*

• Gold Hill Museum (1946), Gold Hill, **Shaftesbury**, Dorset, SP7 8JW. Tel: 01747 852 157. *Hoard of Saxon coins.*

• Weston Park Museum (1875), Western Bank, **Sheffield.** Tel: 0114 278 2600. *Over 5,000 coins of all periods, but mainly English and modern British. European coins, imperial Roman (including three hoards of about 500 coins each), Yorkshire trade tokens, British historical medals, campaign medals. Library.*

• Shrewsbury Museum and Art Gallery, The Music Hall, Market Street, **Shrewsbury.** Tel: 01743 258 885 *Coins minted at Shrewsbury 925-1180, Civil War coinage of 1642, Shropshire tradesmen's tokens, English coins and medals.*

• Atkinson Art Gallery (1878), Lord Street, **Southport,** Lancs. Tel: 01704 53333 *Roman coins.*

• Southwold Museum (1933), 9-11 Victoria Street, **Southwold**, IP18 6HZ. Tel: 07708 781317. *General collection of coins, specialised Suffolk trade tokens.*

• Stockport Museum (1860), 30-31 Market Place, **Stockport**, Cheshire SK1 1ES. Tel: 0161 474 4444 *Miscellaneous collection of coins, tokens and medals.*

• Museum in the Park (1899), Stratford Park, Stratford Road, **Stroud**, Glos GL5 4AF. Tel: 01453 7633 394. *Ancient British, Roman, Saxon, Norman, later medieval English, British coins and Gloucestershire trade tokens.*

• Sunderland Museum and Winter Gardens (1846), Burdon Road, **Sunderland,** Tyne & Wear SR1 1PP. Tel: 0191 553 2323. *Roman imperial, medieval and later English, including examples of the pennies minted at Durham, modern British and foreign coins, 17th-19th century tradesmen's tokens and local medallions.*

• Swansea Museum (1835), Victoria Road, **Swansea**, W. Glamorgan, SA1 1SN. Tel: 01792 653 763. *Coins and medals of local interest.*

T

• Tamworth Castle and Museum (1899), The Holloway, **Tamworth**, Staffs. Tel: 01827 709 626. *Anglo-Saxon coins, medieval English including coins of the Tamworth mint, later English and British coins, tokens, commemorative medallions and medals.*

• The Museum of Somerset, Taunton Castle, Castle Green, **Taunton**, Somerset TA1 4AA. Tel: 01823 255 088. *Celtic, Roman, Anglo-Saxon, early Medieval, tokens, medallions and banknotes. Strong emphasis on locally-found items.*

• Thurrock Museum and Heritage Srvice (1956), Second Floor, Thameside Complex, Orsett Road, Grays, Essex, RM17 5DX. Tel: 01375 413 965. *Roman coins.*

• Royal Cornwall Museum (1818), River Street, **Truro**, Cornwall TR1 2SJ. Tel: 01872 272 205. *Coins, tokens and medals pertaining principally to the county of Cornwall.*

W

• Wakefield Museum (1919), Burton Street, **Wakefield,** West Yorkshire WF1 2EB. Tel: 01924 305 376. *Roman and medieval English silver and copper coins.*

• Epping Forest District Museum, 39/41 Sun Street, **Waltham Abbey**, Essex, EN9 1EL. Tel: 01992 716882 *Ancient British, Roman and medieval coins, Essex tradesmen's tokensof local interest.*

• Warrington Museum and Art Gallery (1848). Bold Street, **Warrington,** Cheshire, WA1 1DR. Tel: 01925 442399. *Coins, medals and tokens.*

• Worcester City Museum (1833), Foregate Street, **Worcester.** Tel: 01905 25371. *Roman, medieval and later coins and tokens. Coins of the Worcester mint.*

• Wells Museum (18903), 8 Cathedral Green, **Wells**, Somerset. Tel: 01749 673 477. *Ancient and modern British and world coins, local trade tokens and medals.*

• Museum of Wigan Life (1878), 41 Library Street, **Wigan**, Lancashire. WN1 1NU Tel: 01942 828 128. *British, Commonwealth and foreign coins from about 1660 to the present. Roman coins from local sites, commemorative medals.*

• City Museum (1851), The Square, **Winchester**, Hants, SO23 9ES. Tel: 01962 863064. *Roman and medieval coins chiefly from local hoards and finds. Hampshire tradesmen's tokens and commemorative medals. Small reference library.*

• Wisbech and Fenland Museum (1835), Museum Square, **Wisbech**, Cambridgeshire, PE13 1ES. Tel: 01945 583 817, *British Roman, medieval and later coins, medals and tokens.*

Y

• York Castle Museum (1938), Eye of York, **York**, YO1 9RY. Tel: 01904 687 687. *English and British coins, campaign medals, orders and decorations, comemorative medals.*

• Jorvik Viking Centre (1984), Coppergate, **York, YO1 9WT.** Tel: 01904 615 505. *Coins and artefacts pertaining to the Viking occupation of York.*

• The Yorkshire Museum (1823), Museum Gardens, **York** YO1 7FR. Tel: 01904 687 687. *Roman imperial, medieval English and later coins, about 12,000 in all.*

Club
directory

Details given here are the names of Numismatic Clubs and Societies, their date of foundation, and their usual venues, days and times of meetings. Meetings are monthly unless otherwise stated. Finally, the telephone number of the club secretary is given; the names and addresses of club secretaries are withheld for security reasons, but full details may be obtained by writing to the Secretary of the British Association of Numismatic Societies, Bill Pugsley, bill@pugsley.co or visiting the website at www.coinclubs.org.uk.

Ayeshire Coin Club 1st Thurs, Oct to April, 19.30. Call for Venue, Tel: 07527 240 016

Banknote Society of Scotland (1994) Meetings are held four times a year in Edinburgh. Email, bnss2006@ntlworld.com

Bath & Bristol Numismatic Society (1950). The Globe Inn, Newton St Loe, Bath BA2 9BB 2nd Thu, 19.30. Email: jagmartin553@gmail.com.

Bedfordshire Numismatic Society (1966). 2nd Mon, call for venue details: 07541 461021

Birmingham Numismatic Society (1964). Friend's Meeting House, Bull Street. Email: bhamns@ hotmail.co.uk.

Matthew Boulton Lunar Society (1994). The Old School House, Chapel Lane, Birmingham, B47 6JX Tel: 01564 821 582.

British Banking History Society. 22 Delamere Road, Gatley, Cheadle, SK8 4PH.

British Numismatic Society (1903). Call for venue and dates; 02070161802.

Cambridgeshire Numismatic Society (1946). Friends' Meeting House, 12 Jesus Lane Cambridge, CB5 8BA. Call for dates. Tel: 01223 332 918.

Chester & North Wales Coin & Banknote Society (1996). Nags Head, Bunbury, Cheshire, CW6 9PB 4th Tue, 20.00. Tel: 01829 260 897.

Crewe & District Coin and Medal Society. Memorial Hall, Church Lane, Wistaston, Crewe, CW2 8ER. 2nd Tue, (exc Jan & July), 19.30 Tel: 07828 602 611.

Derbyshire Numismatic Society The Friends Meeting House, St Helen's Street, Derby. Tel: 01283 211623.

Devon & Exeter Numismatic Society, Courtenay Room, The St James Centre, Stadium Way, Exeter. 3rd Wed. Tel: 01395 568830.

Essex Numismatic Society (1966). Christchurch URC, 164 New London Road. 4th Fri (exc Dec), 20.00. Tel: 01279 814 216.

Glasgow & West of Scotland Numismatic Society (1947). Ibrox Parish Church Halls, Clifford Street, Glasgow, G51 1QH. 2nd Thu, Oct-April, 19.30. Tel: 07949 194036, Email: glasgowcoinclub@aol.com.

Harrow Coin Club (1968). The Scout Building, off Walton Road, Wealdstone, Harrow, HA1 4UX. 2nd Mon, 19.30. Tel: 0208 8952 8765.

Havering Numismatic Society (1967). Fairkytes Arts Centre, Billet Lane, Hornchurch, Essex, RM11 1AX 1st Tue, 19.30. Tel: 0208 5545 486. Email: mail@havering-ns.org.uk

Huddersfield Numismatic Society (1947). Lindley Liberal Club, 36 Occupation Road, Huddersfield, HD3 3EQ. 1st Mon (Sept to June) unless Bank Holiday then following Monday. Tel: 01484 866 814.

International Bank Note Society (London Branch) (1961). Spink, 69 Southampton Row, Bloomsbury, London, WC1B 4ET. Last Thu (exc Sept & Dec), 18.30.

International Bank Note Society (East Mids) , Highfields Community Fire Station, Hassocks Lane, Beeston, Nottingham, NG9 2 GQ. Last Saturday of every odd month. Tel: 0115 928 9720.

Ireland, Numismatic Society of (Northern Branch). Cooke/Instonians RFC, Shaws Bridge Sports Asson, 123 Milltown Road, Belfast. Call for dates; 07843 450597 www.numsocirelandnb.com.

Ireland, Numismatic Society of, Ely House, 8 Ely Place, Dublin 2. For dates and venues visit; 07843 450597, www.numismaticsocietyofireland.com.

Ipswich Coin Club, Archdeacons House, 11 Northgate Street, Ipswich, IP1 3BX. 2nd Weds. Tel; 0789 443 7847, www.ipnumsoc.org.uk.

Lancashire & Cheshire Numismatic Society (1933). Call for venue details. 3rd Sat, 14.00. Tel: 01204 849 469

London Numismatic Club (1947). Call for Venue details and dates; 0208 3030510 Email: g.buddle@btopenworld.com.

Loughborough Coin & Search Society (1964). Rosebery Medical Center, Rosebery Street, Loughborough, Leics, LE11 5DX 1st Thu, 19.30.

Norwich Coin & Medal Society, The White Horse Inn, Trowse, Norwich, NR14 8ST. 3rd Mon. Tel: 01603 617 127.

Numismatic Society of Nottinghamshire (1948). Highfield Fire Station, Hassocks Lane, Beeston, Nottingahm, NG9 2GQ. 2nd Mon (Sep-Apr). Tel: 0115 928 0347.

Orders & Medals Research Society (1942). Spink, 69 Southampton Row, Bloomsbury, London, WC1B 4ET. Last Monday of the month (that is not a Bank Holiday) of the odd numbered months plus April and October. 18.00.

Ormskirk & West Lancashire Numismatic Society (1970). The Eagle & Child, Maltkiln Lane, Bispham Green L40 1SN. 1st Thu, 20.15. Tel: 01704 232 494

Peterborough & District Numismatic Society (1967). Belsize Community Centre, Celta Road Peterborough, Cambs. 4th Tue (exc June, July & Aug), 19.30. Tel: 01733 567 763.

Plymouth Numismatic Society. 3rd Tue. Call for venue details. Tel: 07399 276295.

Reading Coin Club (1964). Abbey Baptist Church, Abbey Square, Reading, RG1 3BE 1st Mon, 19.00. Tel: 01344 774 155.

Royal Numismatic Society (1836). Warburg Institute, Woburn Square, London, WC1H 0AB. (some meetings held at Spink, 69 Southampton Row, Bloomsbury Road, London WC1B 4ET). 3rd Tues 18.00. Email: info@numismatics.org.uk. Tel: 0207 323 8541.

Southampton and District Numismatic Society (1953). Central Baptist Church, Devonshire Road, Polygon, Southampton, SO15 2GY. Email: sue717@btinternet.com.

South Manchester Numismatic Society. Nursery Inn, 258 Green Lane, Heaton Norris, Stockport, SK4 2NA. 1st and 3rd Tue (Mar–Oct), 1st Tue (Nov–Feb). Tel: 07818 422696.

South Wales & Monmouthshire Numismatic Society (1958). 1st Mon (except Bank Holidays when 2nd Mon), 19.30. For venue call Tel: 02920 561 564.

Tyneside Numismatic Society (1954). The Plough Inn, 369 Old Durham Road, Gateshead, NE9 5LA. 2nd Weds, 19.30. Tel: 07867 831 293

Wessex Numismatic Society (1948). Edward Wright Room, Beaufort Community Centre, Southbourne, Bournemouth, Dorset. 1st Tues (exc Aug), 20.00. Tel: 01425 501446.

Wiltshire Numismatic Society (1965). The Raven Inn, Poulshot, Nr. Devizes, Wiltshire. 3rd Weds, (March–Dec), 20.00. Tel: 01225 703143. Email: verityjeffery2@gmail.com.

Worthing & District Numismatic Society (1967). The Chatsworth Hotel, Worthing, BN11 3DU. 2nd Thu, 20.00. www.worthingnumismatics.co.uk.

Yorkshire Numismatic Society (1909). Email for venues and dates. Email: yorkshirenumismaticsociety@gmail.com.

IMPORTANT ORGANISATIONS

ADA
The Antiquities
Dealers Association
Secretary: Susan Hadida, Duke's Court, 32 Duke Street, London SW1Y 6DU

IBNS
International
Bank Note Society
UK Membership Secretary: Kelvin Revere
uk-secretary@theibns.org

ANA
The American
Numismatic Association
818 North Cascade Avenue, Colorado Springs, CO 80903, USA

RNS
Royal Numismatic Society
Dept of Coins & Medals, British Museum, London WC1B 3DG.

BNTA
The British Numismatic
Trade Association
Secretary: Christel Swan 3 Unwin Mansions, Queens Club Gardens, London, W14 9TH

BAMS
British Art Medal Society
Philip Attwood, Dept of Coins & Medals, British Museum, London WC1B 3DG.

IAPN
International Association of
Professional Numismatists
Secretary: Jean-Luc Van der Schueren, 14 Rue de la Bourse, B–1000, Brussels.

BNS
British Numismatic Society
Secretary: Peter Preston-Morley.
Email: secretary@britnumsoc.0rg

**Society activities are featured every month in the "Diary Section" of COIN NEWS magazine—available from all good newsagents or on subscription.
Telephone 01404 46972 for more details or log onto
www.tokenpublishing.com**

How we all missed those heady days of attending fairs in person! There was an enthusiastic return to numismatic events with many organisers reporting bumper attendance of keen, mask-wearing collectors. (A busy view of the Token Congress from previous years. In 2021 it was held in October at the Hilton Hotel in Northampton.)

Directory
of auctioneers

Listed here are the major auction houses which handle coins, medals, banknotes and other items of numismatic interest. Many of them hold regular public auctions, whilst others handle numismatic material infrequently. A number of coin companies also hold regular Postal Auctions—these are marked with a **℗**

2020 Auctions
Tel: 07826 550410, email: info@2020auctions.co.uk.
www.2020auctions.co.uk.

Auction World Company Ltd
1-15-5 Hamamatsucho,Minato-ku,
Tokyo, 105-0013 Japan. www.auction-world.co

Baldwin's Auctions
399 Strand, London, WC2R 0LX.
Tel: 020 7930 6879,
Email: auctions@baldwin.co.uk,
www.baldwin.co.uk.

Biddle & Webb
Icknield Square, Birmingham, B16 0PP.
Tel: 0121 455 8042, www.biddleandwebb.com

Blyth & Co
Arkenstall Center, Haddenham, Cambs, CB6
3XD. Tel: 01353 930 094, www.blyths.com

Bonhams (incorporating Glendinings)
Montpelier Street, Knightsbridge, London,
SW7 1HH. Tel: 020 7393 3914, www.bonhams.com.

BSA Auctions
Units 1/2, Cantilupe Court, Cantilupe Road, Ross on
Wye, Herefordshire, HR9 7AN . Tel: 01989 769 529,
www.the-saleroom.com

cgb.fr
36, Rue Vivienne, 75002, Paris, France.
Email: contact@cgb.fr, www.cgb.fr.

Chilcotts Auctioneers
Silver Street, Honiton, EX14 1QN. Tel: 01404 47783,
email: info@chilcottsauctioneers.co.uk

Christies
8 King Street, St James's, London SW1Y 6QT.
Tel: 020 7839 9060.

Classical Numismatic Group Inc (Seaby Coins)
20 Bloomsbury Street, London, WC1B 3QA.
Tel: 020 7495 1888 ,fax 020 7499 5916,
Email: cng@cngcoins.com,
www.historicalcoins.com. **℗**

The Coin Cabinet
Tel 0800 088 5350, www.thecoincabinet.co.uk.

Corbitts
5 Moseley Sreet, Newcastle upon Tyne NE1 1YE.
Tel: 0191 232 7268, fax 0191 261 4130.
www.corbitts.com

Croydon Coin Auctions
4 Sussex Street, Rhyl LL18 1SG. Tel: 01492 440763,
www.croydoncoinauctions.com.

Davissons Ltd.
PO Box 323, Cold Spring, MN 56320 USA.
Tel: 001 320 685 3835, info@davcoin.com,
www.davcoin.com.

Dix Noonan Webb (IAPN)
16 Bolton Street, Mayfair, London, W1J 8BQ
Tel: 020 7016 1700, auctions@dnw.co.uk,
www.dnw.co.uk.

Duke's
Brewery Square, Dorchester, Dorset DT1 1GA.
Tel: 01305 265 080, enquiries@dukesauctions.
com www.dukes-auctions.com

David Duggleby Auctioneer
The Vine Street Salerooms, Scarborough,
North Yorkshire YO11 1XN. Tel: 01723 507111

English Coin Auctions
3 Elders Street, Scarborough, YO11 1DZ
Tel: 01723 364 760, wwwenglishcoinauctionscom

Jean Elsen & ses Fils s.a.
Avenue de Tervueren 65, B–1040, Brussels.
Tel: 0032 2 734 6356, Email: numismatique@e
lsen.euwww.elsen.eu.

Fellows & Sons
Augusta House, 19 Augusta Street, Hockley,
Birmingham, B18 6JA. Tel: 0121 212 2131,
www.fellows.co.uk.

B. Frank & Son
3 South Avenue, Ryton, Tyne & Wear NE40 3LD.
Tel: 0191 413 8749, Email: bfrankandson@aol.com,
www.bfrankandson.com.

Gadoury
57, rue Grimaldi, 98000 MONACO.
Tel: 0 377 93 25 12 96, Email: contact@gadoury.com,
www.gadoury.com.

Goldberg Coins & Collectibles
11400 W. Olympic Blvd, Suite 800, Los Angeles,
Hills CA 90064. Tel: 001 310.551 2646, info@
goldbergcoins.com, www.goldbergcoins.com.

Gorny & Mosch Gmbh
Giessener Münzhandlung, Maximiliansplatz 20,
80333 Munich. Phone: +49-89/24 22 643-0,
info@gmcoinart.de

Heritage World Coin Auctions
6 Shepherd Street, Mayfair, London, W1J 7JE.
Tel: 001 214 528 3500, Bid@HA.com
www.ha.com).

International Coin Exchange
Charter House, 5 Pembroke Row, Dublin 2. Tel:
00353 8684 93355, email: iceauctiongalleries@
gmail.com, www.ice-auction.com.

Kleeford Coin Auctions
Tel: 01773 528 743, email: kleeford@btinternet.
com 📞

Fritz Rudolf Künker
Nobbenburger, Strasse 4A, 49076, Osnabrüeck,
Germany. Tel: 0049 5419 62020, fax: 0049 541 96 20
222, email: service@kuenker.de, www.kuenker.de

Lawrence Fine Art Auctioneers
The Linen Yard, South Street, Crewkerne, Somerset
TA18 8AB. Tel: 01460 73041, email: enquiries@
lawrences.co.uk, www.lawrences.co.uk.

Lockdale Coins
52 Barrack Square, Martlesham Heath, Ipswich,
Suffolk, IP5 3RF. Tel: 01473 627 110, sales@
lockdales.com, www.lockdales.com.

London Coins
Tel: 01474 871464, email: info@londoncoins.
co.uk, www.londoncoins.co.uk.

Mavin International
20 Kramat Lane, #01-04/05 United House,
Singapore 228773. Tel: +65 6238 7177,

MDC Monaco sarl
Allées Lumières Park Palace, 27 Avenue de la Costa,
98000 Monaco. Tel: +377 93 25 00 42, info@mdc.mc,
www.mdc.mc.

Mitchells
47 Station Road, Cockermouth, Cumbria, CA13 9PZ.
www.mitchellsantiques.co.uk

Morton & Eden Ltd
Nash House, St Georges Street, London W1S
2FQ. Tel: 020 7493 5344, info@mortonandeden.com,
www.mortonandeden.com.

Mowbray Collectables
Private Bag 63000, Wellington 6140, New Zealand
Tel: +64 6 364 8270, email: auctions@mowbrays.nz,
www.mowbraycollectables.com

Myntauktioner i Sverige AB
Banergatan 17, 115 22 Stockholm.

Nesbits Auctioneer & Valuers
7 Clarendon Road, Soouthsea, Hants, PO5 2ED.
Tel: 02392 295568, email: auctions@nesbits.co.uk

Noble Numismatics
169 Macquire Street, Sydney, NSW 2000
Australia. Tel: 0061 2922 34578, fax: 0061 29233
6009, Email: info@noble.com.au, www.noble.com.au.

Numismatica Ars Classica NAC AG
Suite 1, Claridge House, 32 Davies Street,
London W1K 4ND. Tel: 020 7839 7270,
email: info@arsclassicacoins.com.

Numis-Or
4, Rue des Barques 1207, Geneva Switzerland
email: info@numisor.ch, www.numisor.ch.

Pacific Rim Online Auction
P O Box 847, North Sydney, NSW 2060, Australia. Tel
0061 29588 7111,
www.pacificrimonlineauctions.com
Online coin auction.

Penrith, Farmers' & Kidds PLC
Skirsgill Saleroom, Penrith, Cumbria, CA11 0DN.
Tel: 01768 890 781, email: info@pfkauctions.
co.uk,www.pfkauctions.co.uk

Roma Numismatics Ltd
20 Fitzroy Square, London, W1T 6EJ.
Tel: 020 7121 6518. www.romanumismatics.com

Chris Rudd Ltd (IAPN, BNTA)
PO Box 1425, Norwich, NR10 5WS
Tel: 01263 735 007, email: liz@celticcoins.com,
www.celticcoins.com

Simmons Gallery
PO Box 104, Leytonstone, London. Tel: 020 8989
8097. simmonsgallery.co.uk. 📞

Smiths of Newent
The Old Chapel, Culver Street, Newent, GL18 1DB.
Tel: 01531 821 776, email: enquiries@smithsauction-
room.co.uk, www.smithsnewentauctions.co.uk

Sovereign Rarities Ltd (BNTA)
17–19 Maddox Street, London W1S 2QH Tel: 0203
019 1185, www.sovr.co,uk.

Spink & Son Ltd
69 Southampton Row, Bloomsbury, London
WC1B 4ET. Tel: 020 7563 4000, fax 020 7563
4066, email: concierge@spink.com,
www.spink.com.

Stacks, Bowers and Ponterio
1231 East Dyer Road, Suite 100, Santa Ana,
California, 92705, USA. Tel: 001 800 458 4646,
email: info@StacksBowers.com,
www.stacksbowers.com.

St James's Auctions
10 Charles II Street, London, SW1Y 4AA.
Tel: 020 7930 7888, fax 0207 930 8214,
Email: info@sjauctions.com,
www.sjauctions.com.

Tennants Auctioneers
The Auction Centre, Leyburn, North Yorkshire,
DL8 5SG. Tel: 01969 623 780, email: enquiry@
tennants-ltd.co.uk, www.tennants.co.uk.

The-saleroom.com
The Harlequin Building, 65 Southwark Street,
London, SE1 0HR. Tel: 0203 725 555, email: sup
port@auctiontechnologygroup.com,
www.the-saleroom.com.

Thomson Roddick Auctioneers
The Auction Centre, Marconi Road, Carlisle,
CA2 7NA. Tel: 01228 528 939, email: carlisle@
thomsonroddick.com. www.thomsonroddick.com.

Timeline Auctions
The Court House, 363 Main Road, Harwich,
Essex CO12 4DN Tel: 01277 815 121, email:
enquiries@timelineauctions.com
www.timelineauctions.com.

Trevanion and Dean
The Joyce Building, Station Road, Whitchurch, SY13
1RD. Tel: 01948 800 202, email: info@trevanionand
dean.co.uk

Warwick & Warwick
Chalon House, Scarbank, Millers Road, Warwick
CV34 5DB. Tel: 01926 499 031 fax 01926 491 906,
email: richard.beale@warwickandwarwick.com,
www.warwickandwarwick.com.

Whyte's Auctions
38 Molesworth Street, Dublin 2, Ireland.
Tel: +00 3531 676 2888, www.whytes.com.

Peter Wilson Fine Art Auctioneers LLP
Victoria Gallery, Market Street, Nantwich,
Cheshire, CW5 5DG. Tel: 01270 623878, email:
auctions@peterwilson.co.uk, www.peterwilson.
co.uk

Woolley & Wallis
51-61 Castle Street, Salisbury, Wiltshire SP1 3SU.
Tel: 01722 424500, email: nc@woolleyandwallis.co.uk,
www.woolleyandwallis.co.uk

Directory
of fairs

Listed below are the names of the fair organisers, their venue details where known along with contact telephone numbers. Please call the organisers direct for information on dates etc.

Aberdeen
Doubletree by Hilton Hotel Aberdeen TreeTops, Springfield Road, Aderdeen, AB15 7AQ. *Alba Fairs Tel: 07767 020343.*

ANA World's Fair of Money (2021)
Donald E. Stephens Convention Center; Rosemont (Chicago), IL, United States. Organised by the . American Numismatic Association and held in a different venue each year. *www.money.org.*

Berlin. World Money Fair
Estrel Convention Center, Sonnenalle, 12057 Berlin, Germany. *Tel: +41(0)61 3825504.*

Berlin
Messegelände am Funkturm, Hall 11/2, Messedamm 22, 14055 Berlin. Numismata International Tel: +49 (0) 89 268 359.

Birmingham
National Motor Cycle Museum, Bickenhill, Birmingham. *Midland Stamp & Coin Fair Tel: 01694 731 781, www.coinfairs.co.uk.*

Britannia Medal Fair
Carisbrooke Hall, The Victory Services Club, 63/79 Seymour Street, London, W2 2HF. *DNW Tel: 020 7016 1700.*

Cardiff
City Hall, Cathays Park, Cardiff, CF10 3ND. *M. J. Promotions. Tel: 01792 415293.*

Cheltenham
The Regency Hotel, Gloucester Road, GL51 0SS. St Andrews United Reform Church, Montpellier, GL50 1SP. *Mark Grimsley Tel: 0117 962 3203.*

Crewe
Memorial Hall, Church Lane, Wistaston, Crewe. CW2 8ER. Crewe & District Coin & Medal Society. Tel: 01270 661181.

Dublin Coin Fair
Serpentine Hall, RDS, Ballsbridge, Dublin 4. *Mike Kelly Tel: 00353 86 8714 880.*

East Grinstead
Chequer Mead Arts Center, De La Warr Road, East Grinstead, RH19 3BS. *Malcolm Green Tel: 01342 327 554*

Exeter
The America Hall, De La Rue Way, Pinhoe, EX4 8PX. *Michael Hale Collectors Fairs Tel: 01749 677669.*

Frankfurt 2019
Ludwig-Erhard-Anlage1, 60327 Frankfurt, Hesse. *Numismata International Tel: +49 (0) 89 268 359.*

Harrogate
Old Swan Hotel, Swan Road, HG1 2SR. *Bloomsbury Fairs Tel: 01242 898 107.*

Inverness
Kingsmills Hotel, Culcabock Road, Inverness, IV2 3LP. *Alba Fairs Tel: 07767 020343.*

London
Holiday Inn, Coram Street, Bloomsbury, WC1 1HT. London Coin Fair, *Lu Vessid Tel: 01694 731 781*

London
Bloomsbury Hotel, 16-22 Great Russell Street, WC1 3NN. *Bloomsbury Fairs Tel: 01242 898 107.*

London IBNS
Venue as above. *IBNS Web: www.theibns.org*

Maastricht
Maastricht Exhibiton and Convention Center, Forum 100, 6229 GV Maastricht, The Netherlands. *mif events Tel: +32 (0) 89 46 09 33.*

Munich 2020
Lilienthalallee 40, 80939 Munich. *Numismata International Tel: +49 (0) 89 268 359.*

New York International Numismatic Convention 2020
Grand Hyatt Hotel, 109 East 42nd Street, New York 10022, USA. *www.nyinc.info/*

Plymouth
The Guildhall, Armada Way, PL1 2ER. *Peter Jones Tel: 01489 582673.*

Salisbury
City Hall, Salisbury, SP2 7TU. Dauwalders of Salisbury. *Tel: 01722 412100*

Wakefield
Cedar Court Hotel, Denby Dale Road, Calder Grove, Wakefield, WF4 3QZ. *Eddie Smith Tel: 01522 684 681.*

Westcountry Collectors Fair
The Guildhall, Royal Parade, Plymouth, PL1 2EJ. *www.facebook.com/PlymACF*

Weston-super-Mare
Victoria Methodist Church Hall, Station Road, BS23 1XU. *Michael Hale Tel: 01749 677 669*

Worthing
Chatsworth Hotel, The Steyne, Worthing, BN11 3DU. Organised by the Worthing & District Numismatic Society. *Tel: 01903 239867*

York
The Grandstand, York Race Course, YO23 1EX *York Coin Fair, Tel: 01793 513 431 (Chris Rainey), 020 8946 4489 (Kate Puleston).*

THE LONDON COIN FAIR

HOLIDAY INN
London, Bloomsbury,
Coram Street,
WC1N 1HT

2021 dates: 6th November

2022 dates: 5th February,
4th June, 3rd September
& 5th November

70+ dealers in GB
& foreign coins
Ancient coins and antiquities
Medals, tokens and notes

THE MIDLAND COIN FAIR

NATIONAL MOTORCYCLE MUSEUM
Bickenhill, Birmingham,
B92 0EJ

(Opposite the NEC on the M42/A45 junction)

2021 dates: 10th October, 14th
November & 12th December

2022 dates: 9th January,
13th February, 13th March,
10th April, 8th May, 12th June,
10th July, 14th August,
11th September, 9th October,
13th November & 11th December

All dates are dependent on Covid 19 restrictions in place at the time.
Please check our website for up to date information.

For more information please contact:
Lu Veissid, Hobsley House, Frodesley, Shrewsbury SY5 7HD
Tel: 01694 731781   Email: l.veissid@btinternet.com

www.coinfairs.co.uk

Like us on facebook 🄵 @ coin and medal fairs

Dealers
directory

The dealers listed below have comprehensive stocks of coins and medals, unless otherwise stated. Specialities, where known, are noted. Many of those listed are postal dealers only, so to avoid disappointment always make contact by telephone or mail in the first instance, particularly before travelling any distance.

Abbreviations:
ADA — — Antiquities Dealers Association
ANA — American Numismatic Association
BADA — British Antique Dealers Association
BNTA — British Numismatic Trade Association
IAPN — International Association of Professional Numismatists
IBNS — International Bank Note Society
P — — Postal only
L — — Publishes regular lists

ABC Coins & Tokens
  PO Box 52, Alnwick, Northumberland, NE66 1YE.
  Tel: 01665 603 851, www.abccoinsandtokens.com.
  British (particularly Scottish) and world coins, tokens.
Absolutely Banknotes (Chris Burch)
  Tel: 07870 504849, www.absolutelybanknotes.co.uk
  English and Scottish notes. Treasury to modern.
A. Ackroyd (IBNS)
  62 Albert Road, Parkstone, Poole, Dorset BH12 2DB.
  Tel/fax: 01202 739 039, www.AAnotes.com.
  P L *Banknotes and Cheques*
Allgold Coins
  P.O Box 260, Wallington, SM5 4H. Tel:
  0844 544 7952, email: sales@allgoldcoins.co.uk,
  wwwallgoldcoins.co.uk. *Quality Sovereigns.*
A. J. W. Coins
  Tel: 08456 807 087, email: andrewwide@ajw-coins.
  co.uk, www.ajw-coins.com. **P** *Sovereigns and CGS-UK specialist.*
AMR COINS
  PO Box 352, Leeds, LS19 9GG. Tel: 07527 569 308,
  www.amrcoins.com. *Quality English Coins specialising in rare hammered and milled coins of exceptional quality.*
Ancient & Gothic
  Tel: 01202 431 721 **P L** *Greek, Roman, Celtic and Biblical coins. English Hammered Coins & Antiquities.*
Asprey Coins (BNTA)
  Email: info@aspreycoins.co.uk, Tel: 01243 915155.
  www.aspreycoins.co.uk
  British Coins and Banknotes
ARL Collectables
  P O Box 380, Reigate, Surrey, RH2 2BU. Tel: 01737 242 975, www.litherlandcollectables.com.
  Coins, Banknotes, Medallions and Paper Emphemera.

Athens Numismatic Gallery
  Akadimias 39, Athens 10672, Greece. Tel: 0030 210
  364 8386, www.athensnumismaticgallery.com.
  Rare & Common Sovereigns. British & World Coins.
Atlas Numismatics
  Tel: 001 718643 4383, email, info@atlasnumismatics.
  com, www.atlasnumismatics.com
  Ancient, W **ABC Coins & Tokens**
  P and *US Coinage*
ATS Bullion (BNTA)
  2, Savoy Court, Strand. London, WC2R 0EZ.
  Tel: 020 7240 4040, email: sales@atsbullion.com,
  www.atsbullion.com. *Bullion and Modern Coins.*
A. H. Baldwin & Sons Ltd (ANA, BADA, BNTA, IAPN)
  399 The Strand, London WC2R 0LX.
  Tel: 020 7930 6879, fax 020 7930 9450, email:
  coins@baldwin.co.uk *Coins, Tokens, Numismatic Books.*
B & G Coins
  PO Box 1219, Spalding, PE11 9FY. Email: info@
  bandgcoins.co.uk. *Coins, Banknotes and Medals*
Baird & Co
  20 - 21 Gemini Business Park, Hornet Way, London,
  E6 7FF. Tel: 020 7474 1000, www.goldline.co.uk.
  Bullion Merchants
T. Barna
  *64 High Street, Lyndhurst, SO43 7BJ. Email: tbarna_
  and sonuk@hotmail.com. Ancient Greek and Roman Coins.*
Bath Stamp and Coin Shop
  12 -13 Pulteney Bridge, Bath, Avon BA2 4AY.
  Tel: 01225 431 918, *Vintage Coins and Banknotes.*
Michael Beaumont
  PO Box 8, Carlton, Notts NG4 4QZ. Tel: 0115
  9878361.**P** *Gold & Silver bullion, English and Foreign Coins.*
Beaver Coin Room (BNTA)
  57 Philbeach Gardens, London SW5 9ED.
  Tel: 020 7373 4553. **P** *European coins and medals.*
R. P. & P. J. Beckett
  Maes y Derw, Capel Dewi, Llandyssul, Dyfed
  SA44 4PJ. Tel: 01559 395 276, email:
  beckett@xin.co.uk. **P** *Coin Sets and Banknotes.*
Lloyd Bennett (BNTA)
  PO Box 2, Monmouth, Gwent NP25 3YR. Tel:
  07714 284 939, email: Lloydbennett@Coinofbritain.
  biz, www.coinsofbritain.com *English Hammered and Milled Coins.*

Berkshire Coin Centre
35 Castle Street, Reading, RG1 7SB. Tel: 0118 957 5593. *British and World Coins. Militaria.*

Stephen J. Betts
49-63 Spencer Street, Hockley, Birmingham B18 6DE. Tel: 0121 233 2413 **P L**, *Medieval and Modern Coins, Counters, Jetons, Tokens and Countermarks.*

Bigbury Mint
Unit 1 River Park, Ermington, Devon, PL21 9NT. Tel: 01548 830717. *Specialists in reproduction Hammered Coins*

Jon Blyth
Office 63, 2 Lansdowne Row, Mayfair, London W1J 6HL. Tel:07919 307 645, jonblyth@hotmail.com, www.jonblyth.com. *Specialists in quality British Coins*

Bonhams (incorporating Glendinings)
Montpelier Street, Knightsbridge, London, SW7 1HH. Tel: 0207 393 3914, www.bonhams.com.

Barry Boswell and Kate Bouvier
24 Townsend Lane, Upper Boddington, Daventry, Northants, NN11 6DR. Tel: 01327 261 877, email: kate@thebanknotestore.com. *British and World Banknotes.*

James & Chester Brett
jc.brett@btinternet.com **P L** *British and World Coins.*

Stephen Betts
4 Victoria Street, Narborough, Leicester, LE19 2DP. **P L** *World Coins, Tokens, Countermarks, Jettsons, Medallions etc.*

J. Bridgeman Coins
129a Blackburn Road, Accrington, Lancs Tel: 01254 384757. *British & World Coins.*

Brittonum
PO Box 3, 41 Oxford Street, Leamington Spa, CV32 4RA Tel: 07768 645 686, email: info@brittonum.com www.brittonum.com. *British Coins and Medals.*

BRM Coins
3 Minshull Street, Knutsford,Cheshire, WA16 6HG. Tel: 01565 651 480. *British Coins.*

Bucks Coins
St Mary's House, Duke Street, Norwich NR3 1QA Callers by appointment only. Tel: 01603 927 020. *English Milled Coins, Celtic and Roman.*

Iain Burn
2 Compton Gardens, 53 Park Road, Camberley, Surrey GU15 2SP. Tel: 01276 23304. *Bank of England & Treasury Notes.*

Cambridgeshire Coins
12 Signet Court, Swanns Road Cambridge, CB5 8LA. Tel: 01223 503 073, email, info cambridgeshirecoins.com, wwwcambridgeshirecoins.com. *Coins, Banknotes and Accessories.*

Castle Galleries
81 Castle Street, Salisbury, Wiltshire SP1 3SP. Tel: 01722 333 734. *British Coins and collectables.*

Cathedral Coins
23 Kirkgate, Rippon, North Yorkshire, HG4 1PB. Tel: 01765 701 400

Cathedral Court Medals
First Floor Office, 30A Market Place, West Ripon, North Yorks HG4 1BN. Tel: 01765 601 400. *Coin and Medal Sales. Medal Mounting and Framing.*

Cathedral Stamps & Coins
Unit B14, KCR Industrial Estate, Ravensdale Park, Kimmage, Co. Dublin, Ireland. Tel: +353 1 490 6392 *Coins, medals, banknotes & accessories.Stockist of Token Publishing titles in Ireland.*

Central Bank of Ireland
PO Box 559, Dublin 1. Tel: +353 (0) 1248 3605, Ireland. *Issuer of new Coin and Banknote issues of Ireland. Commemorative Coins and Coin Sets*

Lance Chaplin
17 Wanstead Lane, Ilford, Essex IG1 3SB. Tel: 020 8554 7154. www.shaftesburycoins.com. **P L***Roman, Greek, Celtic, Hammered Coins and Antiquities.*

Chard (BNTA)
32-36 Harrowside, Blackpool, FY4 1RJ. Tel: 01253 343081, www.chards.co.uk, *British and World Coins.*

Charing Cross Collectors' Market
Charing Cross, 1, Villiers Street/Northumberland Ave, London.Tel: 07540 144433, www.charingcrossmarket.com, *Market in Central London with dealers offering coins, stamps, postcards, medals & ephemera.*

Jeremy Cheek Coins Ltd
Tel: 01923 450385/07773 872686, email: jeremycoins@aol.com. *Advice, valuation and representation at auctions.*

Simon Chester Coins
196, High Road, London, Farnham, N22 8HH Tel: 07774 886688, email: simosimonchestercoins. com. *British Milled Coins*

Nigel A. Clark
28 Ulundi Road, Blackheath, London SE3 7UG. Tel: 020 8858 4020, email: nigel.a.clark@btinternet. com. **P L** *17th & 19th century Tokens. Farthings.*

Classical Numismatic Group (IAPN)
20 Bloomsbury Street, London, WC1B 3QA. Tel: 020 7495 1888, email cng@cngcoins.com, www.cngcoins.com. **P** *Ancient and world coins. Publishers of the Classical Numismatic Review. Regular High Quality Auctions of Ancient Coins.*

Paul Clayton (BNTA)
PO Box 21, Wetherby, West Yorkshire LS22 5JY. Tel: 01937 582 693. *Modern Gold Coins.*

André de Clermont (BNTA)
10 Charles II Street, London, SW1Y 4AA. Tel: 020 7584 7200. *World Coins, especially Islamic.*

M. Coeshaw
PO Box 115, Leicester LE3 8JJ. Tel: 0116 287 3808. **P** *Coins, Banknotes, Coin Albums and Cases.*

Philip Cohen Numismatics (ANA, BNTA)
20 Cecil Court, Charing Cross Road, London, WC2N 4HE. Tel: 020 7379 0615, www.coinheritage. co.uk

Coin & Collectors Centre
PO Box 22, Pontefract, West Yorkshire WF8 1YT. Tel: 01977 704 112, email sales@coincentre. co.uk, www.coincentre.co.uk. **P***British Coins.*

Coinage of England
P.O. Box 442, Deal, Kent, CT14 4DE Tel: 01304 2712 37, Email: info@coinageofengland. co.uk. *Fine and Rare English Coins.*

Coincraft (ANA, IBNS)
45 Great Russell Street, London, WC1B 3JL. Tel: 020 7636 1188 or 020 7637 8785, fax 020 7323 2860, email: info@coincraft.com. **L** (newspaper format). *Coins and Banknotes.*

Coinote
74 Elwick Road, Hartlepool TS26 9AP. Tel: 01429 890 894. www.coinnote.co.uk. *Coins, Medals, Banknotes and Accessories.*

Coins on a Budget
wwwcoinsonabudget.com. *Incorporating budget stamps. World Coins and Banknotes.*

Coinswap.co.uk
Swap, Sell or Trade Coins.

Coins of Canterbury
PO Box 47, Faversham, Kent,, ME13 7HX. Tel: 01795
531 980. **P** *English Coins.*

Coins of the Realm
PO Box 12131, Harlow, Essex, CM20 9LY.
www.coinsoftherealm.com. *Dealers in Precious and
Historical Coinage*

Colonial Collectables
P.O.Box 35625, Browns Bay, Auckland 0753, New
Zealand. Email: richard@colonialcollectables.com
British & World Coins.

Collectors' World (Mark Ray)
190 Wollaton Road, Wollaton, Nottingham NG8 1HJ.
www.collectorsworld-nottingham.com.
Tel: 01159 280 347. *Coins, Banknotes, Accessories.*

Constania CB
15 Church Road, Northwood, Middlesex, HA6 1AR.
P *Roman and Medieval Hammered Coins.*

Colin Cooke
P.O. Box 602, Altrincham, WA14 5UN. Tel: 0161
927 9524, fax 0161 927 9540, email coins@colin
cooke.com, www.colincooke.com. **L**British Coins.*

Colonial Coins & Medals
218 Adelaide Street, Brisbane, QLD 4001.
Email: coinshop@bigpond.net.au.
Auctions of World Coins.

Coopers Coins
PO Box 12703, Brentwood, Essex, CM14 9RB.
*Tel: 01277 560348, email: jack@cooperscoins.com.
wwwcooperscoins.com. British Coins.*

Copperbark Ltd
Suite 35, 37, St Andrew's Street, Norwich, NR2 4TP.
Tel: 07834 434 780, email: copperbark.ltd@gmail.
com, www.copperbark.com. *English, Russian and
17th Century Tokens.*

Corbitts (BNTA)
5 Mosley Street, Newcastle Upon Tyne NE1 1YE.
Tel: 0191 232 7268, fax: 0191 261 4130. *Dealers and
Auctioneers of all Coins and Medals.*

David Craddock
PO Box 3785, Camp Hill, Birmingham, B11 2NF.
Tel: 0121 733 2259 **L**Crown to Farthings. Copper
and Bronze Specialist. Some foreign.*

Roy Cudworth
8 Park Avenue, Clayton West, Huddersfield HD8
9PT. *British and World Coins.*

Curtis Coin Care
www.curtiscoincare.com. *Numismatic accessories
and storage solutions.*

Paul Dawson
47 The Shambles, York, YO1 7XL. Tel: 01904 654
769, email: pauldawsonyork@hotmail.com, www.
pauldawsonyork.co.uk. *Ancient and British coins,
medals.*

Mark Davidson
PO Box 197, South Croydon, Surrey, CR3 0ZD.
Tel: 020 8651 3890. *Ancient, Hammered & milled
Coinage.*

Paul Davies Ltd (ANA, BNTA, IAPN)
PO Box 17, Ilkley, West Yorkshire LS29 8TZ.
Tel: 01943 603 116, fax 01943 816 326, paul@
pauldaviesltd.co.uk. **P** *World Coins. British Gold
and silver bullion.*

Paul Davis
PO Box 418, Birmingham, B17 0RZ.
Tel: 0121 427 7179. *British and World Coins.*

R. Davis
Tel: 01332 862 755 days / 740828 evenings, email:
robdaviscc@gmail.com. *Maker of Traditional Coin
Cabinets.*

Ian Davison
PO Box 256, Durham DH1 2GW. Tel 0191 3750 808.
L *English Hammered and Milled Coins 1066–1910.*

Davissons
PO Box 323, Cold Spring, MN, 56320, USA.
Tel: (001)320 685 3835, Email: infodavcoin.com,
www.davcoin.com. North American Specialists.
British Coins, Tokens and Medals.*

Patrick Deane
Buckfastleigh, Devon. Tel: 01364 643969.
*Tudors to Victoria. Hammered and milled
gold and silver. 17th, 18th and 19th c. tokens.*

Dei Gratia
PO Box 3568, Buckingham MK18 4ZS Tel: 01280
848 000.**P L** *Pre–Roman to Modern Coins.
Antiquities, Banknotes.*

Den of Antiquity
PO Box 1114, Cambridge, CB25 9WJ. Tel: 01223
863 002, www.denofantiquity.co.uk.)
Ancient and Medieval Coins.

Clive Dennett (BNTA)
66 St Benedicts Street, Norwich, Norfolk, NR2 4AR.
Tel: 01603 624 315, **L** *Specialising in paper money.*

C. J. Denton (ANA, BNTA, FRNS)
PO Box 25, Orpington, Kent BR6 8PU. Tel: 01689
873 690.**P** *Irish Coins.*

Michael Dickinson (ANA, BNTA)
Ramsay House, 825 High Road Finchley, London
N12 8UB. Tel: 0181 441 7175.**P**
British and World Coins.

Douglas Saville
Tel: 0118 918 7628, www.douglassaville.com. *Out
of Print, Second-Hand and Rare Coin and Medal
Books.*

Eagle Coins
Winterhaven, Mourneabbey, Mallow, Co. Cork,
Ireland. Tel: 010 35322 29385.**P L** *Irish Coins.*

East of England Coins
Leprosy Mission Orton Goldhay, Peterborough,
Cambridgeshire, PE2 5GZ. Tel: 01733235277
Coins, Tokens and Banknotes

John Eccles
www.eccleswellington.co.nz. *New Zealand and
Pacific Islands Coins and Banknotes*

Educational Coin Company
Box 892, Highland, New York 12528, USA. Tel:001
845 691 6100. *World Banknotes.*

Christopher Eimer (ANA, BNTA, IAPN)
PO Box 352 London NW11 7RF. Tel; 020 8458 9933,
email: art@christophereimer.co.uk **P**
Commemorative Medals.

Malcolm Ellis Coins
Petworth Road, Witley, Surrey, GU8 5LX. Tel: 01428
685 566, www.malcolmelliscoins.co.uk). *Collectors
and Dealers of British and Foreign Coins*

Elm Hill Collectables
41-43 Elm Hill, Norwich, Norfolk NR3 1HG. Tel:
01603 627 413. *Coins & Banknotes .*

Europa Numismatics (ANA, BNTA)
PO Box 119, High Wycombe, Bucks HP11 1QL.
Tel: 01494 437 307 **P** *European Coins.*

Evesham Stamp & Coin Centre
Magpie Antiques, Manchester House,1 High Street,
Evesham, Worcs WR11 4DA. Tel: 01386 41631.
British Coins.

Robin Finnegan Stamp Shop
83 Skinnergate, Darlington, Co Durham DL3 7LX.
Tel: 01325 489 820/357 674. *World coins.*

Format of Birmingham Ltd (ANA, BNTA, IBNS)
PO Box 1276, Cheltenham, Gloucestershire, GL50
9ZW. Tel: 01242 518 495. *Coins, tokens, medals.*

B. Frank & Son
3 South Avenue, Ryton, Tyne & Wear NE40 3LD.
Tel: 0191 413 8749, Email: bfrankandson@aol.
com, www.bfrankandson.com. *Coins, notes, tokens.*

Galata Coins Ltd (ANA)
The Old White Lion, Market Street, Llanfylin,
Powys SY22 5BX. Tel: 01691 648 765.**P***British and World Coins.*

A. & S. Gillis
59 Roy Kilner Way, Wombwell, Barnsley,
South Yorkshire S73 8DY. Tel: 01226 750 371,
www.gilliscoins.com. *Ancient Coins and Antiquities.*

Richard Gladdle—Northamptonshire
Suite 80, 29/30 Horse Fair, Banbury, Oxfordshire,
OX16 0BW. Tel: 01327 858 511, email: gladdle@
plumpudding.org. *Tokens.* **P L**

GM Coins
Tel: 01242 627 344, email: info@gmcoinsco.
uk, www.gmcoins.co.uk. *Hammered and Milled Coins.*

Adrian Gorka Bond
Tel: 07500 772 080, email: sales@ 1stsovereign.
co.uk, www.1stsovereign.co.uk. *World gold coins*

Goulborn
4 Sussex Street, Rhyl LL18 1SG. Tel: 01745
338 112. *English Coins and Medallions.Organiser of Chester Coin Auctions.*

Ian Gradon
PO Box 359, Durham DH7 6WZ. Tel 0191 3719 700,
email: rarebanknote@gmail.com, www.worldnotes.
co.uk. **L** *World Banknotes.*

Eric Green—Agent in UK for Ronald J. Gillio Inc
1013 State Street, Santa Barbara, California, USA
93101. Tel: 020 8907 0015, Mobile 0468 454948.
Gold Coins, Medals and Paper Money of the World.

Philip Green (GB Classic Coins)
Suite 207, 792 Wilmslow Road, Didsbury,
Manchester M20 6UG. Tel: 0161 440 0685. *Gold Coins.*

Gurnhills of Leicester
8 Nothampton Street, Leicester, LE1 1PA.Tel: 07434
010 925. *British and World Coins and Banknotes.*

Halls Hammered Coins
From early Saxon to late Stuart.
Tel: 07830 019 584 www.hallshammeredcoins.com

Anthony Halse
PO Box 1856, Newport, Gwent NP18 2WA. Tel:
01633 413 238.**P L***English/Foreign coins, tokens.*

A. D. Hamilton & Co (ANA)
7 St Vincent Place, Glasgow, G1 2DW. Tel: 0141
221 5423, email: jefffineman@hotmail.com, www.
adhamilton.co.uk.*British and World Coins.*

Hammered British Coins
PO Box 2330, Salisbury, SP2 2LN. Tel: 07825 226
435, www.hammeredbritishcoins.com. *British Coins.*

Peter Hancock
40–41 West Street, Chichester, West Sussex,
PO19 1RP. Tel: 01243 786 173. *World Coins, Medals and Banknotes.*

Hattons of London
PO Box 3719, Newcastle, ST55 9HH. Tel: 0333 234
3103. Email: enquiries@hattonsoflondon.co.uk **L**
Rare and Exclusive Coins.

Tom Hart Coins
Based in Devon. *Tel: 07745 985 510. Email: woosworlduk@aol.com. Coins, Medals and Antiques.*

Munthandel G. Henzen
PO Box 42, NL – 3958ZT, Amerogngen, Netherlands.
Tel: 0031 343 430564 fax 0031 343 430542,
email: info@henzen.org, www.henzen.org.
L*Ancients, Dutch and Foreign Coins.*

History In Coins
Tel: 07944 374600, email:historyincoins@gmail.com,
www.historyincoins.com. *Hammered to milled, English, Irish and Scottish coins.*

Craig Holmes
6 Marlborough Drive, Bangor, Co Down BT19 1HB.
P L*Low cost Banknotes of the World.*

R. G. Holmes
11 Cross Park, Ilfracombe, Devon EX34 8BJ.
Tel: 01271 864 474. **P L**
Coins, World Crowns and Banknotes.

HTSM Coins
26 Dosk Avenue, Glasgow G13 4LQ. Tel: 0141 562
9530, www.thomasgreaves1.com**P L**
British and foreign coins and Banknotes.

M. J. Hughes Coins
27 Market Street, Alton, Hampshire, GU34 1HA.
Tel: 01420 768 161, email: info@mjhughes.co.uk
World Coins and Bullion.

T. A. Hull
15 Tangmere Crescent, Hornchurch, Essex RM12
5PL.**P L** *British Coins, Farthings, Tokens.*

J. Hume
107 Halsbury Road East, Northolt, Middlesex UB5
4PY. Tel: 020 8864 1731.**P L** *Chinese Coins.*

D. A. Hunter
Email: coins@dahunter.co.uk, www.dahunter.co.uk/
coins. **P L** *UK and World Coins.*

D. D. & A. Ingle
380 Carlton Hill, Nottingham, NG4 1JA. Tel: 0115
987 3325. *World Coins.*

R. Ingram Coins
2 Avonbourne Way, Chandlers Ford, Eastleigh,
SO53 1TF. Tel: 023 8027 5079, email: info@
ringramcoins.com, www.ringramcoins.com.**P L**
Dealers in UK Coins.

F. J. Jeffery & Son Ltd
Haines Croft, Corsham Road, Whitley,
Melksham, Wilts, SN12 8QF. Tel: 01225 703 143.**P**
L*, British, Commonwealth and Foreign Coins.*

Richard W. Jeffery
Tel: 01736 871 263. **P** *British,World Coins, notes.*

JN Coins
PO Box 1030, Ipswich, OP1 9XL. Tel: 07916 145
038, info@jncoins.co.uk, www.jncoins.co.uk).
British Coins from Celtic to Modern.

KB Coins (BNTA)
PO BOX 499, Stevenage, Herts, SG1 9JT. Tel: 01438
312 661, fax 01438 311 990. www.kbcoins.com
L *English coins and medals. Specialists in gold sovereigns, rare dates and varieties.*

Kleeford Coins
Tel: 07484 272 837, kleeford@btinternet.com
www.kleefordcoins.co.uk, . **P** *Monthly Auctions of Coins, Banknotes, Tokens & Medals.*

K&M Coins
PO Box 3662, Wolverhampton WV10 6ZW.
Tel: 0771 238 1880, email: M_Bagguley@hotmail.
com. *English Milled Coins.*

Knightsbridge Coins (ANA, BNTA, IAPN, PNG)
43 Duke Street, St James's, London, SW1Y 6DD.
Tel: 020 7930 8215/7597, info@knightsbridgecoins.
com. *Quality Coins of the World.*

Lancashire Coin and Medal Co
31 Adelaide Street, Fleetwood, Lancs, FY7 6AD. Tel:
01253 779308. **P** *British Coins and Medals.*

Liberty Coins and Bullion
17g Vyse Street, Birmingham, B18 6LE. Tel: 0121
554 4432, www.libertycoinsbullion.co.uk. *Coins and Precious Metals.*

Lindner Publications Ltd (Prinz)
3a Hayle Industrial Park, Hayle, Cornwall TR27 5JR.
Tel: 01736 751 910, email: prinzpublications@gmail.
com. **L** *Coin Albums, accessories.Stockist of the
Lindner range of coin storage solutions.*

Jan Lis (BNTA)
Beaver Coin Room, 57 Philbeach Gardens, London
SW5 9ED. Tel: 020 7373 4553 fax 020 7373 4555.
By appointment only. *European Coins.*

Keith Lloyd
1 Dashwood Close, Pinewood, Ipswich, Suffolk
IP8 3SR. Tel: 01473 403 506.**P L** *Ancient Coins.*

Lockdale Coins (BNTA)
52 Barrack Square, Martlesham Heath, Ipswich,
Suffolk, IP5 3RF. Tel: 01473 627 110, www.lockdales.
com.**L** *World Coins, Medals and Banknotes.*

Stephen Lockett (BNTA)
4–6 Upper Street, New Ash Green, Kent, DA3 8JJ.
Tel: 01474 871464. *British and World Coins.*

The London Coin Company
PO Box 495, Stanmore, Greater London, HA7 9HS
Tel: 0800 085 2933, 020 8343 2231,
www.thelondoncoincompany.com.
Modern Gold and Silver Coins.

The London Mint Office
*Tel: 0330 024 1001, londonmintoffice.org
Gold, Silver and Commemorative Coins*

Mike Longfield Detectors
83 Station Road, Balsall Common, Warks CV7 7FN.
Tel: 01676 533 274. *Metal Detectors.*

MA Shops
www.mashops.com. *On-line coin mall. Coins,
Medals, Banknotes and Accessories.*

Manston Coins of Bath
8 Bartletts St. Antique Centre, Bath. Tel: 01225
487 888. *Coins, Tokens and Medals.*

C. J. Martin Coins (BNTA)
The Gallery, Trent Park Equestrian Centre, Bramley
Road, London, N14 4UW. Tel: 020 8364 4565,
www.ancientart.co.uk.**P L**Bi– *monthly catalogue.
Greek, Roman & English Hammered Coins.*

Maverick Numismatics—Matt Bonaccorsi
07403 111843, www.mattbonaccorsi.com.
Coin and Currency Design.

M. G. Coins & Antiquities
12 Mansfield, High Wych, Herts CM21 0JT. Tel 01279
721 719. **L***Ancient and Hammered Coins,
Antiquities.*

M&H Coins
PO Box 10985, Brentwood, CM14 9JB. Tel: 07504
804 019, www.mhcoins.co.uk. **L** *British Hammered
and Milled Coins.*

Michael Coins
PO Box 3100 Reading RG1 9ZL. *World Coins and
Banknotes.*

Middlesex Coins
www.middlesexcoins.co.uk. Tel: 07753618613,
Email: marksaxby25@hotmail.com.
Quality rare coins specialists since 1999

Timothy Millett
PO Box 20851, London SE22 0YN. Tel: 0208 693
1111, www.historicmedals.com. **L** *Historical
Medals.*

Nigel Mills
PO Box 53126, London, E18 1YR. Email: nigelmills@
onetel.com,
www.nigelmills.net *Coins and Antiquities.*

Monetary Research Institute
PO Box 3174, Houston, TX 77253-3174, Tel: 001
713 827 1796, email: info@mriguide.com. *Bankers
Guide to Foreign Currency*

Moore Antiquities
Unit 12, Ford Lane Industrial Estate, Ford, nr.
Arundel, West Sussex BN18 0AA. Tel: 01243 824
232, email moore.antiquities@virgin.net.
Coins and Artefacts up to the 18th Century.

Mike Morey
19 Elmtrees, Long Crendon, Bucks HP18 9DG.**P L**
British Coins, Halfcrowns to Farthings.

Peter Morris (BNTA, IBNS)
1 Station Concourse, Bromley North Station,
Bromley, BR1 1NN or PO Box 223, Bromley,
BR1 4EQ. Tel: 020 8313 3410,
email: info@petermorris.co.uk,
www.petermorris.co.uk
L *British and World Coins, Proof Sets and
Numismatic Books, Medals and Banknotes.*

Colin Narbeth & Son Ltd (ANA, IBNS)
20 Cecil Court, Leicester Square, London,WC2N.
4HE .Tel: 020 7379 6975, www.colin–narbeth.com
World Banknotes.

Newcastle Coin Dealers
7 Nile Street, North Shields, NE29 0BD. Tel: 07939
999 286, email: newcastlecoin@outlook.com, www.
newcastlecoindealers.co.uk. *Modern British and
World Coins/Banknotes.*

John Newman Coins
P O Box 4890, Worthing, BN119WS. Tel**:** 01903
239 867, email: john@newmancoins.co.uk,
www.johnnewmancoins.co.uk**.** *English hammered
coins, British Milled Coins and British Tokens.*

Peter Nichols Cabinet Makers
The Workshop, 383a High Road,
Chilwell,Nottingham, NG9 5EA. Tel: 0115 922 4149,
email: orders@coincabinets.com,
www.coincabinets.com. *Manufacturers of Bespoke
Mahogany Coin and Medal Cabinets.*

Wayne Nicholls
PO Box 44, Bilston, West Midlands. Tel: 01543
45476. **L** *Choice English Coins.*

North Wales Coins Ltd (BNTA)
1b Penrhyn Road, Colwyn Bay, Clwyd. Tel: 01492
533 023. *British Coins.*

NP Collectables
9 Main Street, Gedney Dyke, Spalding, Lincs PE12
0AJ. Tel: 01406 365 211**P L**. *English Hammered
and Milled Coins.*

NumisCorner
www.NumisCorner.com
Coins, Banknotes, Medals and Tokens

Numitrading.com
Online market place/trading platform.
Tel: 01702 667420, email: info@numitrading.com,
www.numitrading.com.

Odyssey Antiquities
PO Box 61, Southport PR9 0PZ.Tel: 01704 232 494.
*Classical Antiquities, Ancient and Hammered
Coinage.*

Glenn S. Ogden
Tel: 01626 859 350 or 07971 709 427, email:
glennogdencoins@hotmail.com,
www. glennogdencoins.com, **P L** *English Milled
Coinage.*

John Ogden Coins
Hodge Clough Cottage, Moorside, Oldham OL1
4JW. Tel: 0161 678 0709**P L***Ancient and
Hammered.*

Don Oliver Gold Coins
Stanford House, 23 Market Street, Stourbridge,
West Midlands DY8 1AB. Tel: 01384 877 901.
British Gold Coins.

Del Parker
PO Box 310 Richmond Hill, GA 31324.
Tel: + 1 2143521475, Email: irishcoins2000@hotmail.
com www.irishcoins.com. *Irish, American Coins.*

Pavlos S. Pavlou
58 Davies Streer, Mayfair, London W1K 5JF. Tel: 020
7629 9449, email: pspavlou@hotmail.com. *Ancient to Modern.*

PCGS
Tel:+33 (0) 949 833 0600, email:info@pcgs.com,
www.pcgs.com. *Coin Grading and Authentication Service.*

Penrith Coin & Stamp Centre
37 King Street, Penrith, Cumbria CA11 7AY. Tel:
01768 864 185.*World Coins.*

Pentland Coins (IBNS)
Pentland House, 92 High Street, Wick, Caithness
KW14 5L5. ℗ *British and World Coins and Banknotes.*

Philatelic Heritage
35a High Street, Hungerford, RG17 0NF.
Email philatelicheritage@gmx.com. Tel: 01488
684008 Coins & Stamps.

B. C. Pickard
1 Treeside, Christchurch, Dorset BH23 4PF. Tel:
01425 275763, email: bcpickard@fsmail.net). ℗
Stone Age, Greek, Roman Items (inc. coins) for sale.

Pobjoy Mint Ltd (ANA)
Millennium House, Kingswood Park, Bonsor
Drive, Kingswood, Surrey KT20 6AY. Tel: 01737
818 182 fax 01737 818199. Europe's largest private
mint. *New issues.*

George Rankin Coin Co Ltd (ANA)
Tel: 020 7739 1840. rankinsjewellers.co.uk.
World Coins, banknotes, medals, watches.

Mark Rasmussen (BNTA, IAPN)
PO Box 42, Betchworth, Surrey, RH3 7YR. Tel: 01306
884 880, email: mark.rasmussen@rascoins.com,
www.rascoins.com. ℒ *Quality Hammered, Milled Coins.*

Mark T. Ray (see Collectors World)

Rhyl Coin Shop
12 Sussex Street, Rhyl, Clwyd. Tel: 01745 338 112.
World Coins and Banknotes.

Chris Rigby
PO Box 181, Worcester WR1 1YE. Tel: 01905 28028.
℗ ℒ*Modern British Coins.*

Roderick Richardson (BNTA)
The Old Granary Antiques Centre, King's Staithe
Lane, King's Lynn, PE30 1LZ. Tel: 01553 670
833, www.roderickrichardson.com. ℒ *English,
Hammered and Early Milled Coins. High quality lists.*

Charles Riley (BNTA)
PO Box 733, Aylesbury HP22 9AX. Tel: 01296
747 598, charlesrileycoins@gmail.com,
www.charlesriley.co.uk. *Coins and Medallions.*

Robin–on–Acle Coins
193 Main Road Essex CO12 3PH. Tel: 01255
554 440, email: enquiries@robin–on–acle–coins.
co.uk. *Ancient to Modern Coins and Paper Money.*

Roma Numismatics
20 Fitzroy Square, London, W1T 6EJ
Tel: 020 7121 6518, www.romanumismatics.com.
*Dealers and Auctioneers of English, World, Islamic
and Ancient coins..*

Royal Australian Mint
www.ramint.gov.au. *New Coin Issues.*

Royal Gold
PO Box 123, Saxonwold, 2132, South Africa,
Tel: +27 11 483 0161, email: royalg@iafrica.com,
www.royalgold.co.za. *Gold Coins 1874–1902 bought
and sold,*

Colin de Rouffignac (BNTA)
57, Wigan Lane, Wigan, Lancs WN1 2LF. Tel: 01942
237 927. *P. English and Scottish Hammered.*

R. P. Coins
PO Box 367, Prestwich, Manchester, M25 9ZH.
Tel: 07802 713 444, www.rpcoins.co.uk.
Coins, Books, Catalogues and Accessories.

Chris Rudd Ltd (IAPN, BNTA)
PO Box 1425, Norwich, NR10 5WS ℗ ℒ
Tel: 01263 735 007 www.celticcoins.com.
Celtic Coins.

Colin Rumney (BNTA)
PO Box 34, Denbighshire, North Wales, LL16 4YQ.
Tel: 01745 890 621. *All world coins including
ancients.*

R & J Coins
21b Alexandra Street, Southend-on-Sea, Essex, SS1
1DA. Tel: 01702 345 995. *World Coins.*

Safe Albums (UK) Ltd
16 Falcon Business Park, 38 Ivanhoe Road,
Finchampstead, Berkshire RG40 4QQ. Tel: 0118 932
8976 fax 0118 932 8612. *Accessories.*

Saltford Coins
Harcourt, Bath Road, Saltford, Bristol, Avon
BS31 3DQ. Tel: 01225 873 512, email: info@
saltfordcoins.com, www.saltfordcoins.com
℗ *British, Commonwealth, World Coins and
medallions.*

Satin Coins
PO Box 63, Stockport, Cheshire SK4 5BU.
Tel: 07940 393 583 answer machine.

Scotmint Ltd
68 Sandgate, Ayr, Scotland KA7 1BX
Tel: 01292 268 244, email: rob@scotmint.com,
www.scotmint.com. *Coins, Medals and Banknotes.
Retail shop.*

David Seaman
PO Box 449, Waltham Cross, EN9 3WZ. Tel: 01992
719 723, email: davidseamancoins@outlook.com.
℗ ℒ *Hammered, Milled, Maundy.*

Mark Senior
553 Falmer Road, Woodingdean, Brighton, Sussex
Tel: 01273 309 359. By appointment only.
℗ ℒ*Saxon, Norman and English hammered.*

Sharps Pixley
54, St James's Street, London SW1A 1JT Tel: 020
7871 0532, www.sharpspixley.com. *Safe deposit
boxes in St James's, buying and selling Gold Bullion.*

Silbury Coins
PO Box 281, Cirencester, Gloucs GL7 9ET. Tel:
01242 898 107, email: info@silburycoins.com,
www.silburycoins.com. *Iron Age, Roman, Saxon,
Viking, Medieval Coins and later.*

Simmons Gallery (ANA, BNTA, IBNS)
PO Box 104, Leytonstone, London E11 1ND Tel: 020
898 98097, simmonsgallery.co.uk. ℒ *Coins,
Tokens and Medals.*

E. Smith (ANA, IBNS)
PO Box 348, Lincoln LN6 0TX Tel: 01522 684 681 fax
01522 689 528. Organiser of the Wakefield (formally
known as Leeds) monthly coin fair. ℗ *World Coins
and Paper Money.*

Neil Smith
PO Box 774, Lincoln LN4 2WX. Tel: 01522 522 772
fax 01522 689 528. *GB and World Gold Coins 1816
to date, including Modern Proof Issues.*

Jim Smythe
PO Box 6970, Birmingham B23 7WD. Email:
Jimdens@aol.com.℗ ℒ*19th/20th Century British
and World Coins.*

Sovereign Rarities Ltd (BNTA)
17–19 Maddox Street, London W1S 2QH Tel: 0203 019 1185, www.sovr.co,uk. *Quality British and World Coins.*

SP Asimi
Cabinet at The Emporium, 112 High Street, Hungerford, RG17 ONB. Tel: 01488 686959. British Milled Coins 1662-1946

Spink & Son Ltd (ANA, BNTA, IAPN, IBNS)
69 Southampton Row, Bloomsbury, London. WC1B 4ET. Tel: 020 7563 4000, fax 020 7563 4066, email: info@spinkandson.com, www.spink.com. *Ancient to Modern World Coins. Medals, Banknotes.*

Stamford Coins
65–67 Stamford Street, Bradford, West Yorkshire, BD4 8SD. Tel: 07791 873 595, email: stamfordcoins@hotmail.co.uk.

Stamp & Collectors Centre
404 York Town Road, College Town, Camberley, Surrey GU15 4PR. Tel:01276 32587 fax 01276 32505. *World Coins and Medals.*

St Edmunds Coins & Banknotes
PO Box 118, Bury St Edmunds IP33 2NE. Tel: 01284 761 894.

Sterling Coins & Medals
2 Somerset Road, Boscombe, Bournemouth, Dorset BH7 6JH. Tel: 01202 423 881. *World Coins & Medals.*

Drake Sterling Numismatics Pty Ltd
GPO Box 2913, Sydney 2001, Australia. UK callers Tel: 020 7097 1781, www.drakesterling.co.uk. *British and British Colonial Gold Coins.*

Studio Coins (ANA, BNTA)
Studio 111, 80 High Street, Winchester, Hants SO23 9AT. Tel: 01962 853 156 email: stephenmitchell13@ bttconnect.com. **P** *English Coins.*

The Britannia Coin Company
143 High Street, Royal Wootton Bassett,Wilts, SN4 7AB.Tel: 01793 205007.
wwwbritanniacoincompany.com. Ancient, Hammered and Milled, Sovereigns, Investment Gold, Royal Mint New Issues.

The Coin Cabinet
First Floor, 60 St James's Street, London, SW1A 1LE. Tel: 020 3808 5855.
Email: contact@thecoincabinet.com.
www.thecoincabinet.com. World Coin Dealer and Auctioneer.

The Coin House
Tel: 01935 824 878, email: thecoinhouse@ btinternet.com. *Quality Investment Coins and Silver Bars.*

The East India Company
Tel: 0203 205 3394, email: service@ theeastindiacompany.com. *Gold and Silver Coins, retail premises.Gifts and collectables of historic interest.*

The Royal Mint
Llantrisant, Pontyclun, CF72 8YT. Tel: 01443 222111. *New coin minter/issuer. Also historic numismatics.*

Time Line Originals
PO Box 193, Upminster, RM14 3WH. Tel: 01708 222 384/07775 651 218, email: sales@time–lines. co.uk.

Stuart J. Timmins
Smallwood Lodge Bookshop, Newport, Salop. Tel: 01952 813 232. *Numismatic Literature.*

R. Tims
39 Villiers Road, Watford, Herts WD1 4AL.**P L**
Uncirculated World Banknotes.

Michael Trenerry
PO Box 55, Truro, TR1 2YQ. Tel: 01872 277 977, email: veryfinecoins@aol.com. By appointment only. **L** *Roman, Celtic and English Hammered Coins and Tokens.*

Robert Tye
7–9 Clifford Street, York, YO1 9RA. Tel: 0845 4 900 724, email: orders@earlyworlscoins.com. *www.uk–coins.com. Rare Historical Medals*

Vale
Tel: 01322 405 911, email: valecoins@ntlworld.com *British Coins and Medals.*

Van der Schueren, John-Luc (IAPN)
14 Rue de la Borse, 1,000 Bussels, Belgium. Email: iapnsecret@compuserve.com, www.coins.be. . *Coins and Tokens of the World and of the Low Countries.*

M. Veissid & Co (The Collectors Centre)
16 The Parade, St Marys Place, Shrewsbury SY1 1DL Tel: 01743 600951. *Retail shop offering coins, medals, notes and emphemera.*

Victory Coins (BNTA)
PO Box 948, Southsea, Hampshire, PO1 9LZ. Tel: 023 92 751908. *British and World Coins.*

Mark J. Vincenzi (BNTA)
Rylands, Earls Colne, Essex CO6 2LE. Tel: 01787 222 555. **P** *Greek, Roman, Hammered.*

Mike Vosper
PO Box 32, Hockwold, Brandon IP26 4HX. Tel: 01842 828 292, email: mikevosper@vosper4coins. co.uk, www.vosper4coins.co.uk. *Roman, Hammered.*

Weighton Coin Wonders
50 Market Place, Market Weighton, York, Y043 3AL, Tel: 01430 879 740, www.weightoncoin.co.uk. *Modern Gold, Silver Proofs and Sets.*

Wessex Coins
PO Box 482, Southampton, SO30 9FB. Tel: 02380 972 059, email: info@wessexcoins.co.uk, www.wessexcoins.co.uk. *Ancient Greek, Roman, English Hammered Coins and Antiquities, also Shipwreck Treasure.*

Pam West (IBNS, BNTA)
PO Box 257, Sutton, Surrey, SM3 9WW. Tel: 020 8641 3224, email: pam@britishnotes.co.uk, www.britishnotes.co.uk.**P L** *English Banknotes and related publications.*

West Essex Coin Investments (BNTA, IBNS)
Croft Cottage, Station Road, Alderholt, Fordingbridge, Hants SP6 3AZ. Tel: 01425 656 459. *British and World Coins and Paper Money.*

West Wicklow Coins
Blessington, Co Wicklow, Ireland. Tel: 00353 45 858 767, email: westwicklowcoins@hotmail.com. *Irish and World Coins.*

Trevor Wilkin
PO Box 182 Cammeray, NSW 2602, Australia. Tel: 0061 9438 5040, email trevorsnotes@bigpond.com. *World Banknotes.*

Simon Willis Coins
43a St Marys Road, Market Harborough, LE16 7DS. Tel:07908 240 978, swcoins@simonwilliscoins.com, www.simonwilliscoins.com. *Quality Hammered and Early Milled British Coins.*

Worldwide Coins (IBNS)
PO Box 11, Wavertree, Liverpool L15 0FG. Tel: 0845 634 1809, email: sales@worldwidecoins.co.uk, www.worldwidecoins.co.uk. *World Coins and Paper Money.*

World Treasure Books
PO Box 5, Newport, Isle of Wight PO30 5QE. Tel: 01983 740 712. **L** *Coins, Books, Metal Detectors.*

Treasure
and the Law

Until the introduction of the new Treasure Act, the legal position regarding articles of gold, silver or bullion, found long after they were hidden or abandoned, was not as simple and straightforward as it might be supposed. Furthermore, this was a case where the law in England and Wales differed fundamentally from that in Scotland.

Treasure Trove was one of the most ancient rights of the Crown, deriving from the age-old right of the monarch to gold, silver or bullion treasure whose owner was not known. In England and Wales, the law applied only to objects made of, or containing, gold or silver, whether in the form of coin, jewellery, plate or bullion. Moreover, the object had to be shown to have been deliberately hidden with intent to retrieve and the owner could not be readily found. The English law therefore excluded precious stones and jewels set in base metals or alloys such as bronze or pewter. It also took no account of artifacts in pottery, stone, bone, wood or glass which might be of immense antiquarian value.

In recent years, as a result of the rise in metal-detecting as a hobby, the archaeological lobby brought pressure to bear on Parliament to change the law and bring it into line with Scotland where the rules on Treasure Trove were far more rigorously interpreted. In Scotland the Crown is entitled to *all* abandoned property, even if it has not been hidden and is of little value. This applies even to objects dumped in skips on the pavement. Strictly speaking you would be committing a criminal offence if you removed an old chair from a skip without the owner's permission, although in practice such helping oneself rarely proceeds to a prosecution. In 1958 an archaeological expedition from Aberdeen University found several valuable artifacts on St Ninian's Isle, Shetland. These included silver vessels and ornaments, as well as a porpoise bone which had incised decoration on it. The archaeologists challenged the rights of the Crown to this treasure, arguing that the Crown would have to prove that the articles had been deliberately hidden, and that a porpoise bone was in any case not valuable enough to count as treasure. The High Court, however, decided that as long as the property had been abandoned, it belonged automatically to the Crown. Its value, intrinsic or otherwise, or whether or not it was hidden, did

Re-writing history—the unrecorded gold stater of Caratacus discovered by a metal detectorist in Hampshire in 2020 and declared "perhaps the most important single Iron Age coin ever found in this country", sold for a record price of £71,000 when offered by Chris Rudd Auctions in their November 2020 sale.

not make any difference. Since then, as a result of this decision in case law, the criteria for Treasure Trove have been very strictly applied in Scotland. It would have only required a similar test case in England or Wales to result in a similar tightening of the rules. This has been resisted, mainly by the detectorist lobby, but inevitably the government considered legislation to control the use of metal detectors, if not to ban them altogether.

In England and Wales a find of gold or silver coins, artifacts or ornaments, or objects which contain some of these metals, which appears to have been concealed by the original owner, was deemed to be Treasure Trove. It was not even necessary for the articles to be buried in the ground; objects concealed in thatched roofs or under the floorboards of buildings have been judged to be Treasure Trove. Such finds had to be notified immediately to the police who then informed the district coroner. He then convened an inquest which decided whether all or part of the find was Treasure Trove. Establishing the gold or silver content was straightforward, but the coroner's inquest had to decide whether the material was hidden deliberately and not just lost or abandoned, and that the owner could not be located. A gold coin found on or near a country footpath might reasonably have been dropped by the original possessor through a hole in pocket or purse and in such cases it was very unlikely that it would be deemed Treasure Trove, even if the coin turned out to be very rare. In this instance the coroner would then have had to determine who was the lawful owner of the find: the actual finder, the owner of the land where it was found or even the tenant of the land. As a rule, however, it was left to the finder and landowner to decide between them who the owner of the coin should be, and in some cases the matter could only be resolved by referring to a civil court. For this reason

it was vital that metal detectorists should secure permission *in writing* from landowners before going on to their land, defining rights and obligations on both sides, in order to determine the disposal or share-out of any finds or proceeds from the sale of finds, *beforehand*.

If the coroner decided that the articles were deliberately concealed, and declared them to be Treasure Trove, the find automatically reverted to the Crown. In practice the find was considered by the Treasure Trove Reviewing Committee of the Treasury. They might decide that although the articles, *invariably coins*, were gold or silver, they were so common that they were not required by the British Museum or one of the other great national collections, and would return them to the finder to dispose of at their discretion. If some or all of the coins were deemed vital for inclusion in a national collection the finder was recompensed with the full market value of the material. On the other hand, if someone found gold or silver which might be Treasure Trove and failed to declare it at the time, that person was liable to prosecution under the Theft Act 1968 should the find subsequently come to light. Not only could they face a heavy fine but the articles would be forfeit to the Crown, and of course no reward or recompense was then payable either.

The anomalies and inconsistencies of existing law on Treasure Trove were eliminated and the position considerably tightened up by the passage, on July 5, 1996, of the Treasure Act.

Announcing that the Treasure Act had received the Royal Assent, Lord Inglewood, National Heritage Minister, said, "This represents the first legislation on Treasure Trove to be passed in England and Wales and will replace Common Law precedents and practices dating back to the Middle Ages. The Act, which offers a clearer

It is not just the British Isles that can give up its "treasure". Joe McGregor of New Zealand discovered an 1855 Sydney half sovereign in February of 2020 while detecting in the Bay of Plenty in New Zealand. The coin is the first and rarest year of the type with supposedly just 50 examples known. It was sold by Heritage Auctions for an impressive $31,200.

In July 26, 2020 three metal detectorists discovered a huge hoard of coins, probably hidden during the English Civil War, in the 1640s in a field in Suffolk. An impressive 1,061 coins were found along with the shattered remnants of the ceramic container in which they'd been housed. They were a mixture of sixpences, shillings and half-crowns from the reigns of Elizabeth I, James I and Charles I.

(Image courtesy of Treasure Hunting *magazine.)*

definition of treasure and simplified procedures for dealing with finds, will come into force after a code of practice has been drawn up and agreed by both Houses of Parliament". The Act came into force in England, Wales and Northern Ireland on September 24, 1997, replacing the Common Law of Treasure Trove.

The act was introduced as a Private Member's Bill by Sir Anthony Grant, after the failure of an earlier attempt by Lord Perth. For the first time, it would be a criminal offence to fail to report within 14 days the discovery of an item which could be declared Treasure Trove. Finders will continue to be rewarded for reporting their discoveries promptly, while landowners and occupiers will also be eligible for rewards for the first time.

The Treasure Act covers man-made objects and defines treasure as objects other than coins which are at least 300 years old and contain at least 10 per cent by weight of gold or silver; coins more than 300 years old which are found in hoards (a minimum of two coins if the precious metal content is more than 10 per cent, and a minimum of 10 coins if the precious metal content is below 10 per cent). The act also embraces all objects found in clear archaeological association with items which are treasure under the above definitions. It also covers any object which would have been Treasure Trove under the previous definitions (e.g. hoards of 19th century gold or silver coins).

An extension to The Act from January 2003 provides that groups of prehistoric bronze implements are also deemed to be Treasure.

The maximum penalty for failing to report the discovery of treasure within 14 days will be a fine of £5,000 or three months imprisonment, or both.

In Scotland the police pass the goods on to the procurator fiscal who acts as the local representative of the Queen's and Lord Treasurer's Remembrancer. If the articles are of little value, historically or intrinsically, the finder will usually be allowed to keep them. If they are retained for the appropriate national collection then a reward equal to the market value is payable.

A favourite haunt of metal-detectorists these days is the beach, and many hobbyists make quite a lucrative living by sweeping the beaches especially just after a Bank Holiday. It's surprising how much loose change gets lost from pockets and handbags over a holiday weekend. Technically the coins recovered from the beach are lost property, in which case they ought to be surrendered to the police, otherwise the finder may be guilty of theft. In practice, however, the law turns a blind eye to coins, on the sensible grounds that it would be impossible to prove ownership. On the other hand, banknotes are treated as lost property since someone could in theory at least identify a note as his by citing the serial number.

In the case of other objects, such as watches and jewellery, of course the law governing lost property is enforced, and the old adage of "finders keepers" does not apply. Any object of value, identifiable as belonging to someone, that is washed up on the foreshore or found in territorial waters is known technically as "wreck". This includes not just a wrecked ship, but any cargo that was being carried by a ship.

If wreck is not claimed by its owner, it falls to the Crown. In this case it is not necessary to prove deliberate concealment, as in the case of Treasure Trove. This law has a specific numismatic application in the case of the gold and silver coins washed up after storms around our shores, from Shetland to the Scillies. Such coins, emanating from wrecks of Spanish treasure ships and Dutch East Indiamen in particular, are well documented, and any such finds ought to be reported immediately to the police.

Stray finds of coins, as well as other objects of value, on public places, such as the street, a public park or a sports ground, are also subject to law. In this case the finder must take all reasonable steps to locate the owner. Anyone who keeps a coin without making reasonable

effort to find the owner could be prosecuted for theft. As with the beach, however, such "reasonable effort" would clearly be impractical. Finding coins on private premises is another matter. In this case large bodies, such as the Post Office, British Rail, the British Airports Authority, bus companies, municipal authorities, hospitals, the owners of department stores, theatre and cinema proprietors and the like, may have bye-laws, rules and regulations for dealing with lost property found within their precincts, or in their vehicles. If you found a purse or wallet on a bus or train, or in a telephone kiosk or a shop, common sense (and your conscience) would tell you to hand it over to the driver, conductor, shopkeeper or official in charge.

As a rule, unclaimed lost property reverts eventually to the finder, but not always; British Rail and some other organisations have a rule that in such cases the property reverts to the organisation. In any event, failure to disclose the find immediately might render you liable to prosecution for stealing by finding.

In January 2019, detectorists Lisa Grace and Adam Staples (above) located one of the most significant finds in British history near the Chew Valley in Somerset. Illustrated left is just one of the importance pieces unearthed that day, a mule of Edward the Confessor and William I.

Advertisers
directory